Annual Reports 7

COLUMBUS
Mechanicsburg
NEWARK
CAMBRIDGE
St. Clairsville
Reynoldsburg
London
W. Jefferson
ZANESVILLE
Barnesville
Somerset
Jamestown
Mt. Sterling
LANCASTER
Bremen
New Lexington
Caldwell
Woodsfield
McConnelsville
CIRCLEVILLE
WASHINGTON C H
Logan
Nelsonville
Sharpsburg
Chauncey
MARIETTA
Williamstown
CHILLICOTHE
St Marys
Ellenboro
Smithville
Buffington Island
Ravenswood
Lockhart
Pt Pleasant
Mount Alto
Reedy
Grantsville
GALLIPOLIS
Ambrosia
Ripley
Spencer
Arnoldsburg
W Union
PORTSMOUTH
Friendship
OHIO
Ohio
KY
Lisman
Buffalo
Midway
Goldtown
Walton
Tollesburg
Vanceburg
Greenup
IRONTON
Ivydale
ASHLAND
Chesapeake
Winfield
Clendenin
Cattettsburg
Milton
Nitro
Clay
Barboursville
HUNTINGTON
ST ALBANS
S CHARLESTON
CHARLESTON
Olive Hill
Grayson
W Hamlin
Hamlin
Maiden
Rand
Morehead
Wayne
Marmet
Cedar Grove
Gauley Bridge
Ansted
Echo
Ranger
Racine
Sandy Hook
Louisa
Ft Gay
Madison
Dunlow
Fry
Frenchburg
Chapmanville
Whitesville
Oak Hill
W Liberty
Inez
Chief Logan
Kermit
Logan
Naoma
Arnett
Mt. Hope
Staffordsville
Paintsville
Salyersville
Naugatuck
BECKLEY
Prestonsburg
Barnabus
Man
Shady Spring
WILLIAMSON
Sophia
Jackson
Pie
Gilbert
Twin Falls
Pineville
Tralee
Pikeville
Iaeger
Camp Creek
Welch
Northfork
Mouthcard
Big Rock
Bradshaw
Maybeury
Princeton
Hazard
Lothair
Grundy
War
Vicco
Shelby Gap
BLUEFIELD
Vansant
Rocky Gap
Jenkins
Clintwood
Whitesburg
Pound
Tazewell
Cumberland
Richlands
Bland

From the 1998 Progressive Corporation Annual Report
Illustrator: Stephen Frailey
Design Firm: Nesnady and Schwartz

Annual Reports 7

The International Yearbook of Annual Reports
Das internationale Jahrbuch über Jahresberichte
Le Répertoire international des Rapports Annuels

Publisher and Creative Director: B. Martin Pedersen

Contributing Art Director: Lana Rigsby
Art Director: Lauren Slutsky

Contributing Designers: Pamela Zuccker, Thomas Hull, Delfin Chavez
Photographer: Jack Thompson, Alfredo Parraga
Editorial Assistant: Michael Porciello
Production Assistant: Joseph Liotta
Published by Graphis Inc.

This book is dedicated to:
Robert Myles Runyon, who started it all. (1925-)

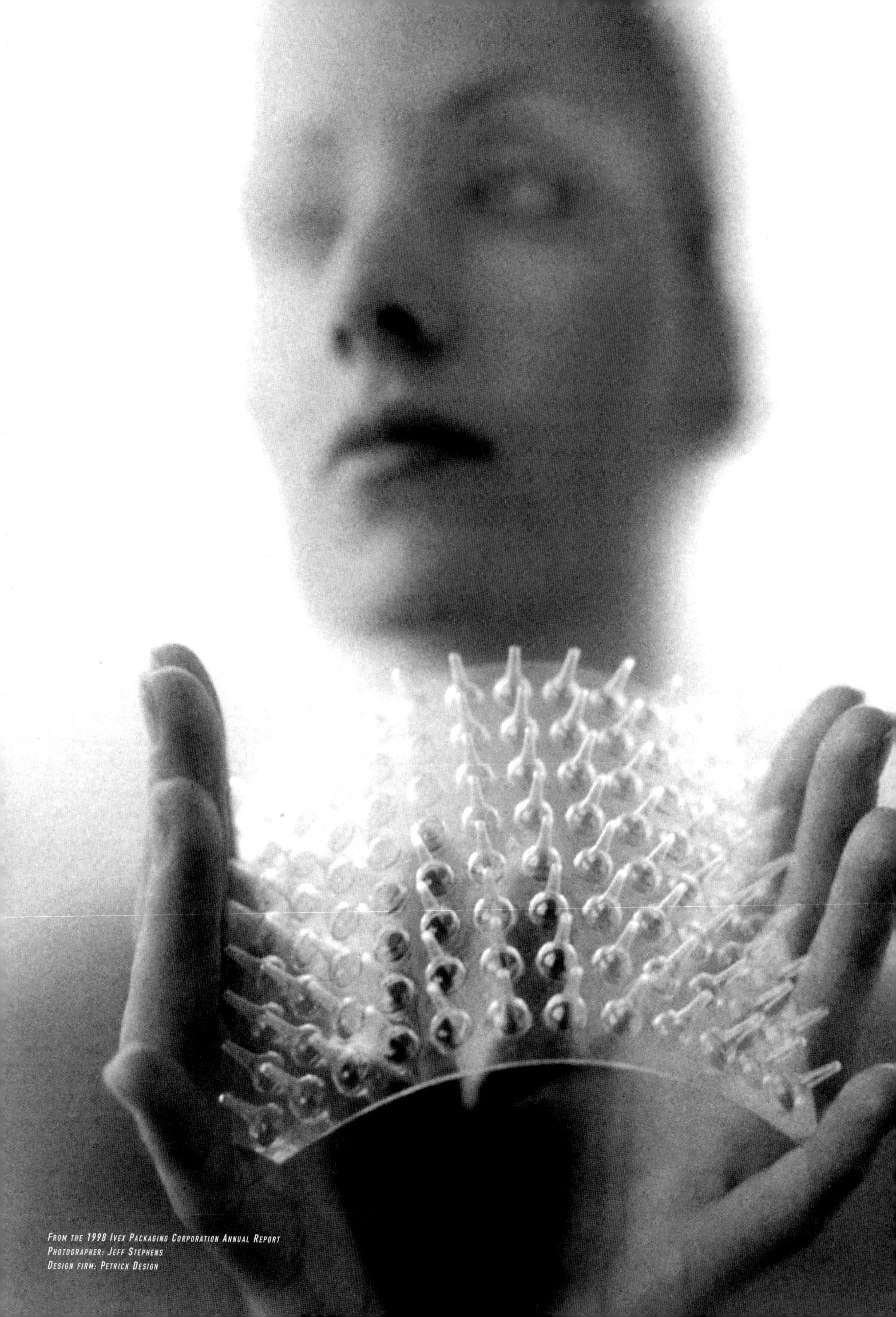

FROM THE 1998 IVEX PACKAGING CORPORATION ANNUAL REPORT
PHOTOGRAPHER: JEFF STEPHENS
DESIGN FIRM: PETRICK DESIGN

Contents Inhalt Sommaire

Remarks: We extend our heartfelt thanks to contributors throughout the world who have made it possible to publish a wide and international spectrum of the best work in this field. Entry instructions for all Graphis Books may be requested from: **Graphis Inc.**, 307 Fifth Avenue, Tenth Floor, New York, NY 10016 or visit our Web site, www.graphis.com

Anmerkungen: Unser Dank gilt den Einsendern aus aller Welt, die es uns durch ihre Beiträge ermøglicht haben, ein breites, internationales Specktrum der besten Arbeiten zu veröffentlichen. Teilnahmebedingungen für die Graphis-Bücher sind erhältlich bei: **Graphis Inc.**, 307 Fifth Avenue, Tenth Floor, New York, NY 10016. Besuchen Sie uns im World Wide Web, www.graphis.com

Remerciements: Toute notre reconnaissance va aux designers du monde entier dont les envois nous ont permis de constituer un vaste panorama international des meilleures création. Les modalités d'inscription peuvent être obtenues auprès de: **Graphis Inc.**, 307 Fifth Avenue, Tenth Floor, New York, NY 10016. Rendez-nous visite sur notre site web: www.graphis.com

ISBN: 1-888001-89-5 Printed by DNP.

Nike's Image Remains Soil
Hit by Asia Labor Woes, Sneaker Maker Still Can't Get Mu
By SAMANTHA MARSHALL
Staff Reporter of THE ASIAN WALL STREET JOURNAL
Dear Mr. Knight –
No more Nike
For me!
Carl Jakimore
Oakland, CA
Women
fights b
Asian fac
says
plants
Labor
Watchdog group slams Nike
HYPOCRISY IS NIKE'S SOLE PURPOSE

Hypocrisy Is Nike's Sole Purpose

THE EVIDENCE is piling up around Nike's well-adorned feet. There are more charges of human-rights abuses in poor countries, and more evidence that Nike would prefer to keep it all quiet.

There's no stopping Nike, of course, and the company knows it. It has purchased the soul of America's youth, as well as most of its famous athletes and an alarming number of its university athletic departments. A few howling cries from the wilderness, from human-rights organizations and newspaper columnists, is a minor nuisance, not a significant threat.

Besides, is this even a sports issue? Does it have anything to do with sports when it is revealed that an independent report — commissioned and paid for by Nike — found the company pays young Vietnamese women $10 a week for up to 65 hours to make shoes that cost $5 to produce and sell for more than $100?

Does it matter that Nike tried to keep the report under wraps, and only acknowledged its existence when a former employee ("disgruntled" is the obligatory adjective) leaked it to the media?

Does it belong on the sports page when that same report, conducted by Ernst and Young, reveals that 77 percent of the workers in one Ho Chi Minh City shoe-manufacturing plant suffer from respiratory problems because their workplaces are insufficiently ventilated and filled with carcinogens?

Of course it does. Nike is more powerful than any individual sports franchise, more

Commentary **Kommentar** Commentaire

Forget the

lottery.

In this era of unprecedented prosperity, the stock market has become Everyman's (and woman's) ticket to undreamed-of wealth. Are annual reports a great place to get the skinny on great companies? Graphis asks the hard questions, and takes a look at one company that's doing it right, right now.

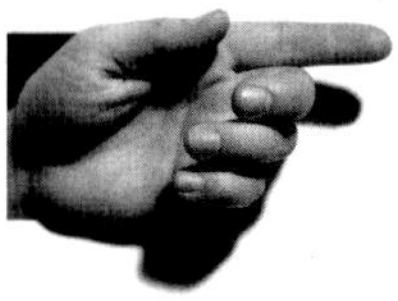

At the rate of about 4 million households annually, people are flocking online to buy and sell stocks and to learn about the companies those stocks represent. What does it all mean for expensive, dated, snail-mail-distributed annual reports? On behalf of those who design and produce them, Graphis ventures a peek at the world of annual reports beyond print.

There's no doubt about it: the Internet has changed everything. The way we shop, study, watch the news, check the weather. It's also changed how corporations operate on every level; it's not surprising that it's changing the way they communicate. But something equally big is going on: a profound shift in the fabric of the marketplace itself—who owns stock in companies, what they want to know about them, and how they want to get the information. These two factors are responsible for a revolution in the way businesses talk to their shareholders.

To understand the whole story, it's important to start at the beginning—in 1792 when the New York Stock Exchange was a handful of rich guys trading investments in the shade of a buttonwood tree on Wall Street. There were no laws governing disclosure, other than gentlemen's rules. Reporting was done—not annually—but in real time, and verbally, as relevant information became available. There were fewer than two dozen traders in the United States.

Measured in Internet years, the market grew veeeerry slowly. In the 1920s, only traders who paid big bucks for a seat on the Exchange could make multiple trades in and out of stocks on a daily basis. It took nearly 150 years for someone to figure out that investors require good, thorough information upon which to make decisions, hence the Securities Act of 1933 requiring full disclosure. It took another 41 years for trading hours to be extended to 4:00 pm (still no Saturdays or before 10:00 am). Until 1994, the vast majority of shareholders were institutions. The market was primarily influenced by fund managers and the analysts that provided them with research, opinions, and recommendations.

Up until now, information has pretty much flowed like this: companies fulfill reporting regulations with SEC filings and an annual report to shareholders. But the good stuff, *the information that that can make a person really rich,* ***is shared far more frequently, in quarterly earnings conference calls. These calls are typically open to a select group of analysts and institutional investors who filter and interpret (and benefit from) what companies disclose.***

Finally...eventually...vital information trickles down to the individual investor. A scurry to buy, sell, or short shares, sadly, comes hours after folks more in-the-know have acted on new knowledge. The price of the stock has already jumped or fallen based on the newly released news. Well-informed sellers profit from less-informed buyers. The practice is known as selective disclosure, and it wasn't a big problem until the number of individuals losing out hit the tipping point in the late 1990s. ≥

A peek at the world beyond print.

by Lana Rigsby

Photography by Jack Thompson, Houston Texas

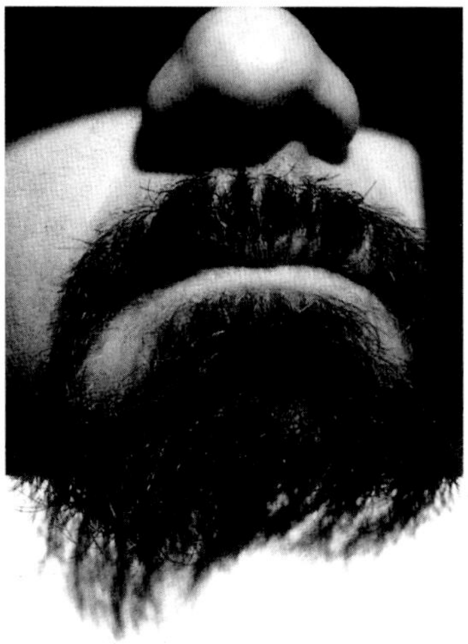
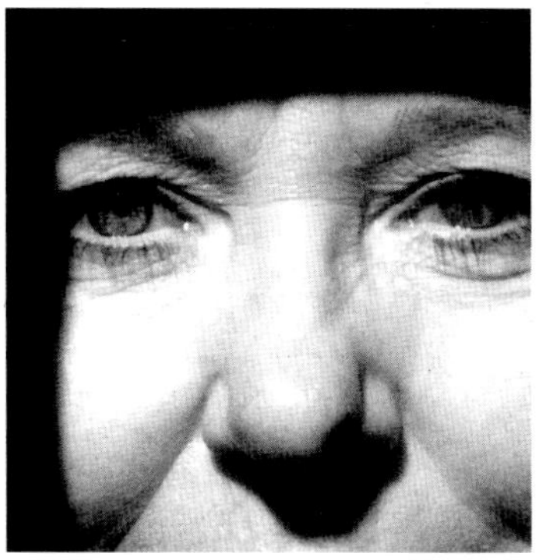
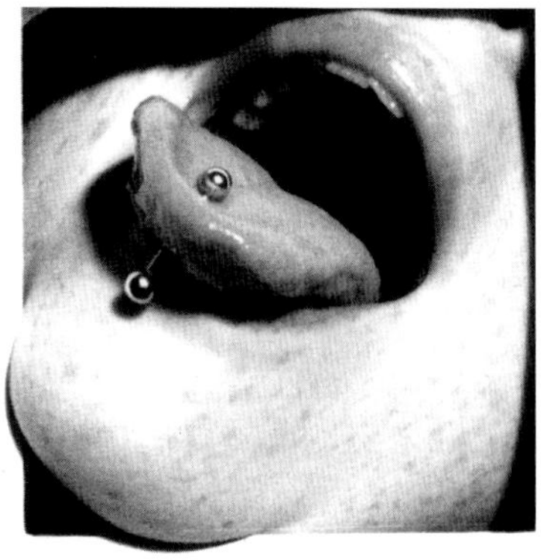

So where have all those individual investors come from? As the longest bull market in history wears on, people have come to see the stock market as a lucrative alternative to savings accounts. Lured by stunning overnight profits, many former professional traders, brokers and financial services pros have quit their jobs to become full time day traders or money managers. And the markets have soared—the Dow recently scored its first billion share day, the Industrial Average its biggest single day gain.

The cheaper and faster it becomes for people to make their own trades, the more of them enter the market. And, all of the sudden, they look a lot more like Ameritrade's Stuart than its Mr. P. They're younger (11% of online traders are under 25); they're more diverse; and the standards to which they hold companies differ wildly from those of a bottom line-driven fund manager. What are the company's labor practices, for example, or its environmental policies? These investors are more than willing to make up their own minds on what they think of the answers to these questions, and are likely to share their opinions with vast online communities.

Suddenly, corporations find themselves required to communicate with an audience whose numbers have exploded, and who want diverse and specific information. Influential content still moves through established channels—analysts and institutions mostly—but individual shareholders are increasingly hard, and costly, to ignore. James Lee, head of the Electronic Trading Association, says "[Direct trading] rocks right to the core of the Wall Street establishment." And the effects have rippled out to everyone involved in helping companies communicate.

The waves are most apparent in the simple economics of production and distribution. Annual report print runs for many companies are becoming bloated beyond recognition, often spiking into the millions. With printing budgets big enough to be visible on the bottom line, many companies are downsizing, replacing the traditional glossy report with less expensive 10k "wraps" or other, cheaper formats. AR design forums applaud reports that are able to cheerfully and creatively pull it off or—better yet—innovatively restructure distribution costs and logistics, as did EAI's landmark 1999 annual for Seagate Technology. (The entire annual was printed as a 4-page ad in the Wall Street Journal.)

But these are all incremental solutions. The real savior, of course, appears to be the Internet. It can disseminate information electronically at a fraction of the cost of print, and to vastly larger audiences. In an odd paradox, the same technology that solves the problem of communicating with infinite constituencies also makes it possible to target messages to smaller, more focused interest groups—or tailor the content for a single user. A company's Web site can be personalized and dynamically updated each time a user logs on, so the news is always fresh.

Webcast conference calls let individuals listen in on conversations between companies, analysts and institutional investors, leveling the playing field between large and small investors. Trades can be placed 24/7, and companies like Eclipse Trading are moving to allow individuals the same access to after-hours investing that professionals have long been allowed. As in the earliest days of Wall Street, communication happens in real time. >

The infrastructure is being built, and they are coming. In 1999, an estimated 40 million people went to the Net in search of investment information; one survey shows 87% of them found what they needed online. Investment pros, who probably value their time more keenly than the average Internet surfer, are logging on too. (93% of sell side analysts and nearly 80% of those on the buy side, according to Rivel Research.) Jeffrey Parker, founder of Thompson's First Call and now CEO of CCBN states flatly "The web will be the standard of disclosure in a few years."

A great migration is indeed underway. But here's the disturbing—and exciting—part: none of this is working the way we thought it would. People aren't flocking online to get the company story from ever-fancier interactive annual reports. They're looking to chat rooms, where the wackiest rumors can send the stock crashing (sometimes irrecoverably) within hours."One-to-many" messages, along with anything that sounds canned, are bypassed in favor of real, one-to-one dialog—with all the messiness and inaccuracy that human communication implies.

What shareholders don't learn from the company itself, they get from a variety of other resources. Or maybe they just make it up, causing stock prices to swing wildly for reasons unrelated to financial performance (as when Qualcomm's stock plummeted in response to rumors that turned out to be unfounded, or when Nike's stock tanked along with its reputation, responding to news and rumors that were apparently based in fact.) And it's practically impossible for a corporate annual report to gloss over bad news. If there's something a company's uncomfortable talking about, you can bet its customers and/or shareholders are ranting about it in a chat room somewhere. Business strategist David Seigel refers to the new no-secrets environment as the "Truth Economy". (Besides honesty, it calls for a sense of humor. Reporting on a disappointing year, one footwear company considered this good-natured opener "We stubbed our toe. Lucky for us we were wearing really good shoes.")

So what does all this really mean for corporate communications in general, and specifically for annual reports? Maybe the big opportunity is for designers and communicators to step back and see that what's changing is something very fundamental about the nature of the conversation itself. An article published on Motley Fool's Web site puts it this way: "Ultimately, investor relations departments must become something more than a tool for public relations, the mere gatekeeping of corporate information, or the stroking of Wall Street analysts. Companies should strive to develop a community of informed investors by becoming more attuned to the opportunities for doing so. A firm's investor relations department should serve the interests of its shareholders."

What's that again? The shareholders? There's probably not an IR department in the world that doesn't claim to puts its shareholders' needs first. But the reality is that corporate annual reports have traditionally served—not investor needs—but the corporation's need to deliver its message in a controlled way. The bad news is that control is an illusion. The near-total availability of information and gossip about anything and everything makes it so. ≥

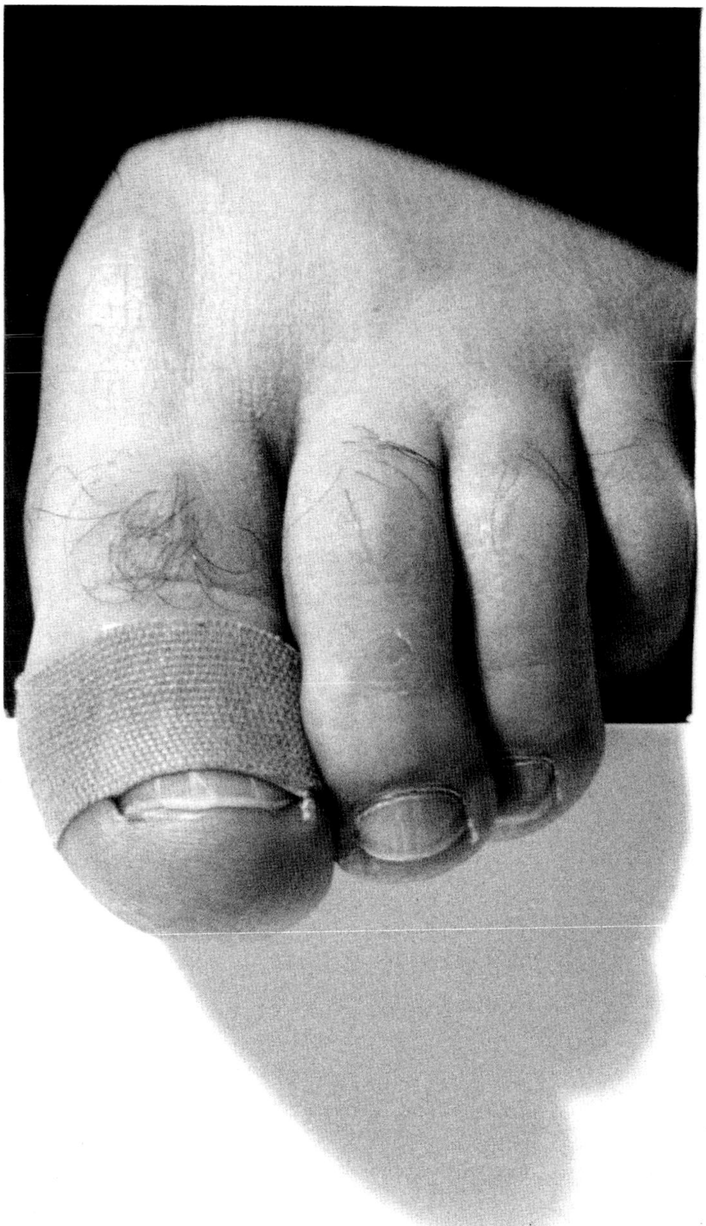

An annual report (or an investor Web site) should be a magnet for investors. A magnet whose pull is the free flow of information through information tools and genuine conversation: between shareholders and companies, between shareholders and other shareholders and anyone else with a financial interest in a company.

The analysis tools, ancillary data, and street buzz that people really use to make investment decisions are generally cobbled together from sources outside of the corporation. Wouldn't it be more useful for companies to anticipate those needs as far as possible and offer up the goods themselves?

There aren't yet many examples of companies that are doing this well. State-of-the-art in mid-2000 still seems to be the transfer of existing documents and processes to the online environment—maybe as more than pdf files, but still as traditional sell-side communications with interactivity or movement or sound thrown in for interest.

But what if the tools were something people really needed, like Microsoft's functionality allowing users to read the AR in one of 11 languages and view income statements in accordance with their own accounting standards, in their local currency? Or Cisco Systems' calendar of events that lets shareholders register for e-mail reminders and promises a personal response to queries within 8 business hours? Or IBM's interactive charting tools, with which folks can view comparisons of only the data that they select? No one has yet installed an investor chat room or message board on a corporate IR site, but it could be a next logical step toward bringing a real exchange of ideas and information closer to home.

Fine books and other printed communications will probably never go away, but expensive, dated, printed annual reports probably will. And soon. Strangely enough, though, it's not because of their expensiveness or their static nature, but because of their one-sidedness and their built-in tendency toward 'spin'. As corporations scramble to build free digital marketplaces, the necessity for real dialog is making these approaches seem quaint and...well, a little naive.

John Heskett, professor at University of Illinois Institute of Technology, spoke at an American Center for Design conference nearly ten years ago. His words sum up the challenges, and the opportunities, for corporate communicators as aptly today as they did then:
"...that is the most fundamental problem: creating a compatibility between reality and image, between integrity and identity, and above all between the truth and what is told. A corporate culture can change with great volatility, whereas real culture follows deep and abiding values. To help shape those values, designers must develop objects and images that express a relationship between what exists inside and what happens outside a company. Those who do so will be seen as leaders..."

His conclusion is particularly poignant for annual report designers:
"We cannot hope to act as changemakers in other people's lives unless we accept change in the design world itself." ■

TR REID >> SENIOR PUBLIC RELATIONS MANAGER

BY >> MIKE NOBLE

DELL COMPUTER CORPORATION >> BE DIRECT

Being direct.

An essay on brevity, clarity and the annual report.
By Mike Noble

There is nothing ostentatious about Dell Computer Corporation's headquarters on the outskirts of Austin. A network of gleaming steel and glass rectangles form a rapidly growing campus. The now familiar corporate identity with its upturned "E" stands out against a seemingly limitless Texas sky; otherwise buildings are labeled simply "1, 2, 3". Everything here seems clean, sharp-angled, geared for efficiency.

As I enter the building I see Michael Dell—at 34 the longest-tenured CEO in the industry—stride purposefully through the lobby and bound up the stairs, taking them two by two. I'm reminded of an old stagecoach drivers' adage: "The speed of the leader is the speed of the team."

One of the planet's most respected and profitable corporations, Dell has a growth story so well-known and well-documented that it hardly needs to be repeated here. Dell's is the top-performing stock in the world for the decade of the '90s and the most successful stock in the history of Nasdaq, with a 10-year return of better than 63,000%. Its growth over the past decade spikes so sharply upward that on a chart, Coke's, Microsoft's, the S&P 500 ...all look like flat lines in comparison. No need to quote current measures of performance, since by the time this essay is published those figures will be far surpassed even if a widely predicted slowdown in Dell's performance occurs.

But in the context of this volume of recent achievements in annual report design, Dell's story is brand new. While other ARs are growing larger and more complex, Dell's is getting smaller, simpler, more focused. And Dell's view of the design process is both instructive and inspiring, even a little scary.

T.R. Reid is the senior public relations manager who turns management's vision into Dell's annual report. He handles a lot more than the annual, and the day I met him his desk was overflowing, his phone ringing constantly. A red ribbon blocked entry to his cubicle, and in the middle of that ribbon was a warning penned in black magic marker: DEADLINE. Reid gets right to the point: "Most annual reports fail," he tells me, "because they try to be all things to all kinds of diverse audiences. We don't have all the answers, but our sense of audience is clear." The audience is Dell customers.

Investors, analysts and employees surely read the annual report, but customers are the primary target. To those customers Dell says one thing, loudly, repeatedly. "Be Direct." That simple and commanding phrase is both business approach and defining brand characteristic; it runs, like an electrical current, through everything the company says and does. No other phrase better explains Dell's inimitable model: selling directly to customers (eliminating distributors, resellers, and dealers); dealing directly with a tight cadre of vendors (again avoiding middlemen); and building every computer only after it's been ordered (in many cases, paid for as well). And nowhere in the company's literature are the model and its benefits so crisply outlined as in the annual report.

In Reid's mind, the key is eliminating anything that conflicts with, obscures or over-embellishes the "Be Direct" message. He eschews the overt themes and abstract metaphors that seem to be the lifeblood of so much award-winning graphic design. Relentless reductionism eventually yields a report with the brevity and wallop of a good ad campaign. Full-page, full-color spreads juxtapose powerful photography against simple headlines. Subtly addressing concerns about Dell's ability to compete globally against other top-tier computer makers, one report asks a series of questions: "How many? 1 or 100 or 1000." "How close? Direct." "Services? Around the world."

A recent Fortune magazine article sums up the approach: "Wall Street likes it simple. Dell keeps its story very simple, as in 'We sell custom-made computers directly to our customers.' Compare that with the complicated stories [other computer companies] must walk analysts through. They are great communicators." And so they are. If "direct" is the Dell business model, it's also the communications model for the annual report. The tempo is fast, easy to grasp, compelling. The letter to shareholders is concise, to the point. (Notably succinct, it's less than half the length of rival IBM's.) For the past two years, the narrative has centered on a handful of tightly phrased case studies that clearly spell out how Dell's model has benefited customers such as AOL, Sony, Wal-Mart, Nasdaq, Microsoft. Dell's online address, www.dell.com, appears on every page of the report and in inch-tall letters on the cover. In even larger type is the unequivocal pronouncement "Be Direct".

But if the type is getting bigger, the book itself is getting smaller. As corporations grow, annual reports often grow along with them, bulked up by increasingly lengthy financial reports, divisional performance reviews and the like. Not Dell's. Last year the printed report was a mere 24 pages. Cost is one consideration; the most recent print run was in the neighborhood of 2 million copies, up from half a million the year before and just over a hundred thousand the year before that.

If Dell continues its pace of 7 stock splits in as many years, the number of shareholders—and the volume of annual reports—is guaranteed to keep rising exponentially. But that's not the primary issue. The question for T.R. Reid is, once again, what is the most direct route to the customer?

Given the velocity with which Dell moves, financial information is out of date before the books even hit the press. Performance is yesterday's news. At the time of writing the '98 annual report, Dell was selling $3 million a day online; by the time the book came out that number had grown to $5 million; today it's closer to $30 million. And besides all that...are customers really using the annual report to review financial performance anyway? Isn't that kind of information much more usable in an electronic format? It took Dell little time to answer those questions, and whack twenty-six pages of financial discussion down to a two-page summary.

BE DIRECT
DELL
www.dell.com
Dell Computer Corporation
Fiscal 1999 in Review
19
98
DELL

Why Be Direct?
you
DELL

The twenty-six pages now appear—in downloadable form—in Dell's online report, along with a full 10-k. The printed piece is freed to focus nearly its entire bulk to the central mission: communicating to customers the benefits of Being Direct.

By moving timely financial information online and using print to express the company's more enduring ideas, Dell demonstrates its usual savvy for matching the medium to the message. There is some recognition that the print and online audiences don't perfectly overlap; individual investors and many portfolio fund managers may use the printed report to learn about the company but look for financial data online. So Dell's online report contains detailed financial information, expanded through interactivity and links to other parts of Dell.com. Quarterly reports and conference calls are webcast in real time.

The print report is amplified online in other ways too: an animated diagram dramatizes the static, printed visualization of how the direct model works. New customer stories supplement case studies featured in the book. But when the suggestion arises that the Internet might one day render printed reports altogether obsolete, Reid disagrees. "As long as there are physical relationships," he says, "we'll need physical tools that help us communicate."

That may be good news to paper companies, but designers should take careful note. The process has changed. Adaptability and speed take precedence over an ability to exact stylistic refinements. In his recent book (entitled, what else? Direct from Dell) Michael Dell remarks that his company's suppliers must have "sprint capability."

Though the key messages presented in the annual report don't change much, bigger, more interesting examples of Dell's success emerge almost daily. New products are announced, new awards won. Communicating a reality in which constant, accelerated change is the status quo is a matter of continual course correction. Not always easy work. And there has been the occasional misstep. One year, Fortune magazine featured the chart mentioned earlier, in which the performance of six bigtime bull-market success stories (including Coke, Microsoft, Cisco and Intel) appear to flatline next to Dell's. An enormously dramatic image, instantly communicating a story that no company on earth could match. At the annual shareholders meeting earlier in the year, Michael Dell had led his presentation with that same chart, to an immediate extended ovation. The design firm proposed several alternative covers featuring the chart, only to be reigned in by Reid's insistence that customers, not financial audiences, are the report's primary target. And that financial performance—no matter how spectacular—is not the primary message of Dell's annual report.

The phone rings yet again. My host has deadlines to meet, my hour is up. In parting, I ask for that one defining statement, his prediction for the future of communications in general and annual reports in particular. He doesn't make one. Instead he patiently repeats his boss' conviction that the Internet will not only change everything, but that it will determine who wins and who loses in the game of global big business. Dell's success has always been fueled by paying close attention to the customer; continuously refining delivery methods to give people what they want, in exactly the form they want it, ever more efficiently. T.R. Reid smiles. "It's simple really. We'll just keep approaching the annual report that same way." ■

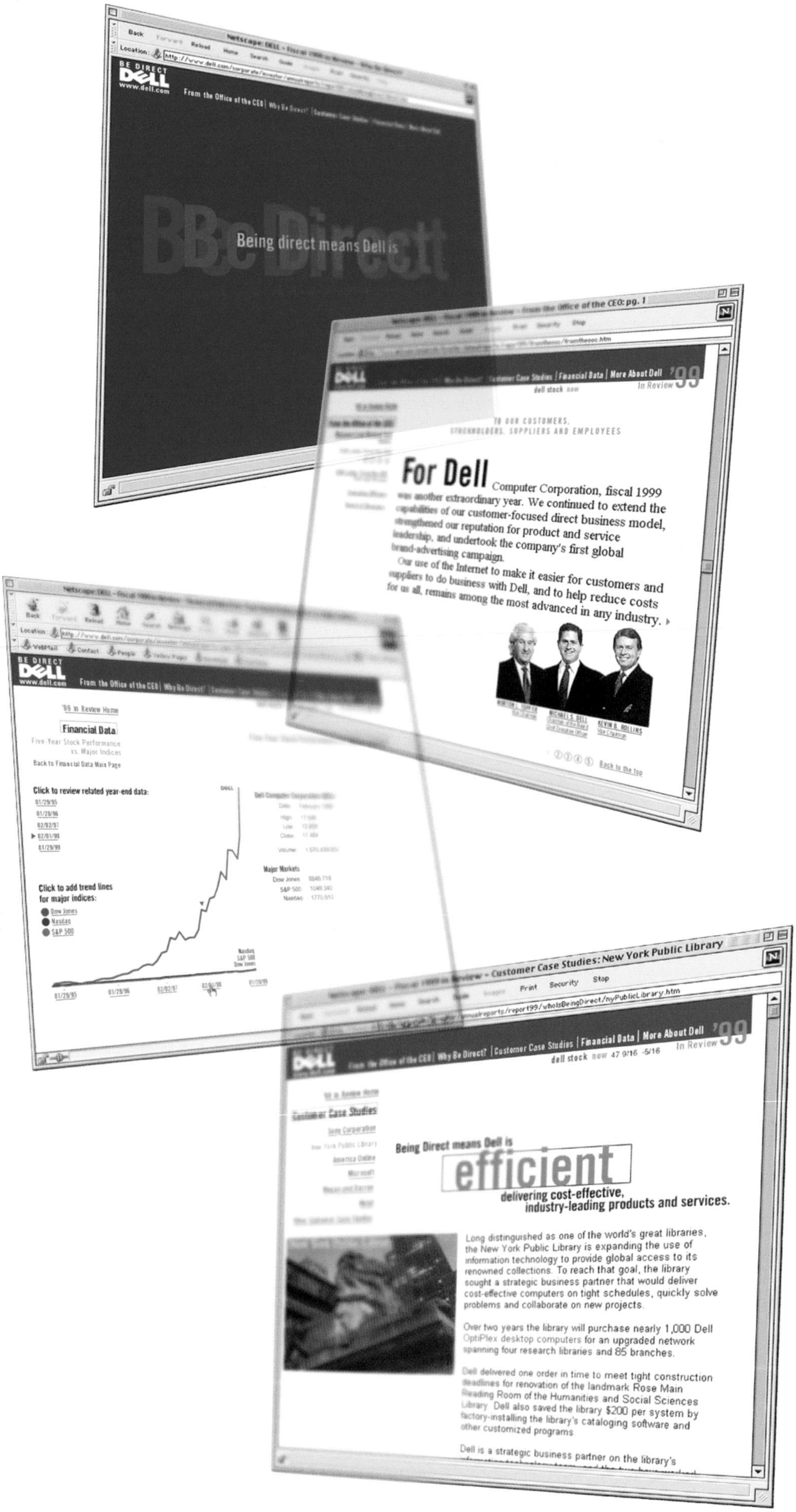
BE DIRECT
DELL
www.dell.com
From the Office of the CEO | Why Be Direct?
Being direct means Dell is
Customer Case Studies | Financial Data | More About Dell
'99 In Review
dell stock
TO OUR CUSTOMERS, STOCKHOLDERS, SUPPLIERS AND EMPLOYEES
For Dell Computer Corporation, fiscal 1999 was another extraordinary year. We continued to extend the capabilities of our customer-focused direct business model, strengthened our reputation for product and service leadership, and undertook the company's first global brand-advertising campaign.
Our use of the Internet to make it easier for customers and suppliers to do business with Dell, and to help reduce costs for us all, remains among the most advanced in any industry.
MICHAEL S. DELL
KEVIN B. ROLLINS
Back to the top
'99 In Review Home
Financial Data
Five-Year Stock Performance vs. Major Indices
Back to Financial Data Main Page
Click to review related year-end data:
01/29/95
01/28/96
02/02/97
02/01/98
01/29/99
Click to add trend lines for major indices:
Dow Jones
Nasdaq
S&P 500
Major Markets
Netscape: DELL - Fiscal 1999 in Review - Customer Case Studies: New York Public Library
Print
Security
Stop
dell stock now 47 9/16 -5/16
Customer Case Studies
Being Direct means Dell is
efficient
delivering cost-effective, industry-leading products and services.
Long distinguished as one of the world's great libraries, the New York Public Library is expanding the use of information technology to provide global access to its renowned collections. To reach that goal, the library sought a strategic business partner that would deliver cost-effective computers on tight schedules, quickly solve problems and collaborate on new projects.
Over two years the library will purchase nearly 1,000 Dell OptiPlex desktop computers for an upgraded network spanning four research libraries and 85 branches.
Dell delivered one order in time to meet tight construction deadlines for renovation of the landmark Rose Main Reading Room of the Humanities and Social Sciences Library. Dell also saved the library $200 per system by factory-installing the library's cataloging software and other customized programs.
Dell is a strategic business partner on the library's

Selected annual reports 1998|99 >

DSP Communications, Inc.
Agency: Jennifer Sterling Design
Art & Creative Director, Designer: Jennifer Sterling
Photographer: Marko Lavrisha, Photonica
Copywriter: Eric Labreque

Outside
It Could Be Anything
9 8

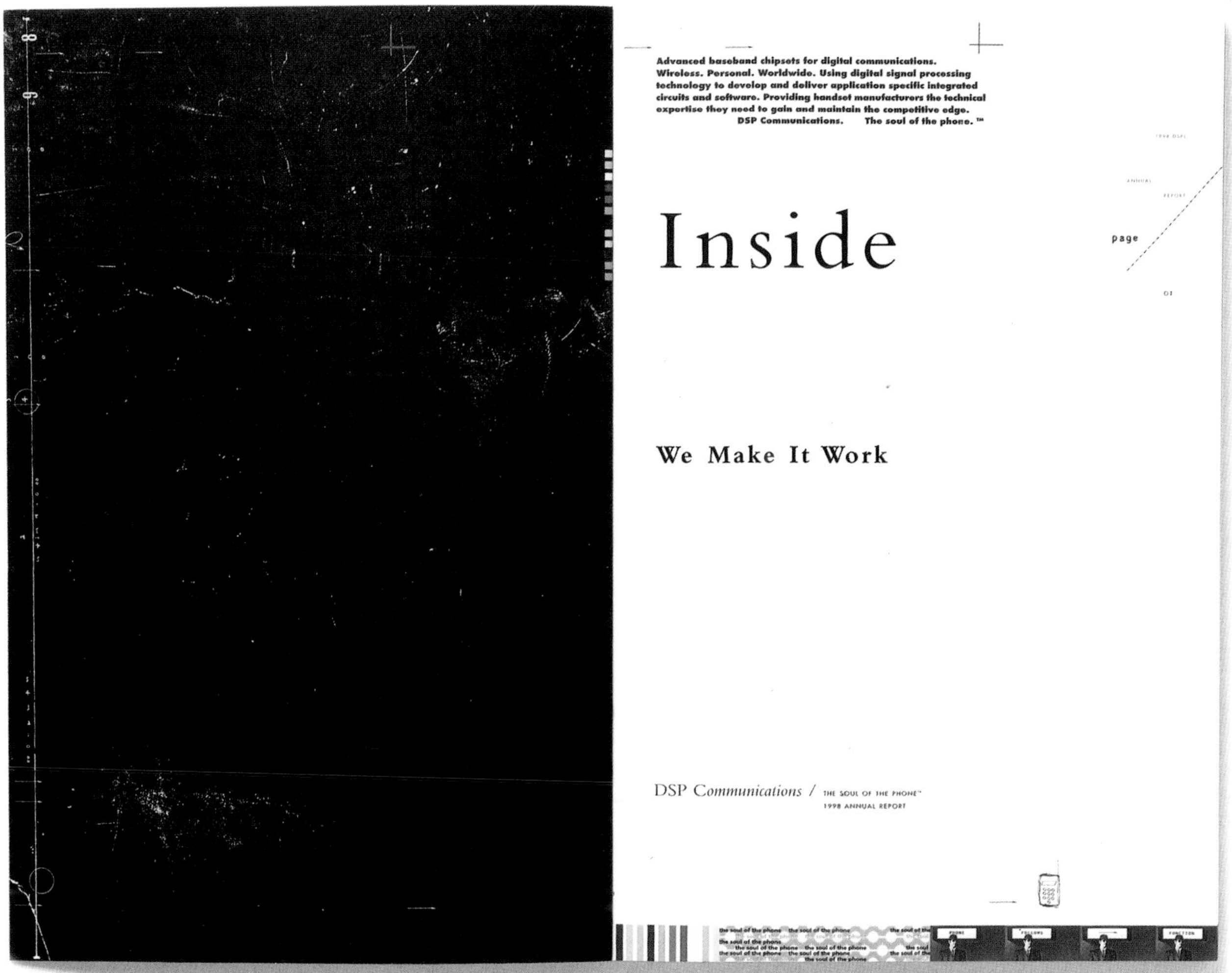
Advanced baseband chipsets for digital communications. Wireless. Personal. Worldwide. Using digital signal processing technology to develop and deliver application specific integrated circuits and software. Providing handset manufacturers the technical expertise they need to gain and maintain the competitive edge.
DSP Communications. The soul of the phone. ™
page
Inside
We Make It Work
DSP Communications / THE SOUL OF THE PHONE™
1998 ANNUAL REPORT

The fun one
1 When we read about the new friendship phones with the cartoon animation screens,
2 we were the first to get them.
Anna and Emily have the exact same one
3 except Anna's is orange and Emily's has stripes.
We can download games or play the ones built in. And our phone lets us play together even when we're sitting far apart.
4 Now everybody wants one.
page
18
page
19
PHONE FOLLOWS FUNCTION

ContrOl

1

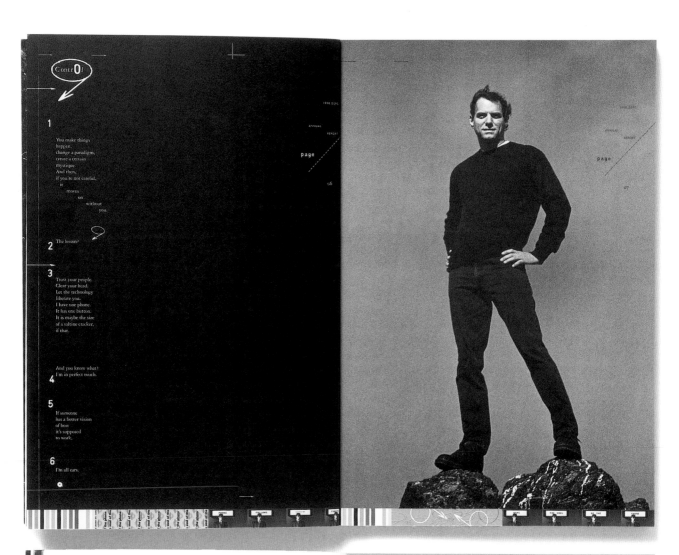

You make things
happen,
change a paradigm,
create a certain
mystique.
And then,
if you're not careful,
it
moves
on
without
you.

2

The lesson?

3

Trust your people.
Clear your head.
Let the technology
liberate you.
I have one phone.
It has one button.
It is maybe the size
of a saltine cracker,
if that.

4

And you know what?
I'm in perfect touch.

5

If someone
has a better vision
of how
it's supposed
to work,

6

I'm all ears.

WHICH PHONE WILL YOU USE TODAY?

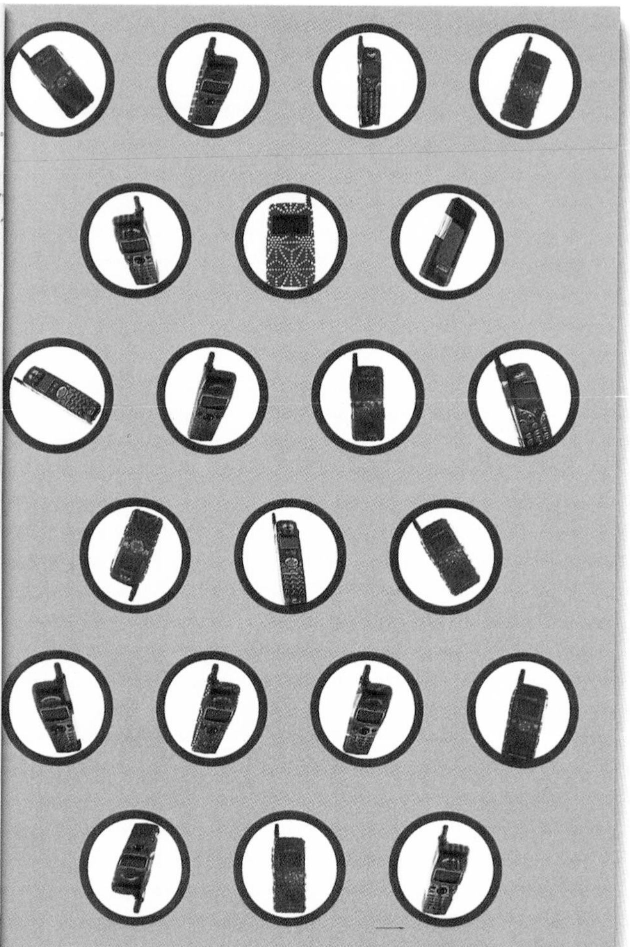

DEVICES ARE DOING MORE.

1998 DSPC ANNUAL REPORT page 26

CELLULAR PHONES ARE BECOMING MORE CAPABLE AND DIVERSE. MANUFACTURERS ARE NOW OFFERING A HOST OF NEW FEATURES IN AN ARRAY OF COMBINATIONS. THESE INCLUDE VOICE COMMAND AND VOICE RECOGNITION, SPEAKERPHONES AND MESSAGING AS WELL AS GAMES AND OTHER DOWNLOADABLE APPLICATIONS. AS THE MARKET MOVES TO A PHONE ON A CHIP, HANDSETS WILL BECOME NOT ONLY MORE VERSATILE, BUT ALSO MORE VARIED IN FORM. SIMPLE, VOICE-ONLY HANDSETS WILL HAVE THE POTENTIAL TO BECOME VERY SMALL. AND HANDSETS WITH SCREENS WILL BECOME COMMONPLACE.

8. Stockholders' Equity (continued)

1995 Director Stock Option Plan (continued)

director of the Company. Thereafter, each nonemployee director shall be granted an option to purchase 8,000 additional shares of common stock on January 1 of each year if, on such date, he or she shall have served on the Company's board of directors for at least six months.

Options granted under the Director Option Plan have an exercise price equal to the fair market value of the common stock on the date of grant and have a term of ten years, unless terminated sooner upon termination of the optionee's status as a director or otherwise pursuant to the Director Option Plan.

1998 Non-Qualified Stock Option Plan

DSPC's 1998 Non-Qualified Stock Option Plan (the "1998 Plan") provides for (i) the grant to employees, consultants and non-employee directors of DSPC of non-qualified stock options, and (ii) the grant of stock options which comply with the applicable requirements of Israeli law to the extent granted to persons who may be subject to income tax in Israel. A total of 5,000,000 shares of common stock have been authorized for issuance under the 1998 Plan.

Options granted under the 1998 Plan have an exercise price no less than the fair market value of the common stock on the date of grant. The period within which the option may be exercised is determined at the time of grant.

Option Exchange Programs

In March 1997, the Company adopted an Option Exchange Program whereby employee options which were previously granted at exercise prices greater than $9.88 and $10.88 per share for non-executives and executives, respectively, were exchanged. The exercise price of the new options for non-executives and executives are: $9.88 and $10.88 per share, respectively. Notwithstanding the original vesting schedule, the new options generally vest over a three year period and have a term of five years. A total of 4.0 million options with a weighted-average exercise price of $21.55 were exchanged and are reflected in the following table as cancellations and grants.

In October 1998, the Company adopted an Option Exchange Program whereby employee options which were previously granted but not previously repriced, at exercise prices greater than $6.13 and $6.69 per share for non-executives and executives, respectively, were exchanged. The exercise price of the new options for non-executives and executives are: $6.13 and $6.69 per share, respectively. Notwithstanding the original vesting schedule of the repriced options for non-executives, the vesting schedule of the new options was amended such that one-sixth (1/6) of the options vest six months after the date of the repricing, and one-thirty-sixth (1/36) of the options vest at the end of each month thereafter for the following 30 months. In addition, certain of these new options are subject to acceleration of vesting upon the occurrence of certain milestones based upon the market price of the Company's common stock. Any of such options whose original termination date was prior to April 7, 2002, were extended to have a termination date of April 7, 2002. The repriced options of executives retained their original vesting schedules, except that the new options are subject to acceleration of vesting upon the occurrence of certain milestones based upon the market price of the Company's common stock. A total of approximately 2.4 million options with a weighted-average exercise price of $15.07 were exchanged and are reflected in the following table as cancellations and grants.

1998 DSPC ANNUAL REPORT page 56

8. Stockholders' Equity (continued)

Share Option Plans

A summary of the Company's stock option activity under all option plans and related information for the years ended December 31 is as follows
(in thousands except per share information):

	Shares Available For Grant	Shares Under Option	Weighted Average Option Price	Weighted Average Fair Value	Options Exercisable
Year ended December 31, 1995	3,416	5,534	$ 2.71		1,360
Authorized	3,000	-	$ -		
Granted	(4,307)	4,307	$ 19.92	$ 8.33	
Exercised	-	(2,077)	$ 1.57		
Canceled and forfeited	374	(374)	$ 3.94		
Year ended December 31, 1996	2,483	7,390	$ 13.00		995
Granted	(6,233)	6,233	$ 11.63	$ 4.85	
Exercised	-	(1,789)	$ 5.50		
Canceled and forfeited	5,214	(5,214)	$ 19.60		
Year ended December 31, 1997	1,464	6,620	$ 8.49		953
Authorized	7,000	-	$ -		
Granted	(6,873)	6,873	$ 8.76	$ 3.22	
Exercised	-	(1,900)	$ 6.60		
Canceled and forfeited	3,549	(3,549)	$ 12.92		
Year ended December 31, 1998	5,140	8,044	$ 7.22		3,329

The options outstanding at December 31, 1998 have been segregated into ranges for additional disclosure as follows
(in thousands except per share information):

	Options Outstanding			Options Exercisable	
Range of Exercise Prices	Options Outstanding at December 31, 1998	Weighted Average Remaining Contractual Life (years)	Weighted Average Exercise Price	Options Currently Exercisable at December 31, 1998	Weighted Average Exercise Price
$ 1.04-$3.88	872	1.64	$ 2.87	663	$ 2.73
$ 5.00-$6.00	646	3.54	$ 5.24	415	$ 5.23
$ 6.13-$6.13	1,570	4.12	$ 6.13	-	$ -
$ 6.68-$6.68	1,978	3.69	$ 6.68	988	$ 6.68
$ 6.81-$9.88	2,037	3.10	$ 9.22	1,056	$ 9.23
$9.94-$19.38	941	4.61	$ 11.32	207	$ 10.82
$1.04-$19.38	8,044	3.49	$ 7.22	3,329	$ 6.87

1998 DSPC ANNUAL REPORT page 57

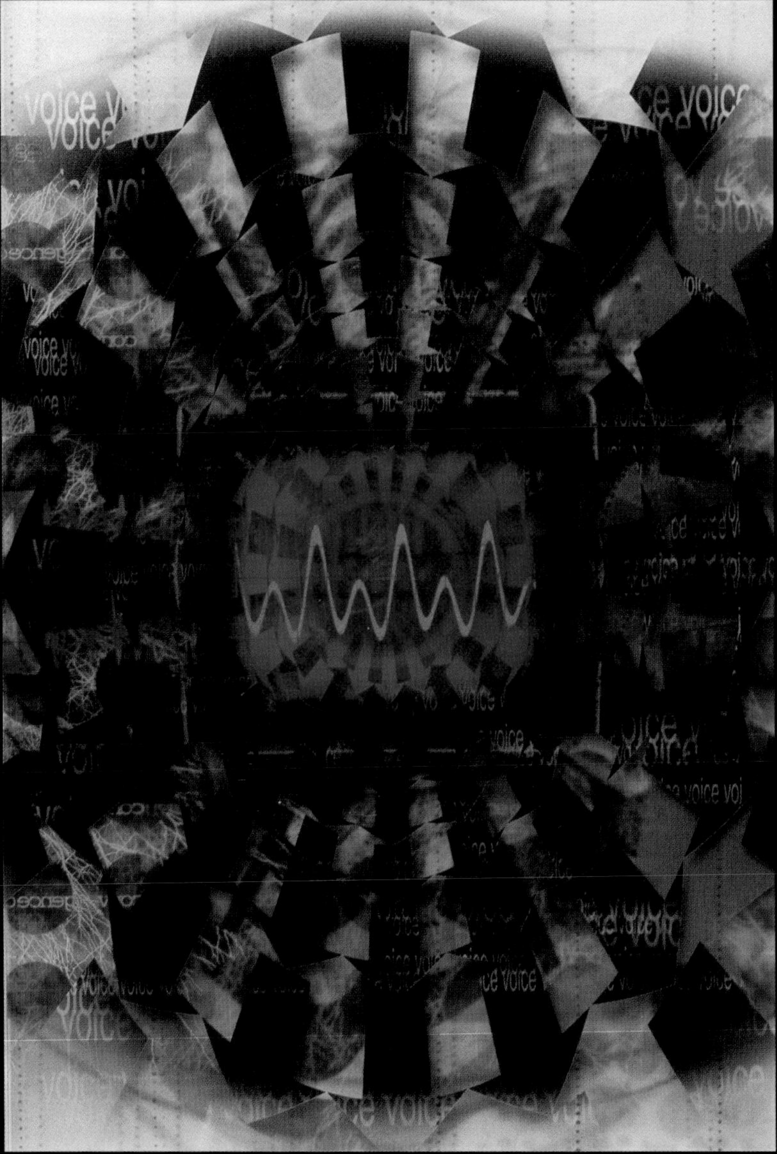
voice
voice voice

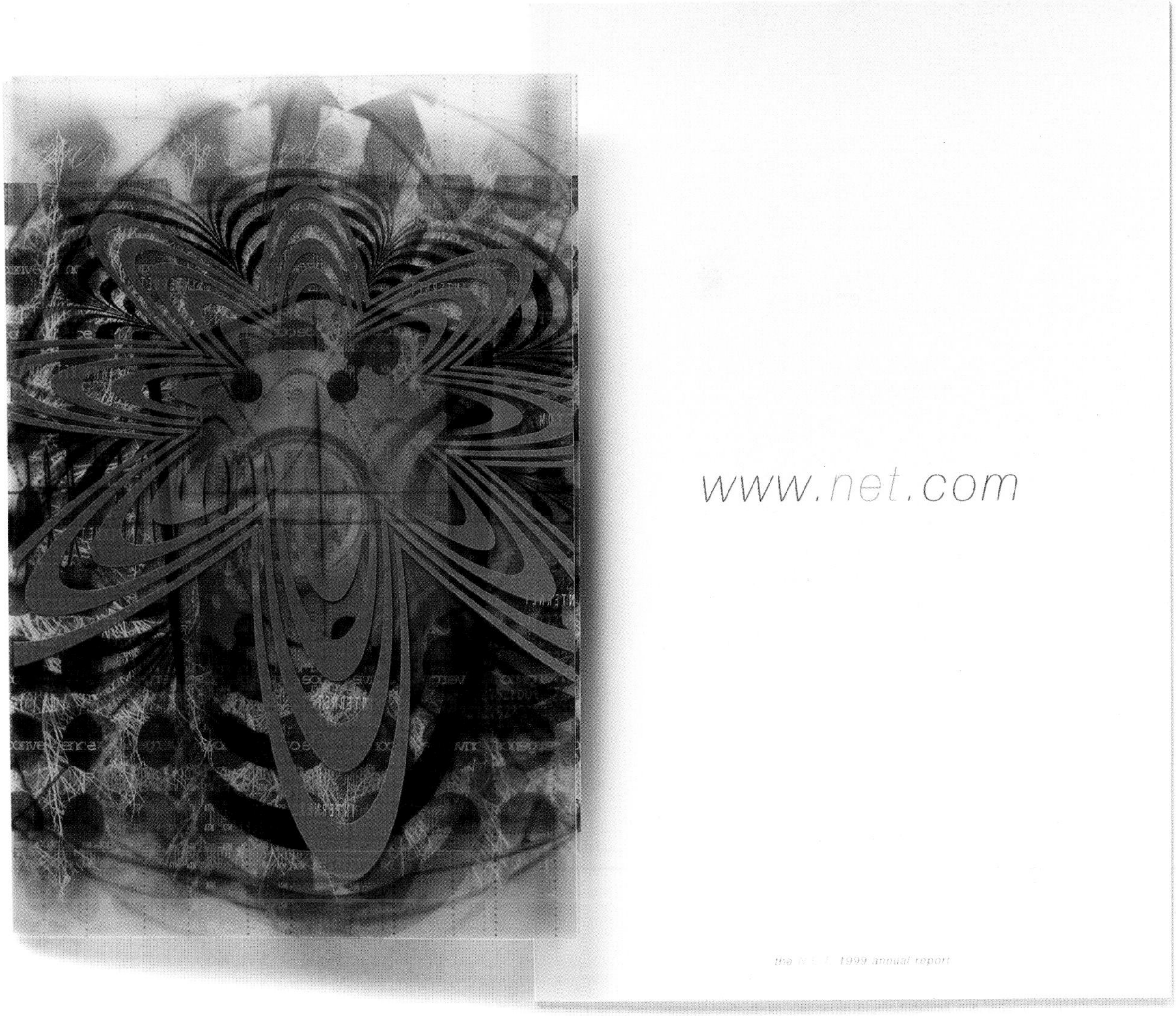
www.net.com
1999 annual report

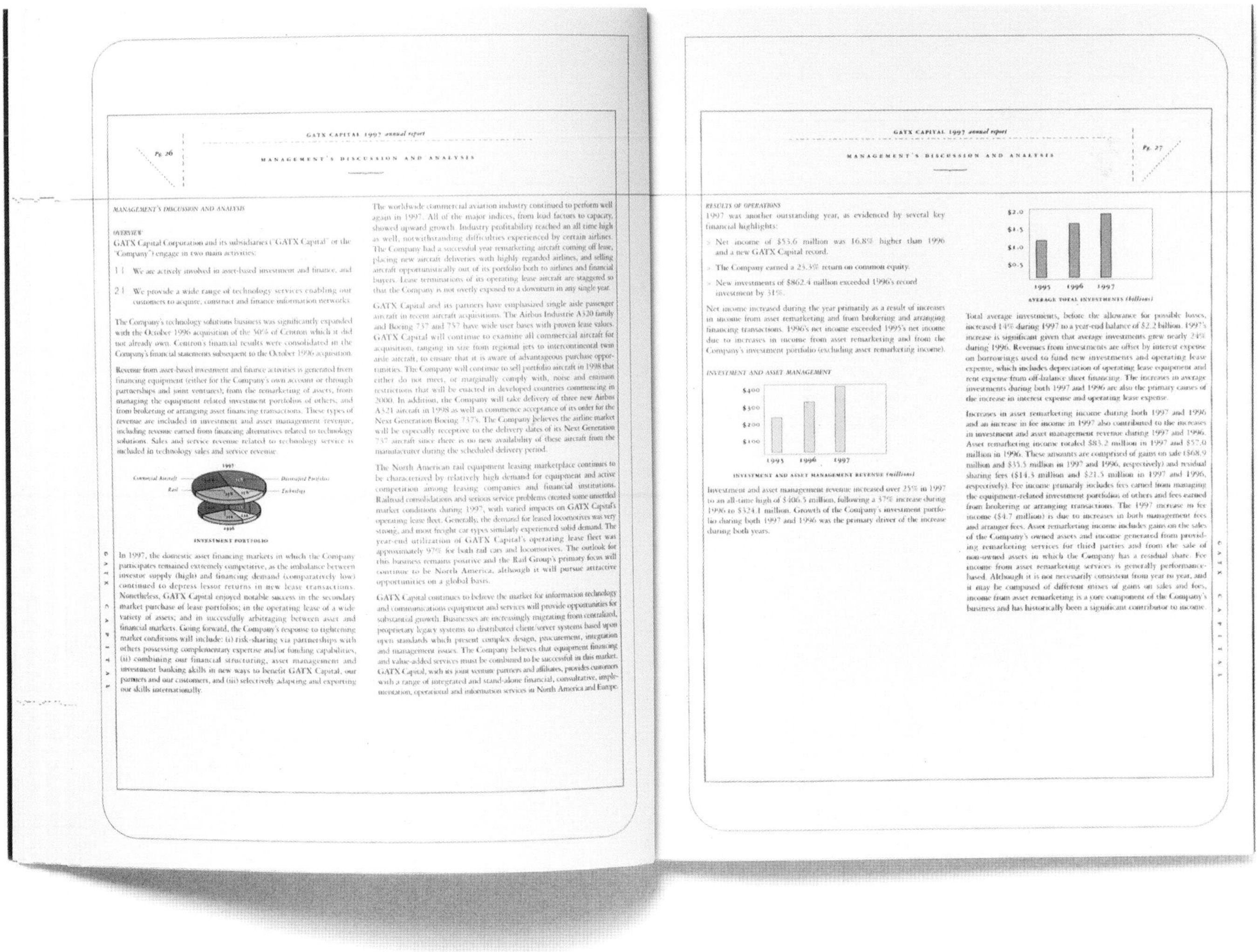
GATX CAPITAL 1997 annual report
Pg. 26
MANAGEMENT'S DISCUSSION AND ANALYSIS
MANAGEMENT'S DISCUSSION AND ANALYSIS
OVERVIEW
GATX Capital Corporation and its subsidiaries ("GATX Capital" or the "Company") engage in two main activities:
INVESTMENT PORTFOLIO
GATX CAPITAL 1997 annual report
Pg. 27
MANAGEMENT'S DISCUSSION AND ANALYSIS
RESULTS OF OPERATIONS
INVESTMENT AND ASSET MANAGEMENT
1995 1996 1997
INVESTMENT AND ASSET MANAGEMENT REVENUE (millions)
AVERAGE TOTAL INVESTMENTS (billions)

the N.E.T. 1999 annual report

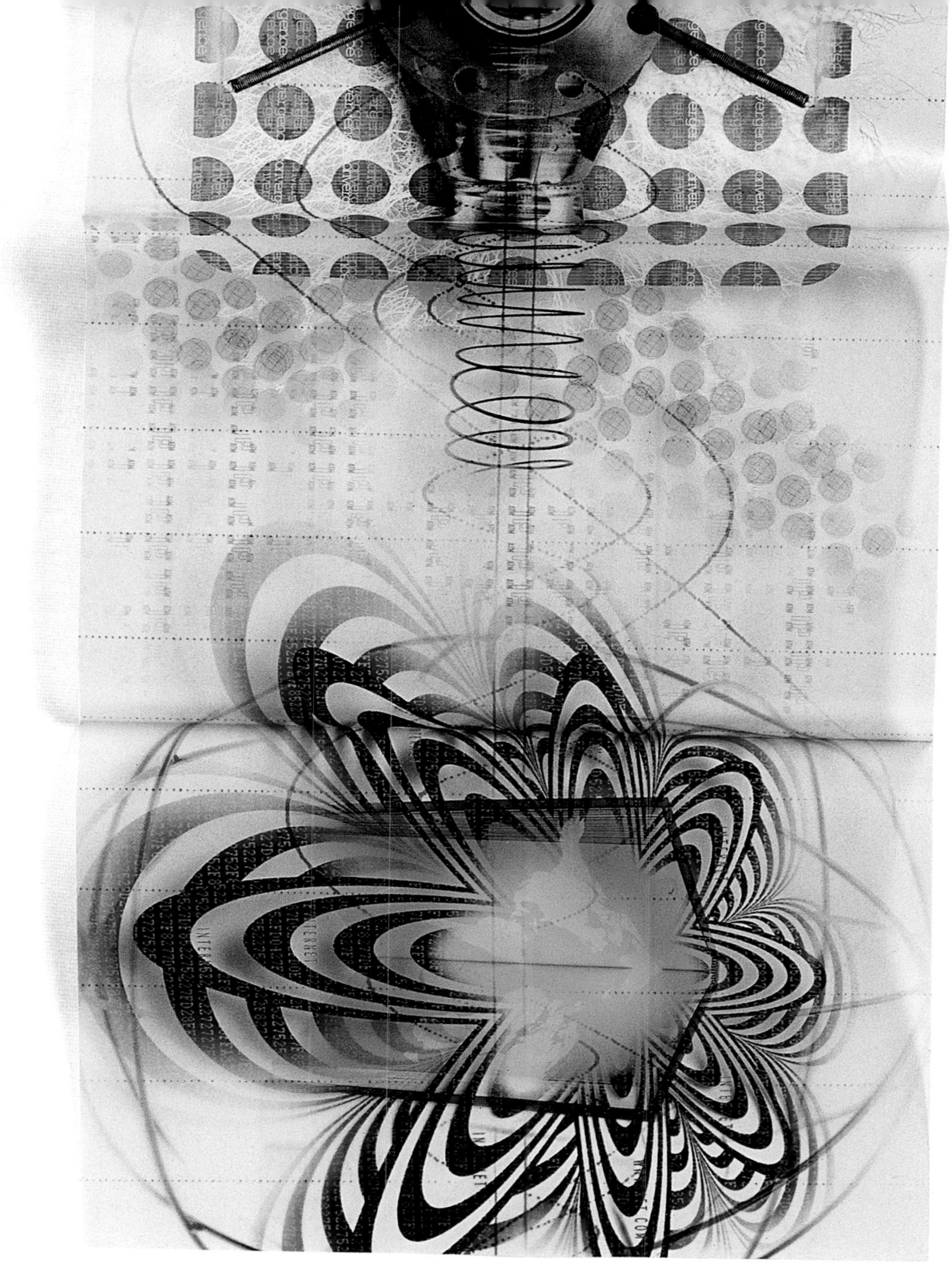

GATX Capital

Agency: Jennifer Sterling Design
Art & Creative Director, Designer: Jennifer Sterling
Photographer: Marko Lavrisha
Illustrator: Jonathan Rosen
Copywriter: Margaret Stangl

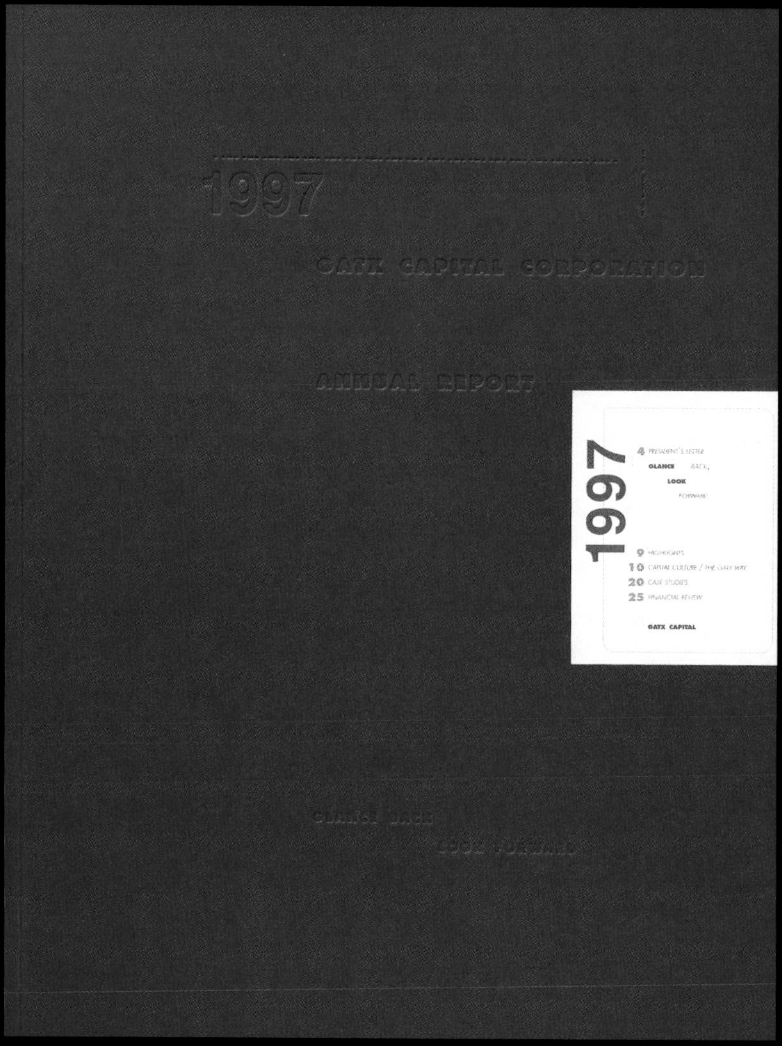
1997
GATX CAPITAL CORPORATION
ANNUAL REPORT
1997
4 PRESIDENT'S LETTER
GLANCE BACK,
LOOK
FORWARD
9 HIGHLIGHTS
10 CAPITAL CULTURE / THE GATX WAY
20 CASE STUDIES
25 FINANCIAL REVIEW
GATX CAPITAL

Pg. 2

Pg. 3

While this report focuses on 1997, we have begun celebrating two significant events in 1998 – the 50th anniversary of GATX Capital and the 100th anniversary of GATX Corporation.
These two anniversaries allow us to reflect on the depth and breadth of our business experience. However, as important as it is to recognize and celebrate our heritage, we are working to bridge the strength of our past to our success in the future.

Hence our theme for this year:

GLANCE BACK, **LOOK** FORWARD

for GATX Capital, the best is yet to come.

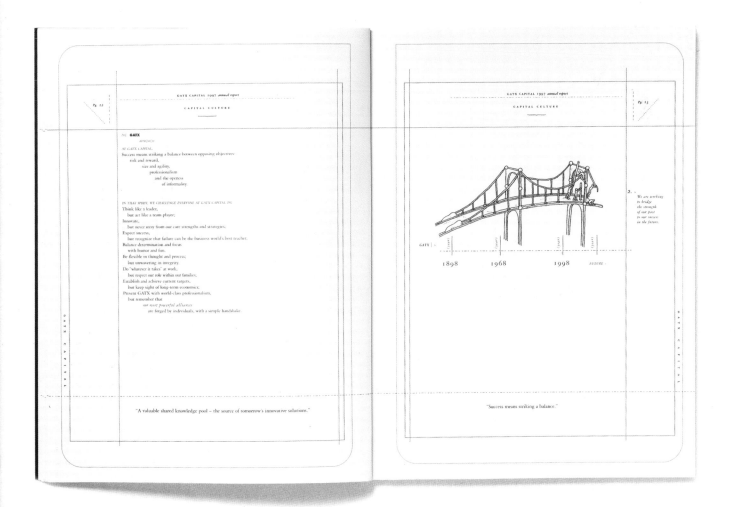

Pg. 12

GATX CAPITAL 1997 *annual report*

CAPITAL CULTURE

THE **GATX** APPROACH

AT GATX CAPITAL,
Success means striking a balance between opposing objectives:
risk and reward,
size and agility,
professionalism
and the openess
of informality.

IN THAT SPIRIT, WE CHALLENGE EVERYONE AT GATX CAPITAL TO:
Think like a leader,
but act like a team player;
Innovate,
but never stray from our core strengths and strategies;
Expect success,
but recognize that failure can be the business world's best teacher;
Balance determination and focus
with humor and fun.
Be flexible in thought and process;
but unwavering in integrity.
Do "whatever it takes" at work,
but respect our role within our families;
Establish and achieve current targets,
but keep sight of long-term economics;
Present GATX with world-class professionalism,
but remember that
our most powerful alliances
are forged by individuals, with a simple handshake.

GATX CAPITAL

"A valuable shared knowledge pool – the source of tomorrow's innovative solutions."

GATX CAPITAL 1997 *annual report*

CAPITAL CULTURE

Pg. 13

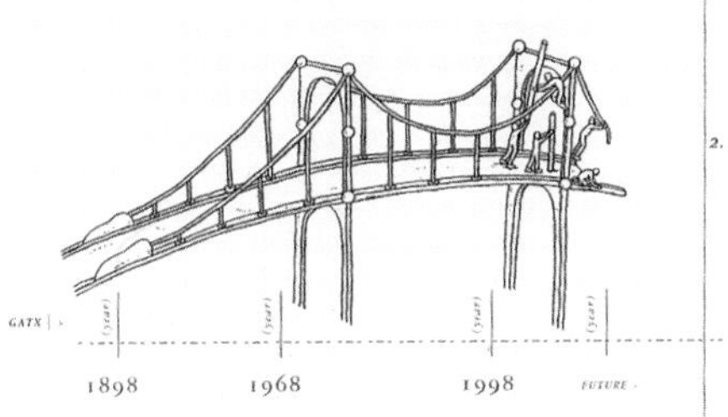
GATX
(year)
(year)
(year)
(year)
1898
1968
1998
FUTURE

2.

*We are working
to bridge
the strength
of our past
to our success
in the future.*

GATX CAPITAL

"Success means striking a balance."

DA Consulting Group
Agency: Pentagram
Art Director: Lowell Williams
Designers: Wendy Carnegie, Julie Hoyt

GOOD
Fortune 500 companies all over the world will spend 3.8 billion dollars
BAD N
Most of them won't know how to use it.
GOOD
We're there to teach them. DACG 1998 Annual Report

NEWS

on ERP software within the year.

NEWS

NEWS

1998 Financial Highlights
DA Consulting Group, Inc.®

(Consolidated amounts in thousands, except per share amounts and number of employees)	1996	1997	1998
			Years ended December 31,
Operating Data:			
Revenue	$26,202	$44,204	$80,132
Operating income*	2,212	2,756	7,090
EBITDA* (Earnings Before Interest, Taxes, Depreciation and Amortization)	2,465	2,990	7,948
Net income*	1,441	1,606	4,299
Number of employees	353	568	863
Balance Sheet Data:			
Cash and cash equivalents	$ 2,199	$ 3,664	$ 9,971
Working capital	1,629	4,101	25,585
Total assets	8,549	20,135	48,903
Total debt	731	3,970	–
Shareholders' equity	3,071	7,943	34,944
Per Share Data (Diluted):			
Net income*	$ 0.32	$ 0.32	$ 0.69
Net income	$ 0.01	$ 0.28	$ 0.69
Weighted average shares outstanding	4,462	5,053	6,233

*Before employee stock-related charges

1998 At A Glance

February	DACG acronym adopted for worldwide marketing use, replacing DA Consulting Group, Inc.
April	**Became a public company on April 24.**
June	Mexico City office opened to service clients in Mexico. Caracas office opened to meet demands in Venezuela and other Latin American countries. **At mid-year, revenue nearly doubled to $19.7 million from $9.9 million in 1997.**
August	Board of Directors elected Nicholas Marriner to Chairman and Patrick Newton to President.
September	Launched "e-learning" for business systems training. New training tool, DA FIT/Fast Implementation Toolkit™, introduced to support demand for faster SAP™ implementations.
October	SAP software selected to manage DACG's internal business information systems.
November	Became SAP AG Global Consulting Partner. Licensed SAP's training tool "InfoDB" and incorporated into DACG training solutions. The Hague sales office opened to serve Belgium, The Netherlands and Luxembourg.
December	Became PeopleSoft Global Education Services Alliance Partner. Dilip Keshu joined DACG as EVP of Asia Pacific Division. **Record year-end revenues of $80.1 million, reflecting an 80% increase over 1997.**

1

MORE

GOOD

NEWS

9

Staying Ahead. As adults, we learn what we have to, when we need to. Add to it the normal, day-to-day workload, and the stress of a new information system, and you understand the drive at DACG to deliver complex information to people using the very best approach. Today, it's e-learning, where an instructor on a headset delivers an audio course from Seattle to employees in Toronto, Dallas, Paris and Johannesburg via the Internet – a sort of training "live-chat." And tomorrow? Could be a virtual university with a course curriculum developed specifically for a client, or delivered directly from DACG. Maybe this, something completely different – as we look for the next, best way to teach within the constraints of time, costs and increasing geographic diversity.

The Fortune 500. Our clients are big, stable and blue chip. We started 1998 with 50 of the Global Fortune 500 companies and ended the year with more than 70. Along with three of the Global Top Ten, they turn to DACG to make sure their software investments are successful. We help employees become more productive faster by streamlining training, sidestepping the common pitfalls and giving them a jumpstart on how new technology will change their company's working patterns. In 1998, we served 216 clients, including Nabisco, Scott Paper Limited, Eastman Kodak, Browning-Ferris Services, Inc., Corning Consumer Products, and McKesson Corporation. With roots in the oil and gas industry, we now do work for nearly all business segments: aerospace, automotive, banking, consumer products, high tech, public sector, pharmaceuticals, telecommunications, utilities and others.

500

We Hear You. "Help" is what we do. To deliver it, we focus on three things: education, change communication and something we call "performance support." Education is customized for each client, depending on needs of the moment. If a key department can't be away for five days of training, we find another way: maybe "distance learning" through the Internet. Change communication means we give our clients hands-on help in conveying the impact of new technology to employees. Ongoing performance support means we don't pack up one day and leave our clients out in the cold. We record complex business policies, processes and procedures and turn it into an on-line help desk. That means employees can get answers from their computers just when they need it.

Help

Financial Section

Selected Combined and Consolidated Financial Data
(In thousands, except per share data)

The following selected consolidated financial statement data as of December 31, 1997 and 1998 and the three year period ended December 31, 1998 is derived from the audited consolidated financial statements of DA Consulting Group, Inc. and its subsidiaries (the "Company") included elsewhere herein. This information should be read in conjunction with such Consolidated Financial Statements and related notes thereto. The selected financial information as of December 31, 1994, 1995 and 1996, and for each of the years in the two year period ended December 31, 1995 has been derived from audited financial statements of the Company that have been previously included in the Company's reports under The Securities Exchange Act of 1934, that are not included herein. See "Management's Discussion and Analysis of Financial Condition and Results of Operations."

	Year Ended December 31, 1994 Combined(1)	Six Months Ended June 30, 1995 Combined(1)	Six Months Ended December 31, 1995 Consolidated(1)	1995 Pro Forma(2)	Years Ended December 31, 1996	1997 Consolidated (1)	**1998**
Income Statement Data:							
Revenue	$7,501	$6,299	$8,319	$14,618	$26,202	$44,204	**$80,132**
Cost of revenue	4,028	3,412	4,249	7,661	14,190	24,063	**40,812**
Gross profit	3,473	2,887	4,070	6,957	12,012	20,141	**39,320**
Selling and marketing expense	450	407	665	1,072	1,953	3,726	**5,184**
Development expense	–	296	411	707	1,250	1,223	**3,091**
General and administrative expense	2,629	1,657	2,357	4,014	6,597	12,436	**23,926**
Amortization expense(3)	–	–	230	459	274	54	**29**
Employee stock-related charge(4)	–	–	–	–	1,858	263	**–**
Operating Income	394	527	407	705	80	2,439	**7,090**
Other (expense) income, net	(77)	(23)	(61)	(84)	95	(135)	**22**
Income before taxes	317	504	346	621	175	2,304	**7,112**
Provision for income taxes	119	189	228	250	141	896	**2,813**
Net income	$ 198	$ 315	$ 118	$ 371	$ 34	$ 1,408	**$ 4,299**
Basic earnings per share(5)	$ 0.05	$ 0.09	$ 0.03	$ 0.10	$ 0.01	$ 0.29	**$ 0.72**
Weighted average shares outstanding	3,623	3,623	3,623	3,623	4,217	4,808	**5,976**
Diluted earnings per share(5)	$ 0.05	$ 0.08	$ 0.03	$ 0.10	$ 0.01	$ 0.28	**$ 0.69**
Weighted average shares outstanding	3,868	3,868	3,868	3,868	4,462	5,053	**6,233**
Balance Sheet Data:							
Cash and cash equivalents	$ 104	$ 585	$ 592		$ 2,199	$ 3,664	**$ 9,971**
Working capital	313	315	761		1,629	4,101	**25,585**
Total assets	1,784	3,211	5,440		8,549	20,135	**48,903**
Total debt	205	445	562		731	3,970	**–**
Shareholders' equity	258	573	1,891		3,071	7,943	**34,944**

Refer to accompanying footnotes on the following page.

Daisytek International
Agency: Eisenberg and Associates
Art Director & Designer: Larry White
Creative Director: Arthur Eisenberg, Saul Torres
Photographer: Phil Hollenbeck
Illustrator: Peter Hoey
Copywriter: Craig McDaniel

DAISYTEK
19 98
The Annual Report Edition
GROWTH
A GAME OF STRATEGY

Computer/Electronic 40, 41

CORPORATE PLAYBOOK
DAISYTEK
19 98
The Annual Report Edition
GROWTH
A GAME OF STRATEGY
DAISYTEK

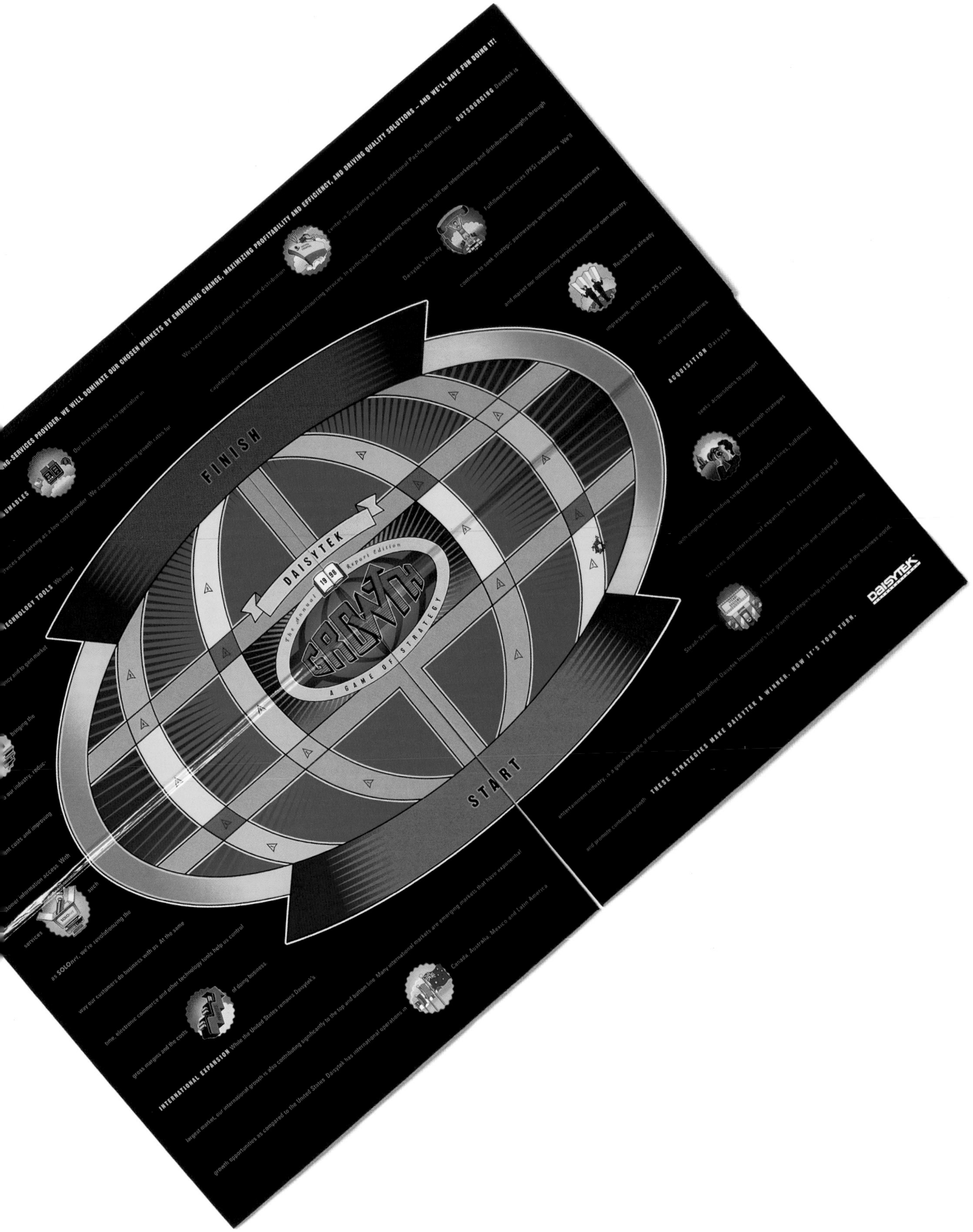
...NG-SERVICES PROVIDER. WE WILL DOMINATE OUR CHOSEN MARKETS BY EMBRACING CHANGE, MAXIMIZING PROFITABILITY AND EFFICIENCY, AND DRIVING QUALITY SOLUTIONS – AND WE'LL HAVE FUN DOING IT!
OUTSOURCING Daisytek is ...
Daisytek's Priority Fulfillment Services (PFS) subsidiary. We'll continue to seek strategic partnerships with existing business partners and market our outsourcing services beyond our own industry. Results are already impressive, with over 75 contracts in a variety of industries.
ACQUISITION Daisytek seeks acquisitions to support these growth strategies with emphasis on finding selected new product lines, fulfillment services and international expansion. The recent purchase of Steadi-Systems, a leading provider of film and videotape media for the entertainment industry, is a good example of our acquisition strategy. Altogether, Daisytek International's five growth strategies help us stay on top of the business world and promote continued growth.
THESE STRATEGIES MAKE DAISYTEK A WINNER. NOW IT'S YOUR TURN.
DAISYTEK
INTERNATIONAL EXPANSION While the United States remains Daisytek's largest market, our international growth is also contributing significantly to the top and bottom line. Many international markets are emerging markets that have exponential growth opportunities as compared to the United States. Daisytek has international operations in Canada, Australia, Mexico and Latin America.
We have recently added a sales and distribution center in Singapore to serve additional Pacific Rim markets.
Capitalizing on the international trend toward outsourcing services. In particular, we're exploring new markets to sell our telemarketing and distribution strengths through
...UMABLES Our first strategy is to specialize in
... We capitalize on strong growth rates for
...vices and serving as a low cost provider.
...ECHNOLOGY TOOLS We invest
...stomer information access. With
... services such as SOLOnet, we're revolutionizing the way our customers do business with us. At the same time, electronic commerce and other technology tools help us control gross margins and the costs of doing business.
FINISH
START
DAISYTEK
The Annual 1998 Report Edition
GROWTH
A GAME OF STRATEGY

OUR WINNING STRATEGIES DAISYTEK INTERNATIONAL WILL BE A LOW-COST, HIGH-GROWTH DISTRIBUTOR AND OUTSOURCING-SERVICES PROVIDER. WE WILL DOMINATE OUR CHOSEN MARKETS BY EMBRACING CHANGE, MAXIMIZING PROFITABILITY AND EFFICIENCY, AND DRIVING QUALITY SOLUTIONS – AND WE'LL HAVE FUN DOING IT! DAISYTEK'S CONTINUED GROWTH IS BASED ON THESE FIVE STRATEGIES.

Focus on the Growing Consumable Computer-Supplies Industry

Daisytek seeks to capitalize on strong growth rates for the products we distribute. Our strategy is to specialize in specific consumable computer supplies that have longer life cycles and a lower risk of technological obsolescence than hardware and software products. The growth in demand for these products remains strong due to the advancement and reduction in price points of printer and computer technologies, which in turn grows the installed base of equipment which consumes the products we distribute. Continuing automation of the workplace and the tremendous growth in color printing technologies that use consumables at higher rates also fuel the demand for our product offering. In addition to a strong product line, we offer these products to our customers using value-added services such as next-business-day delivery, the latest order cutoff times in the industry, our Daisygram order confirmation, product drop-shipping, customized product catalogs, and much more. Daisytek's goal is to increase sales to existing customers – including those in the Contract Stationer, Value-Added Reseller ("VAR"), computer and office-product dealer, and superstore channels. We also seek new customer relationships and new distribution channels such as mass merchants, and grocery and convenience stores. Daisytek is a pioneer in the introduction of consumable computer supplies to those channels. We believe that this consumables focus will help Daisytek capture more market share in the industry's fastest growing segments.

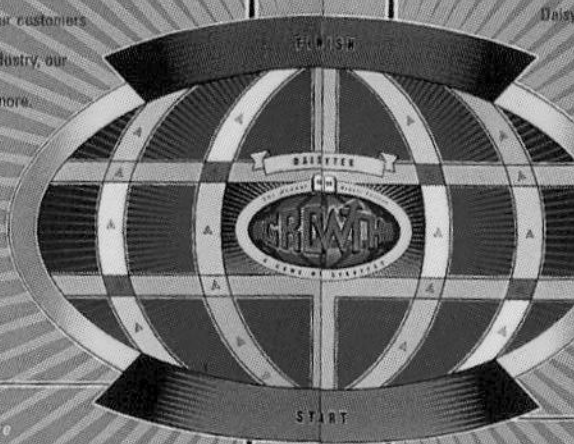
DAISYTEK
START

Leverage Innovative Technology to Capture Market Share

We're investing heavily in technology to continually improve service and efficiency, and gain market share. In fact, Daisytek is bringing the "Electronic Commerce Age" to our industry, reducing order-fulfillment costs and improving customer information access. Daisytek's technology edge brings us higher productivity in telemarketing and distribution. It also provides our customers with the ability to do business with us electronically and allows us to offer a wide array of value-added services such as EDI, advanced order tracking systems and "customer links," which give our customers direct access to their account information. With services such as **SOLO***net* (The System for Online Ordering on the Internet), we're revolutionizing the way our customers do business with us. At the same time, electronic commerce and other technology tools help us control gross margins and the costs of doing business. We believe Daisytek's technology investments enhance our ability to improve efficiency, monitor operations, offer faster and higher levels of service to customers and vendors, and win market share.

Expand International Presence

While the United States remains Daisytek's largest market, our international growth is also contributing significantly to the top and bottom line. Many international markets are emerging markets that have exponentially higher growth opportunities for consumable computer supplies compared with the United States. Presently, Daisytek operates sales and distribution centers in Canada, Australia, and Mexico, and exports products into Latin America, the Far East and throughout the rest of the world. To expand our Pacific Rim presence, we recently added a sales and distribution center in Singapore. We believe our financial strength, consumable-supplies experience and broad product range place Daisytek in a strong competitive position in emerging international markets.

Capitalize on the International Outsourcing Trend

Many companies seek to improve their speed and quality of service while reducing costs by outsourcing key functions that are Daisytek's core strengths. Our subsidiary, Priority Fulfillment Services (PFS), uses our core strengths in distribution and telemarketing to provide our business partners with end-to-end transaction management, which includes warehousing and distribution, telemarketing, order processing, product drop-shipping, receivable financing and other operating and logistical support services. This component of our business strategy offers the potential for higher margins because it is primarily fee- and activity-based. We'll continue to seek strategic partnerships with existing business partners and market our outsourcing services beyond our own industry. Results are already impressive, with more than 25 contracts since 1996 in a variety of industries. We believe that the rapid growth of electronic and Internet commerce will present additional growth opportunities for PFS to offer its services to a wide array of customers across a broad spectrum of markets and industries.

Seek Acquisitions of Selected Product Lines, Fulfillment Services and International Operations

Our acquisition strategy is to add players to the team that will support our growth strategies and capitalize on Daisytek's expertise in call-center management and small-package distribution. This strategy focuses on finding selected new product lines, fulfillment services, and international operations; and on identifying companies with significant market positions and quality management teams. Daisytek seeks to enhance the value of the acquired companies by providing capital, delivering value-added services, and providing operational and logistics expertise. The recent purchase of Steadi-Systems, a leading provider of film and videotape media for the filmed entertainment and multimedia industries, is a good example of our acquisition strategy. We believe our acquisition strategy will support Daisytek's overall game plan for continued growth. Altogether, Daisytek International's five growth strategies help us stay on top of the business world, and promote continued growth.

DAISYTEK

THE FOLLOWING SELECTED CONSOLIDATED STATEMENT OF INCOME DATA FOR EACH OF THE FISCAL YEARS ENDED MARCH 31, 1998, 1997 AND 1996, AND THE SELECTED CONSOLIDATED BALANCE SHEET DATA AS OF MARCH 31, 1998 AND 1997, HAVE BEEN DERIVED FROM DAISYTEK INTERNATIONAL CORPORATION'S AUDITED CONSOLIDATED FINANCIAL STATEMENTS, AND SHOULD BE READ IN CONJUNCTION WITH THOSE STATEMENTS, WHICH ARE INCLUDED IN THE COMPANY'S FORM 10-K FOR ITS FISCAL YEAR ENDED MARCH 31, 1998. THE SELECTED CONSOLIDATED STATEMENT OF INCOME DATA FOR THE FISCAL YEARS ENDED MARCH 31, 1995 AND 1994, AND THE SELECTED CONSOLIDATED BALANCE SHEET DATA AS OF MARCH 31, 1996, 1995 AND 1994, HAVE BEEN DERIVED FROM THE COMPANY'S AUDITED CONSOLIDATED FINANCIAL STATEMENTS, AND SHOULD BE READ IN CONJUNCTION WITH THOSE STATEMENTS, WHICH ARE INCLUDED IN THE COMPANY'S PREVIOUSLY FILED FORM 10-K's. THE SELECTED CONSOLIDATED FINANCIAL DATA SHOULD BE READ IN CONJUNCTION WITH "MANAGEMENT'S DISCUSSION AND ANALYSIS OF FINANCIAL CONDITION AND RESULTS OF OPERATIONS" AND THE CONSOLIDATED FINANCIAL STATEMENTS AND NOTES THERETO WHICH ARE INCLUDED IN THE COMPANY'S FORM 10-K FOR ITS FISCAL YEAR ENDED MARCH 31, 1998.

	FISCAL YEARS ENDED MARCH 31,				
	1998	1997	1996	1995	1994
	(in thousands, except per share data)				
CONSOLIDATED STATEMENT OF INCOME DATA:					
Net sales	$757,027	$603,814	$464,169	$352,953	$276,699
Cost of sales	679,726	543,848	416,199	316,982	247,480
Provision for losses from disposal of software and hardware inventory	–	–	–	–	402
Gross profit	77,301	59,966	47,970	35,971	28,817
Selling, general and administrative expenses	47,684	36,630	29,024	23,260	20,338
Acquisition integration costs	735	–	–	–	–
Income from operations	28,882	23,336	18,946	12,711	8,479
Interest expense	2,698	1,677	1,482	2,050	1,726
Income before income taxes	26,184	21,659	17,464	10,661	6,753
Provision for income taxes	10,024	8,292	6,697	4,165	2,496
Net income	$ 16,160	$ 13,367	$ 10,767	$ 6,496	$ 4,257
PER SHARE DATA (1):					
Net income per common share:					
Basic	$ 1.19	$ 1.03	$ 0.85	$ 0.68	$ 0.49
Diluted	$ 1.13	$ 0.97	$ 0.80	$ 0.59	$ 0.40
Weighted average common shares outstanding:					
Basic	13,566	12,934	12,602	9,558	8,676
Weighted average common shares and common share equivalents outstanding:					
Diluted	14,343	13,826	13,514	11,084	10,576

	AS OF MARCH 31,				
	1998	1997	1996	1995	1994
	(in thousands)				
CONSOLIDATED BALANCE SHEET DATA:					
Working capital	$122,318	$ 80,248	$ 56,663	$ 43,427	$ 28,167
Total assets	246,651	175,288	128,601	94,421	67,385
Long-term debt, net of current maturities	12,656	30,454	16,419	11,334	19,640
Shareholders' equity	139,370	67,193	51,661	40,817	15,937

(1) In February 1998, the Company's Board of Directors approved a two-for-one stock split effected in the form of a stock dividend paid on March 2, 1998 to stockholders of record on February 16, 1998. Share data is based upon the weighted average common shares and share equivalents outstanding for each period, adjusted to reflect the split.

DAISYTEK

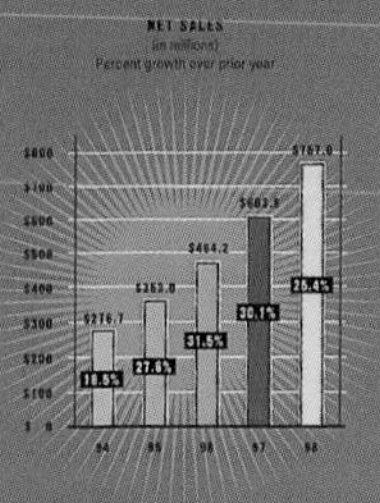
NET SALES
(in millions)
Percent growth over prior year
$800
$700
$600
$500
$400
$300
$200
$100
$ 0
$276.7
$353.0
$464.2
$603.8
$757.0
18.5%
27.6%
31.5%
30.1%
25.4%
94
95
96
97
98

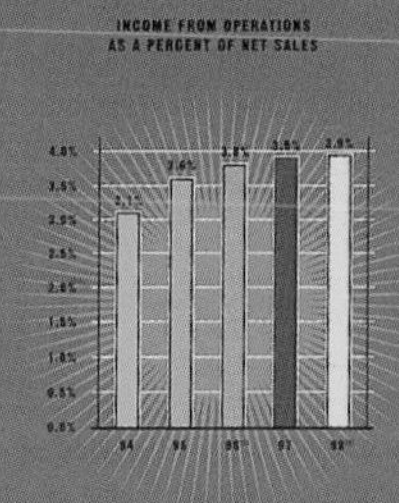
INCOME FROM OPERATIONS
AS A PERCENT OF NET SALES
4.0%
3.5%
3.0%
2.5%
2.0%
1.5%
1.0%
0.5%
0.0%
94
95
97

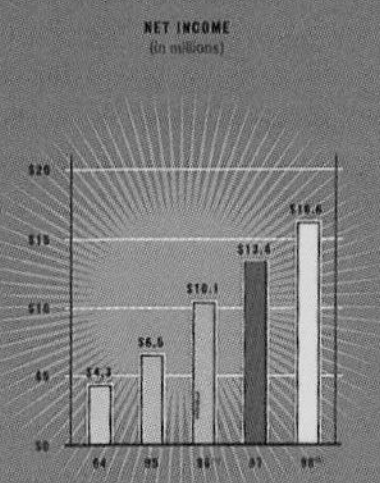
NET INCOME
(in millions)
$20
$15
$10
$5
$0
$4.3
$6.5
$10.1
$13.4
94
95
97

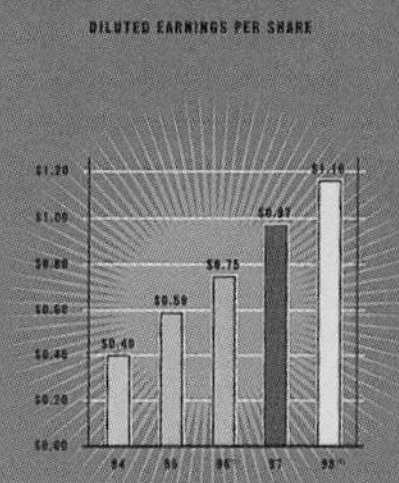
DILUTED EARNINGS PER SHARE
$1.20
$1.00
$0.80
$0.60
$0.40
$0.20
$0.00
$0.40
$0.59
$0.75
$0.97
94
95
97

(1) As adjusted to exclude the benefit of certain one-time inventory purchase actions prior to manufacturer price increases. See Management's Discussion and Analysis in Daisytek's March 31, 1998 Form 10-K.
(2) As adjusted to include the effects of one-time acquisition integration costs relating to the Steadi-Systems acquisition. See Management's Discussion and Analysis.

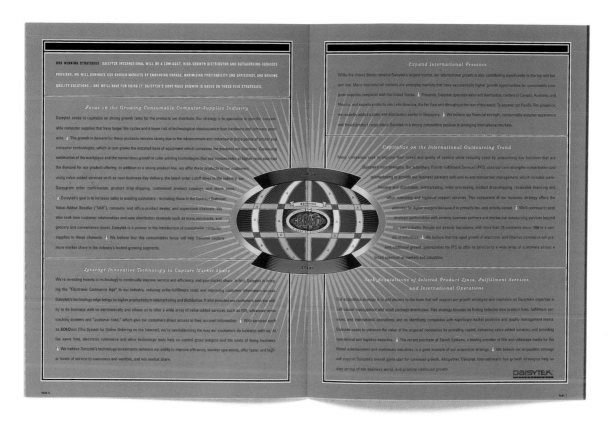

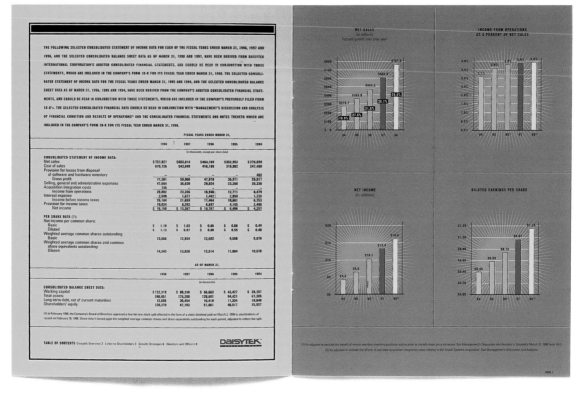

Adaptec
Agency: Turner & Associates
Creative Director: Stephen Turner
Designer: Laurie Carrigan
Photographer: Stephen Austin Welch

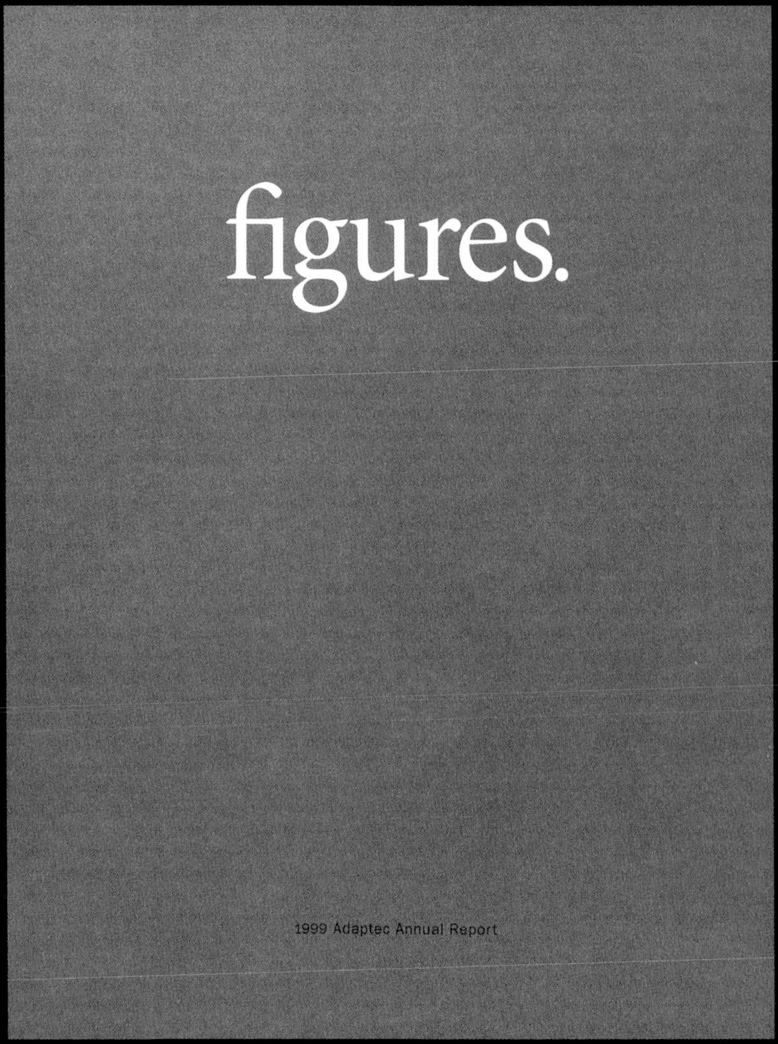
figures.
1999 Adaptec Annual Report

A close examination of the numbers shows that they are all going in the same direction:

Ours.

Windows NT® Server Unit Compound Annual Growth Rate:

24% [01.A]

RAID Controller Unit Compound Annual Growth Rate:

38% [01.B]

CD-R/RW and DVD Drive Unit Compound Annual Growth Rate:

74% [01.C]

ONE

Number of US private aircraft with GPS navigation systems on board:

82,235 [06.A]

Number of farm tractors with GPS navigation systems on board:

40,789

Number of times this year that Al Nunley couldn't find his way back to the barn:

five

SIX HOST I/O

INFORMATION — WHEN YOU NEED IT — IS WHAT IT'S ALL ABOUT. You need more information today than you did yesterday. Tomorrow, even more. And faster. Adaptec host I/O products connect you to your data speedily, reliably — and without your ever having to worry about it. No matter how much data you have, or how much more you need.

So when a farmer in Iowa needs to examine a digitized map of plant yields by row over eight different slope exposures on his 1,678-acre spread, Adaptec makes sure he doesn't have to wait for his computer to load all that data. Thanks to the speed of the Adaptec host adapter in his PC workstation, it all appears in the blink of an eye. Or when Justine's mother orders a Beanie Baby® on the Internet, she's assured a fast delivery, because the I/O performance of the distributor's computer gives instantaneous access to a nationwide inventory database. Adaptec's fast I/O performance means her on-line order is confirmed and delivered to the warehouse in just a matter of seconds.

Why do the world's major information technology makers build Adaptec's high-speed host I/O solutions into products? Because you need your data, and you want it now.

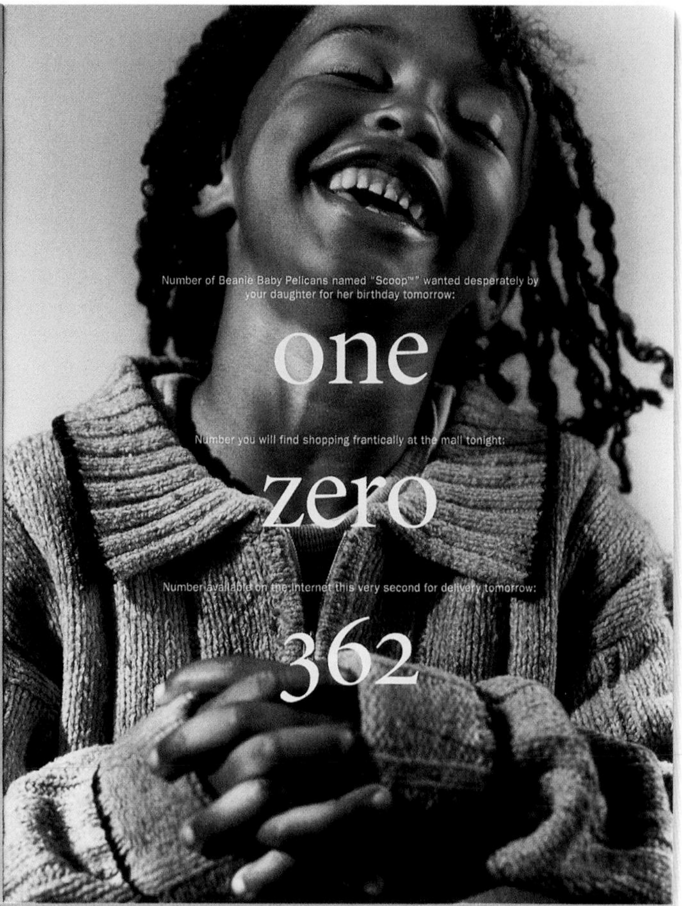
Number of Beanie Baby Pelicans named "Scoop™" wanted desperately by your daughter for her birthday tomorrow:
one
Number you will find shopping frantically at the mall tonight:
zero
Number available on the Internet this very second for delivery tomorrow:
362

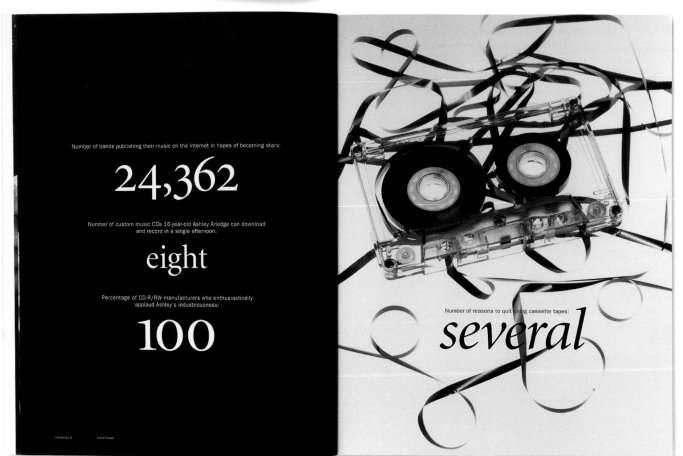

Number of bands publishing their music on the Internet in hopes of becoming stars:

24,362

Number of custom music CDs 16-year-old Ashley Arledge can download and record in a single afternoon:

eight

Percentage of CD-R/RW manufacturers who enthusiastically applaud Ashley's industriousness:

100

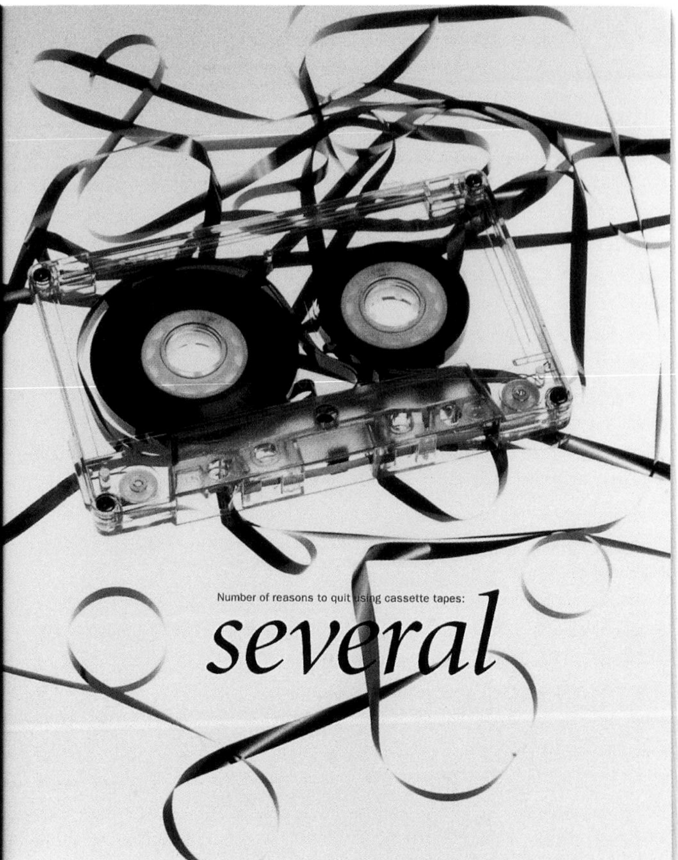
Number of reasons to quit using cassette tapes:
several

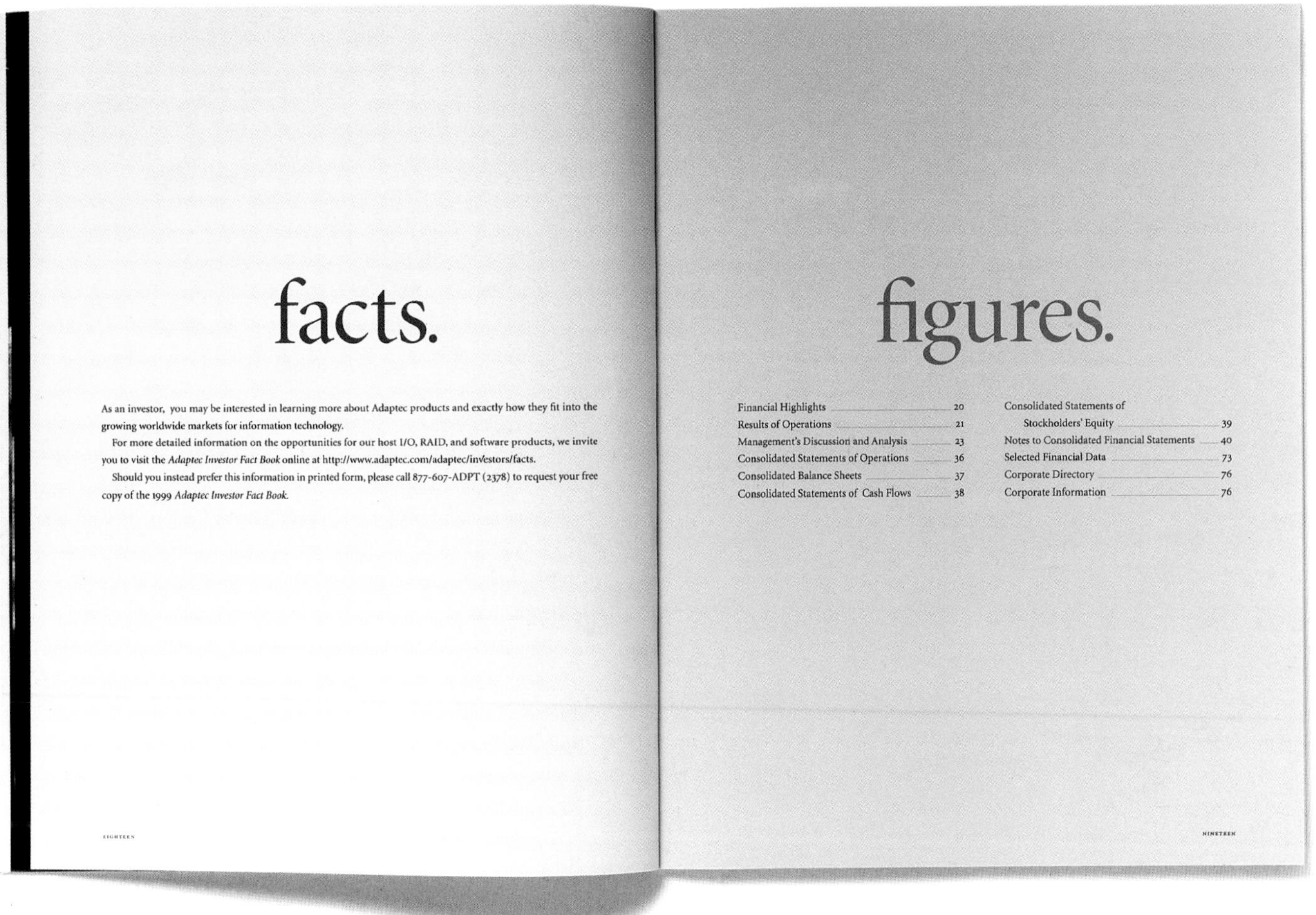

facts.

As an investor, you may be interested in learning more about Adaptec products and exactly how they fit into the growing worldwide markets for information technology.

For more detailed information on the opportunities for our host I/O, RAID, and software products, we invite you to visit the *Adaptec Investor Fact Book* online at http://www.adaptec.com/adaptec/investors/facts.

Should you instead prefer this information in printed form, please call 877-607-ADPT (2378) to request your free copy of the 1999 *Adaptec Investor Fact Book.*

EIGHTEEN

figures.

NINETEEN

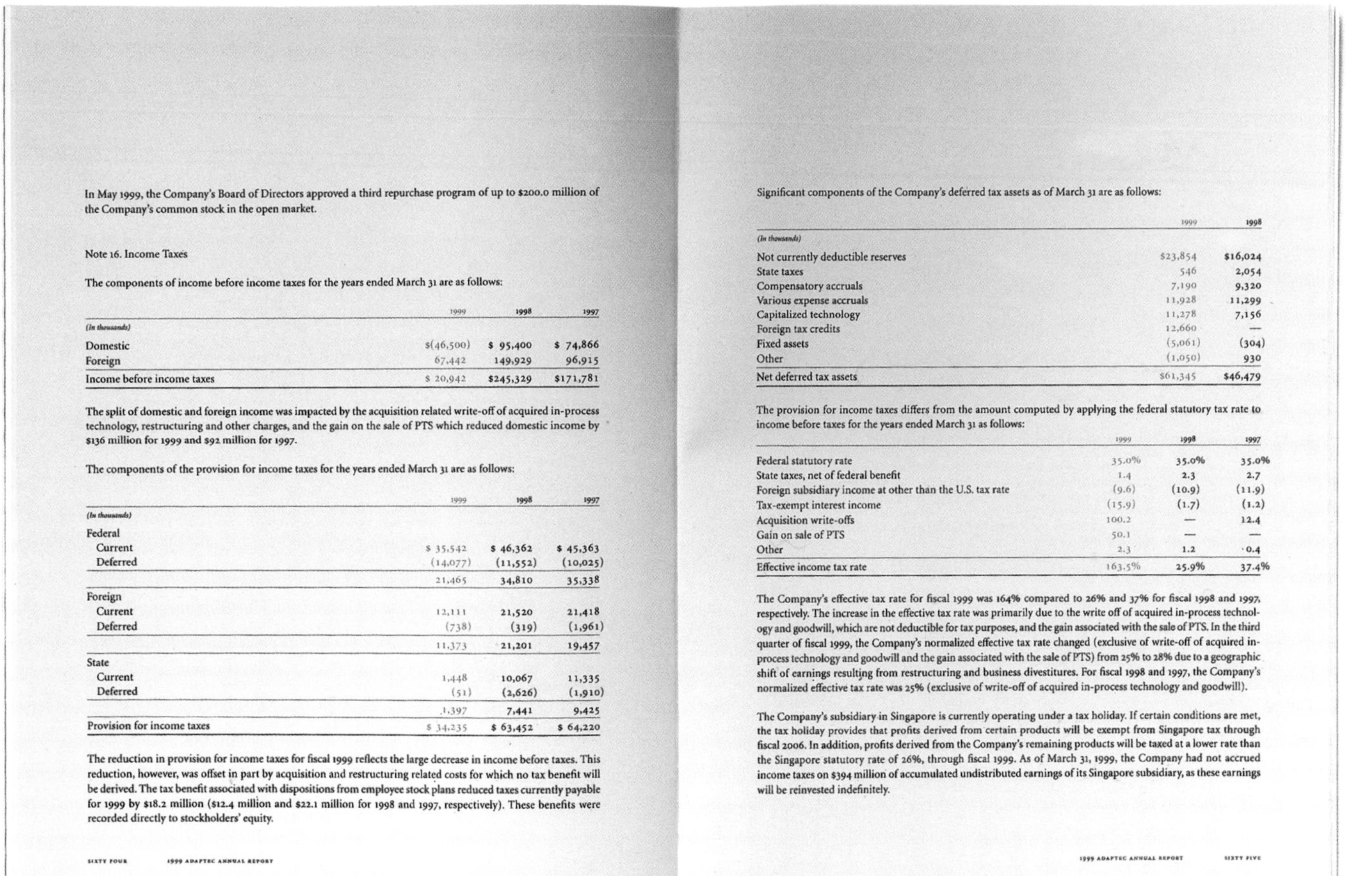

In May 1999, the Company's Board of Directors approved a third repurchase program of up to $200.0 million of the Company's common stock in the open market.

Note 16. Income Taxes

The components of income before income taxes for the years ended March 31 are as follows:

(In thousands)	1999	1998	1997
Domestic	$(46,500)	$ 95,400	$ 74,866
Foreign	67,442	149,929	96,915
Income before income taxes	$ 20,942	$245,329	$171,781

The split of domestic and foreign income was impacted by the acquisition related write-off of acquired in-process technology, restructuring and other charges, and the gain on the sale of PTS which reduced domestic income by $136 million for 1999 and $92 million for 1997.

The components of the provision for income taxes for the years ended March 31 are as follows:

(In thousands)	1999	1998	1997
Federal			
Current	$ 35,542	$ 46,362	$ 45,363
Deferred	(14,077)	(11,552)	(10,025)
	21,465	34,810	35,338
Foreign			
Current	12,111	21,520	21,418
Deferred	(738)	(319)	(1,961)
	11,373	21,201	19,457
State			
Current	1,448	10,067	11,335
Deferred	(51)	(2,626)	(1,910)
	1,397	7,441	9,425
Provision for income taxes	$ 34,235	$ 63,452	$ 64,220

The reduction in provision for income taxes for fiscal 1999 reflects the large decrease in income before taxes. This reduction, however, was offset in part by acquisition and restructuring related costs for which no tax benefit will be derived. The tax benefit associated with dispositions from employee stock plans reduced taxes currently payable for 1999 by $18.2 million ($12.4 million and $22.1 million for 1998 and 1997, respectively). These benefits were recorded directly to stockholders' equity.

SIXTY FOUR 1999 ADAPTEC ANNUAL REPORT

Significant components of the Company's deferred tax assets as of March 31 are as follows:

(In thousands)	1999	1998
Not currently deductible reserves	$23,854	$16,024
State taxes	546	2,054
Compensatory accruals	7,190	9,320
Various expense accruals	11,928	11,299
Capitalized technology	11,278	7,156
Foreign tax credits	12,660	—
Fixed assets	(5,061)	(304)
Other	(1,050)	930
Net deferred tax assets	$61,345	$46,479

The provision for income taxes differs from the amount computed by applying the federal statutory tax rate to income before taxes for the years ended March 31 as follows:

	1999	1998	1997
Federal statutory rate	35.0%	35.0%	35.0%
State taxes, net of federal benefit	1.4	2.3	2.7
Foreign subsidiary income at other than the U.S. tax rate	(9.6)	(10.9)	(11.9)
Tax-exempt interest income	(15.9)	(1.7)	(1.2)
Acquisition write-offs	100.2	—	12.4
Gain on sale of PTS	50.1	—	—
Other	2.3	1.2	0.4
Effective income tax rate	163.5%	25.9%	37.4%

The Company's effective tax rate for fiscal 1999 was 164% compared to 26% and 37% for fiscal 1998 and 1997, respectively. The increase in the effective tax rate was primarily due to the write off of acquired in-process technology and goodwill, which are not deductible for tax purposes, and the gain associated with the sale of PTS. In the third quarter of fiscal 1999, the Company's normalized effective tax rate changed (exclusive of write-off of acquired in-process technology and goodwill and the gain associated with the sale of PTS) from 25% to 28% due to a geographic shift of earnings resulting from restructuring and business divestitures. For fiscal 1998 and 1997, the Company's normalized effective tax rate was 25% (exclusive of write-off of acquired in-process technology and goodwill).

The Company's subsidiary in Singapore is currently operating under a tax holiday. If certain conditions are met, the tax holiday provides that profits derived from certain products will be exempt from Singapore tax through fiscal 2006. In addition, profits derived from the Company's remaining products will be taxed at a lower rate than the Singapore statutory rate of 26%, through fiscal 1999. As of March 31, 1999, the Company had not accrued income taxes on $394 million of accumulated undistributed earnings of its Singapore subsidiary, as these earnings will be reinvested indefinitely.

1999 ADAPTEC ANNUAL REPORT SIXTY FIVE

Overland Data

Agency: Mentus, Inc.
Art Director & Designer: Christy Van Deman
Creative Director: Tracy Mitsunaga
Copywriter: Scott Reiger

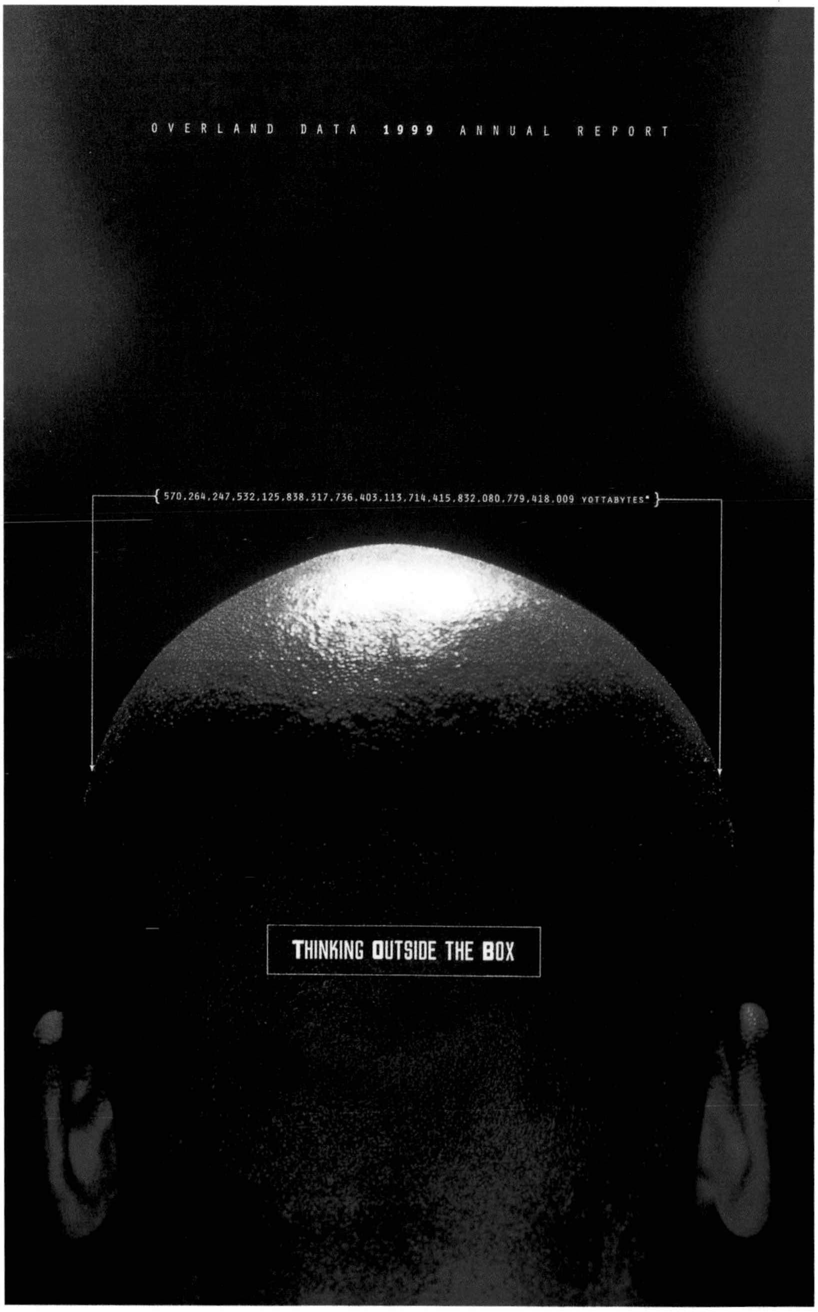
OVERLAND DATA 1999 ANNUAL REPORT
{570.264.247.532.125.838.317.736.403.113.714.415.832.080.779.418.009 YOTTABYTES*}
THINKING OUTSIDE THE BOX

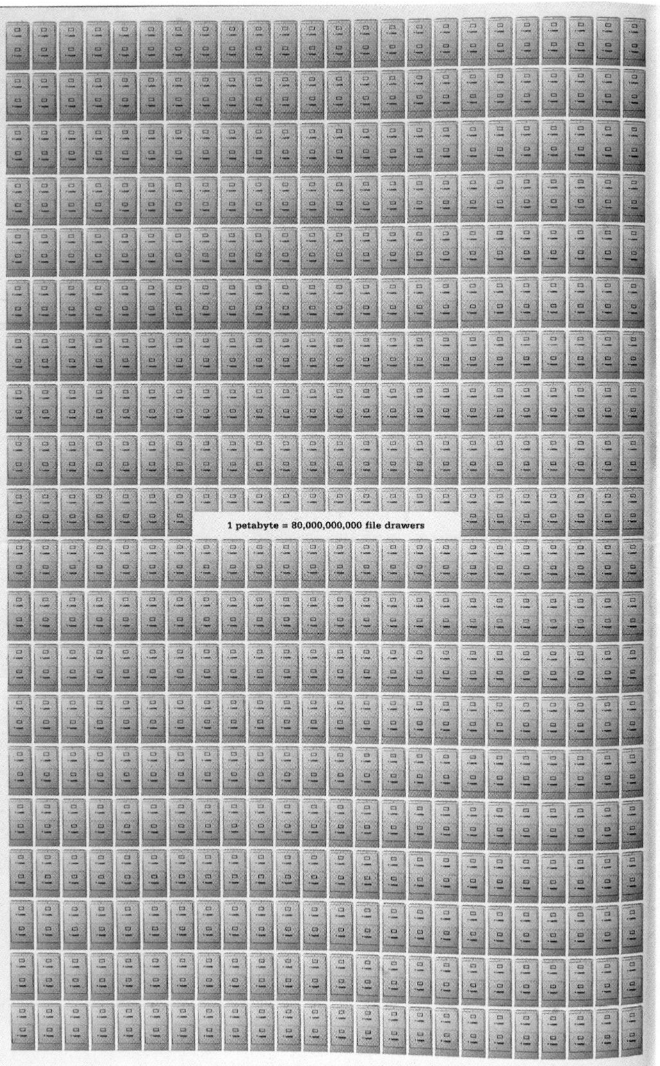
1 petabyte = 80,000,000,000 file drawers

INCREASED DATA

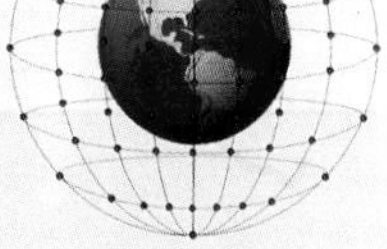

There are currently over 200 petabytes of information on distributed networks in the world. Each petabyte is the equivalent of 1,000 terabytes. One terabyte holds the equivalent of the information that would be stored in 40 million two-drawer file cabinets. That equals enough information to fill 16 trillion file drawers. Or at least it was at last count. By the time you read this page, enough data will have been generated to fill another 600,000 drawers.

INCREASED CAPACITY

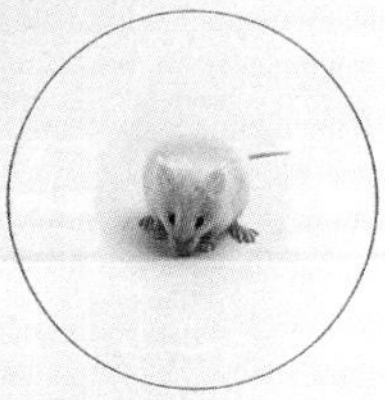

Given the tidal wave of data being generated today, what was once a manageable annoyance has now become a beastly burden. Total disk capacity shipped in calendar year 1995 was a mere 15 petabytes. In the year 2000, total disk capacity shipped is expected to exceed 400 petabytes. **If stored on paper, that would equate to two trillion pounds, or the equivalent of a herd of 200 million lumbering elephants. By the year 2002, total disk capacity shipped is expected to reach 1,300 petabytes, equating to a compound annual growth rate of 90% since 1995.**

Following the World Trade Center bombing in New York City, over 50% of the businesses that did not have off-site data recovery went out of business. After the San Francisco earthquake, 60% of the businesses that could not restore data in two weeks failed. Chances are, however, most businesses won't lose their data to a disaster. In fact, odds are considerably greater that data will be lost to simple hardware failure or power loss. And probably at the worst possible time. Clearly, given the potential risks, reliable storage and retrieval of vital data is essential in today's highly competitive business world.

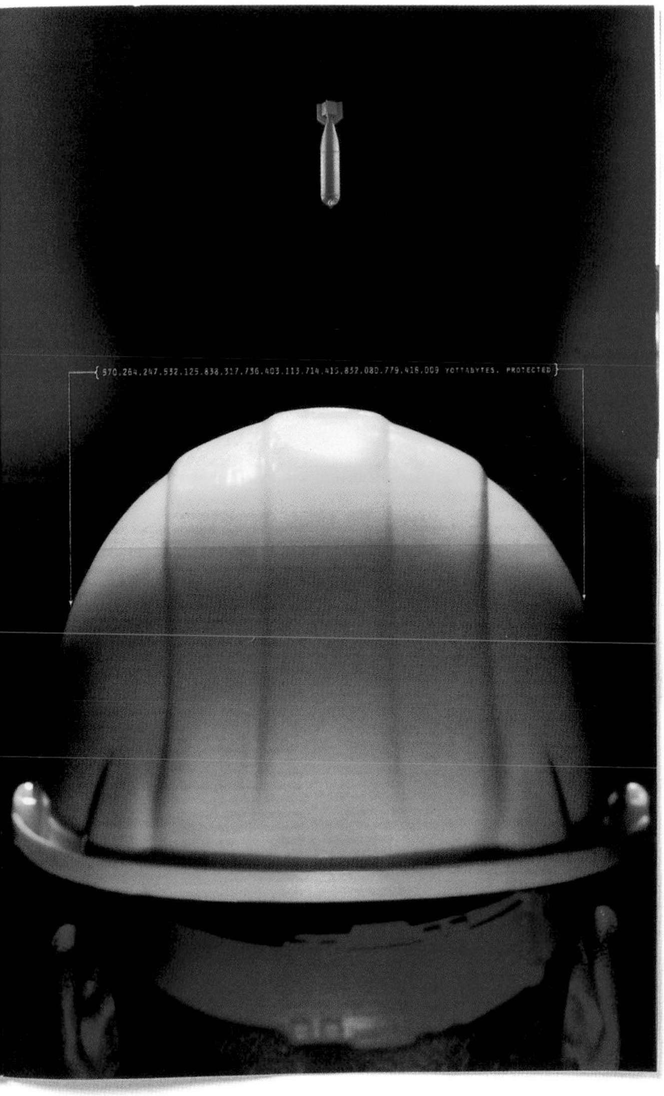
{970.264.247.532.125.838.317.736.403.113.714.415.832.080.779.418.009 YOTTABYTES. PROTECTED}

Kopin Corporation
Agency: Weymouth Design
Art & Creative Director: Tom Laidlaw
Designer: Jonathan Grove
Photographer: Michael Weymouth
Copywriter: Kopin Corporation

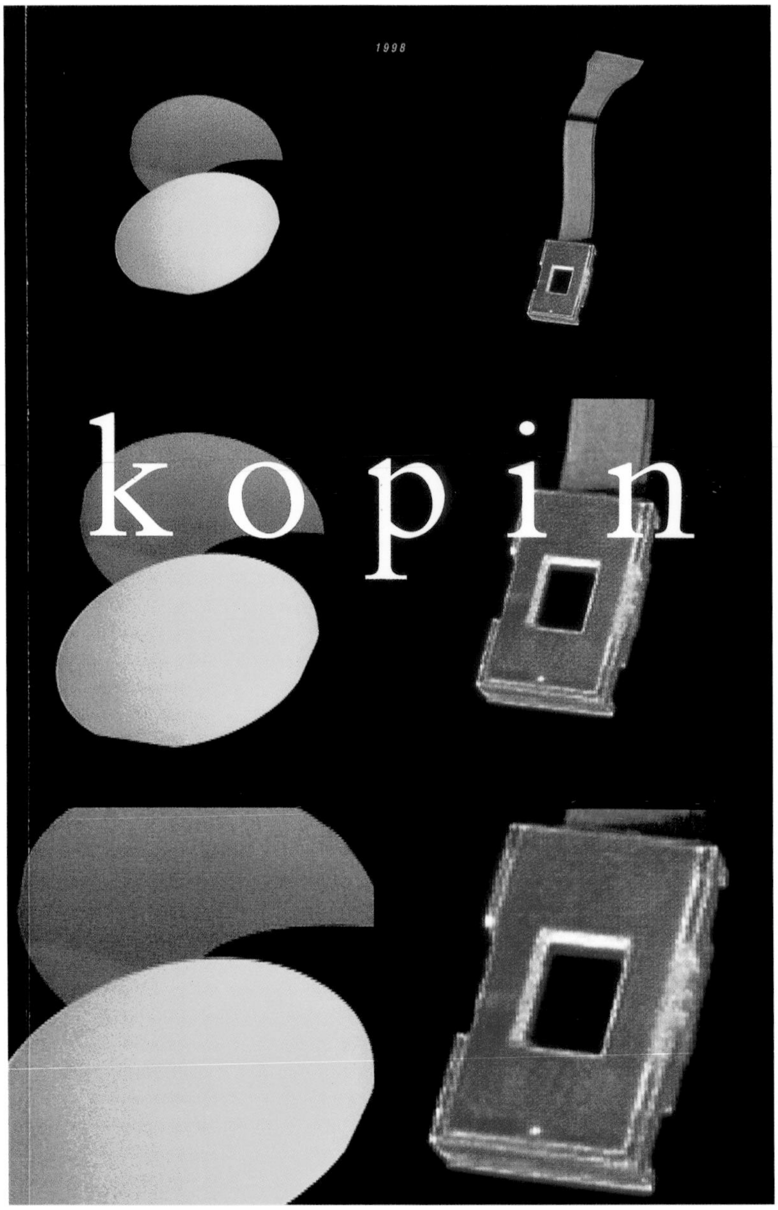
1998
kopin

Founded in 1984, Kopin holds over 125 patents and patent applications for technological breakthroughs in device wafer and flat panel display technology. Kopin applies these technologies in its fast growing businesses to develop and market products that enhance the delivery and presentation of video, voice and data.

Wireless telecommunication providers are using Kopin's device wafers for high performance integrated circuits used primarily in advanced cellular phones. Original equipment manufacturers are using Kopin's CyberDisplay family of miniature, high resolution displays to enable a new generation of ultra-portable personal communications and consumer electronics products.

Financial Highlights (in thousands, except per share data)

for the years ending dec. 31st	1998	1997	1996
Product revenues	$23,225	$13,140	$11,727
Research and development revenues	3,680	3,283	6,291
Gross profit	7,716	4,474	2,218
Net loss	(2,968)	(6,258)	(21,996)
Net loss per share	(.25)	(.57)	(1.98)

Product Revenues (dollars in millions)

for the years ending dec. 31st	
1998	$23.2
1997	$13.1
1996	$9.2
1995	$3.6
1994	$2.8

Gross Profit (dollars in millions)

for the years ending dec. 31st	
1998	$7.7
1997	$4.5
1996	$2.5
1995	$.8
1994	$.8

image

The Kopin CyberDisplay products provide the manufacturers of camcorders and digital cameras with the benefits of high resolution, low power consumption and small form factor. Preview, review and status information (for example, remaining battery life), functions which are currently provided by multiple displays, can be provided by a single CyberDisplay. The CyberDisplay's ability to provide these features will allow for the redesign of existing camcorder and digital cameras into smaller devices with superior performance.

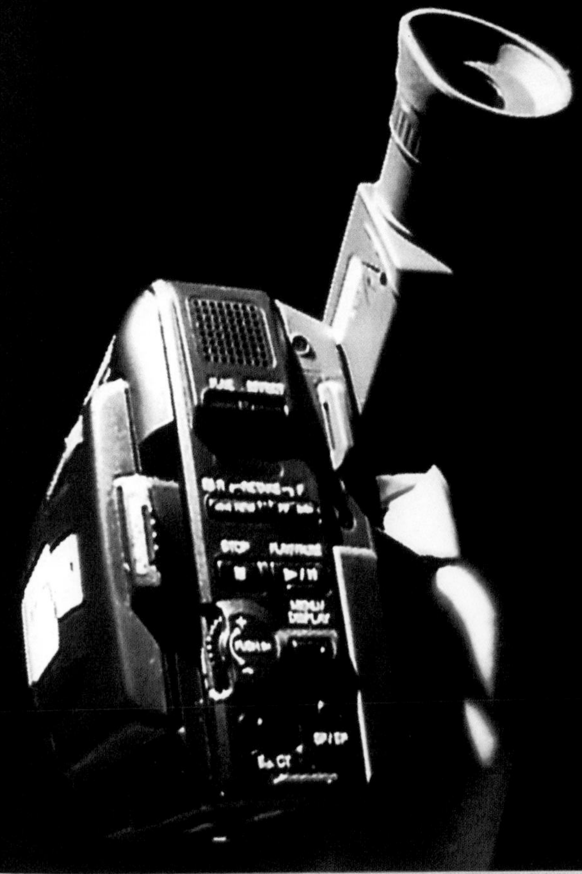

d a t a

Significant resources worldwide are being devoted to provide users of wireless telecommunications with access to data, be it e-mail, internet or other sources. Kopin's products are uniquely positioned for this convergence. Our HBT device wafers provide the performance features critical for clear signal and low power consumption. Our CyberDisplay provides the high resolution, low power consumption and small form factor to be uniquely suited as the display for data viewing on mobile communication products.

Boston

1998

Selected Consolidated Financial Data (in thousands, except per share data)

for the years ending dec. 31st	1998	1997	1996	1995	1994
Statement of Operations Data					
Total revenues	$26,905	$16,393	$ 18,018	$15,789	$13,283
Gross profit	7,716	4,474	2,238	1,102	849
Net loss	(2,968)	(6,258)	(21,596)	(8,991)	(6,694)
Net loss per share	$ (.25)	$ (.57)	$ (1.98)	$ (.95)	$ (.72)
Weighted average number of shares outstanding	12,068	11,010	10,921	9,462	9,267
Balance Sheet Data					
Cash and equivalents and marketable securities	$36,808	$19,046	$ 27,072	$41,997	$28,728
Working capital	39,359	21,466	27,687	44,727	30,566
Total assets	61,906	43,394	53,746	76,160	52,836
Long-term obligations	4,209	1,959	2,793	1,605	2,235
Stockholders' equity	51,846	35,869	40,271	61,842	43,451

Unaudited Quarterly Financial Information (in thousands, except per share data)

for the year 1998	1st Qtr.	2nd Qtr.	3rd Qtr.	4th Qtr.
Total revenues	$ 5,466	$ 6,684	$ 7,836	$ 6,919
Gross profit	1,937	2,155	2,831	793
Net loss	(611)	(175)	454	(2,636)
Net loss per share	(.05)	(.01)	.03	(.22)
Common stock prices:				
High	22 3/8	22 3/8	21	21 1/4
Low	14	16	11 7/16	11 1/2

for the year 1997	1st Qtr.	2nd Qtr.	3rd Qtr.	4th Qtr.
Total revenues	$ 3,714	$ 3,881	$ 3,908	$ 4,890
Gross profit	771	1,145	1,050	1,508
Net loss	(2,101)	(1,689)	(1,489)	(979)
Net loss per share	(.19)	(.15)	(.13)	(.09)
Common stock prices:				
High	15 3/4	16 3/4	24 5/8	29
Low	9 7/8	10 1/2	14 1/4	16 5/8

The Company has never paid dividends on its common stock and has no present plans to do so. As of December 31, 1998, there were 237 stockholders of record of the Company's Common Stock. These numbers do not reflect persons or entities who hold their stock through nominee or "street" name.

Bellwether Explorations Corporation
Agency: Squires & Company
Designer: Brandon Murphy
Photographer: Jay Rusovich
Copywriter: Rob Bensch

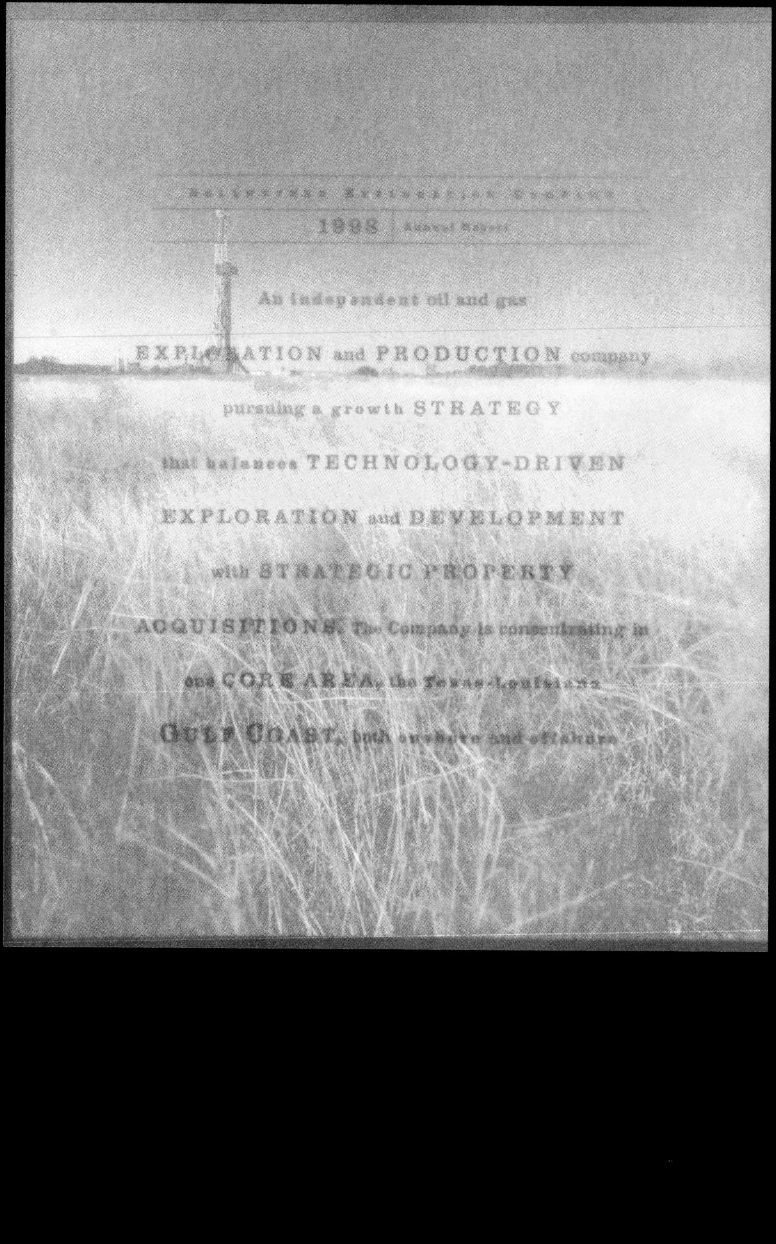
1998
An independent oil and gas
EXPLORATION and PRODUCTION company
pursuing a growth STRATEGY
that balances TECHNOLOGY-DRIVEN
EXPLORATION and DEVELOPMENT
with STRATEGIC PROPERTY
ACQUISITIONS. The Company is concentrating in
one CORE AREA, the Texas-Louisiana
GULF COAST, both onshore and offshore

Bellwether Exploration Company

1998 | Annual Report

An independent oil and gas EXPLORATION and PRODUCTION company pursuing a growth STRATEGY that balances TECHNOLOGY-DRIVEN EXPLORATION and DEVELOPMENT with STRATEGIC PROPERTY ACQUISITIONS. The Company is concentrating in one CORE AREA, the Texas-Louisiana GULF COAST, both onshore and offshore.

Performance Highlights

Dollar amounts in thousands, except per unit data

Financial Data	Fiscal years ended June 30, 1994	1995	1996	1997	Six-month transition period ended December 31, 1997	1998
Total revenue	$ 6,686	$ 13,231	$ 19,316	$ 42,760	$ 45,576	$ 75,767
Net income (loss)	$ 814	$ 941	$ 992	$ 4,645	$ 3,548	$ (77,251)
EBITDA	$ 4,158	$ 7,636	$ 10,833	$ 27,281	$ 27,992	$ 41,048
Cash flow from operations, before working capital changes	$ 3,494	$ 6,443	$ 9,072	$ 23,251	$ 21,840	$ 30,372
Earnings (loss) per share	$ 0.35	$ 0.12	$ 0.11	$ 0.46	$ 0.26	$ (5.50)
Cash flow per share	$ 1.49	$ 0.84	$ 1.00	$ 2.28	$ 1.57	$ 2.16
Weighted average common and common equivalent shares outstanding	2,322	7,716	9,052	10,201	13,876	$ 14,039
Capital expenditures	$ 11,876	$ 42,191	$ 6,977	$ 155,766	$ 20,845	$ 40,868
Current assets	$ 4,319	$ 6,627	$ 8,504	$ 35,731	$ 28,877	$ 18,184
Total assets	$ 35,870	$ 74,650	$ 67,225	$ 222,648	$ 214,757	$ 131,196
Long term debt	$ 12,797	$ 16,525	$ 13,048	$ 115,300	$ 100,000	$ 104,400
Stockholders' equity	$ 18,372	$ 45,447	$ 46,597	$ 87,924	$ 91,669	$ 14,489
Oil & gas revenues per Mcfe	$ 2.27	$ 2.01	$ 2.21	$ 2.49	$ 2.52	$ 2.09
LOE per Mcfe	$ 0.79	$ 0.68	$ 0.75	$ 0.73	$ 0.79	$ 0.72
G&A per Mcfe	$ 0.39	$ 0.41	$ 0.34	$ 0.23	$ 0.21	$ 0.24
Operating cash flow per Mcfe	$ 1.09	$ 0.92	$ 1.12	$ 1.53	$ 1.52	$ 1.13
DD&A per Mcfe	$ 0.95	$ 0.92	$ 0.98	$ 0.94	$ 0.90	$ 1.10
Operating income per Mcfe	$ 0.14	$ –	$ 0.14	$ 0.59	$ 0.62	$ 0.03
Credit Statistics						
EBITDA/Interest expense	$ 6.11	$ 6.40	$ 6.86	$ 6.76	$ 5.58	$ 3.68
Long-term Debt/EBITDA	$ 3.08	$ 2.43	$ 1.20	$ 4.23	$ 3.57	$ 2.49
Long-term Debt/Book Capitalization	$ 0.41	$ 0.29	$ 0.22	$ 0.57	$ 0.52	$ 0.88
Long-term Debt/Market Capitalization	$ 0.63	$ 0.34	$ 0.21	$ 0.83	$ 0.65	$ 1.49
Long-term Debt/PV-10	$ 1.06	$ 0.50	$ 0.27	$ 0.55	$ 0.50	$ 0.90
Long-term Debt/Bcfe	$ 7.84	$ 4.38	$ 1.84	$ 7.36	$ 5.71	$ 2.98

Operational Data	1994	1995	1996	1997	1997	1998
Average daily production						
Oil (Bbl)	195	592	913	2,339	5,729	6,295
Gas (Mcf)	3,304	8,033	13,932	28,910	60,829	58,362
Gas equivalent (Mcfe)	4,474	11,585	19,410	42,944	95,203	96,132
% Natural Gas	74%	69%	72%	67%	64%	61%
Average price						
Oil per Bbl	$ 15.27	$ 16.89	$ 17.81	$ 17.41	$ 19.34	$ 11.34
Gas per Mcf	$ 2.17	$ 1.66	$ 2.02	$ 2.29	$ 2.56	$ 2.05
Reserves						
Oil & liquids (MBbl)	393	2,597	1,808	16,030	14,809	10,061
Gas (MMcf)	10,671	30,169	33,194	127,940	125,960	111,585
Gas equivalent (MMcfe)	13,029	45,741	44,042	224,120	214,814	171,951
% Natural Gas	82%	66%	75%	57%	59%	65%
SEC PV-10 value (pre-tax)	$ 12,044	$ 37,291	$ 48,140	$ 210,715	$ 200,232	$ 115,960

Core Area of Operations

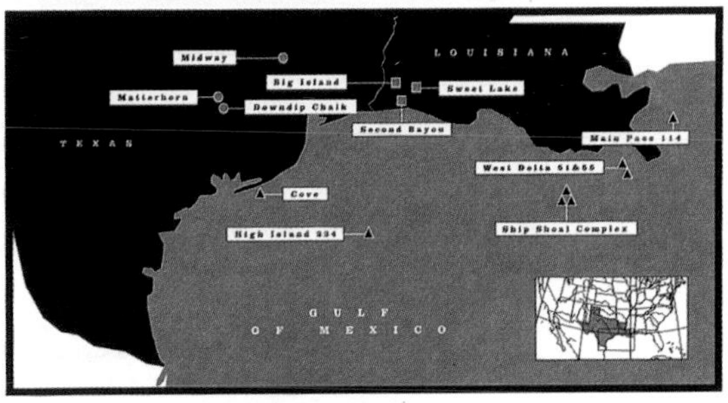
Midway
Matterhorn
Big Island
Downdip Chalk
Sweet Lake
Second Bayou
LOUISIANA
TEXAS
Main Pass 114
West Delta 51&55
Cove
High Island 334
Ship Shoal Complex
GULF OF MEXICO

Exploration Prospect Inventory

	Operator	Number of Prospects	Expected Spud Date	Expected WI%	Risk Cost ($MM)	Unrisked Net Potential (Bcfe)
Texas Gulf Coast						
Matterhorn	Bellwether	1	April 1999	50	0.44	59
Downdip Chalk	Bellwether	2	August 1999	40	1.60	41
Midway	Bellwether	1	June 1999	50	0.45	25
South Louisiana						
Big Island	Mayne & Mertz	4	June 1999	25	1.91	47
Second Bayou	Newfield	2	May 1999	15-33	2.21	26
Sweet Lake	Clayton Williams	6	January 2000	19	3.42	21
Offshore Gulf of Mexico						
West Delta 51	CXY	1	January 2000	50	1.50	38
Cove	Bellwether	2	August 1999	20-90	2.38	33
Main Pass 114	Bellwether	1	March 2000	35	0.78	28
High Island 334	Spirit 76	1	October 1999	25	1.00	21
West Delta 55	Bellwether	1	July 1999	17	0.50	13
Ship Shoal Complex	Kerr McGee	3	July 1999	22	1.23	11
Other						
Mist	Enerfin	10	May 1999	50	1.25	10
Totals		35			18.87	373

Bellwether Exploration Company | 1 | 1998 Annual Report To Shareholders

OIL COUNTRY

Since the $141 million producing property acquisition completed in April 1997, Bellwether has pursued a more balanced growth strategy emphasizing technology-driven exploration and development and strategic property acquisitions. In implementing its strategy, the Company has focused on developing core areas, concentrating its activities in a reduced number of mostly operated, higher value properties and building an inventory of impactful, internally generated exploration prospects. **The Company currently has one core area, the Texas-Louisiana Gulf Coast, both onshore and in shallow waters offshore.** Through its focus on core areas, operatorship of major properties and internal prospect generation, Bellwether can better utilize its existing infrastructure and technical database, superior technical expertise and experience and demonstrated regional business know-how. This strategy enhances Bellwether's leverage to create and develop business opportunities and ultimately lower its finding and development costs. **A favorable acquisition marketplace is developing.** Low oil and gas prices have resulted in a tight capital market and a number of companies with distressed balance sheets. These companies have a need to merge or sell assets. In addition, the recent trend of mergers within the energy business and employee layoffs at many major oil companies will likely spur more asset sales. Bellwether is well positioned to take advantage of improving acquisition economics. The Company has more than $50 million of capacity under its bank credit facility and acquisitions are a core competency. The Company has grown historically primarily through a series of successful acquisitions and mergers. Our acquisition efforts will target opportunities within our core area, where value is predominantly in operated properties with identified upside.

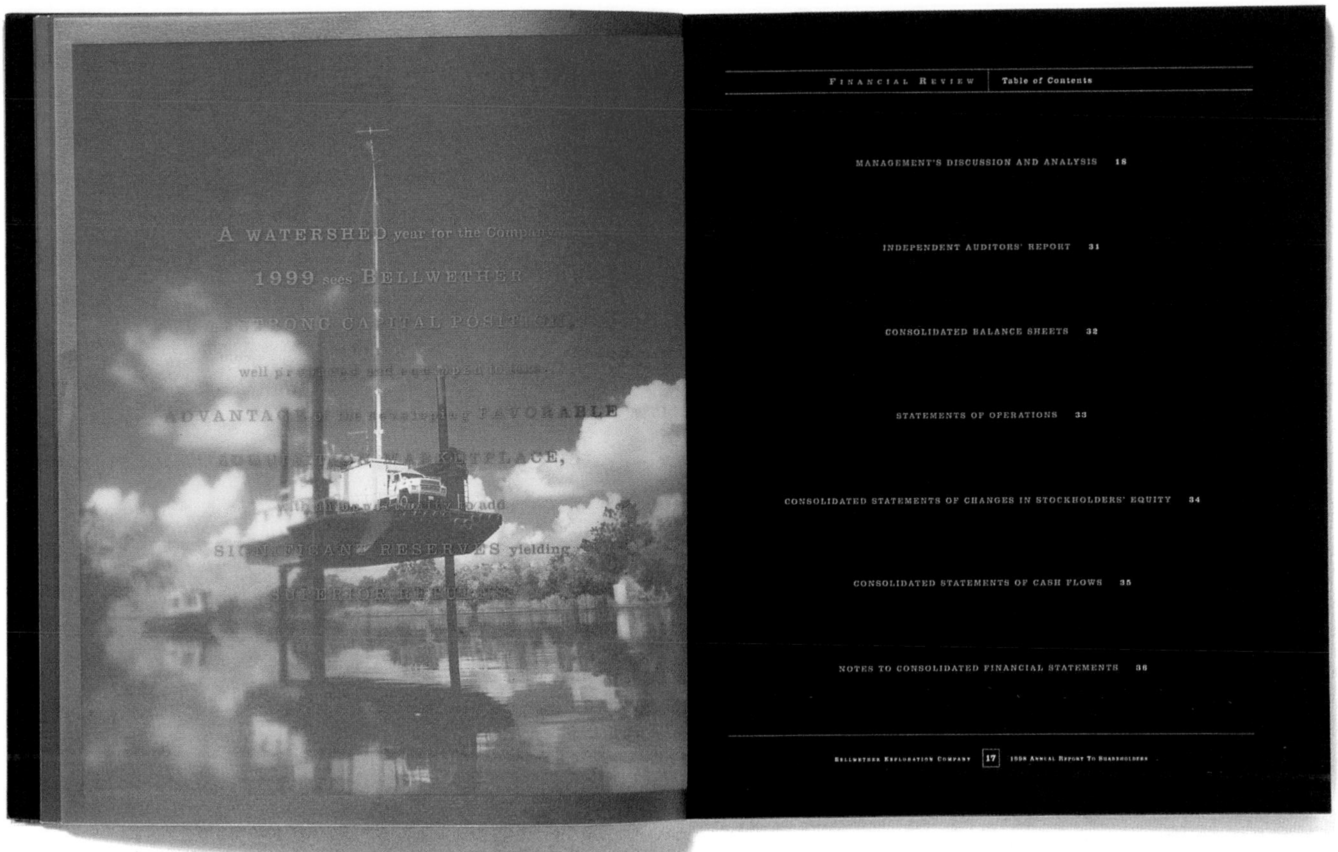
A WATERSHED year for the Company
1999 sees BELLWETHER
FINANCIAL REVIEW
Table of Contents
MANAGEMENT'S DISCUSSION AND ANALYSIS 18
INDEPENDENT AUDITORS' REPORT 31
CONSOLIDATED BALANCE SHEETS 32
STATEMENTS OF OPERATIONS 33
CONSOLIDATED STATEMENTS OF CHANGES IN STOCKHOLDERS' EQUITY 34
CONSOLIDATED STATEMENTS OF CASH FLOWS 35
NOTES TO CONSOLIDATED FINANCIAL STATEMENTS 36
17

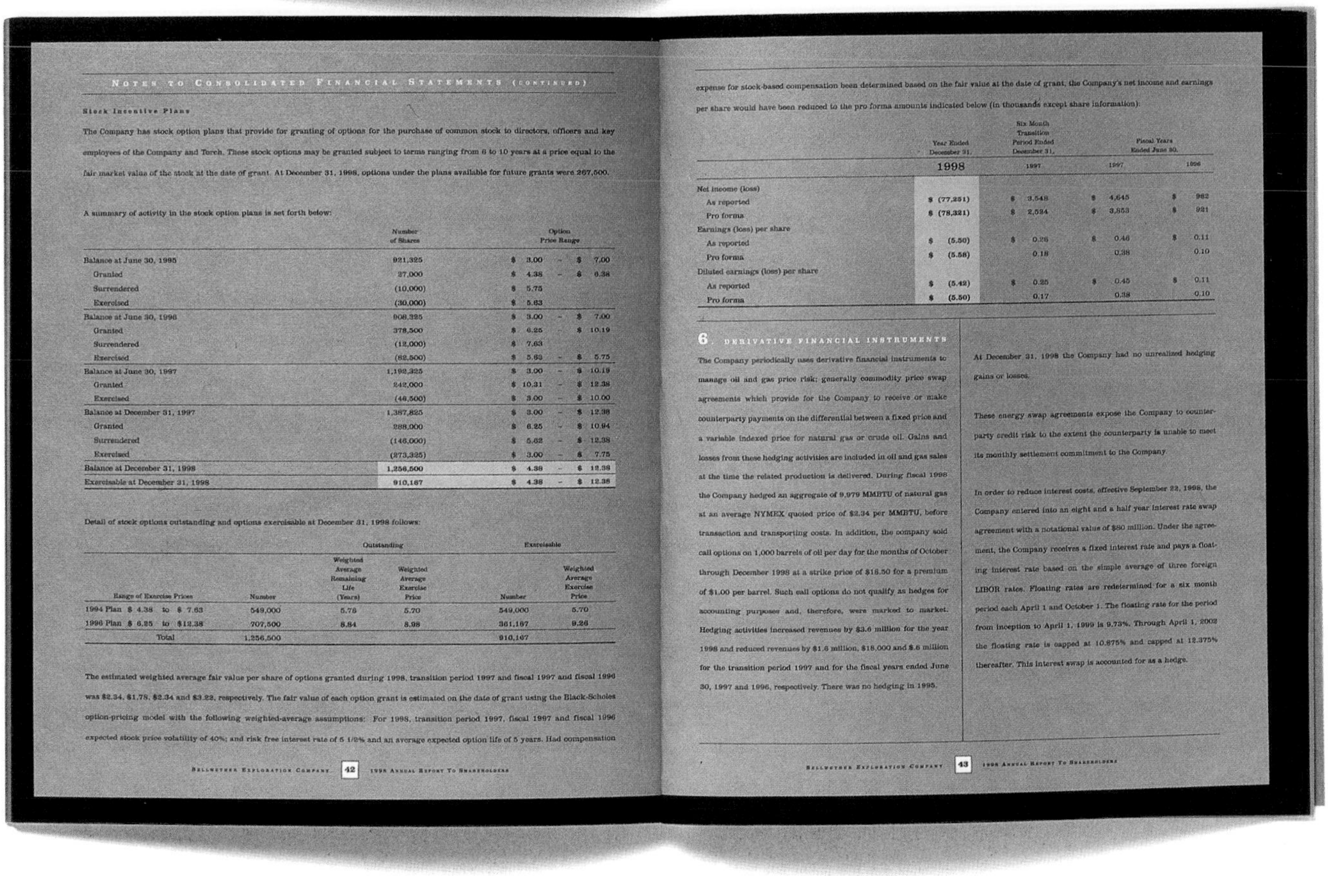
NOTES TO CONSOLIDATED FINANCIAL STATEMENTS (CONTINUED)
1998
6. DERIVATIVE FINANCIAL INSTRUMENTS
42
43

Nike

Agency: Nike, Inc.
Art Director: David Odusanya
Creative Director: Greg Hoffman
Designers: David Odusanya, Adam Cohn
Photographers: Jim Appleton, Numerov
Copywriter: Stanley Hainsworth

nike
ANNUAL
REPORT
.99
LEAN

ANNUAL
nike REPORT
.99
LEAN

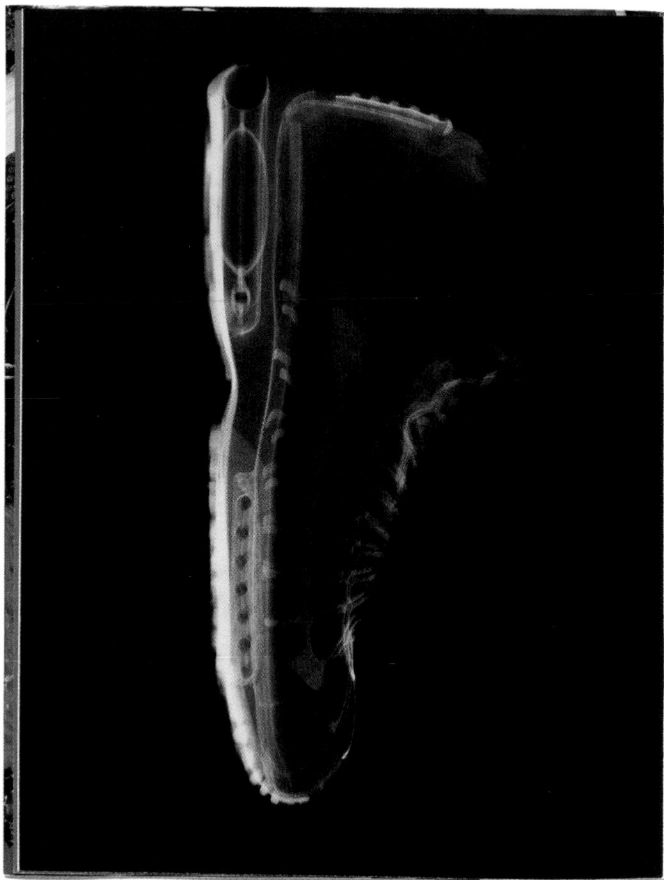

Self-Examination

When asked to describe our fiscal 1999 financial performance, our President, COO and chief soccer junkie Tom Clarke characterized the year as "a hard-fought draw." Revenues decreased for the first time since 1994, down eight percent for the year. Three of our four regions were down in revenues with Europe the only exception. Revenues in Japan fell by one third. Michael Jordan retired. The National Basketball Association was forced to truncate its season due to a prolonged labor dispute.

Sounds like a recipe for disappointment and things certainly were headed in that direction if we hadn't chosen the path of vigilant self-examination. In our life as a public company, we have endured sales declines on several occasions. During those cycles we would put our heads down and plow ahead, firm in the belief that our vision was correct, but the execution may have gone a bit astray.

In fiscal 1999, we recognized that bumps in the road for a $9 billion company have a greater capacity to permanently injure than they did a few years back. Our size had become our greatest challenge. Running the same offense that we did in the past was not going to put us back on the path of growth.

So if fiscal 1998 was spent in the emergency room, fiscal 1999 was spent partially in post-op and partially in rehab. We put our organization under the microscope, seeking to define what NIKE needed to look like on the precipice of a new century. And while we may not feel totally healed, we believe strongly in our future and our ability to make it happen.

We cut operating expenses by almost $200 million, enabling us to bring net income in relatively flat for the year when you factor out the restructuring charges. Every nook and cranny was examined. One result was an additional nine percent reduction in headcount. Not fun stuff, but necessary measures regardless.

Corporate 62, 63

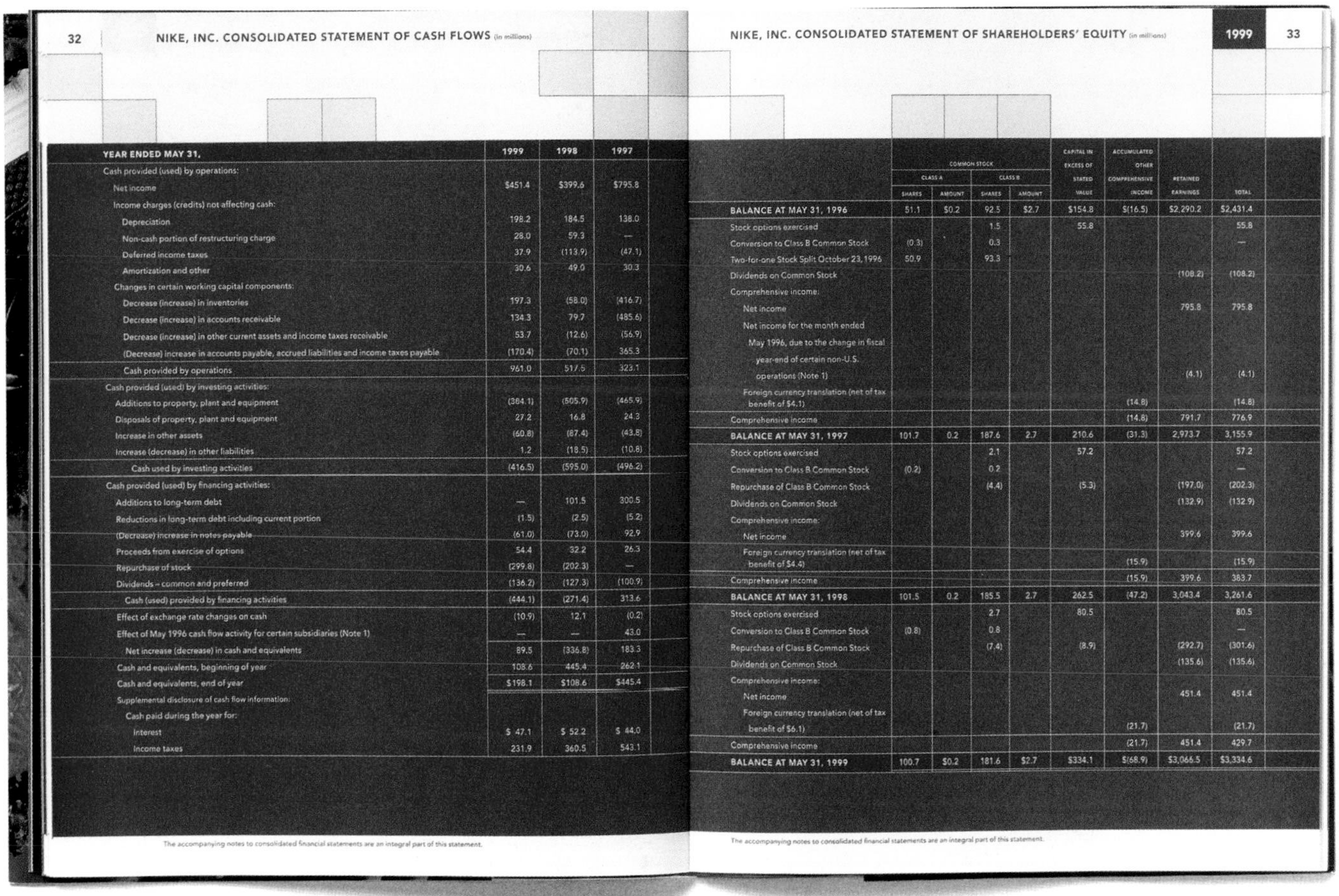

32 NIKE, INC. CONSOLIDATED STATEMENT OF CASH FLOWS (in millions)

YEAR ENDED MAY 31,	1999	1998	1997
Cash provided (used) by operations:			
Net income	$451.4	$399.6	$795.8
Income charges (credits) not affecting cash:			
Depreciation	198.2	184.5	138.0
Non-cash portion of restructuring charge	28.0	59.3	—
Deferred income taxes	37.9	(113.9)	(47.1)
Amortization and other	30.6	49.0	30.3
Changes in certain working capital components:			
Decrease (increase) in inventories	197.3	(58.0)	(416.7)
Decrease (increase) in accounts receivable	134.3	79.7	(485.6)
Decrease (increase) in other current assets and income taxes receivable	53.7	(12.6)	(56.9)
(Decrease) increase in accounts payable, accrued liabilities and income taxes payable	(170.4)	(70.1)	365.3
Cash provided by operations	961.0	517.5	323.1
Cash provided (used) by investing activities:			
Additions to property, plant and equipment	(384.1)	(505.9)	(465.9)
Disposals of property, plant and equipment	27.2	16.8	24.3
Increase in other assets	(60.8)	(87.4)	(43.8)
Increase (decrease) in other liabilities	1.2	(18.5)	(10.8)
Cash used by investing activities	(416.5)	(595.0)	(496.2)
Cash provided (used) by financing activities:			
Additions to long-term debt	—	101.5	300.5
Reductions in long-term debt including current portion	(1.5)	(2.5)	(5.2)
(Decrease) increase in notes payable	(61.0)	(73.0)	92.9
Proceeds from exercise of options	54.4	32.2	26.3
Repurchase of stock	(299.8)	(202.3)	—
Dividends – common and preferred	(136.2)	(127.3)	(100.9)
Cash (used) provided by financing activities	(444.1)	(271.4)	313.6
Effect of exchange rate changes on cash	(10.9)	12.1	(0.2)
Effect of May 1996 cash flow activity for certain subsidiaries (Note 1)	—	—	43.0
Net increase (decrease) in cash and equivalents	89.5	(336.8)	183.3
Cash and equivalents, beginning of year	108.6	445.4	262.1
Cash and equivalents, end of year	$198.1	$108.6	$445.4
Supplemental disclosure of cash flow information:			
Cash paid during the year for:			
Interest	$ 47.1	$ 52.2	$ 44.0
Income taxes	231.9	360.5	543.1

The accompanying notes to consolidated financial statements are an integral part of this statement.

NIKE, INC. CONSOLIDATED STATEMENT OF SHAREHOLDERS' EQUITY (in millions) 1999 33

	COMMON STOCK				CAPITAL IN EXCESS OF STATED VALUE	ACCUMULATED OTHER COMPREHENSIVE INCOME	RETAINED EARNINGS	TOTAL
	CLASS A		CLASS B					
	SHARES	AMOUNT	SHARES	AMOUNT				
BALANCE AT MAY 31, 1996	51.1	$0.2	92.5	$2.7	$154.8	$(16.5)	$2,290.2	$2,431.4
Stock options exercised			1.5		55.8			55.8
Conversion to Class B Common Stock	(0.3)		0.3					—
Two-for-one Stock Split October 23, 1996	50.9		93.3					
Dividends on Common Stock							(108.2)	(108.2)
Comprehensive income:								
Net income							795.8	795.8
Net income for the month ended May 1996, due to the change in fiscal year-end of certain non-U.S. operations (Note 1)							(4.1)	(4.1)
Foreign currency translation (net of tax benefit of $4.1)						(14.8)		(14.8)
Comprehensive income						(14.8)	791.7	776.9
BALANCE AT MAY 31, 1997	101.7	0.2	187.6	2.7	210.6	(31.3)	2,973.7	3,155.9
Stock options exercised			2.1		57.2			57.2
Conversion to Class B Common Stock	(0.2)		0.2					—
Repurchase of Class B Common Stock			(4.4)		(5.3)		(197.0)	(202.3)
Dividends on Common Stock							(132.9)	(132.9)
Comprehensive income:								
Net income							399.6	399.6
Foreign currency translation (net of tax benefit of $4.4)						(15.9)		(15.9)
Comprehensive income						(15.9)	399.6	383.7
BALANCE AT MAY 31, 1998	101.5	0.2	185.5	2.7	262.5	(47.2)	3,043.4	3,261.6
Stock options exercised			2.7		80.5			80.5
Conversion to Class B Common Stock	(0.8)		0.8					—
Repurchase of Class B Common Stock			(7.4)		(8.9)		(292.7)	(301.6)
Dividends on Common Stock							(135.6)	(135.6)
Comprehensive income:								
Net income							451.4	451.4
Foreign currency translation (net of tax benefit of $6.1)						(21.7)		(21.7)
Comprehensive income						(21.7)	451.4	429.7
BALANCE AT MAY 31, 1999	100.7	$0.2	181.6	$2.7	$334.1	$(68.9)	$3,066.5	$3,334.6

The accompanying notes to consolidated financial statements are an integral part of this statement.

Yageo Corporation
Agency: JRV International
Creative Director: Van So
Designer: Pacey Chao
Photographer: Leung Ka Tai
Copywriters: Chan Wei-Shiung, R.V. Dougherty

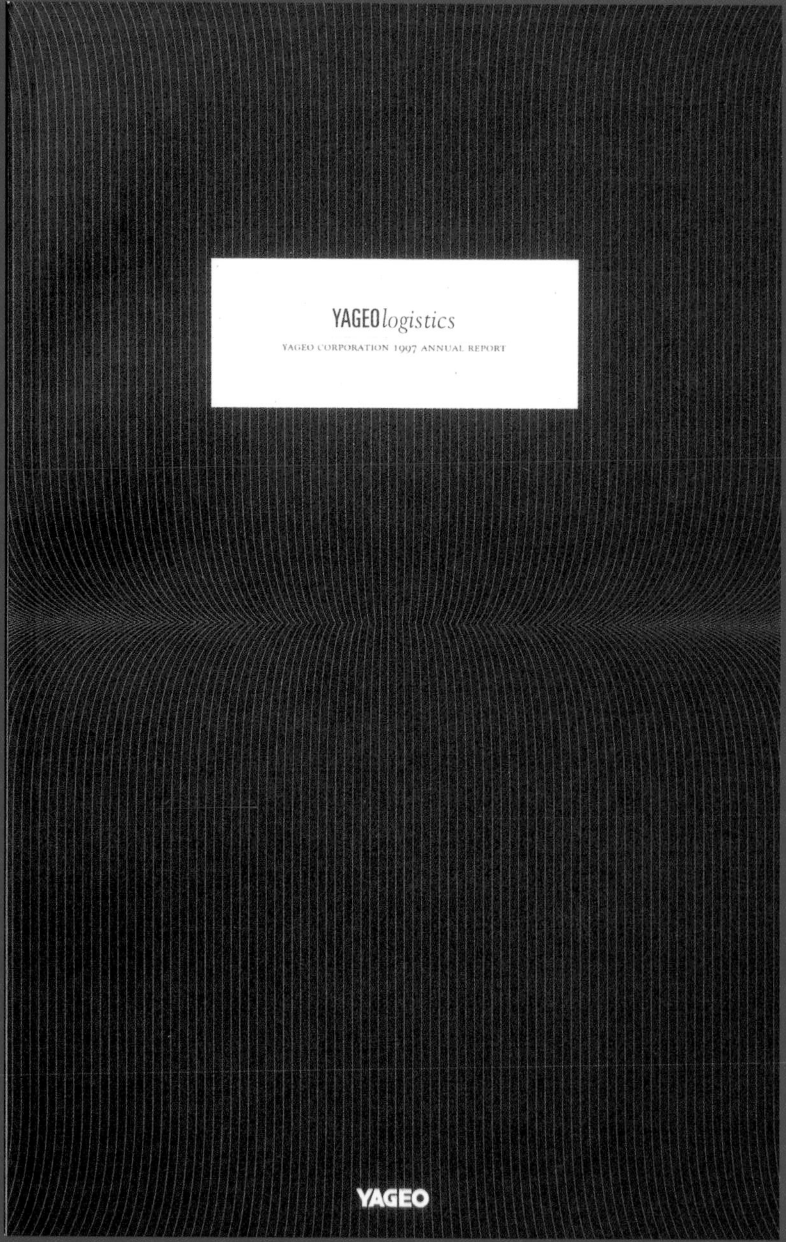
YAGEO logistics
YAGEO CORPORATION 1997 ANNUAL REPORT
YAGEO

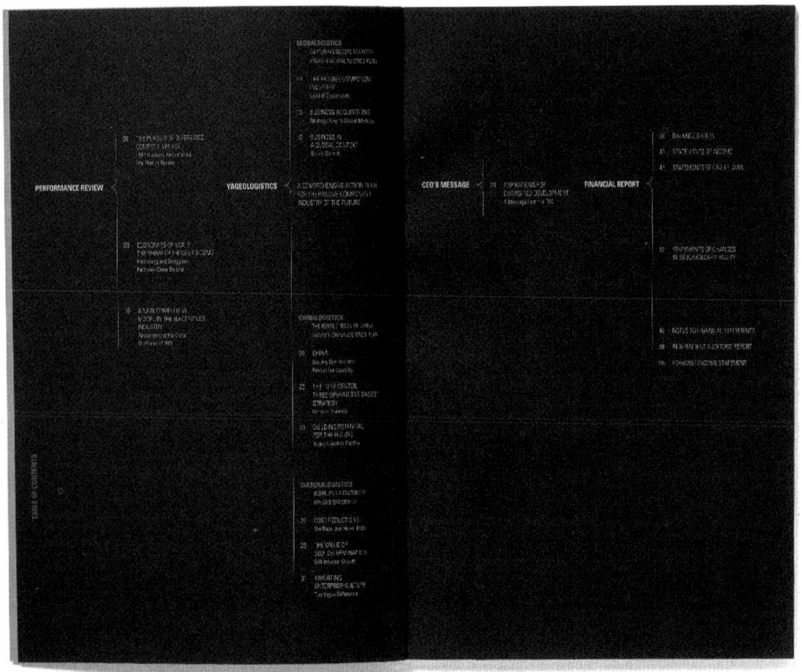
PERFORMANCE REVIEW
YAGEOLOGISTICS
CEO'S MESSAGE
FINANCIAL REPORT

Shorewood Packaging
Agency: Addison
Art & Creative Director: David Kohler
Designer: Anna Tan
Photographer: William Vasquez
Copywriter: Elaine Bennett

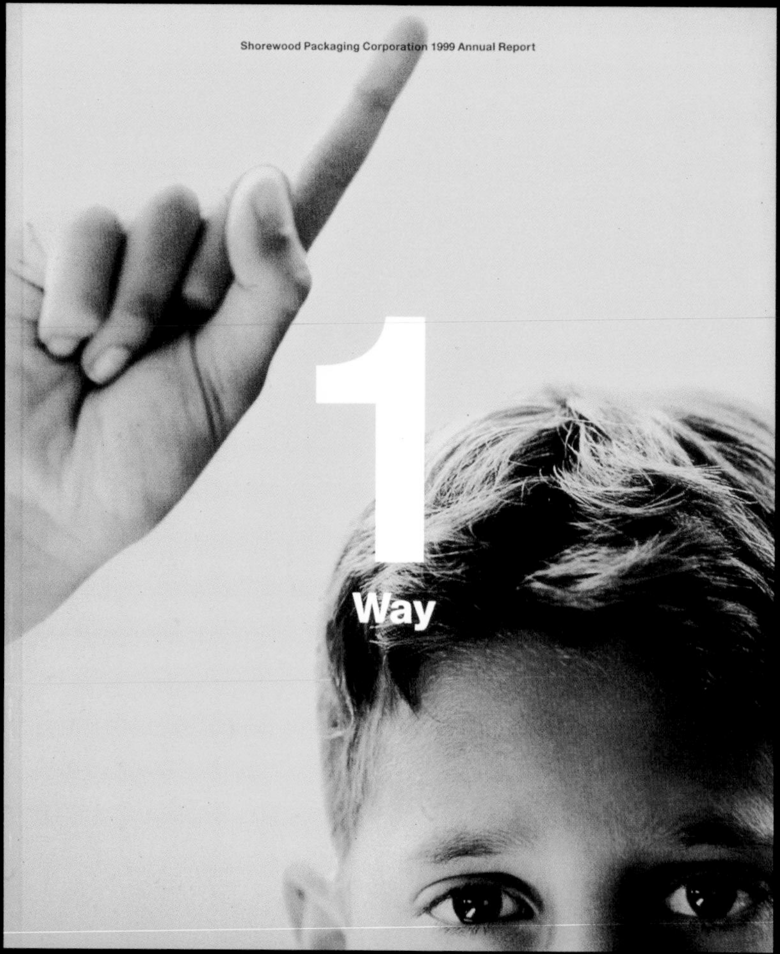

Shorewood Packaging Corporation 1999 Annual Report
1
Way

1
World
Whomever we serve – manufacturers of software, cosmetics, tobacco, sporting goods, pharmaceuticals, or music... Whatever task we undertake – creating unique structural designs for packaging, developing new technology, ensuring the quality of every job we run...Wherever in the world we operate...We do things 1 Way – the Shorewood Way.
To serve our global customer base, we operate 16 plants in the United States, Canada, and China – featuring the most advanced equipment. Digital prepress technology and a digital network linking our plants together mean that we can run a job in China or in North America with identical results.

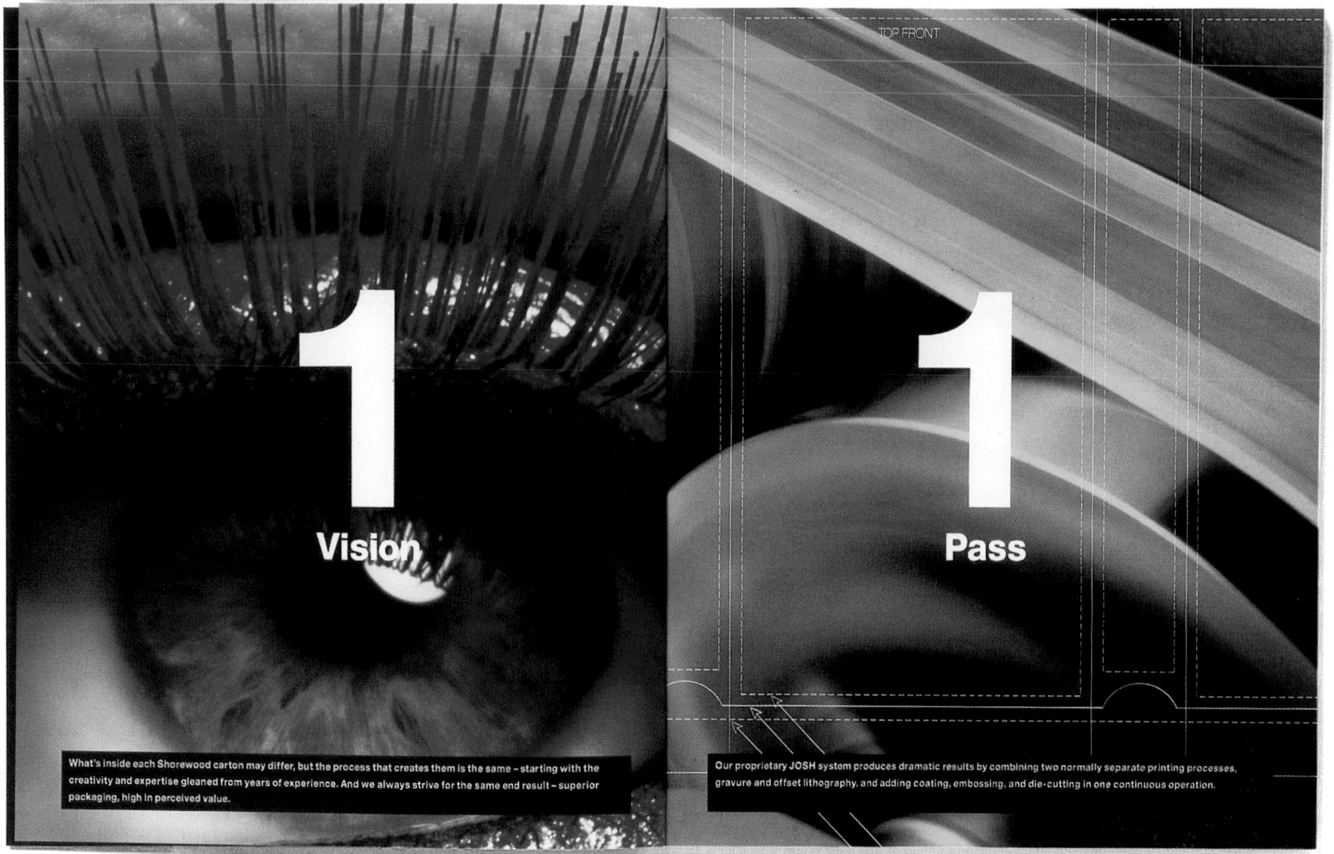
1
Vision
What's inside each Shorewood carton may differ, but the process that creates them is the same – starting with the creativity and expertise gleaned from years of experience. And we always strive for the same end result – superior packaging, high in perceived value.
TOP FRONT
1
Pass
Our proprietary JOSH system produces dramatic results by combining two normally separate printing processes, gravure and offset lithography, and adding coating, embossing, and die-cutting in one continuous operation.

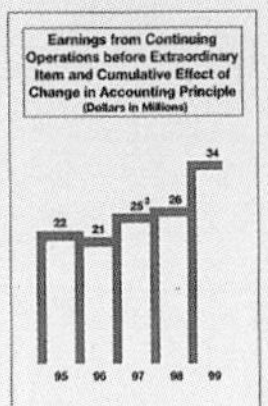
Earnings from Continuing Operations before Extraordinary Item and Cumulative Effect of Change in Accounting Principle
(Dollars in Millions)
22
21
25[2]
26
34
95
96
97
98
99

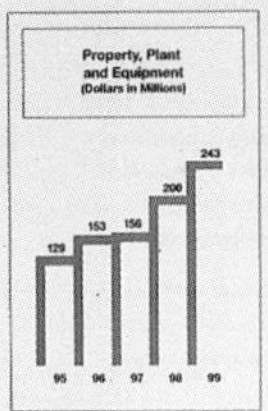
Property, Plant and Equipment
(Dollars in Millions)
129
153
156
200
243
95
96
97
98
99

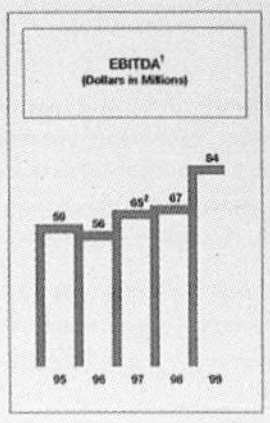
EBITDA[1]
(Dollars in Millions)
59
56
65[2]
67
84
95
96
97
98
99

[1]Earnings from operations (before $3.5 million of equipment write-down in 1999) plus depreciation and amortization.
[2]1997 was a 53-week year.

While China is certainly a new challenge for us, it is also a market of enormous potential. China will arguably become one of the world's major packaging markets. It has always been our intent to find an experienced partner to help us take advantage of opportunities there. Westvaco provides a perfect strategic fit for several reasons. From a financial perspective, Westvaco purchased a 45% interest in our Guangzhou plant for $22.7 million including a $5 million premium above our cost. The proceeds from this transaction were used to pay down debt. Westvaco also brings great value to Shorewood in terms of their knowledge of the China market. For two decades, Westvaco has been doing business in China exporting paper, paperboard and specialty chemicals to Chinese customers. We look forward to working with Westvaco on new marketing and product development programs.

1 WAY, THE SHOREWOOD WAY

Innovation is at the core of Shorewood's success and has been so for the last 32 years. Since our breakthrough development of the Shorepak® record jacket, we have embraced the newest technologies and invested heavily in Research and Development and hard-core capital expenditures. In today's world especially, we operate in a very competitive marketplace with a continually changing landscape. Fueled by our strong operating cash flow, Shorewood's commitment to technological advances has enabled us to surpass our competitors by providing superior and revolutionary packaging.

Today, we are without question the largest manufacturer of printed packaging for the entertainment and multimedia markets in North America. To support our customers worldwide, we have expanded to China and are looking at opportunities in Europe and South America.

At the same time, we must continually improve and implement changes to serve our existing customers and ensure our future growth together. With this in mind, we have broadened the number of services

we offer – unique services, like our Shorewood Technology Center and award-winning structural design from Shorewood Creative. Some of our innovations, like the JOSH system and Shorebrite inks, have yet to be duplicated by our competitors.

Shorewood Packaging of today – nearly 3,800 employees strong on two continents – may be dramatically larger than ever envisioned by its founder, but we are motivated by the same principles:

- ☐ Listen to our customers
- ☐ Create unique and effective packaging solutions
- ☐ Implement the latest advances in printing and manufacturing technology
- ☐ Train our people for advancement
- ☐ Ensure quality and consistency of our product
- ☐ Meet our commitments on time
- ☐ Satisfy our customers

This is the Shorewood Way, the one and only way we do business. While respecting our roots as a family business, we have developed into a very unique entrepreneurial company that has taken on global proportions. And, as dramatic as our growth has been in the last 13 years since becoming a public company, we have that much more opportunity ahead of us. With our seasoned infrastructure of professionals, we are stronger and better positioned than ever before.

On the pages that follow, you will see the Shorewood Way illustrated, with concrete examples of packaging solutions created for our customers. You will also see why we are so proud of the men and women of Shorewood Packaging who are dedicated to growing our first-rate business: their hard work and unfailing commitment are evident in every package we create.

Marc P. Shore
Chairman of the Board and
Chief Executive Officer

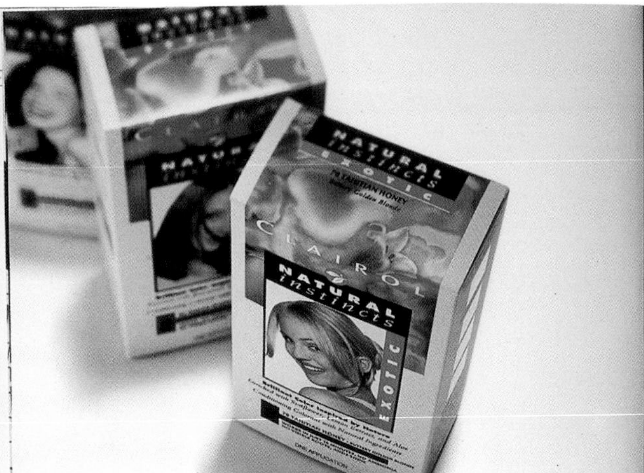
CLAIROL
NATURAL instincts
EXOTIC

MARKET:
Hair Coloring
CLIENT:
Clairol
PRODUCT:
Natural Instincts *Exotic* Hair Color

CHALLENGE:
Produce packaging for a line of subtly different hair colors – and get the colors exactly right each time.

SOLUTION:
We used direct-to-plate technology to provide maximum color consistency for this complex, 14-color, double-coated carton, which required three passes through the press.

CASE: 3

NIKE PRECISION
DISTANCE
MAXIMUM LINEAR FLIGHT

MARKET:
Sporting Goods
CLIENT:
Nike, Inc.
PRODUCT:
Nike Precision Distance golf balls

CHALLENGE:
Develop packaging in strict confidentiality for maximum impact at product launch.

SOLUTION:
We tightened security at both the Shorewood Technology Center and our manufacturing plant – temporarily enclosing the production line. Confidentiality was kept for nine months, at which time the product was released in a complex package that included windowing, embossing, metallic inks and UV coating.

CASE: 4

MOTOROLA
Tonka
SEARCH & RESCUE
MARKET:
Consumer Electronics
CLIENT:
Motorola
PRODUCT:
Iridium Satellite cell phone
CHALLENGE:
Create an electronics package that reflects the cutting-edge technology of the product inside.
SOLUTION:
Working closely with the client's design firm, Lipson, Alport, Glass & Associates, we suggested using rainbow holographic laminated stock to provide a high-impact, high-tech look.
1999 Clio Award (Silver).
CASE: 5
16
MARKET:
Multimedia
CLIENT:
Sonopress for Hasbro Interactive
PRODUCT:
Children's games on CD-ROM
CHALLENGE:
Present durable, child-safe, nontoxic packaging for children's CD-ROM games.
SOLUTION:
The Q-Pack. Its high-impact polystyrene and paperboard construction won't shatter, crack, or fall apart like the traditional CD jewel box. Autoloads on standard equipment. The Q-Pack won the 1994 IDEA Award (Bronze) from IDSA/Business Week.
CASE: 6
17

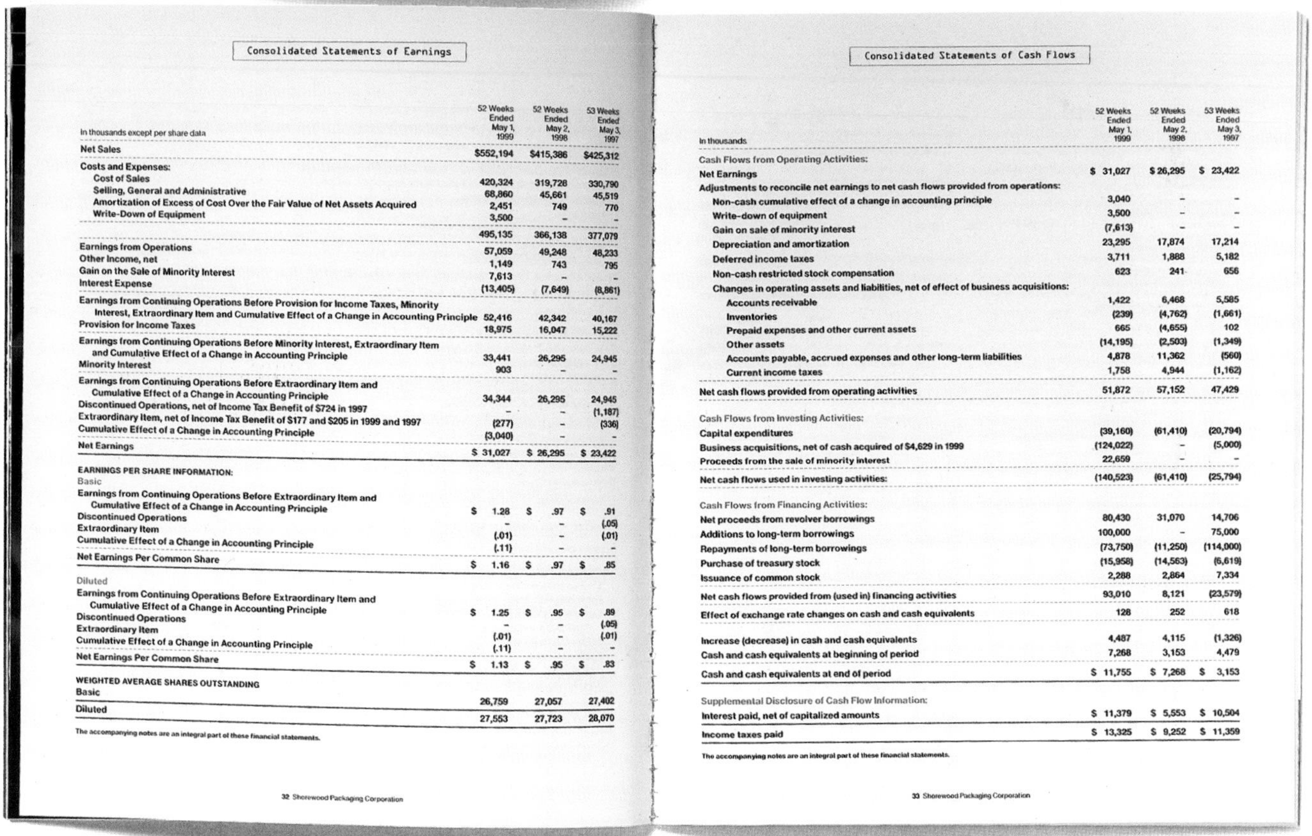

Consolidated Statements of Earnings

In thousands except per share data	52 Weeks Ended May 1, 1999	52 Weeks Ended May 2, 1998	53 Weeks Ended May 3, 1997
Net Sales	$552,194	$415,386	$425,312
Costs and Expenses:			
Cost of Sales	420,324	319,728	330,790
Selling, General and Administrative	68,860	45,661	45,519
Amortization of Excess of Cost Over the Fair Value of Net Assets Acquired	2,451	749	770
Write-Down of Equipment	3,500	-	-
	495,135	366,138	377,079
Earnings from Operations	57,059	49,248	48,233
Other Income, net	1,149	743	795
Gain on the Sale of Minority Interest	7,613	-	-
Interest Expense	(13,405)	(7,649)	(8,861)
Earnings from Continuing Operations Before Provision for Income Taxes, Minority Interest, Extraordinary Item and Cumulative Effect of a Change in Accounting Principle	52,416	42,342	40,167
Provision for Income Taxes	18,975	16,047	15,222
Earnings from Continuing Operations Before Minority Interest, Extraordinary Item and Cumulative Effect of a Change in Accounting Principle	33,441	26,295	24,945
Minority Interest	903	-	-
Earnings from Continuing Operations Before Extraordinary Item and Cumulative Effect of a Change in Accounting Principle	34,344	26,295	24,945
Discontinued Operations, net of Income Tax Benefit of $724 in 1997	-	-	(1,187)
Extraordinary Item, net of Income Tax Benefit of $177 and $205 in 1999 and 1997	(277)	-	(336)
Cumulative Effect of a Change in Accounting Principle	(3,040)	-	-
Net Earnings	$ 31,027	$ 26,295	$ 23,422
EARNINGS PER SHARE INFORMATION:			
Basic			
Earnings from Continuing Operations Before Extraordinary Item and Cumulative Effect of a Change in Accounting Principle	$ 1.28	$ .97	$ .91
Discontinued Operations	-	-	(.05)
Extraordinary Item	(.01)	-	(.01)
Cumulative Effect of a Change in Accounting Principle	(.11)	-	-
Net Earnings Per Common Share	$ 1.16	$ .97	$ .85
Diluted			
Earnings from Continuing Operations Before Extraordinary Item and Cumulative Effect of a Change in Accounting Principle	$ 1.25	$ .95	$ .89
Discontinued Operations	-	-	(.05)
Extraordinary Item	(.01)	-	(.01)
Cumulative Effect of a Change in Accounting Principle	(.11)	-	-
Net Earnings Per Common Share	$ 1.13	$ .95	$ .83
WEIGHTED AVERAGE SHARES OUTSTANDING			
Basic	26,759	27,057	27,402
Diluted	27,553	27,723	28,070

The accompanying notes are an integral part of these financial statements.

32 Shorewood Packaging Corporation

Consolidated Statements of Cash Flows

In thousands	52 Weeks Ended May 1, 1999	52 Weeks Ended May 2, 1998	53 Weeks Ended May 3, 1997
Cash Flows from Operating Activities:			
Net Earnings	$ 31,027	$ 26,295	$ 23,422
Adjustments to reconcile net earnings to net cash flows provided from operations:			
Non-cash cumulative effect of a change in accounting principle	3,040	-	-
Write-down of equipment	3,500	-	-
Gain on sale of minority interest	(7,613)	-	-
Depreciation and amortization	23,295	17,874	17,214
Deferred income taxes	3,711	1,888	5,182
Non-cash restricted stock compensation	623	241	656
Changes in operating assets and liabilities, net of effect of business acquisitions:			
Accounts receivable	1,422	6,468	5,585
Inventories	(239)	(4,762)	(1,661)
Prepaid expenses and other current assets	665	(4,655)	102
Other assets	(14,195)	(2,503)	(1,349)
Accounts payable, accrued expenses and other long-term liabilities	4,878	11,362	(560)
Current income taxes	1,758	4,944	(1,162)
Net cash flows provided from operating activities	51,872	57,152	47,429
Cash Flows from Investing Activities:			
Capital expenditures	(39,160)	(61,410)	(20,794)
Business acquisitions, net of cash acquired of $4,629 in 1999	(124,022)	-	(5,000)
Proceeds from the sale of minority interest	22,659	-	-
Net cash flows used in investing activities:	(140,523)	(61,410)	(25,794)
Cash Flows from Financing Activities:			
Net proceeds from revolver borrowings	80,430	31,070	14,706
Additions to long-term borrowings	100,000	-	75,000
Repayments of long-term borrowings	(73,750)	(11,250)	(114,000)
Purchase of treasury stock	(15,958)	(14,563)	(6,619)
Issuance of common stock	2,288	2,864	7,334
Net cash flows provided from (used in) financing activities	93,010	8,121	(23,579)
Effect of exchange rate changes on cash and cash equivalents	128	252	618
Increase (decrease) in cash and cash equivalents	4,487	4,115	(1,326)
Cash and cash equivalents at beginning of period	7,268	3,153	4,479
Cash and cash equivalents at end of period	$ 11,755	$ 7,268	$ 3,153
Supplemental Disclosure of Cash Flow Information:			
Interest paid, net of capitalized amounts	$ 11,379	$ 5,553	$ 10,504
Income taxes paid	$ 13,325	$ 9,252	$ 11,359

The accompanying notes are an integral part of these financial statements.

33 Shorewood Packaging Corporation

Art & Creative Director: Tom Laidlaw
Designer: Robert Krivicich
Photographers: Chip Fanelli, Michael Indresano
Copywriter: John Temple

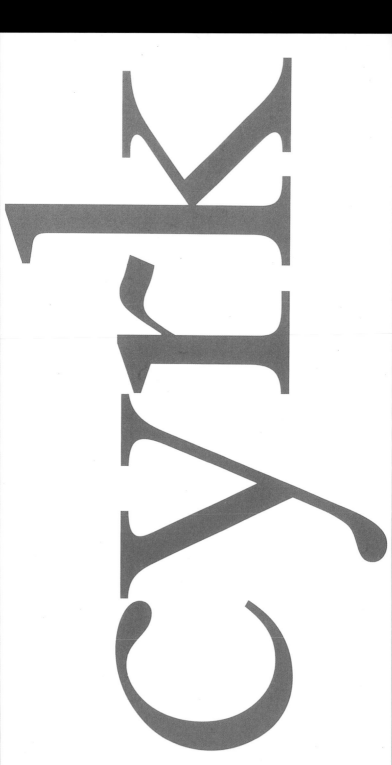

cyrk

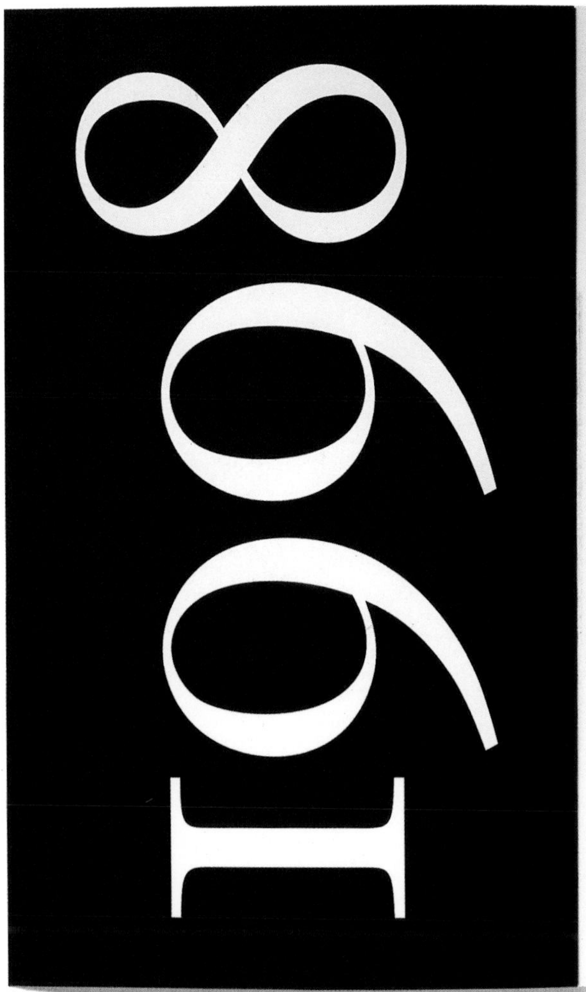
1998

A successful restructuring, a significant increase in sales, and recognition as the worldwide leader in the business of corporate promotions made 1998 a very important year for Cyrk.

Building on the best design, manufacturing and fulfillment resources in the industry, we continued to deliver integrated, high-impact programs and products for the largest brands in the world while staking out new territory in the exploding marketplace of the Internet.

Our challenge for 1999 is to leverage these extraordinary assets with increasing efficiency to build long-term shareholder value by making every success as predictable, replicable and profitable as possible.

The year's results reflect this work in progress. For the year ending December 31, 1998, net sales were $757.9 million, an increase of 36% over the 1997 figure of $558.6 million. Adjusted full-year earnings totaled $1.7 million, or $0.12 per diluted share, excluding restructuring and nonrecurring events. Unadjusted, the year's results included a net loss of $3.0 million, or $0.20 per diluted share, compared with net income of $3.2 million, or $0.25 per diluted share, for 1997.

On a qualitative basis, 1998's achievements were absolutely our best ever. Simon Marketing, our wholly owned Los Angeles-based subsidiary, continued to rack up stunning promotional victories around the world for a blue-chip client base including McDonald's,® Blockbuster® and Chevron Corporation. Simon's creative flair and command of the nuances of kid and family marketing and sales promotion are unique in the industry; equally important, they are masters of the production and delivery of millions of toys each year. Our Corporate Promotions Group achieved significant sales growth by applying its proprietary blend of marketing insight, product design and sourcing, catalog expertise and outstanding service to industries ranging from food to pharmaceuticals to financial services. And our Custom Product and Licensing organization continued to deliver strong performance for many companies including Philip Morris and Ty Inc., the Beanie Babies® company.

As the Internet seized the attention of companies and consumers all over the world, we expanded our capabilities in Web design and marketing while evaluating several strategic options to leverage internal resources and maximize our ability to create new business for ourselves and our clients. Our March 1999 investment in ThingWorld.com,™ described

BrandExperience	Coca-Cola®
I	No terrain is too tough, no challenge too great for the combined power of the Coca-Cola® brand and Cyrk's expertise in specialized branded product. The Coca-Cola Company's worldwide market leadership is now reinforced in 52 European countries through a multi-year specialty merchandise supplier agreement with Cyrk. With Coca-Cola®-branded catalogs going to all bottlers and national offices throughout Europe, there's total integration with the Coca-Cola® look, feel, system and philosophy.

consumer promotion marketing

A decade of leadership in consumer promotions was capped in 1997 by Cyrk's acquisition of Simon Marketing, the world's premier family marketing and sales promotion agency. Since then the Cyrk-Simon combination has

eam
that
rld.

tive
mer
s to
and
bil-
t to
yrk
her,
duct
per-
have
con-

The relationship between Simon Marketing, a wholly owned subsidiary of Cyrk, and McDonald's has spanned more than 20 years and billions of Happy Meal® toys for children in more than 50 countries.

custom product and licensing
In an industry traditionally dominated by off-
the-shelf giveaways of no lasting value, Cyrk
pioneered the use of original products and collections that work together to systematically
enhance brands and build value for years. The
Over the last few years, Beanie Babies have emerged as one of the biggest brand phenomenons in the history of the toy industry.

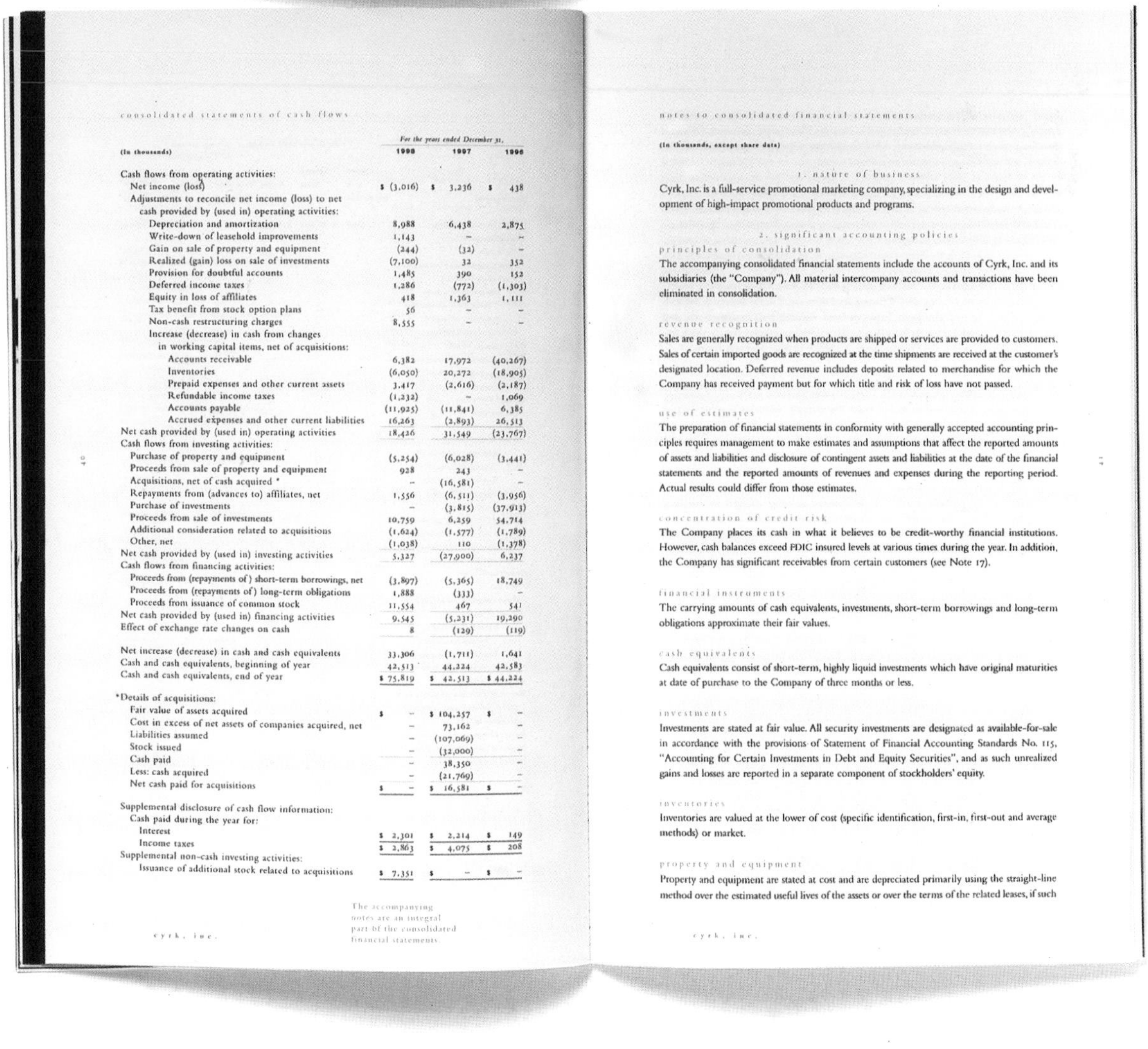

consolidated statements of cash flows

(In thousands)	1998	1997	1996
	For the years ended December 31,		
Cash flows from operating activities:			
Net income (loss)	$ (3,016)	$ 3,236	$ 438
Adjustments to reconcile net income (loss) to net cash provided by (used in) operating activities:			
Depreciation and amortization	8,988	6,438	2,875
Write-down of leasehold improvements	1,143	–	–
Gain on sale of property and equipment	(244)	(32)	–
Realized (gain) loss on sale of investments	(7,100)	32	352
Provision for doubtful accounts	1,485	390	152
Deferred income taxes	1,286	(772)	(1,303)
Equity in loss of affiliates	418	1,363	1,111
Tax benefit from stock option plans	56	–	–
Non-cash restructuring charges	8,555	–	–
Increase (decrease) in cash from changes in working capital items, net of acquisitions:			
Accounts receivable	6,382	17,972	(40,267)
Inventories	(6,050)	20,272	(18,905)
Prepaid expenses and other current assets	3,417	(2,616)	(2,187)
Refundable income taxes	(1,232)	–	1,069
Accounts payable	(11,925)	(11,841)	6,385
Accrued expenses and other current liabilities	16,263	(2,893)	26,513
Net cash provided by (used in) operating activities	18,426	31,549	(23,767)
Cash flows from investing activities:			
Purchase of property and equipment	(5,254)	(6,028)	(3,441)
Proceeds from sale of property and equipment	928	243	–
Acquisitions, net of cash acquired *	–	(16,581)	–
Repayments from (advances to) affiliates, net	1,556	(6,511)	(3,956)
Purchase of investments	–	(3,815)	(37,913)
Proceeds from sale of investments	10,759	6,259	54,714
Additional consideration related to acquisitions	(1,624)	(1,577)	(1,789)
Other, net	(1,038)	110	(1,378)
Net cash provided by (used in) investing activities	5,327	(27,900)	6,237
Cash flows from financing activities:			
Proceeds from (repayments of) short-term borrowings, net	(3,897)	(5,365)	18,749
Proceeds from (repayments of) long-term obligations	1,888	(333)	–
Proceeds from issuance of common stock	11,554	467	541
Net cash provided by (used in) financing activities	9,545	(5,231)	19,290
Effect of exchange rate changes on cash	8	(129)	(119)
Net increase (decrease) in cash and cash equivalents	33,306	(1,711)	1,641
Cash and cash equivalents, beginning of year	42,513	44,224	42,583
Cash and cash equivalents, end of year	$ 75,819	$ 42,513	$ 44,224
*Details of acquisitions:			
Fair value of assets acquired	$ –	$ 104,257	$ –
Cost in excess of net assets of companies acquired, net	–	73,162	–
Liabilities assumed	–	(107,069)	–
Stock issued	–	(32,000)	–
Cash paid	–	38,350	–
Less: cash acquired	–	(21,769)	–
Net cash paid for acquisitions	$ –	$ 16,581	$ –
Supplemental disclosure of cash flow information:			
Cash paid during the year for:			
Interest	$ 2,301	$ 2,214	$ 149
Income taxes	$ 2,863	$ 4,075	$ 208
Supplemental non-cash investing activities:			
Issuance of additional stock related to acquisitions	$ 7,351	$ –	$ –

The accompanying notes are an integral part of the consolidated financial statements.

cyrk, inc.

notes to consolidated financial statements

(In thousands, except share data)

1. nature of business

Cyrk, Inc. is a full-service promotional marketing company, specializing in the design and development of high-impact promotional products and programs.

2. significant accounting policies

principles of consolidation

The accompanying consolidated financial statements include the accounts of Cyrk, Inc. and its subsidiaries (the "Company"). All material intercompany accounts and transactions have been eliminated in consolidation.

revenue recognition

Sales are generally recognized when products are shipped or services are provided to customers. Sales of certain imported goods are recognized at the time shipments are received at the customer's designated location. Deferred revenue includes deposits related to merchandise for which the Company has received payment but for which title and risk of loss have not passed.

use of estimates

The preparation of financial statements in conformity with generally accepted accounting principles requires management to make estimates and assumptions that affect the reported amounts of assets and liabilities and disclosure of contingent assets and liabilities at the date of the financial statements and the reported amounts of revenues and expenses during the reporting period. Actual results could differ from those estimates.

concentration of credit risk

The Company places its cash in what it believes to be credit-worthy financial institutions. However, cash balances exceed FDIC insured levels at various times during the year. In addition, the Company has significant receivables from certain customers (see Note 17).

financial instruments

The carrying amounts of cash equivalents, investments, short-term borrowings and long-term obligations approximate their fair values.

cash equivalents

Cash equivalents consist of short-term, highly liquid investments which have original maturities at date of purchase to the Company of three months or less.

investments

Investments are stated at fair value. All security investments are designated as available-for-sale in accordance with the provisions of Statement of Financial Accounting Standards No. 115, "Accounting for Certain Investments in Debt and Equity Securities", and as such unrealized gains and losses are reported in a separate component of stockholders' equity.

inventories

Inventories are valued at the lower of cost (specific identification, first-in, first-out and average methods) or market.

property and equipment

Property and equipment are stated at cost and are depreciated primarily using the straight-line method over the estimated useful lives of the assets or over the terms of the related leases, if such

cyrk, inc.

Nintendo Corporation, Ltd.

Agency: Leimer Cross Design
Art & Creative Director: Kerry Leimer
Designers: Kerry Leimer, Marianne Li
Photographer: Jeff Engelstadt
Illustrators: Haydn Cornner, Nintendo EAD
Copywriter: Don Varyu

Nintendo 1999

Nintendo Co., Ltd.
and consolidated subsidiaries

Financial Highlights

Years ended March 31,	¥ : millions 1999	¥ : millions 1998	$US : thousands[A] 1999	$US : thousands[A] 1998
Net sales	¥572,440	¥534,325	$4,730,906	$4,415,908
Net income	85,817	83,697	709,234	691,710
Total assets	893,374	848,607	7,383,255	7,013,279
Shareholders' equity	700,292	633,083	5,787,541	5,232,095
AMOUNTS PER SHARE				
Net income[B]	¥ 605.77	¥ 590.80	$ 5.01	$ 4.88
Cash dividends	120	120	0.99	0.99

A The amounts presented herein are expressed in Japanese yen and, solely for the convenience of the readers, have been translated into United States dollars at the rate of ¥121 = US$1, the approximate exchange rate on March 31, 1999.

B See Note 2K to consolidated financial statements.

To Our Shareholders,

In the fiscal year just ended, profits reached their highest level in six years on strong worldwide sales. This performance was particularly gratifying because it occurred in the face of several negative forces.

While America continued to enjoy robust growth, Europe began to display the first signs of an economic slowdown. Also, continuing economic difficulties in Japan, characterized by growing unemployment and reduced personal spending, worked against virtually all entertainment companies. Additionally, since the yen was appreciated higher at the end of March 1999 in comparison with one year ago, it was necessary to book a significant amount of exchange loss.

We believe our ability to overcome these forces stems from significant moves to diversify our business and our unrelenting commitment to the quality of our games.

Revenues for total Nintendo 64 software, led by the enthusiastic worldwide reception for *The Legend of Zelda: Ocarina of Time,* have increased steadily. Game Boy hardware featuring our first color handheld display technology and boosted by the insatiable appetite for Pokémon products, has not shown any

POKÉMON **IT'S JUST A GROUP OF 150 CREATURES THAT FIT INTO A SIMPLE GAME BOY CARTRIDGE AND HAVE UNLEASHED ENOUGH MARKETING POWER TO TAKE OVER THE WORLD. TOGETHER THEY'VE CONQUERED TWO OF THE WORLD'S BIGGEST CONSUMER MARKETS – JAPAN AND, IN ONLY 9 MONTHS, NORTH AMERICA.** AND AS THE PHENOMENON CROSSES THE ATLANTIC THIS YEAR, WILL EUROPE BE ABLE TO RESIST THE ALLURE OF THESE UNIQUE CREATURES? POKÉMON IS FRIENDLY COMPETITION, COOPERATION, AND FUN. They've played their way into family rooms, schoolyards, lunchboxes, and the hearts and minds of children everywhere. Two Game Boy games, the "RED" and "BLUE" versions, have spawned a rash of trading cards, plush toys, a number-one rated cartoon, CD, and a new feature film. The phenomenon appears to be unstoppable. "Gotta Catch 'Em All!" continues to be the chant heard as millions of players set their sights on collecting, training, trading, and mastering Pokémon.

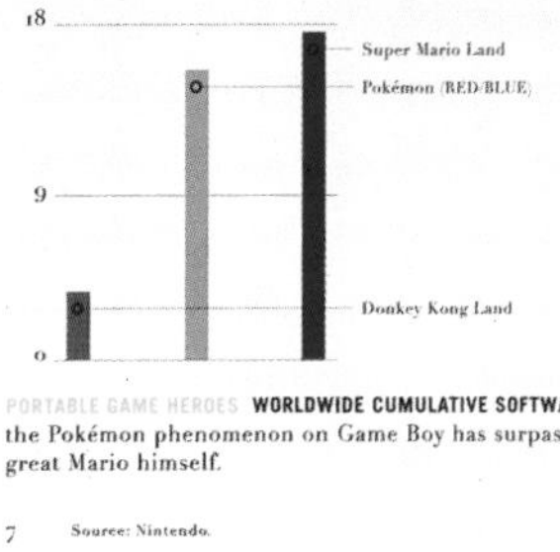
18
9
0
Super Mario Land
Pokémon (RED/BLUE)
Donkey Kong Land

PORTABLE GAME HEROES **WORLDWIDE CUMULATIVE SOFTWARE UNIT SALES – MILLIONS** In less than 37 months, the Pokémon phenomenon on Game Boy has surpassed game sales for every portable hero except the great Mario himself.

7 Source: Nintendo.

sign of sales decline. These facts illustrate the first benefit of diversification. Our commitment to fully back Game Boy, now into its second decade of category leadership, acts as a powerful buffer to the traditionally highly competitive nature of the dedicated console business. Secondly, because many of our products appeal seamlessly to a worldwide audience, we are able to better withstand the economic hardships in one part of the globe with robust sales in other more prosperous territories.

NINTENDO FAVORITES: MARIO, DONKEY KONG AND YOSHI

Thirdly, we have leveraged the family popularity of games featuring Mario, Yoshi, and Donkey Kong to intensify our appeal among more targeted audiences. For example, Pokémon is particularly attractive to grade school players, while titles like *Zelda* and *GoldenEye* have proven extremely popular with older consumers.

Finally, we also have diversified the development of our games. Once our internal teams in Japan created virtually all first-party products, but that work now reaches to the talented developers at Rare Limited in England, and to several groups in the U.S., including our recently-formed Nintendo Software Technology Corporation at our North American headquarters.

JET FORCE GEMINI™ AND JOANNA DARK IN *PERFECT DARK™* COMING IN 1999

But while we continue to diversify and decentralize some operations, we will not retreat in any way from our historic insistence on industry-leading quality. The ability of Nintendo to aggressively compete in each successive generation of technology – 8-bit, 16-bit, handheld and 64-bit – is a testament to our insistence that our products simply entertain better. The public is unerring in its ability to quickly identify and demand those products which meet their standards of excellence. To lose touch with their reality is often a fatal oversight.

Of course, periodically it is necessary to improve the technology on which games are produced in order to meet public expectations. We will soon reach another of these moments. Although the vast majority of sales will continue to derive from current systems for the coming fiscal year, there will be a decided switch to new machines as we move into 2001.

GAME BOY COLOR IN AN INDUSTRY WHERE MOST PRODUCT LIFE CYCLES ARE MEASURED IN WEEKS OR MONTHS, GAME BOY CELEBRATES ITS 10TH ANNIVERSARY WITH STAGGERING LIFETIME WORLDWIDE SALES OF MORE THAN 80 MILLION UNITS. NOW WITH A WHOLE NEW LOOK INSIDE-AND-OUT, GAME BOY COLOR MAKES FOR A WHOLE NEW GAME. It's anytime, anywhere portable entertainment starring Mario and Wario, Pokémon, Zelda, Bugs Bunny, Ken Griffey Jr., and many more. Since its release last November, Game Boy Color has broken sales records every month, making it one of the most successful product lines in history. And, if you look closer, you'll probably find a Berry, Kiwi, Teal or Dandelion somewhere in your home, too.

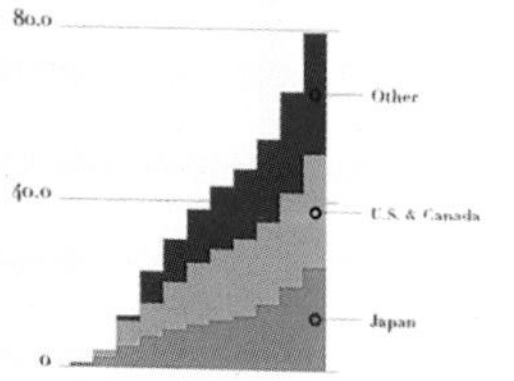
80.0
40.0
0
Other
U.S. & Canada
Japan

GAME BOY LIFETIME HARDWARE UNIT SALES MILLIONS OF UNITS 1989-1999 In year 10, Game Boy set an all time record for worldwide sales. Then last year, it beat that number by better than 20%.

 Source: Nintendo.

GAME BOY COLOR
GAME BOY COLOR
GAME BOY COLOR
GAME BOY COLOR
GAME BOY COLOR
© 1999 Infogrames. Looney Tunes, characters, names, and all related indicia are trademarks of Warner Bros. © 1999.

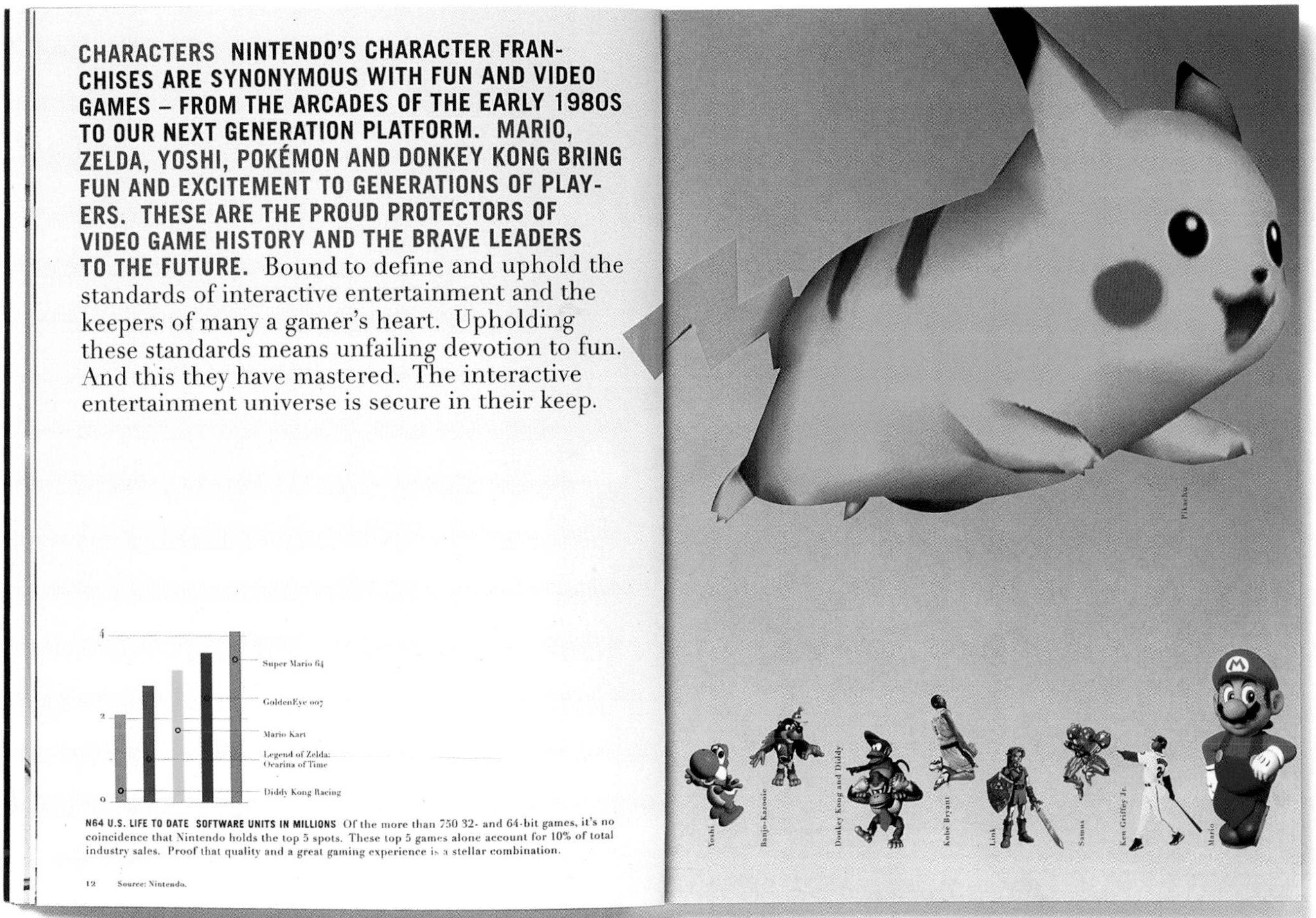

CHARACTERS NINTENDO'S CHARACTER FRANCHISES ARE SYNONYMOUS WITH FUN AND VIDEO GAMES – FROM THE ARCADES OF THE EARLY 1980S TO OUR NEXT GENERATION PLATFORM. MARIO, ZELDA, YOSHI, POKÉMON AND DONKEY KONG BRING FUN AND EXCITEMENT TO GENERATIONS OF PLAYERS. THESE ARE THE PROUD PROTECTORS OF VIDEO GAME HISTORY AND THE BRAVE LEADERS TO THE FUTURE. Bound to define and uphold the standards of interactive entertainment and the keepers of many a gamer's heart. Upholding these standards means unfailing devotion to fun. And this they have mastered. The interactive entertainment universe is secure in their keep.

4
2
0
Super Mario 64
GoldenEye 007
Mario Kart
Legend of Zelda: Ocarina of Time
Diddy Kong Racing

N64 U.S. LIFE TO DATE SOFTWARE UNITS IN MILLIONS Of the more than 750 32- and 64-bit games, it's no coincidence that Nintendo holds the top 5 spots. These top 5 games alone account for 10% of total industry sales. Proof that quality and a great gaming experience is a stellar combination.

12 Source: Nintendo.

Pikachu
Yoshi
Banjo-Kazooie
Donkey Kong and Diddy
Kobe Bryant
Link
Samus
Ken Griffey Jr.
Mario

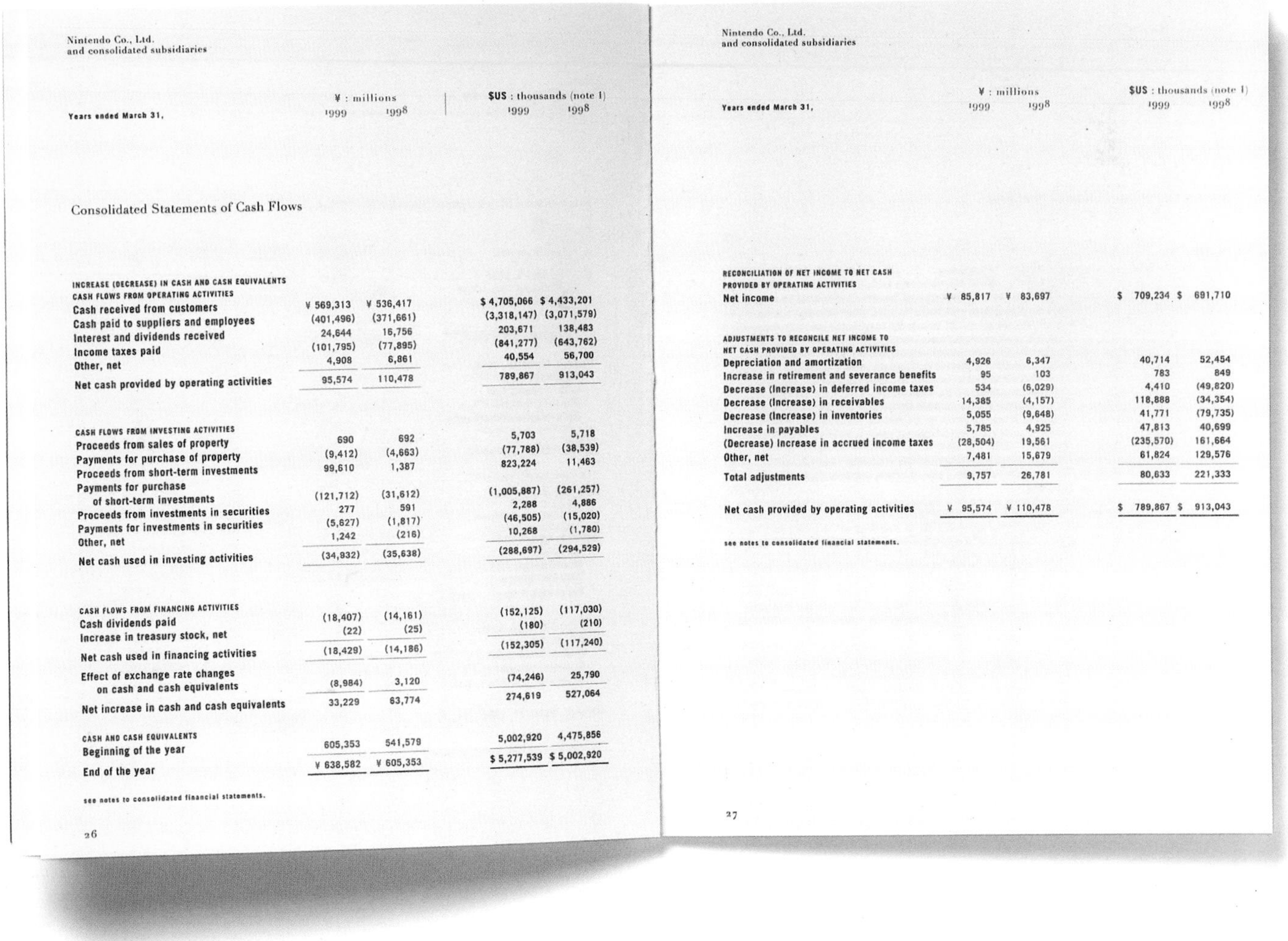

Nintendo Co., Ltd.
and consolidated subsidiaries

Consolidated Statements of Cash Flows

Years ended March 31,	¥ : millions 1999	1998	$US : thousands (note 1) 1999	1998
INCREASE (DECREASE) IN CASH AND CASH EQUIVALENTS				
CASH FLOWS FROM OPERATING ACTIVITIES				
Cash received from customers	¥ 569,313	¥ 536,417	$ 4,705,066	$ 4,433,201
Cash paid to suppliers and employees	(401,496)	(371,661)	(3,318,147)	(3,071,579)
Interest and dividends received	24,644	16,756	203,671	138,483
Income taxes paid	(101,795)	(77,895)	(841,277)	(643,762)
Other, net	4,908	6,861	40,554	56,700
Net cash provided by operating activities	95,574	110,478	789,867	913,043
CASH FLOWS FROM INVESTING ACTIVITIES				
Proceeds from sales of property	690	692	5,703	5,718
Payments for purchase of property	(9,412)	(4,663)	(77,788)	(38,539)
Proceeds from short-term investments	99,610	1,387	823,224	11,463
Payments for purchase of short-term investments	(121,712)	(31,612)	(1,005,887)	(261,257)
Proceeds from investments in securities	277	591	2,288	4,886
Payments for investments in securities	(5,627)	(1,817)	(46,505)	(15,020)
Other, net	1,242	(216)	10,268	(1,780)
Net cash used in investing activities	(34,932)	(35,638)	(288,697)	(294,529)
CASH FLOWS FROM FINANCING ACTIVITIES				
Cash dividends paid	(18,407)	(14,161)	(152,125)	(117,030)
Increase in treasury stock, net	(22)	(25)	(180)	(210)
Net cash used in financing activities	(18,429)	(14,186)	(152,305)	(117,240)
Effect of exchange rate changes on cash and cash equivalents	(8,984)	3,120	(74,246)	25,790
Net increase in cash and cash equivalents	33,229	63,774	274,619	527,064
CASH AND CASH EQUIVALENTS				
Beginning of the year	605,353	541,579	5,002,920	4,475,856
End of the year	¥ 638,582	¥ 605,353	$ 5,277,539	$ 5,002,920

see notes to consolidated financial statements.

26

Nintendo Co., Ltd.
and consolidated subsidiaries

Years ended March 31,	¥ : millions 1999	1998	$US : thousands (note 1) 1999	1998
RECONCILIATION OF NET INCOME TO NET CASH PROVIDED BY OPERATING ACTIVITIES				
Net income	¥ 85,817	¥ 83,697	$ 709,234	$ 691,710
ADJUSTMENTS TO RECONCILE NET INCOME TO NET CASH PROVIDED BY OPERATING ACTIVITIES				
Depreciation and amortization	4,926	6,347	40,714	52,454
Increase in retirement and severance benefits	95	103	783	849
Decrease (Increase) in deferred income taxes	534	(6,029)	4,410	(49,820)
Decrease (Increase) in receivables	14,385	(4,157)	118,888	(34,354)
Decrease (Increase) in inventories	5,055	(9,648)	41,771	(79,735)
Increase in payables	5,785	4,925	47,813	40,699
(Decrease) Increase in accrued income taxes	(28,504)	19,561	(235,570)	161,664
Other, net	7,481	15,679	61,824	129,576
Total adjustments	9,757	26,781	80,633	221,333
Net cash provided by operating activities	¥ 95,574	¥ 110,478	$ 789,867	$ 913,043

see notes to consolidated financial statements.

27

Nelvana

Agency: Tudhope
Creative Director: Ian C. Tudhope
Designer: Chistopher Campbell
Illustrator: Nelvana
Copywriters: Tudhope, Tony Leighton

Nelvana
Our 1998 Annual Report

NELVANA IS AN INTEGRATED FAMILY ENTERTAINMENT COMPANY, WITH OPERATIONS IN TELEVISION AND FEATURE FILM PRODUCTION AND DISTRIBUTION, MERCHANDISE LICENSING, AND PUBLISHING. SINCE ITS FOUNDING IN 1971, NELVANA HAS COMPLETED OVER 40 PRODUCTIONS AT ITS TORONTO STUDIO AND DISTRIBUTES ITS OWN PROGRAMMING WORLDWIDE TO OVER 160 COUNTRIES THROUGH SALES OFFICES IN TORONTO, LOS ANGELES, LONDON AND PARIS. THE COMPANY OWNS THE MERCHANDISE LICENSING RIGHTS TO A BROAD BASE OF CLASSIC AND CONTEMPORARY CHARACTERS, INCLUDING SUCH WELL-KNOWN PROPERTIES AS BABAR, LITTLE BEAR, FRANKLIN AND RUPERT. NELVANA ALSO OWNS KIDS CAN PRESS, CANADA'S LARGEST ENGLISH-LANGUAGE CHILDREN'S BOOK PUBLISHER, WITH A BACKLIST OF OVER 250 TITLES.
18 TO OUR SHAREHOLDERS, EMPLOYEES AND FRIENDS
29 IMAGINE
46 PROGRAM LIBRARY
48 PROGRAM PRODUCTION COMMITMENTS – 1999/2000
50 MANAGEMENT'S DISCUSSION AND ANALYSIS
74 MANAGEMENT'S RESPONSIBILITY FOR FINANCIAL REPORTING AND AUDITORS' REPORT
76 CONSOLIDATED BALANCE SHEETS
77 CONSOLIDATED STATEMENTS OF EARNINGS
78 CONSOLIDATED STATEMENTS OF CHANGES IN FINANCIAL POSITION
79 NOTES TO CONSOLIDATED FINANCIAL STATEMENTS
94 QUARTERLY FINANCIAL INFORMATION
95 COMMON STOCK INFORMATION
96 SUPPLEMENTARY FINANCIAL INFORMATION
98 DIRECTORS AND OFFICERS
100 CORPORATE INFORMATION
Imagine all your favourite Nelvana friends
>

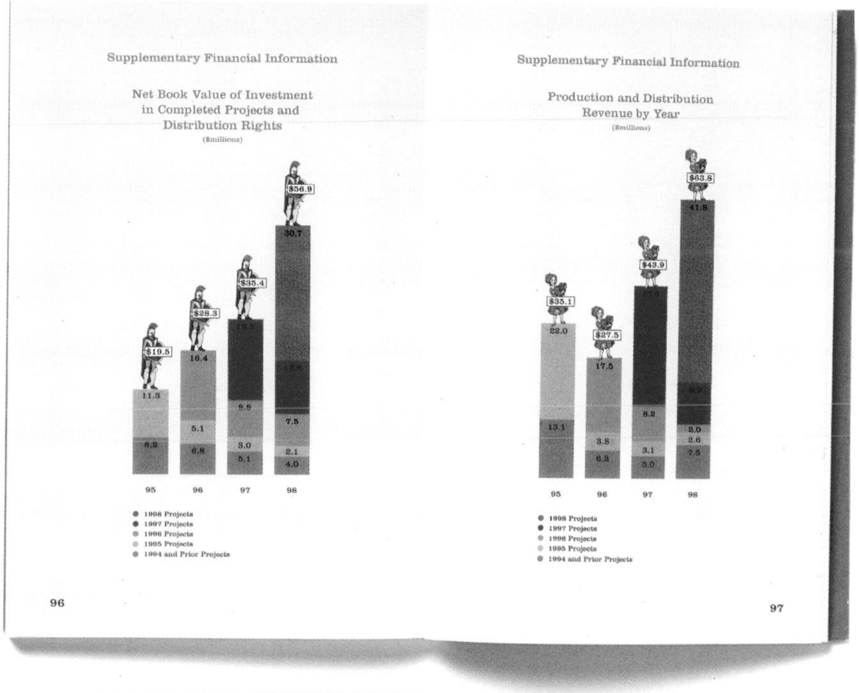
Supplementary Financial Information
Net Book Value of Investment in Completed Projects and Distribution Rights
($millions)
$19.5
$28.3
$35.4
$56.9
95
96
97
98
1998 Projects
1997 Projects
1996 Projects
1995 Projects
1994 and Prior Projects
96
Supplementary Financial Information
Production and Distribution Revenue by Year
($millions)
$35.1
$27.5
$43.9
$63.8
95
96
97
98
1998 Projects
1997 Projects
1996 Projects
1995 Projects
1994 and Prior Projects
97

big and small,
ROLIE POLIE OLIE

Tropical Sportswear International Coporation
Agency: Sibley Peteet Design
Art Director: Rex Peteet
Illustrator: Peter Krämer

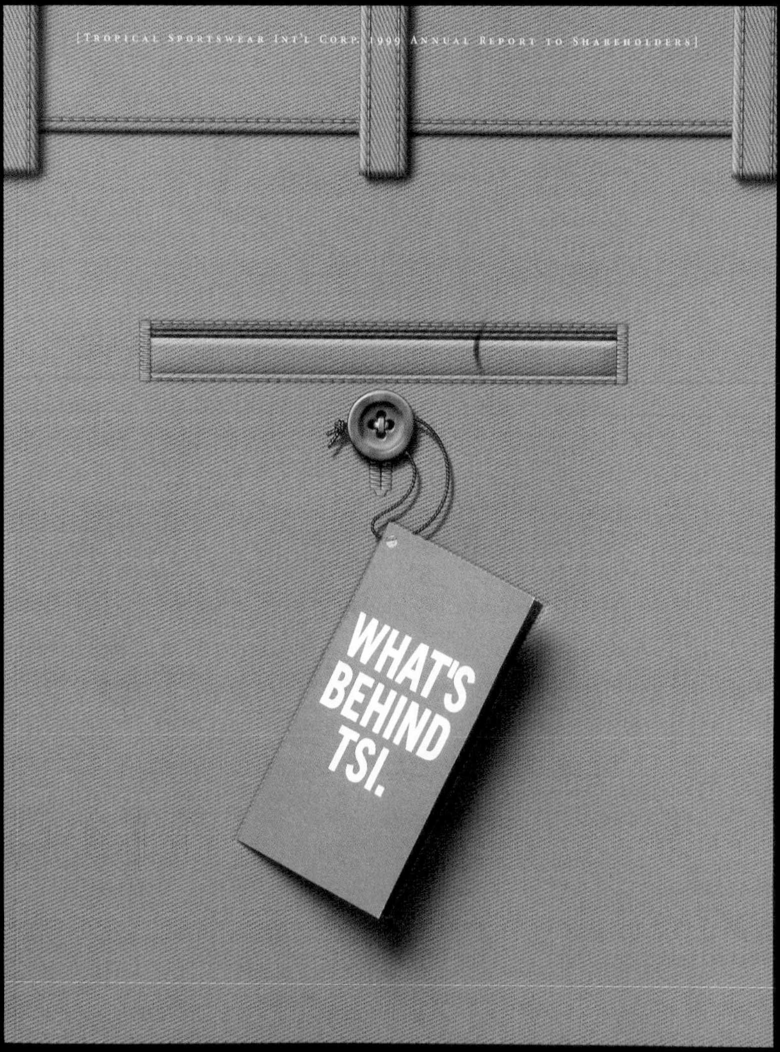
[Tropical Sportswear Int'l Corp. 1999 Annual Report to Shareholders]
WHAT'S BEHIND TSI.

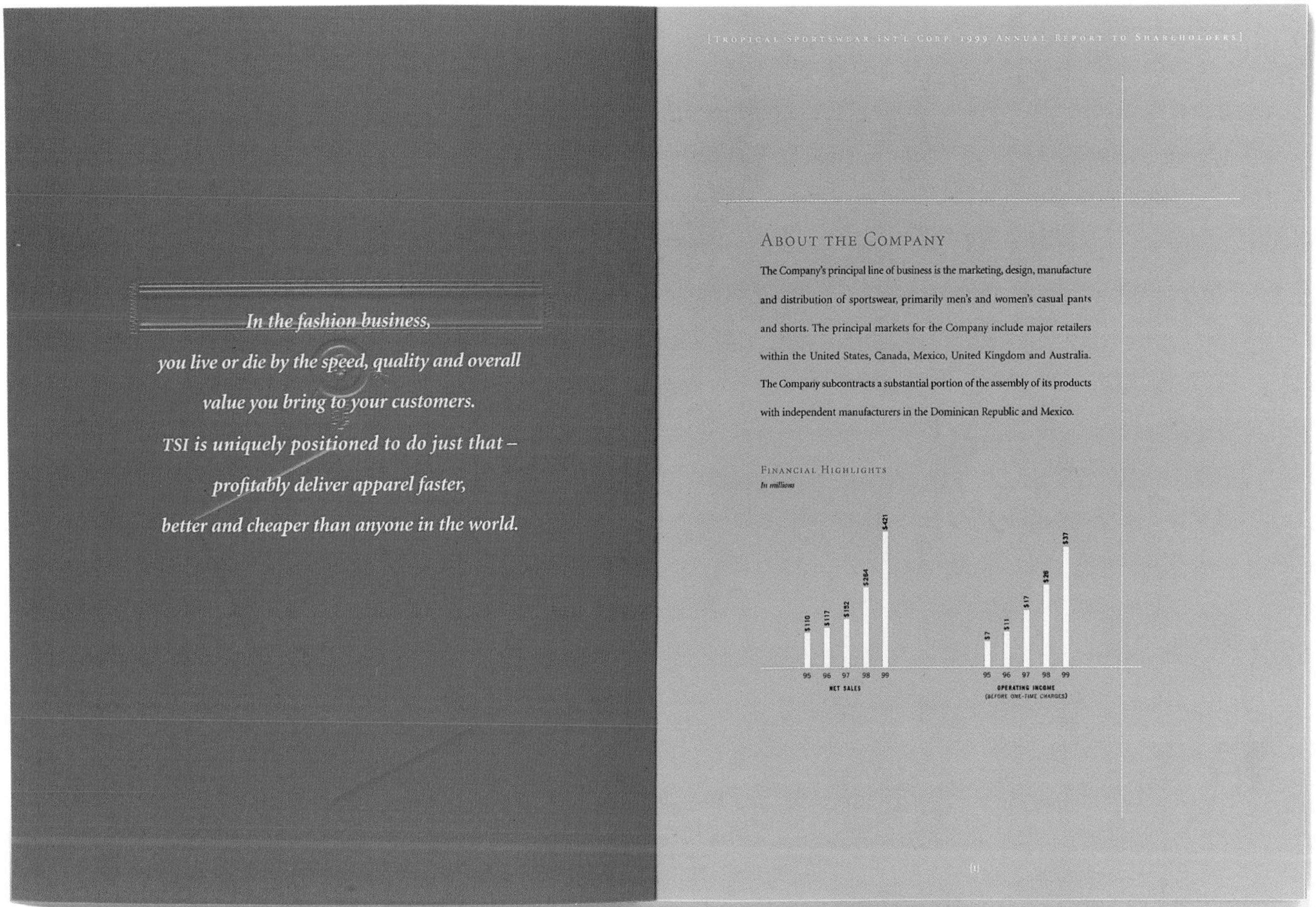
In the fashion business,
you live or die by the speed, quality and overall
value you bring to your customers.
TSI is uniquely positioned to do just that –
profitably deliver apparel faster,
better and cheaper than anyone in the world.
[Tropical Sportswear Int'l Corp. 1999 Annual Report to Shareholders]
About the Company
The Company's principal line of business is the marketing, design, manufacture and distribution of sportswear, primarily men's and women's casual pants and shorts. The principal markets for the Company include major retailers within the United States, Canada, Mexico, United Kingdom and Australia. The Company subcontracts a substantial portion of the assembly of its products with independent manufacturers in the Dominican Republic and Mexico.
Financial Highlights
In millions
$110 $117 $152 $264 $421
95 96 97 98 99
NET SALES
$7 $11 $17 $26 $37
95 96 97 98 99
OPERATING INCOME
(BEFORE ONE-TIME CHARGES)

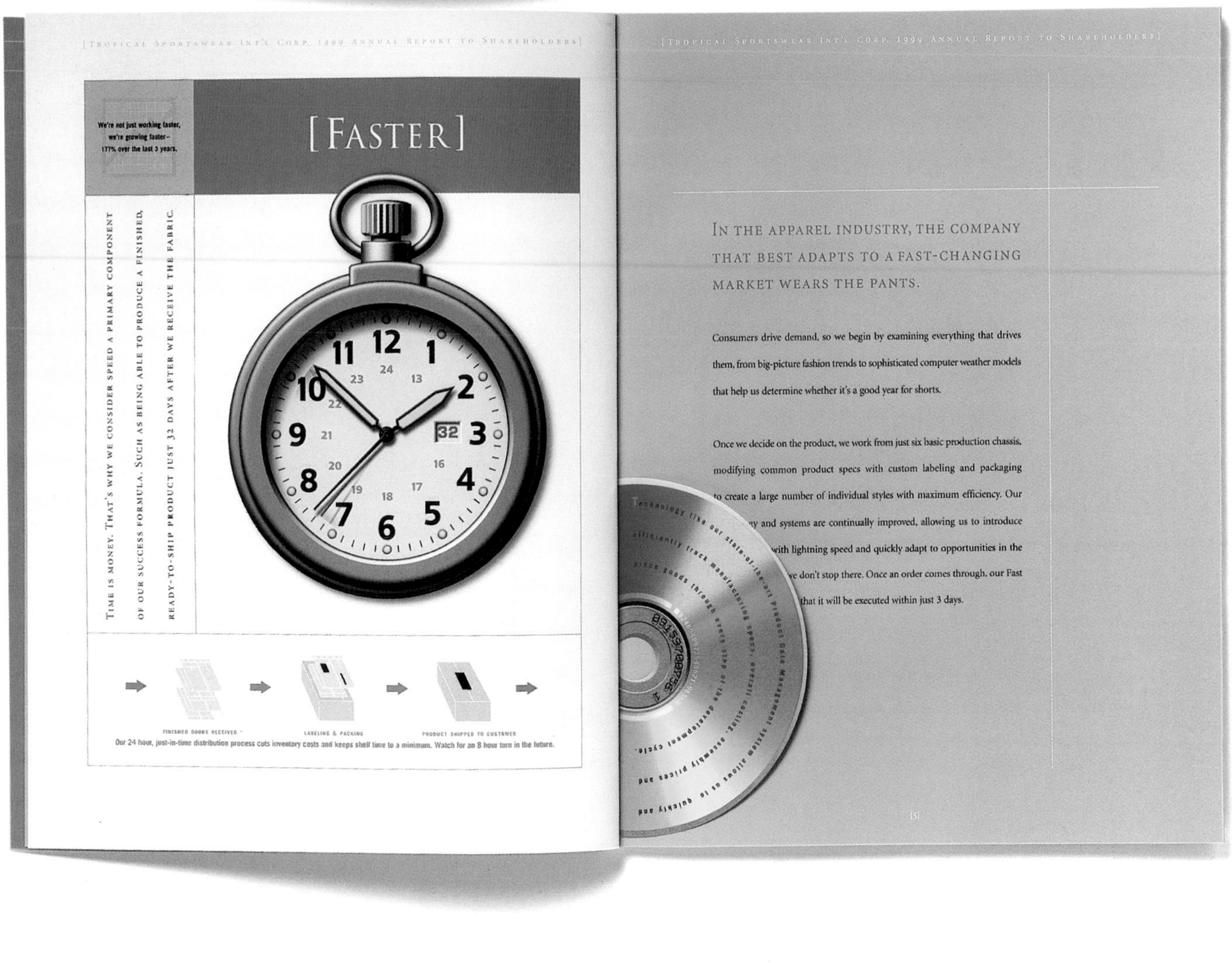
[Tropical Sportswear Int'l Corp. 1999 Annual Report to Shareholders]
We're not just working faster, we're growing faster– 177% over the last 3 years.
[Faster]
Time is money. That's why we consider speed a primary component of our success formula. Such as being able to produce a finished, ready-to-ship product just 32 days after we receive the fabric.
FINISHED GOODS RECEIVED
LABELING & PACKING
PRODUCT SHIPPED TO CUSTOMER
Our 24 hour, just-in-time distribution process cuts inventory costs and keeps shelf time to a minimum. Watch for an 8 hour turn in the future.
[Tropical Sportswear Int'l Corp. 1999 Annual Report to Shareholders]
In the apparel industry, the company that best adapts to a fast-changing market wears the pants.
Consumers drive demand, so we begin by examining everything that drives them, from big-picture fashion trends to sophisticated computer weather models that help us determine whether it's a good year for shorts.
Once we decide on the product, we work from just six basic production chassis, modifying common product specs with custom labeling and packaging to create a large number of individual styles with maximum efficiency. Our
and systems are continually improved, allowing us to introduce
with lightning speed and quickly adapt to opportunities in the
we don't stop there. Once an order comes through, our Fast
that it will be executed within just 3 days.

[Tropical Sportswear Int'l Corp. 1999 Annual Report to Shareholders]

Keeping an eye on the little things has enabled us to grow to global proportions.

[Better]

At TSI, "good enough" will never be enough for us. Every aspect of our operations is designed to create total customer satisfaction by taking customer service to an entirely unexpected new level.

Platinum · Standard ·

From brass zippers, to cross stitched buttons, to stronger thread, every TSI product is packed with quality features. Because details count.

[Tropical Sportswear Int'l Corp. 1999 Annual Report to Shareholders]

Talk about buttoned up. At TSI, we can consistently replenish a retailer's stock with what their customer is demanding, and do it on time.

Our vision and execution begin with our experienced management team. Our associates contribute their drive, creativity and talents. Thanks to our continuous process improvement initiatives, we have a strong competitive position. And with our unique production strategy, we can offer retailers of all sizes a complete range of both branded and private label products.

Regardless of the product, existing and potential customers alike know they can count on TSI's reputation for workmanship, technological innovation and consistent quality. Not to mention outstanding service and support, with complete fixturing programs, inventory management and advertising to build consumer … demand.

Inspected By

99

Our quality control associates are the best, accounting for our defect return rate of only .5%. That means over 99% of our carefully crafted apparel is wearing very well, right now.

[7]

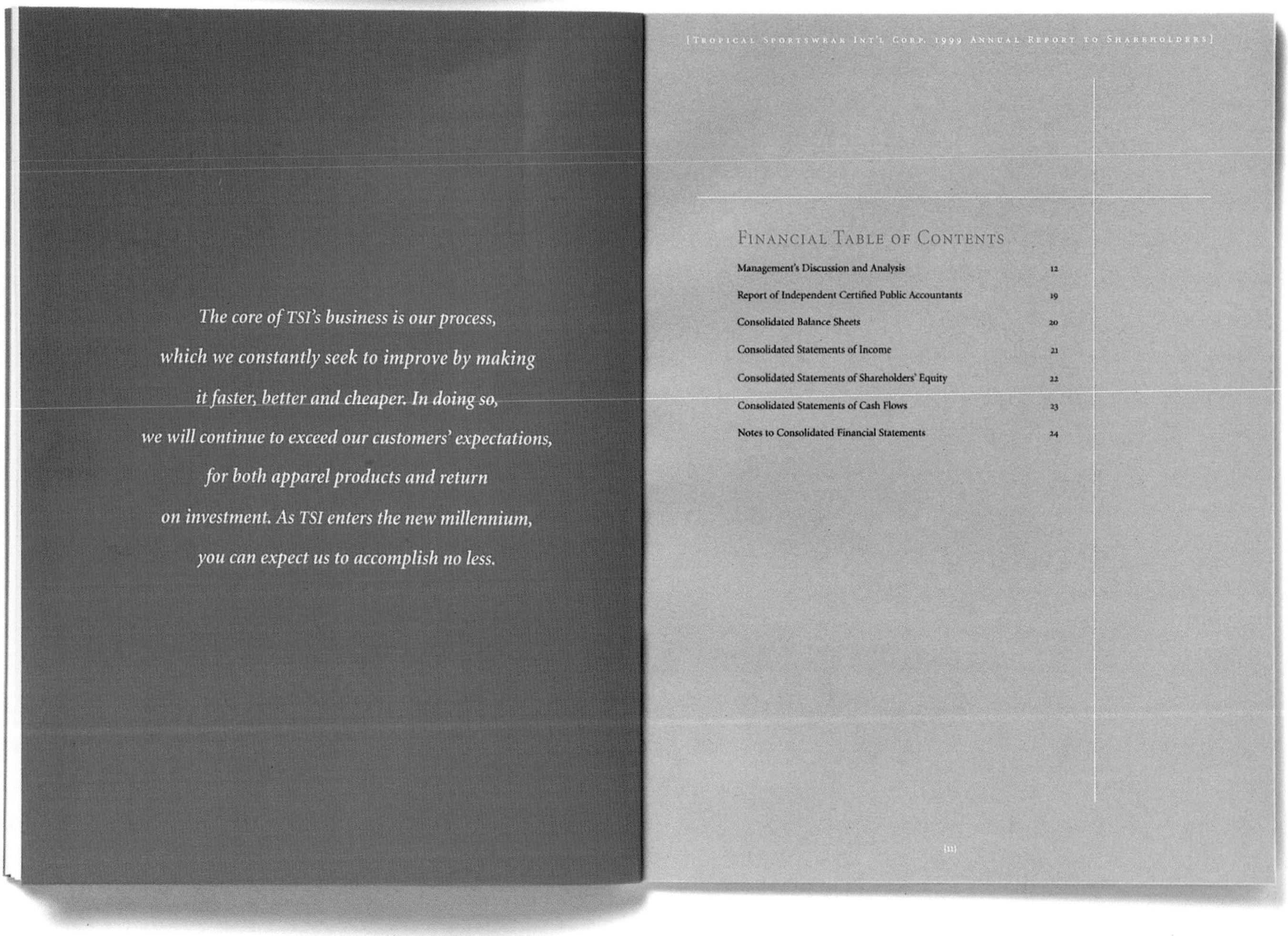
The core of TSI's business is our process, which we constantly seek to improve by making it faster, better and cheaper. In doing so, we will continue to exceed our customers' expectations, for both apparel products and return on investment. As TSI enters the new millennium, you can expect us to accomplish no less.

[Tropical Sportswear Int'l Corp. 1999 Annual Report to Shareholders]

Financial Table of Contents

Management's Discussion and Analysis	12
Report of Independent Certified Public Accountants	19
Consolidated Balance Sheets	20
Consolidated Statements of Income	21
Consolidated Statements of Shareholders' Equity	22
Consolidated Statements of Cash Flows	23
Notes to Consolidated Financial Statements	24

[11]

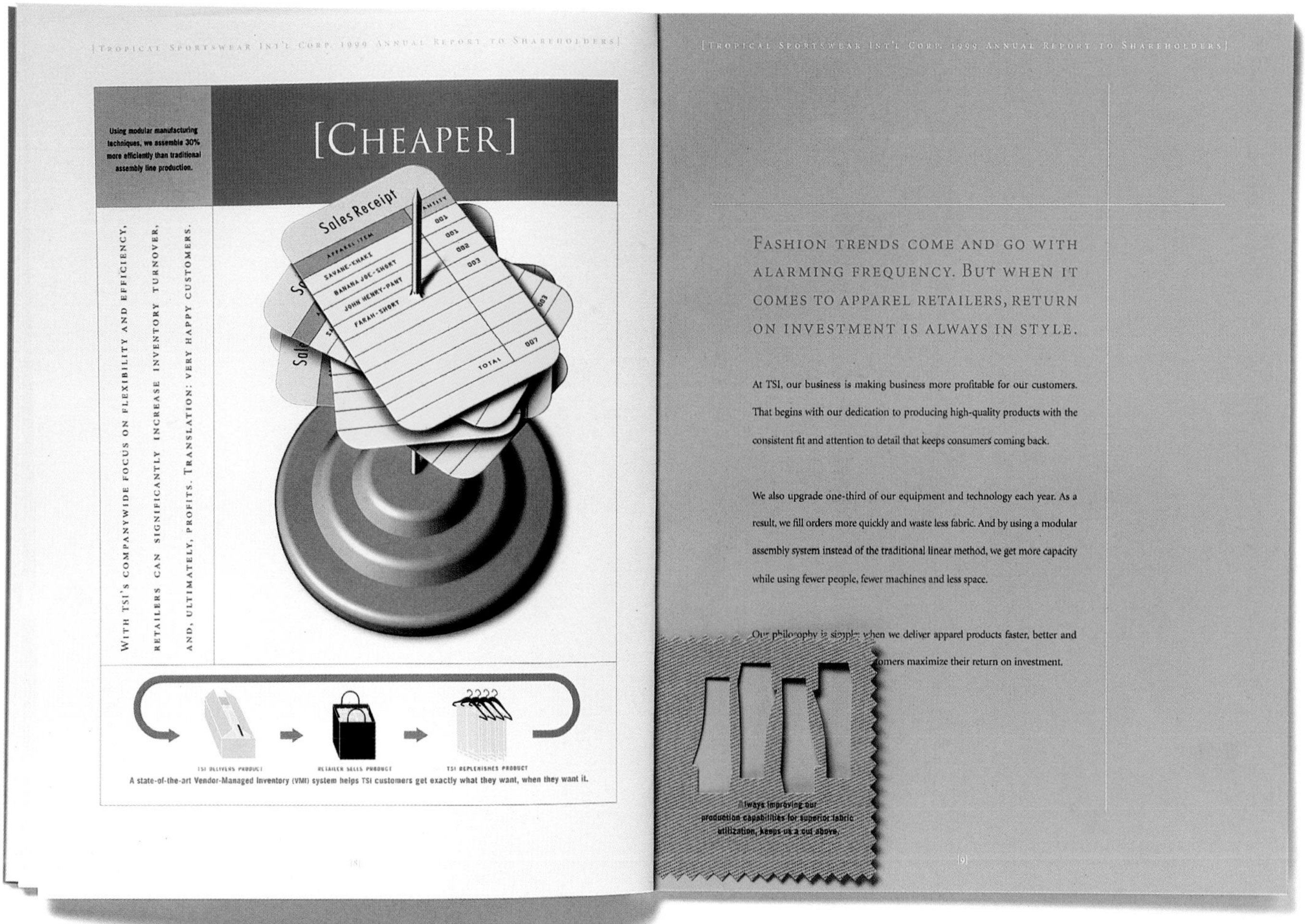

[Tropical Sportswear Int'l Corp. 1999 Annual Report to Shareholders]

Using modular manufacturing techniques, we assemble 30% more efficiently than traditional assembly line production.

[CHEAPER]

WITH TSI'S COMPANYWIDE FOCUS ON FLEXIBILITY AND EFFICIENCY, RETAILERS CAN SIGNIFICANTLY INCREASE INVENTORY TURNOVER, AND, ULTIMATELY, PROFITS. TRANSLATION: VERY HAPPY CUSTOMERS.

Sales Receipt
SAVANE-KHAKI
BANANA JOE-SHORT
JOHN HENRY-PANT
FARAH-SHORT
TOTAL
TSI DELIVERS PRODUCT
RETAILER SELLS PRODUCT
TSI REPLENISHES PRODUCT

A state-of-the-art Vendor-Managed Inventory (VMI) system helps TSI customers get exactly what they want, when they want it.

[Tropical Sportswear Int'l Corp. 1999 Annual Report to Shareholders]

FASHION TRENDS COME AND GO WITH ALARMING FREQUENCY. BUT WHEN IT COMES TO APPAREL RETAILERS, RETURN ON INVESTMENT IS ALWAYS IN STYLE.

At TSI, our business is making business more profitable for our customers. That begins with our dedication to producing high-quality products with the consistent fit and attention to detail that keeps consumers coming back.

We also upgrade one-third of our equipment and technology each year. As a result, we fill orders more quickly and waste less fabric. And by using a modular assembly system instead of the traditional linear method, we get more capacity while using fewer people, fewer machines and less space.

Our philosophy is simple: when we deliver apparel products faster, better and ... omers maximize their return on investment.

Always improving our production capabilities for superior fabric utilization, keeps us a cut above.

[9]

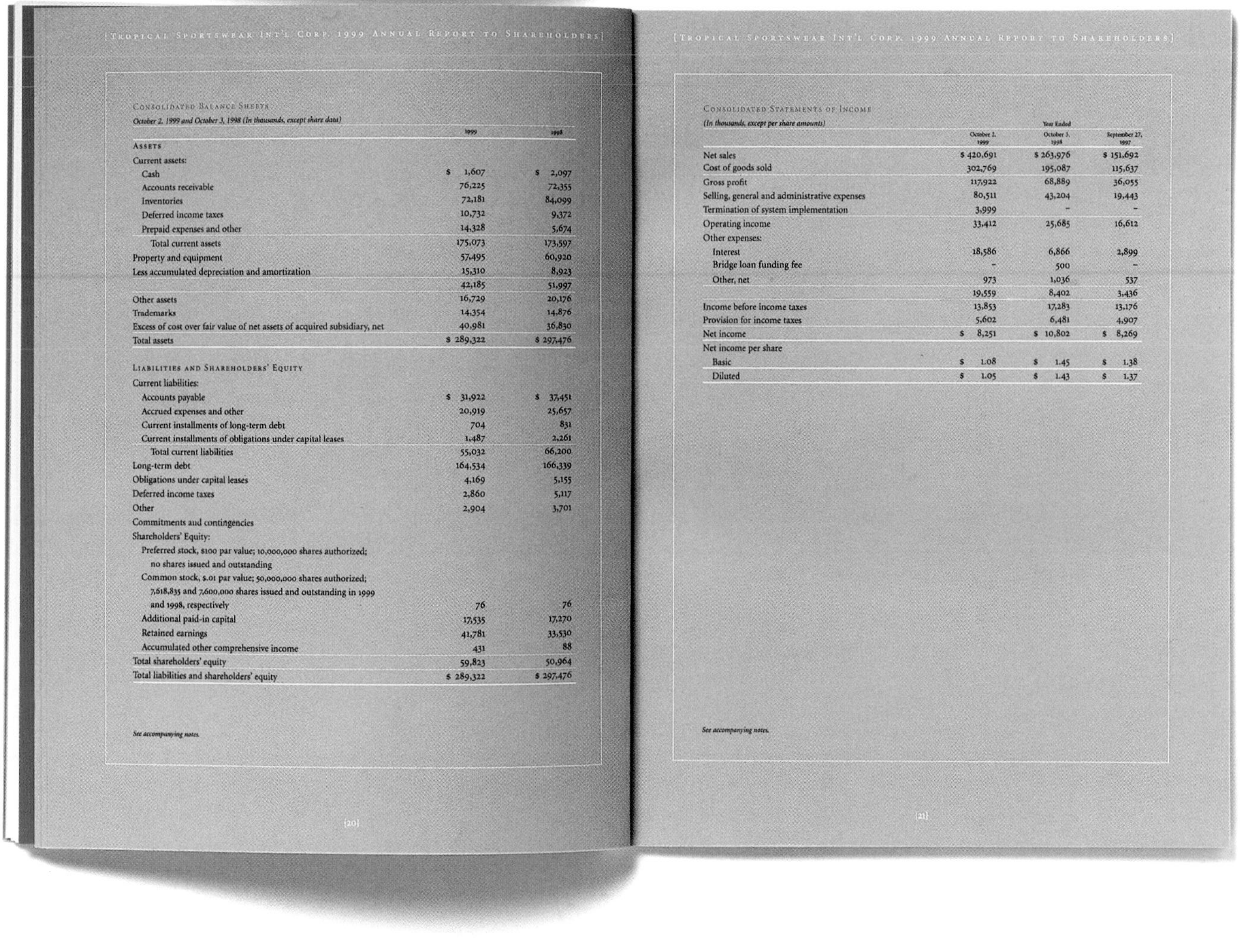

[Tropical Sportswear Int'l Corp. 1999 Annual Report to Shareholders]

CONSOLIDATED BALANCE SHEETS

October 2, 1999 and October 3, 1998 (In thousands, except share data)

	1999	1998
ASSETS		
Current assets:		
Cash	$ 1,607	$ 2,097
Accounts receivable	76,225	72,355
Inventories	72,181	84,099
Deferred income taxes	10,732	9,372
Prepaid expenses and other	14,328	5,674
Total current assets	175,073	173,597
Property and equipment	57,495	60,920
Less accumulated depreciation and amortization	15,310	8,923
	42,185	51,997
Other assets	16,729	20,176
Trademarks	14,354	14,876
Excess of cost over fair value of net assets of acquired subsidiary, net	40,981	36,830
Total assets	$ 289,322	$ 297,476
LIABILITIES AND SHAREHOLDERS' EQUITY		
Current liabilities:		
Accounts payable	$ 31,922	$ 37,451
Accrued expenses and other	20,919	25,657
Current installments of long-term debt	704	831
Current installments of obligations under capital leases	1,487	2,261
Total current liabilities	55,032	66,200
Long-term debt	164,534	166,339
Obligations under capital leases	4,169	5,155
Deferred income taxes	2,860	5,117
Other	2,904	3,701
Commitments and contingencies		
Shareholders' Equity:		
Preferred stock, $100 par value; 10,000,000 shares authorized; no shares issued and outstanding		
Common stock, $.01 par value; 50,000,000 shares authorized; 7,618,835 and 7,600,000 shares issued and outstanding in 1999 and 1998, respectively	76	76
Additional paid-in capital	17,535	17,270
Retained earnings	41,781	33,530
Accumulated other comprehensive income	431	88
Total shareholders' equity	59,823	50,964
Total liabilities and shareholders' equity	$ 289,322	$ 297,476

See accompanying notes.

[20]

[Tropical Sportswear Int'l Corp. 1999 Annual Report to Shareholders]

CONSOLIDATED STATEMENTS OF INCOME

(In thousands, except per share amounts)

	Year Ended		
	October 2, 1999	October 3, 1998	September 27, 1997
Net sales	$ 420,691	$ 263,976	$ 151,692
Cost of goods sold	302,769	195,087	115,637
Gross profit	117,922	68,889	36,055
Selling, general and administrative expenses	80,511	43,204	19,443
Termination of system implementation	3,999	–	–
Operating income	33,412	25,685	16,612
Other expenses:			
Interest	18,586	6,866	2,899
Bridge loan funding fee	–	500	–
Other, net	973	1,036	537
	19,559	8,402	3,436
Income before income taxes	13,853	17,283	13,176
Provision for income taxes	5,602	6,481	4,907
Net income	$ 8,251	$ 10,802	$ 8,269
Net income per share			
Basic	$ 1.08	$ 1.45	$ 1.38
Diluted	$ 1.05	$ 1.43	$ 1.37

See accompanying notes.

[21]

Art Directors: Tim Hale, Casey McGarr, Stephen Zhang
Creative Director: Tim Hale
Designer: Stephen Zhang
Photographer: Dave McCormick
Illustrators: Ellen Tanner, John Vineyard, Paula Wallace, Andrea Haynes, Jennifer Burk, Susie Stampley
Copywriter: Fossil

Fossil
1998 Annual Report

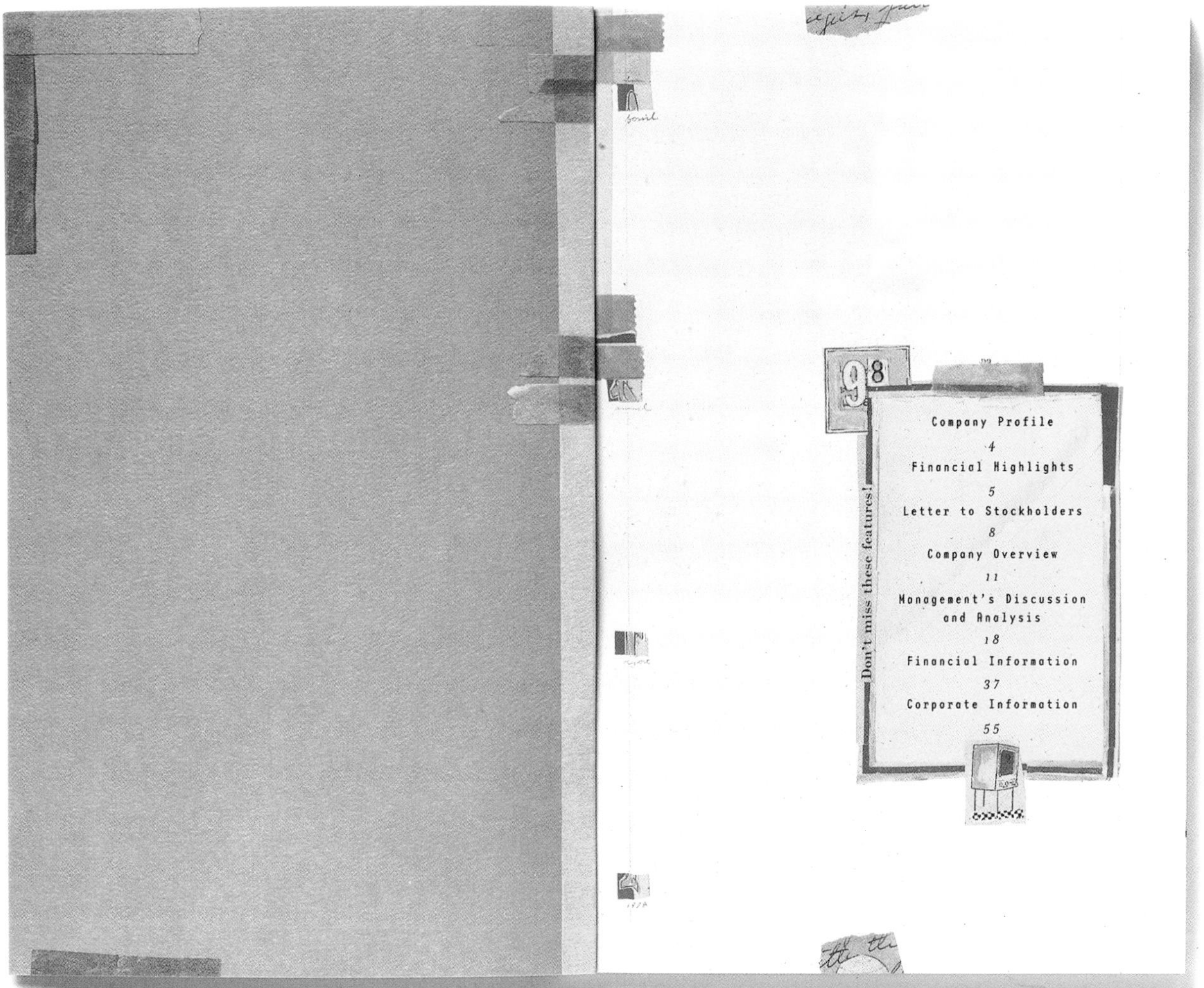
Don't miss these features!
Company Profile
4
Financial Highlights
5
Letter to Stockholders
8
Company Overview
11
Management's Discussion and Analysis
18
Financial Information
37
Corporate Information
55

KINDLY PLACE ONE LABEL ON EACH F... THE PACKAGE
FOSSIL JAPAN Inc.
TEL03-3263-6341
WWW.fossil.com
LONDON
AUTHENTIC FOSSIL
FOSSIL (EUROPE) GMBH
83278 TRAUNSTEIN
TEL. 0861-98983-0
FAX 0861-98983-28
FOSSIL GENUINE CLASSIC
COMPANY overview
11
The Company's long-term goal is to capitalize on the strength of its growing consumer brand recognition and capture an increasing share of a growing number of markets by providing consumers with fashionable, high quality, value-driven products. The FOSSIL brand continued to be one of the leading fashion watch brands in 1998, while continuing to gain momentum in sales of non-watch products and increasing its brand presence globally.
Watches: The FOSSIL brand continued to build market share in department stores in 1998. New product introductions throughout the year contributed to driving comparable store sales to record levels. The introduction of FOSSIL BIG TIC in the fall was highly successful and FOSSIL Steel solid stainless steel watches continued to build momentum after their 1997 debut. FOSSIL BLUE water-resistant sport watches continued to increase market share and FOSSIL BLUE TEQ chronograph-styled watches were strong throughout the year. FOSSIL F2 women's dress watches performed well all year and continued to maintain a leadership position in the dress classification at department stores.
Leathers: The leather division continued to exhibit strong sales and earnings growth in 1998. Handbags continued to increase market share and enhance the visibility and sales of the Company's other leather categories, including men's and women's small leather goods and belts. A new line of FOSSIL nylon handbags was introduced in 1998 in addition to a group of bags with a sporty feel and look. Strong growth should continue in the leather product category during 1999 as key basic collections continue sales increases fueled by new lines of more classic, less ornamented styles providing a fresh and exciting product assortment.
Sunglasses: FOSSIL sunwear rebounded in 1998 with double-digit increases in the midst of continued turmoil in the sunglass market. The overall success of the division was spurred by significant growth in optical and specialty stores such as Lenscrafters and Sunglass Hut. Strong international sales, particularly in northern Europe, played a role in the growth of this product category. A new collection of more popularly-priced sunglasses provided increased market share and retail sales in the Company's department store distribution channel, prompting the introduction of two new collections in the third quarter. FOSSIL Steel sunwear, featuring polarized polycarbonate lenses and stainless steel frames, and FOSSIL BLUE sunwear, crafted from a technologically advanced plastic material that floats, complement the quality and value of the FOSSIL brand perfectly.

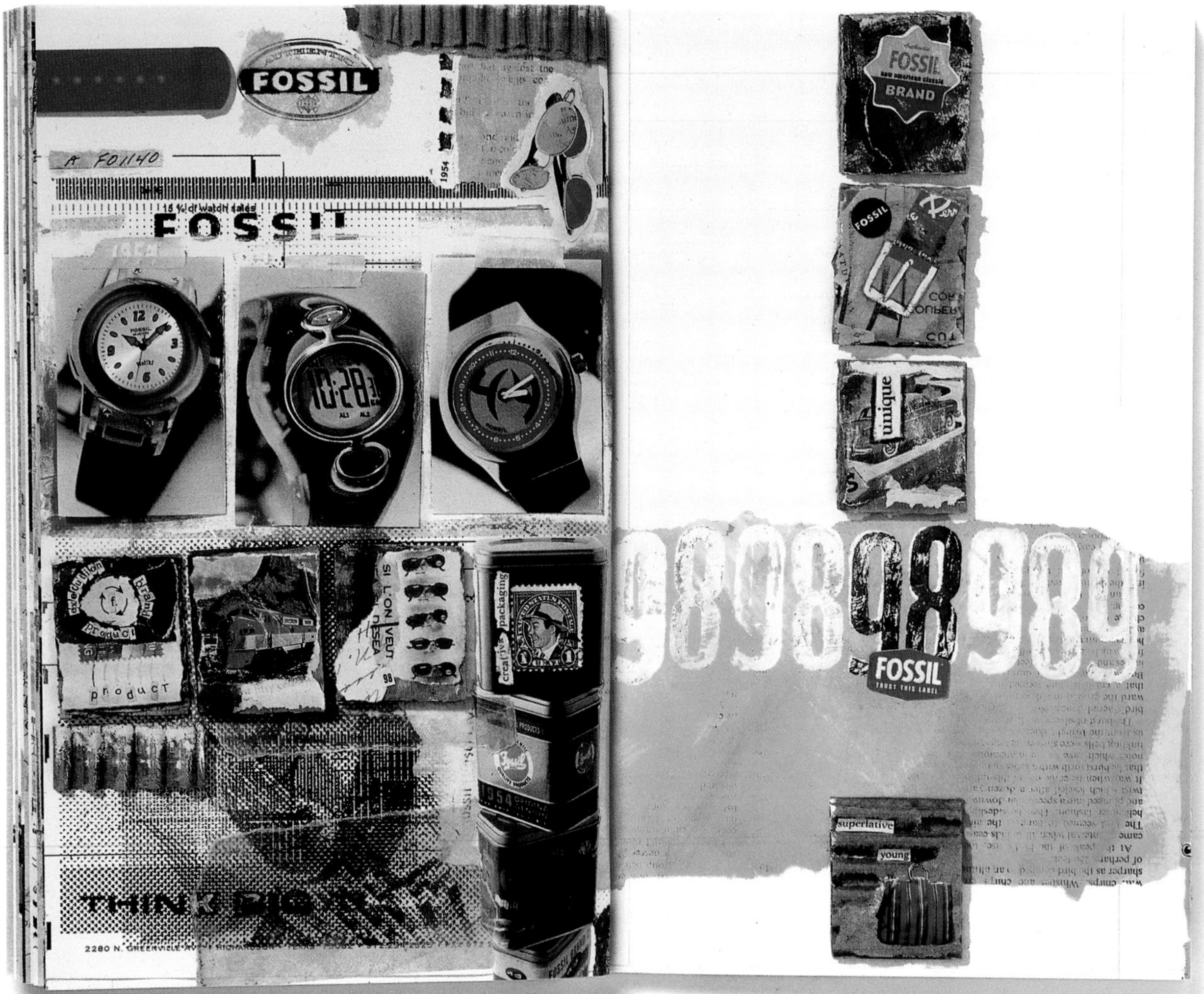
FOSSIL
A FO1140
FOSSIL
1954
product
creative packaging
superlative
young
FOSSIL
TRUST THIS LABEL
unique
BRAND

International: Increasing demand for FOSSIL products worldwide, coupled with the expansion of the EMPORIO ARMANI licensed line of watches, helped broaden the Company's business tremendously across the globe. The FOSSIL brand is available in over 80 countries around the world through the Company's six subsidiary operations and a network of independent distributors. The Company began distribution in five additional markets in 1998, including Argentina, Uruguay, Egypt, Israel and Korea Duty Free. In addition, FOSSIL retail stores and kiosks grew from 40 international locations in 1997 to over 80 locations in 1998. These stores and kiosks are principally owned and operated by independent distributors. International distribution will continue to offer excellent growth opportunities for the Company in 1999.

Relic: The RELIC brand displayed strong sales in 1998, due primarily to an improved product assortment and a new store image and visual presentation. The RELIC brand featured an assortment of four primary categories: RELIC Wet (water-resistant sport watches), RELIC Adjust-A-Link (women's metal dress watches with easily adjustable links), RELIC Stainless Steel (100% solid stainless steel cases and bracelets), and RELIC Pocket Watches (geared toward the young, casual consumer). The RELIC division unveiled a new image and visual presentation — upscale look featuring natural wood, black and white photography, and the strong red RELIC logo. These new displays were installed in over 1,000 doors during 1998, and due to the excellent sales results, another 1,000 doors are currently scheduled to receive the new look in 1999.

Emporio Armani: The Company has a worldwide, multi-year licensing agreement with Giorgio Armani for Emporio Armani Orologi, a line of watches featuring distinctive interpretations of retro and modern design. Throughout the collection, the Emporio Armani name and Eagle logo are used as a background element on the dials, etched into the casings, or incorporated more subtly into the band designs. Available in Emporio Armani Boutiques, better department stores, specialty stores and select jewelry stores, the line continues to grow in sales and distribution worldwide. New markets continue to open as the product continues to perform well at retail.

Licensing: The Company continues to test new products bearing the FOSSIL mark by utilizing license agreements with select partners. The Company is careful to limit the size and penetration of these product categories to be sure that the products are consistent with the brand image and desirable to end consumers. FOSSIL brand outerwear and optical frames will be launched in 1999. The Company will continue to evaluate additional license arrangements as a mechanism for product expansion as suitable products and partners are identified.

Private Label: In addition to building its own brand, the Company also designs and manufactures private label products for some of the most prestigious companies in the world, including national retailers, entertainment companies and theme restaurants. The Company continues to expand its core private label watch business as well as integrate other product categories such as leather goods and eyewear. In 1998, the Company's premium/incentive division continued to utilize its sourcing, design, and development expertise to translate many corporate themes, events, or promotions into a comprehensive custom program.

FOSSIL General Stores: The Company was operating nine FOSSIL stores at the end of 1998, adding three new locations during the year. New stores were opened in North Miami, Florida (Aventura Mall), Scottsdale, Arizona (Scottsdale Fashion Square), and Los Angeles, California (Universal Studios City Walk). The FOSSIL stores continue to provide an exciting and profitable format in which to display the Company's increasing product assortments and to convey the FOSSIL brand image. The Company also operates 28 outlet stores coast-to-coast, allowing the Company to control the timely liquidation of discontinued styles while maintaining the integrity of the FOSSIL brand.

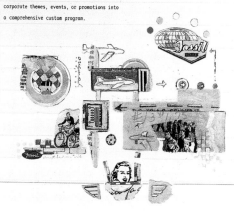

Fossil

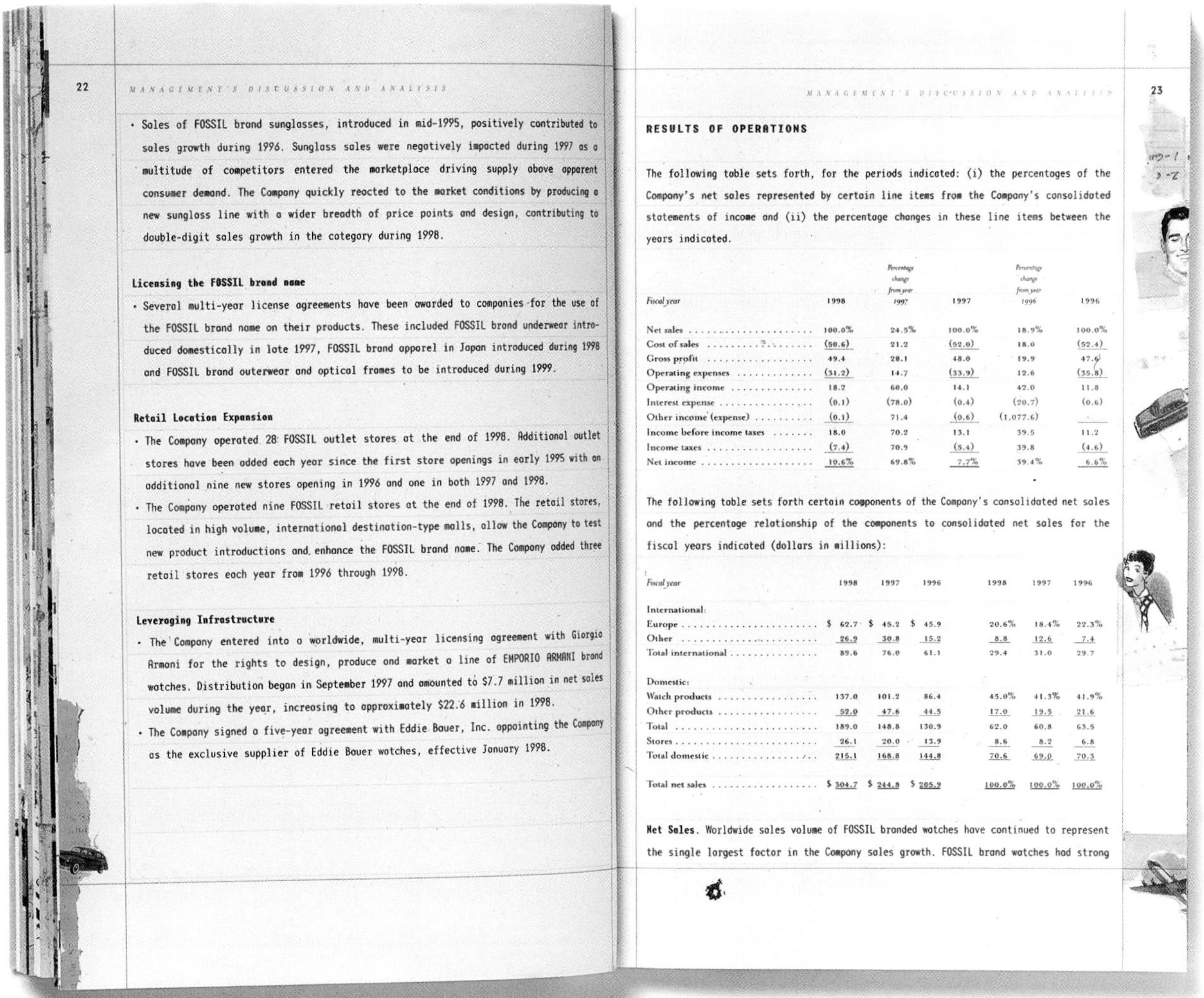

22 MANAGEMENT'S DISCUSSION AND ANALYSIS

- Sales of FOSSIL brand sunglasses, introduced in mid-1995, positively contributed to sales growth during 1996. Sunglass sales were negatively impacted during 1997 as a multitude of competitors entered the marketplace driving supply above apparent consumer demand. The Company quickly reacted to the market conditions by producing a new sunglass line with a wider breadth of price points and design, contributing to double-digit sales growth in the category during 1998.

Licensing the FOSSIL brand name

- Several multi-year license agreements have been awarded to companies for the use of the FOSSIL brand name on their products. These included FOSSIL brand underwear introduced domestically in late 1997, FOSSIL brand apparel in Japan introduced during 1998 and FOSSIL brand outerwear and optical frames to be introduced during 1999.

Retail Location Expansion

- The Company operated 28 FOSSIL outlet stores at the end of 1998. Additional outlet stores have been added each year since the first store openings in early 1995 with an additional nine new stores opening in 1996 and one in both 1997 and 1998.
- The Company operated nine FOSSIL retail stores at the end of 1998. The retail stores, located in high volume, international destination-type malls, allow the Company to test new product introductions and enhance the FOSSIL brand name. The Company added three retail stores each year from 1996 through 1998.

Leveraging Infrastructure

- The Company entered into a worldwide, multi-year licensing agreement with Giorgio Armani for the rights to design, produce and market a line of EMPORIO ARMANI brand watches. Distribution began in September 1997 and amounted to $7.7 million in net sales volume during the year, increasing to approximately $22.6 million in 1998.
- The Company signed a five-year agreement with Eddie Bauer, Inc. appointing the Company as the exclusive supplier of Eddie Bauer watches, effective January 1998.

MANAGEMENT'S DISCUSSION AND ANALYSIS 23

RESULTS OF OPERATIONS

The following table sets forth, for the periods indicated: (i) the percentages of the Company's net sales represented by certain line items from the Company's consolidated statements of income and (ii) the percentage changes in these line items between the years indicated.

Fiscal year	1998	Percentage change from year 1997	1997	Percentage change from year 1996	1996
Net sales	100.0%	24.5%	100.0%	18.9%	100.0%
Cost of sales	(50.6)	21.2	(52.0)	18.0	(52.4)
Gross profit	49.4	28.1	48.0	19.9	47.6
Operating expenses	(31.2)	14.7	(33.9)	12.6	(35.8)
Operating income	18.2	60.0	14.1	42.0	11.8
Interest expense	(0.1)	(78.0)	(0.4)	(20.7)	(0.6)
Other income (expense)	(0.1)	71.4	(0.6)	(1,077.6)	-
Income before income taxes	18.0	70.2	13.1	39.5	11.2
Income taxes	(7.4)	70.9	(5.4)	39.8	(4.6)
Net income	10.6%	69.8%	7.7%	39.4%	6.6%

The following table sets forth certain components of the Company's consolidated net sales and the percentage relationship of the components to consolidated net sales for the fiscal years indicated (dollars in millions):

Fiscal year	1998	1997	1996	1998	1997	1996
International:						
Europe	$ 62.7	$ 45.2	$ 45.9	20.6%	18.4%	22.3%
Other	26.9	30.8	15.2	8.8	12.6	7.4
Total international	89.6	76.0	61.1	29.4	31.0	29.7
Domestic:						
Watch products	137.0	101.2	86.4	45.0%	41.3%	41.9%
Other products	52.0	47.6	44.5	17.0	19.5	21.6
Total	189.0	148.8	130.9	62.0	60.8	63.5
Stores	26.1	20.0	13.9	8.6	8.2	6.8
Total domestic	215.1	168.8	144.8	70.6	69.0	70.3
Total net sales	$ 304.7	$ 244.8	$ 205.9	100.0%	100.0%	100.0%

Net Sales. Worldwide sales volume of FOSSIL branded watches have continued to represent the single largest factor in the Company sales growth. FOSSIL brand watches had strong

BRAND
PRODUCT
EXECUTION
FOSSIL
AUTHENTIC FOSSIL ORIGINAL
TOLEDO VALVES
19
98

Polo Ralph Lauren
Agency: EAI
Creative Director: Matt Rollins
Designers: David Cannon, Nicole Riekki
Copywriter: Lindsay Beaman

RL-99

WHAT I SEE
AN INSIDE VIEW OF POLO RALPH LAUREN

RL-99

which lets us extend the original Polo concept across a broad range of apparel and other consumer product segments. Our brand also applies with equal success to exclusive premium items and to lines with mass market appeal. From Collection to Lauren, and Purple Label to Chaps, our brand carries the essence of the original Polo lifestyle vision to all product lines — with faithful consistency. Likewise, focusing on lifestyle allows us to apply our design principles and brand imagery in fragrances, home concepts and furnishings, and just about any other lifestyle category.

In this way, we have proven our ability to attract new Polo consumers, yet retain an enduring appeal by remaining faithful to the traditional Polo customer's sensibilities. That strategy drove our results before we went public and we believe it will continue to guide our growth in the future.

Our Company has a strong and committed management team. I work alongside a talented group of people who bring strong leadership and creative depth to both the operations and design side of Polo Ralph Lauren. Many members of our management team have been with Polo for 10, 15, and even 25 years, which gives us uncommon stability in a volatile industry. Over the years, we have also added new professionals from other industries who are attracted to the Polo brand strength. Management's combination of loyalty, longevity, and experience is a great advantage for our performance.

Regarding teamwork, I would be remiss if I did not thank our 6,800 employees worldwide for their hard work. With their energetic support and dedication, I see no limits to what we can achieve. As their executive, as your fellow shareholder, and personally, I intend to do everything necessary for Polo Ralph Lauren to maintain its visibility as one of the world's leading lifestyle brands.

I began this letter in terms of Polo's growth and performance, and I will end it the same way: Our Company is stronger than it was a year ago. Polo Ralph Lauren is growing, with an ever-increasing number of its products either in the launch or early growth phase of their cycle. We will continue to innovate, leveraging the brand into new lifestyle categories and markets. As we enter fiscal 2000, we are on course to meet the expectations that shareholders have of us, and that we have of ourselves.

Ralph Lauren
RALPH LAUREN
Chairman of the Board
Chief Executive Officer

1999
WORLDWIDE WHOLESALE NET SALES

POLO RALPH LAUREN

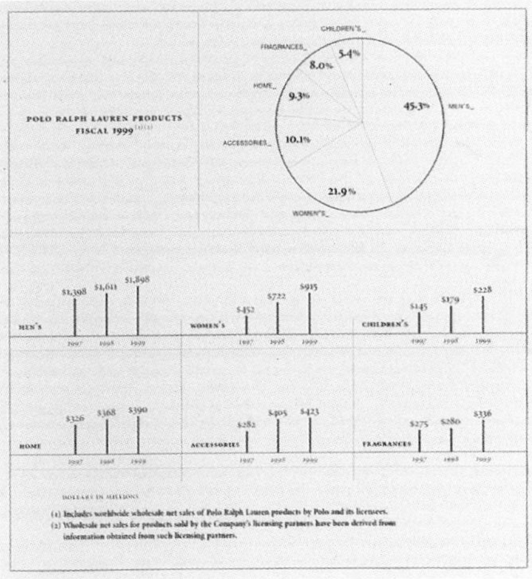
POLO RALPH LAUREN PRODUCTS
FISCAL 1999
CHILDREN'S
FRAGRANCES
HOME
ACCESSORIES
WOMEN'S
MEN'S
5.4%
8.0%
9.3%
10.1%
21.9%
45.3%
MEN'S
$1,398
$1,611
$1,898
WOMEN'S
$452
$722
$915
CHILDREN'S
$145
$179
$228
HOME
$326
$368
$390
ACCESSORIES
$282
$405
$423
FRAGRANCES
$275
$280
$336
DOLLARS IN MILLIONS
(1) Includes worldwide wholesale net sales of Polo Ralph Lauren products by Polo and its licensees.
(2) Wholesale net sales for products sold by the Company's licensing partners have been derived from information obtained from such licensing partners.

RALPH LAUREN
Chairman of the Board
Chief Executive Officer

I SEE A COMPANY THAT IS — LITERALLY AND FIGURATIVELY — A PUBLIC COMPANY, AS PASSIONATE ABOUT DELIVERING **SHAREHOLDER VALUE** AS IT IS ABOUT ENSURING BRAND STRENGTH AND PRODUCT QUALITY.

DEAR FELLOW SHAREHOLDERS In 1999, strong growth across all segments of Polo Ralph Lauren resulted in record revenue performance for our Company. We launched exciting new lines and expanded our markets geographically. However, despite top-line growth, our performance in terms of margin, operating income, and return on equity was below our expectations.

Last year in our inaugural annual report, I described to you how this Company was founded 31 years ago as a line of ties. That story of our modest beginnings often is repeated as it underscores the significance of what Polo Ralph Lauren has become: a global brand inspired by a vision for living, expressed over and over again in timeless elements of style. From that original line of ties, we have gone on to design whole worlds. And we make those worlds accessible to consumers with products that are original, elegant, and classic.

Equally important in that story, but often overlooked, is the insight it offers into our resolve and commitment to build and manage our brand. Establishing Polo Ralph Lauren as one of the most widely recognized global brands with worldwide wholesale net sales of $4.2 billion in fiscal 1999 has required us to face and overcome many challenges. That is particularly significant given the extent to which we have altered the world's perception of American quality and style, and how steadfastly we have maintained our brand integrity.

Upon this foundation, we have built our brand into an industry leader. Yet despite its worldwide presence and name recognition, ours is still very much a young brand. Like the business that pilots it, our brand is full of tremendous growth potential, which we have only just begun to tap.

That potential is there because we always meant for our brand to look beyond fashion for its opportunities. In fact, I do not consider Polo to be a fashion company. We derive our brand equity from concentrating on style — and how people want to live. Lifestyle is how you present yourself in all aspects of life — at work, home, when traveling, and at play. We position Polo as a global lifestyle brand associated with value and quality.

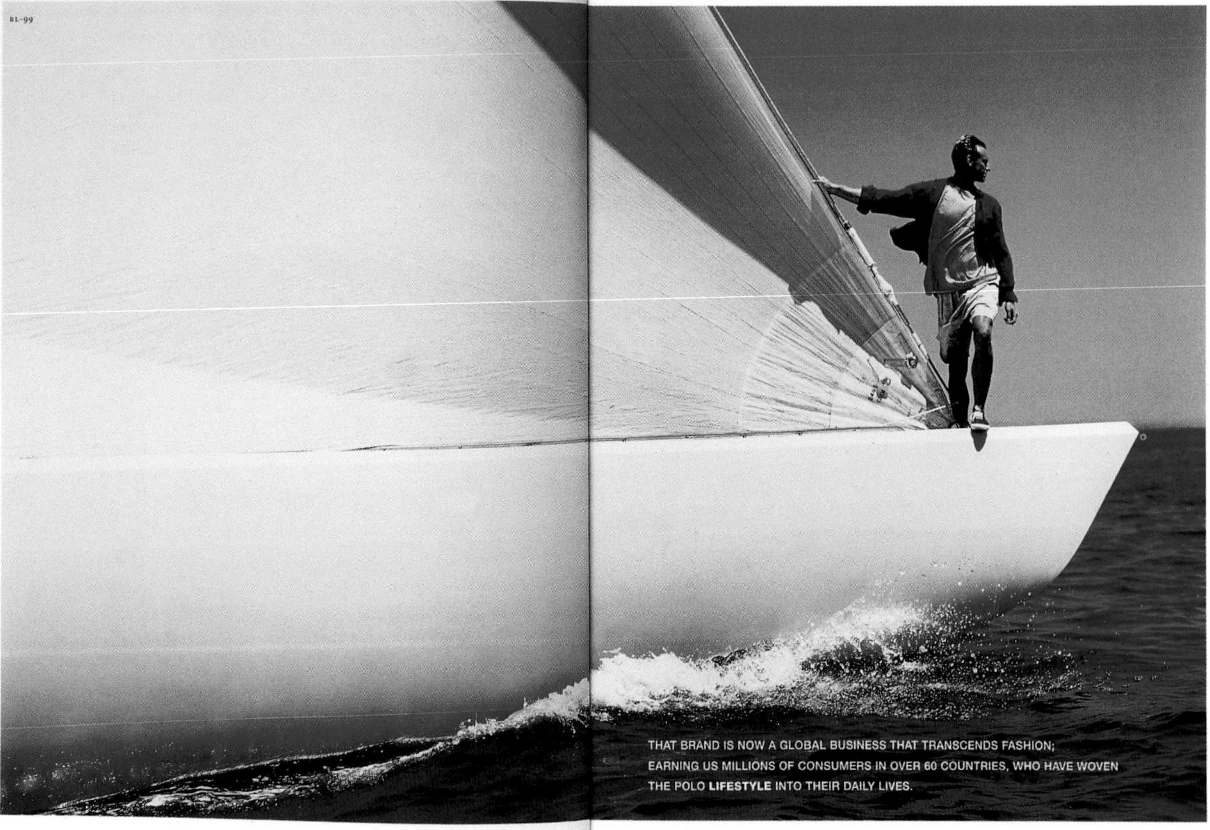
THAT BRAND IS NOW A GLOBAL BUSINESS THAT TRANSCENDS FASHION;
EARNING US MILLIONS OF CONSUMERS IN OVER 60 COUNTRIES, WHO HAVE WOVEN
THE POLO LIFESTYLE INTO THEIR DAILY LIVES.

RL-99
I SEE TREMENDOUS GROWTH POTENTIAL AHEAD, THANKS TO A BUSINESS MODEL THAT
LEVERAGES OUR BRAND ACROSS PRODUCT CATEGORIES AND GEOGRAPHIC REGIONS.
9.

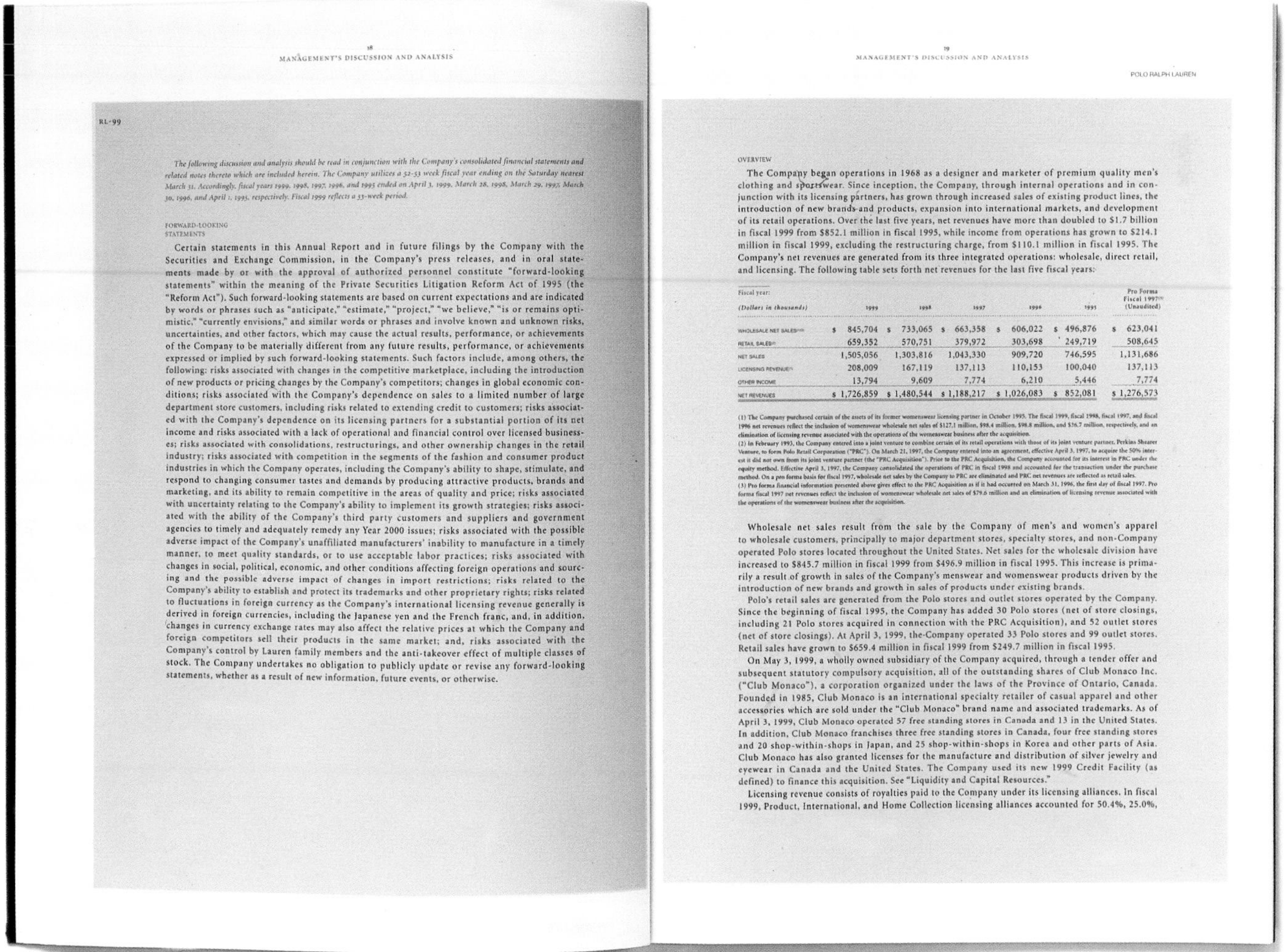

18
MANAGEMENT'S DISCUSSION AND ANALYSIS

RL-99

The following discussion and analysis should be read in conjunction with the Company's consolidated financial statements and related notes thereto which are included herein. The Company utilizes a 52-53 week fiscal year ending on the Saturday nearest March 31. Accordingly, fiscal years 1999, 1998, 1997, 1996, and 1995 ended on April 3, 1999, March 28, 1998, March 29, 1997, March 30, 1996, and April 1, 1995, respectively. Fiscal 1999 reflects a 53-week period.

FORWARD-LOOKING STATEMENTS

Certain statements in this Annual Report and in future filings by the Company with the Securities and Exchange Commission, in the Company's press releases, and in oral statements made by or with the approval of authorized personnel constitute "forward-looking statements" within the meaning of the Private Securities Litigation Reform Act of 1995 (the "Reform Act"). Such forward-looking statements are based on current expectations and are indicated by words or phrases such as "anticipate," "estimate," "project," "we believe," "is or remains optimistic," "currently envisions," and similar words or phrases and involve known and unknown risks, uncertainties, and other factors, which may cause the actual results, performance, or achievements of the Company to be materially different from any future results, performance, or achievements expressed or implied by such forward-looking statements. Such factors include, among others, the following: risks associated with changes in the competitive marketplace, including the introduction of new products or pricing changes by the Company's competitors; changes in global economic conditions; risks associated with the Company's dependence on sales to a limited number of large department store customers, including risks related to extending credit to customers; risks associated with the Company's dependence on its licensing partners for a substantial portion of its net income and risks associated with a lack of operational and financial control over licensed businesses; risks associated with consolidations, restructurings, and other ownership changes in the retail industry; risks associated with competition in the segments of the fashion and consumer product industries in which the Company operates, including the Company's ability to shape, stimulate, and respond to changing consumer tastes and demands by producing attractive products, brands and marketing, and its ability to remain competitive in the areas of quality and price; risks associated with uncertainty relating to the Company's ability to implement its growth strategies; risks associated with the ability of the Company's third party customers and suppliers and government agencies to timely and adequately remedy any Year 2000 issues; risks associated with the possible adverse impact of the Company's unaffiliated manufacturers' inability to manufacture in a timely manner, to meet quality standards, or to use acceptable labor practices; risks associated with changes in social, political, economic, and other conditions affecting foreign operations and sourcing and the possible adverse impact of changes in import restrictions; risks related to the Company's ability to establish and protect its trademarks and other proprietary rights; risks related to fluctuations in foreign currency as the Company's international licensing revenue generally is derived in foreign currencies, including the Japanese yen and the French franc, and, in addition, changes in currency exchange rates may also affect the relative prices at which the Company and foreign competitors sell their products in the same market; and, risks associated with the Company's control by Lauren family members and the anti-takeover effect of multiple classes of stock. The Company undertakes no obligation to publicly update or revise any forward-looking statements, whether as a result of new information, future events, or otherwise.

19
MANAGEMENT'S DISCUSSION AND ANALYSIS

POLO RALPH LAUREN

OVERVIEW

The Company began operations in 1968 as a designer and marketer of premium quality men's clothing and sportswear. Since inception, the Company, through internal operations and in conjunction with its licensing partners, has grown through increased sales of existing product lines, the introduction of new brands and products, expansion into international markets, and development of its retail operations. Over the last five years, net revenues have more than doubled to $1.7 billion in fiscal 1999 from $852.1 million in fiscal 1995, while income from operations has grown to $214.1 million in fiscal 1999, excluding the restructuring charge, from $110.1 million in fiscal 1995. The Company's net revenues are generated from its three integrated operations: wholesale, direct retail, and licensing. The following table sets forth net revenues for the last five fiscal years:

Fiscal year: (Dollars in thousands)	1999	1998	1997	1996	1995	Pro Forma Fiscal 1997(3) (Unaudited)
WHOLESALE NET SALES(1)(2)	$ 845,704	$ 733,065	$ 663,358	$ 606,022	$ 496,876	$ 623,041
RETAIL SALES(2)	659,352	570,751	379,972	303,698	249,719	508,645
NET SALES	1,505,056	1,303,816	1,043,330	909,720	746,595	1,131,686
LICENSING REVENUE(1)	208,009	167,119	137,113	110,153	100,040	137,113
OTHER INCOME	13,794	9,609	7,774	6,210	5,446	7,774
NET REVENUES	$ 1,726,859	$ 1,480,544	$ 1,188,217	$ 1,026,083	$ 852,081	$ 1,276,573

(1) The Company purchased certain of the assets of its former womenswear licensing partner in October 1995. The fiscal 1999, fiscal 1998, fiscal 1997, and fiscal 1996 net revenues reflect the inclusion of womenswear wholesale net sales of $127.1 million, $98.4 million, $98.8 million, and $36.7 million, respectively, and an elimination of licensing revenue associated with the operations of the womenswear business after the acquisition.
(2) In February 1993, the Company entered into a joint venture to combine certain of its retail operations with those of its joint venture partner, Perkins Shearer Venture, to form Polo Retail Corporation ("PRC"). On March 21, 1997, the Company entered into an agreement, effective April 3, 1997, to acquire the 50% interest it did not own from its joint venture partner (the "PRC Acquisition"). Prior to the PRC Acquisition, the Company accounted for its interest in PRC under the equity method. Effective April 3, 1997, the Company consolidated the operations of PRC in fiscal 1998 and accounted for the transaction under the purchase method. On a pro forma basis for fiscal 1997, wholesale net sales by the Company to PRC are eliminated and PRC net revenues are reflected as retail sales.
(3) Pro forma financial information presented above gives effect to the PRC Acquisition as if it had occurred on March 31, 1996, the first day of fiscal 1997. Pro forma fiscal 1997 net revenues reflect the inclusion of womenswear wholesale net sales of $79.6 million and an elimination of licensing revenue associated with the operations of the womenswear business after the acquisition.

Wholesale net sales result from the sale by the Company of men's and women's apparel to wholesale customers, principally to major department stores, specialty stores, and non-Company operated Polo stores located throughout the United States. Net sales for the wholesale division have increased to $845.7 million in fiscal 1999 from $496.9 million in fiscal 1995. This increase is primarily a result of growth in sales of the Company's menswear and womenswear products driven by the introduction of new brands and growth in sales of products under existing brands.

Polo's retail sales are generated from the Polo stores and outlet stores operated by the Company. Since the beginning of fiscal 1995, the Company has added 30 Polo stores (net of store closings, including 21 Polo stores acquired in connection with the PRC Acquisition), and 52 outlet stores (net of store closings). At April 3, 1999, the Company operated 33 Polo stores and 99 outlet stores. Retail sales have grown to $659.4 million in fiscal 1999 from $249.7 million in fiscal 1995.

On May 3, 1999, a wholly owned subsidiary of the Company acquired, through a tender offer and subsequent statutory compulsory acquisition, all of the outstanding shares of Club Monaco Inc. ("Club Monaco"), a corporation organized under the laws of the Province of Ontario, Canada. Founded in 1985, Club Monaco is an international specialty retailer of casual apparel and other accessories which are sold under the "Club Monaco" brand name and associated trademarks. As of April 3, 1999, Club Monaco operated 57 free standing stores in Canada and 13 in the United States. In addition, Club Monaco franchises three free standing stores in Canada, four free standing stores and 20 shop-within-shops in Japan, and 25 shop-within-shops in Korea and other parts of Asia. Club Monaco has also granted licenses for the manufacture and distribution of silver jewelry and eyewear in Canada and the United States. The Company used its new 1999 Credit Facility (as defined) to finance this acquisition. See "Liquidity and Capital Resources."

Licensing revenue consists of royalties paid to the Company under its licensing alliances. In fiscal 1999, Product, International, and Home Collection licensing alliances accounted for 50.4%, 25.0%,

Maconde
Agency: João Machado Design, Lda
Art & Creative Director, Designer: João Machado
Copywriter: Maconde

MACONDE
CONFECÇÕES S.A.

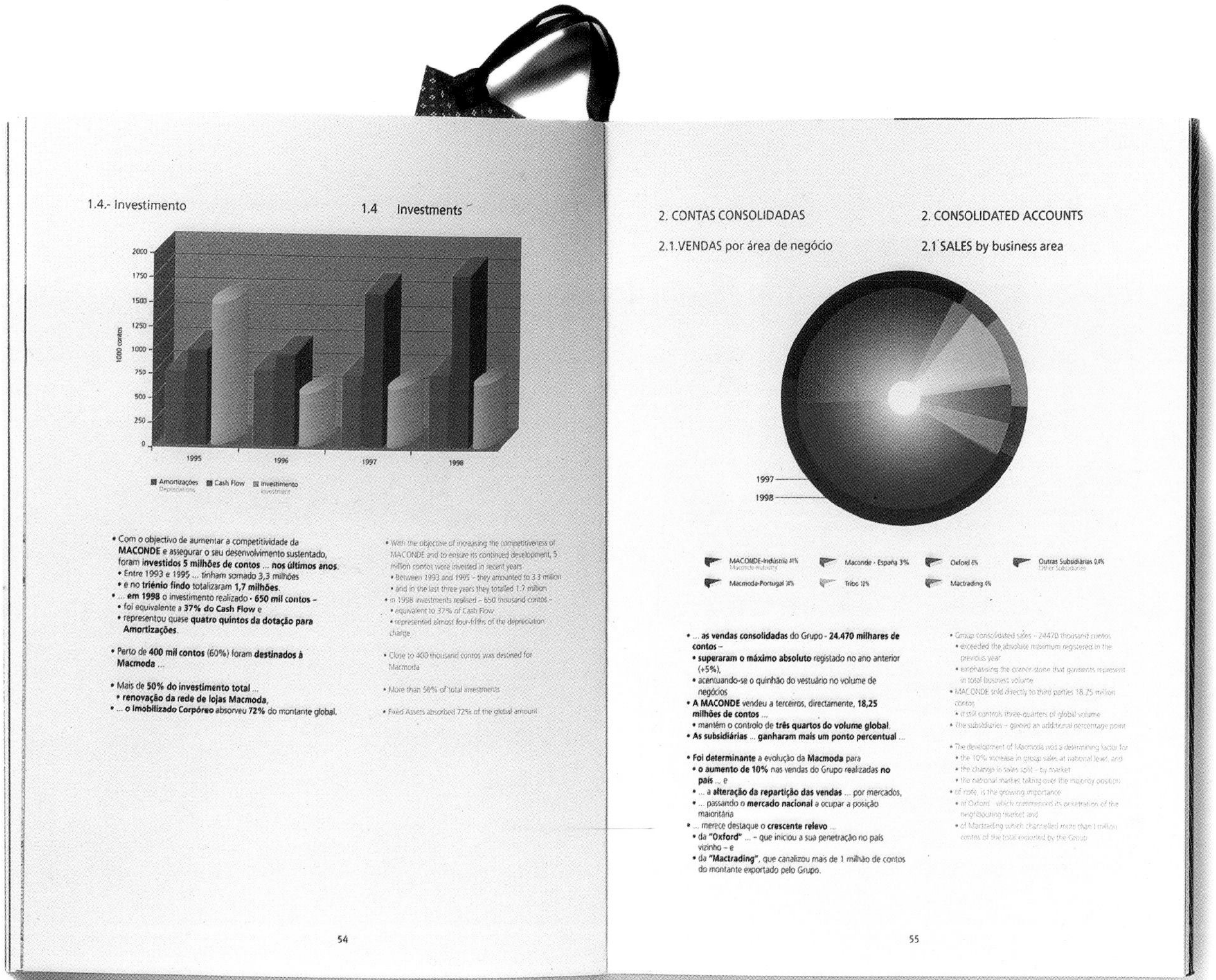
1.4.- Investimento
1.4 Investments
1995
1996
1997
1998
2. CONTAS CONSOLIDADAS
2. CONSOLIDATED ACCOUNTS
2.1.VENDAS por área de negócio
2.1 SALES by business area
1997
1998
54
55

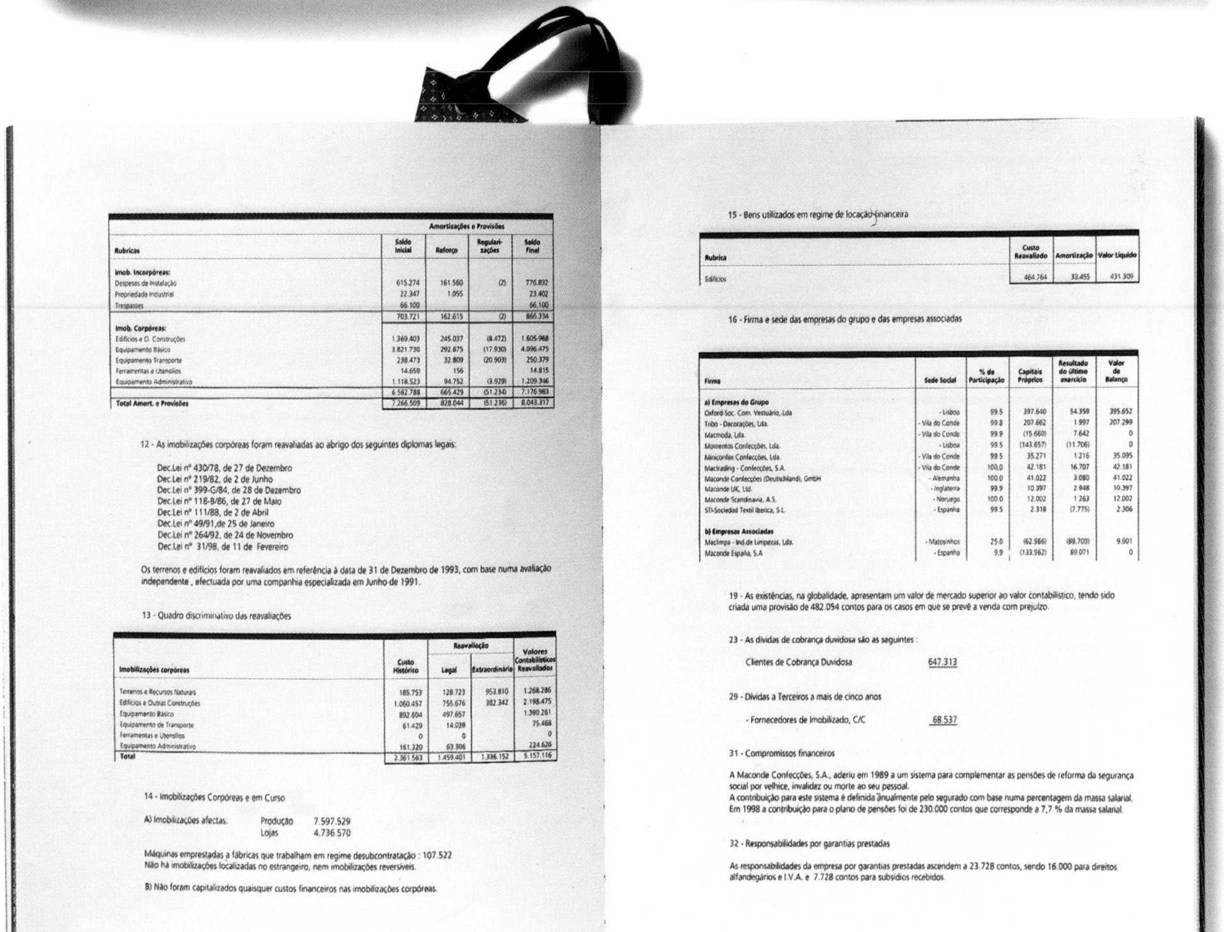
15 - Bens utilizados em regime de locação financeira
16 - Firma e sede das empresas do grupo e das empresas associadas
38
39

The 1998 Annual Report of the Chicago Board of Trade

THE FUTURE BELONGS TO YOU

The Annual Report of the Chicago Board of Trade
THE FUTURE BELONGS TO YOU
YOU
YOU, THE MEMBERS, reaffirm every day what the world has known for more than 150 years — that Chicago Board of Trade members are serious about their business and they will take the necessary risk to compete. And they will always be...

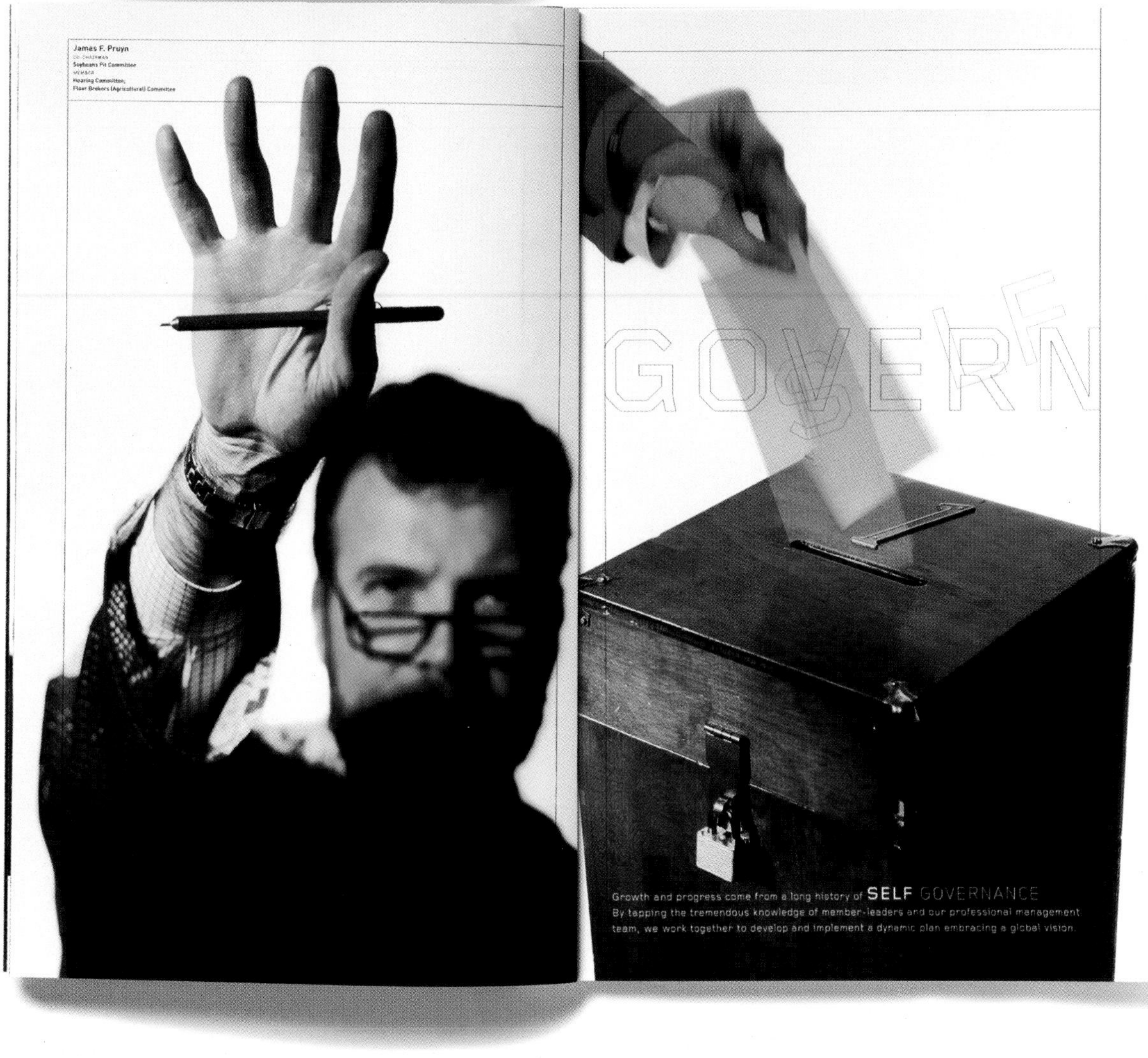
James F. Pruyn
CO-CHAIRMAN
Soybeans Pit Committee
MEMBER
Hearing Committee;
Floor Brokers (Agricultural) Committee
GOVERN
SELF
Growth and progress come from a long history of SELF GOVERNANCE
By tapping the tremendous knowledge of member-leaders and our professional management team, we work together to develop and implement a dynamic plan embracing a global vision.

Joel R. Riechers
CHAIRMAN
Floor Agricultural Subcommittee
CO-VICE CHAIRMAN
Floor Executive Committee
MEMBER
Floor Governors Committee;
Floor Brokers (Agricultural) Committee
Enhancing OUR WAY OF DOING BUSINESS: The Chicago Board of Trade rededicated itself to maximizing order execution and efficiency by expanding use of electronic order routing, resulting in fewer outtrades, faster fills, and low administration costs.

1998 Board of Directors
BOARD OF TRADE OF THE CITY OF CHICAGO, SUBSIDIARIES AND AFFILIATES
Robert H. Michel
Former Republican Leader
U.S. House of Representatives
Senior Advisor for Corporate & Government Affairs
Hogan & Hartson
Ronald M. Hersch
Executive Vice President
Bear Stearns Securities Co.
Paul R. T. Johnson, Jr.
Senior Vice President
ING Securities & Options, Inc.
President
LSU Trading Co.
Nicholas C. Zagotta
Sole Proprietor
Zagotta Grain
James J. O'Connor
Chairman / Chief Executive Officer
Unicom Corporation (Retired)
Charles P. Carey, Jr.
Independent Trader
Gov. James R. Thompson
Partner and Chairman of the Executive Committee
Winston & Strawn
Jack R. Frymire
Vice President / Secretary
Iowa Grain Co.
Dr. Robert S. Hamada
Edward Eagle Brown Distinguished Professor of Finance
Dean
University of Chicago Graduate School of Business
34
1998 Board of Directors
BOARD OF TRADE OF THE CITY OF CHICAGO, SUBSIDIARIES AND AFFILIATES
Wallace G. Weisenborn
President
ING (U.S.) Securities, Futures and Options, Inc.
Peter C. Lee
Managing Director
Exchange-Traded Derivatives
Global Execution Services
Merrill Lynch
Michael A. Manning
Executive Vice President
Rand Financial Services, Inc.
Michael Patrick Ryan
Independent Trader and Floor Broker
Thomas M. Marsh
Independent Trader
Charles P. Nastro
Managing Director
Lehman Brothers, Inc.
James E. Cashman
Independent Trader
Jay S. Sorkin
Independent Trader
Harold I. Richard
President / Chief Executive Officer
Farmers Commodities Corporation
Ralph H. Weems
Past President
American Soybean Association
James F. Curley
Chairman / Chief Executive Officer
Cresvale International (U.S.) L.L.C.
35

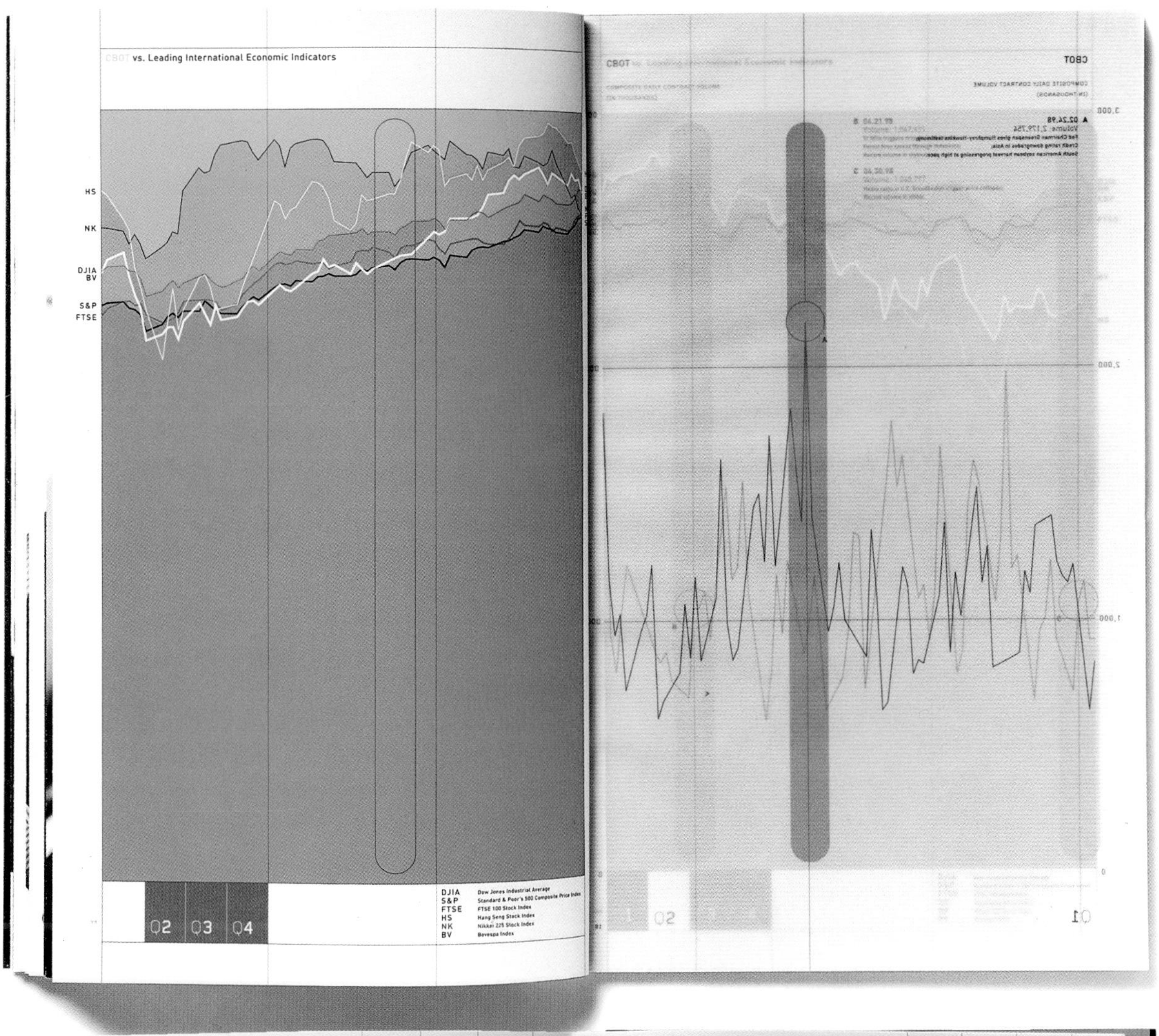

CBOT vs. Leading International Economic Indicators
HS
NK
DJIA
BV
S&P
FTSE
Q2
Q3
Q4
DJIA Dow Jones Industrial Average
S&P Standard & Poor's 500 Composite Price Index
FTSE FTSE 100 Stock Index
HS Hang Seng Stock Index
NK Nikkei 225 Stock Index
BV Bovespa Index
CBOT
Q2

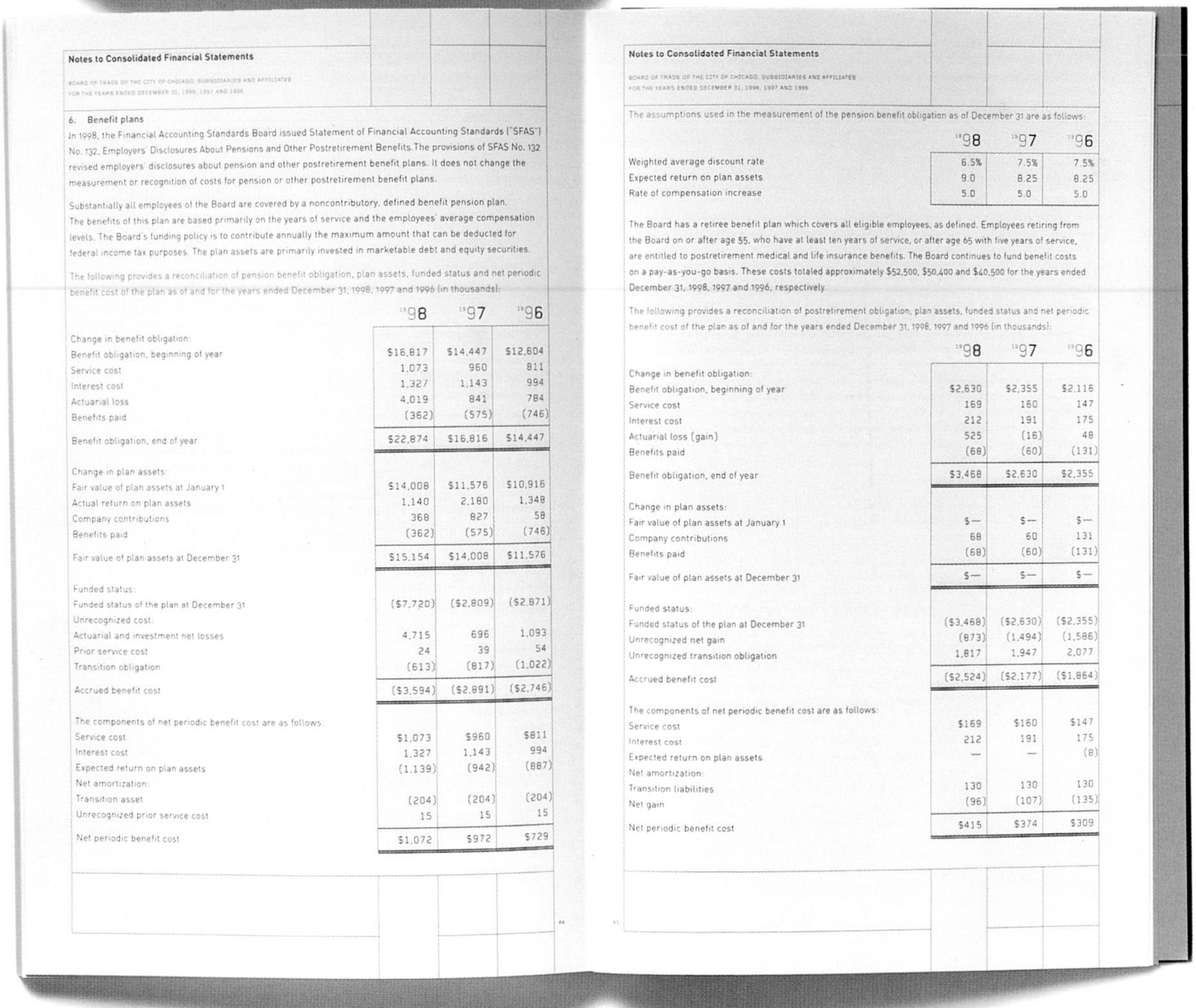

Notes to Consolidated Financial Statements

BOARD OF TRADE OF THE CITY OF CHICAGO, SUBSIDIARIES AND AFFILIATES
FOR THE YEARS ENDED DECEMBER 31, 1998, 1997 AND 1996

6. **Benefit plans**

In 1998, the Financial Accounting Standards Board issued Statement of Financial Accounting Standards ("SFAS") No. 132, Employers' Disclosures About Pensions and Other Postretirement Benefits. The provisions of SFAS No. 132 revised employers' disclosures about pension and other postretirement benefit plans. It does not change the measurement or recognition of costs for pension or other postretirement benefit plans.

Substantially all employees of the Board are covered by a noncontributory, defined benefit pension plan. The benefits of this plan are based primarily on the years of service and the employees' average compensation levels. The Board's funding policy is to contribute annually the maximum amount that can be deducted for federal income tax purposes. The plan assets are primarily invested in marketable debt and equity securities.

The following provides a reconciliation of pension benefit obligation, plan assets, funded status and net periodic benefit cost of the plan as of and for the years ended December 31, 1998, 1997 and 1996 (in thousands):

	1998	1997	1996
Change in benefit obligation:			
Benefit obligation, beginning of year	$16,817	$14,447	$12,604
Service cost	1,073	960	811
Interest cost	1,327	1,143	994
Actuarial loss	4,019	841	784
Benefits paid	(362)	(575)	(746)
Benefit obligation, end of year	$22,874	$16,816	$14,447
Change in plan assets:			
Fair value of plan assets at January 1	$14,008	$11,576	$10,916
Actual return on plan assets	1,140	2,180	1,348
Company contributions	368	827	58
Benefits paid	(362)	(575)	(746)
Fair value of plan assets at December 31	$15,154	$14,008	$11,576
Funded status:			
Funded status of the plan at December 31	($7,720)	($2,809)	($2,871)
Unrecognized cost:			
Actuarial and investment net losses	4,715	696	1,093
Prior service cost	24	39	54
Transition obligation	(613)	(817)	(1,022)
Accrued benefit cost	($3,594)	($2,891)	($2,746)
The components of net periodic benefit cost are as follows:			
Service cost	$1,073	$960	$811
Interest cost	1,327	1,143	994
Expected return on plan assets	(1,139)	(942)	(887)
Net amortization:			
Transition asset	(204)	(204)	(204)
Unrecognized prior service cost	15	15	15
Net periodic benefit cost	$1,072	$972	$729

Notes to Consolidated Financial Statements

BOARD OF TRADE OF THE CITY OF CHICAGO, SUBSIDIARIES AND AFFILIATES
FOR THE YEARS ENDED DECEMBER 31, 1998, 1997 AND 1996

The assumptions used in the measurement of the pension benefit obligation as of December 31 are as follows:

	1998	1997	1996
Weighted average discount rate	6.5%	7.5%	7.5%
Expected return on plan assets	9.0	8.25	8.25
Rate of compensation increase	5.0	5.0	5.0

The Board has a retiree benefit plan which covers all eligible employees, as defined. Employees retiring from the Board on or after age 55, who have at least ten years of service, or after age 65 with five years of service, are entitled to postretirement medical and life insurance benefits. The Board continues to fund benefit costs on a pay-as-you-go basis. These costs totaled approximately $52,500, $50,400 and $40,500 for the years ended December 31, 1998, 1997 and 1996, respectively.

The following provides a reconciliation of postretirement obligation, plan assets, funded status and net periodic benefit cost of the plan as of and for the years ended December 31, 1998, 1997 and 1996 (in thousands):

	1998	1997	1996
Change in benefit obligation:			
Benefit obligation, beginning of year	$2,630	$2,355	$2,116
Service cost	169	160	147
Interest cost	212	191	175
Actuarial loss (gain)	525	(16)	48
Benefits paid	(68)	(60)	(131)
Benefit obligation, end of year	$3,468	$2,630	$2,355
Change in plan assets:			
Fair value of plan assets at January 1	$—	$—	$—
Company contributions	68	60	131
Benefits paid	(68)	(60)	(131)
Fair value of plan assets at December 31	$—	$—	$—
Funded status:			
Funded status of the plan at December 31	($3,468)	($2,630)	($2,355)
Unrecognized net gain	(873)	(1,494)	(1,586)
Unrecognized transition obligation	1,817	1,947	2,077
Accrued benefit cost	($2,524)	($2,177)	($1,864)
The components of net periodic benefit cost are as follows:			
Service cost	$169	$160	$147
Interest cost	212	191	175
Expected return on plan assets	—	—	(8)
Net amortization:			
Transition liabilities	130	130	130
Net gain	(96)	(107)	(135)
Net periodic benefit cost	$415	$374	$309

Statement of Values

USTrust is a community oriented, full service commercial bank. Our principal business is providing high quality financial services to individuals and commercial customers in the eastern Massachusetts area. We add significant value for our constituencies while holding to the highest standards of ethical business practice.

Balance in serving our four constituencies is the best assurance of superior performance.

We treat our customers as our most important constituency. As the alternative to small and larger banks, we provide essential products and services that are high quality, responsive to customer needs, and attractively priced. We are relationship bankers who consistently meet our customers' everyday and specialized needs.

We recognize employees as our most important asset. We are a knowledgeable and diverse team who serve each other and

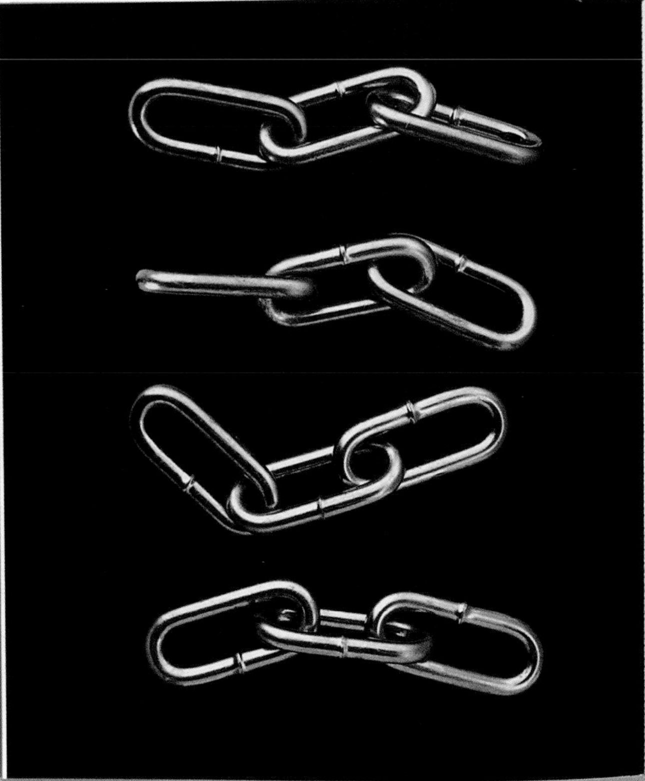

Insurance

A blacksmith was given four segments of chain and asked to join them together to make a circle. How could he do this while cutting the fewest possible links?

Private Banking and Investment Management

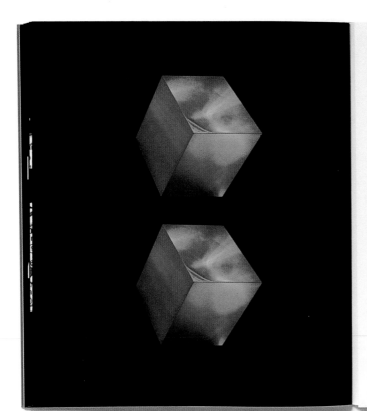

How would you cut a hole in one cube to enable another identically-sized cube to pass through it?

15 80 100 112 1000

ATMs

What is the minimum number of arrows needed to score exactly 1312 on this target?

with all 87 branches flying the colors of USTrust and embracing common values, products, practices, and technology.

Net income for the year, excluding merger-related and restructuring charges, was $70.5 million, or $1.63 per diluted share, compared with $61.7 million, or $1.44 per diluted share, for 1997, excluding merger-related and restructuring charges. Net income after deducting these charges was $55.3 million, or $1.28 per diluted share, in 1998, up from $50.2 million, or $1.18 per diluted share, in 1997.

A Community-oriented, Full-service Commercial Bank

With the completion of our acquisitions of Somerset Savings Bank and Affiliated Community Bancorp, Inc., and its two subsidiaries, Lexington Savings Bank and The Federal Savings Bank, USTrust became a significantly larger player in eastern Massachusetts. Meeting growing service needs across an extended geographic market while realizing the cost reductions implicit in bank acquisitions is an art as well as a science, and we have been improving our knowledge and skills for

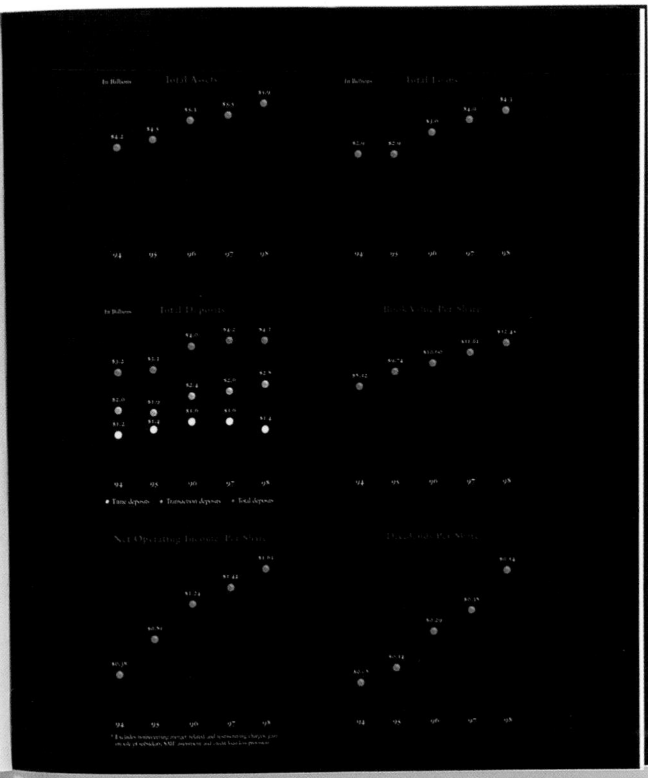

Financial Highlights

(Dollars in thousands, except per share amounts)	1998	1997
For the Year		
Net interest income	$ 252,315	$ 230,530
Provision for possible loan losses	2,239	3,100
Noninterest income	48,804	41,674
Noninterest expense	209,233	190,244
Operating income*	70,491	61,674
Net income	55,286	50,216
Per Share		
Operating income*	$ 1.63	$ 1.44
Net income (diluted)	1.28	1.18
Stockholders' investment	12.45	11.49
Dividends declared	0.54	0.38
At Year End		
Total assets	$ 5,900,877	$ 5,532,978
Total deposits	4,233,671	4,165,540
Loans, net of unearned discount	4,296,103	3,967,529
Reserve for possible loan losses	65,274	68,539
Stockholders' investment	533,545	489,056
Other		
Shares outstanding for book value calculation	42,871,000	42,574,000
Common stock price:		
High	$ 30.187	$ 29.625
Low	16.500	18.125
Year end close	23.563	27.750

*Excludes merger related and restructuring charges, net of tax.

To Our Shareholders

By most measures, 1998 proved the value of UST Corp.'s strategic approach and years of execution. With an asset base approaching $6 billion, we became the #3 banking franchise in metropolitan Boston. For an organization of our original size to accomplish this in one of America's best markets is something that we are proud of and that we have worked hard to make happen.

Our quantitative achievements for 1998 are summarized in the graphs accompanying this letter. The story also stands up when you drill down into the numbers. After allowing for merger-related and restructuring charges in a year notable for the scale of these activities, we stayed on course with 10% growth in net income and healthy increases in new deposit accounts, lending activity, and ATM/debit card transaction volumes. Equally important, we succeeded in forging a single, integrated organization

The Finova Group, Inc.
Agency: CFD Design
Art Director & Designer: John Havel
Photographer: Scott Baxter
Illustrator: Dave Plunkert

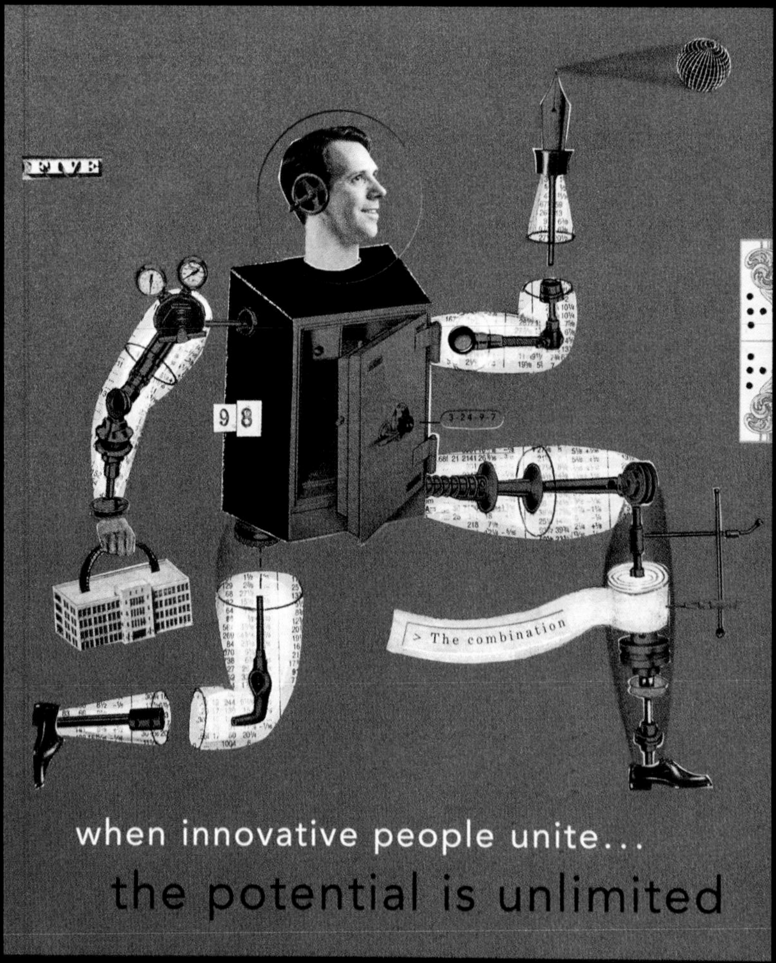
FIVE
98
3-24-9-7
> The combination
when innovative people unite...
the potential is unlimited

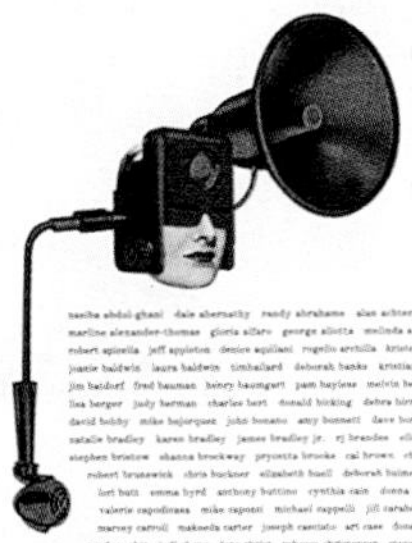

My goal is to get prospects as excited about being a customer as I am about being an employee.

Bruce Sim
VP Syndications & International Ops, Corporate Finance

together, the people

of FINOVA have built one of the largest and most successful financial services companies in the U.S. Our specialty is addressing the financing needs of midsize business – a diverse, dynamic and underserved market. With innovative minds and methods, uncommon focus and skillful execution, we continue to produce exceptional results for our clients and shareowners alike.

welcome to FINOVA

a focused strategy

keeps FINOVA and its people committed to providing custom-tailored solutions

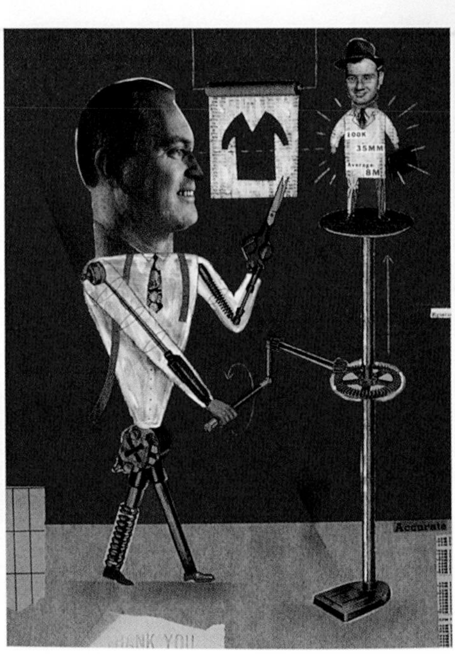

FINOVA's target market
650,000 midsize companies in the U.S.
($2–200 million annual sales or 10–1,000 employees)

that address the unique financing requirements of midsize business. This dynamic and underserved market of more than 650,000 companies leads the U.S. economy in growth, yet is one whose options are limited by the one-size-fits-all approach of smaller lenders and banks or overlooked altogether by larger lenders. So, at FINOVA, we have assembled a broad product line and the attendant underwriting expertise to thoughtfully structure almost any financing accommodation a midsize company may require.

FINOVA's middle market leadership is refined by our product or industry niche approach. Specialized underwriting and collateral expertise and in-depth industry knowledge enable us to be not only the preferred source of financing for our clients, but a key component in their continuing success. And with possibly the largest selection of financing products focused on the middle market, FINOVA's ability to be a 'one-stop' financing source continues to win acceptance. In fact, 24% of our clients were on FINOVA's books with more than one financing product in 1998, up from 6% in 1996, and 36% of our new loan volume, or $1.4 billion, was derived from cross-selling.

In addition to FINOVA's comprehensive product capability, our people provide the personal touch that distinguishes our product – money – from that of other lenders. **"I owned a small business myself, so I really do sweat all the details in crafting a financing package for a customer,"** says Bruce Sim (pictured left), a vice president with FINOVA Corporate Finance in Atlanta. "You'll never convince me that money is a commodity. For our midsize clients, proper structuring and flexible terms can make all the difference in the world."

Our focus on midsize business extends to a significant nonprofit partnership, The FINOVA Alliance for Midsize Business at The University of Arizona. Since 1996, this FINOVA-funded initiative has produced unique economic research, including The FINOVA Quarterly newsletter, notable academic studies and an annual gathering of business leaders, policy experts and scholars. By accenting key business issues within the context of the middle market and bringing greater prominence to an often overlooked yet crucial sector of the U.S. economy, FINOVA continues to add value for its clients as The Capital Source for Midsize Business.

a high-performance culture is a hallmark of FINOVA.

our people, the 'financial innovators'

8

for whom the company is named, operate in an environment oriented toward high standards, aggressive goals and generous rewards, as evidenced by FINOVA's #12 ranking in *FORTUNE* magazine's "100 Best Companies To Work For."

Our product – money – is no different than any other lender's, but how our people package and deliver it is. So, at FINOVA, we do everything possible to attract, develop and retain the best people in the commercial finance industry. From The FINOVA Institute, a mini-MBA program developed with the University of Arizona that advances a common culture and business philosophy companywide, to leading-edge technology systems that increase knowledge-sharing, improve decision-making and reduce 'red tape,' our people are prepared to serve our clients in an uncompromising manner. At FINOVA Franchise Finance in Paramus, N.J., Marketing V.P. Mike Vallorosi and Contract Administration Director Christine Currens (pictured right) expertly manage FINOVA's business development and loan approval processes to quickly and seamlessly deliver innovative financing solutions.

Reaping the benefits are clients like Ron and Marcia York of Southwest Florida Restaurant Investments Inc., which opened the first '50s-themed Denny's Classic Diner concept in the U.S. and has since expanded. "Opportunities like these come together very quickly, so communication, trust and teamwork between our sales, credit and documentation functions is critical," Mike notes. "Our clients are comforted in knowing FINOVA delivers on its commitments." Relentlessly rethinking and refining what we do and how we do it, FINOVA people move quickly to understand and address the changing needs of midsize businesses while maintaining our market leadership and low-cost advantage. Independently administered customer surveys provide objective feedback to improve our performance, and 'stealth visits' at the client's business strengthen relationships and introduce new opportunities.

As the millennium approaches, our exceptional people and unique culture will continue powering FINOVA's emergence as The Capital Source for Midsize Business.

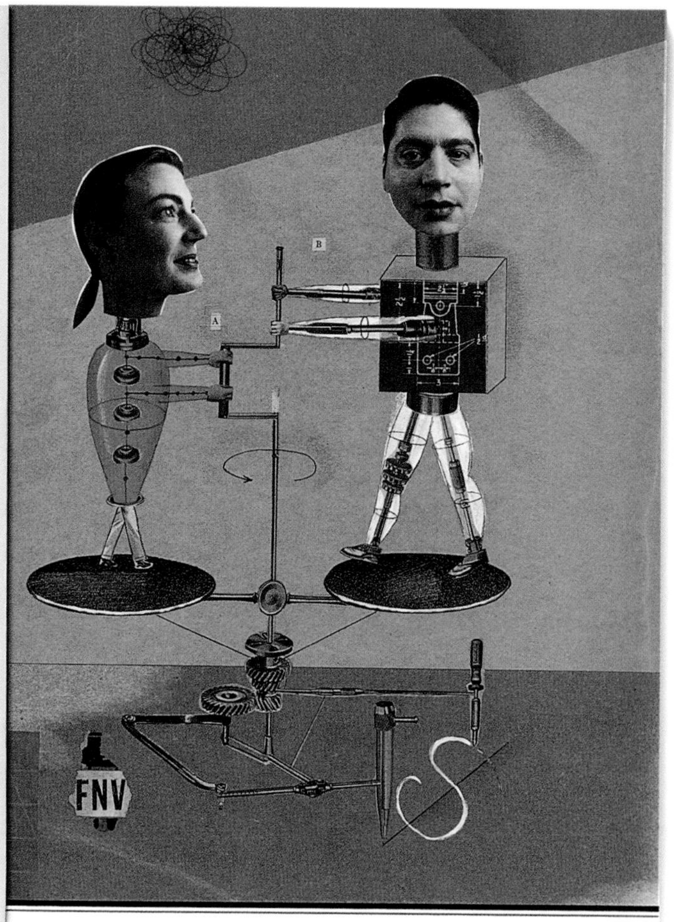

B
A
FNV

a balanced approach

that combines diverse yet complementary businesses with a disciplined methodology

10

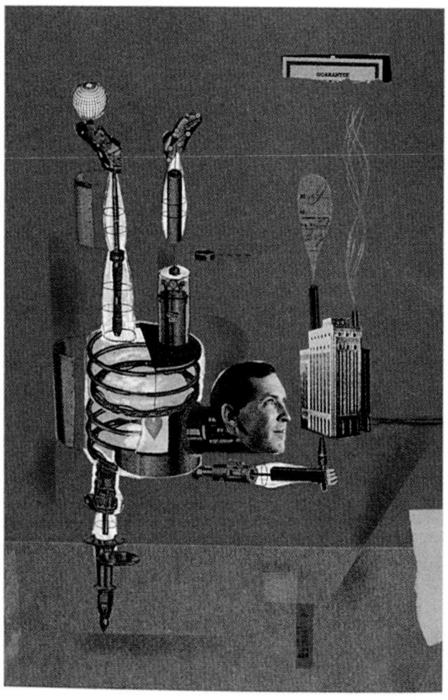

for managing our portfolio has created FINOVA, a dynamic commercial finance franchise optimized to deliver consistent, sustainable growth through a variety of market conditions.

FINOVA's broad-based distribution system of 200 highly cross-trained marketing officers calls on midsize companies throughout the U.S., Canada and select international locations, self-generating more than two-thirds of our new business and minimizing dependence on outside referral sources. At the same time, we supplement strong internal growth with attractive acquisitions that enhance existing businesses or improve our ability to serve our midsize clients. Our October 1998 acquisition of United Credit Corp. marked the birth of FINOVA Growth Finance, a new platform for elongating our relationship with midsize businesses by financing them earlier in their growth cycle. The subsequent acquisition of Electronic Payment Systems, Inc., now FINOVA Loan Administration, brought in-house servicing and collections capabilities to FINOVA Realty Capital's commercial mortgage loan business.

FINOVA's marketing prowess is married to a rigorous credit discipline. Employees like Ward Carr (pictured left), a vice president in FINOVA's Portfolio Management Group in Phoenix, take **a credit-first approach to evaluating new business and monitoring and collecting on existing business.** This helps assure that our portfolio quality remains at near-flawless levels even as our new-business volume and managed assets rise to record levels.

FINOVA is well-diversified by industry and geography, so when market conditions are less favorable in one area, they typically are counterbalanced by more favorable conditions elsewhere. Matched funding of all financing transactions – fixed loans with fixed debt and floating loans with floating debt – helps maintain a healthy, stable operating margin and insulates FINOVA from interest-rate volatility.

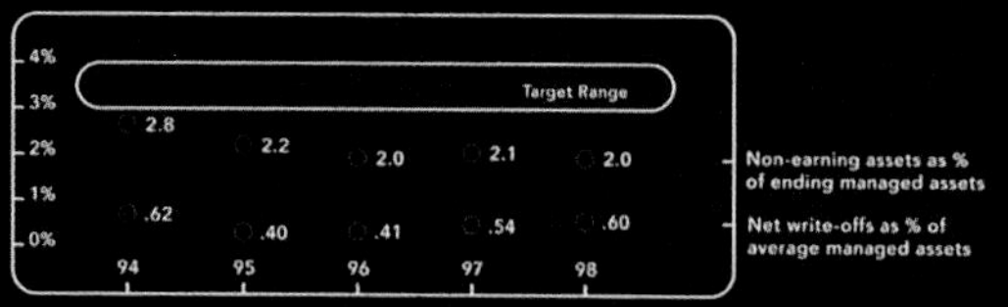

4%
3%
2%
1%
0%
Target Range
2.8
2.2
2.0
2.1
2.0
.62
.40
.41
.54
.60
94
95
96
97
98
Non-earning assets as % of ending managed assets
Net write-offs as % of average managed assets

Strong credit discipline delivers exceptional portfolio quality

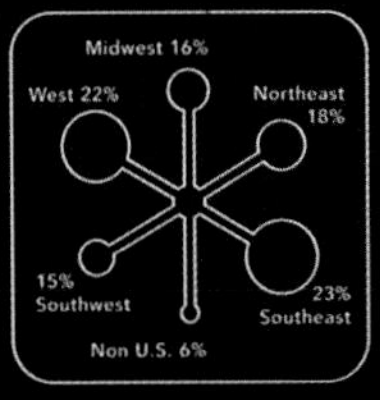
Midwest 16%
West 22%
Northeast 18%
15% Southwest
23% Southeast
Non U.S. 6%

Geographic portfolio distribution

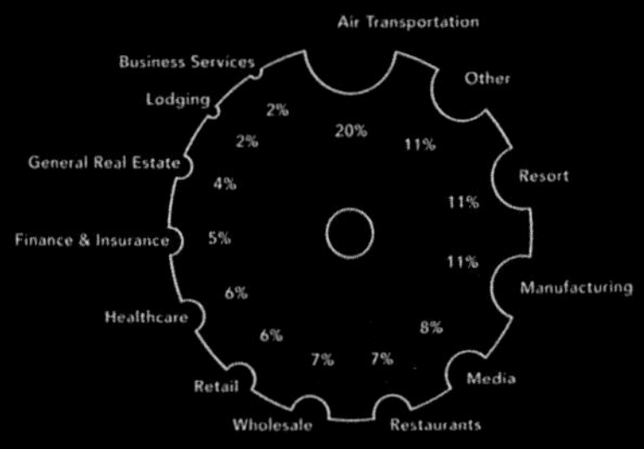
Air Transportation
Business Services
Lodging
Other
General Real Estate
Resort
Finance & Insurance
Manufacturing
Healthcare
Retail
Media
Wholesale
Restaurants
2%
2%
20%
11%
4%
11%
5%
11%
6%
6%
8%
7%
7%

Industry portfolio distribution

FINOVA's highly diversified and complementary businesses reach all corners of the middle market, facilitating consistently strong growth that is largely insulated from changing economic conditions or customer demands.

index to financial statements

statements of consolidated shareowners' equity

	Common Stock	Additional Capital	Retained Income	Accumulated Other Comprehensive (Deficit)/Income	Common Stock in Treasury	Shareowners' Equity	Comprehensive Income
Balance, January 1, 1996	$ 568	$ 686,098	$ 184,381	$ (5,686)	$ (40,177)	$ 825,184	
Comprehensive income:							
Net income			117,000			117,000	$ 117,000
Foreign currency translation							6,694
Other comprehensive income				6,694		6,694	6,694
Comprehensive income							$ 123,694
Net change in unamortized amount of restricted stock		(1,816)				(1,816)	
Dividends			(25,230)			(25,230)	
Shares issued in connection with employee benefit plans		(21)			7,780	7,759	
Balance, December 31, 1996	568	684,261	276,151	1,008	(32,397)	929,591	
Comprehensive income:							
Net income			139,098			139,098	$ 139,098
Foreign currency translation							(1,018)
Other comprehensive income				(1,018)		(1,018)	(1,018)
Comprehensive income							$ 138,080
Issuance of common stock	17	77,521				77,538	
Net change in unamortized amount of restricted stock		(1,558)				(1,558)	
Dividends			(28,584)			(28,584)	
Purchase of shares					(37,296)	(37,296)	
Shares issued in connection with employee benefit plans		4,301			8,382	12,683	
Balance, December 31, 1997	585	764,525	386,665	(10)	(61,311)	1,090,454	
Comprehensive income:							
Net income			169,737			169,737	$ 169,737
Unrealized holding gains							3,422
Foreign currency translation							(208)
Other comprehensive income				3,214		3,214	3,214
Comprehensive income							$ 172,951
Net change in unamortized amount of restricted stock		(1,053)				(1,053)	
Dividends			(33,749)			(33,749)	
Purchase of shares					(63,271)	(63,271)	
Shares issued in connection with employee benefit plans		1,578			10,435	12,013	
Balance, December 31, 1998	$ 585	$ 765,050	$ 522,653	$ 3,204	$ (114,147)	$ 1,177,345	

See notes to consolidated financial statements.

statements of consolidated cash flows

Years Ended December 31, (Dollars in Thousands)	1998	1997	1996
operating activities:			
Net income	$ 169,737	$ 139,098	$ 117,000
Adjustments to reconcile net income to net cash provided by operating activities:			
Provision for credit losses	82,200	69,200	41,751
Depreciation and amortization	93,830	90,396	76,471
Gains on disposal of assets	(55,024)	(30,261)	(12,949)
Deferred income taxes	72,612	30,553	29,356
Gains on dispositions of discontinued operations, net			(3,521)
Change in assets and liabilities, net of effects from acquisitions:			
Increase in other assets	(134,559)	(48,610)	(61,694)
(Decrease) increase in accounts payable and accrued expenses	(1,180)	20,800	(16,009)
Increase (decrease) in interest payable	12,582	(34)	5,853
Other	1,819	(603)	6,153
Net cash provided by operating activities	242,017	270,539	182,411
investing activities:			
Proceeds from sales of assets	129,324	178,413	102,945
Proceeds from sales of securitized assets	99,967	36,565	100,000
Proceeds from sales of commercial mortgage backed securities ("CMBS") assets	869,296		
Principal collections on financing transactions	2,181,364	2,087,619	1,781,985
Expenditures for financing transactions	(3,282,348)	(2,507,822)	(2,221,363)
Expenditures for CMBS transactions	(1,005,373)		
Net change in short-term financing transactions	(631,478)	(844,584)	(624,952)
Acquisitions, net of cash acquired	(61,164)	(120,883)	(7,455)
Sales of discontinued operations			616,434
Other	2,307	2,399	3,296
Net cash used for investing activities	(1,698,105)	(1,168,293)	(249,110)
financing activities:			
Net borrowings under commercial paper and short-term loans	739,515	649,653	62,156
Long-term borrowings	1,580,000	1,080,625	564,988
Repayment of long-term borrowings	(689,176)	(817,892)	(681,401)
Proceeds from exercise of stock options	12,013	12,683	7,759
Net proceeds from sale of company-obligated mandatory redeemable convertible preferred securities of subsidiary trust solely holding convertible debentures of FINOVA ("TOPrS")			111,550
Common stock purchased for treasury	(63,271)	(37,296)	
Dividends	(33,749)	(28,584)	(25,230)
Net change in due to clients	(72,916)	40,495	(32,143)
Net cash provided by financing activities	1,472,416	899,684	7,679
Increase (decrease) in cash and cash equivalents	16,328	1,930	(59,020)
Cash and cash equivalents, beginning of year	33,190	31,260	90,280
Cash and cash equivalents, end of year	$ 49,518	$ 33,190	$ 31,260

See notes to consolidated financial statements.

Silicon Valley Bank

Agency: Cahan & Associates
Art & Creative Director: Bill Cahan
Designer: Sharrie Brooks
Photographer: Tony Stromberg
Illustrator: Jason Holley
Copywriter: Tim Peters

The Art of Success
Silicon Valley Bancshares
1998 Year in Review

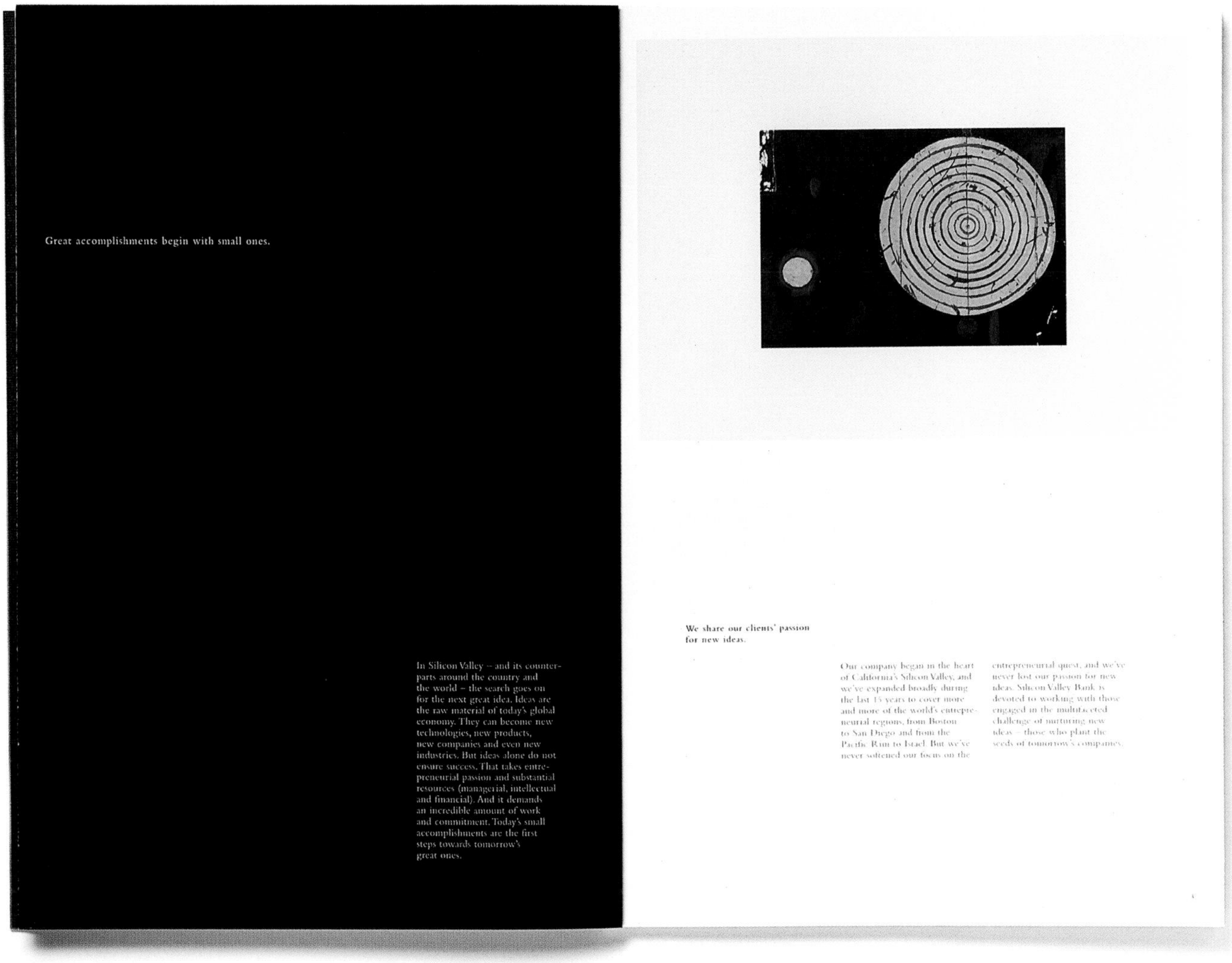
Great accomplishments begin with small ones.
In Silicon Valley – and its counterparts around the country and the world – the search goes on for the next great idea. Ideas are the raw material of today's global economy. They can become new technologies, new products, new companies and even new industries. But ideas alone do not ensure success. That takes entrepreneurial passion and substantial resources (managerial, intellectual and financial). And it demands an incredible amount of work and commitment. Today's small accomplishments are the first steps towards tomorrow's great ones.
We share our clients' passion for new ideas.
Our company began in the heart of California's Silicon Valley, and we've expanded broadly during the last 15 years to cover more and more of the world's entrepreneurial regions, from Boston to San Diego and from the Pacific Rim to Israel. But we've never softened our focus on the entrepreneurial quest, and we've never lost our passion for new ideas. Silicon Valley Bank is devoted to working with those engaged in the multifaceted challenge of nurturing new ideas – those who plant the seeds of tomorrow's companies.

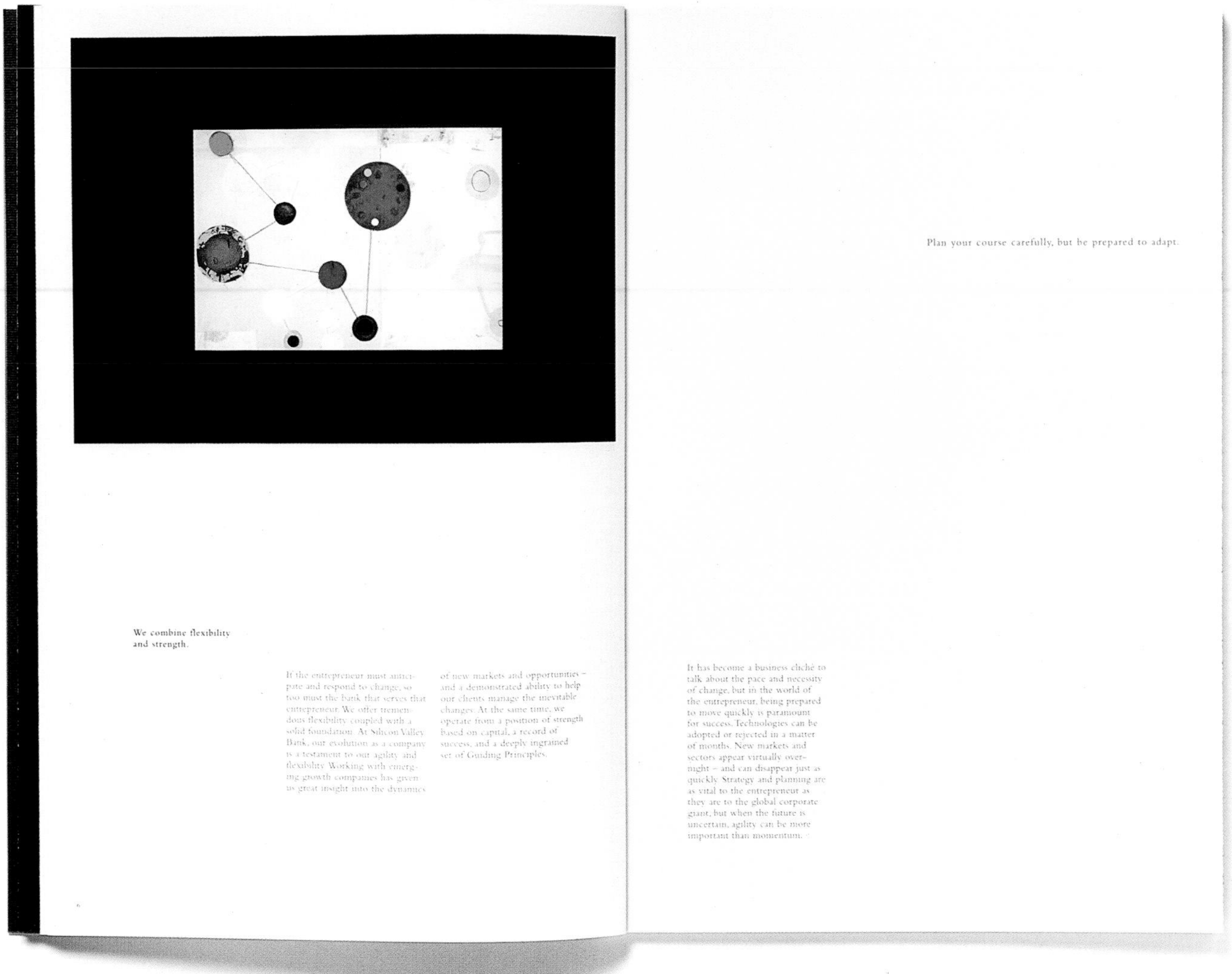
We combine flexibility and strength.
If the entrepreneur must anticipate and respond to change, so too must the bank that serves that entrepreneur. We offer tremendous flexibility coupled with a solid foundation. At Silicon Valley Bank, our evolution as a company is a testament to our agility and flexibility. Working with emerging growth companies has given us great insight into the dynamics of new markets and opportunities – and a demonstrated ability to help our clients manage the inevitable changes. At the same time, we operate from a position of strength based on capital, a record of success, and a deeply ingrained set of Guiding Principles.
Plan your course carefully, but be prepared to adapt.
It has become a business cliché to talk about the pace and necessity of change, but in the world of the entrepreneur, being prepared to move quickly is paramount for success. Technologies can be adopted or rejected in a matter of months. New markets and sectors appear virtually overnight – and can disappear just as quickly. Strategy and planning are as vital to the entrepreneur as they are to the global corporate giant, but when the future is uncertain, agility can be more important than momentum.

Study the past for what it reveals of the future.

Entrepreneurs don't anticipate or even predict the future – *they create it*. But they know that looking back can be useful. Everyone engaged in building the future can learn from the past – triumphs and tribulations.

Our experience is a resource.

Turning a great idea into tomorrow's successful company requires the efforts and the wisdom of many – a collection of skills, talents and experience. At Silicon Valley Bank, each banker's personal experience, along with the experiences we've distilled from working with clients over the past 15 years, is a tremendous resource for every client and every relationship. Experience doesn't automatically generate answers, but it definitely helps us chart a course for the journey ahead, and it strengthens our confidence in anticipating the future.

11

The Life Cycle of Emerging Growth Companies

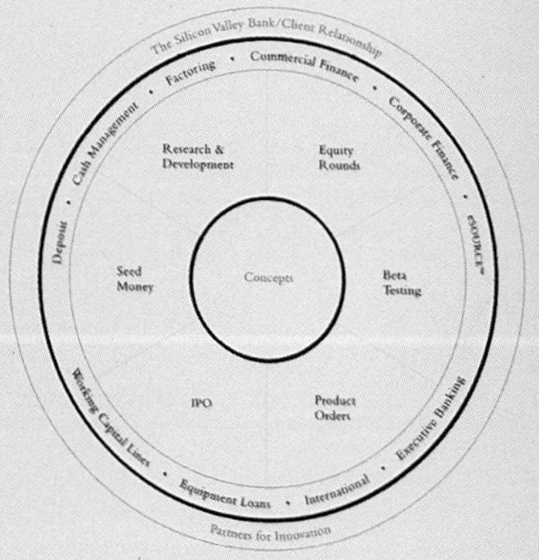

The Silicon Valley Bank/Client Relationship
Factoring • Commercial Finance • Corporate Finance • eSOURCE™
Executive Banking • International • Equipment Loans • Working Capital Lines
Deposit • Cash Management
Research & Development
Equity Rounds
Seed Money
Concepts
Beta Testing
IPO
Product Orders
Partners for Innovation

We are with you every step of the way.

In the popular imagination, the evolution of an entrepreneurial company begins in the prototypical garage and ends with an initial public offering. There's an element of truth in that depiction, but the reality is more complex and much more interesting. Companies begin and develop in a great variety of ways, in a great variety of places, and at a great variety of speeds. Still, the life cycle of emerging growth companies can be mapped to some degree, as this chart illustrates. We use this dynamic as a blueprint for building relationships with emerging growth companies and for guiding the development and deployment of specialized products and services.

17

Unite with allies to ensure success.

We are partners in your growth.

Silicon Valley Bank embodies the ideas of teamwork and partnership. We work together to address the needs of our clients. We work with our clients to build relationships of trust and value; we are eager to become a part of their growing enterprise. Moreover, we have built a growing network of resources that we apply to the needs of our clients, resources that address a huge range of issues and challenges for entrepreneurial clients. Our role is more than mere matchmaking; we always seek to add value to clients, to apply our knowledge, our relationship, and our insight in their quest for resources to help them reach their goals.

The dream of the entrepreneur begins with an individual and an idea, but building a business is a team effort. In today's world, the concept of teamwork has been greatly extended, as companies seek partnerships, alliances, joint ventures, and other relationships to create enterprises of vendors, suppliers and customers. These are allies in the pursuit of success.

Selected Financial Data

Years Ended December 31, (Dollars and numbers in thousands, except per share amounts)	1998	1997	1996	1995
Income Statement Summary:				
Net interest income	$ 146,615	$ 110,824	$ 87,275	$ 73,952
Provision for loan losses	37,159	10,067	10,426	8,737
Noninterest income	23,162	13,265	11,609	12,565
Noninterest expense	83,645	66,301	52,682	47,925
Income before taxes	48,973	47,721	35,776	29,855
Income tax expense	20,117	20,043	14,310	11,702
Net income	28,856	27,678	21,466	18,153
Common Share Summary:				
Basic earnings per share	$ 1.42	$ 1.43	$ 1.17	$ 1.04
Diluted earnings per share	1.38	1.36	1.11	0.99
Book value per share	10.42	8.75	7.26	5.86
Weighted average shares outstanding	20,268	19,370	18,426	17,494
Weighted average diluted shares outstanding	20,923	20,338	19,382	18,288
Year-End Balance Sheet Summary:				
Loans, net of unearned income	$1,611,921	$1,174,645	$ 863,492	$ 738,405
Assets	3,545,452	2,625,123	1,924,544	1,407,587
Deposits	3,269,753	2,432,407	1,774,304	1,290,060
Shareholders' equity	215,865	174,481	135,400	104,974

Years Ended December 31, (Dollars and numbers in thousands, except per share amounts)	1998	1997	1996	1995
Average Balance Sheet Summary:				
Loans, net of unearned income	$1,318,826	$ 973,637	$ 779,655	$ 681,255
Assets	2,990,548	2,140,630	1,573,903	1,165,004
Deposits	2,746,041	1,973,118	1,441,360	1,060,333
Shareholders' equity	198,675	152,118	119,788	91,710
Capital Ratios:				
Total risk-based capital ratio	11.5%	11.5%	11.5%	11.9%
Tier 1 risk-based capital ratio	10.3%	10.2%	10.2%	10.6%
Tier 1 leverage ratio	7.6%	7.1%	7.7%	8.0%
Average shareholders' equity to average assets	6.6%	7.1%	7.6%	7.9%
Selected Financial Ratios:				
Return on average assets	1.0%	1.3%	1.4%	1.6%
Return on average shareholders' equity	14.5%	18.2%	17.9%	19.8%
Efficiency ratio	53.8%	55.9%	55.9%	60.6%
Net interest margin	5.2%	5.6%	6.1%	7.1%

Central Power
Agency: Origin Design Company, Ltd.
Creative Director: Robert Achten
Designer: Julia Parkinson
Photographer: Michael Hall

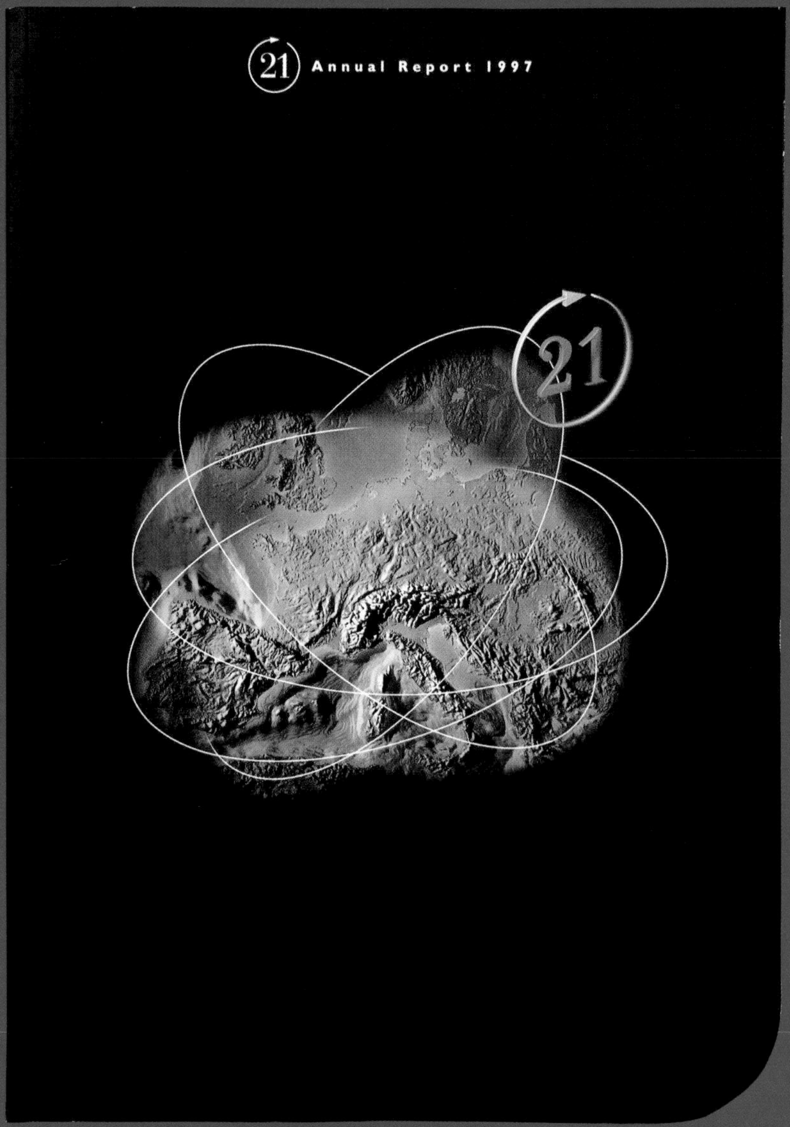
21 Annual Report 1997
21

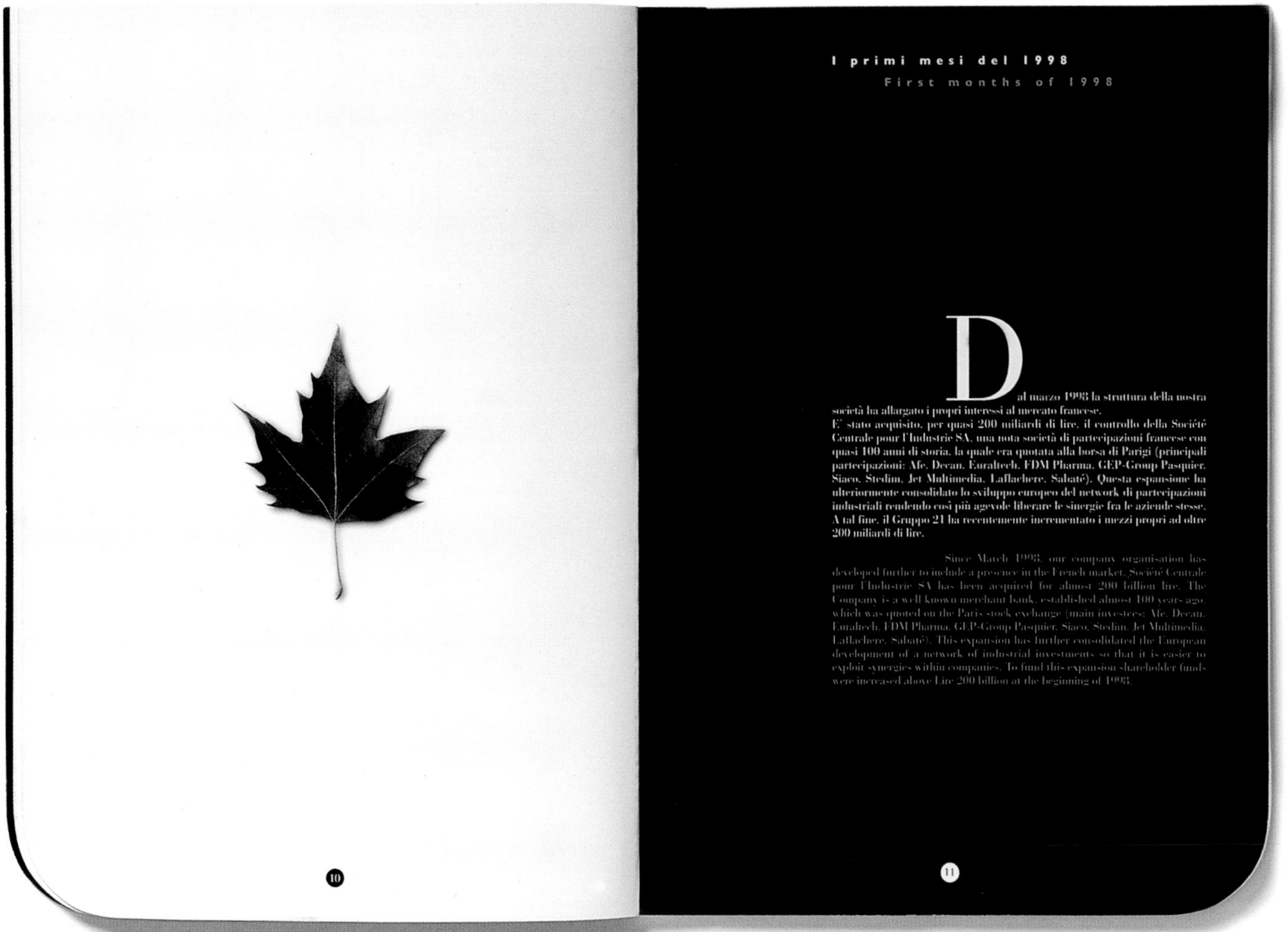

I primi mesi del 1998

First months of 1998

Dal marzo 1998 la struttura della nostra società ha allargato i propri interessi al mercato francese.
E' stato acquisito, per quasi 200 miliardi di lire, il controllo della Société Centrale pour l'Industrie SA, una nota società di partecipazioni francese con quasi 100 anni di storia, la quale era quotata alla borsa di Parigi (principali partecipazioni: Afe, Decan, Euraltech, FDM Pharma, GEP-Group Pasquier, Siaco, Stedim, Jet Multimedia, Laflachere, Sabaté). Questa espansione ha ulteriormente consolidato lo sviluppo europeo del network di partecipazioni industriali rendendo così più agevole liberare le sinergie fra le aziende stesse. A tal fine, il Gruppo 21 ha recentemente incrementato i mezzi propri ad oltre 200 miliardi di lire.

Since March 1998, our company organisation has developed further to include a presence in the French market. Société Centrale pour l'Industrie SA has been acquired for almost 200 billion lire. The Company is a well known merchant bank, established almost 100 years ago, which was quoted on the Paris stock exchange (main investees: Afe, Decan, Euraltech, FDM Pharma, GEP-Group Pasquier, Siaco, Stedim, Jet Multimedia, Laflachere, Sabaté). This expansion has further consolidated the European development of a network of industrial investments so that it is easier to exploit synergies within companies. To fund this expansion shareholder funds were increased above Lire 200 billion at the beginning of 1998.

10

11

Lit/bil.
100
75
50
25
0
1994 1995 1996 1997 1998 B
Lire/mld.

Founded in 1973 by three specialised engineers as a well recognised brand in the heating and burners industry. The founders started with the production of burners and reinvested the profits to fund the growth of the Company and to diversify the product range. Today Ecoflam ranks second in the Italian market. It employs 191 people and its products are known for their technical innovation. Ecoflam invited the 21 Group to invest in the capital of the company in order to strengthen the balance sheet and exploit its brand recognition, by diversifying the product range and developing the Company internationally.
In January 1996, the 21 Group acquired a 28.5% shareholding. 21 Group personnel became responsible, together with the management, for reorganising the Company finances allowing Ecoflam access to medium term financial sources of funding. The 21 Group contributed to the growth of the management culture of the Company and was instrumental in redesigning the marketing strategy. Joint-ventures agreements were established in order to incorporate Ecoflam branches in the UK and Spain. Foreign branches were established with local entrepreneurs who utilized their local skills in the development of Ecoflam products. The sales growth demonstrates the results of the Business Development Plan implemented by 21 Group.

Ecoflam Group

Ecoflam Group SpA

Opera nel settore del riscaldamento civile ed industriale con un marchio molto conosciuto. E' stata fondata nel 1973 da tre ingegneri specializzati, inizialmente per la produzione di bruciatori; reinvestendo successivamente i profitti realizzati, la società ha iniziato a diversificare la propria gamma di prodotti.
Oggi Ecoflam occupa il secondo posto nel mercato italiano del settore. Ha 191 dipendenti e i suoi prodotti sono conosciuti per l'innovazione tecnologica. Ecoflam ha chiesto al Gruppo 21 di investire nel capitale della società al fine di consolidare il bilancio e rafforzare il marchio, diversificando la gamma prodotti e sviluppando la società a livello internazionale.
Nel gennaio 1996, il Gruppo 21 ha acquisito il 28,5% di partecipazione e insieme al management della società ha messo allo studio un progetto di riorganizzazione finanziaria che permetta ad Ecoflam di accedere a risorse finanziarie a medio termine. Il Gruppo 21 ha contribuito alla crescita manageriale della società e ne ha ridisegnato le strategie di marketing. Sono stati stipulati degli accordi di joint venture per incorporare le filiali inglesi e spagnole. Le filiali estere sono state incorporate insieme agli imprenditori locali che hanno mostrato grandi capacità nello sviluppare il business dei prodotti Ecoflam. Il tasso di incremento del fatturato è un chiaro risultato del Piano di Sviluppo studiato dal Gruppo 21.

Ecoflam

28

29

Nando's

Agency: Cross Colours

Creative Director: Joanina Pastoll, Janine Rech

Designer: Joanina Pastoll

Photographer: David Pastoll

Copywriter: Craig Wapnick

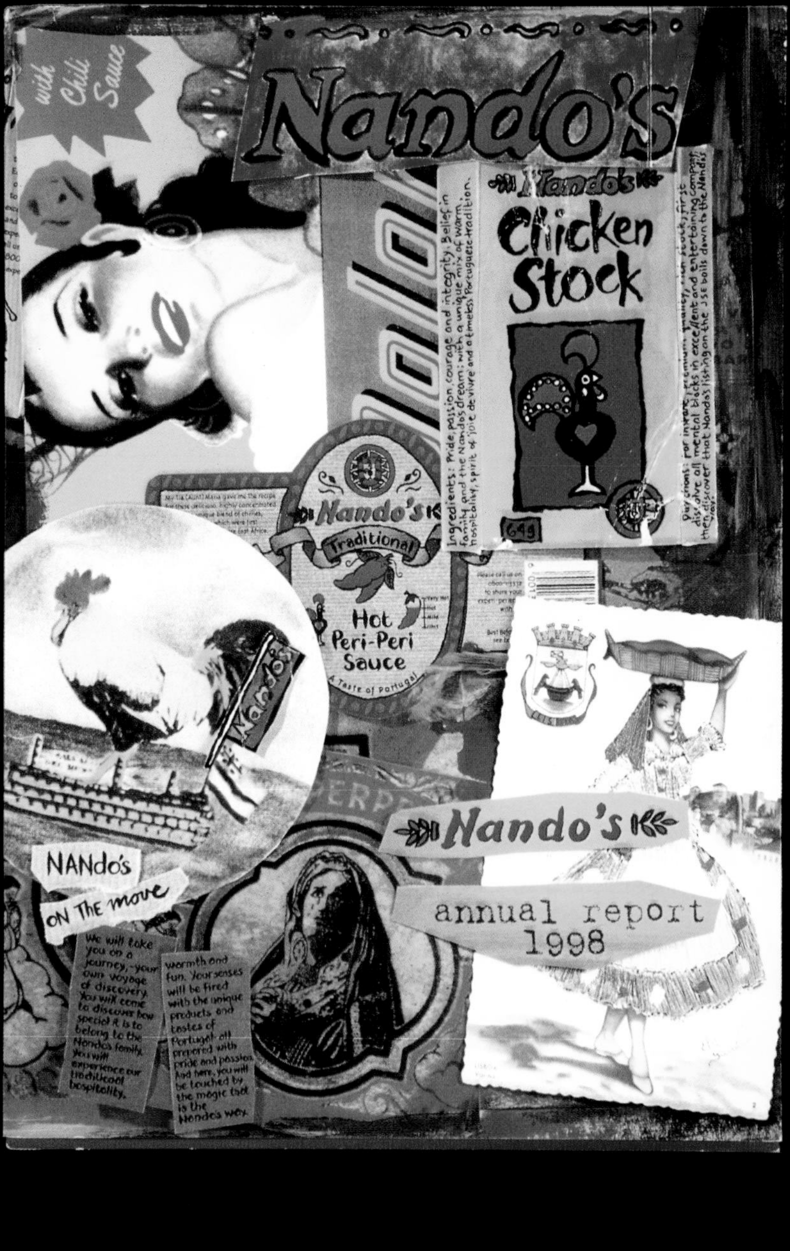

with Chili Sauce
Nando's
Nando's
Chicken Stock
Nando's
Traditional
Hot Peri-Peri Sauce
Nando's
annual report 1998
NANDo's
ON THE move

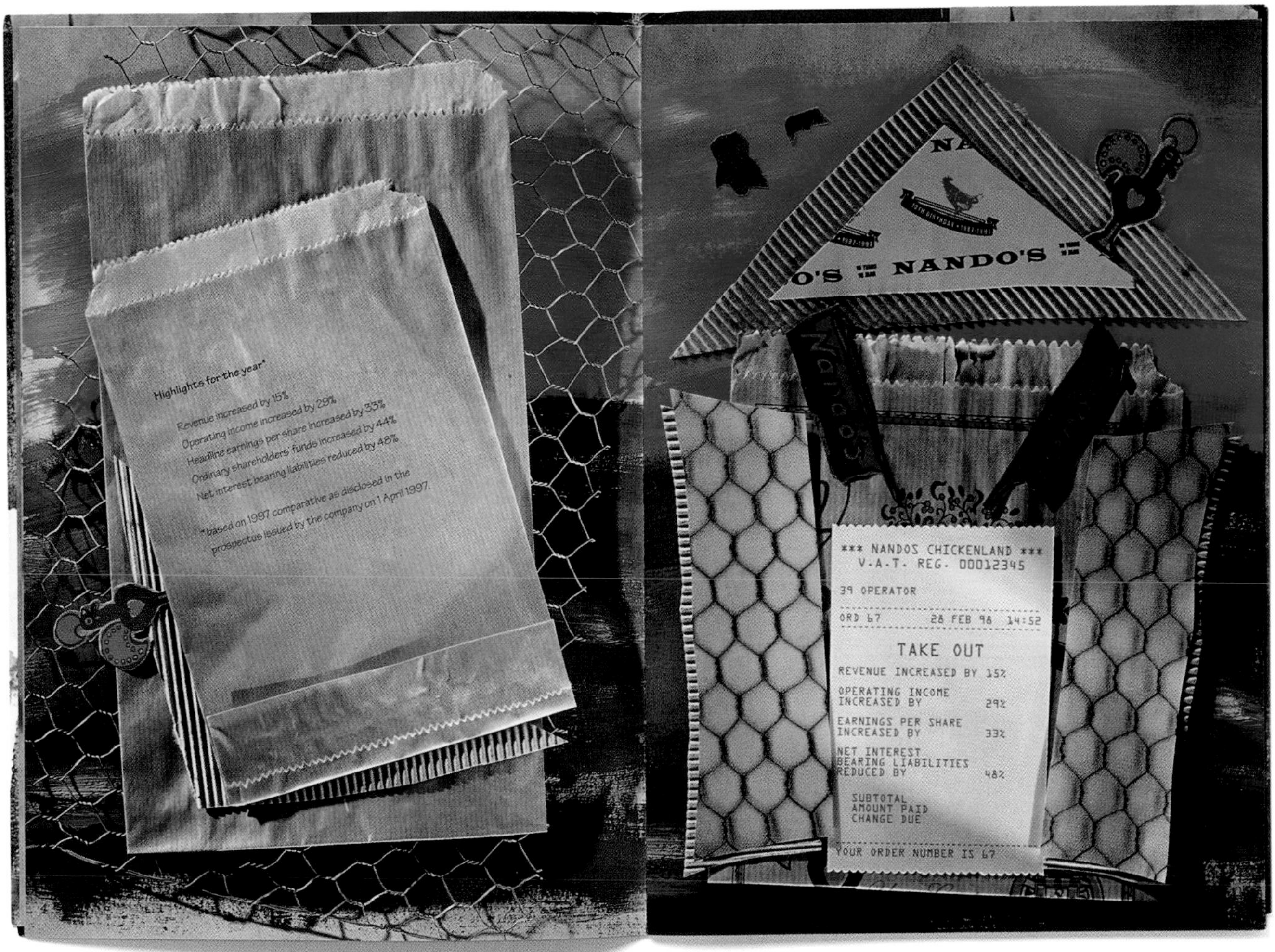
Highlights for the year*
Revenue increased by 15%
Operating income increased by 29%
Headline earnings per share increased by 33%
Ordinary shareholders' funds increased by 44%
Net interest bearing liabilities reduced by 48%
*based on 1997 comparative as disclosed in the prospectus issued by the company on 1 April 1997.
NANDO'S
*** NANDOS CHICKENLAND ***
V.A.T. REG. 00012345
39 OPERATOR
ORD 67 28 FEB 98 14:52
TAKE OUT
REVENUE INCREASED BY 15%
OPERATING INCOME INCREASED BY 29%
EARNINGS PER SHARE INCREASED BY 33%
NET INTEREST BEARING LIABILITIES REDUCED BY 48%
SUBTOTAL
AMOUNT PAID
CHANGE DUE
YOUR ORDER NUMBER IS 67

Nando's Chickenland
Nando's
Nando's is not about chicken.
It's never been just about chicken.
It's about pride, passion, courage, integrity, and most of all, family.
Corporate objectives
The Nando's mission is to be recognised as a global brand that consistently delivers quality, value and commitment to its customer base. These objectives underpin the economic value of the Nando's brand, ensuring future sustainable growth in headline earnings.

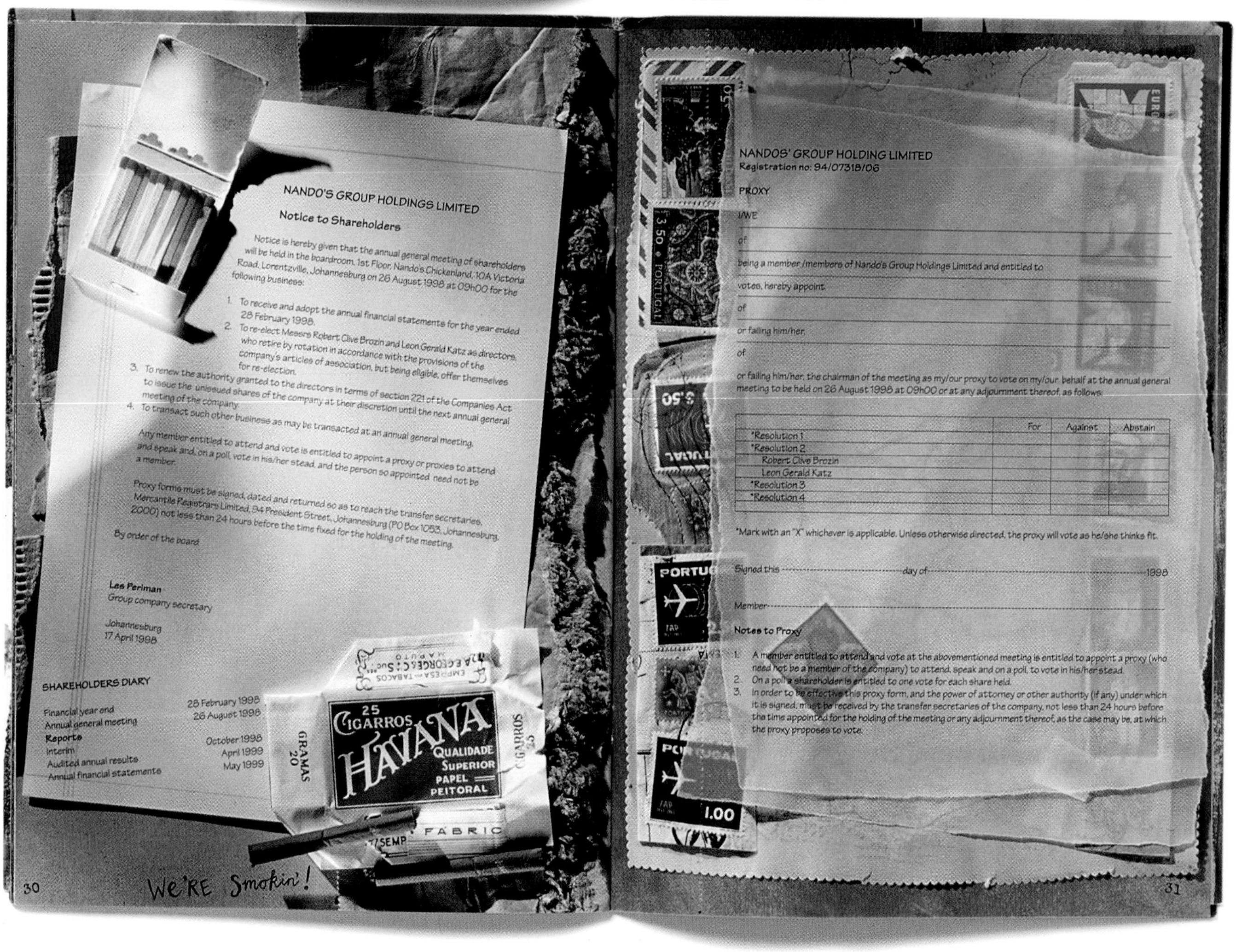

NANDO'S GROUP HOLDINGS LIMITED

Notice to Shareholders

Notice is hereby given that the annual general meeting of shareholders will be held in the boardroom, 1st Floor, Nando's Chickenland, 10A Victoria Road, Lorentzville, Johannesburg on 26 August 1998 at 09h00 for the following business:

1. To receive and adopt the annual financial statements for the year ended 28 February 1998.
2. To re-elect Messrs Robert Clive Brozin and Leon Gerald Katz as directors, who retire by rotation in accordance with the provisions of the company's articles of association, but being eligible, offer themselves for re-election.
3. To renew the authority granted to the directors in terms of section 221 of the Companies Act to issue the unissued shares of the company at their discretion until the next annual general meeting of the company.
4. To transact such other business as may be transacted at an annual general meeting.

Any member entitled to attend and vote is entitled to appoint a proxy or proxies to attend and speak and, on a poll, vote in his/her stead, and the person so appointed need not be a member.

Proxy forms must be signed, dated and returned so as to reach the transfer secretaries, Mercantile Registrars Limited, 94 President Street, Johannesburg (PO Box 1053, Johannesburg, 2000) not less than 24 hours before the time fixed for the holding of the meeting.

By order of the board

Les Perlman
Group company secretary

Johannesburg
17 April 1998

SHAREHOLDERS DIARY

Financial year end	28 February 1998
Annual general meeting	26 August 1998
Reports	
Interim	October 1998
Audited annual results	April 1999
Annual financial statements	May 1999

NANDOS' GROUP HOLDING LIMITED
Registration no: 94/07318/06

PROXY

I/WE

of

being a member /members of Nando's Group Holdings Limited and entitled to

votes, hereby appoint

of

or failing him/her,

of

or failing him/her, the chairman of the meeting as my/our proxy to vote on my/our behalf at the annual general meeting to be held on 26 August 1998 at 09h00 or at any adjournment thereof, as follows:

	For	Against	Abstain
*Resolution 1			
*Resolution 2			
Robert Clive Brozin			
Leon Gerald Katz			
*Resolution 3			
*Resolution 4			

*Mark with an "X" whichever is applicable. Unless otherwise directed, the proxy will vote as he/she thinks fit.

Signed this ------------------------ day of ------------------------ 1998

Member ------------------------

Notes to Proxy

1. A member entitled to attend and vote at the abovementioned meeting is entitled to appoint a proxy (who need not be a member of the company) to attend, speak and on a poll, to vote in his/her stead.
2. On a poll a shareholder is entitled to one vote for each share held.
3. In order to be effective this proxy form, and the power of attorney or other authority (if any) under which it is signed, must be received by the transfer secretaries of the company, not less than 24 hours before the time appointed for the holding of the meeting or any adjournment thereof, as the case may be, at which the proxy proposes to vote.

25 CIGARROS HAVANA
QUALIDADE SUPERIOR
PAPEL PEITORAL
GRAMAS 20
FÁBRIC
We're Smokin'!

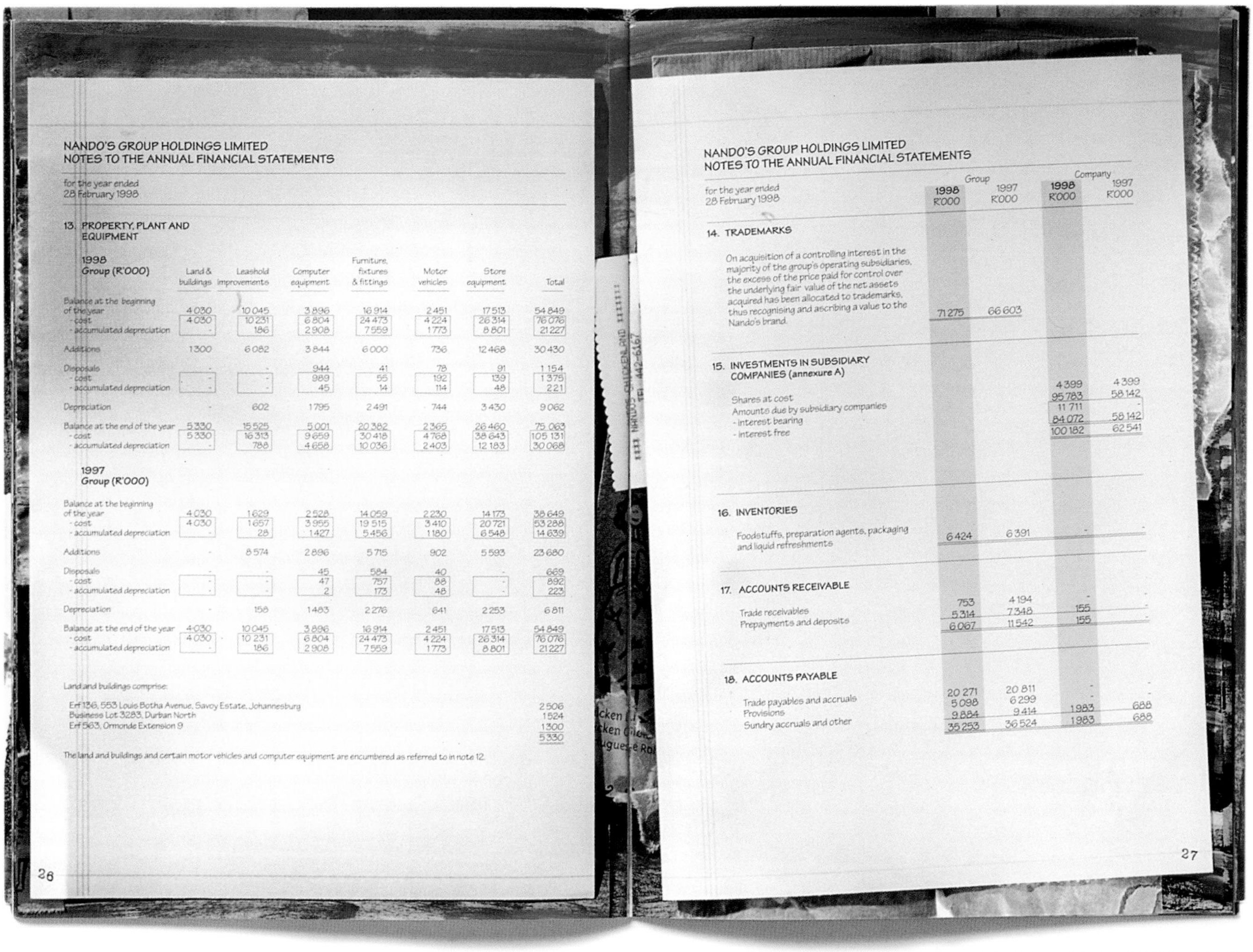

NANDO'S GROUP HOLDINGS LIMITED
NOTES TO THE ANNUAL FINANCIAL STATEMENTS

for the year ended
28 February 1998

13. PROPERTY, PLANT AND EQUIPMENT

1998
Group (R'000)

	Land & buildings	Leasehold improvements	Computer equipment	Furniture, fixtures & fittings	Motor vehicles	Store equipment	Total
Balance at the beginning of the year	4 030	10 045	3 896	16 914	2 451	17 513	54 849
- cost	4 030	10 231	6 804	24 473	4 224	26 314	76 076
- accumulated depreciation	-	186	2 908	7 559	1 773	8 801	21 227
Additions	1300	6 082	3 844	6 000	736	12 468	30 430
Disposals	-	-	944	41	78	91	1 154
- cost	-	-	989	55	192	139	1 375
- accumulated depreciation	-	-	45	14	114	48	221
Depreciation	-	602	1 795	2 491	744	3 430	9 062
Balance at the end of the year	5 330	15 525	5 001	20 382	2 365	26 460	75 063
- cost	5 330	16 313	9 659	30 418	4 768	38 643	105 131
- accumulated depreciation	-	788	4 658	10 036	2 403	12 183	30 068

1997
Group (R'000)

	Land & buildings	Leasehold improvements	Computer equipment	Furniture, fixtures & fittings	Motor vehicles	Store equipment	Total
Balance at the beginning of the year	4 030	1 629	2 528	14 059	2 230	14 173	38 649
- cost	4 030	1 657	3 955	19 515	3 410	20 721	53 288
- accumulated depreciation	-	28	1 427	5 456	1 180	6 548	14 639
Additions	-	8 574	2 896	5 715	902	5 593	23 680
Disposals	-	-	45	584	40	-	669
- cost	-	-	47	757	88	-	892
- accumulated depreciation	-	-	2	173	48	-	223
Depreciation	-	158	1 483	2 276	641	2 253	6 811
Balance at the end of the year	4 030	10 045	3 896	16 914	2 451	17 513	54 849
- cost	4 030	10 231	6 804	24 473	4 224	26 314	76 076
- accumulated depreciation	-	186	2 908	7 559	1 773	8 801	21 227

Land and buildings comprise:

Erf 136, 553 Louis Botha Avenue, Savoy Estate, Johannesburg	2 506
Business Lot 3283, Durban North	1 524
Erf 563, Ormonde Extension 9	1 300
	5 330

The land and buildings and certain motor vehicles and computer equipment are encumbered as referred to in note 12.

26

NANDO'S GROUP HOLDINGS LIMITED
NOTES TO THE ANNUAL FINANCIAL STATEMENTS

for the year ended 28 February 1998	Group 1998 R'000	Group 1997 R'000	Company 1998 R'000	Company 1997 R'000
14. TRADEMARKS				
On acquisition of a controlling interest in the majority of the group's operating subsidiaries, the excess of the price paid for control over the underlying fair value of the net assets acquired has been allocated to trademarks, thus recognising and ascribing a value to the Nando's brand.	71 275	66 603		
15. INVESTMENTS IN SUBSIDIARY COMPANIES (annexure A)				
Shares at cost			4 399	4 399
Amounts due by subsidiary companies			95 783	58 142
- interest bearing			11 711	-
- interest free			84 072	58 142
			100 182	62 541
16. INVENTORIES				
Foodstuffs, preparation agents, packaging and liquid refreshments	6 424	6 391	-	-
17. ACCOUNTS RECEIVABLE				
Trade receivables	753	4 194	-	-
Prepayments and deposits	5 314	7 348	155	-
	6 067	11 542	155	-
18. ACCOUNTS PAYABLE				
Trade payables and accruals	20 271	20 811	-	-
Provisions	5 098	6 299	-	-
Sundry accruals and other	9 884	9 414	1 983	688
	35 253	36 524	1 983	688

27

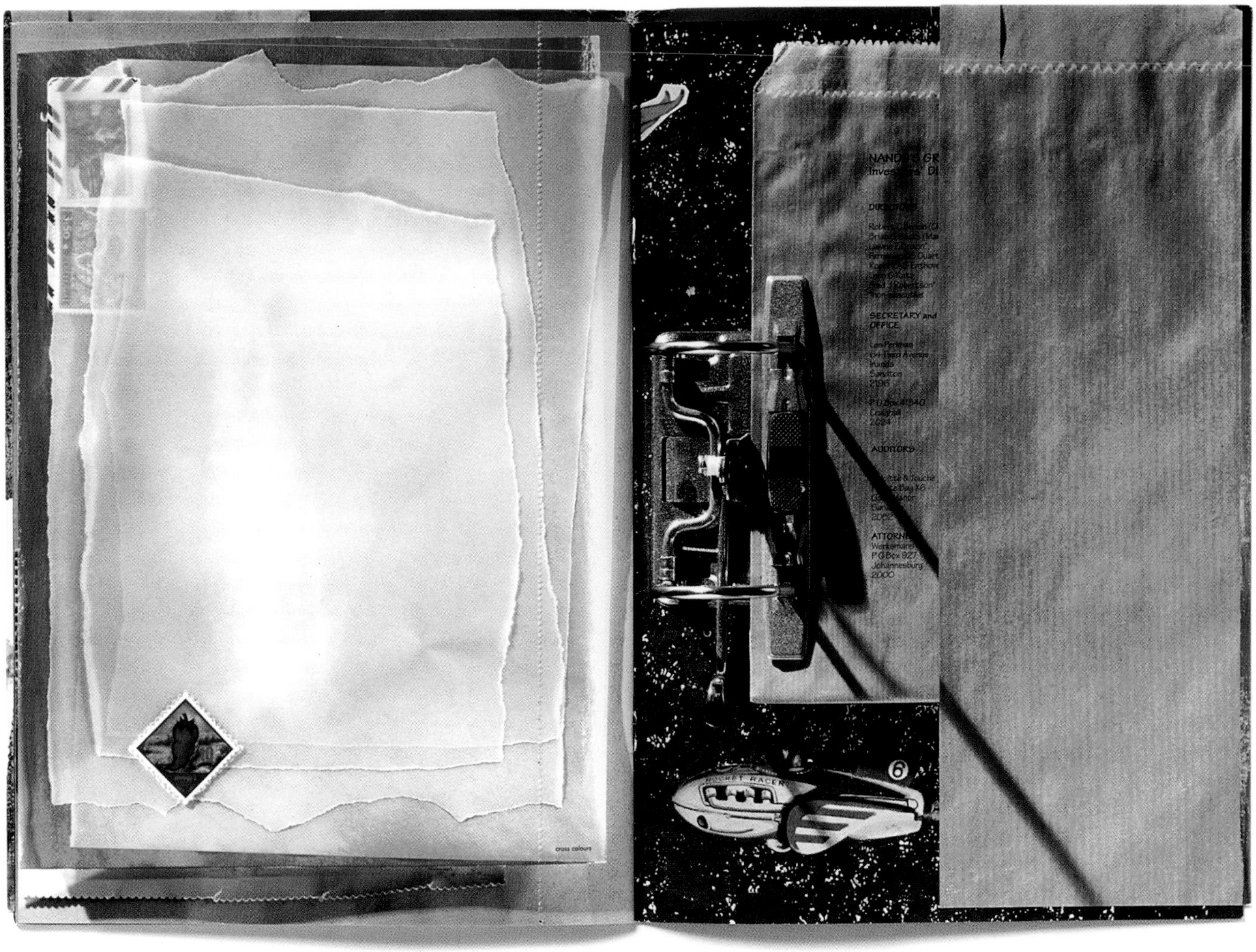
DIRECTORS
AUDITORS
ROCKET RACER
cross colours

Aurora Foods

Agency: Cahan & Associates
Art & Creative Director: Bill Cahan
Designer: Lian Ng
Photographers: Deborah Jones, Tony Stromberg
Copywriter: Aurora Foods

Recipes for Success
AURORA
FOODS INC.
You may not be familiar with our name,
but you are with our faces.

Recipes for Success
AURORA

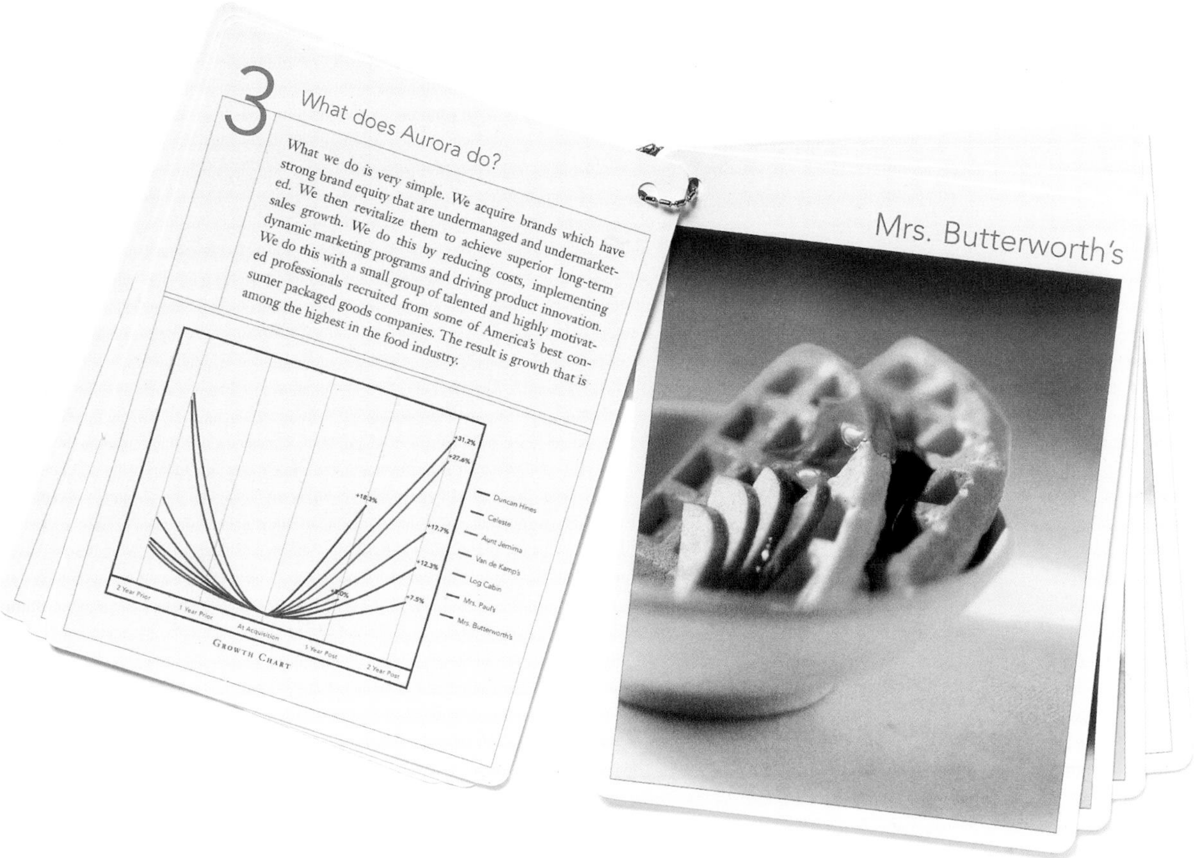
3
What does Aurora do?
What we do is very simple. We acquire brands which have strong brand equity that are undermanaged and undermarketed. We then revitalize them to achieve superior long-term sales growth. We do this by reducing costs, implementing dynamic marketing programs and driving product innovation. We do this with a small group of talented and highly motivated professionals recruited from some of America's best consumer packaged goods companies. The result is growth that is among the highest in the food industry.
Duncan Hines
Celeste
Aunt Jemima
Van de Kamp's
Log Cabin
Mrs. Paul's
Mrs. Butterworth's
2 Year Prior
1 Year Prior
At Acquisition
1 Year Post
2 Year Post
Growth Chart
Mrs. Butterworth's

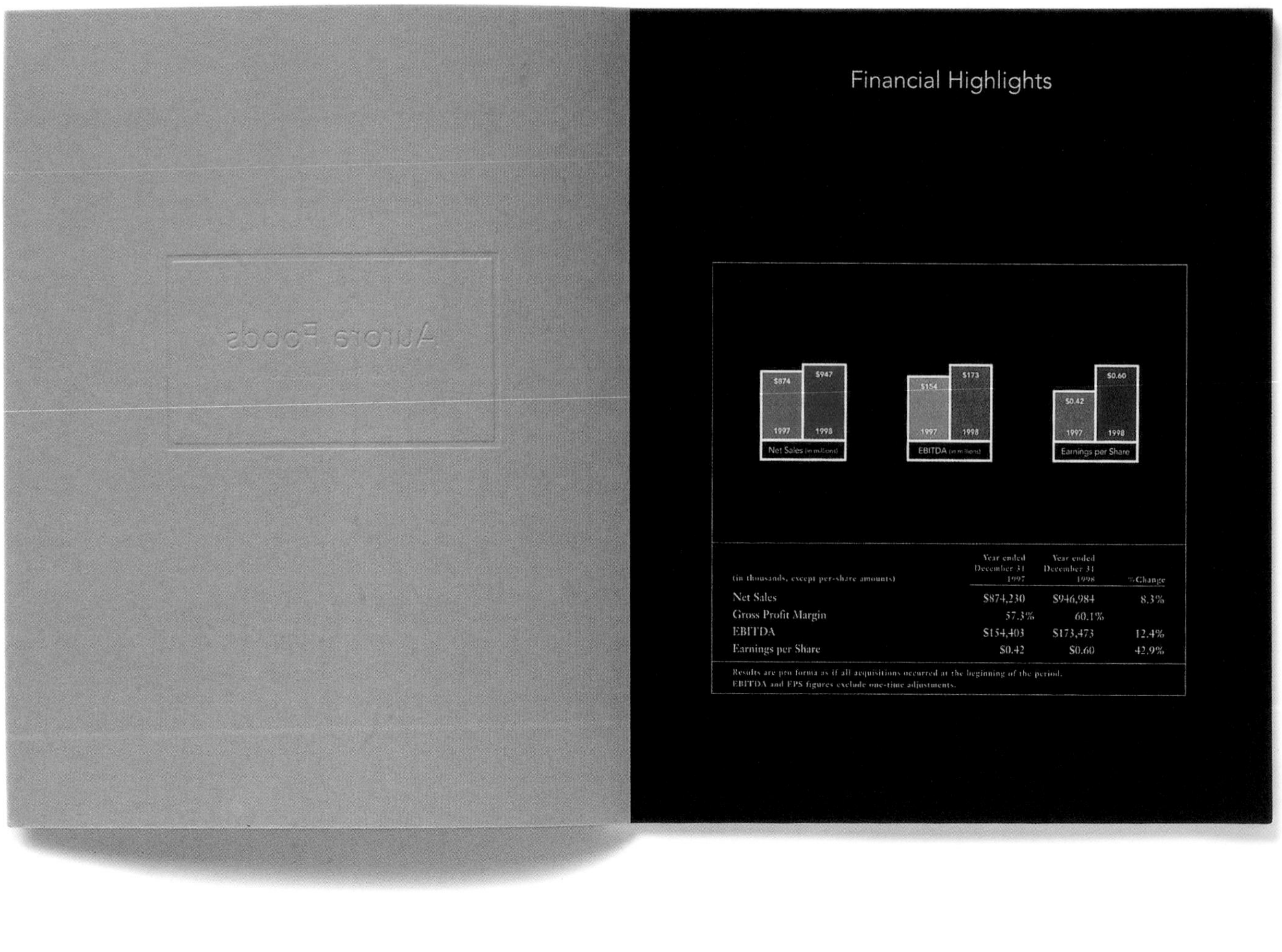
Aurora Foods
Financial Highlights
$874
$947
1997
1998
Net Sales (in millions)
$154
$173
1997
1998
EBITDA (in millions)
$0.42
$0.60
1997
1998
Earnings per Share
(in thousands, except per-share amounts) | Year ended December 31 1997 | Year ended December 31 1998 | %Change
Net Sales | $874,230 | $946,984 | 8.3%
Gross Profit Margin | 57.3% | 60.1% |
EBITDA | $154,403 | $173,473 | 12.4%
Earnings per Share | $0.42 | $0.60 | 42.9%
Results are pro forma as if all acquisitions occurred at the beginning of the period.
EBITDA and EPS figures exclude one-time adjustments.

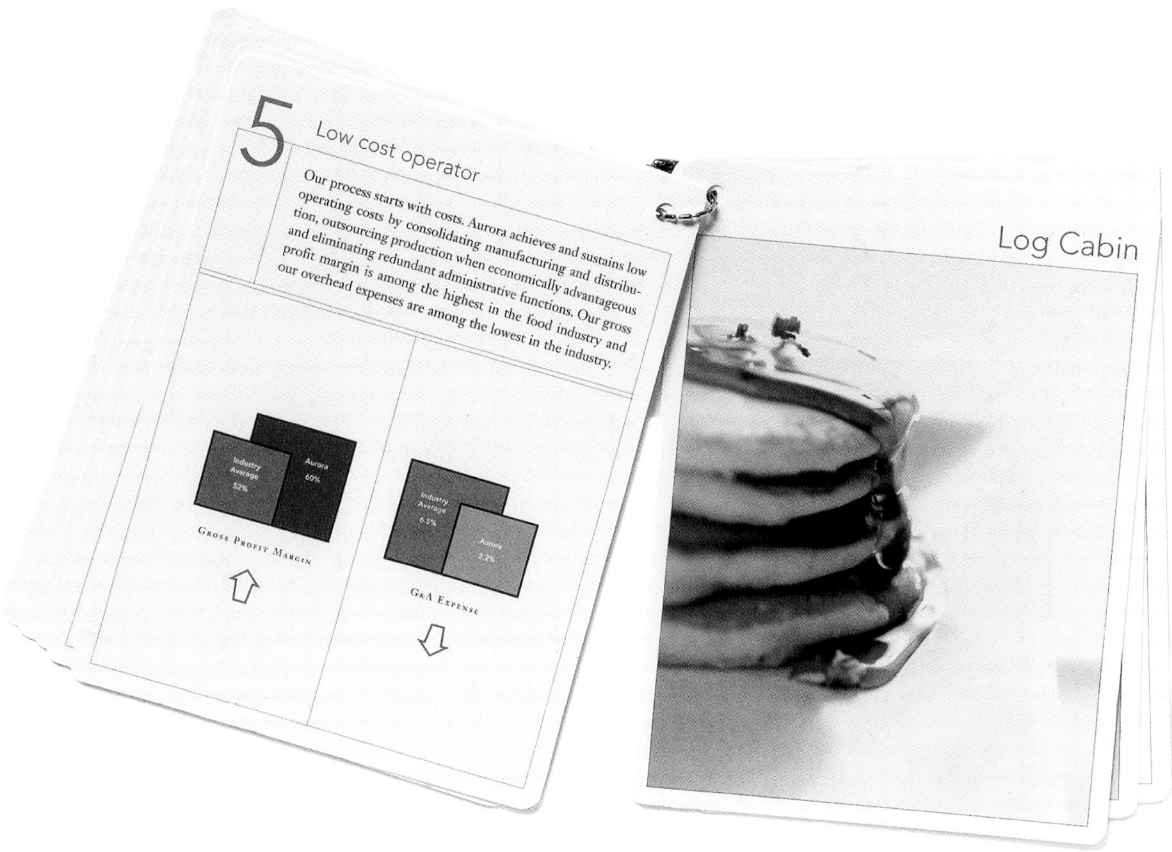
5
Low cost operator
Our process starts with costs. Aurora achieves and sustains low operating costs by consolidating manufacturing and distribution, outsourcing production when economically advantageous and eliminating redundant administrative functions. Our gross profit margin is among the highest in the food industry and our overhead expenses are among the lowest in the industry.
Industry Average 52%
Aurora 60%
Gross Profit Margin
Industry Average 6.5%
Aurora 3.2%
G&A Expense
Log Cabin

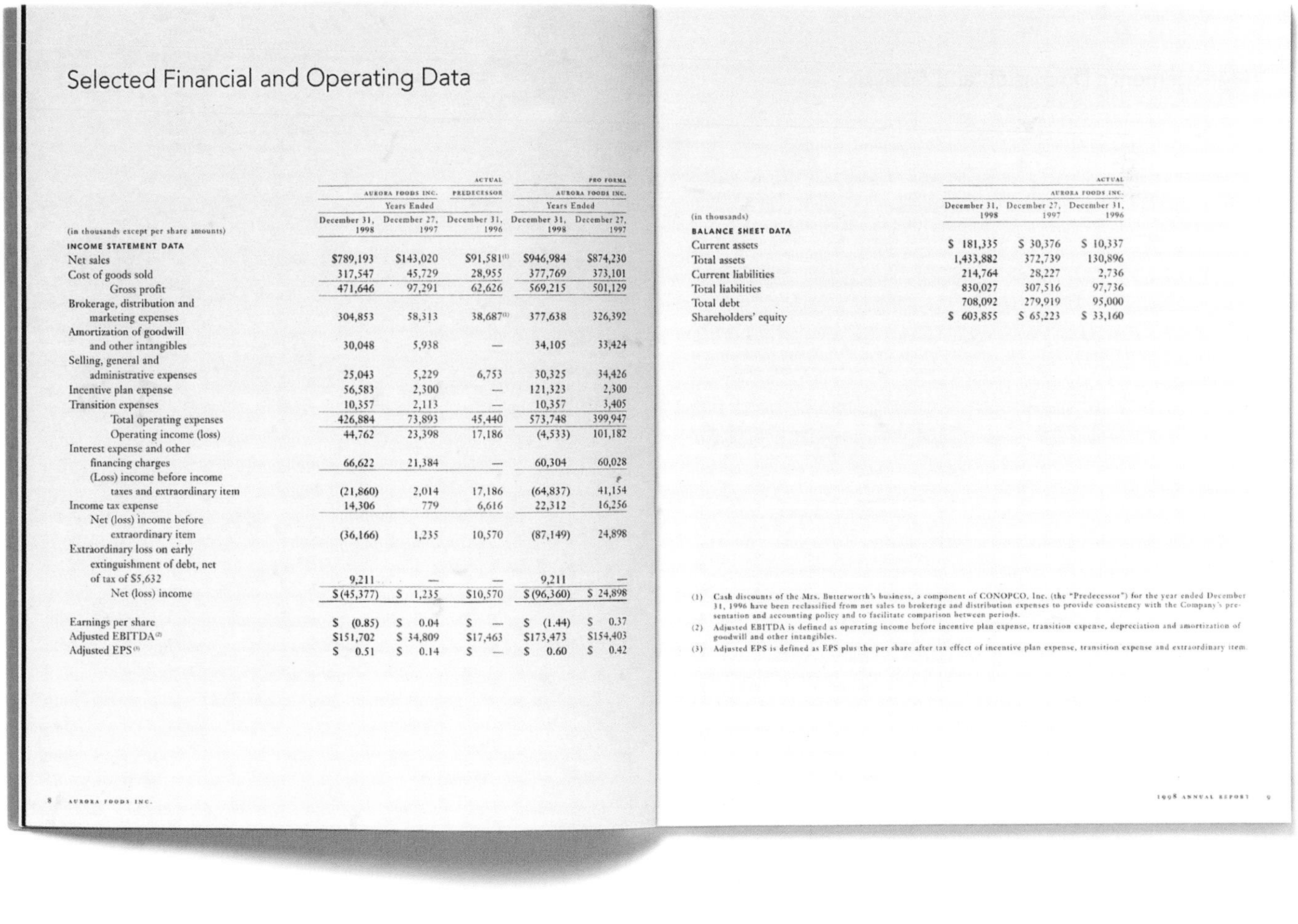

Selected Financial and Operating Data

(in thousands except per share amounts)	December 31, 1998	December 27, 1997	December 31, 1996	December 31, 1998	December 27, 1997
	ACTUAL			PRO FORMA	
	AURORA FOODS INC. Years Ended		PREDECESSOR	AURORA FOODS INC. Years Ended	
INCOME STATEMENT DATA					
Net sales	$789,193	$143,020	$91,581(1)	$946,984	$874,230
Cost of goods sold	317,547	45,729	28,955	377,769	373,101
Gross profit	471,646	97,291	62,626	569,215	501,129
Brokerage, distribution and marketing expenses	304,853	58,313	38,687(1)	377,638	326,392
Amortization of goodwill and other intangibles	30,048	5,938	—	34,105	33,424
Selling, general and administrative expenses	25,043	5,229	6,753	30,325	34,426
Incentive plan expense	56,583	2,300	—	121,323	2,300
Transition expenses	10,357	2,113	—	10,357	3,405
Total operating expenses	426,884	73,893	45,440	573,748	399,947
Operating income (loss)	44,762	23,398	17,186	(4,533)	101,182
Interest expense and other financing charges	66,622	21,384	—	60,304	60,028
(Loss) income before income taxes and extraordinary item	(21,860)	2,014	17,186	(64,837)	41,154
Income tax expense	14,306	779	6,616	22,312	16,256
Net (loss) income before extraordinary item	(36,166)	1,235	10,570	(87,149)	24,898
Extraordinary loss on early extinguishment of debt, net of tax of $5,632	9,211	—	—	9,211	—
Net (loss) income	$(45,377)	$ 1,235	$10,570	$(96,360)	$ 24,898
Earnings per share	$ (0.85)	$ 0.04	$ —	$ (1.44)	$ 0.37
Adjusted EBITDA(2)	$151,702	$ 34,809	$17,463	$173,473	$154,403
Adjusted EPS(3)	$ 0.51	$ 0.14	$ —	$ 0.60	$ 0.42

8 AURORA FOODS INC.

(in thousands)	December 31, 1998	December 27, 1997	December 31, 1996
	ACTUAL AURORA FOODS INC.		
BALANCE SHEET DATA			
Current assets	$ 181,335	$ 30,376	$ 10,337
Total assets	1,433,882	372,739	130,896
Current liabilities	214,764	28,227	2,736
Total liabilities	830,027	307,516	97,736
Total debt	708,092	279,919	95,000
Shareholders' equity	$ 603,855	$ 65,223	$ 33,160

(1) Cash discounts of the Mrs. Butterworth's business, a component of CONOPCO, Inc. (the "Predecessor") for the year ended December 31, 1996 have been reclassified from net sales to brokerage and distribution expenses to provide consistency with the Company's presentation and accounting policy and to facilitate comparison between periods.

(2) Adjusted EBITDA is defined as operating income before incentive plan expense, transition expense, depreciation and amortization of goodwill and other intangibles.

(3) Adjusted EPS is defined as EPS plus the per share after tax effect of incentive plan expense, transition expense and extraordinary item.

1998 ANNUAL REPORT 9

Starbucks Coffee Company
Agency: Starbucks Design Group
Art Director & Designer: John Cannell
Creative Director: Ted Jacobs
Photographer: Nancy LeVine
Illustrator: Martina Witte
Copywriter: Alice Meadows

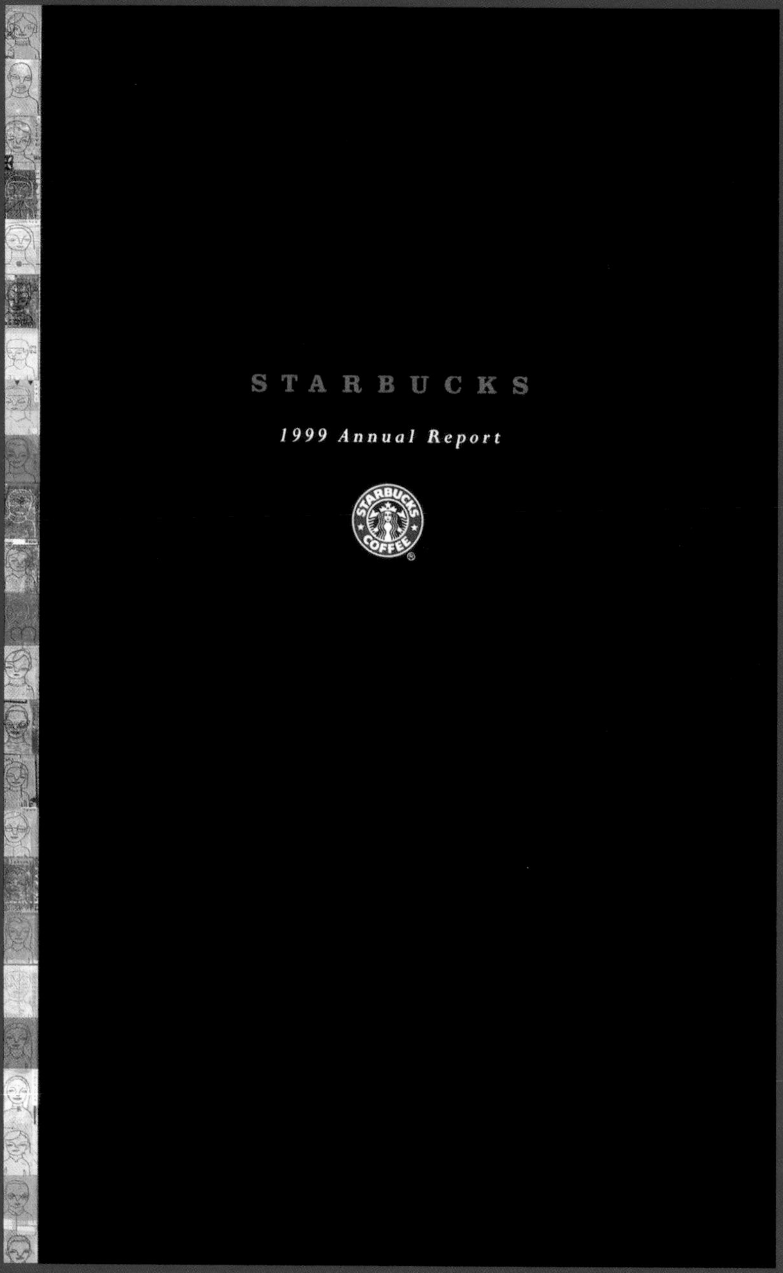
STARBUCKS
1999 Annual Report
STARBUCKS COFFEE

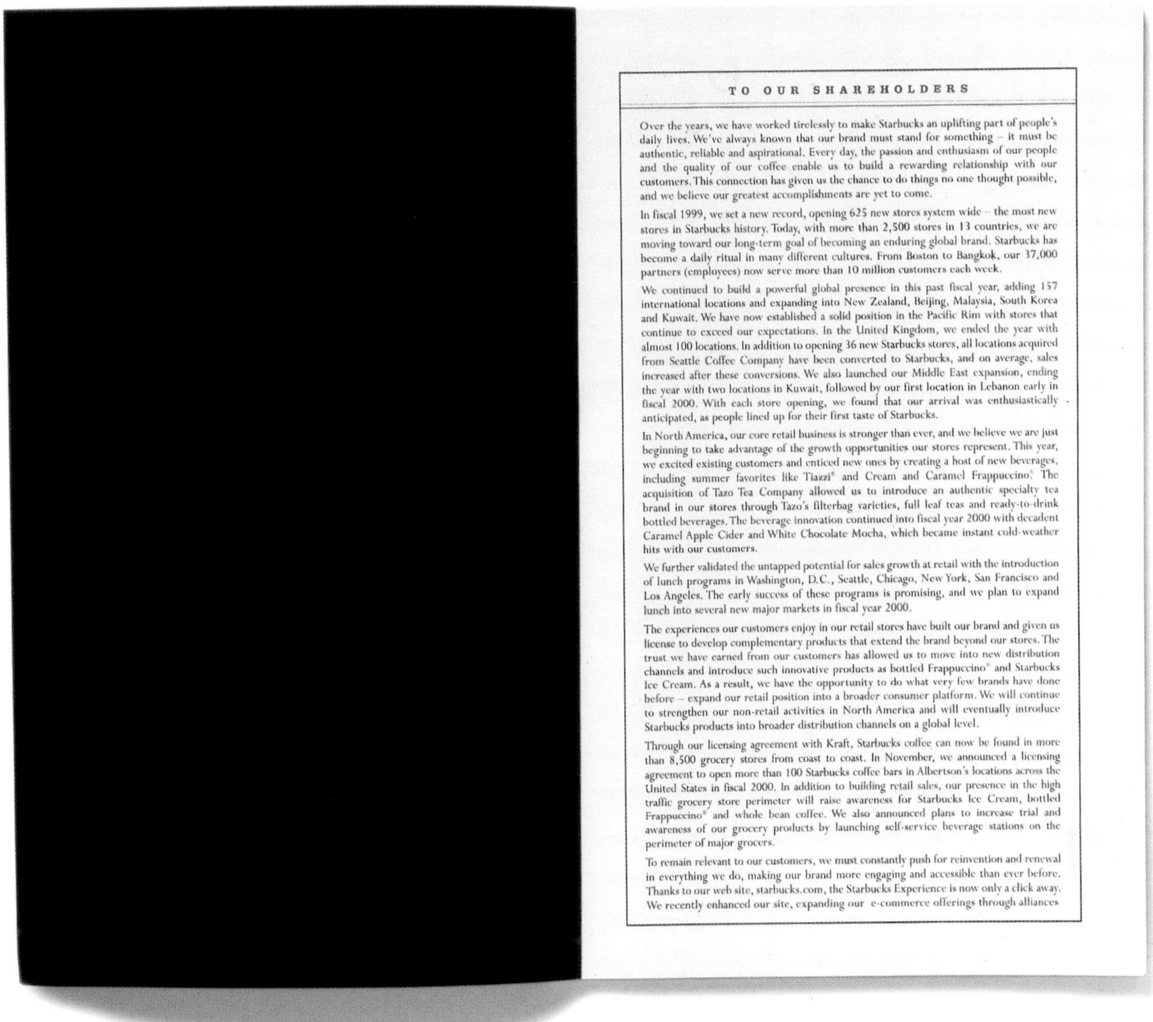

TO OUR SHAREHOLDERS

Over the years, we have worked tirelessly to make Starbucks an uplifting part of people's daily lives. We've always known that our brand must stand for something – it must be authentic, reliable and aspirational. Every day, the passion and enthusiasm of our people and the quality of our coffee enable us to build a rewarding relationship with our customers. This connection has given us the chance to do things no one thought possible, and we believe our greatest accomplishments are yet to come.

In fiscal 1999, we set a new record, opening 625 new stores system wide – the most new stores in Starbucks history. Today, with more than 2,500 stores in 13 countries, we are moving toward our long-term goal of becoming an enduring global brand. Starbucks has become a daily ritual in many different cultures. From Boston to Bangkok, our 37,000 partners (employees) now serve more than 10 million customers each week.

We continued to build a powerful global presence in this past fiscal year, adding 157 international locations and expanding into New Zealand, Beijing, Malaysia, South Korea and Kuwait. We have now established a solid position in the Pacific Rim with stores that continue to exceed our expectations. In the United Kingdom, we ended the year with almost 100 locations. In addition to opening 36 new Starbucks stores, all locations acquired from Seattle Coffee Company have been converted to Starbucks, and on average, sales increased after these conversions. We also launched our Middle East expansion, ending the year with two locations in Kuwait, followed by our first location in Lebanon early in fiscal 2000. With each store opening, we found that our arrival was enthusiastically anticipated, as people lined up for their first taste of Starbucks.

In North America, our core retail business is stronger than ever, and we believe we are just beginning to take advantage of the growth opportunities our stores represent. This year, we excited existing customers and enticed new ones by creating a host of new beverages, including summer favorites like Tiazzi® and Cream and Caramel Frappuccino®. The acquisition of Tazo Tea Company allowed us to introduce an authentic specialty tea brand in our stores through Tazo's filterbag varieties, full leaf teas and ready-to-drink bottled beverages. The beverage innovation continued into fiscal year 2000 with decadent Caramel Apple Cider and White Chocolate Mocha, which became instant cold-weather hits with our customers.

We further validated the untapped potential for sales growth at retail with the introduction of lunch programs in Washington, D.C., Seattle, Chicago, New York, San Francisco and Los Angeles. The early success of these programs is promising, and we plan to expand lunch into several new major markets in fiscal year 2000.

The experiences our customers enjoy in our retail stores have built our brand and given us license to develop complementary products that extend the brand beyond our stores. The trust we have earned from our customers has allowed us to move into new distribution channels and introduce such innovative products as bottled Frappuccino® and Starbucks Ice Cream. As a result, we have the opportunity to do what very few brands have done before – expand our retail position into a broader consumer platform. We will continue to strengthen our non-retail activities in North America and will eventually introduce Starbucks products into broader distribution channels on a global level.

Through our licensing agreement with Kraft, Starbucks coffee can now be found in more than 8,500 grocery stores from coast to coast. In November, we announced a licensing agreement to open more than 100 Starbucks coffee bars in Albertson's locations across the United States in fiscal 2000. In addition to building retail sales, our presence in the high traffic grocery store perimeter will raise awareness for Starbucks Ice Cream, bottled Frappuccino® and whole bean coffee. We also announced plans to increase trial and awareness of our grocery products by launching self-service beverage stations on the perimeter of major grocers.

To remain relevant to our customers, we must constantly push for reinvention and renewal in everything we do, making our brand more engaging and accessible than ever before. Thanks to our web site, starbucks.com, the Starbucks Experience is now only a click away. We recently enhanced our site, expanding our e-commerce offerings through alliances

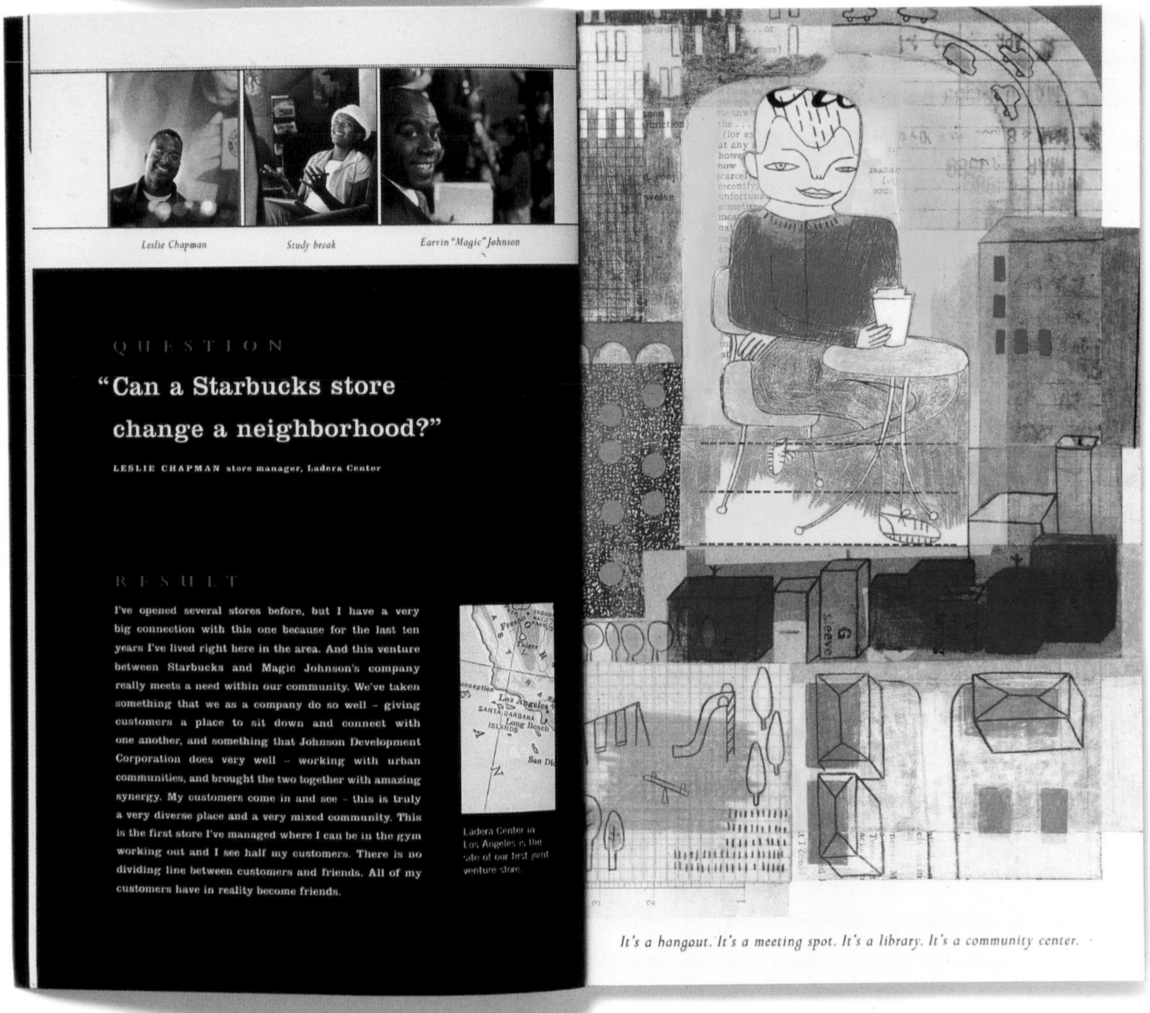

Leslie Chapman *Study break* *Earvin "Magic" Johnson*

QUESTION

"Can a Starbucks store change a neighborhood?"

LESLIE CHAPMAN store manager, Ladera Center

RESULT

I've opened several stores before, but I have a very big connection with this one because for the last ten years I've lived right here in the area. And this venture between Starbucks and Magic Johnson's company really meets a need within our community. We've taken something that we as a company do so well – giving customers a place to sit down and connect with one another, and something that Johnson Development Corporation does very well – working with urban communities, and brought the two together with amazing synergy. My customers come in and see – this is truly a very diverse place and a very mixed community. This is the first store I've managed where I can be in the gym working out and I see half my customers. There is no dividing line between customers and friends. All of my customers have in reality become friends.

Ladera Center in Los Angeles is the site of our first joint venture store.

It's a hangout. It's a meeting spot. It's a library. It's a community center.

Sharleen Chao *Afternoon meeting* *Taipei barista*

QUESTION

"What about Starbucks remains constant and what can be adapted to different cultures?"

SHARLEEN CHAO merchandising manager for Taiwan

RESULT

The good coffee, the high standard of quality control, the passion of the baristas, these things are the same. Of course we know the market is different – the morning is very slow for us, that is a very traditional time at home. We are not ready to change that. And so eighty percent of sales happen after 11:00 am. That is the time to come to Starbucks. The Taiwanese young people, they are so sensitive to all things American. They are welcoming – they are very open – to all kinds of new things. And coffee is a very fashionable thing to try. Here it is a very social drink – for after dinner, for dating – people come here together. That shows with each transaction – the average is 2.5 beverages per purchase. So we are well received. Our first store opened a year and a half ago, and now there are twenty-five.

Our cup, the symbol of Starbucks, is the same in Taiwan as it is in the U.S.

中杯那堤
Double Tall Latte

Kwang-Fu Store. Hsin-Nan Store. Chung-Chin Store. San-Ming Store. Jen-Ai Store.

Jazz. Cuban. Blues. Classical. Country. Opera. Folk. Celtic.

Holly Hinton *Songs for the road* *Ray Brown, live at Starbucks*

QUESTION

"Why would a coffeehouse create its own music compilations?"

HOLLY HINTON music specialist

RESULT

It's our customers who give us permission to try something new – something beyond coffee. Like Starbucks music, which we created in response to their requests for the music we were playing in our stores. We started with mostly jazz and some blues collections, but recently we've discovered that we can walk out a bit further. And these little surprises can be one of the most rewarding things for customers. So we're beginning to introduce different genres – Celtic, alternative country, Cuban. It's niche music that people don't get through regular commercial channels, but they're intrigued by it. Maybe they're reading about it in their Sunday paper and yet they're not the kind of person to wade through the stacks at their local record store to figure out where it is. But they'll see it at Starbucks and it's easy to get at – a natural.

Last year's compilations reflect the diversity of our customers' tastes.

To think and question and push and try. This is what the partners of Starbucks strive for every single day. Some things will work, some things won't. But if we weren't so passionate about what we do, we could never *become the enduring company we aspire to be.*

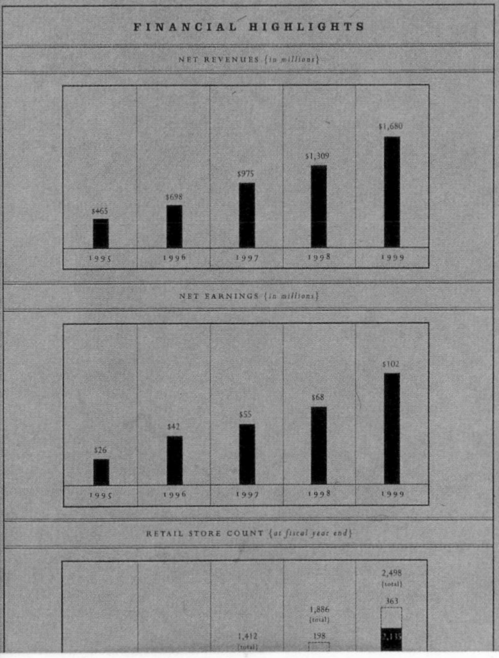
FINANCIAL HIGHLIGHTS
NET REVENUES {in millions}
$465
$698
$975
$1,309
$1,680
1995
1996
1997
1998
1999
NET EARNINGS {in millions}
$26
$42
$55
$68
$102
1995
1996
1997
1998
1999
RETAIL STORE COUNT {at fiscal year end}
1,412 {total}
1,886 {total}
198
2,498 {total}
363
2,135

TEAR ALONG PERFORATION TO REMOVE COUPON

FOR YOU. FROM US.

GOOD FOR ONE 12-OUNCE BEVERAGE OF YOUR CHOICE.

Redeemable only at participating Starbucks Coffee stores in the continental U.S., Canada and the United Kingdom. No cash value. EXPIRES 10/1/00. *Barista please ring as* DISCT 12

To further reduce its exposure to rising coffee costs, the Company may, from time to time, enter into futures contracts to hedge price-to-be-established coffee purchase commitments. The specific risks associated with these activities are described below in "Financial Risk Management."

In addition to fluctuating coffee prices, management believes that the Company's future results of operations and earnings could be significantly impacted by other factors such as increased competition within the specialty coffee industry, the Company's ability to find optimal store locations at favorable lease rates, increased costs associated with opening and operating retail stores and the Company's continued ability to hire, train and retain qualified personnel.

FINANCIAL RISK MANAGEMENT

The Company maintains investment portfolio holdings of various issuers, types and maturities. These securities are classified as available-for-sale and are recorded on the balance sheet at fair value with unrealized gains or losses reported as a separate component of accumulated other comprehensive income. As of October 3, 1999, approximately 76% of the total portfolio was invested in short-term marketable debt securities with maturities of less than one year. An additional 15% was invested in long-term U.S. Government obligations with maturities of 12 to 18 months and the remaining 9% was invested in marketable equity securities. The Company does not hedge its interest rate exposure.

The Company is subject to foreign currency exchange rate exposure, primarily related to its foreign retail operations in Canada and the United Kingdom. Historically, this exposure has had a minimal impact on the Company. At the present time, the Company does not hedge foreign currency risk, but may do so in the future.

The Company may, from time to time, enter into futures contracts to hedge price-to-be-fixed coffee purchase commitments with the objective of minimizing cost risk due to market fluctuations. The Company does not hold or issue derivative instruments for trading purposes. In accordance with Statement of Financial Accounting Standards ("SFAS") No. 80, "Accounting for Futures Contracts," these futures contracts meet the hedge criteria and are accounted for as hedges. Accordingly, gains and losses are deferred and recognized as adjustments to the carrying value of coffee inventory when purchased and recognized in results of operations as coffee products are sold. Gains and losses are calculated based on the difference between the cost basis and the market value of the coffee contracts. The market risk related to coffee futures is substantially offset by changes in the costs of coffee purchased.

SEASONALITY AND QUARTERLY RESULTS

The Company's business is subject to seasonal fluctuations. Significant portions of the Company's net revenues and profits are realized during the first quarter of the Company's fiscal year, which includes the December holiday season. In addition, quarterly results are affected by the timing of the opening of new stores, and the Company's rapid growth may conceal the impact of other seasonal influences. Because of the seasonality of the Company's business, results for any quarter are not necessarily indicative of the results that may be achieved for the full fiscal year.

NEW ACCOUNTING STANDARDS

In June 1998, the Financial Accounting Standards Board ("FASB") issued SFAS No. 133, "Accounting for Derivative Instruments and Hedging Activities." This pronouncement will require the Company to recognize derivatives on its balance sheet at fair value. Changes in the fair values of derivatives that qualify as cash-flow hedges will be recognized in accumulated other comprehensive income until the hedged item is recognized in earnings. The Company is in the process of evaluating the impact of this new accounting standard and does not expect that it will have a significant effect on its results of operations. The FASB subsequently issued SFAS No. 137, "Accounting for Derivative Instruments and Hedging Activities – Deferral of the Effective Date of FASB Statement No. 133," which postpones initial application until fiscal years beginning after June 15, 2000. The Company expects to adopt SFAS No. 133 in fiscal 2001.

CONSOLIDATED BALANCE SHEETS

In thousands, except share data

	OCT 3, 1999	SEPT 27, 1998
ASSETS		
Current assets		
Cash and cash equivalents	$ 66,419	$ 101,663
Short-term investments	51,367	21,874
Accounts receivable	47,646	50,972
Inventories	180,886	143,118
Prepaid expenses and other current assets	19,049	11,205
Deferred income taxes, net	21,133	8,448
Total current assets	386,500	337,280
Joint ventures and other investments	68,060	38,917
Property, plant and equipment, net	760,289	600,794
Deposits and other assets	23,474	15,685
Goodwill, net	14,191	79
Total	$ 1,252,514	$ 992,755
LIABILITIES AND SHAREHOLDERS' EQUITY		
Current liabilities		
Accounts payable	$ 56,108	$ 49,861
Checks drawn in excess of bank balances	64,211	33,634
Accrued compensation and related costs	43,872	35,941
Accrued occupancy costs	23,017	17,526
Accrued taxes	30,752	18,323
Other accrued expenses	33,637	24,190
Total current liabilities	251,597	179,475
Deferred income taxes, net	32,886	18,983
Long-term debt	7,018	–
Commitments and contingencies (notes 5, 9 and 13)		
SHAREHOLDERS' EQUITY		
Common stock – Authorized, 300,000,000 shares; issued and outstanding, 183,282,095 and 179,266,956 shares, respectively (includes 848,550 common stock units in both years)	651,020	589,214
Retained earnings	313,939	212,246
Accumulated other comprehensive loss	(3,946)	(7,163)
Total shareholders' equity	961,013	794,297
Total	$ 1,252,514	$ 992,755

See Notes to Consolidated Financial Statements.

Del Monte Foods

Agency: Howry Design Associates
Art & Creative Director: Jill Howry
Designer: Ty Whittington
Photographer: Stuart Schwartz
Copywriter: Lindsay Beaman

DEL MONTE: CREATIVE SOLUTIONS FOR BUSY LIFESTYLES

Del Monte Foods Company

1999 ANNUAL REPORT

WELCOME TO DEL MONTE FOODS' INAUGURAL ANNUAL REPORT. WE ARE PROUD TO HAVE BECOME A PUBLIC COMPANY THIS YEAR. ALTHOUGH, IN A SENSE WE ALREADY HAVE BEEN A PUBLIC COMPANY IN THE MARKETPLACE FOR OVER A CENTURY. EVERY DAY, CONSUMERS INVEST THEIR TRUST IN OUR BRAND BY PURCHASING SOME 7 MILLION DEL MONTE PRODUCTS, WHICH MAKE THEIR WAY TO OVER 80% OF AMERICAN HOUSEHOLDS. THE FRUITS — AND VEGETABLES AND TOMATOES — OF OUR LABORS ARE PART OF EVERYDAY LIFE, MAKING WHOLESOME, FLAVORFUL MEALS EASIER AND QUICKER TO PREPARE. LOOKING AHEAD, WE INTEND TO EXPAND THAT ROLE, WITH PRODUCTS THAT FIT WITH TODAY'S LIFESTYLE, AND A BUSINESS THAT BUILDS SHAREHOLDER VALUE.

QUICK

ADD IMAGINATION AND

WHAT'S FOR DE$$ERT?

SELECTED FINANCIAL DATA

The following table sets forth historical consolidated financial information of the Company. The statement of operations data for each of the fiscal years in the two-year period ended June 30, 1996 and the balance sheet data as of June 30, 1996 and 1995 have been derived from consolidated financial statements of the Company audited by Ernst & Young LLP, independent auditors. The statement of operations data for each of the fiscal years in the three-year period ended June 30, 1999 and the balance sheet data as of June 30, 1999, 1998 and 1997 have been derived from consolidated financial statements of the Company audited by KPMG LLP, independent auditors. The table should be read in conjunction with "Management's Discussion and Analysis of Financial Condition and Results of Operations," the consolidated financial statements of the Company and related notes and other financial information included in the Company's Annual Report on Form 10-K.

	Fiscal Year Ended June 30,				
(In millions, except share data)	1999	1998	1997	1996	1995
STATEMENT OF OPERATIONS DATA:					
Net sales	$ 1,505	$ 1,313	$ 1,217	$ 1,305	$ 1,527
Cost of products sold	999	898	819	984	1,183
Selling, administrative and general expense[a]	375	316	327	239	264
Special charges related to plant consolidation	17	10	—	—	—
Acquisition expense	1	7	—	—	—
Operating income	113	82	71	82	80
Interest expense	78	77	52	67	76
Loss (gain) on sale of divested assets[b]	—	—	5	(123)	—
Other (income) expense[c]	2	(1)	30	3	(11)
Income (loss) before income taxes, minority interest, extraordinary item and cumulative effect of accounting change	33	6	(16)	135	15
Provision for income taxes	—	1	—	11	2
Minority interest in earnings of subsidiary	—	—	—	3	1
Income (loss) before extraordinary item and cumulative effect of accounting change	33	5	(16)	121	12
Extraordinary loss[d]	19	—	42	10	7
Cumulative effect of accounting change[e]	—	—	—	7	—
Net income (loss)	$ 14	$ 5	$ (58)	$ 104	$ 5
Net income (loss) attributable to common shares	$ 10	$ —	$ (128)	$ 22	$ (66)
Net income (loss) per common share[f]	$ 0.23	$ 0.01	$ (2.07)	$ 0.29	$ (0.85)
Weighted average number of shares outstanding	41,979,665	31,619,642	61,703,436	75,047,353	76,671,294

	Fiscal Year Ended June 30,				
(In millions)	1999	1998	1997	1996	1995
OTHER DATA:					
Adjusted EBITDA:[g]					
EBIT	$ 111	$ 83	$ 36	$ 202	$ 91
Depreciation and amortization[h]	34	29	24	26	35
EBITDA of Divested Operations[i]	—	—	—	(22)	(35)
Asset write-down/impairment[j]	—	—	7	—	—
Loss (gain) on sale of Divested Operations[b]	—	—	5	(123)	—
Terminated transactions[k]	2	—	—	—	(22)
Benefit costs[l]	—	3	—	—	7
Headcount reduction and relocation[m]	—	—	—	9	—
Recapitalization expenses[a][c]	—	—	47	—	—
Special charges related to plant consolidation	17	10	—	—	—
Expenses of acquisitions[n]	1	7	—	—	—
Inventory write-up[n]	3	3	—	—	—
Adjusted EBITDA	$ 168	$ 135	$ 119	$ 92	$ 76
Adjusted EBITDA margin[g]	11.2%	10.3%	10.2%	8.6%	6.9%
Cash flows provided by operating activities	$ 97	$ 97	$ 25	$ 60	$ 63
Cash flows provided by (used in) investing activities	(87)	(222)	37	170	(21)
Cash flows provided by (used in) financing activities	(10)	127	(63)	(224)	(44)
Capital expenditures	55	32	20	16	24
SELECTED RATIOS:					
Ratio of earnings to fixed charges[o]	1.4x	1.1x	—	2.8x	1.2x
Deficiency of earnings to cover fixed charges[o]	—	—	$ 16	—	—

	Fiscal Year Ended June 30,				
(In millions)	1999	1998	1997	1996	1995
BALANCE SHEET DATA:					
Working capital	$ 188	$ 210	$ 118	$ 209	$ 99
Total assets	872	844	667	736	960
Total debt	544	709	610	373	576
Redeemable preferred stock	—	33	32	213	215
Stockholders' equity (deficit)	(118)	(350)	(398)	(288)	(393)

(a) In connection with the Company's recapitalization, which was consummated on April 18, 1997, expenses of approximately $25 million were incurred primarily for management incentive payments and, in part, for severance payments.

(b) In the fiscal quarter ended December 1996, the Company sold Del Monte Latin America. The combined sales price of $80 million, reduced by $2 million of related transaction expenses, resulted in a loss of $5 million. In November 1995, the Company sold its pudding business for $89 million, net of $4 million of related transaction fees. The sale resulted in a gain of $71 million. In March 1996, the Company sold its 50.1% ownership interest in Del Monte Philippines for $100 million, net of $2 million of related transaction fees. The sale resulted in a gain of $52 million.

```
Aeron, cames, Equa, seating, systems, environments, facilities, design, alternative work places, technology integration
REL=stylesheet HREF="/piglet.css" TYPE="text/css"><SCRIPT LANGUAGE=JavaScript><!-(store_on = "";hmhome_on ="";he
"";sqa_on = "";products_on = "";service_on = "";research_on = "";design_on = "";news_on = "";investors_on = "";gsa_
broadview_on = "";mapOn = "";juggle_on = "";juggleNew_on = "";searchOn = "";contactOn = "";usOn = "";youOn = "";buy
= "";us_on = "";you_on = ""; contact_on="";buy_on="";on = new Image();on.src = '/graphics/bullet.GIF';var toys_ro =
Image();toys_ro.src = "/neocon/things/graphics/toys_ro.GIF";var brochure_ro = new Image();brochure_ro.src = "/neoc
things/graphics/brochure_ro.GIF";)off = new Image();off.src = '/graphics/bullet0.GIF';a=8;b=9;rand = Math.floor((Math
10)) % b + 1; rand2 = Math.floor((Math.random() * 10) % a; var topbar = new Array("graphics/top1.GIF","graphics/top2.
graphics/top2.GIF","graphics/top3.GIF","graphics/top4.GIF","graphics/top5.GIF","graphics/top6.GIF","graphics/top7.GIF","
top8.GIF");var storebar = "graphics/store" + rand + ".GIF"juggleNew_on = new Image();juggleNew_on.src = '/graphics/
function preLoad(){store_on = new Image();store_on.src = storebar;hmhome_on = new Image();hmhome_on.src = '/graph
hmhome.JPG';healthcare_on = new Image();healthcare_on.src = '/graphics/healthcare.GIF';sqa_on = new Image();sqa_on
'/graphics/sqa.GIF';products_on = new Image();products_on.src = '/graphics/products.GIF';service_on = new Image();s
= '/graphics/services.GIF';research_on = new Image();research_on.src = '/graphics/research.GIF';design_on = new Ima
design_on.src ='/graphics/design.GIF';news_on = new Image();news_on.src = '/graphics/news_front.GIF';investors_on =
Image();investors_on.src = '/graphics/investors.GIF';gsa_on = new Image();gsa_on.src = '/graphics/gsa.GIF';juggle_on
Image();juggle_on.src = '/graphics/jugglezine.GIF';contact_on = new Image();contact_on.src = "/graphics/contact3.GIF
us_on = new Image();us_on.src = "/graphics/us3.GIF";you_on = new Image();you_on.src = "/graphics/you3.GIF";buy_o
Image();buy_on.src = "/graphics/buy3.GIF";contactOn = new Image();contactOn.src = "/includes/graphics/contact2.GIF
new Image();usOn.src = "/includes/graphics/us2.GIF";youOn = new Image();youOn.src = "/includes/graphics/you2.GIF";
new Image();buyOn.src = "/includes/graphics/buy2.GIF";searchOn = new Image();searchOn.src = "/graphics/search2.GI
mapOn = new Image();mapOn.src = "/graphics/sitemap2.GIF";}function searching(){if(document.searchOut.arg.value == "
(document.location = "overview.html")else(document.searchOut.submit())}//-></SCRIPT></HEAD><BODY MARGINWIDTH=0 M
HEIGHT=0 LEFTMARGIN=0 TOPMARGIN=0 BGCOLOR="#FFFFFF" ONLOAD="if (parent.frames.length != 0) (open (URL, '_top'));
()"><!-Created by BBK Studio (web@bbkstudio.com) for Herman Miller on Monday, March 29, 1999, last revised August 13
<IMG SRC=graphics/top6.GIF ALT='Herman Miller Inc.' WIDTH=600 HEIGHT=150 HSPACE=0 VSPACE=0 BORDER=0><TABLE BC
CELLSPACING=0 CELLPADDING=0><TR><TD WIDTH=200><TABLE WIDTH=200 BORDER=0 CELLSPACING=0 CELLPADDING=0><TR V
TOP><TD ALIGN=LEFT VALIGN=TOP><IMG SRC="/graphics/gray.GIF" ALT="" HSPACE=0 VSPACE=0 BORDER=0 WIDTH=17 HEIG
<IMG SRC="/graphics/bullet0.GIF" NAME="d1" ALT="" HSPACE=0 VSPACE=0 BORDER=0 WIDTH=17 HEIGHT=10><BR><IMG SRC
graphics/bullet0.GIF" NAME="d2" ALT="" HSPACE=0 VSPACE=0 BORDER=0 WIDTH=17 HEIGHT=10><BR><IMG SRC="/graphics
ALT="" NAME="d3" HSPACE=0 VSPACE=0 BORDER=0 WIDTH=17 HEIGHT=10><BR><IMG SRC="/graphics/bullet0.GIF" NAME="d
HSPACE=0 VSPACE=0 BORDER=0 WIDTH=17 HEIGHT=10><BR><IMG SRC="/graphics/bullet0.GIF" NAME="d5" ALT="" HSPACE=
BORDER=0 WIDTH=17 HEIGHT=10><BR><IMG SRC="/graphics/bullet0.GIF" NAME="d6" ALT="" HSPACE=0 VSPACE=0 BORDER=
HEIGHT=10><BR><IMG SRC="/graphics/bullet0.GIF" NAME="d7" ALT="" HSPACE=0 VSPACE=0 BORDER=0 WIDTH=17 HEIGHT=
SRC="/graphics/bullet0.GIF" NAME="d8" ALT="" HSPACE=0 VSPACE=0 BORDER=0 WIDTH=17 HEIGHT=10><BR><IMG SRC="/g
let0.GIF" NAME="d9" ALT="" HSPACE=0 VSPACE=0 BORDER=0 WIDTH=17 HEIGHT=10><BR><IMG SRC="/graphics/bullet0.GIF
ALT="" HSPACE=0 VSPACE=0 BORDER=0 WIDTH=17 HEIGHT=10><BR><IMG SRC="/graphics/bullet0.GIF" NAME="d11" ALT=""
VSPACE=0 BORDER=0 WIDTH=17 HEIGHT=10><BR><IMG SRC="/graphics/bullet0.GIF" NAME="d12" ALT="" HSPACE=0 VSPACE
WIDTH=17 HEIGHT=10></TD><TD ALIGN=LEFT VALIGN=TOP><IMG SRC="/graphics/dbase.GIF" ALT="" WIDTH=183 HEIGHT=121
VSPACE=0 BORDER=0 USEMAP="#stroll" ISMAP></TD></TR></TABLE></TD><TD WIDTH=400 ALIGN=TOP VALIGN=LEFT><A HREF=
```

HermanMiller MAKE CONNECTIONS >>

```
WIDTH=47 HEIGHT=10></A><BR><A HREF="outline.html"><IMG SRC="/graphics/sitemap3.GIF" ALT="" WIDTH=47 HEIGHT=10
</A><BR><A HREF="/extras/legal.html"><IMG SRC="/graphics/legal.GIF" ALT="" WIDTH=47 HEIGHT=10 BORDER=0></A></F
</TD></TABLE></TD><TD WIDTH="399" ALIGN="left" VALIGN="top"><IMG SRC="/graphics/black.GIF" ALT="" HSPACE="0" VS
BORDER="0" WIDTH="1" HEIGHT="200" ALIGN="left"><TABLE BORDER=0 CELLSPACING=0 CELLPADDING=0 ALIGN=LEFT><TR V
VALIGN=TOP><A HREF="/contact/" ONMOUSEOUT="Image9.src='/includes/graphics/contact.GIF';Guido.src=store_on.src" (
="Image9.src=contactOn.src;Guido.src=contact_on.src"><IMG NAME="Image9" BORDER=0 SRC="/includes/graphics/contac
WIDTH=100 HEIGHT=43 ALIGN=TOP VSPACE=0 HSPACE=0></A></TD></TR><TR><TD><A HREF="/company/" ONMOUSEOUT="Ima
includes/graphics/us.GIF';Guido.src=store_on.src" ONMOUSEOVER="Image10.src=usOn.src;Guido.src=us_on.src"><IMG NAM
BORDER=0 SRC="/includes/graphics/us.GIF" WIDTH=50 HEIGHT=15 ALIGN=TOP VSPACE=0 HSPACE=0></A><A HREF="/conta
ONMOUSEOUT="Image11.src='/includes/graphics/you.GIF';Guido.src=store_on.src" ONMOUSEOVER="Image11.src=youOn.src
Guido.src=you_on.src"><IMG NAME="Image11" BORDER=0 SRC="/includes/graphics/you.GIF" WIDTH=50 HEIGHT=15 ALIGN=
HSPACE=0></A></TD></TR><TR VALIGN=BOTTOM ALIGN=LEFT><TD><A HREF="/contact/buy.html" ONMOUSEOUT="Image12.src=
graphics/buy.GIF';Guido.src=store_on.src" ONMOUSEOVER="Image12.src=buyOn.src;Guido.src=buy_on.src"><IMG NAME="Im
DER=0 SRC="/includes/graphics/buy.GIF" WIDTH=100 HEIGHT=42 ALIGN=TOP HSPACE=0 VSPACE=0></A></TD></TR></TABL
SRC="/graphics/gray.GIF" ALT="" HSPACE=0 VSPACE=0 BORDER=0 WIDTH=1 HEIGHT=200 ALIGN=left><TABLE BORDER=0 CE
CELLPADDING=0 width=299><TR ALIGN=left VALIGN=top><TD VALIGN=top ALIGN=LEFT><A HREF="/neocon99/things/index.h
SRC="/graphics/arrow.GIF" ALT="" WIDTH=30 HEIGHT=30 HSPACE=0 VSPACE=0 BORDER=0 ALIGN=middle></A></TD><TD AL
VALIGN=top><P CLASS=left><A HREF="/neocon99/things/index.html">Things That Matter</A>. Maybe you've seen our color
can play with their digital entity. </TD></TR><TR ALIGN=left VALIGN=top></TR><TR><TD ALIGN=left COLSPAN=2><IMG SRC=
gray.GIF" ALT="" HSPACE=0 VSPACE=0 BORDER=0 WIDTH=298 HEIGHT=1 ALIGN=left></TD></TR><TR ALIGN=left VALIGN=to
VALIGN=top ALIGN=LEFT><A HREF="http://www.jugglezine.com"><IMG SRC="/graphics/arrow.GIF" ALT="" WIDTH=30 HEIGH
HSPACE=0 VSPACE=0 BORDER=0 ALIGN=middle></A></TD><TD ALIGN=left VALIGN=top><P CLASS=left>Work. Family. Life. <A
HREF="http://www.jugglezine.com">Jugglezine</A>. Now better than ever.</TD></TR><TR ALIGN=left VALIGN=top></TR><TR
ALIGN=left COLSPAN=2><IMG SRC="/graphics/gray.GIF" ALT="" HSPACE=0 VSPACE=0 BORDER=0 WIDTH=298 HEIGHT=1 AL
</TD></TR><TR ALIGN=left VALIGN=top><TD ALIGN=left VALIGN=top><A HREF="/neocon99/"><IMG SRC="/graphics/arrow.G
WIDTH=30 HEIGHT=30 HSPACE=0 VSPACE=0 BORDER=0 ALIGN=left></A></TD><TD ALIGN=left VALIGN=top><P CLASS=left>M
HREF="/neocon99/">Neocon 99</A>? Go back to the future by visiting our virtual showroom.</TD></TR><TR><TD ALIGN=le
COLSPAN=2><IMG SRC="/graphics/gray.GIF" ALT="" HSPACE=0 VSPACE=0 BORDER=0 WIDTH=298 HEIGHT=1 ALIGN=left></
ALIGN=left VALIGN=top><TD ALIGN=left VALIGN=top><A HREF="/news/99/06.30.html"><IMG SRC="/graphics/arrow.GIF" A
WIDTH=30 HEIGHT=30 HSPACE=0 VSPACE=0 BORDER=0 ALIGN=left></A></TD><TD ALIGN=left VALIGN=top><P CLASS=left>S
orders and profits for <A HREF="/news/99/06.30.html" NAME="News Desk">Fourth Quarter of Fiscal Year 1999</A>.</TD
<TR><TD ALIGN=left COLSPAN=2><IMG SRC="/graphics/gray.GIF" ALT="" HSPACE=0 VSPACE=0 BORDER=0 WIDTH=298 HEIG
ALIGN=left></TD></TR><TR ALIGN=left VALIGN=top><TD ALIGN=left VALIGN=top><A HREF="/news/99/6.17.html"><IMG SRC=
/arrow.GIF" ALT="" WIDTH=30 HEIGHT=30 HSPACE=0 VSPACE=0 BORDER=0 ALIGN=left></A></TD><TD ALIGN=left VALIGN=
<P CLASS=left>Herman Miller, Inc., announces Mazda <A HREF="/news/99/6.17.html">"Summer of Style"</A> (Aeron chair
Giveaway.</TD></TR><TR><TD ALIGN=left COLSPAN=2><IMG SRC="/graphics/gray.GIF" ALT="" HSPACE=0 VSPACE=0 BORDER
WIDTH=298 HEIGHT=1 ALIGN=left></TD></TR></TABLE></TD></TR></TABLE><MAP NAME="stroll"><AREA SHAPE=rect COORDS=
111,181,119" HREF="http://www.jugglezine.com/" onMouseOver="Guido.src=juggle_on.src;d12.src=on.src;" onMouseOut="(
=store_on.src;d12.src=off.src"><AREA SHAPE=rect COORDS="2,101,181,110" HREF="/investors/" onMouseOver="d11.src=o
Guido.src=investors_on.src" onMouseOut="d11.src=off.src"><AREA SHAPE=rect COORDS="2,91,181,100" HREF="/news/" on
="d10.src=on.src;Guido.src=news_on.src" onMouseOut="d10.src=off.src"><AREA SHAPE=rect COORDS="2,81,181,90" HREF=
onMouseOver="d9.src=on.src;Guido.src=design_on.src" onMouseOut="d9.src=off.src"><AREA SHAPE=rect COORDS="2,71,18
HREF="/research/" onMouseOver="d8.src=on.src;Guido.src=research_on.src" onMouseOut="d8.src=off.src"><AREA SHAPE=
COORDS="2,61,181,70" HREF="/services/" onMouseOver="d7.src=on.src;Guido.src=service_on.src" onMouseOut="d7.src=o
```

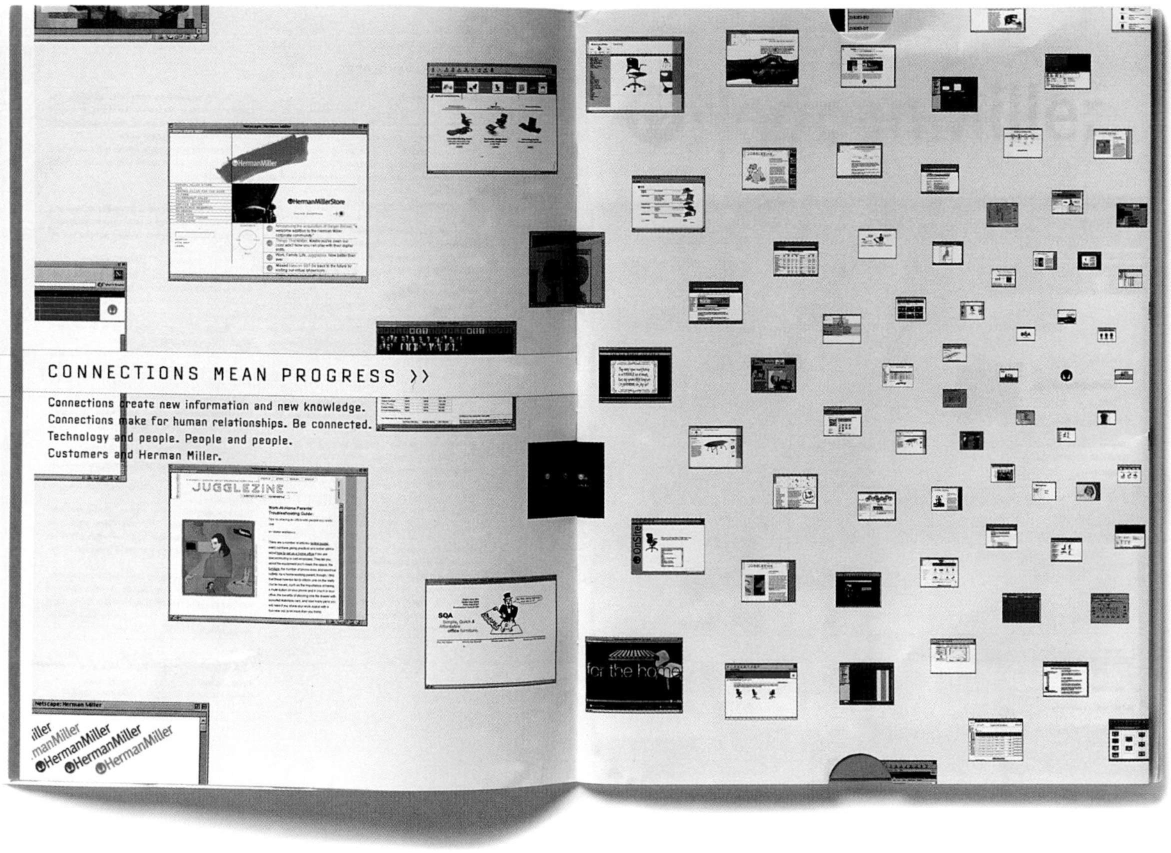
CONNECTIONS MEAN PROGRESS >>
Connections create new information and new knowledge.
Connections make for human relationships. Be connected.
Technology and people. People and people.
Customers and Herman Miller.
JUGGLEZINE
HermanMiller

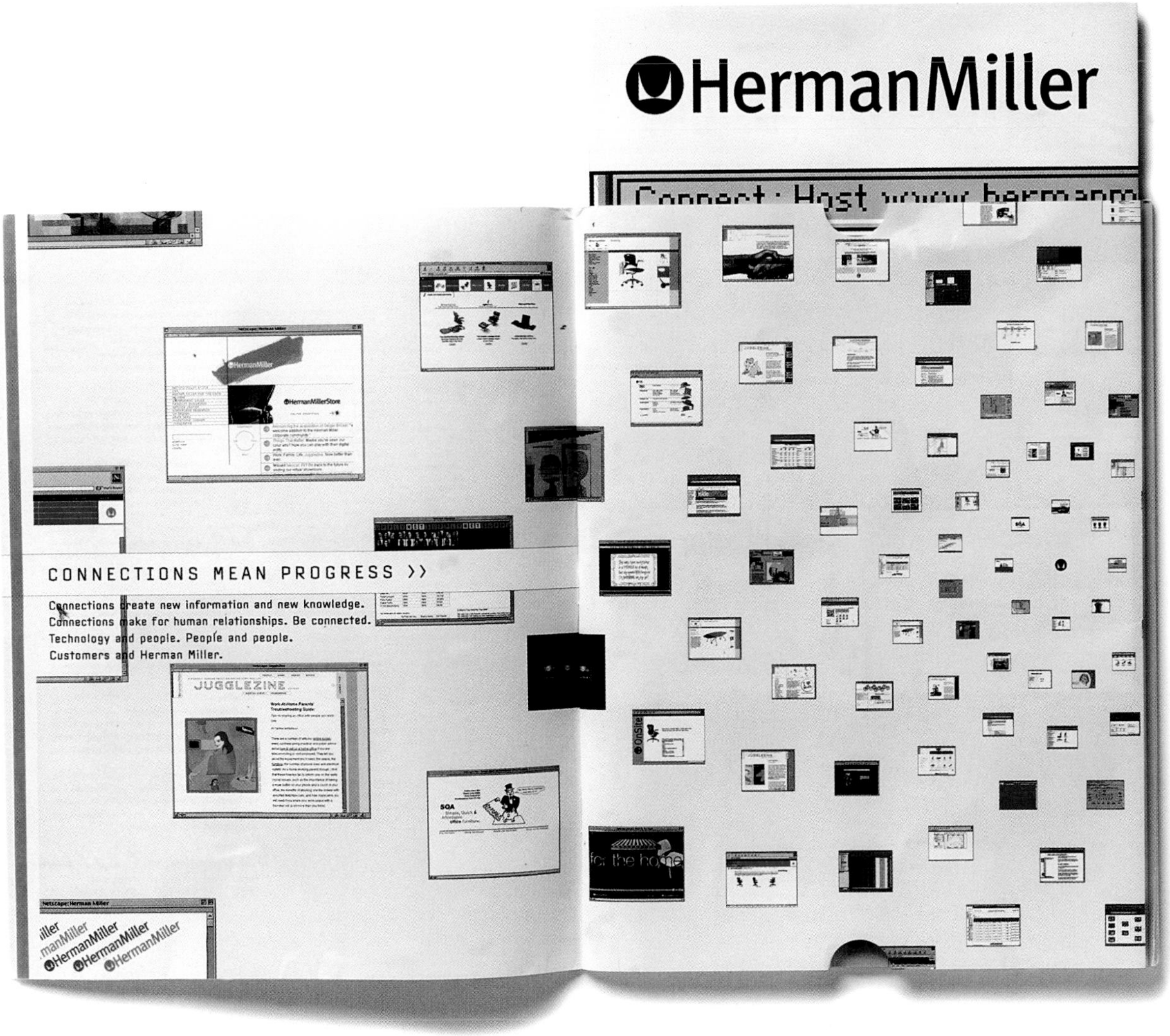
HermanMiller
CONNECTIONS MEAN PROGRESS >>
Connections create new information and new knowledge.
Connections make for human relationships. Be connected.
Technology and people. People and people.
Customers and Herman Miller.
JUGGLEZINE

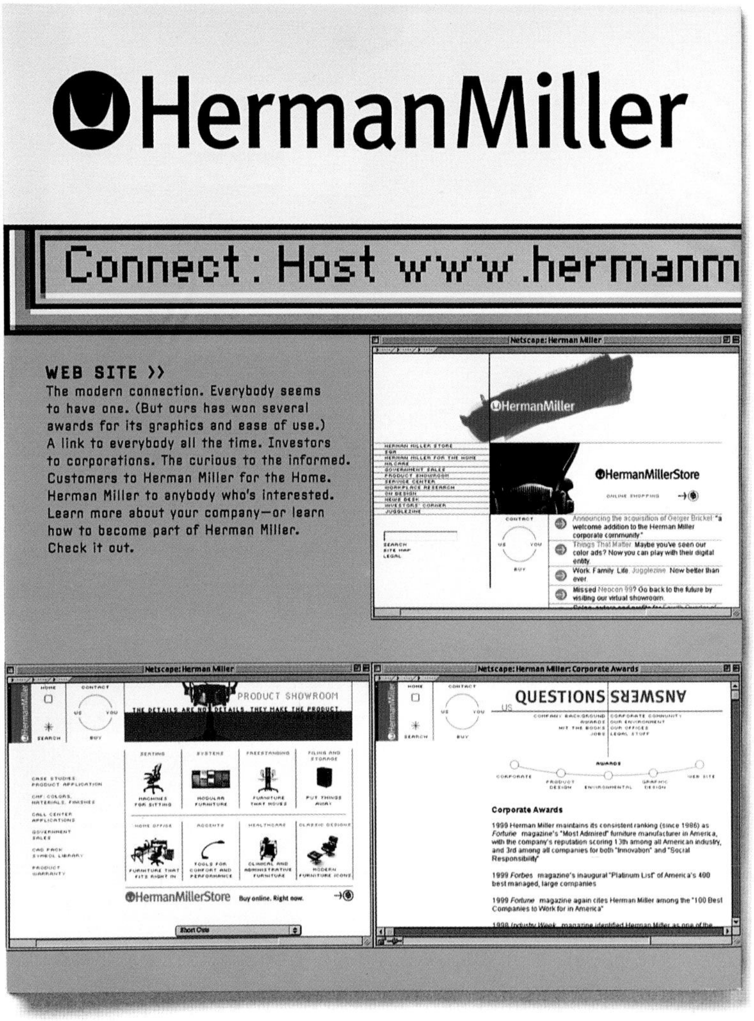
HermanMiller
Connect : Host www.hermanm
WEB SITE >>
The modern connection. Everybody seems to have one. (But ours has won several awards for its graphics and ease of use.) A link to everybody all the time. Investors to corporations. The curious to the informed. Customers to Herman Miller for the Home. Herman Miller to anybody who's interested. Learn more about your company—or learn how to become part of Herman Miller. Check it out.
Netscape: Herman Miller
HermanMillerStore
PRODUCT SHOWROOM
QUESTIONS ANSWERS
Corporate Awards
HermanMillerStore Buy online. Right now.

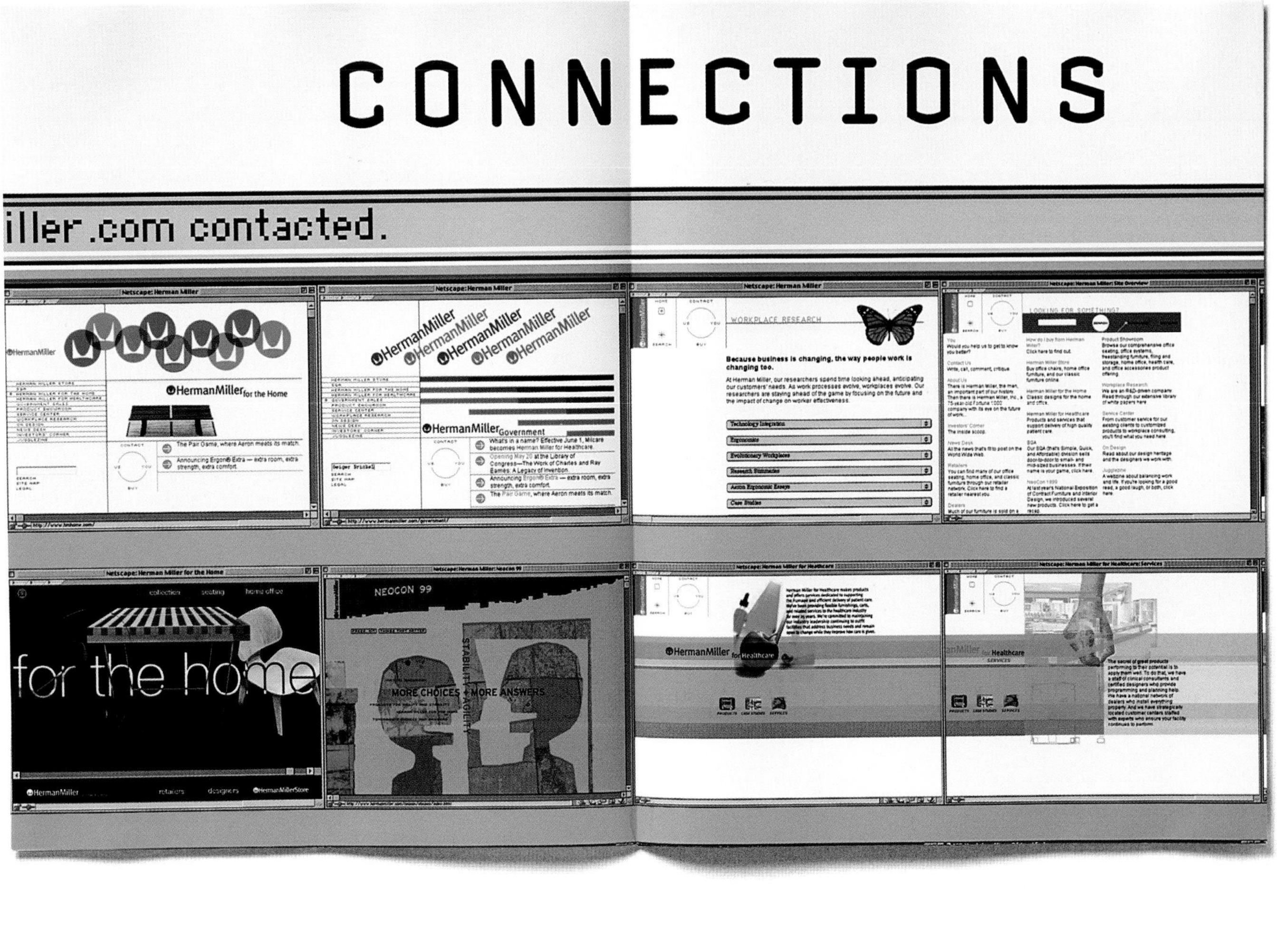
CONNECTIONS
iller.com contacted.
Netscape: Herman Miller
HermanMiller for the Home
HermanMiller Government
WORKPLACE RESEARCH
Because business is changing, the way people work is changing too.
for the home
NEOCON 99
MORE CHOICES + MORE ANSWERS
HermanMiller for Healthcare

Good Works
Connect
Netscape: Herman Miller
HermanMiller for the Home
Netscape: Herman Miller: Investors' Center
Netscape: Herman Miller
HermanMiller

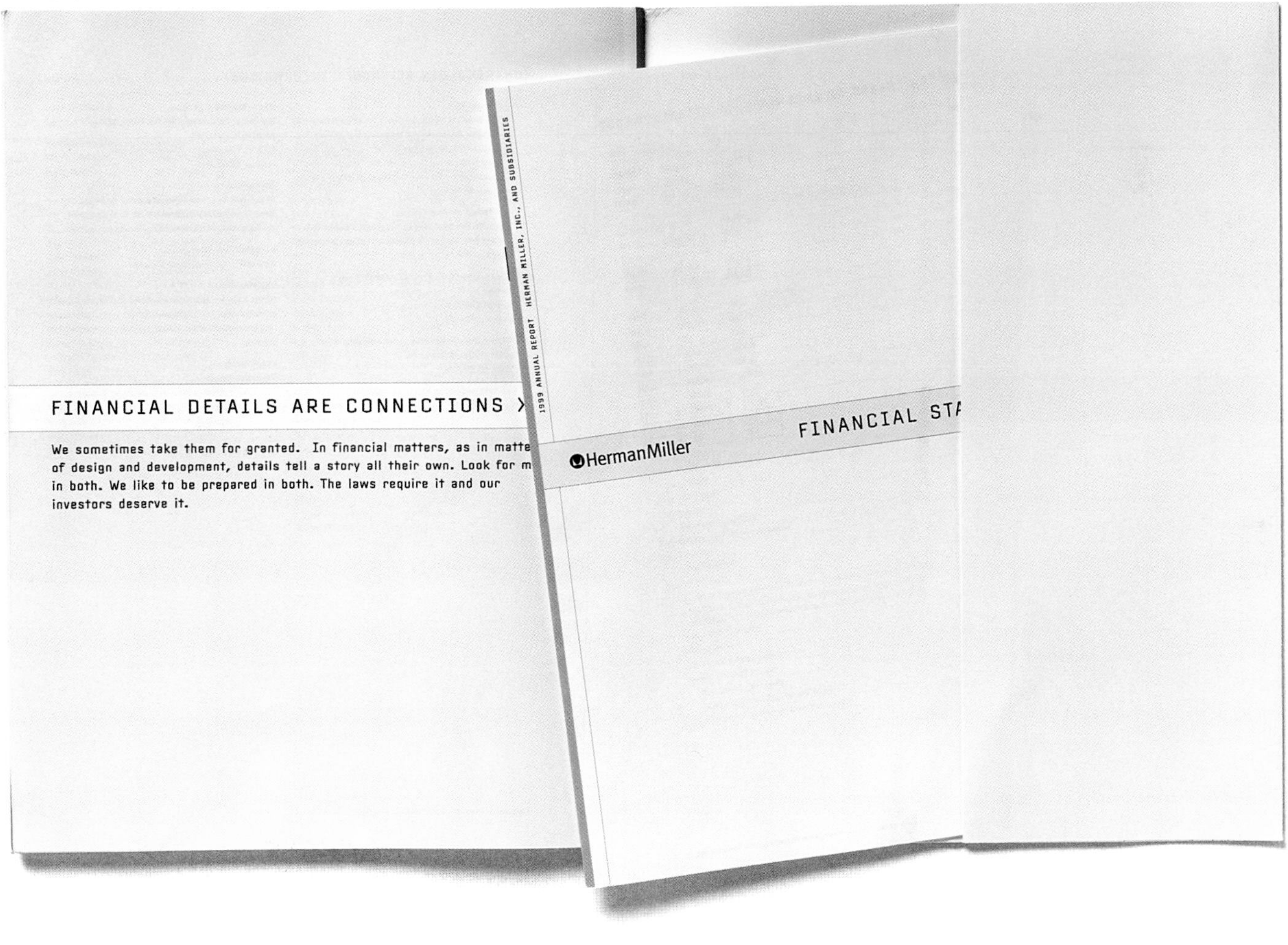
FINANCIAL DETAILS ARE CONNECTIONS >
We sometimes take them for granted. In financial matters, as in matte
of design and development, details tell a story all their own. Look for m
in both. We like to be prepared in both. The laws require it and our
investors deserve it.
1999 ANNUAL REPORT HERMAN MILLER, INC., AND SUBSIDIARIES
HermanMiller
FINANCIAL STA

Williams-Sonoma

Agency: Eleven, Inc./Goodby, Silverstein & Partners
Art Director: Keith Anderson
Creative Directors: Paul Curtin, Rob Price
Designer: Druanne Cummins
Photographer: William Abrenowicz
Copywriter: Stephanie Marlis

WILLIAMS-SONOMA, INC.
1998 ANNUAL REPORT

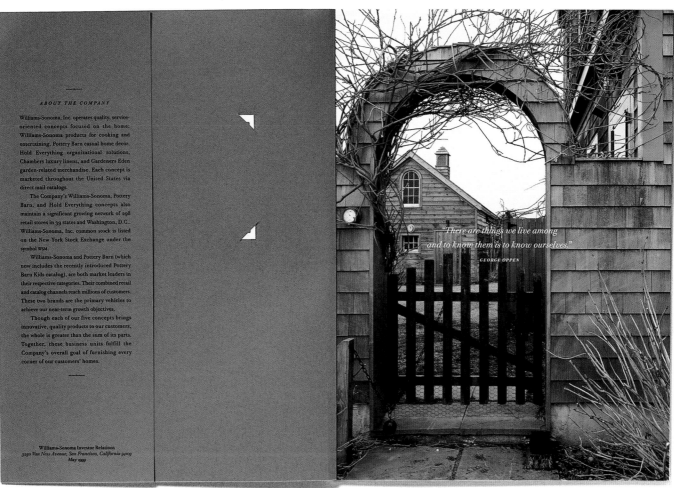

ABOUT THE COMPANY

Williams-Sonoma, Inc. operates quality, service-oriented concepts focused on the home: Williams-Sonoma products for cooking and entertaining, Pottery Barn casual home decor, Hold Everything organizational solutions, Chambers luxury linens, and Gardeners Eden garden-related merchandise. Each concept is marketed throughout the United States via direct mail catalogs.

The Company's Williams-Sonoma, Pottery Barn, and Hold Everything concepts also maintain a significant growing network of 298 retail stores in 39 states and Washington, D.C.. Williams-Sonoma, Inc. common stock is listed on the New York Stock Exchange under the symbol WSM.

Williams-Sonoma and Pottery Barn (which now includes the recently introduced Pottery Barn Kids catalog), are both market leaders in their respective categories. Their combined retail and catalog channels reach millions of customers. These two brands are the primary vehicles to achieve our near-term growth objectives.

Though each of our five concepts brings innovative, quality products to our customers, the whole is greater than the sum of its parts. Together, these business units fulfill the Company's overall goal of furnishing every corner of our customers' homes.

Williams-Sonoma Investor Relations
3250 Van Ness Avenue, San Francisco, California 94109
May 1999

"There are things we live among
and to know them is to know ourselves."
GEORGE OPPEN

5 YEAR FINANCIAL HIGHLIGHTS

Dollars in thousands except per share data	Fiscal Year 1998	1997	1996	1995	1994
Net Sales	$ 1,103,954	$933,257	$ 811,758	$644,653	$528,543
Net Earnings	54,897	41,347	22,742	2,536	19,572
Net Earnings Per Share[1]	.96	.75	.43	.05	.37
Stockholders' Equity	$ 302,030	$193,198	$146,038	$ 121,653	$ 118,216
Return on Assets	10.7%	10.2%	7.7%	2.6%	10.8%
Return on Equity	22.2%	24.4%	17.0%	2.1%	18.3%
Operating Margin	8.3%	7.9%	5.4%	1.4%	6.6%

[1] *Per share amounts have been restated to reflect the 3-for-2 stock splits in February 1994 and September 1994, as well as the 2-for-1 stock split in May 1998.*

NET SALES 1994-1998

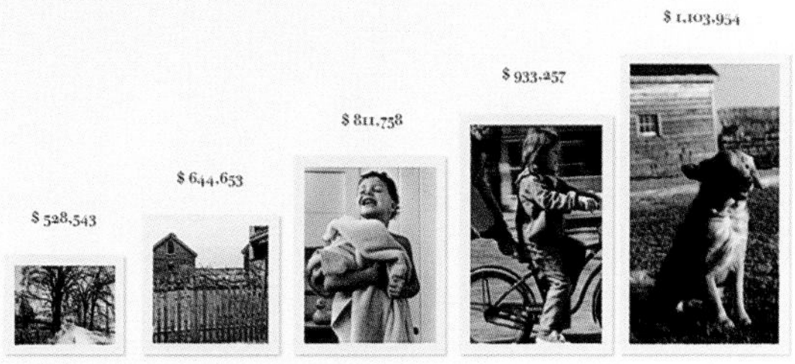
$ 528,543
$ 644,653
$ 811,758
$ 933,257
$ 1,103,954
1994
1995
1996
1997
1998

Williams–Sonoma continues its long history of strong performance. In fiscal 1998, sales exceeded $1 billion, while compound sales growth for the past five years reached 22%.

As Americans have enriched their culinary interests, we've enriched our offerings. Knowing what people are cooking and serving in their homes is our business. This past year, we held a cooks' symposium with 24 experts, including well-known chefs, cookbook publishers, and editors from leading publications. We called this our "Kitchen Cabinet," and together we took a look at what's going on in American kitchens and dining rooms. When it comes to food and entertaining, Williams-Sonoma is a pacesetter and the leader in our market niche.

WILLIAMS-SONOMA, INC. ONLINE

We set up our first website in January, and by this summer, we will offer our Williams-Sonoma in-store bridal and gift registry on-line. According to Boston Consulting, a specialist in the field, the most successful websites have been those of established retailers. With many years of direct-to-consumer marketing experience, we are optimistic about our opportunities on the Internet.

BUILDING DOMINANT BRANDS

Brand recognition is what matters; the majority of the decisions we made in 1998 contributed to establishing our concepts as top-of-mind, world-class brands for the home. The same opportunities that existed in the apparel market a number of years ago, when a few insightful, vertically-integrated companies successfully targeted the baby boomer generation, are present in the home furnishings market now. These consumers are now a bit older; they've bought homes, and purchasing items for the home has become one of their highest priorities. This past year, we continued to focus on developing recognizable styles,

When purchasing furniture, today's upscale homeowners consider quality and design the most important factors.'
(It's a good time to be Williams-Sonoma, Inc.)

A family's home
is not something that can
be created overnight.
It comes together over time;
piece by piece, memory by memory.
In ways small and large,
Pottery Barn has helped furnish
millions of families' homes
—and their memories.

WILLIAMS-SONOMA, INC.

FIVE-YEAR SELECTED FINANCIAL DATA

Dollars and amounts in thousands except percentages, per share amounts and retail stores data	Jan. 31, 1999	Feb. 1, 1998	Feb. 2, 1997[2]	Jan. 28, 1996	Jan. 29, 1995
RESULTS OF OPERATIONS					
Net Sales	$ 1,103,954	$ 933,257	$ 811,758	$ 644,653	$ 528,543
Earnings before income taxes	90,745	70,022	39,197	4,373	33,435
Net earnings	54,897	41,347	22,742	2,536	19,572
Basic net earnings per share[1]	1.01	.81	.45	.05	.39
Diluted net earnings per share[1]	$ .96	$ .75	$ .43	$ .05	$ .37
Financial Position					
Working capital	$ 172,866	$ 134,524	$ 96,568	$ 39,076	$ 49,506
Long-term debt and other liabilities	44,649	89,789	89,319	46,757	6,781
Total assets	576,245	477,229	404,417	319,096	217,878
Shareholders' equity per share (book value)[1]	$ 5.42	$ 3.74	$ 2.86	$ 2.39	$ 2.35
Debt-to-equity ratio	16.9%	46.5%	61.2%	38.4%	5.7%
Retail Stores					
Store Count					
Williams-Sonoma	163	152	145	139	120
Classic	65	78	89	97	105
Grand Cuisine	98	74	56	42	15
Pottery Barn	96	88	76	67	57
Classic	19	34	43	47	53
Design Studio	77	54	33	20	4
Hold Everything	33	32	32	32	35
Outlets	6	4	3	2	2
Number of stores at year-end	298	276	256	240	214
Comparable store sales growth	5.0%	2.8%	4.6%	3.4%	16.5%
Store selling area at year-end (sq. ft.)	1,217,047	1,015,778	839,112	690,256	537,969
Gross leasable area at year-end (sq. ft.)	1,887,560	1,553,137	1,264,531	1,023,003	746,683
Catalog Sales					
Catalogs mailed in year	163,067	154,475	136,489	131,800	126,833
Catalog sales growth	15.7%	11.2%	19.1%	16.2%	55.0%
Catalog sales as percent of total sales	34.8%	35.5%	36.7%	38.8%	40.8%

[1] *Per share amounts have been restated to reflect the 3-for-2 stock splits in February 1994 and September 1994, as well as reflect the 2-for-1 stock split in May 1998.*

[2] *The year ended February 2, 1997 includes 53 weeks.*

furniture for the future of business

Teknion

1998 ANNUAL REPORT

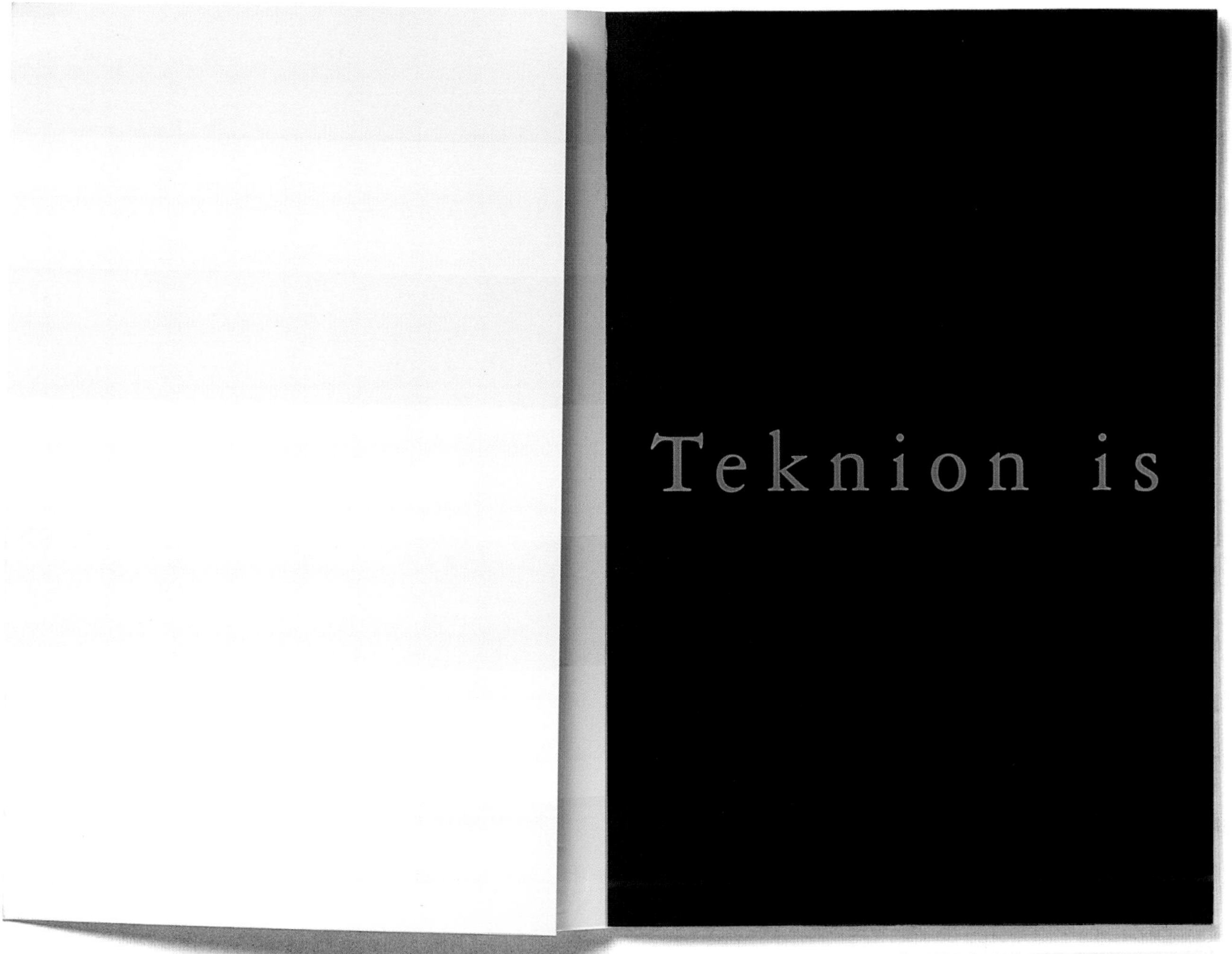
Teknion is

agile

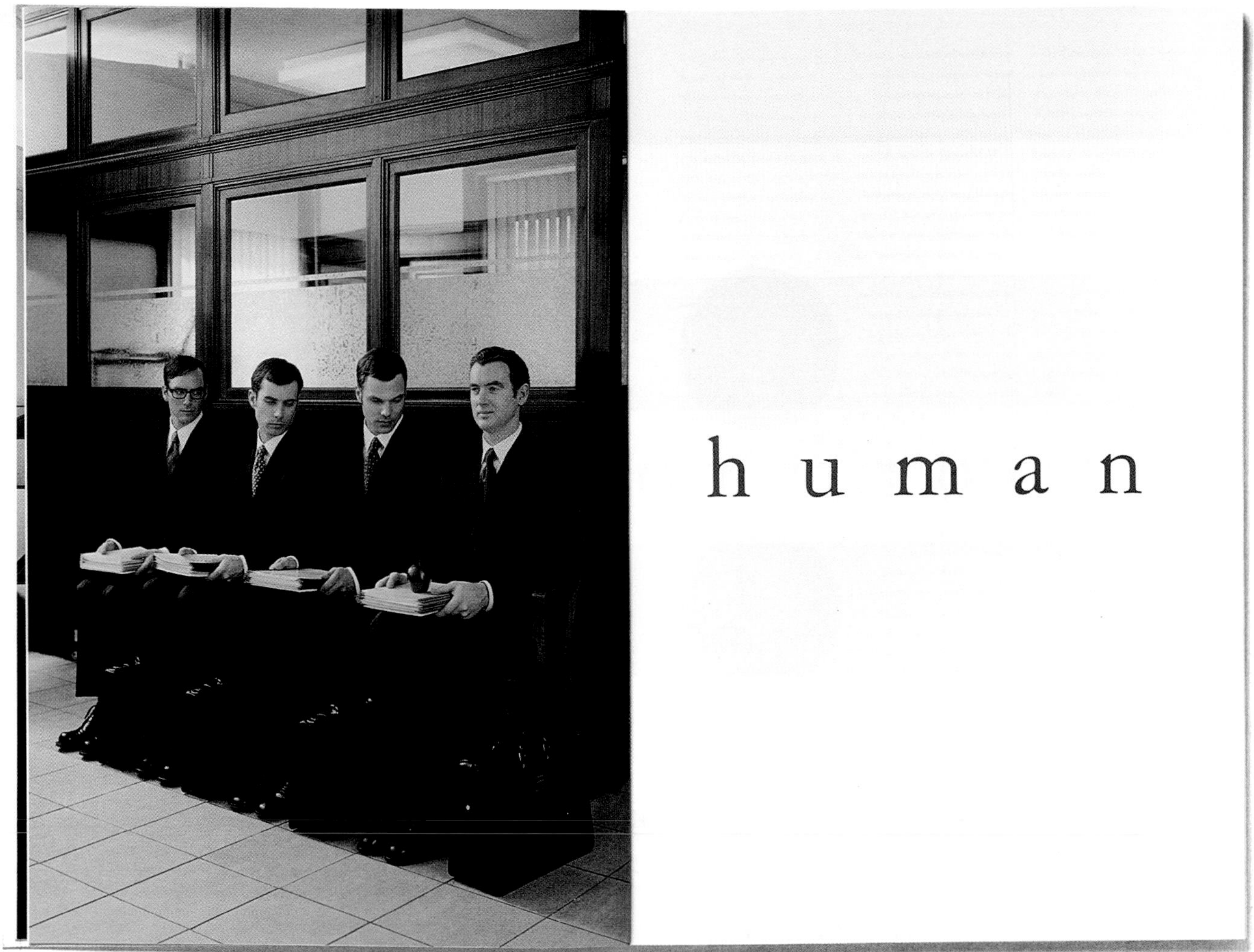
human

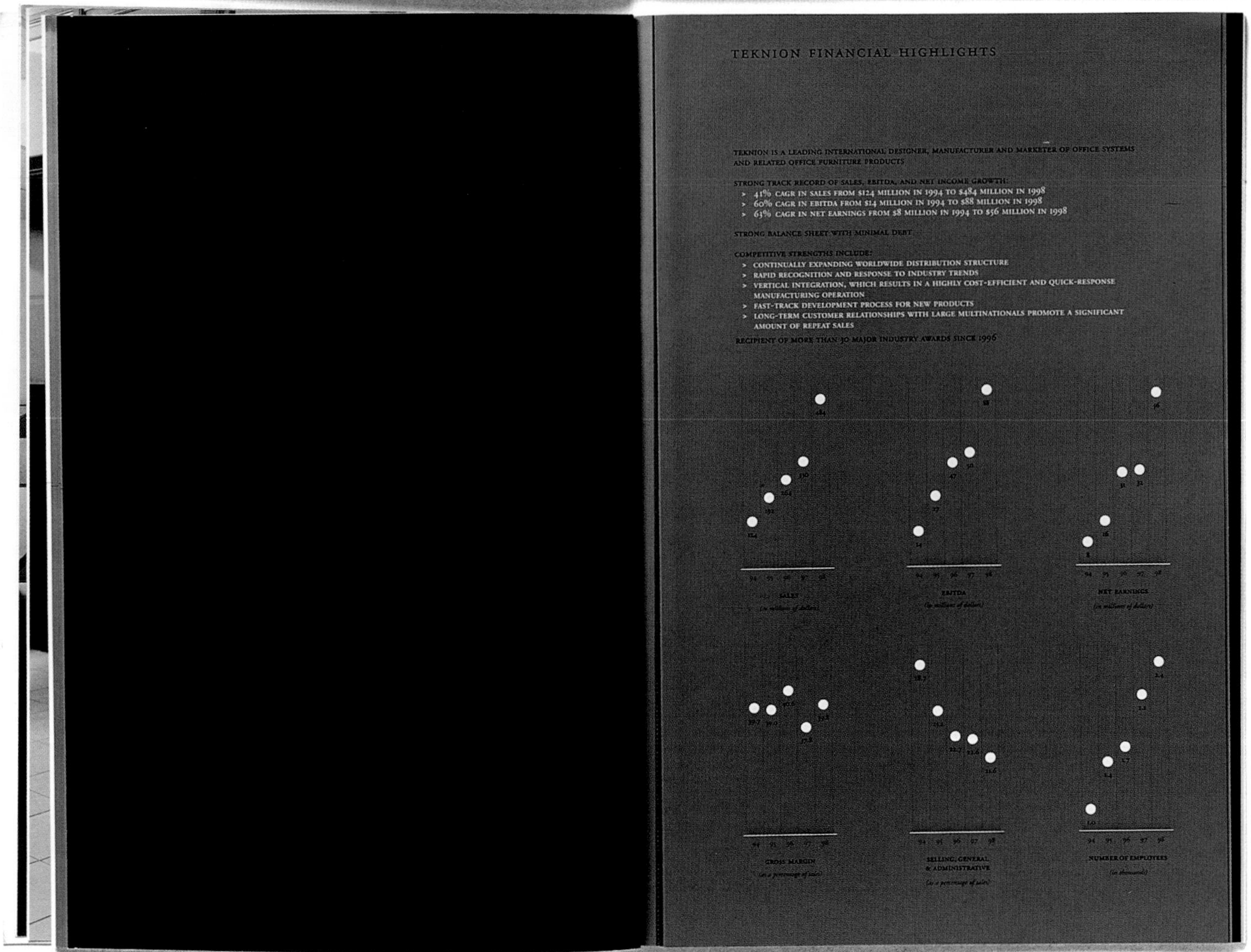
TEKNION FINANCIAL HIGHLIGHTS

TEKNION IS A LEADING INTERNATIONAL DESIGNER, MANUFACTURER AND MARKETER OF OFFICE SYSTEMS AND RELATED OFFICE FURNITURE PRODUCTS

STRONG TRACK RECORD OF SALES, EBITDA, AND NET INCOME GROWTH:
> 41% CAGR IN SALES FROM $124 MILLION IN 1994 TO $484 MILLION IN 1998
> 60% CAGR IN EBITDA FROM $14 MILLION IN 1994 TO $88 MILLION IN 1998
> 63% CAGR IN NET EARNINGS FROM $8 MILLION IN 1994 TO $56 MILLION IN 1998

STRONG BALANCE SHEET WITH MINIMAL DEBT

COMPETITIVE STRENGTHS INCLUDE:
> CONTINUALLY EXPANDING WORLDWIDE DISTRIBUTION STRUCTURE
> RAPID RECOGNITION AND RESPONSE TO INDUSTRY TRENDS
> VERTICAL INTEGRATION, WHICH RESULTS IN A HIGHLY COST-EFFICIENT AND QUICK-RESPONSE MANUFACTURING OPERATION
> FAST-TRACK DEVELOPMENT PROCESS FOR NEW PRODUCTS
> LONG-TERM CUSTOMER RELATIONSHIPS WITH LARGE MULTINATIONALS PROMOTE A SIGNIFICANT AMOUNT OF REPEAT SALES

RECIPIENT OF MORE THAN 30 MAJOR INDUSTRY AWARDS SINCE 1996

94 95 96 97 98
SALES
(in millions of dollars)
94 95 96 97 98
EBITDA
(in millions of dollars)
94 95 96 97 98
NET EARNINGS
(in millions of dollars)
94 95 96 97 98
GROSS MARGIN
(as a percentage of sales)
94 95 96 97 98
SELLING, GENERAL & ADMINISTRATIVE
(as a percentage of sales)
94 95 96 97 98
NUMBER OF EMPLOYEES
(in thousands)

SYNOPSIS
VENTURE
HARRINGTON
SEATING
AMICUS
STORAGE
SYSTEMS STORAGE
CHRONICLE
EXECUTIVE
HALCON
LEIF JACOBSEN

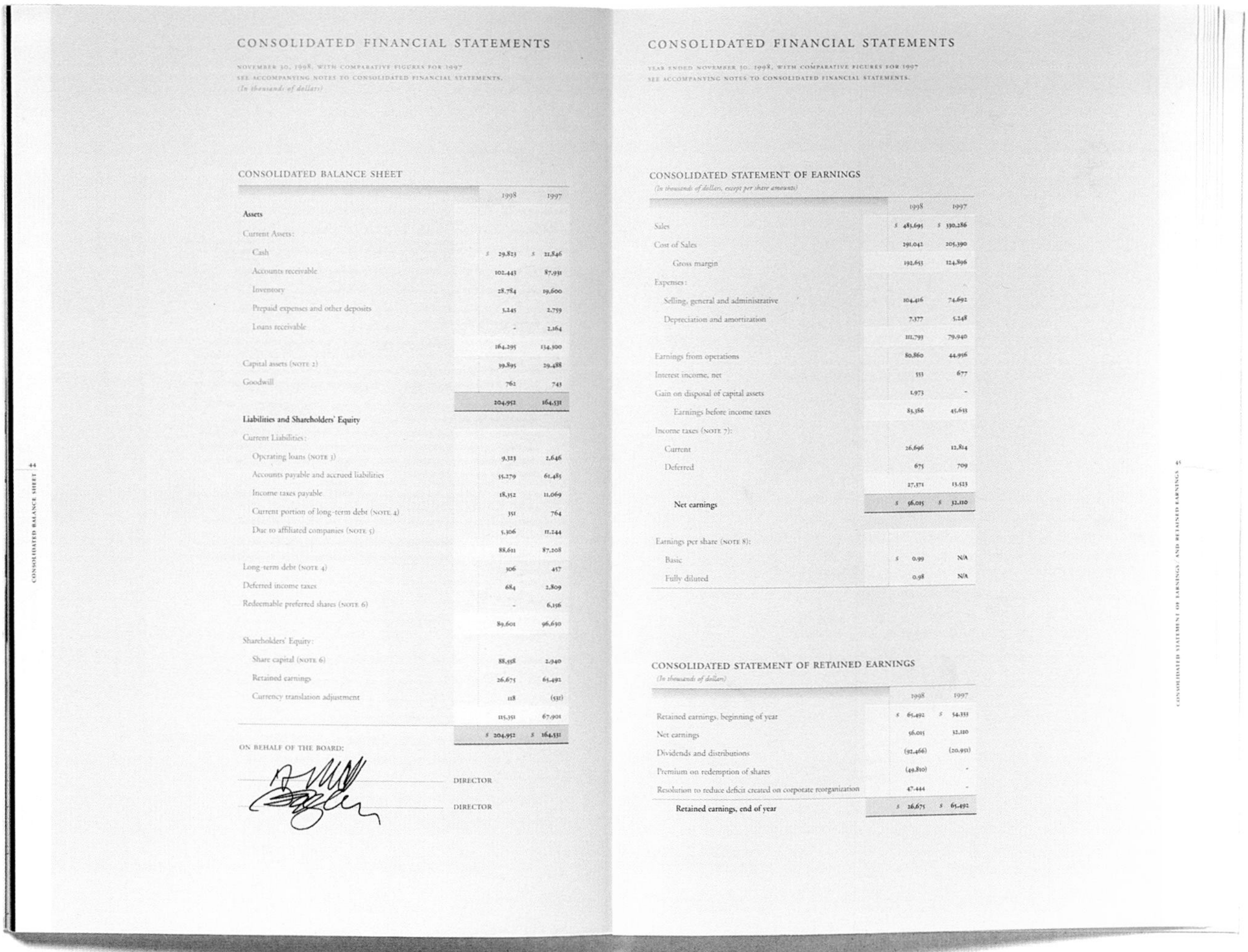

CONSOLIDATED FINANCIAL STATEMENTS

NOVEMBER 30, 1998, WITH COMPARATIVE FIGURES FOR 1997
SEE ACCOMPANYING NOTES TO CONSOLIDATED FINANCIAL STATEMENTS.
(In thousands of dollars)

CONSOLIDATED BALANCE SHEET

	1998	1997
Assets		
Current Assets:		
Cash	$ 29,823	$ 21,846
Accounts receivable	102,443	87,931
Inventory	28,784	19,600
Prepaid expenses and other deposits	3,245	2,759
Loans receivable	-	2,164
	164,295	134,300
Capital assets (NOTE 2)	39,895	29,488
Goodwill	762	743
	204,952	164,531
Liabilities and Shareholders' Equity		
Current Liabilities:		
Operating loans (NOTE 3)	9,323	2,646
Accounts payable and accrued liabilities	55,279	61,485
Income taxes payable	18,352	11,069
Current portion of long-term debt (NOTE 4)	351	764
Due to affiliated companies (NOTE 5)	5,306	11,244
	88,611	87,208
Long-term debt (NOTE 4)	306	457
Deferred income taxes	684	2,809
Redeemable preferred shares (NOTE 6)	-	6,156
	89,601	96,630
Shareholders' Equity:		
Share capital (NOTE 6)	88,558	2,940
Retained earnings	26,675	65,492
Currency translation adjustment	118	(531)
	115,351	67,901
	$ 204,952	$ 164,531

ON BEHALF OF THE BOARD:

DIRECTOR

DIRECTOR

44 CONSOLIDATED BALANCE SHEET

CONSOLIDATED FINANCIAL STATEMENTS

YEAR ENDED NOVEMBER 30, 1998, WITH COMPARATIVE FIGURES FOR 1997
SEE ACCOMPANYING NOTES TO CONSOLIDATED FINANCIAL STATEMENTS.

CONSOLIDATED STATEMENT OF EARNINGS
(In thousands of dollars, except per share amounts)

	1998	1997
Sales	$ 483,695	$ 330,286
Cost of Sales	291,042	205,390
Gross margin	192,653	124,896
Expenses:		
Selling, general and administrative	104,416	74,692
Depreciation and amortization	7,377	5,248
	111,793	79,940
Earnings from operations	80,860	44,956
Interest income, net	553	677
Gain on disposal of capital assets	1,973	-
Earnings before income taxes	83,386	45,633
Income taxes (NOTE 7):		
Current	26,696	12,814
Deferred	675	709
	27,371	13,523
Net earnings	$ 56,015	$ 32,110
Earnings per share (NOTE 8):		
Basic	$ 0.99	N/A
Fully diluted	0.98	N/A

CONSOLIDATED STATEMENT OF RETAINED EARNINGS
(In thousands of dollars)

	1998	1997
Retained earnings, beginning of year	$ 65,492	$ 54,333
Net earnings	56,015	32,110
Dividends and distributions	(92,466)	(20,951)
Premium on redemption of shares	(49,810)	-
Resolution to reduce deficit created on corporate reorganization	47,444	-
Retained earnings, end of year	$ 26,675	$ 65,492

45 CONSOLIDATED STATEMENT OF EARNINGS AND RETAINED EARNINGS

Blue Shield of California
Agency: Jennifer Sterling Design
Art & Creative Director, Designer: Jennifer Sterling
Copywriters: Lisa Citron, Jennifer Sterling

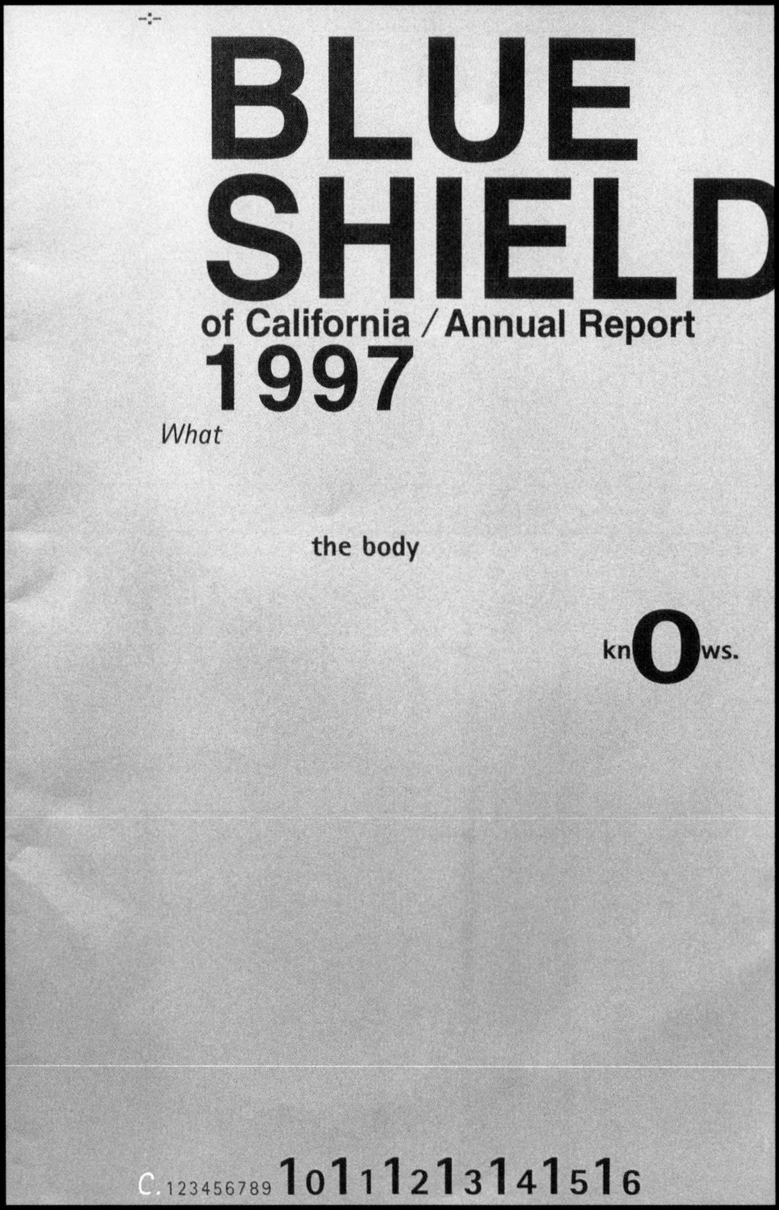
BLUE
SHIELD
of California / Annual Report
1997
What
the body
knOws.
C. 123456789 10 11 12 13 14 15 16

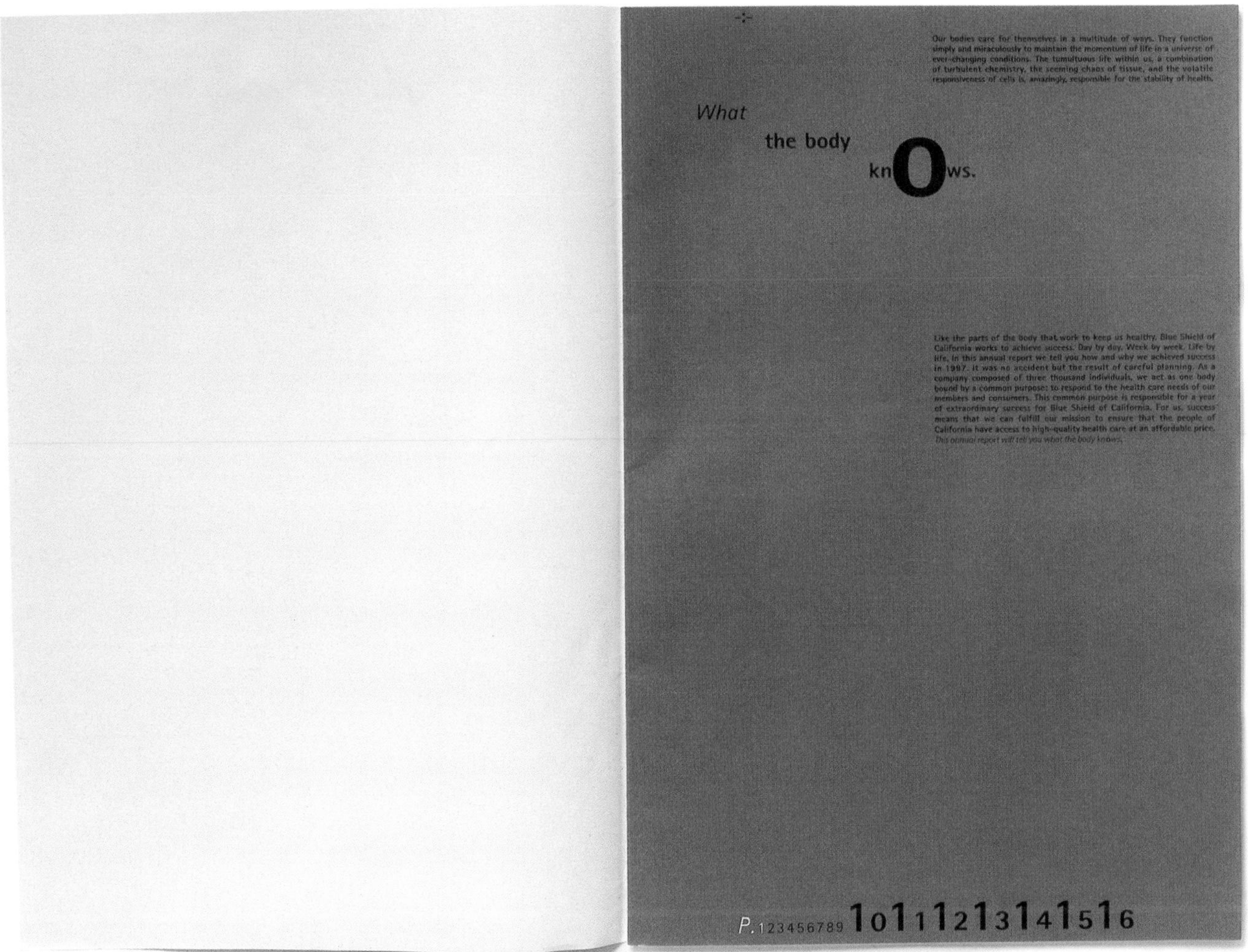

Our bodies care for themselves in a multitude of ways. They function simply and miraculously to maintain the momentum of life in a universe of ever-changing conditions. The tumultuous life within us, a combination of turbulent chemistry, the seeming chaos of tissue, and the volatile responsiveness of cells is, amazingly, responsible for the stability of health.

What
the body
knOws.

Like the parts of the body that work to keep us healthy, Blue Shield of California works to achieve success. Day by day. Week by week. Life by life. In this annual report we tell you how and why we achieved success in 1997. It was no accident but the result of careful planning. As a company composed of three thousand individuals, we act as one body bound by a common purpose: to respond to the health care needs of our members and consumers. This common purpose is responsible for a year of extraordinary success for Blue Shield of California. For us, success means that we can fulfill our mission to ensure that the people of California have access to high-quality health care at an affordable price.
This annual report will tell you what the body knows.

P. 1 2 3 4 5 6 7 8 9 10 11 12 13 14 15 16

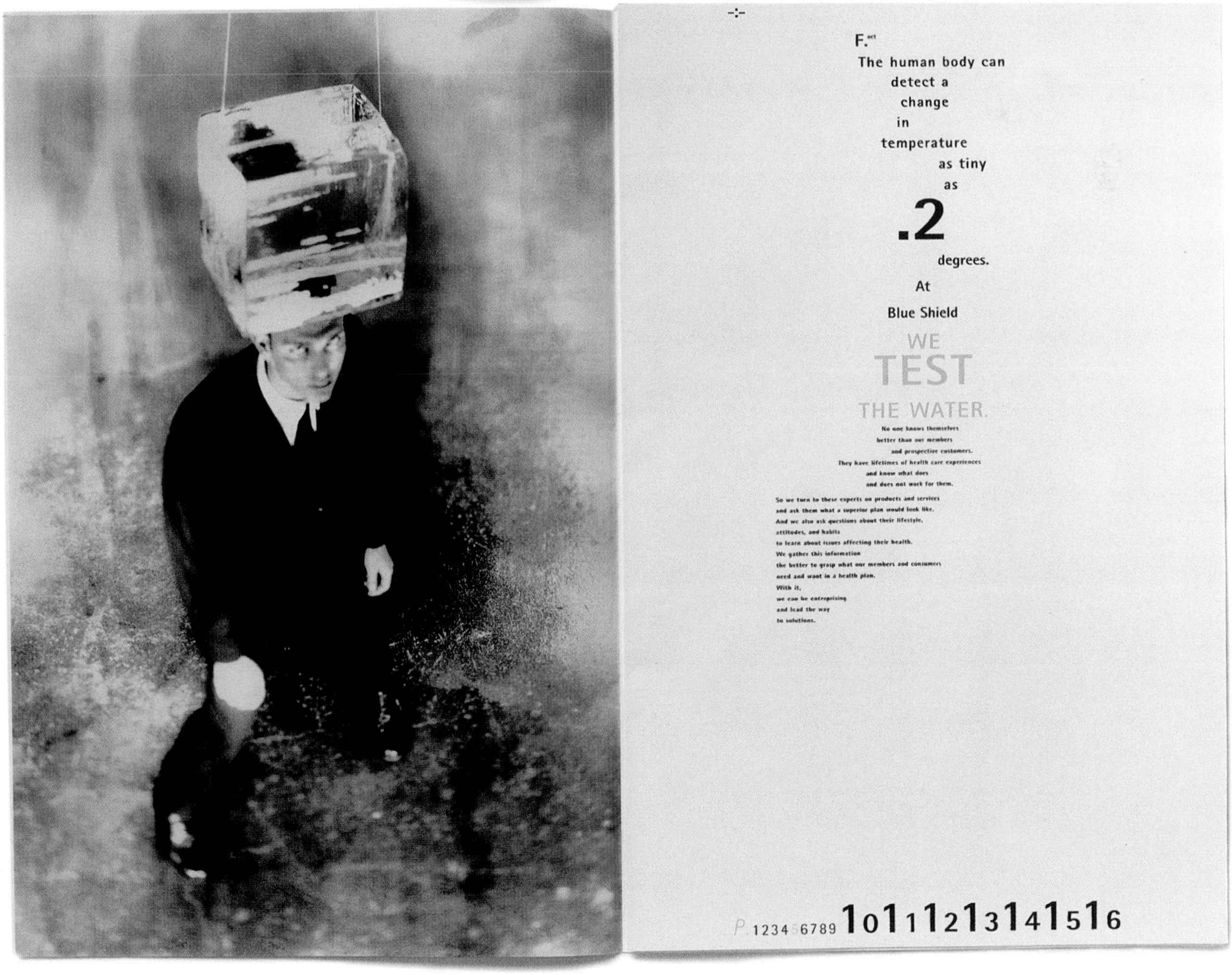

F.act
The human body can
detect a
change
in
temperature
as tiny
as
.2
degrees.
At
Blue Shield
WE
TEST
THE WATER.

No one knows themselves
better than our members
and prospective customers.
They have lifetimes of health care experiences
and know what does
and does not work for them.

So we turn to these experts on products and services
and ask them what a superior plan would look like.
And we also ask questions about their lifestyle,
attitudes, and habits
to learn about issues affecting their health.
We gather this information
the better to grasp what our members and consumers
need and want in a health plan.
With it,
we can be enterprising
and lead the way
to solutions.

P. 1 2 3 4 5 6 7 8 9 10 11 12 13 14 15 16

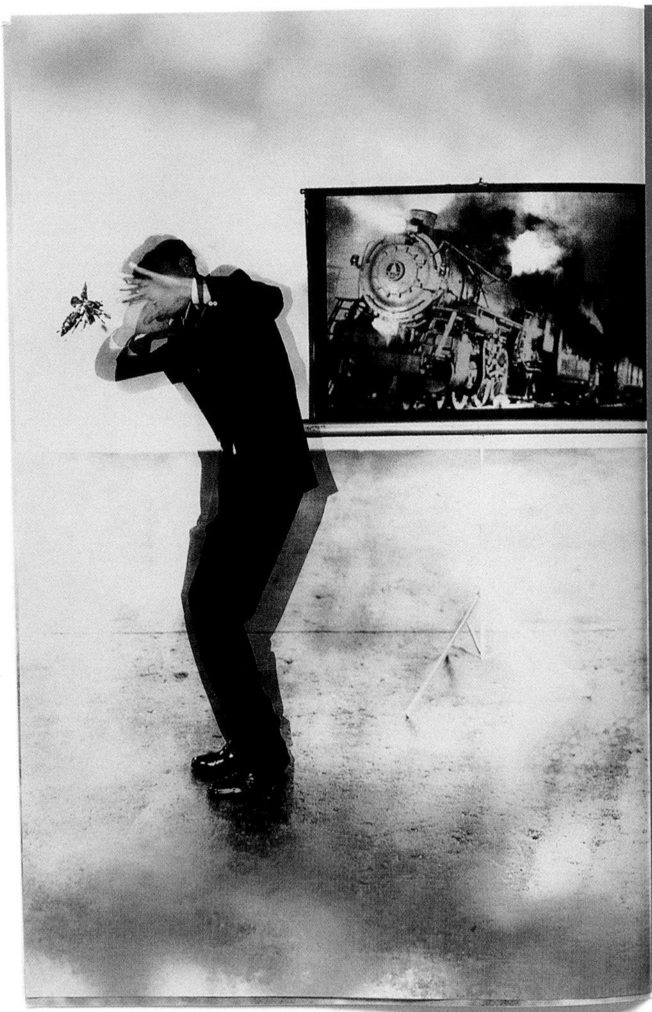

F.act

AT ANY DIFFERENCE GREATER THAN TEN THOUSANDTHS OF A SECOND, ONE EAR CAN DETECT THE ARRIVAL OF SOUND BEFORE THE OTHER EAR.

AT BLUE SHIELD WE HEAR WHAT'S IMPORTANT.

We learn from our members and consumers. We listen as they tell us their good and bad experiences: the child who waited too long for authorization to see a specialist, the doctor who went the extra mile, the elderly parent released from the hospital who had trouble caring for himself, the nurse who taught useful preventive health information. We sort through what our members and potential members describe to us. We assess what it means and identify emerging issues. We heard when consumers wanted direct access to specialists, a broad selection of high-quality doctors, and alternative health and wellness services. These affordable options make sense. With this information in hand, we design unique products, services, and health management capabilities.

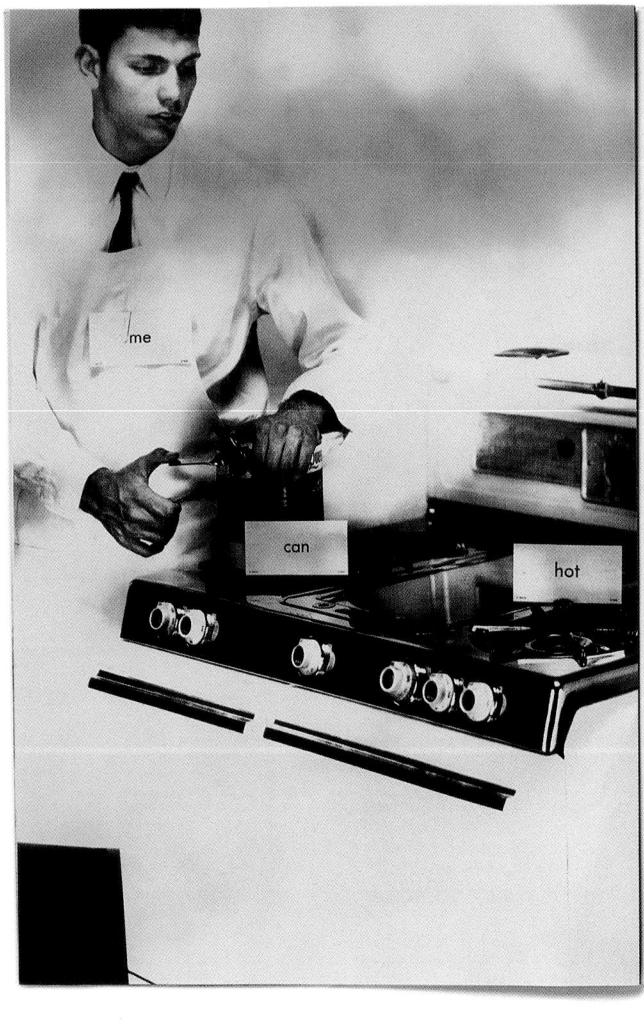

me
can
hot

F.act

Humans possess an estimated 1 trillion neurons,
plus 70 trillion synaptic connections between them.

A single neuron may have
as many as 10,000 synapses,

but during the process of memory formation
perhaps only 12 synapses will be strengthened,

while another 100 will be weakened.
The sum of these changes,

multiplied neuron by neuron,
creates a circuit that amounts to a memory.

At Blue Shield

we

listen to

our

members

and

don't

fOrget

what's

important.

Our members' health and well-being extend beyond their physical selves into the environment in which they live.

We support their communities by investing in research, education, and service programs. In 1997 we confronted the critical public health problem of domestic violence by creating a program for both employees and employers. In addition, we continue to support important health care research programs.

In October, Blue Shield of California introduced its Domestic Violence Prevention Program, a public service initiative designed to provide resources to businesses and health care providers throughout the state. The program includes a powerful video, *Thirty Seconds at a Time: What Corporate America Can Do About Domestic Violence,* and a resource kit, *Domestic Violence Doesn't Stay at Home When a Woman Goes to Work.* Materials include human resource guidelines to help supervisors and co-workers identify the signs of domestic abuse, and suggestions on how to support endangered individuals. These resource packets are offered to brokers to take to their business customers. Health care providers are offered training to screen, diagnose, document, and make referrals for domestic violence.

Blue Shield of California is funding health research under way at the Stanford Center for Research in Disease Prevention, an internationally recognized institution. Our support fosters interdisciplinary research in the prevention and control of chronic disease.

Using a nurse-managed model Stanford developed for reducing coronary disease risk, Blue Shield of California funded three projects to demonstrate how effective it is in real-life workplaces. In the first project, participants had outstanding results, with significant improvements in blood pressure, total cholesterol and LDL cholesterol, stress management, nutrition, weight, and blood sugar. The other two programs are still ongoing, but we can clearly see that the Stanford model works. The upshot of the studies is that we will create our own nurse-managed cardiovascular risk reduction program for our PPO members with cardiovascular disease.

In another Stanford study, Blue Shield of California requested our Medicare HMO Shield 65 members to participate in a survey on their use of alternative medicine therapies. In this way, we will learn more about the needs of aging people, the most rapidly growing population in the nation.

F.[01]

The nervous system, hormones, and cells
keep the body's chemistry
adjusted within a few parts per million.
At Blue Shield
we cOOrdinate
our response
to
best
serve
our
members.

A body works diligently,
cell by cell, second by second,
to function properly and maintain its health.
We at Blue Shield work in much the same way,
doing what's right for our members.
Blue Shield of California makes choices daily
about how to best protect our members and the community at large.
This began when Blue Shield of California
started the first medically sponsored prepaid health plan
in the nation in 1939.
Our mission and purpose
as a not-for-profit health plan has always made us
fundamentally different from most of our competitors.

We continue to grow and to
protect our Blue Shield of California
members as we focus on the best solutions
in their interests,
unconstrained by the
demands of investors.
As we look to the future,
our continued success hinges on
our concept of who we are
and what we stand for.
Blue Shield of California
has created a new role
in the marketplace:
to make the most
of our competitive presence
by acting as a catalyst
for positive changes
in health care.
History shows us
that not-for-profit health plans
provide
unique solutions
to
community
health
care
needs.

P.123456789 10 11 12 13 14 15 16

.97 1997 Annual Report
Blue Shield of California
(California Physicians' Service)
and Subsidiaries

Financial highlights

DEC. 31, 1997 AND 1996 (DOLLARS IN THOUSANDS)

		1997		1996
Cash and investments	$	707,253	$	707,151
Receivables		134,481		134,524
Fixed assets		77,577		45,870
Other assets		166,121		6,826
TOTAL ASSETS		1,105,887		917,098
Accrued health care costs and experience rated credits		356,318		285,818
Accounts payable and accrued expenses		145,269		121,572
Unearned subscriber dues		86,289		48,225
Postretirement benefit accrual		28,294		28,143
STABILIZATION FUND		487,996		431,643

P.123456789 10 11 12 13 14 15 16

.97 1997 Annual Report
Blue Shield of California
(California Physicians' Service)
and Subsidiaries

Financial highlights

DEC. 31, 1997 AND 1996 (DOLLARS IN THOUSANDS)

		1997		1996
TOTAL REVENUE	$	1,716,463	$	1,418,973
Health care services		1,344,411		1,132,984
Marketing, selling, general, and administrative expenses		377,413		314,296
INVESTMENT INCOME		54,862		53,895
NET INCOME		39,383		18,693
Net increase (*decrease*) in market value of investments		16,970		(7,939)

SPECIAL NOTE *These financial highlights are derived from the audited financial statements of Blue Shield of California. For a complete copy of the audited financial statements, please contact our Public Affairs Department at* (415)229.5090. *OFFICES* Blue Shield of California 50 Beale Street San Francisco, CA 94105-1808 *TELEPHONE NO.* (415)229.5090. *FAX* (415)229.5070. http://www.blueshieldca.com

P.123456789 10 11 12 13 14 15 16

COR Therapeutics
Agency: Cahan & Associates
Art & Creative Director: Bill Cahan
Designer: Michael Braley
Photographer: William Mercer McLeod
Copywriters: Michael Braley, NCI Worldwide, Jackie Jeffries

He watched one more inning.

He continued to wait on table seven.

She tried to finish the set.

He thought it was heartburn.

TOPS
INSTALLED
COVERS
EAT COVERS
ATS OUR BUSINESS
Replaced
OPEN
WALLY
CARPETS

He couldn't afford to close the shop.

They had to turn back.

She dropped everything...

COR Therapeutics, Inc. is a company dedicated to the discovery, development, and commercialization of novel pharmaceutical products to establish new standards of care for the treatment and prevention of severe cardiovascular diseases. Since the Company's inception in 1988, our research has focused on advancing the basic understanding of the molecular and cellular mechanisms underlying the development of cardiovascular diseases. This targeted scientific strategy, when combined with the Company's multi-disciplinary approach to drug discovery and design, has resulted in a series of novel molecules with the potential to treat a wide range of cardiovascular disorders. Today, COR has multiple new product development programs underway—each designed to address unmet clinical needs in the management of patients suffering from disorders such as unstable angina, complications associated with coronary angioplasty, acute myocardial infarction, stroke, and deep vein thrombosis.

and lived.

CORPORATE HIGHLIGHTS

The first product from our own research labs, INTEGRILIN™ (eptifibatide) Injection, was approved and launched in the United States.

INTEGRILIN is the parenteral GP IIb-IIIa inhibitor approved with the broadest range of indications in the U.S.

COR recruited and trained a dedicated cardiovascular sales force.

PURSUIT trial results were published in the New England Journal of Medicine.

In February 1999, the Committee for Proprietary Medicinal Products (CPMP) of the European Agency for the Evaluation of Medicinal Products (EMEA) gave a positive opinion recommending the approval of INTEGRILIN.

INTEGRILIN is being studied as an adjunct to thrombolytics in a Phase II clinical program for the treatment of acute myocardial infarction.

INTEGRILIN sales by COR and Key were $12.2 million from June-December 1998.

Cromafiban, our oral GP IIb-IIIa inhibitor, progressed to Phase II clinical trials.

Phase I and early Phase II data were presented at the American College of Cardiology meeting held in March 1999.

ACUTE MARKET PROFILE

Number of patients discharged from U.S. hospitals per year Source: 1997 SMG HPD database and 1999 AHA Heart and Stroke Data

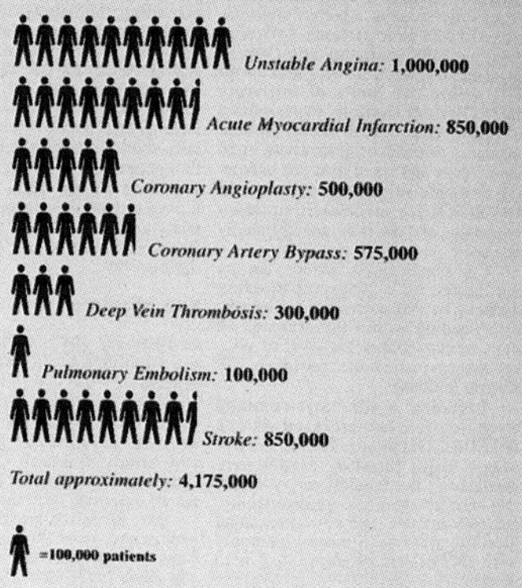
Unstable Angina: 1,000,000
Acute Myocardial Infarction: 850,000
Coronary Angioplasty: 500,000
Coronary Artery Bypass: 575,000
Deep Vein Thrombosis: 300,000
Pulmonary Embolism: 100,000
Stroke: 850,000
Total approximately: 4,175,000
=100,000 patients

RESEARCH AND DEVELOPMENT PIPELINE

Product/Candidate	Therapeutic Target	Development Status
Cromafiban	ACS and Stroke	Clinical
Factor Xa Inhibitor	Venous Thrombosis	Preclinical
Growth Factor Inhibitor	Restenosis	Preclinical
Thrombin Receptor Inhibitor	ACS, Restenosis, Stroke Prevention	Research and Development
Platelet ADP Receptor	ACS, Restenosis, Stroke Prevention	Research and Development
Myocardial Signal Transduction	Congestive Heart Failure	Research and Development
Integrin Signaling	Multiple	Research and Development

FINANCIAL HIGHLIGHTS

	YEAR ENDED DECEMBER 31,				
	1998	1997	1996	1995	1994
Statement of Operations Data: (in thousands, except per share amounts)					
Total revenues	$ 41,963	$ 22,190	$ 18,755	$ 31,850	$ 522
Total expenses	$ 73,192	$ 57,898	$ 58,094	$ 43,421	$ 44,774
Loss from operations	$ (31,229)	$ (35,708)	$ (39,339)	$ (11,571)	$ (44,252)
Net loss	$ (27,614)	$ (33,492)	$ (36,546)	$ (7,531)	$ (39,537)
Basic and diluted net loss per share	$ (1.14)	$ (1.60)	$ (1.86)	$ (0.39)	$ (2.07)
Shares used in computing basic and diluted net loss per share	24,141	20,952	19,636	19,360	19,091

	AT DECEMBER 31,				
	1998	1997	1996	1995	1994
Balance Sheet Data: (in thousands)					
Cash, cash equivalents and short-term investments	$ 75,205	$ 82,569	$ 53,134	$ 84,834	$ 94,432
Total assets	$ 103,093	$ 95,385	$ 71,245	$ 100,906	$ 106,367
Total long-term obligations	$ 3,261	$ 2,817	$ 3,365	$ 4,574	$ 4,669
Total liabilities	$ 48,497	$ 16,987	$ 20,803	$ 18,669	$ 19,636
Total stockholders' equity	$ 54,596	$ 78,398	$ 50,442	$ 82,237	$ 86,731

MGM Grand, Inc.

Agency: Young & Rubicam/RPM Design
Creative Director: Sue Zeifman
Designer: Lenore Bartz
Photographer: Steven Rothfeld
Copywriter: Delphine Hirasuna

MGM GRAND, INC.
Annual Report
19
98

Financial *Highlights*

MGM GRAND, INC.

Our Mission

MGM Grand consistently provides the premier entertainment experience while maximizing value and opportunity for our guests, cast members, business partners and shareholders.

MGM Grand is a premier owner, developer and operator of entertainment/gaming destination resorts in the United States, Australia and South Africa. The Company owns the MGM Grand's "City of Entertainment," the New York-New York Hotel and Casino on the Las Vegas Strip and other properties in Nevada acquired from Primadonna Resorts. A temporary casino is scheduled to open in Detroit, Michigan, this year, and planning continues on a resort hotel/casino in Atlantic City, New Jersey.

To our *Stockholders* and *Owners.*

With a commitment to build the world's most successful gaming and entertainment company, MGM Grand, Inc. devoted 1998 to setting the stage for global expansion and growth. Key to this strategy was ensuring that your Company's balance sheet remained the strongest in the gaming industry. * Through concentrated effort over the past two years, we have achieved that goal. We have prudently reduced operating costs, improved profit margins, streamlined systems and raised approximately $500 million in low-interest, long-term fixed debt. Our debt-to-capital ratio now stands at 36% at a time when our peer group averages 60%. In 1998, we further enhanced shareholder value by buying back 6 million shares of MGM Grand stock at $35 a share and our Board of Directors has granted us the authority to repurchase an additional 6 million shares in the future.

* With a superior cash flow position and our strong balance sheet, we were able to move aggressively on the $570-million Master Plan, transforming our flagship property in Las Vegas into "The City of Entertainment." Bringing together the amenities of a four-star hotel experience with an unparalleled panoply of entertainment choices, we now offer a combination of attractions unavailable anywhere else. In April 1998, we opened a new 380,000 square-foot conference center, which has been operating at near capacity ever since. This state-of-the-art facility has generated group business that has significantly improved our midweek occupancy, traditionally a slower period in the resort hotel industry. Equally beneficial, our conference guests have contributed to increased casino, entertainment and food and beverage revenue and have generated higher room rates. * We

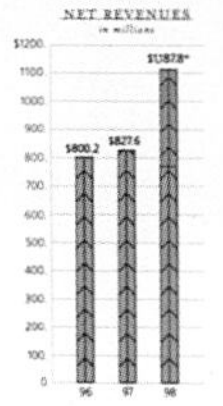
NET REVENUES
in millions
$1200
1100
1000
900
800
700
600
500
400
300
200
100
0
$800.2
$827.6
$1187.8*
96
97
98

*Represents the proforma impact for the twelve months ended December 31, 1998 of MGM Grand, Inc.'s merger with Primadonna Resorts, Inc.

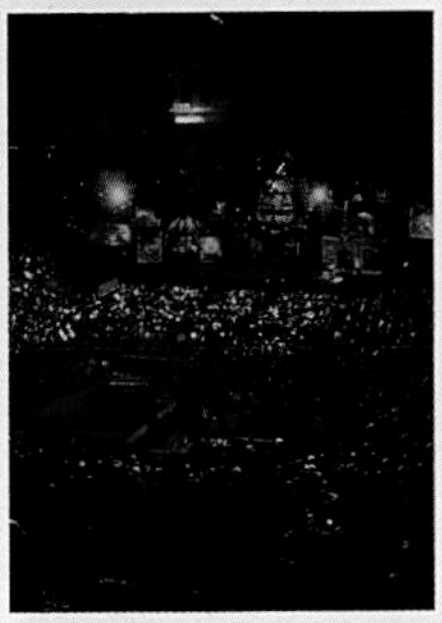

have also taken steps to maintain and improve our leadership in the high-end segment of the market by providing our guests with the finest facilities available in Las Vegas. To this end, the opulent Mansion at the MGM Grand, opening this spring, features 29 palatial villas with private pools, and perfectly manicured European gardens, all contained inside an envelope of romance. Mansion guests will be treated as royalty — which they often are. * The MGM Grand is renowned for its world-class entertainment. In 1998, we oversaw the successful opening of the Studio 54 nightclub, a luxury spa and 6.6-acre pool complex, and new celebrity chef restaurants and retail stores on Studio Walk. An interactive Lion Habitat attraction situated in the middle of our casino will open in the spring. Headliners at our Grand Garden Arena in 1998 included a dazzling array of entertainment legends, among them Elton John, Janet Jackson and Rod Stewart. * In the first quarter of 1999, we completed the acquisition of Primadonna Resorts, which brings to your Company the remaining 50% of New York-New York and other profitable assets located on the California-Nevada state line, including three hotel-casinos and two championship golf courses. The most spectacular profile on the Las Vegas Strip skyline, New York-New York continues to be the most profitable resort in its market segment. The Primadonna transaction gives us a multi-property presence on the Strip, diversifies our revenues and Nevada assets, and enhances our profitability. * In 1998, we made major strides in Detroit as well, after your Company and its Detroit partners were selected as one of three operators to develop a casino-based resort in that city.

*Represents the proforma impact for the twelve months ended December 31, 1998 of MGM Grand, Inc.'s merger with Primadonna Resorts, Inc.

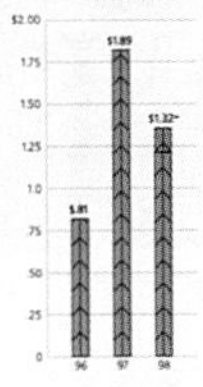
DILUTED E.P.S.
$2.00
1.75
1.50
1.25
1.0
.75
.50
.25
0
$.81
$1.89
$1.32*
96
97
98

Evenings and *entertainment.*

A night on the town in "The City of Entertainment" means a choice of the world's finest entertainment and dining attractions. The MGM Grand has not just one but several live theatres and a concert/sports arena where superstars such as the Rolling Stones, Elton John and Celine Dion have appeared in concert. Our nightly show is the $45-million EFX stage extravaganza now featuring the dazzling talents of Tony Award-winner Tommy Tune. The latest draw is the spectacular Studio 54, open for dancing and cocktails. It overlooks our elegant casino, one of the largest in the world. Dining choices are equally grand at our Las Vegas resort, with celebrity-chef and signature restaurants that range from Hollywood's legendary Brown Derby to Emeril Lagasse's New Orleans Fish House. In every way, The City of Entertainment lives up to its name.

NEW ORL
FISH HO

MGM GRAND'S WORLD-CLASS GAMING CASINO IS MATCHED BY WORLD-CLASS RESTAURANTS FEATURING RENOWNED CHEFS.

GLAMOROUS TRENDSETTERS LOVE TO HANG OUT AT THE ULTRA-CHIC STUDIO 54 NIGHT CLUB, FEATURING FOUR DANCE FLOORS, NUMEROUS BARS, AN EXCLUSIVE GUEST AREA AND SEMI-PRIVATE LOUNGES.

STUDIO

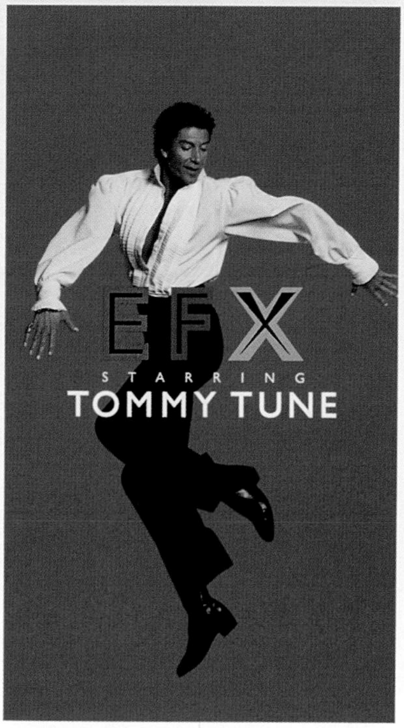
EFX
STARRING
TOMMY TUNE

FROM ELTON JOHN TO ROD STEWART, THE GRAND GARDEN ARENA SHOWCASES LEGENDS IN ENTERTAINMENT AND SPORTS.

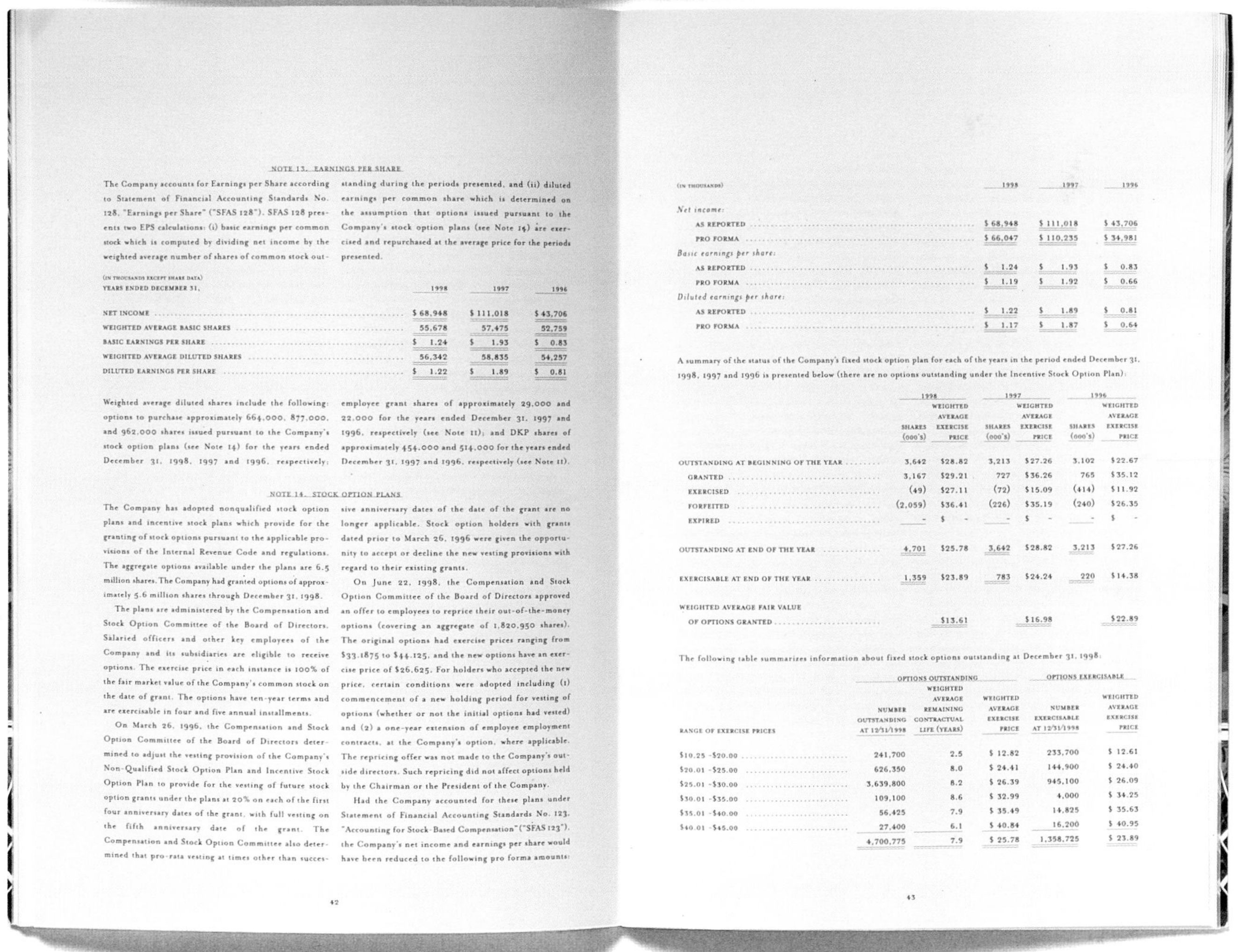

NOTE 13. EARNINGS PER SHARE

The Company accounts for Earnings per Share according to Statement of Financial Accounting Standards No. 128, "Earnings per Share" ("SFAS 128"). SFAS 128 presents two EPS calculations: (i) basic earnings per common stock which is computed by dividing net income by the weighted average number of shares of common stock outstanding during the periods presented, and (ii) diluted earnings per common share which is determined on the assumption that options issued pursuant to the Company's stock option plans (see Note 14) are exercised and repurchased at the average price for the periods presented.

(IN THOUSANDS EXCEPT SHARE DATA) YEARS ENDED DECEMBER 31,	1998	1997	1996
NET INCOME	$ 68,948	$ 111,018	$ 43,706
WEIGHTED AVERAGE BASIC SHARES	55,678	57,475	52,759
BASIC EARNINGS PER SHARE	$ 1.24	$ 1.93	$ 0.83
WEIGHTED AVERAGE DILUTED SHARES	56,342	58,835	54,257
DILUTED EARNINGS PER SHARE	$ 1.22	$ 1.89	$ 0.81

Weighted average diluted shares include the following: options to purchase approximately 664,000, 877,000, and 962,000 shares issued pursuant to the Company's stock option plans (see Note 14) for the years ended December 31, 1998, 1997 and 1996, respectively; employee grant shares of approximately 29,000 and 22,000 for the years ended December 31, 1997 and 1996, respectively (see Note 11); and DKP shares of approximately 454,000 and 514,000 for the years ended December 31, 1997 and 1996, respectively (see Note 11).

NOTE 14. STOCK OPTION PLANS

The Company has adopted nonqualified stock option plans and incentive stock plans which provide for the granting of stock options pursuant to the applicable provisions of the Internal Revenue Code and regulations. The aggregate options available under the plans are 6.5 million shares. The Company had granted options of approximately 5.6 million shares through December 31, 1998.

The plans are administered by the Compensation and Stock Option Committee of the Board of Directors. Salaried officers and other key employees of the Company and its subsidiaries are eligible to receive options. The exercise price in each instance is 100% of the fair market value of the Company's common stock on the date of grant. The options have ten-year terms and are exercisable in four and five annual installments.

On March 26, 1996, the Compensation and Stock Option Committee of the Board of Directors determined to adjust the vesting provision of the Company's Non-Qualified Stock Option Plan and Incentive Stock Option Plan to provide for the vesting of future stock option grants under the plans at 20% on each of the first four anniversary dates of the grant, with full vesting on the fifth anniversary date of the grant. The Compensation and Stock Option Committee also determined that pro-rata vesting at times other than successive anniversary dates of the date of the grant are no longer applicable. Stock option holders with grants dated prior to March 26, 1996 were given the opportunity to accept or decline the new vesting provisions with regard to their existing grants.

On June 22, 1998, the Compensation and Stock Option Committee of the Board of Directors approved an offer to employees to reprice their out-of-the-money options (covering an aggregate of 1,820,950 shares). The original options had exercise prices ranging from $33.1875 to $44.125, and the new options have an exercise price of $26.625. For holders who accepted the new price, certain conditions were adopted including (1) commencement of a new holding period for vesting of options (whether or not the initial options had vested) and (2) a one-year extension of employee employment contracts, at the Company's option, where applicable. The repricing offer was not made to the Company's outside directors. Such repricing did not affect options held by the Chairman or the President of the Company.

Had the Company accounted for these plans under Statement of Financial Accounting Standards No. 123, "Accounting for Stock-Based Compensation" ("SFAS 123"), the Company's net income and earnings per share would have been reduced to the following pro forma amounts:

42

(IN THOUSANDS)	1998	1997	1996
Net income:			
AS REPORTED	$ 68,948	$ 111,018	$ 43,706
PRO FORMA	$ 66,047	$ 110,235	$ 34,981
Basic earnings per share:			
AS REPORTED	$ 1.24	$ 1.93	$ 0.83
PRO FORMA	$ 1.19	$ 1.92	$ 0.66
Diluted earnings per share:			
AS REPORTED	$ 1.22	$ 1.89	$ 0.81
PRO FORMA	$ 1.17	$ 1.87	$ 0.64

A summary of the status of the Company's fixed stock option plan for each of the years in the period ended December 31, 1998, 1997 and 1996 is presented below (there are no options outstanding under the Incentive Stock Option Plan):

	1998		1997		1996	
	SHARES (000'S)	WEIGHTED AVERAGE EXERCISE PRICE	SHARES (000'S)	WEIGHTED AVERAGE EXERCISE PRICE	SHARES (000'S)	WEIGHTED AVERAGE EXERCISE PRICE
OUTSTANDING AT BEGINNING OF THE YEAR	3,642	$28.82	3,213	$27.26	3,102	$22.67
GRANTED	3,167	$29.21	727	$36.26	765	$35.12
EXERCISED	(49)	$27.11	(72)	$15.09	(414)	$11.92
FORFEITED	(2,059)	$36.41	(226)	$35.19	(240)	$26.35
EXPIRED	-	$ -	-	$ -	-	$ -
OUTSTANDING AT END OF THE YEAR	4,701	$25.78	3,642	$28.82	3,213	$27.26
EXERCISABLE AT END OF THE YEAR	1,359	$23.89	783	$24.24	220	$14.38
WEIGHTED AVERAGE FAIR VALUE OF OPTIONS GRANTED		$13.61		$16.98		$22.89

The following table summarizes information about fixed stock options outstanding at December 31, 1998:

	OPTIONS OUTSTANDING			OPTIONS EXERCISABLE	
RANGE OF EXERCISE PRICES	NUMBER OUTSTANDING AT 12/31/1998	WEIGHTED AVERAGE REMAINING CONTRACTUAL LIFE (YEARS)	WEIGHTED AVERAGE EXERCISE PRICE	NUMBER EXERCISABLE AT 12/31/1998	WEIGHTED AVERAGE EXERCISE PRICE
$10.25 - $20.00	241,700	2.5	$ 12.82	233,700	$ 12.61
$20.01 - $25.00	626,350	8.0	$ 24.41	144,900	$ 24.40
$25.01 - $30.00	3,639,800	8.2	$ 26.39	945,100	$ 26.09
$30.01 - $35.00	109,100	8.6	$ 32.99	4,000	$ 34.25
$35.01 - $40.00	56,425	7.9	$ 35.49	14,825	$ 35.63
$40.01 - $45.00	27,400	6.1	$ 40.84	16,200	$ 40.95
	4,700,775	7.9	$ 25.78	1,358,725	$ 23.89

43

National Insurance Crime Bureau
Agency: Froeter Design Co.
Art Director: Chris Froeter
Designer: Heather Crosby
Photographer: Francois Robert
Copywriter: National Insurance Crime Bureau

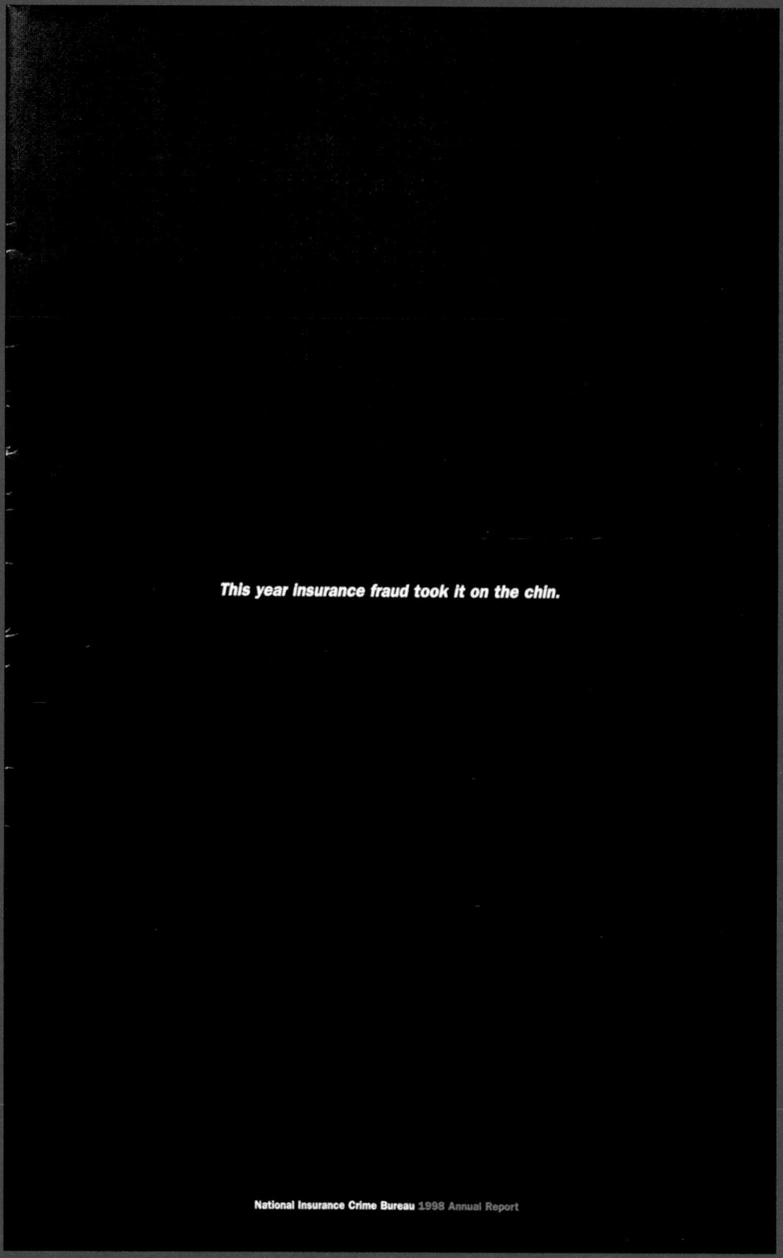
This year insurance fraud took it on the chin.

National Insurance Crime Bureau 1998 Annual Report

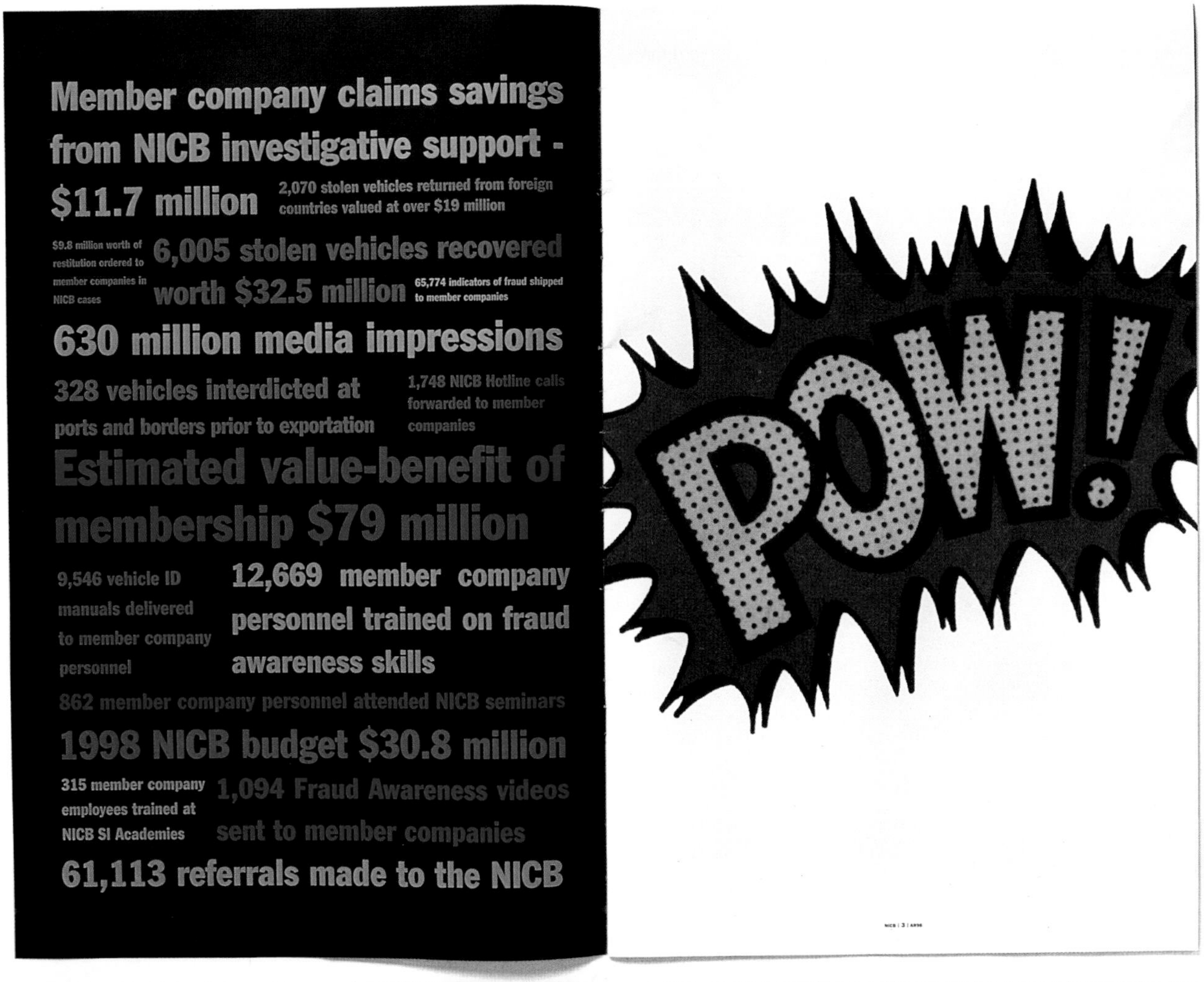
Member company claims savings from NICB investigative support - $11.7 million
2,070 stolen vehicles returned from foreign countries valued at over $19 million
$9.8 million worth of restitution ordered to member companies in NICB cases
6,005 stolen vehicles recovered worth $32.5 million
65,774 indicators of fraud shipped to member companies
630 million media impressions
328 vehicles interdicted at ports and borders prior to exportation
1,748 NICB Hotline calls forwarded to member companies
Estimated value-benefit of membership $79 million
9,546 vehicle ID manuals delivered to member company personnel
12,669 member company personnel trained on fraud awareness skills
862 member company personnel attended NICB seminars
1998 NICB budget $30.8 million
315 member company employees trained at NICB SI Academies
1,094 Fraud Awareness videos sent to member companies
61,113 referrals made to the NICB
POW!
NICB | 3 | AR98

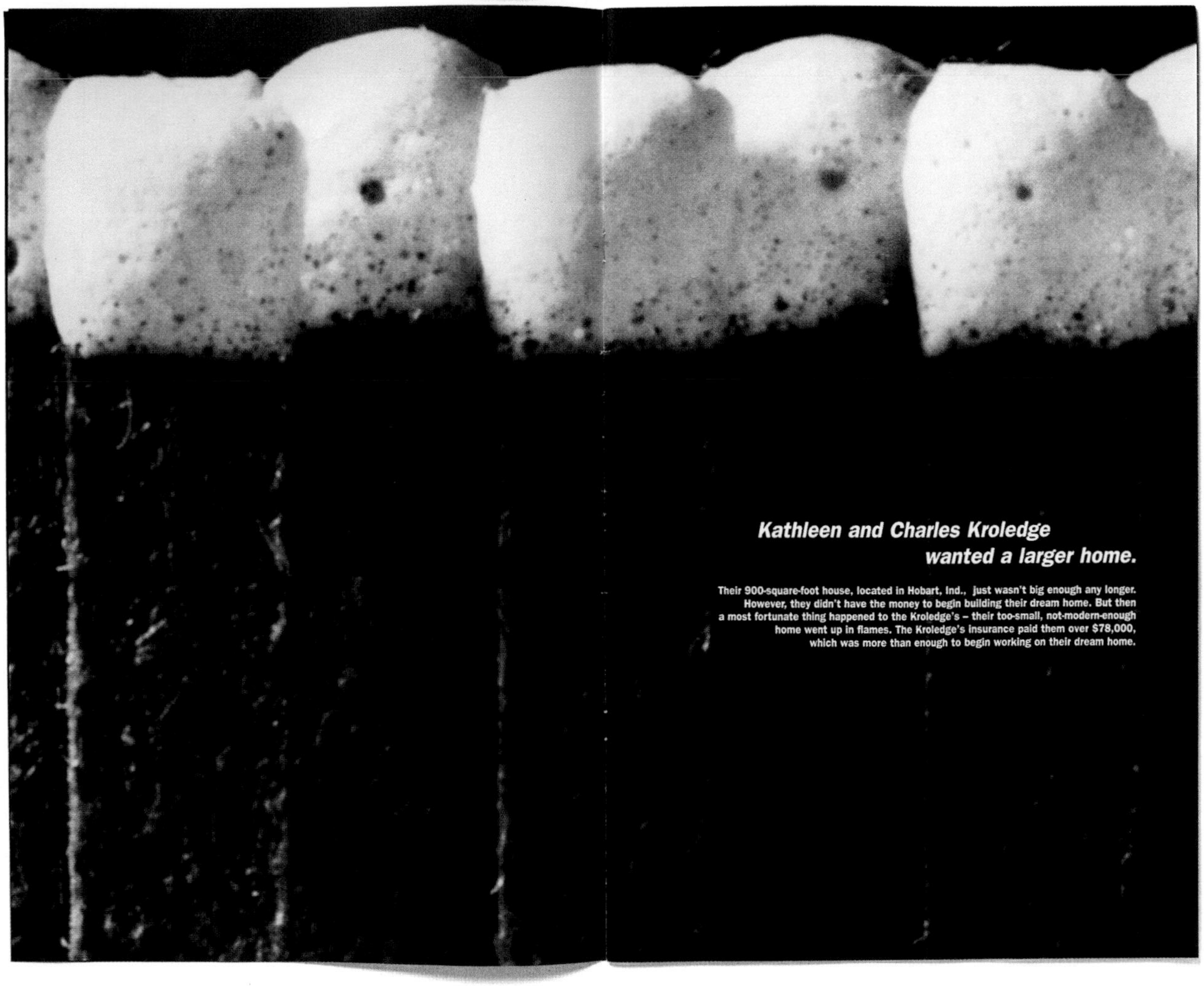
Kathleen and Charles Kroledge wanted a larger home.
Their 900-square-foot house, located in Hobart, Ind., just wasn't big enough any longer. However, they didn't have the money to begin building their dream home. But then a most fortunate thing happened to the Kroledge's – their too-small, not-modern-enough home went up in flames. The Kroledge's insurance paid them over $78,000, which was more than enough to begin working on their dream home.

We couldn't stop the fire,
but we did douse the fraudulent claims.
Investigative Services
Training
AGHH!
NICB | 7 | AR98

Jane and Michael Brown appeared to be just
like any other middle-class family from Queens–
which included a mountain of bills: a mortgage, car payments and credit card debts, to name a few. They also wanted to provide their son with all the necessities in life including a good education at an expensive school. So they worked even harder. And the harder they worked, the more money they made. Only working harder for this typical middle-class family didn't mean staying late at the office or working on Saturdays....

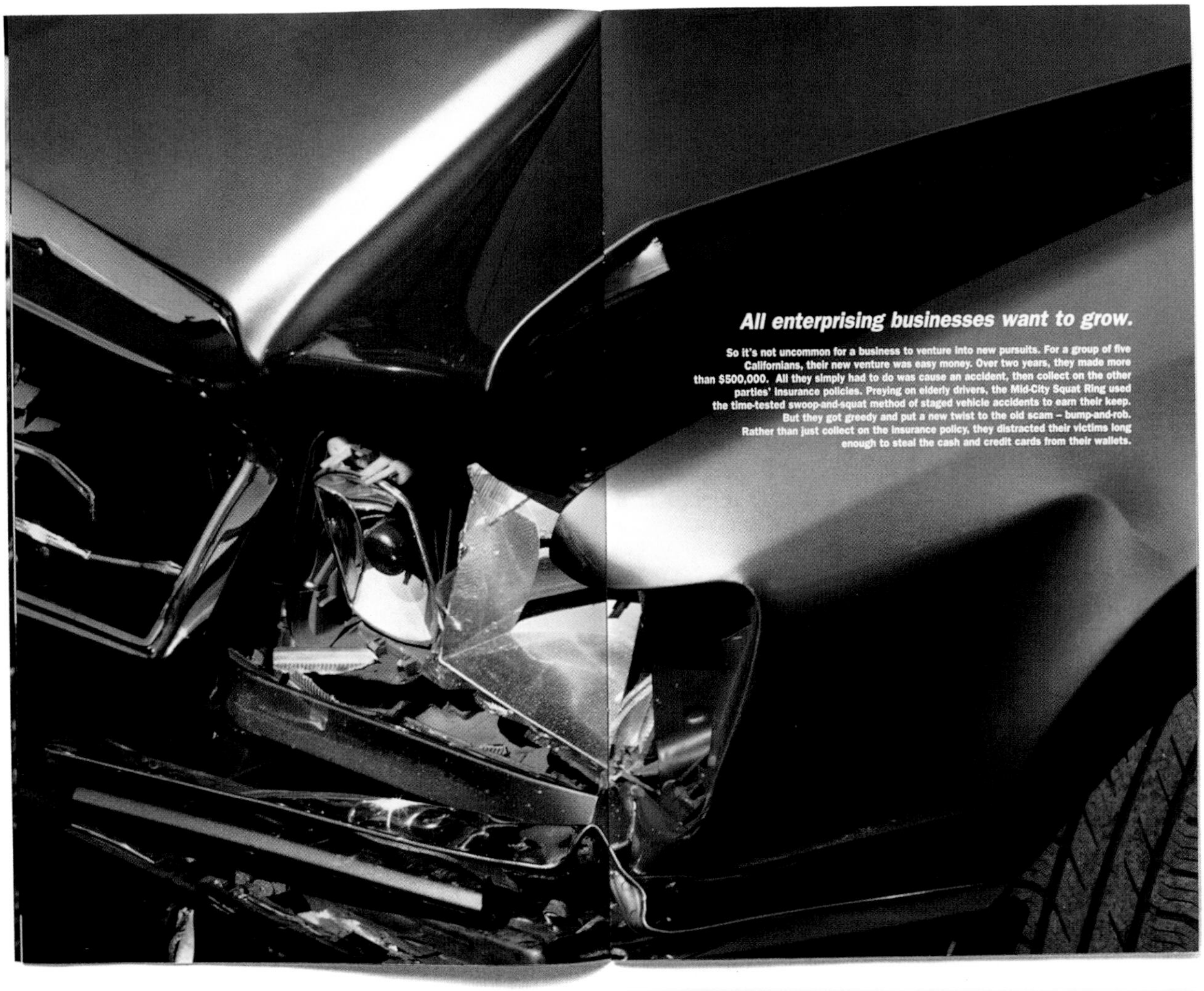
All enterprising businesses want to grow.
So it's not uncommon for a business to venture into new pursuits. For a group of five Californians, their new venture was easy money. Over two years, they made more than $500,000. All they simply had to do was cause an accident, then collect on the other parties' insurance policies. Preying on elderly drivers, the Mid-City Squat Ring used the time-tested swoop-and-squat method of staged vehicle accidents to earn their keep. But they got greedy and put a new twist to the old scam – bump-and-rob. Rather than just collect on the insurance policy, they distracted their victims long enough to steal the cash and credit cards from their wallets.

FINANCIAL STATEMENTS

Statements of Financial Position

For the year ended June 30, 1998 and the six months ended June 30, 1997

	1998	1997
Assets		
Current assets	$ 1,905,777	$ 1,128,968
Investments	15,475,545	12,335,517
Property and equipment (net)	3,884,470	6,312,028
Prepaid pension cost	2,107,288	1,045,106
Due from NICB-FACTA, Inc. (net)	733,997	809,923
Other assets	37,559	19,108
TOTAL ASSETS	$24,144,636	$21,650,650
Liabilities and Net Assets		
Current liabilities (including assessment reduction)	$ 5,054,228	$ 4,569,600
Note payable (net of current portion)	–	290,278
Capital lease obligations (net current portion)	168,740	1,902,183
Accrued pension cost	355,639	826,636
Accrued supplemental pension	50,869	476,939
Accrued postretirement benefits	3,589,000	2,449,000
TOTAL LIABILITIES	$ 9,218,476	$10,514,636
Unrestricted Net Assets	14,926,160	11,136,014
TOTAL LIABILITIES AND UNRESTRICTED NET ASSETS	$24,144,636	$21,650,650

Statements of Activities

	1998	1997
Revenues		
Assessments	$32,476,212	$17,022,343
Investment income	888,001	357,398
Net realized and unrealized gain on investment	678,788	304,235
Gain (loss) on the sale of fixed assets	(29,633)	1,326
TOTAL REVENUES	$34,013,368	$17,685,302
Expenses		
Salaries	$15,060,970	$ 7,976,255
Other employee benefits	2,262,730	1,192,327
Automobile operations	1,814,863	980,780
Postretirement benefits	1,431,215	689,005
Depreciation and amortization	1,380,719	961,604
Telecommunications	1,315,225	706,861
Payroll taxes	1,218,168	688,851
Travel and group meetings	1,117,631	549,004
Office expense	755,514	354,339
Bad debt expense	748,387	68
Technical fees and services	679,093	122,570
Other	3,037,916	2,006,480
TOTAL EXPENSES	$30,822,431	$16,228,144
Other Changes		
Gain on sale of database	$ 3,800,000	$ –
Refund of sale proceeds to member companies	(3,200,791)	–
Change in Unrestricted Net Assets	3,790,146	1,457,158
Unrestricted net assets, beginning of period	11,136,014	9,678,856
Unrestricted net assets, end of period	$14,926,160	$11,136,014

These financial statements have been prepared by management in conformity with generally accepted accounting principles and include all adjustments which, in the opinion of management, are necessary to reflect a fair presentation. This presentation represents a summarization from audited financial statements. Certain reclassification of prior year amounts have been made to conform with the current year presentation.

NOTES TO FINANCIAL STATEMENTS

Change in Year End
NICB changed its year end from December 31 to June 30, effective for the six-month period ended June 30, 1997. This change was made to coincide with member company premium information and the annual budget review.

Related Party Transactions
NICB-FACTA, Inc. ("FACTA") was incorporated on July 13, 1995 as a charitable and educational organization under section 501(c)(3) of the Internal Revenue Code ("IRC"). FACTA was formed to facilitate the development of the National Motor Vehicle Title Information System and the National Stolen Passenger Motor Vehicle System. During the year ended June 30, 1998 and the six months ended June 30, 1997, the NICB incurred expenses of $658,071 and $252,762 to set-up and commence FACTA operations. The reimbursement of these costs has been reflected as a receivable; however, the recoverability of the receivable is uncertain. FACTA is not producing revenues and future activities and revenues are currently unknown. Due to the uncertain future of FACTA, NICB has created an allowance of $733,997 as of June 30, 1998 against the receivable balance of $1,467,994.

Under guidance from Statement of Position 94-3, "Reporting of Related Entities by Not-For-Profit Organizations," FACTA has not been consolidated with the NICB because the required characteristics have not been met.

Insurance Services Office, Inc. Transaction
Insurance Services Office, Inc. purchased most of the assets and liabilities associated with NICB's claims database on February 20, 1998 for net cash proceeds of $3,860,481. NICB's Board of Governors resolved to return these proceeds, net of $659,690 of related expenses, to NICB member companies in May 1998.

Member Assessment Reduction
As a result of the sale of the database, the budget for member assessments was reduced. The portion of the reduction that was associated with the current fiscal year is $2,071,648. This amount has been reflected as a liability for the year ended June 30, 1998, and was deducted from subsequent member assessment billings (July and October, 1998).

Tax Status
NICB has received a favorable determination letter from the Internal Revenue Service, dated September 9, 1991 stating that it qualifies as a not-for-profit corporation as described in Section 501(c)(4) of the IRC and, as such, is exempt from federal income taxes on related income pursuant to section 501(a) of the IRC. NICB continues to qualify as a not-for-profit corporation under section 501(c)(4).

1998 BOARD OF GOVERNORS

Frank R. Haines
Chairman
Claims Vice President
State Farm Mutual Automobile Insurance Company

Christopher Cawley
Vice Chairman
Vice President, Claims
MetLife Auto & Home

William J. Breslin
Immediate Past Chairman
Senior Vice President, Claims/Service
GEFA/Colonial Penn Group

Terrance W. Gainer
Executive Assistant Chief
Metropolitan Police Department
Washington D.C.

James Gilmartin
Vice President, Insurance Claims
Automobile Club of Southern California

Dean K. Harring
Senior Vice President,
Chief Claim Officer
Zurich U.S./Zurich Small Business

H. Peter Hudson
Chairman
Monroe Guaranty Insurance Company

David J. LaBrec, Esq.
Strasburger & Price, L.L.P.

Robert M. Lindemann
Senior Vice President
Lumbermens Mutual Casualty Co.

Stanton F. Long
Vice Chairman
Travelers Property Casualty Corp.

Jeffrey A. Ludrof
Senior Vice President, Claims Division
Erie Insurance Group

Kathleen J. Robinson
Vice President, Claims and Operations
Chrysler Insurance Company

John E. "Eddie" Ryan
Senior Vice President,
Property and Casualty Claims
USAA

Rubin Snowden
Vice President
Farmers Group, Inc.

Eldon A. Zeigler
Vice President, Compliance/Claims
Legal/Enterprise SIU
Nationwide Insurance Enterprise

ADVISORS TO THE BOARD

John J. McHale
President, IASIU
Director - Claims Investigations
Farmers Insurance Group of Companies

Lynne Hunt
Section Chief, Financial Crimes Section
Federal Bureau of Investigations

Delta Lloyd Verzekeringsgroep nv
Agency: UNA (Amsterdam) designers
Designers: Will De L'ecluse, Hans Bockting, Sabine Reinhardt
Photographer: Reiner Gerritsen

Camilla Andersen
*5. 3. 1980, Hillerød, Danmark

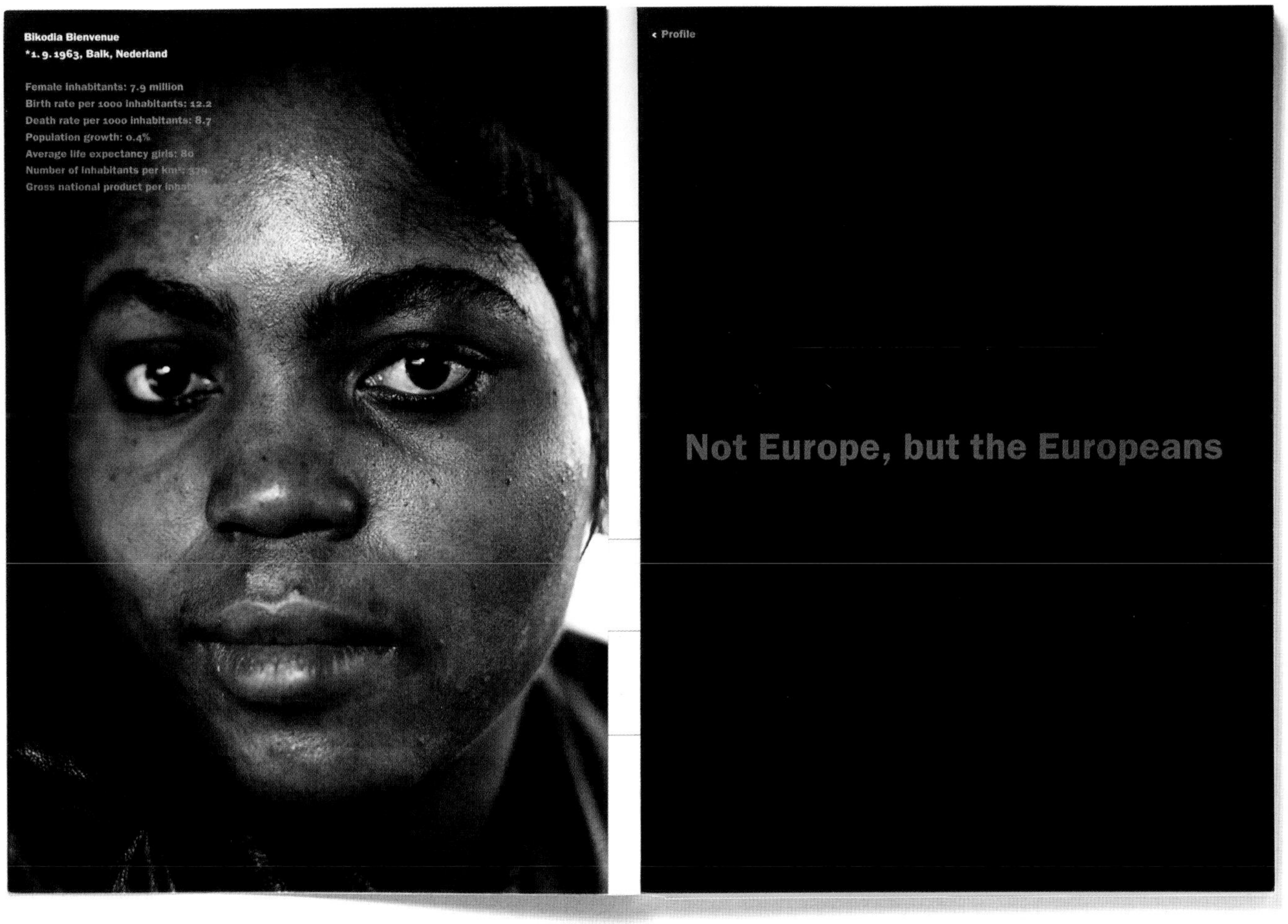
Bikodia Bienvenue
*1. 9. 1963, Balk, Nederland
Female inhabitants: 7.9 million
Birth rate per 1000 inhabitants: 12.2
Death rate per 1000 inhabitants: 8.7
Population growth: 0.4%
Average life expectancy girls: 80
Number of inhabitants per km
Gross national product per inh
‹ Profile
Not Europe, but the Europeans

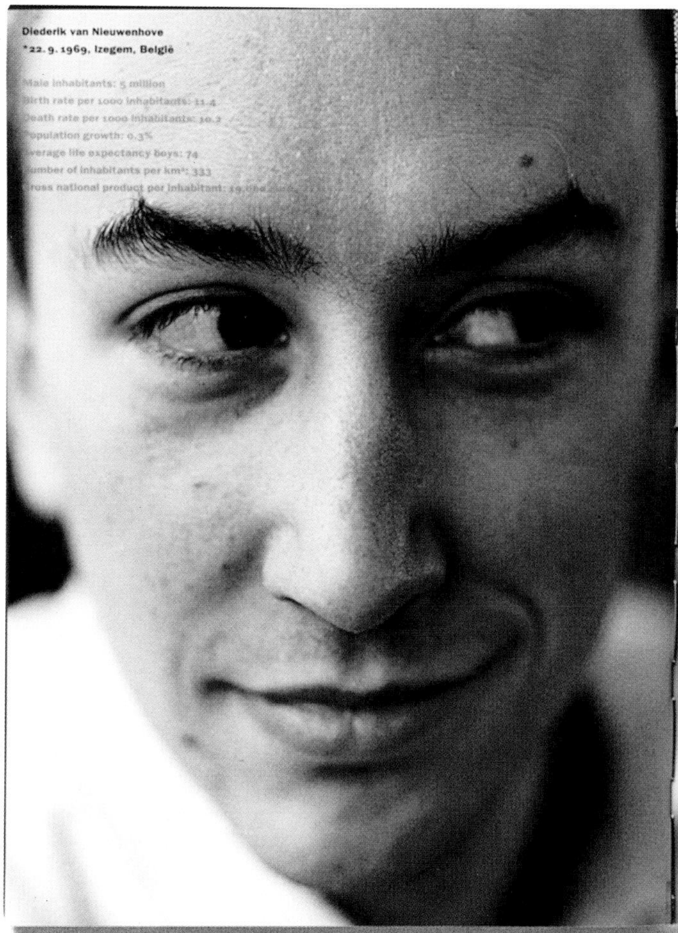
Diederik van Nieuwenhove
*22. 9. 1969, Izegem, België

Sabine Reinhardt
*1. 3. 1969, Bielefeld, Deutschland

Financial results 1998 was a good financial year for Delta Lloyd. Net profits were in line with outlook, they increased by more than 9% to NLG 503 million. The overall gross premium income rose sharply, from NLG 3,431 million to NLG 4,923 million (+44%). Revenue increased by 40% to NLG 8,126 million. This considerable increase was due partly to the take-over of German Berlinische Leben in the summer of 1998. Total operating expenses increased by 40%, due partly to the take-over of Berlinische Leben and extra capital expenditure in IT. Staff number rose to 3,452, caused by various take-overs. Shareholders' funds fell from NLG 4,395 million to NLG 4,087 million. An amount of about NLG 700 million was written off for goodwill in connection with the acquisition of, inter alia, Berlinische Leben and Smeets Securities. This was a restraint on the growth of shareholders' funds.

Delta Lloyd Verzekeringsgroep nv In NLG million	1998	1997
Revenue	8,126.1	5,810.3
– Gross premium incom	4,923.4	3,430.7
– Return on investment	3,140.4	2,351.6
– Other activities	62.3	28.0
Result (before tax)	636.7	623.7
Shareholders' funds	4,086.8	4,394.7
Staff numbers	3,452	2,319

Delta Lloyd Verzekerings-groep nv

J.E. Jansen N.W. Hoek C.H. Tesselhoff S.M. Slottke (Substitute member)

Insurance 158, 159

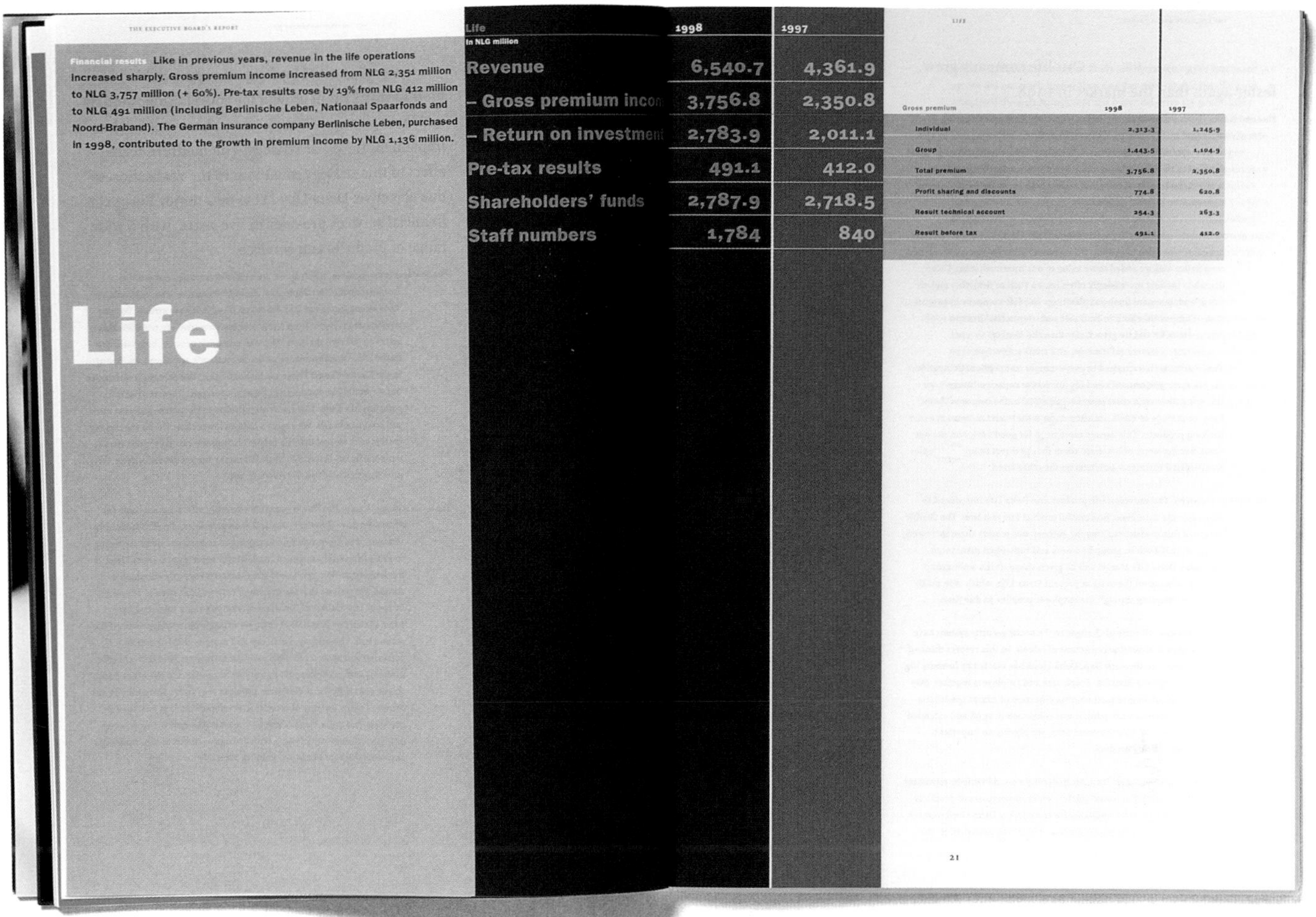
THE EXECUTIVE BOARD'S REPORT
Financial results Like in previous years, revenue in the life operations increased sharply. Gross premium income increased from NLG 2,351 million to NLG 3,757 million (+ 60%). Pre-tax results rose by 19% from NLG 412 million to NLG 491 million (including Berlinische Leben, Nationaal Spaarfonds and Noord-Braband). The German insurance company Berlinische Leben, purchased in 1998, contributed to the growth in premium income by NLG 1,136 million.
Life
Life
In NLG million
1998
1997
Revenue 6,540.7 4,361.9
– Gross premium incon 3,756.8 2,350.8
– Return on investmen 2,783.9 2,011.1
Pre-tax results 491.1 412.0
Shareholders' funds 2,787.9 2,718.5
Staff numbers 1,784 840
LIFE
Gross premium 1998 1997
Individual 2,313.3 1,245.9
Group 1,443.5 1,104.9
Total premium 3,756.8 2,350.8
Profit sharing and discounts 774.8 620.8
Result technical account 254.3 263.3
Result before tax 491.1 412.0
21

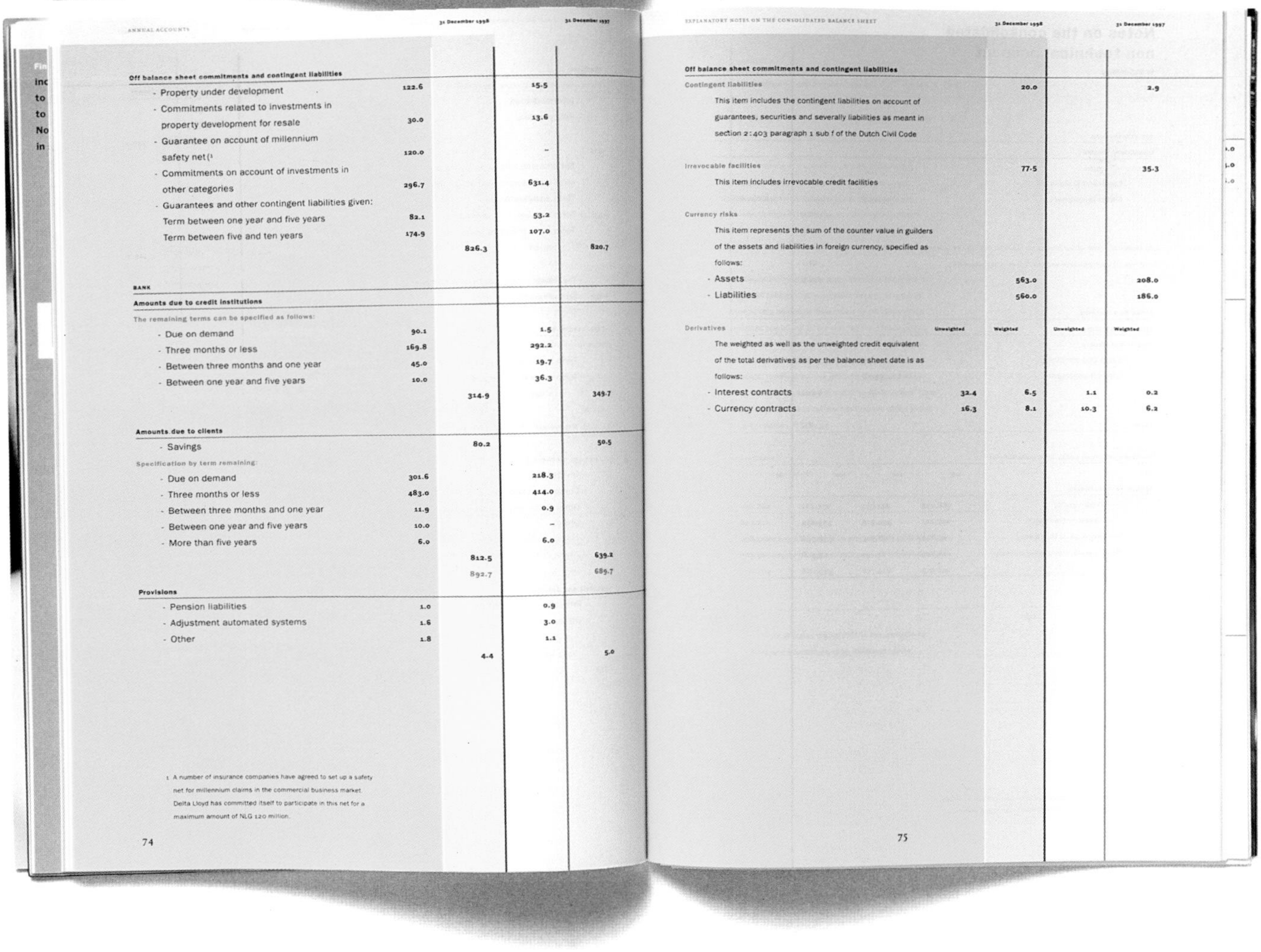
ANNUAL ACCOUNTS
31 December 1998
31 December 1997
Off balance sheet commitments and contingent liabilities
Property under development 122.6 15.5
Commitments related to investments in property development for resale 30.0 13.6
Guarantee on account of millennium safety net 120.0 –
Commitments on account of investments in other categories 296.7 631.4
Guarantees and other contingent liabilities given:
Term between one year and five years 82.1 53.2
Term between five and ten years 174.9 107.0
826.3 820.7
BANK
Amounts due to credit institutions
The remaining terms can be specified as follows:
Due on demand 90.1 1.5
Three months or less 169.8 292.2
Between three months and one year 45.0 19.7
Between one year and five years 10.0 36.3
314.9 349.7
Amounts due to clients
Savings 80.2 50.5
Specification by term remaining:
Due on demand 301.6 218.3
Three months or less 483.0 414.0
Between three months and one year 11.9 0.9
Between one year and five years 10.0 –
More than five years 6.0 6.0
812.5 639.1
892.7 689.7
Provisions
Pension liabilities 1.0 0.9
Adjustment automated systems 1.6 3.0
Other 1.8 1.1
4.4 5.0
1 A number of insurance companies have agreed to set up a safety net for millennium claims in the commercial business market. Delta Lloyd has committed itself to participate in this net for a maximum amount of NLG 120 million.
74
EXPLANATORY NOTES ON THE CONSOLIDATED BALANCE SHEET
31 December 1998
31 December 1997
Off balance sheet commitments and contingent liabilities
Contingent liabilities 20.0 2.9
This item includes the contingent liabilities on account of guarantees, securities and severally liabilities as meant in section 2:403 paragraph 1 sub f of the Dutch Civil Code
Irrevocable facilities 77.5 35.3
This item includes irrevocable credit facilities
Currency risks
This item represents the sum of the counter value in guilders of the assets and liabilities in foreign currency, specified as follows:
Assets 563.0 208.0
Liabilities 560.0 186.0
Derivatives Unweighted Weighted Unweighted Weighted
The weighted as well as the unweighted credit equivalent of the total derivatives as per the balance sheet date is as follows:
Interest contracts 32.4 6.5 1.1 0.2
Currency contracts 16.3 8.1 10.3 6.2
75

Allianz Lebensversicherungs AG
Agency: Claus Koch Corporate Communications
Art Directors: Petra Mehl, Patrick Koch
Creative Director: Claus Koch
Photographers: Oliver Helbig, Nina Pohl
Copywriter: Allianz Lebensversicherungs AG

Allianz 1997

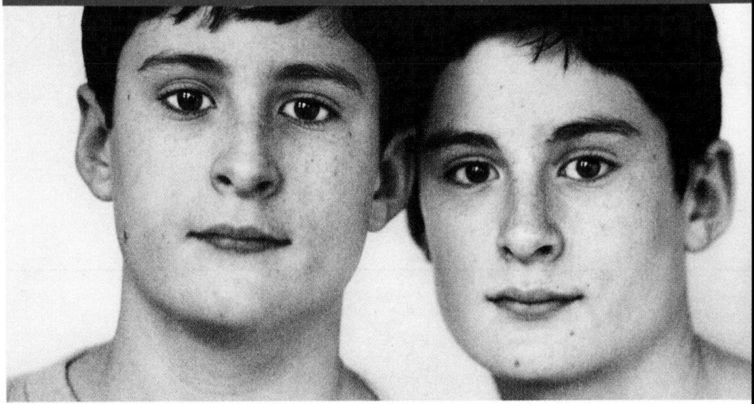

Allianz Lebensversicherungs-Aktiengesellschaft Geschäftsbericht 1997

Geschäftsentwicklung

Das Geschäftsjahr 1997 war für Allianz Leben erfolgreich. Obwohl von der gesamtwirtschaftlichen Entwicklung keine Wachstumsimpulse für die Lebensversicherungswirtschaft ausgingen, konnten die Beitragseinnahmen um 4,7 Prozent auf 12,5 Milliarden DM gesteigert werden. Die Neubeiträge sind mit 8,2 Prozent kräftiger gewachsen als im Branchendurchschnitt. Dadurch hat sich der Marktanteil der Allianz Leben im Neugeschäft erhöht.

Finanzierung

Das umlagefinanzierte System der gesetzlichen Altersvorsorge steht vor einer großen Herausforderung. Ohne umfassende Reformen wird die Finanzierung zu einer erdrückenden Last für zukünftige Generationen. Den kapitalgedeckten Formen der betrieblichen und privaten Altersvorsorge muß eine größere Bedeutung zukommen.

Privatrente

Wir leben immer länger. Und wir leben immer häufiger alleine. Kein Wunder also, daß die Absicherung der Angehörigen im Todesfall in der Lebensplanung vieler Menschen in Deutschland an Bedeutung verliert, die finanzielle Absicherung des Alters dagegen immer wichtiger wird. Das Allianz Privatrenten-Programm bietet dafür einen umfassenden Risikoschutz und bedarfsgerechte Lösungen, sei es für den 30jährigen Single, den 50jährigen Familienvater oder die 65jährige Rentnerin.

Allianz

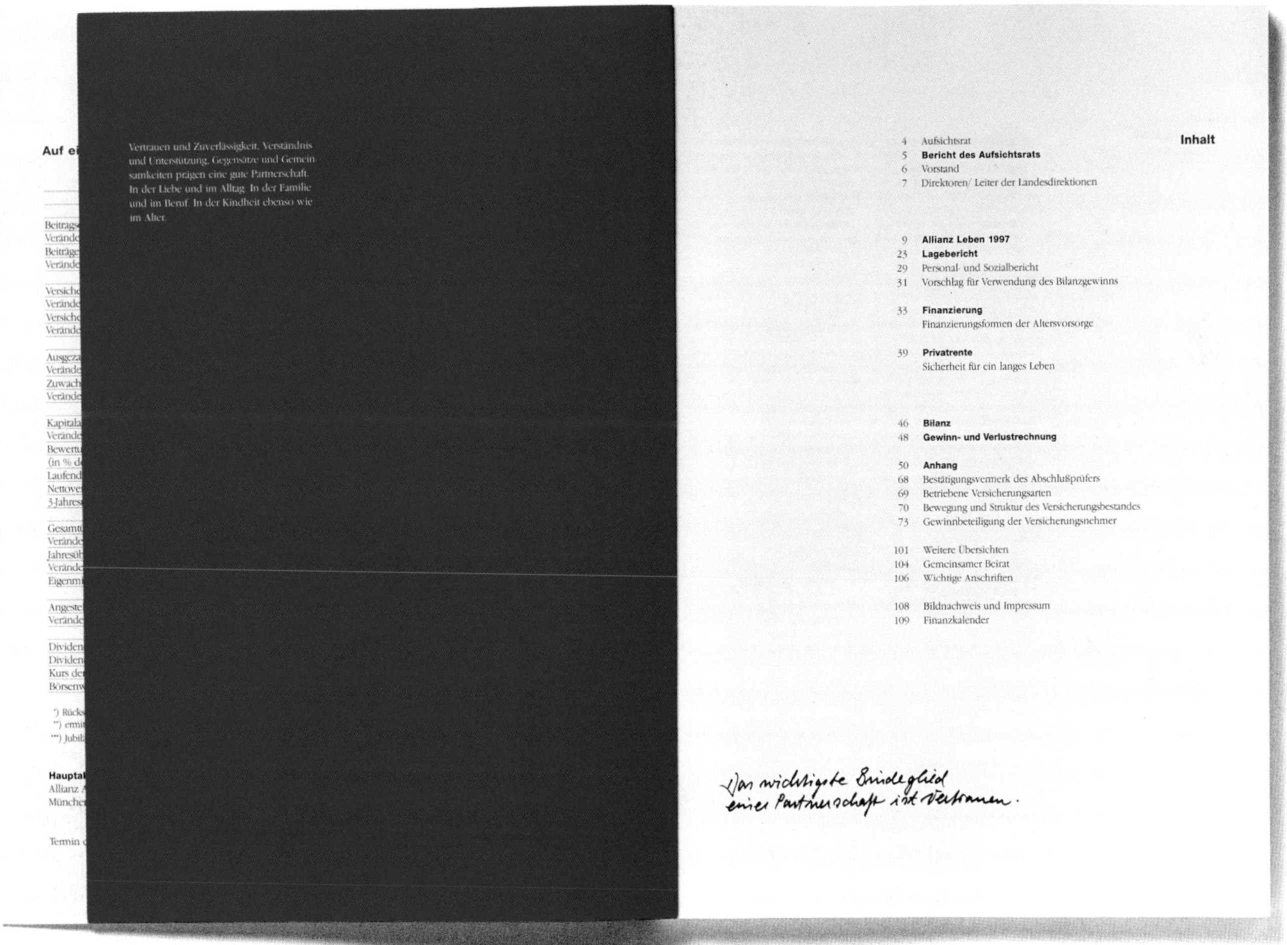
Vertrauen und Zuverlässigkeit. Verständnis und Unterstützung. Gegensätze und Gemeinsamkeiten prägen eine gute Partnerschaft. In der Liebe und im Alltag. In der Familie und im Beruf. In der Kindheit ebenso wie im Alter.
Inhalt
4 Aufsichtsrat
5 Bericht des Aufsichtsrats
6 Vorstand
7 Direktoren/ Leiter der Landesdirektionen
9 Allianz Leben 1997
23 Lagebericht
29 Personal- und Sozialbericht
31 Vorschlag für Verwendung des Bilanzgewinns
33 Finanzierung
Finanzierungsformen der Altersvorsorge
39 Privatrente
Sicherheit für ein langes Leben
46 Bilanz
48 Gewinn- und Verlustrechnung
50 Anhang
68 Bestätigungsvermerk des Abschlußprüfers
69 Betriebene Versicherungsarten
70 Bewegung und Struktur des Versicherungsbestandes
73 Gewinnbeteiligung der Versicherungsnehmer
101 Weitere Übersichten
104 Gemeinsamer Beirat
106 Wichtige Anschriften
108 Bildnachweis und Impressum
109 Finanzkalender
Das wichtigste Bindeglied einer Partnerschaft ist Vertrauen.

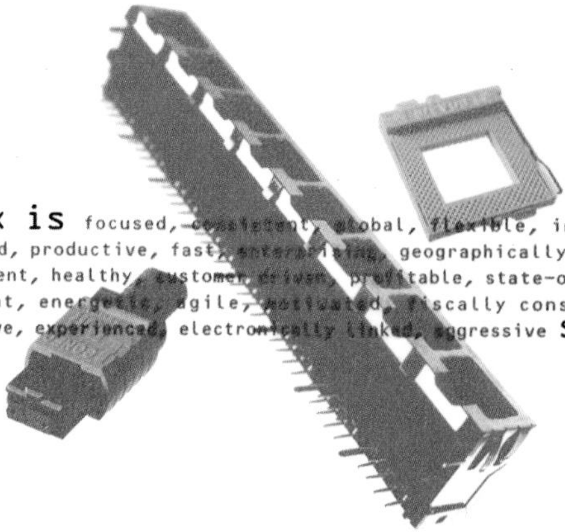

Molex is focused, consistent, global, flexible, innovative, committed, productive, fast, enterprising, geographically balanced, independent, healthy, customer driven, profitable, state-of-the-art, efficient, energetic, agile, motivated, fiscally conservative, responsive, experienced, electronically linked, aggressive **strong**

molex

Molex Incorporated 1999 Annual Report

Financial Highlights

(in thousands, except per share data)

	1999	1998	Change
Operations			
Net revenue	$ 1,711,649	$ 1,622,975	5%
Income before income taxes and minority interest	230,214	274,823	(16)%
Net income	178,029	182,243	(2)%
Net income as a percent of net revenue	10.4%	11.2%	—
Return on beginning shareholders' equity	14.1%	14.7%	—
Per Share			
Net income:			
Basic	$ 1.15	$ 1.16	(1)%
Diluted	1.14	1.15	(1)%
Dividends per common share	.06	.06	—
Book value	9.65	8.06	20%
Outstanding shares of stock:			
Basic	155,472	156,600	—
Diluted	156,505	158,377	—
Number of shareholders:			
Common Stock	5,533	6,404	—
Class A Common Stock	6,333	5,921	—
Financial Position			
Total assets	$ 1,902,012	$ 1,639,634	16%
Working capital	538,897	531,516	1%
Long-term debt	20,148	5,566	262%
Backlog	243,366	231,039	5%
Shareholders' equity	1,500,537	1,261,570	19%
Long-term debt as a percent of shareholders' equity	1.3%	0.4%	—
Number of employees at June 30	14,700	12,455	18%
Current ratio	2.6/1	2.6/1	—

Use of Net Revenue

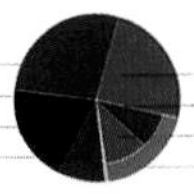
27.6% Materials
21.2% Energy, Rent, Insurance, Interest, etc.
5.1% Taxes: Business, Income and Payroll
0.5% Dividends
Wages, Salaries, Benefits 25.3%
Depreciation and Amortization 9.9%
Net Income 10.4%
Reinvested in Business 20.3%

Molex Sales by Region

39.4% Americas $673.8 Million
21.3% Far East North $364.6 Million
Far East South $341.5 Million 19.9%
Europe $331.7 Million 19.4%

Molex Sales by Industry

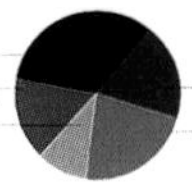
35% Computer/Business Equipment
15% Automotive
10% Other
Consumer Products 19%
Telecommunications 21%

Molex Incorporated is a 61-year-old global manufacturer of electronic, electrical and fiber optic interconnection products and systems; switches; value-added assemblies; and application tooling. The company operates 50 plants in 21 countries and employs 14,700 people. In fiscal 1999, products manufactured and sold outside the U.S. generated 66% of sales.

Molex serves original equipment manufacturers in industries that include automotive, computer, computer peripheral, business equipment, telecommunications, consumer products and premise wiring. We offer more than 100,000 products to our customers, primarily through direct salespeople and authorized distributors.

The worldwide market for electronic connectors, cable assemblies and backplanes is estimated at $27.1 billion. With a 6.3% market share, Molex is the second-largest connector manufacturer in the world in what is a fragmented but highly competitive industry.

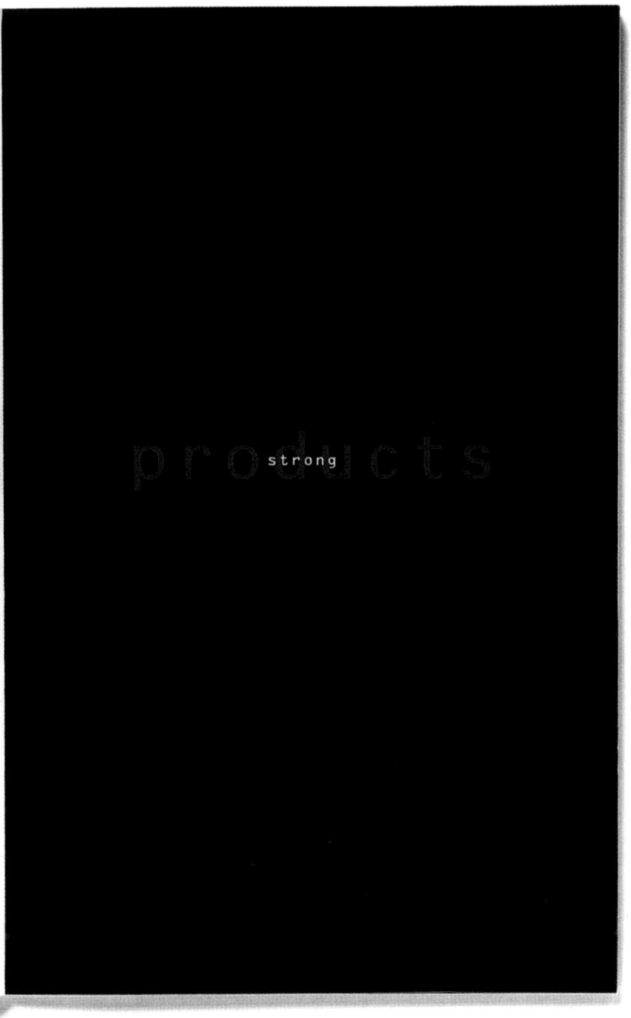
products
strong

Introduced
350
new product families
Breakthrough thinking, coupled with more rapid commercialization, propelled Molex product launches to one of the highest levels in our history.
Molex 1999 2
31%
of 1999 revenue derived from products released in the past 36 months
An unflagging emphasis on new product development keeps our customers supplied with a steady stream of innovative solutions.
Molex 1999 3

Molex ■ 1999

High speed, High performance

Use of specialized contact geometries has spurred numerous Molex innovations in connector design for high speed applications. As the leader in this area, we wrote the standards others follow.

markets strong

#1 in electronic games

In 1999, with more than 30% share, we expanded our position in the game industry as the leading connector supplier to the big three manufacturers.

Molex ■ 1999

2x and counting

From Detroit to Tokyo, we've made steady inroads in the automotive industry. Today, the average new vehicle contains twice as many Molex connectors as three years ago. Driving our increased presence are connectors for sophisticated instrumentation like Global Navigation Systems, safety devices such as ABS brakes and airbags, and specialized connectors for power trains, comfort controls and entertainment systems.

$1.1
billion
for capital
improvements
That's how much we've invested in facilities and equipment in the past five years. In 1999, we expanded factories in the U.S., Germany and France and continued construction in China of what is soon to be Molex's largest plant. All together, we operate 50 manufacturing sites in 21 countrie
Molex 1999 18
strategies
strong

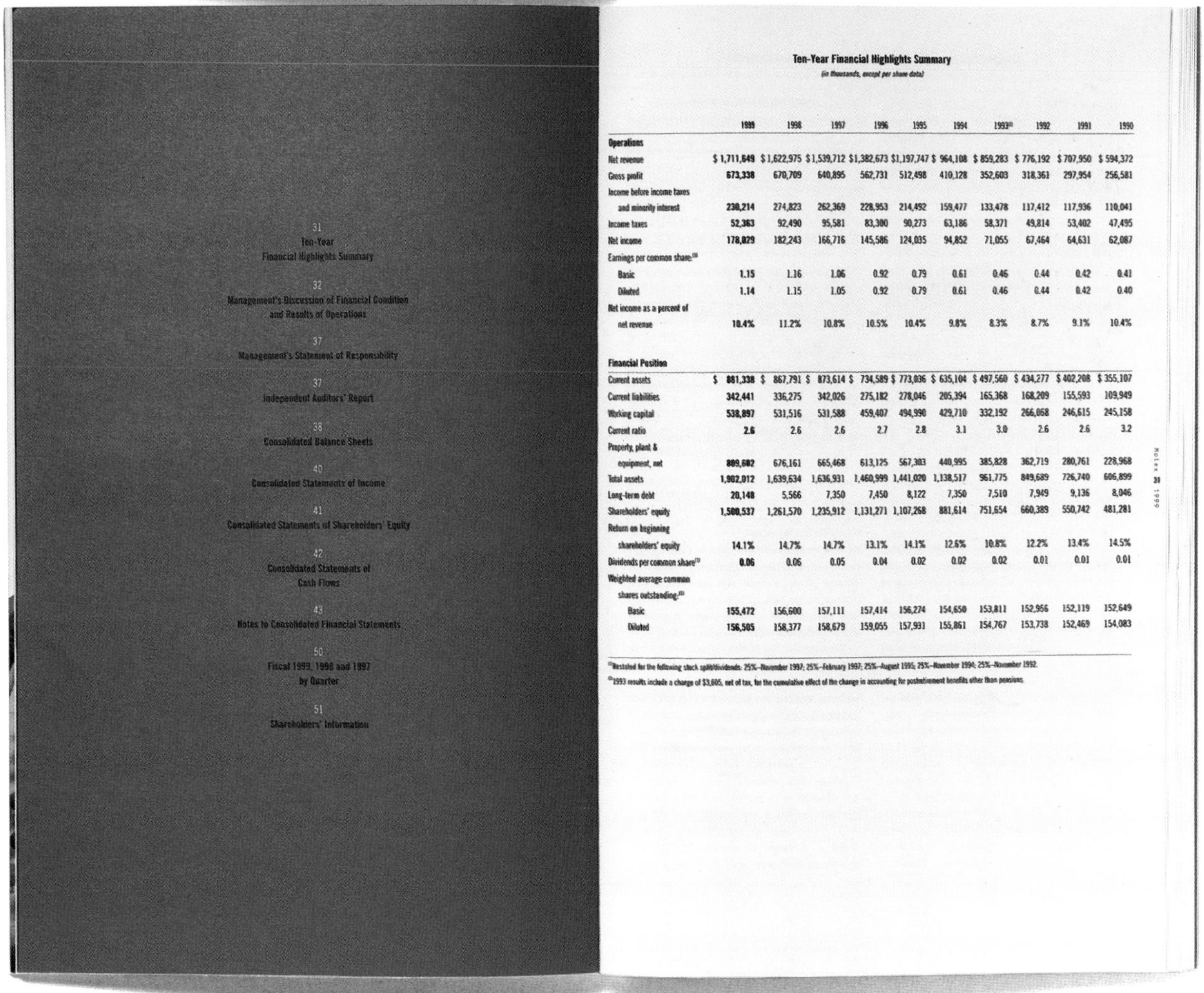

Ten-Year Financial Highlights Summary

(in thousands, except per share data)

	1999	1998	1997	1996	1995	1994	1993[2]	1992	1991	1990
Operations										
Net revenue	**$ 1,711,649**	$ 1,622,975	$ 1,539,712	$ 1,382,673	$ 1,197,747	$ 964,108	$ 859,283	$ 776,192	$ 707,950	$ 594,372
Gross profit	**673,338**	670,709	640,895	562,731	512,498	410,128	352,603	318,361	297,954	256,581
Income before income taxes and minority interest	**230,214**	274,823	262,369	228,953	214,492	159,477	133,478	117,412	117,936	110,041
Income taxes	**52,363**	92,490	95,581	83,300	90,273	63,186	58,371	49,814	53,402	47,495
Net income	**178,029**	182,243	166,716	145,586	124,035	94,852	71,055	67,464	64,631	62,087
Earnings per common share:[1]										
Basic	**1.15**	1.16	1.06	0.92	0.79	0.61	0.46	0.44	0.42	0.41
Diluted	**1.14**	1.15	1.05	0.92	0.79	0.61	0.46	0.44	0.42	0.40
Net income as a percent of net revenue	**10.4%**	11.2%	10.8%	10.5%	10.4%	9.8%	8.3%	8.7%	9.1%	10.4%
Financial Position										
Current assets	**$ 881,338**	$ 867,791	$ 873,614	$ 734,589	$ 773,036	$ 635,104	$ 497,560	$ 434,277	$ 402,208	$ 355,107
Current liabilities	**342,441**	336,275	342,026	275,182	278,046	205,394	165,368	168,209	155,593	109,949
Working capital	**538,897**	531,516	531,588	459,407	494,990	429,710	332,192	266,068	246,615	245,158
Current ratio	**2.6**	2.6	2.6	2.7	2.8	3.1	3.0	2.6	2.6	3.2
Property, plant & equipment, net	**809,602**	676,161	665,468	613,125	567,303	440,995	385,828	362,719	280,761	228,968
Total assets	**1,902,012**	1,639,634	1,636,931	1,460,999	1,441,020	1,138,517	961,775	849,689	726,740	606,899
Long-term debt	**20,148**	5,566	7,350	7,450	8,122	7,350	7,510	7,949	9,136	8,046
Shareholders' equity	**1,500,537**	1,261,570	1,235,912	1,131,271	1,107,268	881,614	751,654	660,389	550,742	481,281
Return on beginning shareholders' equity	**14.1%**	14.7%	14.7%	13.1%	14.1%	12.6%	10.8%	12.2%	13.4%	14.5%
Dividends per common share[1]	**0.06**	0.06	0.05	0.04	0.02	0.02	0.02	0.01	0.01	0.01
Weighted average common shares outstanding:[1]										
Basic	**155,472**	156,600	157,111	157,414	156,274	154,650	153,811	152,956	152,119	152,649
Diluted	**156,505**	158,377	158,679	159,055	157,931	155,861	154,767	153,738	152,469	154,083

[1]Restated for the following stock splits/dividends: 25%–November 1997; 25%–February 1997; 25%–August 1995; 25%–November 1994; 25%–November 1992.

[2]1993 results include a charge of $3,605, net of tax, for the cumulative effect of the change in accounting for postretirement benefits other than pensions.

Robertson-Ceco Corporation

Agency: Oh Boy, A Design Company
Art & Creative Director: David Salanitro
Designer: Ted Bluey
Photographer: Hunter L. Wimmer
Copywriters: Pat McNolte, Ron Stevens, David Salanitro

THIS IS NOT A METAL BUILDING.
Robertson-Ceco Corporation
1998 Annual Report

NEITHER IS THIS.

NOPE.

THIS IS QUALITY.

Only the finest function-matched materials are used to manufacture Robertson-Ceco buildings. High-strength steel for structural members, precoated coiled sheeting for roof and wall panels and specially tempered material for floating roof clips all contribute to the strongest, most durable structures around.

THIS IS PRODUCTION.

Robertson-Ceco's ongoing capital improvement program has helped us create some of the most efficient manufacturing facilities in the industry. Information is electronically downloaded to automated machinery, minimizing errors and misfabrications. Where hand-welding is necessary, it is performed by certified welders. Our Tennessee plant to be completed in the fall of 1999 will represent the latest in technological advances in manufacturing and will be the most efficient in the industry.

ELIZABETHTON, TENNESSEE
FALL 1999
ELIZABETHTON, TENNI
FALL 1999

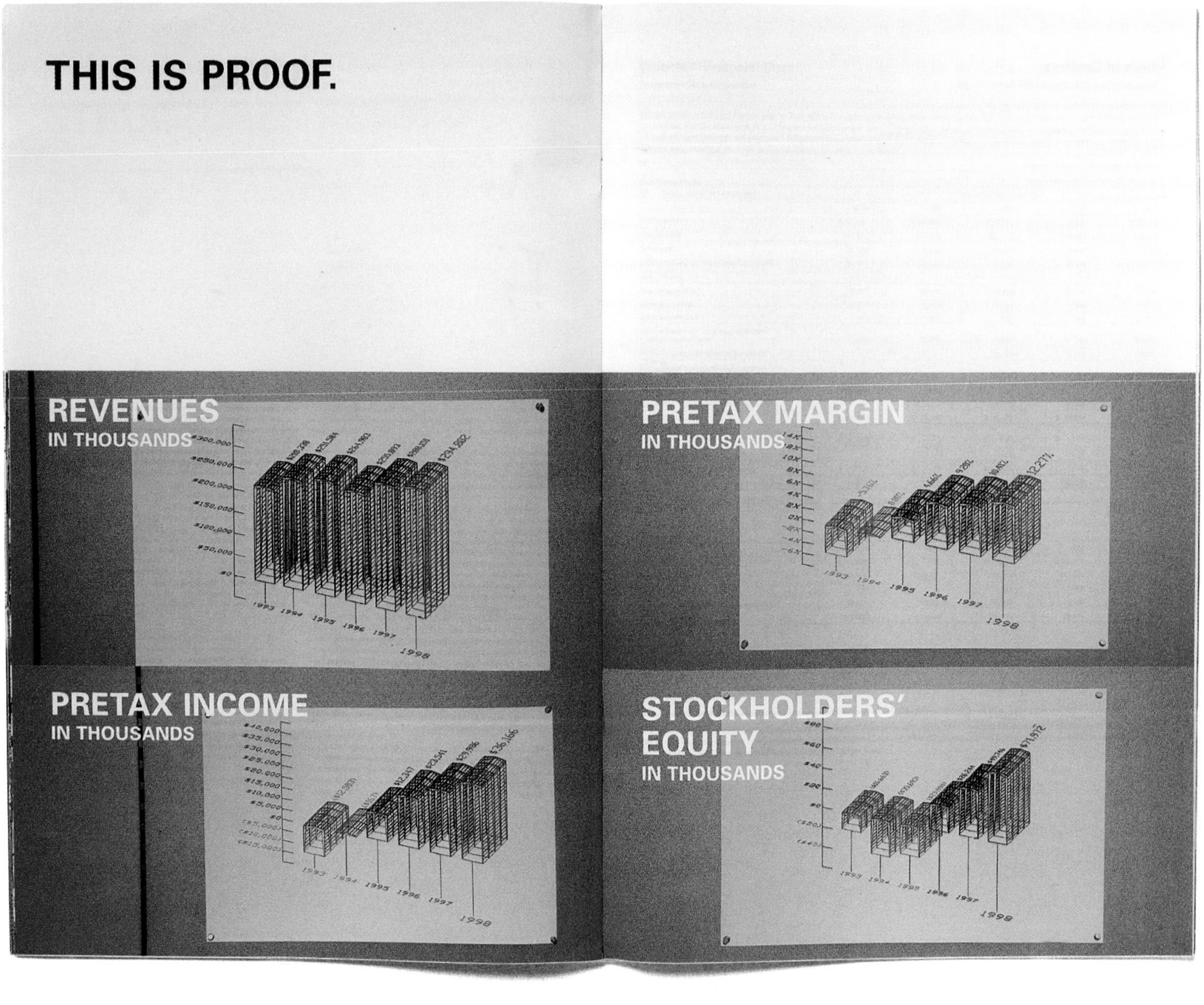

THIS IS PROOF.

REVENUES
IN THOUSANDS
1993
1994
1995
1996
1997
1998
PRETAX MARGIN
IN THOUSANDS
1993
1994
1995
1996
1997
1998
PRETAX INCOME
IN THOUSANDS
1993
1994
1995
1996
1997
1998
STOCKHOLDERS' EQUITY
IN THOUSANDS
1993
1994
1995
1996
1997
1998

THIS IS 7,000 STRUCTURES PER YEAR.

About 70 percent of low-rise commercial and industrial buildings are custom-engineered metal buildings. We are the fastest-growing segment of the construction industry.

AND BUILDING...

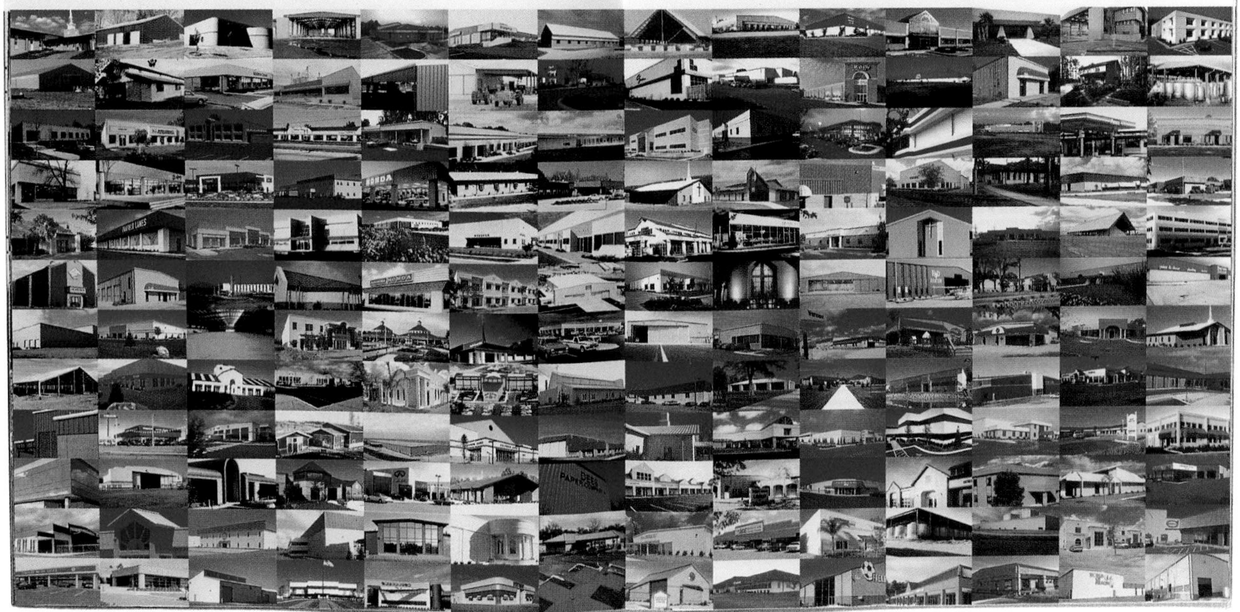

Financial Statements

Robertson-Ceco Corporation
Consolidated Statements of Income

(In thousands, except per share data)	Year Ended December 31 1996	1997	1998
Net revenues	$255,893	$288,151	$294,802
Cost of sales	201,478	233,284	234,913
Gross profit	54,415	54,867	59,889
Selling, general and administrative expenses	27,549	24,126	24,651
Operating income	26,866	30,741	35,238
Other income (expense):			
Interest expense	(4,166)	(1,659)	(1,062)
Other income, net	841	904	1,990
	(3,325)	(755)	928
Income before provision (credit) for taxes on income	23,541	29,986	36,166
Provision (credit) for taxes on income	(29,067)	11,200	13,647
Income before extraordinary item	52,608	18,786	22,519
Extraordinary gain (loss) on debt redemption	(1,315)	4,568	—
Net income	$ 51,293	$ 23,354	$ 22,519
Basic/diluted earnings per common share:			
Income before extraordinary item	$ 3.28	$ 1.17	$ 1.40
Extraordinary item	(.08)	.28	—
Net income	$ 3.20	$ 1.45	$ 1.40
Weighted average number of common shares outstanding	16,017	16,056	16,060

See Notes to Consolidated Financial Statements.

Robertson-Ceco Corporation
Consolidated Statements of Cash Flows

(In thousands)	Year Ended December 31 1996	1997	1998
Cash flows from operating activities:			
Income before extraordinary item	$ 52,608	$ 18,786	$ 22,519
Adjustments to reconcile income before extraordinary item to net cash provided by operating activities:			
Depreciation	3,272	3,660	4,152
Amortization	2,140	933	1,071
Changes in assets and liabilities:			
(Increase) decrease in accounts and notes receivable	2,876	(6,864)	(1,629)
(Increase) decrease in inventories	(2,329)	2,115	2,184
(Increase) decrease in deferred tax assets	(29,067)	11,200	13,647
Increase (decrease) in accounts payable	(5,507)	631	(1,869)
Net changes in other assets and liabilities	(2,206)	(974)	1,736
Net cash provided by operating activities	21,787	30,487	41,811
Net cash used for discontinued operations	(8,160)	(2,918)	(2,935)
Cash flows from investing activities:			
Capital expenditures	(3,366)	(7,267)	(5,134)
Net cash used for investing activities	(3,366)	(7,267)	(5,134)
Cash flows from financing activities:			
Proceeds from long-term borrowings	—	20,000	—
Payments on long-term debt	(5,000)	(32,731)	(15,000)
Payments of capitalized interest on 12% Notes	(2,704)	(338)	—
Net cash used for financing activities	(7,704)	(13,069)	(15,000)
Net increase in cash and cash equivalents	2,557	7,236	18,742
Cash and cash equivalents—beginning of period	9,668	12,225	19,461
Cash and cash equivalents—end of period	$ 12,225	$ 19,461	$ 38,203
Supplemental cash flow data			
Cash payments made for:			
Interest	$ 4,767	$ 1,936	$ 882
Income taxes	$ —	$ —	$ —

See Notes to Consolidated Financial Statements.

Robertson-Ceco Corporation
Consolidated Balance Sheets

(In thousands, except share data)	December 31 1997	1998
ASSETS		
Current assets:		
Cash and cash equivalents	$ 19,461	$ 38,203
Accounts and notes receivable, less allowance for doubtful accounts: 1997, $1,690; 1998, $1,795	28,249	29,876
Inventories	13,702	11,518
Deferred taxes, current	15,688	4,476
Other current assets	557	621
Total current assets	77,657	84,696
Property, plant and equipment—at cost:		
Land	1,654	1,654
Buildings and improvements	11,136	11,550
Machinery and equipment	33,037	38,309
Construction in progress	3,581	1,596
	49,408	53,109
Less accumulated depreciation	(22,902)	(25,900)
Property, plant and equipment—net	26,506	27,209
Excess of cost over net assets of acquired businesses, less accumulated amortization: 1997, $6,741; 1998, $7,569	25,783	24,965
Deferred taxes, non-current	12,329	12,373
Other non-current assets	1,269	758
Total assets	$143,544	$149,991
LIABILITIES AND STOCKHOLDERS' EQUITY		
Current liabilities:		
Current portion of long-term debt	$ 5,000	$ —
Accounts payable	13,209	11,340
Accrued payroll and benefits	7,525	8,137
Other accrued liabilities	16,796	14,156
Total current liabilities	42,530	33,633
Long-term debt, less current portion	10,000	—
Deferred income taxes	5,891	5,830
Other long-term liabilities	35,377	38,556
Commitments and contingencies		
Stockholders' equity:		
Common stock Par value per share $.01 Authorized shares: 30,000,000 Issued and outstanding shares: 1997—16,111,550; 1998—16,096,550	161	161
Capital surplus	178,256	178,233
Accumulated deficit	(128,173)	(105,654)
Deferred compensation	(160)	(105)
Accumulated other comprehensive income	(338)	(863)
Stockholders' equity	49,740	71,972
Total liabilities and stockholders' equity	$143,544	$149,991

See Notes to Consolidated Financial Statements.

Esterline Technologies
Agency: Leimer Cross Design
Art & Creative Director: Kerry Leimer
Designers: Kerry Leimer, Marianne Li
Photographers: Jeff Corwin, Tyler Boley
Copywriters: Kerry Leimer, Brian Keogh

ESTERLINE TECHNOLOGIES
1998
NYSE
ESL
ANNUAL REPORT

To Our Shareholders.

left | Robert W. Cremin
President and Chief Operating Officer

right | Wendell P. Hurlbut
Chairman and Chief Executive Officer

Esterline had a great year. Fiscal 1998 not only produced record sales and earnings for our company, but also marked the fourth consecutive year of double-digit earnings growth.

The results are largely due to our long-term strategy:

We leverage Esterline's well-balanced structure to best take advantage of the business cycles in the markets we serve. Basically, we're a group of specialized manufacturing operations providing both growth and value opportunities.

We maintain an unremitting focus on operating effectiveness in order to grow the company from within. Our managers are disciplined to make the necessary investments in timely new products, new or expanded facilities, new equipment or systems, and the most highly qualified people available.

And we are committed to seek out acquisitions that fit our strategy, preferably manufacturers of engineered products, serving industrial customers, and operating within a market niche where we can be a significant player. We also look for synergy with our existing companies or with markets those companies serve.

This strategy has proved to be particularly effective. Certainly we have the advantages of the classic diversified company, where we are able to balance the ups and downs of inherent cycles that affect our markets. Unlike most diversified companies, however, Esterline is highly focused. We offer specialized, highly engineered products that are at, or near, the top of their market niches.

During the year, this approach resulted in a number of noteworthy achievements.

> **Aerospace Markets Again Led the Way**

As with last year's performance, our companies serving aerospace markets led the way again in 1998.

Commercial airline passenger and air cargo traffic continues to grow, leaving most carriers solidly profitable. In addition, record shipments of new aircraft by the original equipment manufacturers, and a solid defense base, created opportunity and we acted on it.

Possibly the most noteworthy event of the year was the acquisition of Kirkhill Rubber Co. in August. This acquisition was the largest of seven (four companies and three product lines) completed by Esterline during fiscal 1998.

3

ATTRIBUTES

❶ specialized

We are specialists. Specialization requires a discipline that has clearly defined our product lines and capabilities. All are strictly aligned with specific market needs. This focus has helped us build a depth of understanding that reaches beyond what competitors can offer. It has made our market-driven research and development efforts highly efficient. Across our family of Esterline companies you'll find the same discipline and focus, the same determination to offer results that can only be derived from a thorough understanding of the details behind each market we serve.

VALUABLE ATTRIBUTES FOR GROWTH >

• Specialized, engineered solutions are the common denominator among all our markets. Our products are essential for aerospace, electronics and general manufacturing companies that want to make the most of their products and their operations, especially where accuracy, reliability, efficiency and productivity are factors. Specialization also offers us a tactical advantage: because of our focus, our components are often written in to the base specifications of our customers' products. This positions Esterline to build long-term relationships with that customer. We are also in the best position to continue to innovate and evolve our products to meet the emerging needs of our markets, adding to the depth of our understanding and the growing range of our opportunities.

14.

❷ balanced ❸ leadership

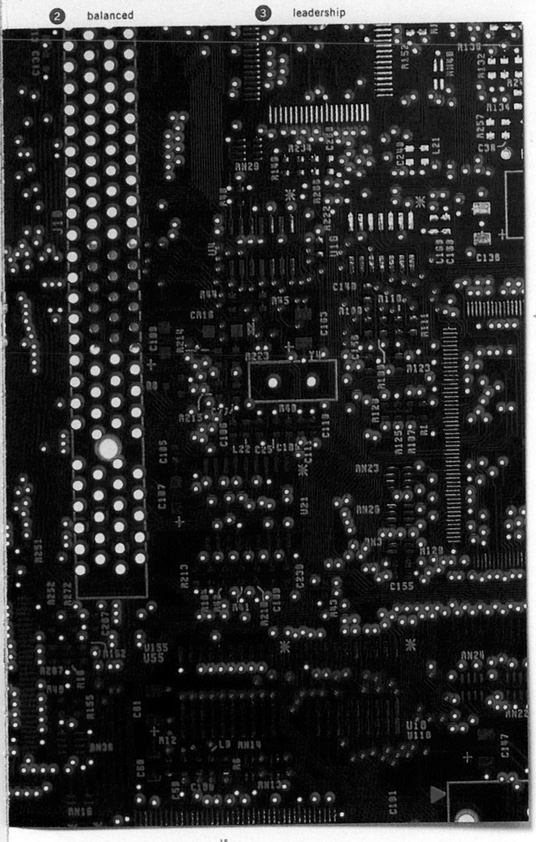

15.

images

color:
Printed circuit board hole diameters continue to shrink as electronic devices get smaller and more powerful. (Photo magnified 2.5 times.)

b&w:
Esterline produces a wide range of specialized products for the aerospace industry.

Results.

1994 - 1998 in millions, except as noted

Sales

$453.9

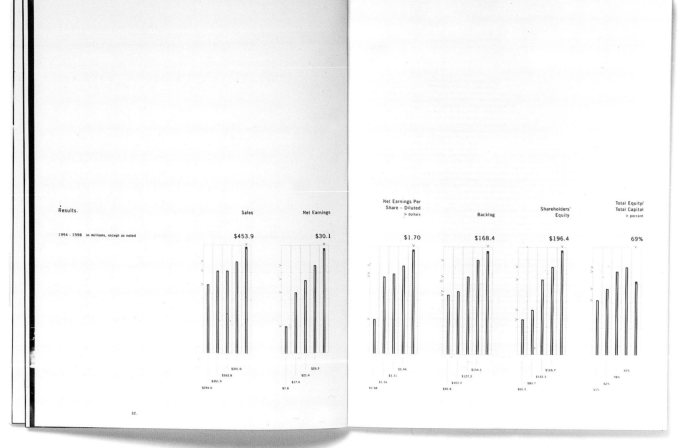

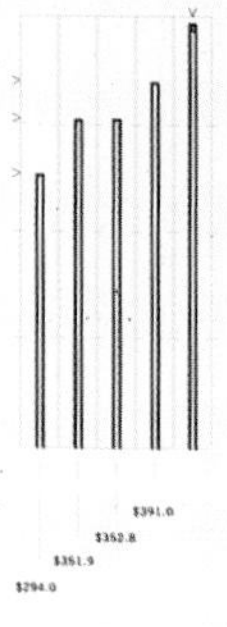
$391.0
$352.8
$351.9
$294.0

Net Earnings

$30.1

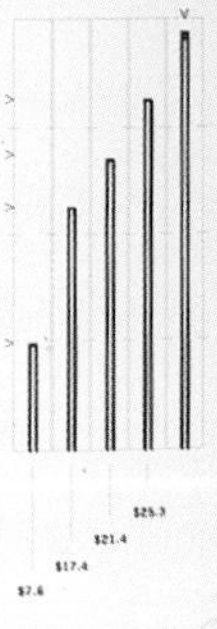
$25.3
$21.4
$17.4
$7.6

Net Earnings Per Share – Diluted
> dollars

$1.70

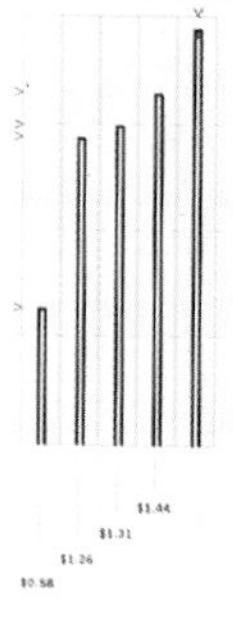
$1.44
$1.31
$1.26
$0.58

Backlog

$168.4

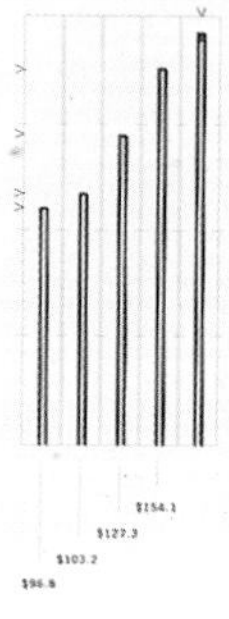
$154.1
$127.3
$103.2
$96.6

Shareholders' Equity

$196.4

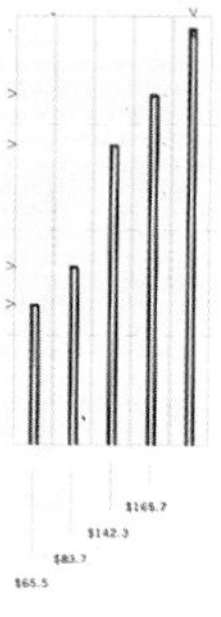
$165.7
$142.3
$83.7
$65.5

Total Equity/ Total Capital
> percent

69%

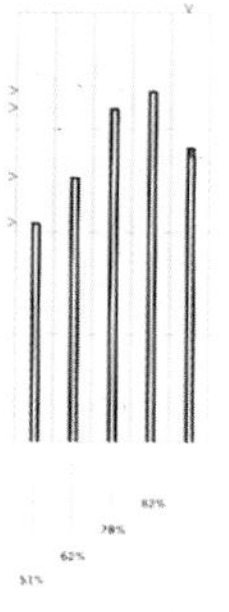
82%
78%
62%
51%

Note 8. Stock Option Plans >

The Company provides a non-qualified stock option plan for officers and key employees. At October 31, 1998, the Company had 1,849,500 shares reserved for issuance to officers and key employees, of which 536,250 shares were available to be granted in the future. The Board of Directors authorized the Compensation and Stock Option Committee to administer option grants and their terms. Awards under the plan may be granted to eligible employees of the Company over a 10-year period ending March 4, 2007. Options granted become exercisable over a period of four years following the date of grant and expire on the tenth anniversary of the grant. Option exercise prices are equal to the fair value of the Company's common stock on the date of grant.

The following table summarizes the changes in outstanding options granted under the Company's stock option plans:

	1998		1997		1996	
	Shares	Weighted Average Price	Shares	Weighted Average Price	Shares	Weighted Average Price
Outstanding, beginning of year	1,190,000	$ 8.472	1,516,250	$ 6.089	1,509,250	$ 4.893
Granted	187,000	18.644	271,000	14.304	258,000	11.155
Exercised	(63,750)	4.261	(589,750)	5.086	(243,500)	4.112
Cancelled	–	–	(7,500)	3.750	(7,500)	3.813
Outstanding, end of year	1,313,250	$ 10.125	1,190,000	$ 8.472	1,516,250	$ 6.089
Exercisable, end of year	741,500	$ 6.893	574,750	$ 5.511	950,500	$ 4.946

The Company accounts for its stock-based compensation plans in accordance with Accounting Principles Board Opinion No. 25. Additional disclosures as required under the Statement of Financial Accounting Standards ("SFAS") No. 123, "Accounting for Stock-Based Compensation," are included below. The Black-Scholes option-pricing model was used to calculate the estimated compensation expense that would have been recognized under these guidelines.

If only options granted after 1995 were included, as prescribed by SFAS No. 123, pro forma net income would have been $28,971,000, $24,517,000 and $21,089,000, respectively. Basic earnings per share for 1998, 1997 and 1996 would have been $1.68, $1.43 and $1.33, respectively. Diluted earnings per share for 1998, 1997 and 1996 would have been $1.64, $1.40 and $1.29, respectively.

The pro forma disclosures presented below include the fair value compensation expense for all options that would have been amortized during 1998, 1997 and 1996.

in thousands, except per share amounts years ended October 31,	1998	1997	1996
Net earnings as reported	$ 30,084	$ 25,321	$ 21,354
Pro forma net earnings	28,928	24,400	20,852
Basic earnings per share as reported	$ 1.74	$ 1.48	$ 1.35
Pro forma basic earnings per share	$ 1.67	$ 1.43	$ 1.32
Diluted earnings per share as reported	$ 1.70	$ 1.44	$ 1.31
Pro forma diluted earnings per share	$ 1.63	$ 1.39	$ 1.28

The weighted average Black-Scholes value of options granted during 1998, 1997 and 1996 was $10.870, $7.320 and $6.012, respectively. The assumptions used in the Black-Scholes option-pricing model for 1998, 1997, and 1996 were as follows:

	1998	1997	1996
Volatility	55.3%	41.6%	44.6%
Risk-free interest rate	4.1 – 4.57%	5.73 – 5.92%	6.12 – 6.38%
Expected life (years)	5 – 8	5 – 8	5 – 8
Dividends	–	–	–

The following table summarizes information for stock options outstanding at October 31, 1998:

	Options Outstanding			Options Exercisable	
Range of Exercise Prices	Shares	Weighted Average Remaining Life (years)	Weighted Average Price	Shares	Weighted Average Price
$ 3.6875 – 4.3750	278,000	4.74	$ 4.0226	278,000	$ 4.0226
4.5000 – 6.4375	295,000	4.92	5.9820	252,500	5.9053
6.9375 – 11.6875	286,000	7.38	10.8433	147,000	10.7700
13.2500 – 17.8125	261,250	8.33	14.0308	57,500	13.7310
18.2500 – 19.8750	193,000	9.16	18.8964	6,500	19.8750

1 2 2 3 7 3 5 1 8 1

5 4 6 0 9 8 1 0 2 6

3 0 2 1 4 2 5 5 9 3

2 7 6 0 2 3 9 1 1 4

1 5 1 8 9 6 2 0 STRENGTH IN NUMBERS 3

6 3 2 3 5 1 4 5 4 1

3 2 0 1 0 4 9 1 9 6

9 1 1 0 2 6 0 3 5 2

2 5 0 6 9 2 5 4 1 9

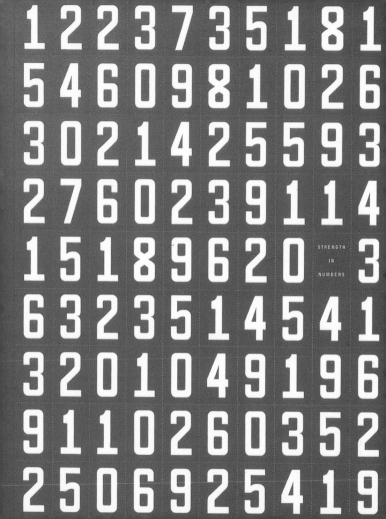

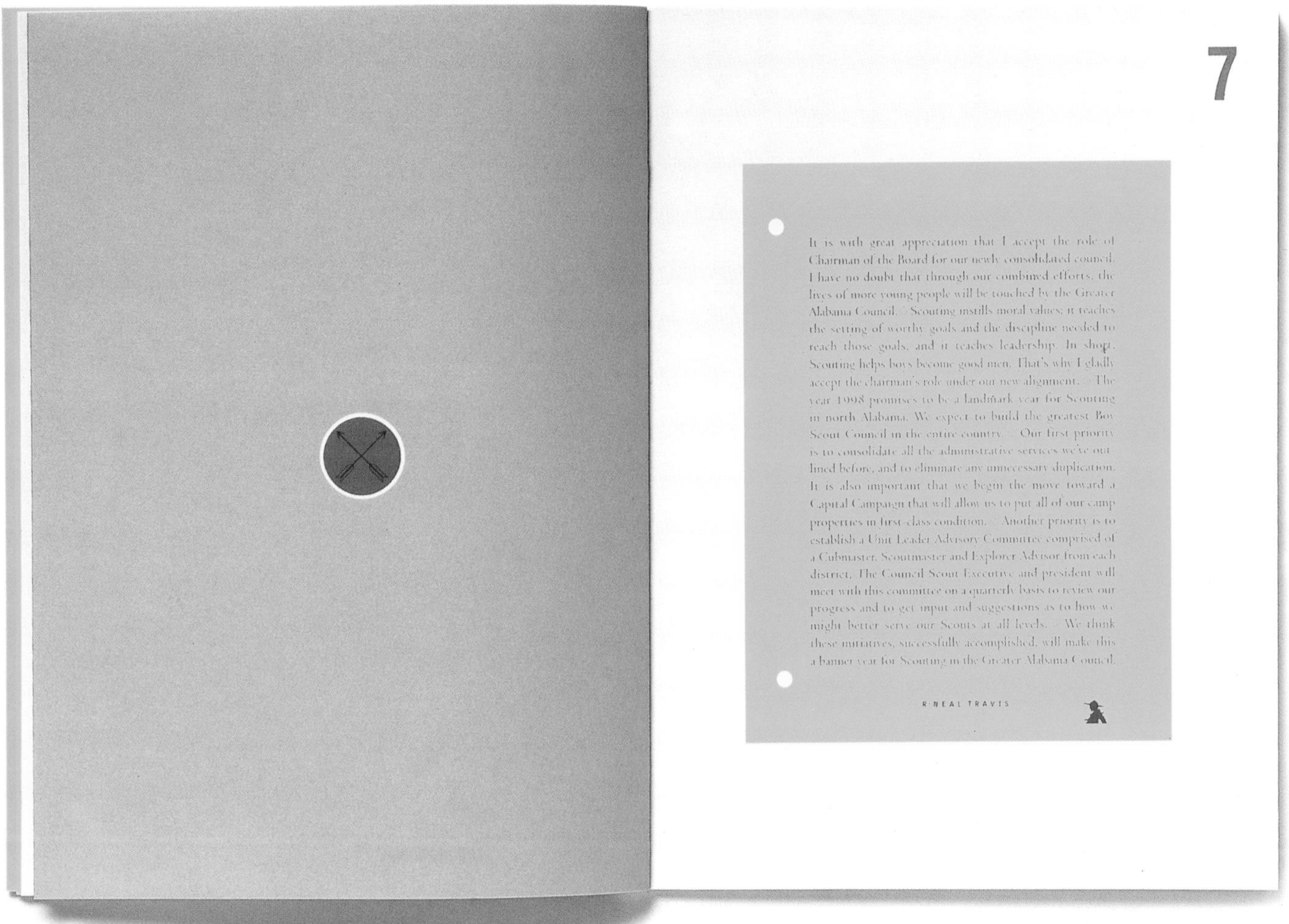

7

It is with great appreciation that I accept the role of Chairman of the Board for our newly consolidated council. I have no doubt that through our combined efforts, the lives of more young people will be touched by the Greater Alabama Council. Scouting instills moral values; it teaches the setting of worthy goals and the discipline needed to reach those goals, and it teaches leadership. In short, Scouting helps boys become good men. That's why I gladly accept the chairman's role under our new alignment. The year 1998 promises to be a landmark year for Scouting in north Alabama. We expect to build the greatest Boy Scout Council in the entire country. Our first priority is to consolidate all the administrative services we've outlined before, and to eliminate any unnecessary duplication. It is also important that we begin the move toward a Capital Campaign that will allow us to put all of our camp properties in first-class condition. Another priority is to establish a Unit Leader Advisory Committee comprised of a Cubmaster, Scoutmaster and Explorer Advisor from each district. The Council Scout Executive and president will meet with this committee on a quarterly basis to review our progress and to get input and suggestions as to how we might better serve our Scouts at all levels. We think these initiatives, successfully accomplished, will make this a banner year for Scouting in the Greater Alabama Council.

R NEAL TRAVIS

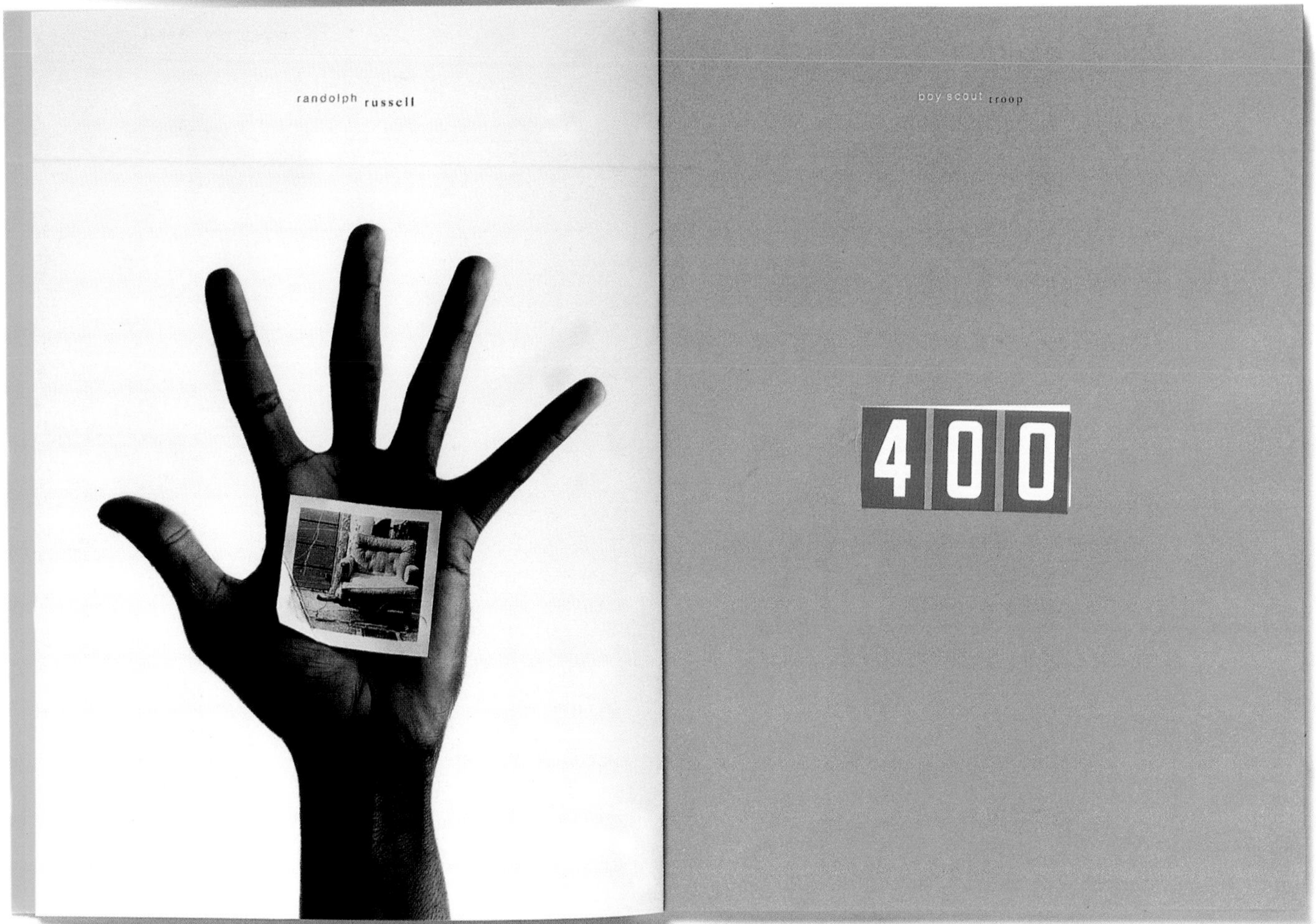
randolph russell
boy scout troop
400

dillon townsel

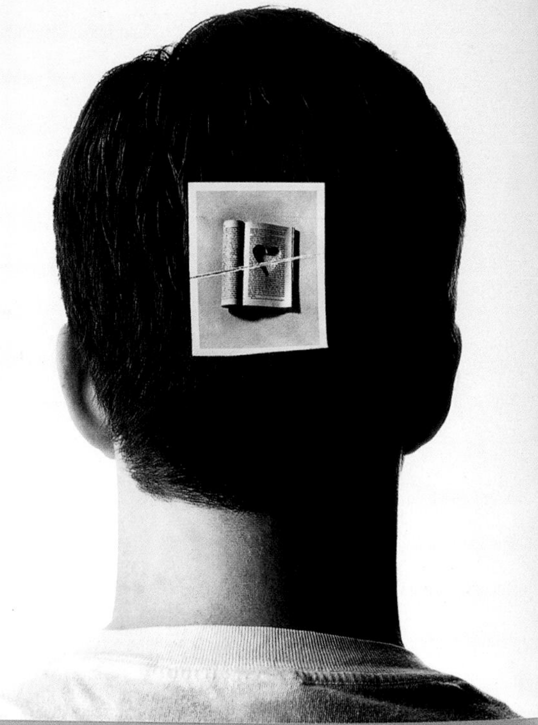

boy scout troop

288

Positive

Programs

nathan fowler

boy scout troop

260

our earnings

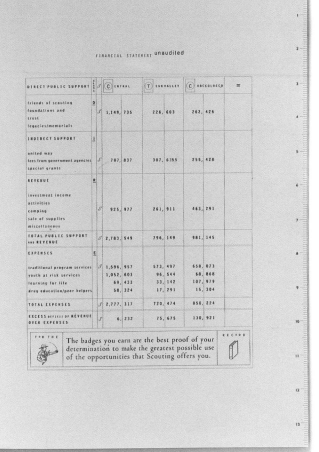

FINANCIAL STATEMENT unaudited

DIRECT PUBLIC SUPPORT	CLASS	$	CENTRAL	TENVALLEY	CROCCOLOCCO	=
friends of scouting foundations and trust legacies/memorials	D	$	1,149, 735	226, 603	262, 426	
INDIRECT SUPPORT	I					
united way fees from government agencies special grants		$	707, 837	307, 6355	255, 428	
REVENUE	R					
investment income activities camping sale of supplies miscellaneous		$	925, 977	261, 911	463, 291	
TOTAL PUBLIC SUPPORT AND REVENUE		$	2,783, 549	796, 149	981, 145	
EXPENSES	E					
traditional program services		$	1,596, 957	573, 497	658, 073	
youth at risk services			1,052, 603	96, 544	68, 868	
learning for life			69, 433	33, 142	107, 979	
drug education/peer helpers			58, 324	17, 291	15, 304	
TOTAL EXPENSES		$	2,777, 317	720, 474	850, 224	
EXCESS DEFICIT OF REVENUE OVER EXPENSES		$	6, 232	75, 675	130, 921	

FOR THE — The badges you earn are the best proof of your determination to make the greatest possible use of the opportunities that Scouting offers you. — RECORD

Greater Alabama Council of Boy Scouts
Agency: Slaughter Hanson
Designer: Marion English
Photographer: Don Harbor
Illustrator: David Webb
Copywriter: Kathy Oldham

help

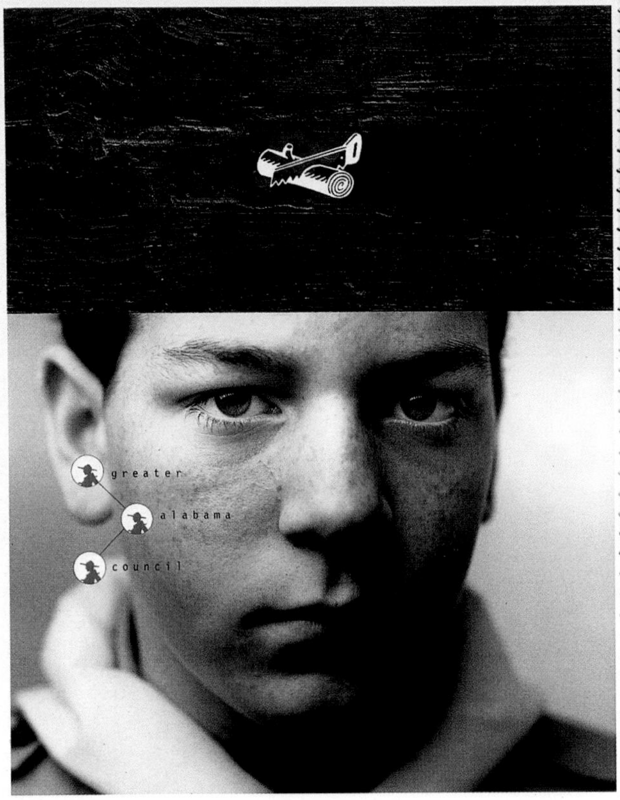
greater
alabama
council

FOR CLOSE TO A CENTURY, SCOUTING HAS HELPED BOYS REALIZE THEIR OWN POTENTIAL, SHOWING THEM THE GREATNESS THAT IS WITHIN THEIR GRASP. SCOUTS LEARN THAT, NO MATTER WHO THEY ARE, NO MATTER WHAT THEIR CIRCUMSTANCES, THEY TOO ARE CAPABLE OF MAKING A POSITIVE IMPACT ON THE WORLD. SCOUTING HAS SHAPED THEIR CHARACTER, INSTILLING TRAITS THAT WILL LEAD THEM TO DO EXTRAORDINARY THINGS. FOR THESE INDIVIDUALS, INCLUDING THE FIVE PROFILED IN THIS ANNUAL REPORT, SCOUTING HAS BECOME A HANDBOOK FOR LIFE. A HANDBOOK FOR CHARACTER.

CLAY

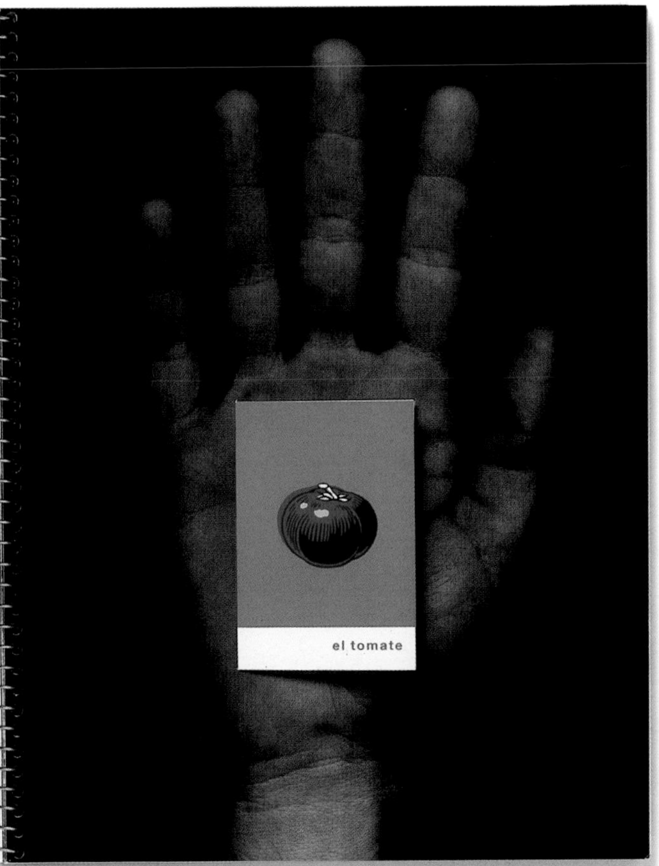
el tomate

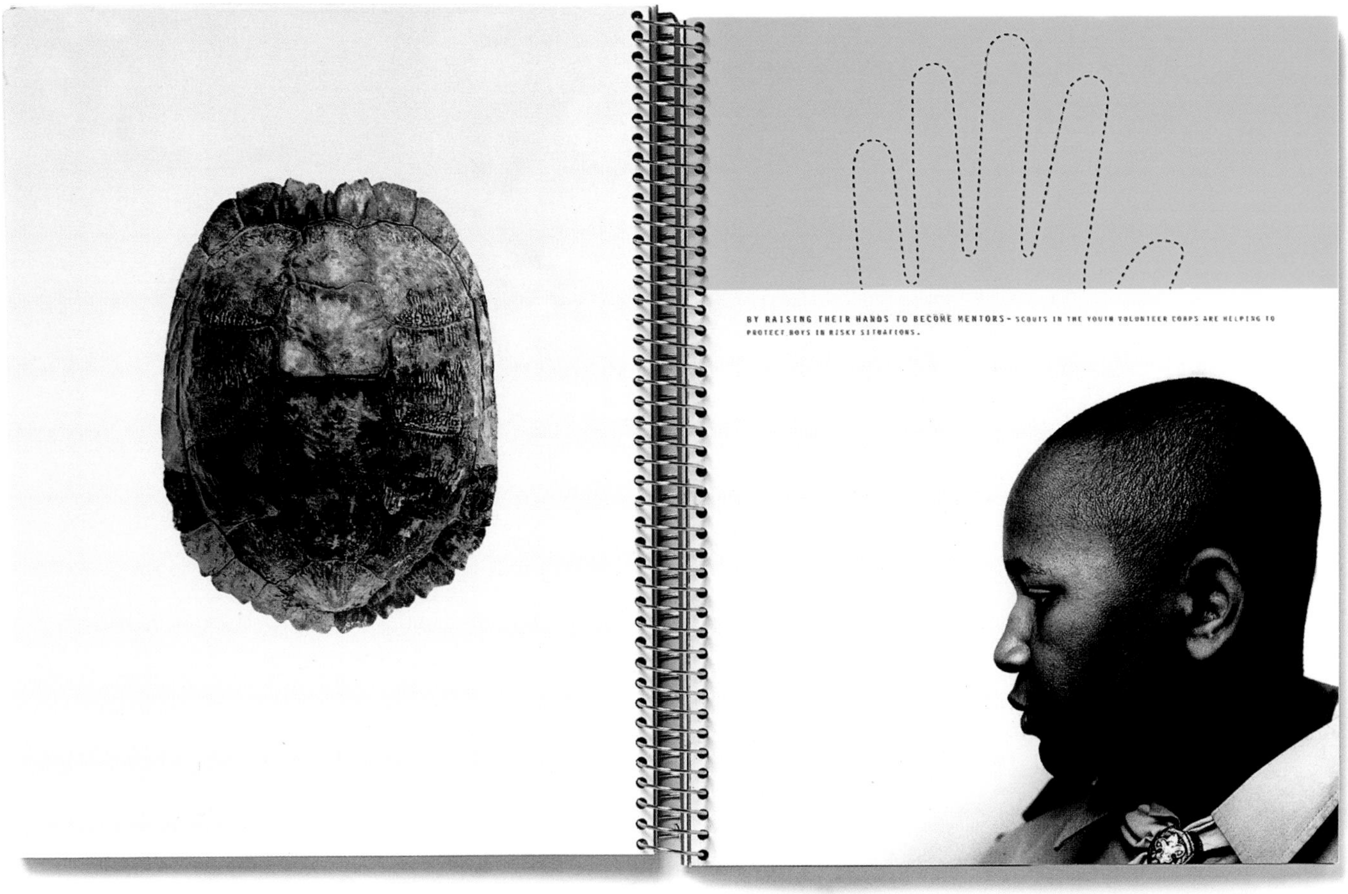
BY RAISING THEIR HANDS TO BECOME MENTORS– SCOUTS IN THE YOUTH VOLUNTEER CORPS ARE HELPING TO PROTECT BOYS IN RISKY SITUATIONS.

98

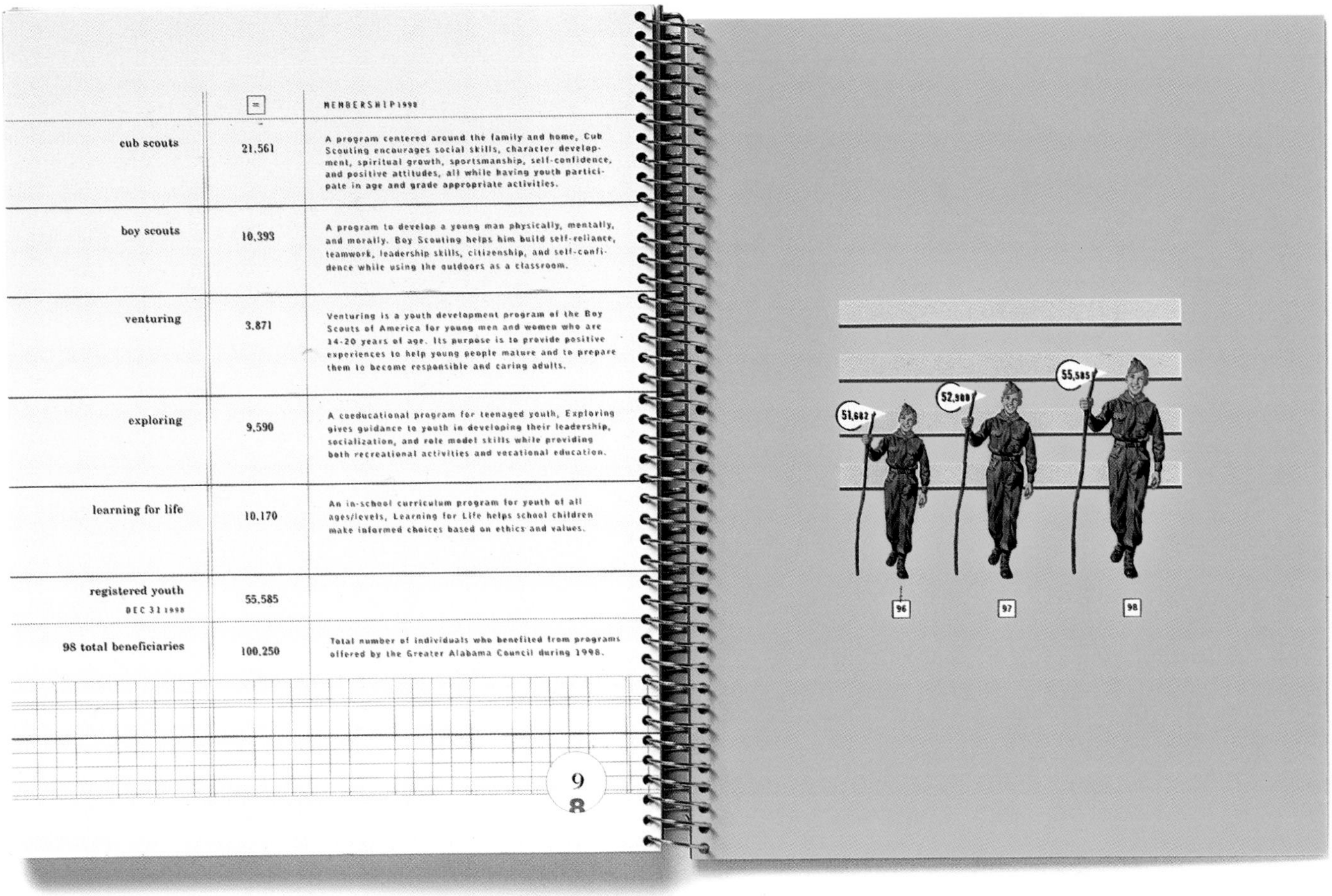

	=	MEMBERSHIP 1998
cub scouts	21,561	A program centered around the family and home, Cub Scouting encourages social skills, character development, spiritual growth, sportsmanship, self-confidence, and positive attitudes, all while having youth participate in age and grade appropriate activities.
boy scouts	10,393	A program to develop a young man physically, mentally, and morally. Boy Scouting helps him build self-reliance, teamwork, leadership skills, citizenship, and self-confidence while using the outdoors as a classroom.
venturing	3,871	Venturing is a youth development program of the Boy Scouts of America for young men and women who are 14-20 years of age. Its purpose is to provide positive experiences to help young people mature and to prepare them to become responsible and caring adults.
exploring	9,590	A coeducational program for teenaged youth, Exploring gives guidance to youth in developing their leadership, socialization, and role model skills while providing both recreational activities and vocational education.
learning for life	10,170	An in-school curriculum program for youth of all ages/levels, Learning for Life helps school children make informed choices based on ethics and values.
registered youth DEC 31 1998	55,585	
98 total beneficiaries	100,250	Total number of individuals who benefited from programs offered by the Greater Alabama Council during 1998.

9 8

51,682
52,980
55,585
96
97
98

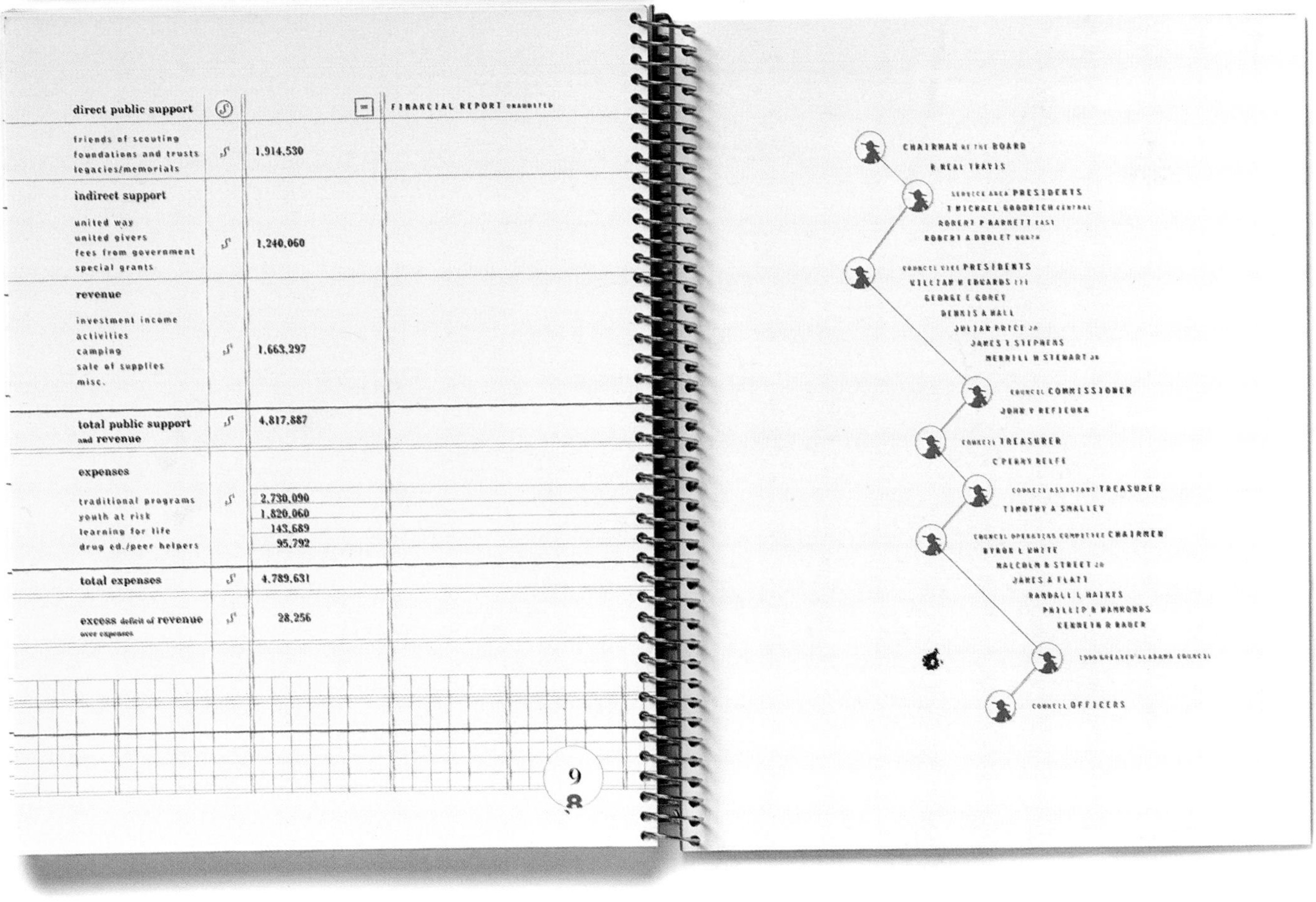

direct public support	$		FINANCIAL REPORT UNAUDITED
friends of scouting foundations and trusts legacies/memorials	$	1,914,530	
indirect support united way united givers fees from government special grants	$	1,240,060	
revenue investment income activities camping sale of supplies misc.	$	1,663,297	
total public support and revenue	$	4,817,887	
expenses			
traditional programs	$	2,730,090	
youth at risk		1,820,060	
learning for life		143,689	
drug ed./peer helpers		95,792	
total expenses	$	4,789,631	
excess deficit of **revenue** over expenses	$	28,256	

9 8

CHAIRMAN OF THE BOARD
R NEAL TRAVIS
SERVICE AREA PRESIDENTS
T MICHAEL GOODRICH CENTRAL
ROBERT P BARNETT EAST
ROBERT A DROLET NORTH
COUNCIL VICE PRESIDENTS
DENNIS A HALL
JULIAN PRICE JR
JAMES T STEPHENS
MERRILL H STEWART JR
COUNCIL COMMISSIONER
COUNCIL TREASURER
C PERRY RELFE
COUNCIL ASSISTANT TREASURER
TIMOTHY A SMALLEY
COUNCIL OPERATING COMMITTEE CHAIRMEN
BYRON L WHITE
MALCOLM B STREET JR
JAMES A PLATT
RANDALL L HAINES
PHILLIP B HAMMONDS
KENNETH R BAUER
1998 GREATER ALABAMA COUNCIL
COUNCIL OFFICERS

Potlatch Corporation
Agency: Pentagram Design
Art & Creative Director: Kit Hinrichs
Designer: Belle How
Photographer: Tom Tracey
Copywriter: Delphine Hirasuna

Potlatch 1999 Annual Report

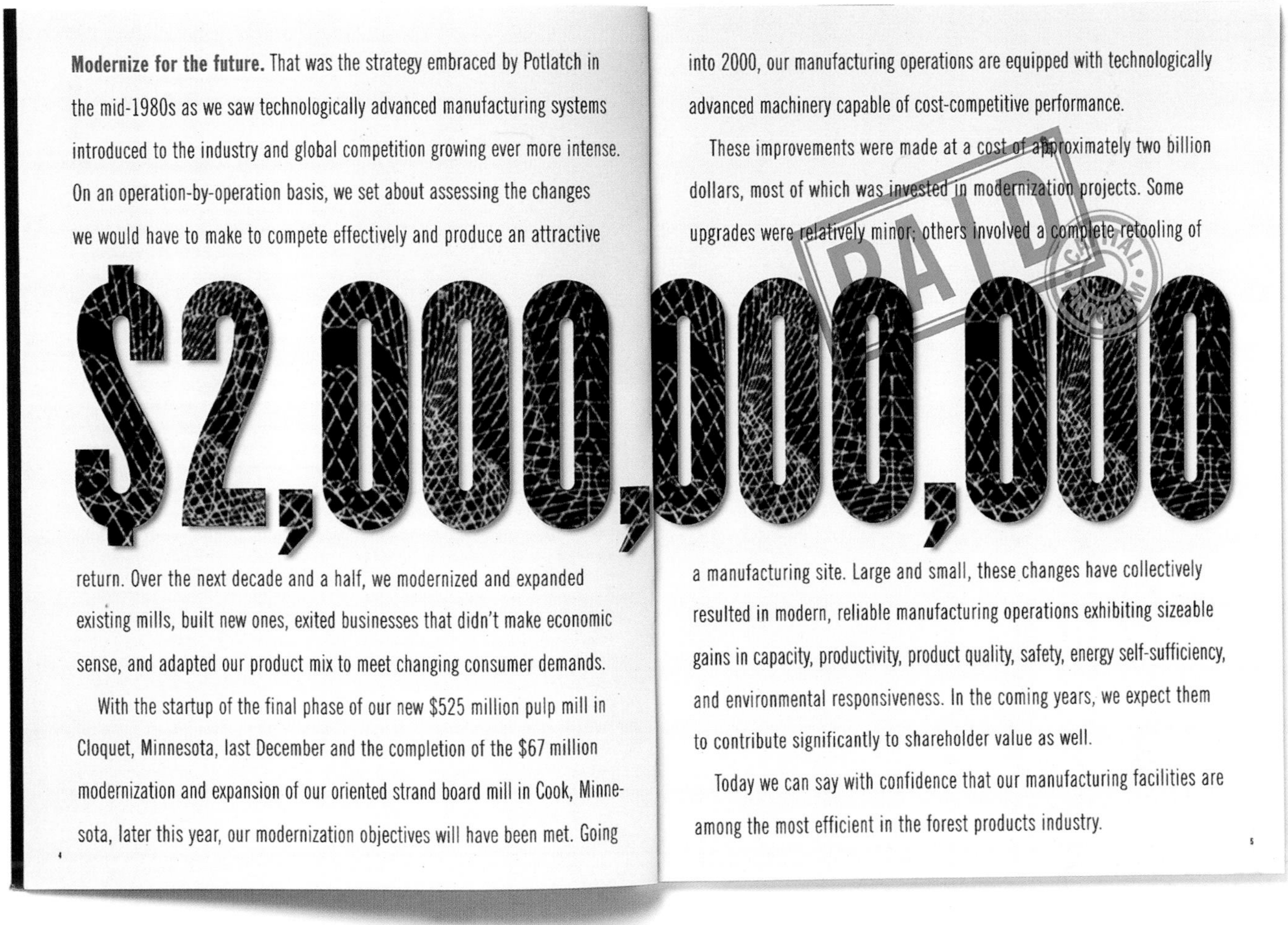

Modernize for the future. That was the strategy embraced by Potlatch in the mid-1980s as we saw technologically advanced manufacturing systems introduced to the industry and global competition growing ever more intense. On an operation-by-operation basis, we set about assessing the changes we would have to make to compete effectively and produce an attractive return. Over the next decade and a half, we modernized and expanded existing mills, built new ones, exited businesses that didn't make economic sense, and adapted our product mix to meet changing consumer demands.

With the startup of the final phase of our new $525 million pulp mill in Cloquet, Minnesota, last December and the completion of the $67 million modernization and expansion of our oriented strand board mill in Cook, Minnesota, later this year, our modernization objectives will have been met. Going into 2000, our manufacturing operations are equipped with technologically advanced machinery capable of cost-competitive performance.

These improvements were made at a cost of approximately two billion dollars, most of which was invested in modernization projects. Some upgrades were relatively minor; others involved a complete retooling of a manufacturing site. Large and small, these changes have collectively resulted in modern, reliable manufacturing operations exhibiting sizeable gains in capacity, productivity, product quality, safety, energy self-sufficiency, and environmental responsiveness. In the coming years, we expect them to contribute significantly to shareholder value as well.

Today we can say with confidence that our manufacturing facilities are among the most efficient in the forest products industry.

$2,000,000,000
PAID

4

5

PREMIUM EQUALS HIGHER MARGIN$
ENERGY
MILK
Super
MARKET
ABC
PRINTING

Aseptic paperboard packaging offers shelf-stable qualities.

Potlatch industrial plywood is used in the construction of recreational vehicles.

Potlatch tissue offers premium quality for the private-label market.

Part of our modernization strategy has been directed toward gaining entry into less cyclical and higher value-added markets. Installation of a new three-ply tissue machine in Lewiston (1992) allowed us to provide private-label customers with premium products unsurpassed by leading national brands. Machine modifications at the St. Maries and Jaype plywood plants in Idaho (1995) enabled production of higher value 5- and 7-ply industrial plywood, used for concrete forms and recreational vehicles. New machinery and upgrades at our Cloquet and Brainerd coated paper mills made it possible to create a new bright-white printing grade called Potlatch McCoy™, now one of Minnesota Paper's top sellers. Installation of two new coaters (1999) at our Lewiston paperboard operation gives us the ability to produce a new aseptic packaging board that assures a longer shelf life – without refrigeration – for liquids such as milk and juice. All of these are attractive markets noted for their good returns.

Bright-white Potlatch McCoy paper is an industry best-seller.

14

15

When it comes to profits, the difference is sometimes in how you slice it. It used to be that any defective piece trimmed off a board of lumber in the grading process went straight to the chipper to be made into chips for pulp. But today two-foot board "trims" are being set aside for sale to manufacturers of finger-joint lumber and specialty craft applications such as birdhouses and dollhouses. At the Lewiston sawmill alone, these two-foot trims now add up to about 3,000,000 board feet of lumber a year – or the equivalent of 75 truckloads. Offering higher revenues than wood chips, the two-foot trim products have produced additional operating income of more than $250,000 per year.

+78%

2000 vs. 1988

(increased capacity of one paper machine vs. three old machines)

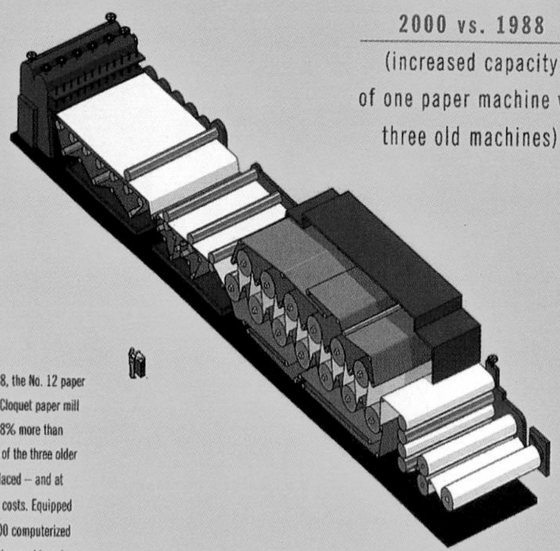

Installed in 1988, the No. 12 paper machine at the Cloquet paper mill now produces 78% more than the total output of the three older machines it replaced – and at greatly reduced costs. Equipped with nearly 2,000 computerized control points, the machine gives operators the ability to monitor and control minute shifts in the manufacturing process, ensuring consistent product quality, timely preventive maintenance and significant savings from reduced downtime.

–50%

1999 vs. 1989

(decrease in OSHA recordable injury accidents)

Potlatch's investment in the development and implementation of a companywide behavioral safety program, led and monitored by employees, contributed to a 50% reduction in injury incidents, as reported to the Occupational Safety & Health Administration (OSHA) over the past decade. The company emphasizes its all-out support of the program through annual safety conferences, safety-based objectives and annual safety reviews.

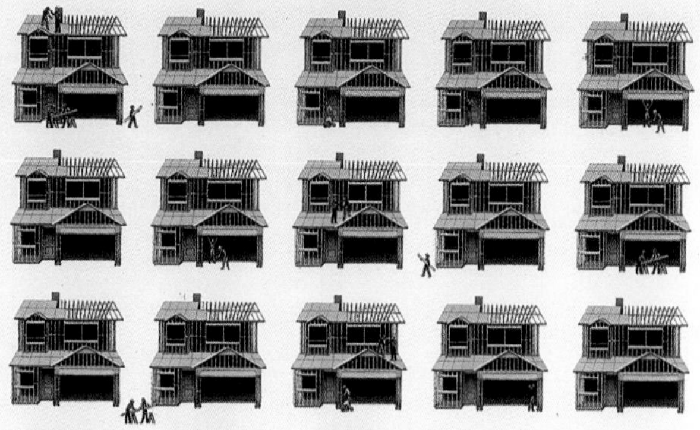

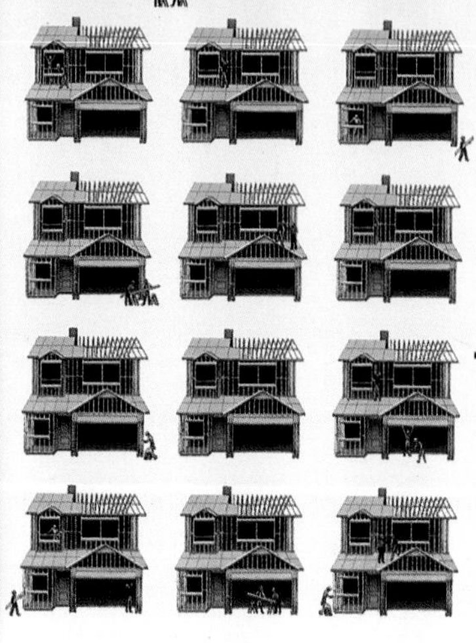

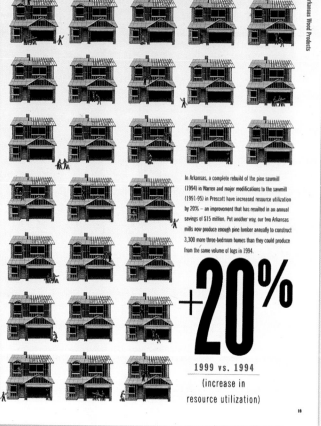

In Arkansas, a complete rebuild of the pine sawmill (1994) in Warren and major modifications to the sawmill (1991-95) in Prescott have increased resource utilization by 20% – an improvement that has resulted in an annual savings of $15 million. Put another way, our two Arkansas mills now produce enough pine lumber annually to construct 3,300 more three-bedroom homes than they could produce from the same volume of logs in 1994.

+20%

1999 vs. 1994

(increase in resource utilization)

With the completion of major construction projects and in anticipation of lower maintenance costs, we expect our cash requirements to be less than in past years and well below our noncash charges (i.e., depreciation, depletion, amortization and deferred taxes). We believe this will result in a dramatic gain in free cash flow, even without market improvements, and provide us with additional funds to pay down debt, invest in opportunities that will bring greater returns to our existing facilities, and repurchase stock to strengthen shareholder return.

15-YEAR COMPARISON OF AVERAGE ANNUAL NONCASH CHARGES AND CAPITAL EXPENDITURES

1990-1994
-$20 million free cash flow
$120 million noncash charges
$140 million capital expenditures*

1995-1999
$12 million free cash flow
$167 million noncash charges
$155 million capital expenditures*

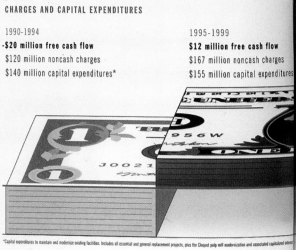

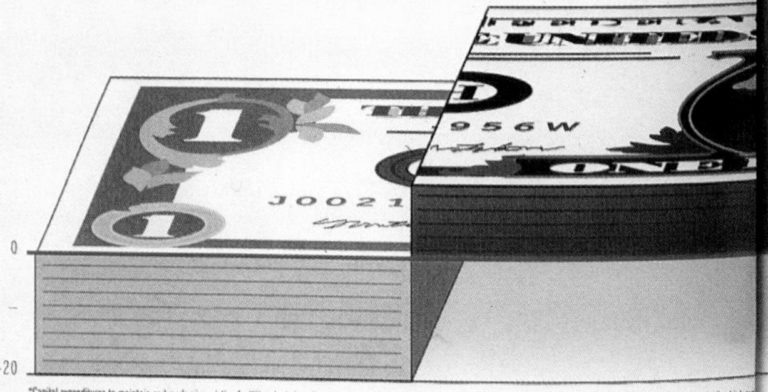
0
-20

$119
MILLION
FREE CASH FLOW
$207 million noncash charges
$88 million capital expenditures*
119
0
-20

*Capital expenditures to maintain and modernize existing facilities. Includes all essential and general replacement projects, plus the Cloquet pulp mill modernization and associated capitalized interes

Eleven-Year Record

For the years ended December 31 (Dollars in thousands – except per-share amounts)	1999	1998	1997	1996	1995	1994	1993	1992	1991	1990	1989
Eleven-Year Summary of Consolidated Operations											
Net sales	$1,676,838	$1,565,878	$1,568,870	$1,554,449	$1,605,206	$1,471,258	$1,368,854	$1,326,612	$1,236,988	$1,252,906	$1,227,622
Costs and expenses:											
Depreciation, amortization and cost of fee timber harvested	150,253	150,278	149,785	141,521	137,031	138,251	123,544	107,165	96,924	86,154	77,294
Materials, labor and other operating expenses	1,284,432	1,195,449	1,219,665	1,186,127	1,158,002	1,121,491	1,064,260	1,006,887	945,888	924,303	856,176
Selling, general and administrative expenses	130,160	120,944	106,450	104,114	90,569	82,799	83,958	83,409	74,998	66,967	67,107
	1,564,845	1,466,671	1,475,900	1,431,762	1,385,602	1,342,541	1,271,762	1,197,461	1,117,810	1,077,424	1,000,577
Earnings from operations	111,993	99,207	92,970	122,687	219,604	128,717	97,092	129,151	119,178	175,482	227,045
Interest expense	(45,442)	(49,744)	(46,124)	(43,869)	(47,976)	(51,137)	(46,230)	(34,902)	(28,882)	(30,775)	(28,246)
Other income (expense), net	(507)	8,712	7,789	7,508	(689)	(1,619)	14,142	30,365	(5,101)	7,631	9,763
Earnings before taxes on income, cumulative effect of accounting changes and extraordinary item	66,044	58,175	54,635	86,326	170,939	75,961	65,004	124,614	85,195	152,338	208,562
Provision for taxes on income	25,097	20,943	18,576	24,792	62,393	26,966	26,665	45,700	29,393	53,726	71,847
Tax rate	38.0%	36.0%	34.0%	28.7%	36.5%	35.5%	41.0%	36.7%	34.5%	35.3%	34.4%
Net earnings before cumulative effect of accounting changes and extraordinary item	40,947	37,232	36,059	61,534	108,546	48,995	38,339	78,914	55,802	98,612	136,715
Cumulative effect of accounting changes, net of tax	–	–	–	–	–	–	(50,292)	–	–	–	–
Extraordinary item, net of tax	–	–	–	(3,445)	–	–	–	–	–	–	–
Net earnings (loss)	40,947	37,232	36,059	58,089	108,546	48,995	(11,953)	78,914	55,802	98,612	136,715
Preferred dividends	–	–	–	–	–	–	–	–	–	–	6
Net earnings (loss) available for common stockholders	$ 40,947	$ 37,232	$ 36,059	$ 58,089	$ 108,546	$ 48,995	$ (11,953)	$ 78,914	$ 55,802	$ 98,612	$ 136,709
Financial returns											
Percent return on beginning of the year common stockholders' equity[1]	4.4%	3.9%	3.8%	6.2%	12.0%	5.4%	4.0%	8.6%	6.2%	11.9%	20.3%
Percent return on net sales[1]	2.4%	2.4%	2.3%	3.7%	6.8%	3.3%	2.8%	5.9%	4.5%	7.9%	11.1%
Per common share											
Basic net earnings[1]	$ 1.41	$ 1.28	$ 1.25	$ 2.01	$ 3.72	$ 1.68	$ 1.31	$ 2.71	$ 1.92	$ 3.41	$ 4.79
Net cash provided by operations, excluding working capital changes	$ 7.25	$ 6.94	$ 6.69	$ 7.91	$ 9.38	$ 6.77	$ 5.85	$ 5.71	$ 5.35	$ 6.77	$ 8.44
Cash dividends	$ 1.74	$ 1.74	$ 1.71	$ 1.67	$ 1.615	$ 1.57	$ 1.515	$ 1.425	$ 1.34	$ 1.23	$ 1.08
Common stockholders' equity at year end	$ 31.79	$ 32.19	$ 32.82	$ 33.06	$ 32.59	$ 30.85	$ 30.86	$ 32.79	$ 31.51	$ 30.93	$ 28.74
Common shares (in thousands)											
Average shares outstanding	28,947	29,000	28,930	28,888	29,157	29,217	29,184	29,110	29,012	28,935	28,513
Outstanding at year end, net of treasury stock	28,972	28,919	28,995	28,866	28,962	29,224	29,199	29,144	29,033	28,971	28,859
Approximate number of common stockholders at year end	3,200	3,400	3,600	3,700	3,300	3,500	3,600	3,600	3,800	4,000	4,100
Price range of common stock											
High	$ 45.50	$ 48.38	$ 52.75	$ 44.88	$ 44.13	$ 49.50	$ 51.88	$ 50.00	$ 47.00	$ 44.50	$ 38.63
Low	$ 32.50	$ 31.00	$ 39.00	$ 35.13	$ 37.13	$ 35.50	$ 38.25	$ 36.75	$ 27.75	$ 23.00	$ 30.75
Employment											
Approximate number of employees at year end	7,000	6,800	6,700	6,700	6,600	6,700	7,000	7,000	7,400	7,700	7,400
Wages, salaries and cost of employee benefits	$ 465,730	$ 437,601	$ 417,422	$ 410,052	$ 405,016	$ 391,160	$ 389,597	$ 376,537	$ 356,796	$ 338,888	$ 320,337
Selected production statistics (in thousands)											
Oriented strand board (square feet, 3/8" basis)	1,101,000	1,077,000	977,000	1,017,000	1,063,000	1,080,000	1,078,000	1,066,000	964,000	645,000	474,000
Lumber, domestic (board feet, dry)	608,000	577,000	534,000	491,000	441,000	408,000	420,000	406,000	324,000	367,000	358,000
Plywood, domestic (square feet, 3/8" basis)	222,000	191,000	254,000	240,000	289,000	298,000	312,000	331,000	310,000	307,000	307,000
Particleboard (square feet, 3/4" basis)	70,000	69,000	67,000	63,000	67,000	67,000	64,000	68,000	65,000	62,000	70,000
Printing papers (tons)	375	359	372	354	344	341	322	317	305	311	297
Pulp (air-dry tons)	925	953	899	878	873	816	811	845	870	869	863
Paperboard (tons)	596	620	614	575	582	549	545	563	562	574	560
Tissue paper (tons)	162	154	160	143	144	135	131	86	85	87	86

1 The 1993 return on equity, return on sales and loss per share after accounting changes were (1.2)%, (.9)% and $(.41), respectively

The Mead Corporation
Agency: NUFORIA
Art Director: Darren Namaye
Creative Directors: Howard Belk, Darren Namaye
Designers: Darren Namaye, Hitomi Murai

Mead
98
BALANCE
The Mead Corporation 1998 Annual Report

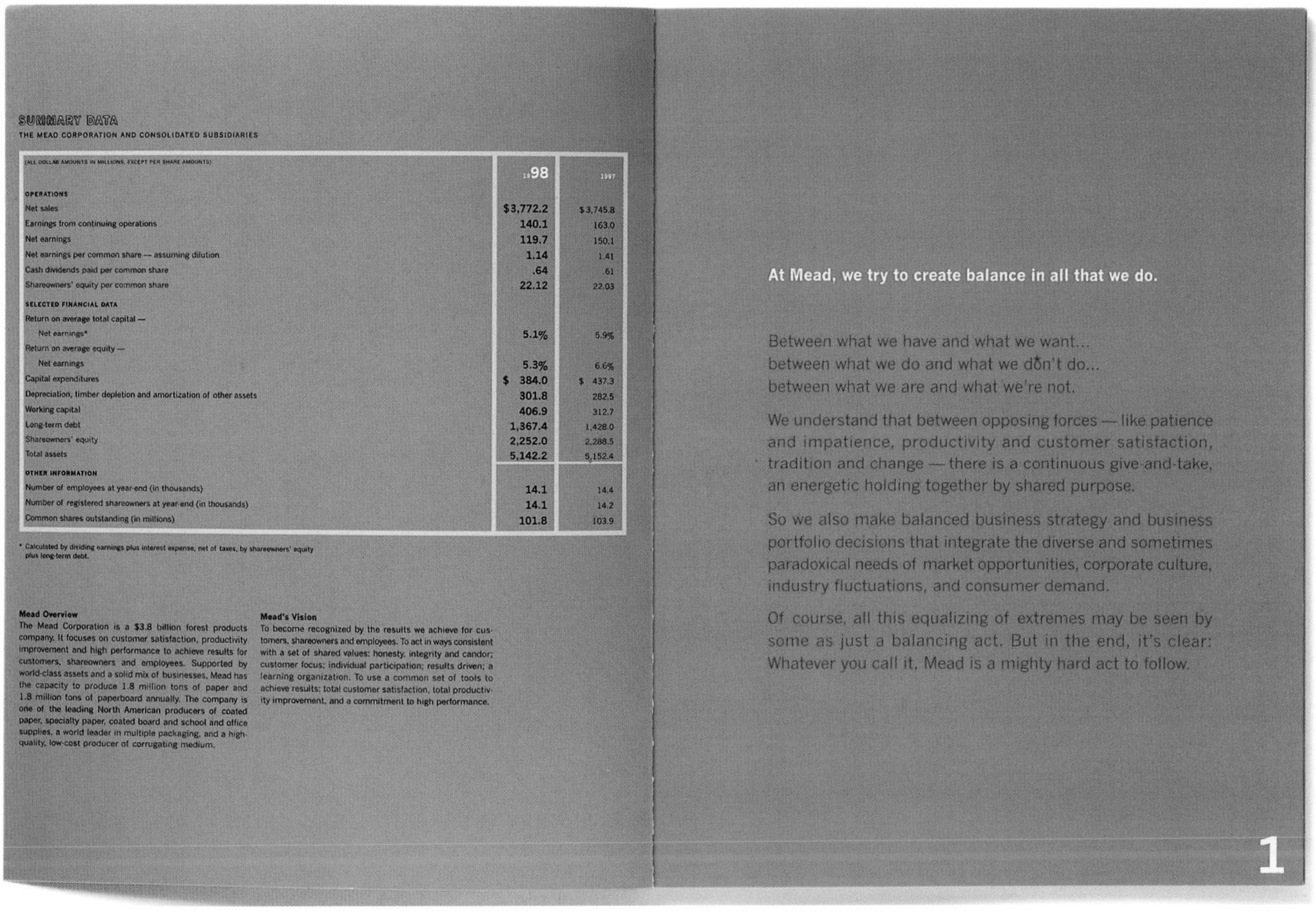

SUMMARY DATA

THE MEAD CORPORATION AND CONSOLIDATED SUBSIDIARIES

(ALL DOLLAR AMOUNTS IN MILLIONS, EXCEPT PER SHARE AMOUNTS)	1998	1997
OPERATIONS		
Net sales	$3,772.2	$3,745.8
Earnings from continuing operations	140.1	163.0
Net earnings	119.7	150.1
Net earnings per common share — assuming dilution	1.14	1.41
Cash dividends paid per common share	.64	.61
Shareowners' equity per common share	22.12	22.03
SELECTED FINANCIAL DATA		
Return on average total capital —		
Net earnings*	5.1%	5.9%
Return on average equity —		
Net earnings	5.3%	6.6%
Capital expenditures	$ 384.0	$ 437.3
Depreciation, timber depletion and amortization of other assets	301.8	282.5
Working capital	406.9	312.7
Long-term debt	1,367.4	1,428.0
Shareowners' equity	2,252.0	2,288.5
Total assets	5,142.2	5,152.4
OTHER INFORMATION		
Number of employees at year-end (in thousands)	14.1	14.4
Number of registered shareowners at year-end (in thousands)	14.1	14.2
Common shares outstanding (in millions)	101.8	103.9

* Calculated by dividing earnings plus interest expense, net of taxes, by shareowners' equity plus long-term debt.

Mead Overview

The Mead Corporation is a $3.8 billion forest products company. It focuses on customer satisfaction, productivity improvement and high performance to achieve results for customers, shareowners and employees. Supported by world-class assets and a solid mix of businesses, Mead has the capacity to produce 1.8 million tons of paper and 1.8 million tons of paperboard annually. The company is one of the leading North American producers of coated paper, specialty paper, coated board and school and office supplies, a world leader in multiple packaging, and a high-quality, low-cost producer of corrugating medium.

Mead's Vision

To become recognized by the results we achieve for customers, shareowners and employees. To act in ways consistent with a set of shared values: honesty, integrity and candor; customer focus; individual participation; results driven; a learning organization. To use a common set of tools to achieve results: total customer satisfaction, total productivity improvement, and a commitment to high performance.

At Mead, we try to create balance in all that we do.

Between what we have and what we want...
between what we do and what we don't do...
between what we are and what we're not.

We understand that between opposing forces — like patience and impatience, productivity and customer satisfaction, tradition and change — there is a continuous give-and-take, an energetic holding together by shared purpose.

So we also make balanced business strategy and business portfolio decisions that integrate the diverse and sometimes paradoxical needs of market opportunities, corporate culture, industry fluctuations, and consumer demand.

Of course, all this equalizing of extremes may be seen by some as just a balancing act. But in the end, it's clear: Whatever you call it, Mead is a mighty hard act to follow.

1

Merry
Christmas

PATIENCE

But patience, we know, is a virtue. We recognize that long-term gain often requires long-term planning. We also understand that forward-thinking strategies demand step-by-step implementation. Therefore, we stay focused on our core businesses of coated and specialty papers, packaging and paperboard, and school and office products. We also continue to identify and implement initiatives designed to enhance our financial performance immediately and over the long-term. Our patient impatience has helped us transform Mead from an average company in 1992 to one of the best performing in the forest products industry today.

13

CHANGE

While our traditions provide a very stable foundation for the company, we also recognize the need for constant change. Long-term success requires us to continually adapt our products and services to meet the changing demands of a global marketplace. We're successful because of our ability to anticipate and respond to customer needs, introduce new products, seize new business opportunities, invest in new technologies, and listen to and implement the best ideas from any source.

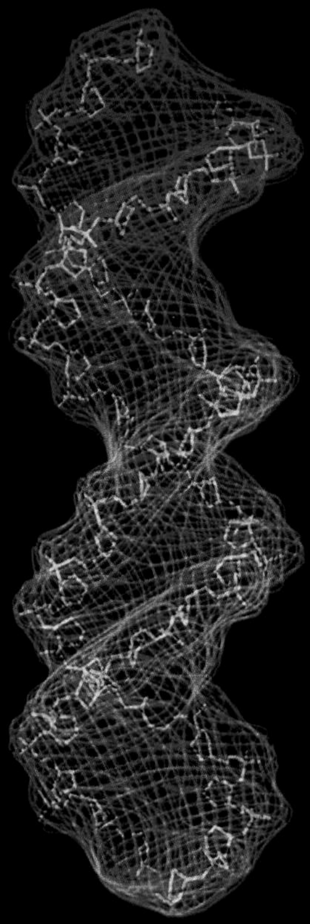

FOREST

Each of our 2.1 million acres of forests is managed under the Sustainable Forestry Initiative℠ of the American Forest & Paper Association. In short, we plant more trees than we harvest. We protect special areas and are always on the lookout for rare species of plants and animals. Where we cut timber, we help the earth regenerate. Our foresters are true environmentalists who protect the land for future generations. Balancing our production of paper with sustainable forests is more than a living — it's a living commitment to what matters most.

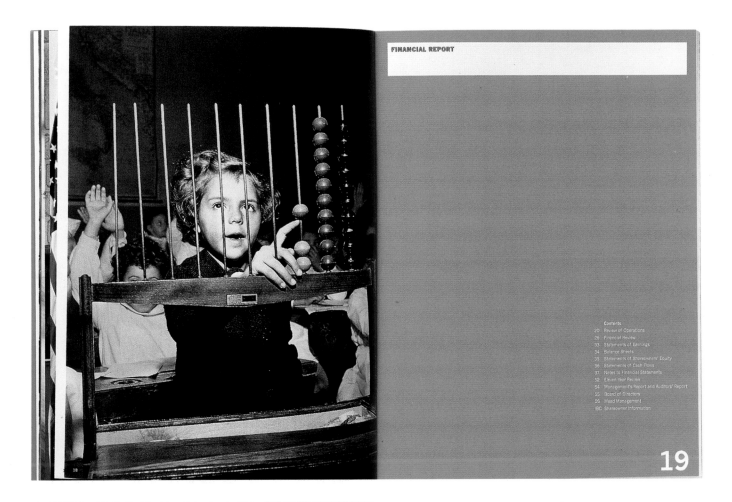

FINANCIAL REPORT

Contents

ELEVEN-YEAR REVIEW

(ALL DOLLAR AMOUNTS IN MILLIONS, EXCEPT PER SHARE AMOUNTS)	1998	1997	1996	1995
OPERATIONS				
Net sales	$3,772.2	$3,745.8	$3,303.9	$3,402.8
Cost of products sold	3,049.5	3,008.5	2,578.2	2,521.6
Gross profit	722.7	737.3	725.7	881.2
Selling and administrative expenses	422.3	404.4	393.4	370.8
Earnings from operations	300.4	332.9	332.3	510.4
Other revenues (expenses) — net	34.2	7.3	9.4	31.9
Interest and debt expense	(109.0)	(98.2)	(57.7)	(69.4)
Earnings from continuing operations before income taxes	225.6	242.0	284.0	472.9
Income taxes	83.7	87.9	104.5	178.0
Earnings from continuing operations before equity in net earnings (loss) of investees	141.9	154.1	179.5	294.9
Equity in net earnings (loss) of investees	(1.8)	8.9	4.3	39.0
Earnings from continuing operations	140.1	163.0	183.8	333.9
Discontinued operations	(20.4)	(12.9)	11.5	16.1
Extraordinary item				
Cumulative effect of change in accounting principle				
Net earnings	$ 119.7	$ 150.1	$ 195.3	$ 350.0
PER COMMON SHARE — ASSUMING DILUTION				
Earnings from continuing operations	$ 1.34	$ 1.53	$ 1.73	$ 3.02
Discontinued operations	(.20)	(.12)	.11	.15
Extraordinary item				
Cumulative effect of change in accounting principle				
Net earnings	$ 1.14	$ 1.41	$ 1.84	$ 3.17
PER SHARE AMOUNTS				
Cash dividends paid	$ .64	$ .61	$ .59	$ .55
Book value	22.12	22.03	21.55	20.42
Price range:				
High	37.31	37.69	30.69	32.07
Low	25.94	24.88	24.25	24.32
FINANCIAL POSITION				
Current assets	$1,086.4	$ 951.2	$ 958.6	$1,135.4
Investments and other assets	683.1	644.6	617.2	580.2
Timber and timberlands — net	381.0	362.5	366.2	233.7
Land and land improvements, plant and equipment — net	2,991.7	2,911.3	2,718.4	2,094.6
Net assets of discontinued operations		282.8	245.5	240.1
	$5,142.2	$5,152.4	$4,905.9	$4,284.0
Current liabilities	$ 679.5	$ 638.5	$ 678.5	$ 734.2
Long-term debt	1,367.4	1,428.0	1,239.7	694.8
Deferred items	843.3	797.4	741.3	694.8
Shareowners' equity	2,252.0	2,288.5	2,246.4	2,160.2
	$5,142.2	$5,152.4	$4,905.9	$4,284.0
ADDITIONAL DATA				
Capital expenditures	$ 384.0	$ 437.3	$ 428.7	$ 261.0
Depreciation, depletion and amortization	301.8	282.5	244.4	230.8
Average shares outstanding — assuming dilution (in millions)[1]	104.9	106.4	106.3	110.6
Number of employees at year end (in thousands)	14.1	14.4	14.1	13.0
Number of registered shareowners at year-end (in thousands)	14.1	14.2	14.9	15.7

(ALL DOLLAR AMOUNTS IN MILLIONS, EXCEPT PER SHARE AMOUNTS)	1994	1993	1992	1991	1990	1989	1988
OPERATIONS							
Net sales	$3,012.0	$2,806.9	$2,800.4	$2,675.2	$2,737.5	$2,660.0	$2,675.7
Cost of products sold	2,436.6	2,284.7	2,300.5	2,202.7	2,210.8	2,112.8	2,048.6
Gross profit	575.4	522.2	499.9	472.5	526.7	547.2	627.1
Selling and administrative expenses	364.7	304.6	396.3	309.3	355.8	254.0	268.5
Earnings from operations	210.7	217.6	103.6	163.2	170.9	293.2	358.6
Other revenues (expenses) — net	(40.6)	6.6	(5.0)	17.1	20.3	53.8	242.2
Interest and debt expense	(101.1)	(94.6)	(99.5)	(112.9)	(92.0)	(81.3)	(69.1)
Earnings from continuing operations before income taxes	69.0	129.6	(.9)	67.4	99.2	265.7	531.7
Income taxes	29.1	54.7	(1.3)	20.5	32.9	94.3	207.0
Earnings from continuing operations before equity in net earnings (loss) of investees	39.9	74.9	.4	46.9	66.3	171.4	324.7
Equity in net earnings (loss) of investees	59.8	18.4	6.0	(18.1)	11.7	44.1	28.8
Earnings from continuing operations	99.7	93.3	6.4	28.8	78.0	215.5	353.5
Discontinued operations	607.3	30.9	31.2	36.8	(46.3)	.3	(.7)
Extraordinary item	(11.3)				6.9		
Cumulative effect of change in accounting principle			34.0	(58.7)			
Net earnings	$ 695.7	$ 124.2	$ 71.6	$ 6.9	$ 38.6	$ 215.8	$ 352.8
PER COMMON SHARE — ASSUMING DILUTION							
Earnings from continuing operations	$ .84	$ .78	$ .05	$ .25	$ .63	$ 1.66	$ 2.69
Discontinued operations	4.85	.26	.27	.31	(.37)	.01	
Extraordinary item	(.09)				.05		
Cumulative effect of change in accounting principle			.29	(.50)			
Net earnings	$ 5.60	$ 1.04	$ .61	$ .06	$ .31	$ 1.67	$ 2.69
PER SHARE AMOUNTS							
Cash dividends paid	$ .50	$ .50	$ .50	$ .50	$ .49	$ .43	$ .37
Book value	18.61	13.33	12.73	12.67	13.14	13.21	11.91
Price range:							
High	26.63	24.25	20.82	18.63	19.75	23.32	24.75
Low	19.57	18.75	16.57	12.25	9.75	17.13	14.50
FINANCIAL POSITION							
Current assets	$1,596.1	$ 739.8	$ 773.5	$ 691.5	$ 593.8	$ 604.2	$ 566.1
Investments and other assets	592.2	390.7	305.1	279.1	275.3	335.0	559.9
Timber and timberlands — net	224.7	219.3	213.1	212.6	217.0	213.9	173.9
Land and land improvements, plant and equipment — net	2,048.2	1,974.5	1,900.3	1,928.7	1,919.0	1,662.2	1,311.4
Net assets of discontinued operations	301.1	659.9	641.3	698.7	714.9	710.4	729.0
	$4,762.3	$3,984.2	$3,833.3	$3,810.6	$3,720.0	$3,525.7	$3,340.3
Current liabilities	$ 987.8	$ 541.0	$ 547.4	$ 587.0	$ 537.6	$ 532.4	$ 513.1
Long-term debt	957.7	1,360.0	1,317.5	1,300.4	1,245.0	947.7	920.4
Deferred items	634.2	505.2	473.0	444.8	406.1	364.8	394.3
Shareowners' equity	2,182.6	1,578.0	1,495.4	1,478.4	1,531.3	1,680.8	1,512.5
	$4,762.3	$3,984.2	$3,833.3	$3,810.6	$3,720.0	$3,525.7	$3,340.3
ADDITIONAL DATA							
Capital expenditures	$ 314.0	$ 301.8	$ 212.7	$ 225.9	$ 416.4	$ 542.1	$ 301.6
Depreciation, depletion and amortization	219.6	247.1	234.6	222.0	182.1	158.3	160.5
Average shares outstanding — assuming dilution (in millions)[1]	125.1	119.2	118.0	117.1	124.4	134.7	134.5
Number of employees at year end (in thousands)	13.7	13.2	14.0	15.0	15.0	15.0	14.8
Number of registered shareowners at year-end (in thousands)	16.7	17.3	18.0	20.3	23.2	23.1	23.3

1 Includes 5.2 million shares in 1994 and 8.4 million shares in 1989 and 1988 of common stock equivalents relating to outstanding convertible debentures.

Sociedade de Distribuição de Papel
Agency: João Machado Design, Lda
Art & Creative Director, Designer, Illustrator: João Machado

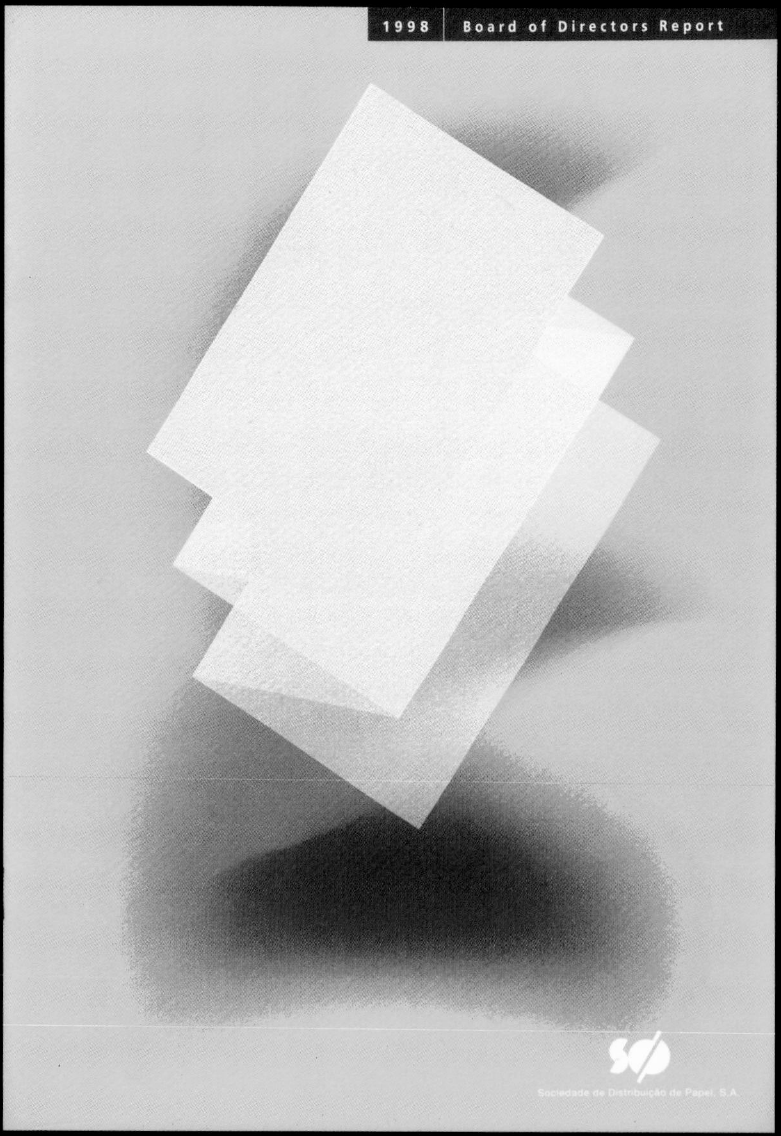
1998
Board of Directors Report
Sociedade de Distribuição de Papel, S.A.

FOREWORD

Profitability on sales can be considered normal and fair despite the continuing trend of price reduction.

As the warehouse at Vale Flores in Sintra became fully operational, the consolidation and adaptation to new working methods was also an important feature of this financial year.

The new warehouse at Sintra was officially inaugurated in the presence of numerous clients and suppliers, as well as friends and other dignitaries who wished to be associated with the event.

COMMERCIAL ACTIVITY

Close monitoring of the market meant that the basic variables of the business could be adjusted when necessary, resulting in a good performance.

The three operating companies, Papéis Carreira, Fernandes Distribuição and Sacopel and the three sales units – Comercial 4, Special Accounts and Board Department – placed a total of 39.975 tons of paper and board, 1.327 thousand M2 of self-adhesive paper and 128.940 units of one thousand envelopes in the market (direct invoicing and agent sales).

Comercial 4 and Special Accounts presented exceptional growth in relation to the previous year. The total volume of sales increased by approximately 18,8%, 9,4% above the market growth.

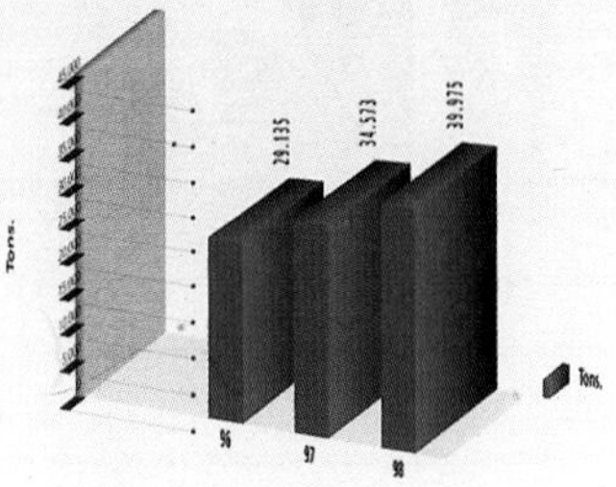
Tons.
28.135
34.573
39.975
96
97
98
Tons.

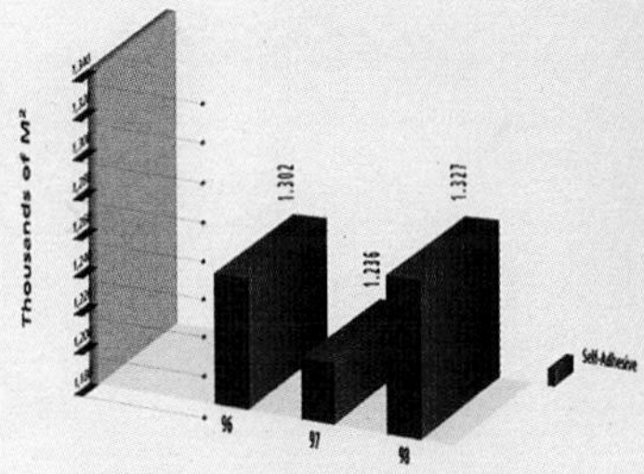
Thousands of M²
1.302
1.236
1.327
96
97
98
Self-Adhesive

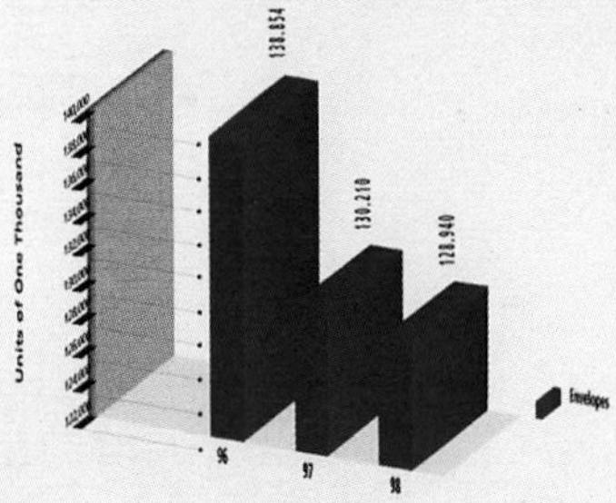
Units of One Thousand
138.854
130.210
128.940
96
97
98
Envelopes

Operations in the Autonomous Region of Madeira were consolidated by Papéis Carreira Madeira, Lda., with marginal profits for the year.

Sacopel, Lda. and Comercial 4 successfully initiated commercial operations in the north of the country.

MAIN SUPPLIERS OF SDP DURING 1998

National	Foreign
A. Vaz dos Santos	Abitibi
Cávado	Arjo Wiggins
Conpapel	Aussedat Rey
Fabrica de Papel do Caima	Cartiera di Crusinallo
I. P. T. (Porto Cavaleiros)	Champion
Indústrias J. F. Couto	Clariana
Kores	Colombier
P. F. I. C.	Curtis Fine Papers
Papéis Dinha	Divipa
Papéis Inapa	Echezarreta
Prado	Fedrigoni
Renova	Forest Alliance
Valpel	Intermills
	Koehler
	Manter
	Miquel & Costas y Miquel
	Munkedals
	Neusiedler
	Norske Skog
	Papelera Amaroz
	Reacto
	Sappi Europe
	Sarrió
	Scheufelen
	Smith Anderson
	Smurfit-Condat
	Stora
	Tullis Russel
	UPM – Kymmene
	Van Leer
	Walki

FINANCIAL ACTIVITY

Business and economic results were extremely positive in 1998. Thus sales volume measured by tons grew by approximately 18,8% (direct invoicing) and 0,9% (agent sales), whilst the increase in total income from sales reached 11,7%. It must be noted however that sales prices decreased during the period under review.

Sales profitability held at the satisfactory level of 20,6%. This clearly shows that the evolution of this important indicator was closely monitored with the introduction of price corrections, as and when the market permitted.

Net profits of 262.556 contos, as well as healthy operating results contributed to net cash generated by operations of 340.077 contos.

An investment of 2.025.000 contos in negotiable securities during the financial year should also be highlighted.

Particular importance was given to the development of current assets and it was established that provisions for bad debts would not be reinforced as the previous years figure was deemed sufficient to cover credit risk.

Justifications for the significant expansion in stock levels compared to the previous year were twofold: opportunity provisioning and the storage of a substantial quantity of paper belonging to a client in our warehouse.

Valentis
Agency: Cahan & Associates
Art & Creative Director: Bill Cahan
Designer: Sharrie Brooks
Copywriter: Bennet Weintraub

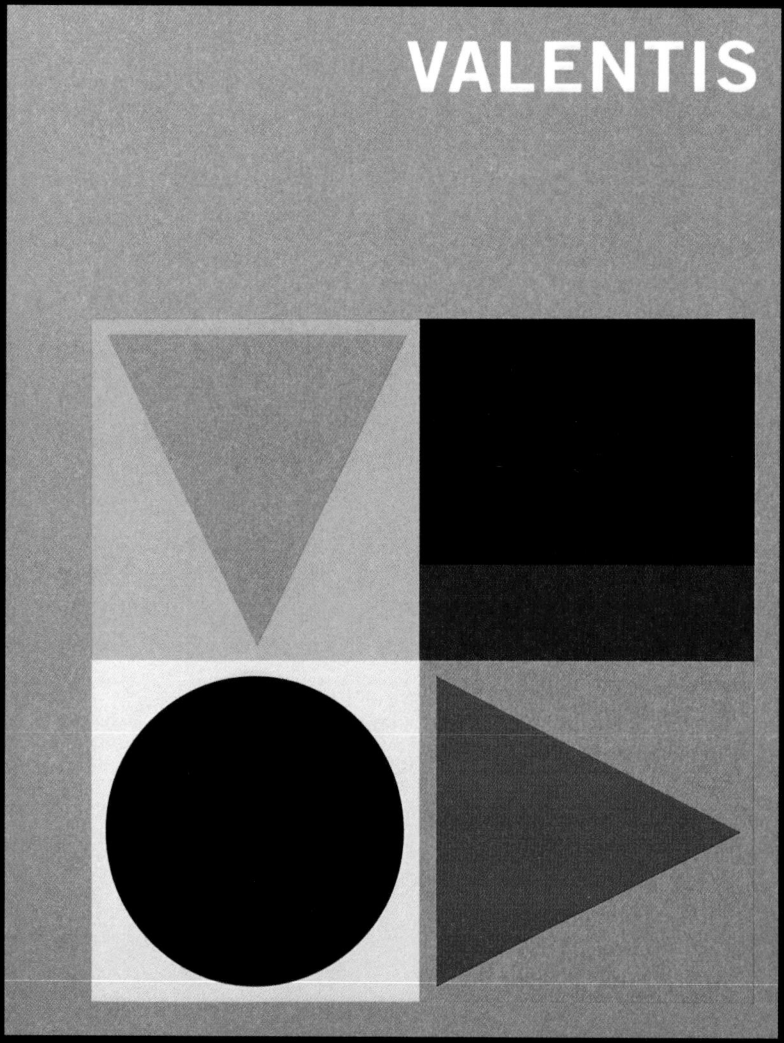
VALENTIS

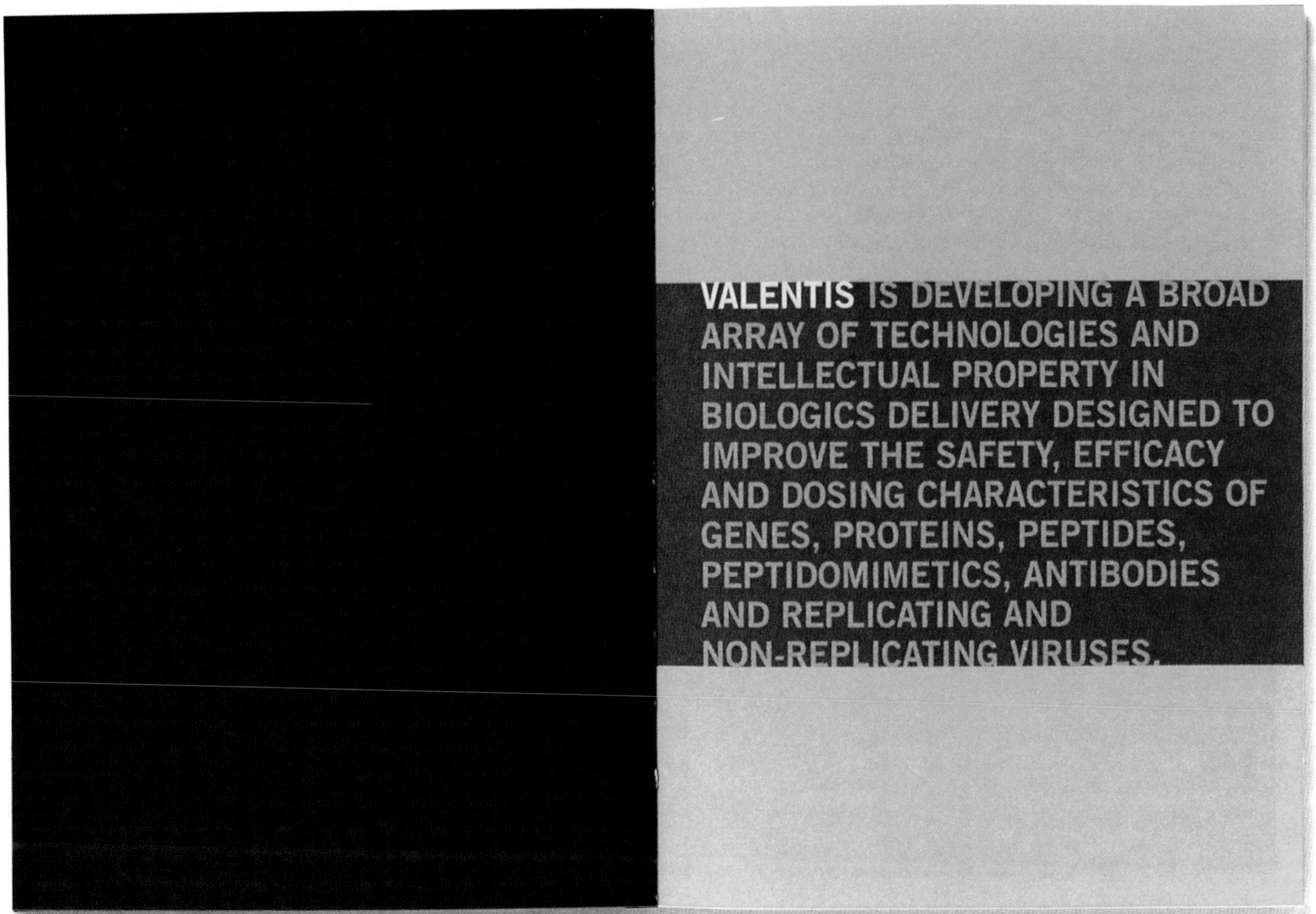
VALENTIS IS DEVELOPING A BROAD ARRAY OF TECHNOLOGIES AND INTELLECTUAL PROPERTY IN BIOLOGICS DELIVERY DESIGNED TO IMPROVE THE SAFETY, EFFICACY AND DOSING CHARACTERISTICS OF GENES, PROTEINS, PEPTIDES, PEPTIDOMIMETICS, ANTIBODIES AND REPLICATING AND NON-REPLICATING VIRUSES.

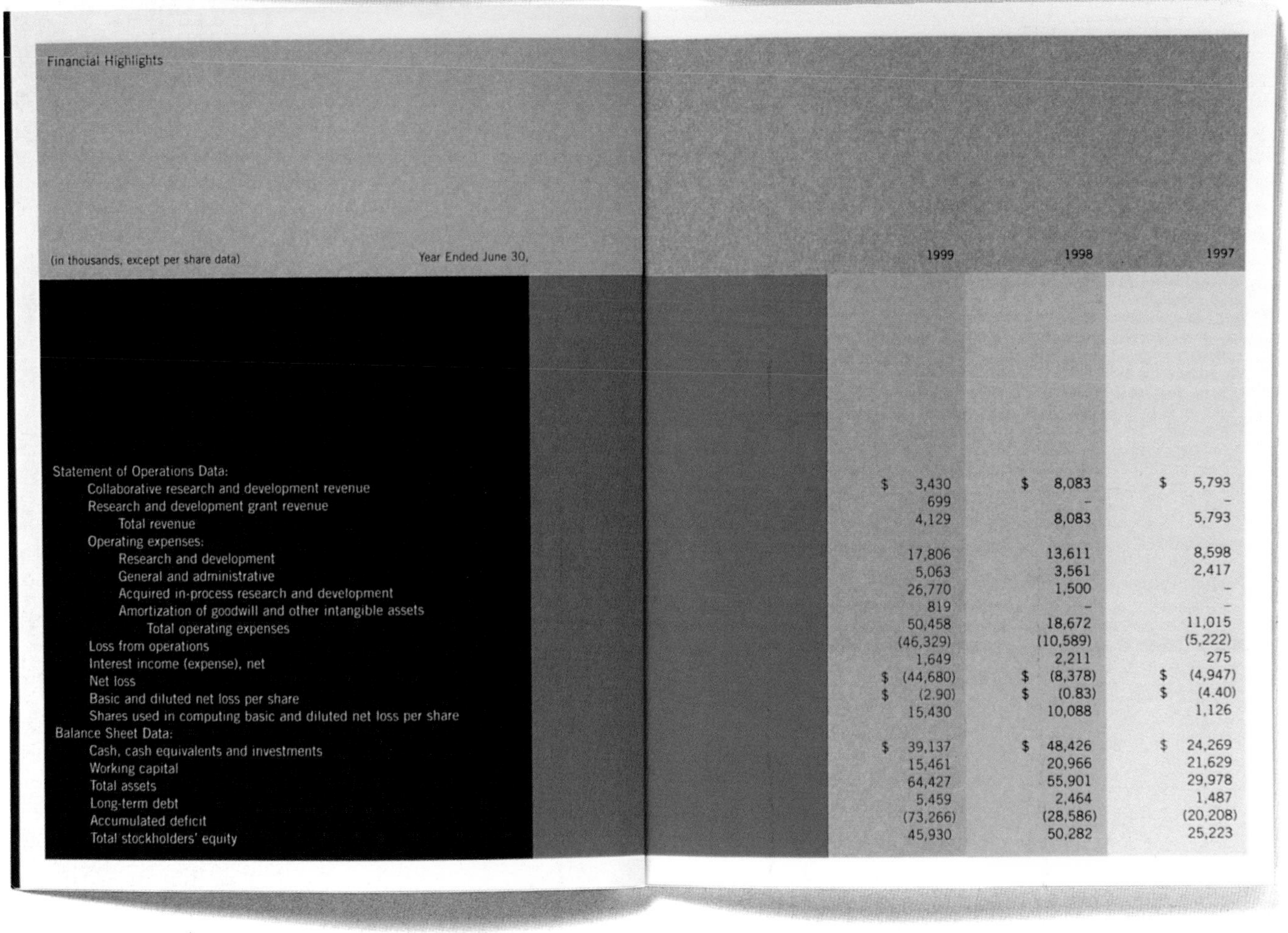

Financial Highlights

(in thousands, except per share data) Year Ended June 30,	1999	1998	1997
Statement of Operations Data:			
Collaborative research and development revenue	$ 3,430	$ 8,083	$ 5,793
Research and development grant revenue	699	–	–
Total revenue	4,129	8,083	5,793
Operating expenses:			
Research and development	17,806	13,611	8,598
General and administrative	5,063	3,561	2,417
Acquired in-process research and development	26,770	1,500	–
Amortization of goodwill and other intangible assets	819	–	–
Total operating expenses	50,458	18,672	11,015
Loss from operations	(46,329)	(10,589)	(5,222)
Interest income (expense), net	1,649	2,211	275
Net loss	$ (44,680)	$ (8,378)	$ (4,947)
Basic and diluted net loss per share	$ (2.90)	$ (0.83)	$ (4.40)
Shares used in computing basic and diluted net loss per share	15,430	10,088	1,126
Balance Sheet Data:			
Cash, cash equivalents and investments	$ 39,137	$ 48,426	$ 24,269
Working capital	15,461	20,966	21,629
Total assets	64,427	55,901	29,978
Long-term debt	5,459	2,464	1,487
Accumulated deficit	(73,266)	(28,586)	(20,208)
Total stockholders' equity	45,930	50,282	25,223

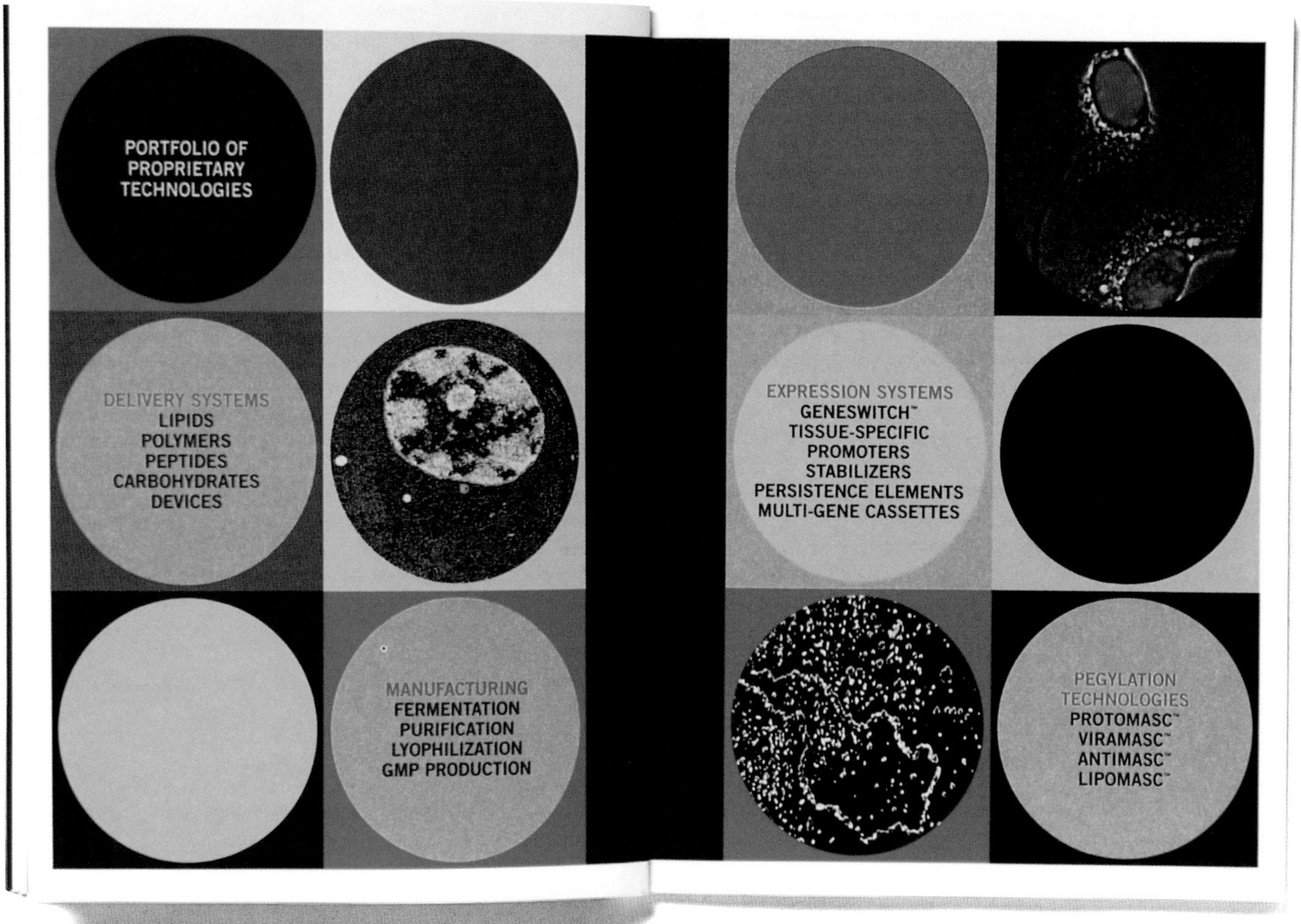
PORTFOLIO OF PROPRIETARY TECHNOLOGIES
DELIVERY SYSTEMS
LIPIDS
POLYMERS
PEPTIDES
CARBOHYDRATES
DEVICES
MANUFACTURING
FERMENTATION
PURIFICATION
LYOPHILIZATION
GMP PRODUCTION
EXPRESSION SYSTEMS
GENESWITCH™
TISSUE-SPECIFIC
PROMOTERS
STABILIZERS
PERSISTENCE ELEMENTS
MULTI-GENE CASSETTES
PEGYLATION TECHNOLOGIES
PROTOMASC™
VIRAMASC™
ANTIMASC™
LIPOMASC™

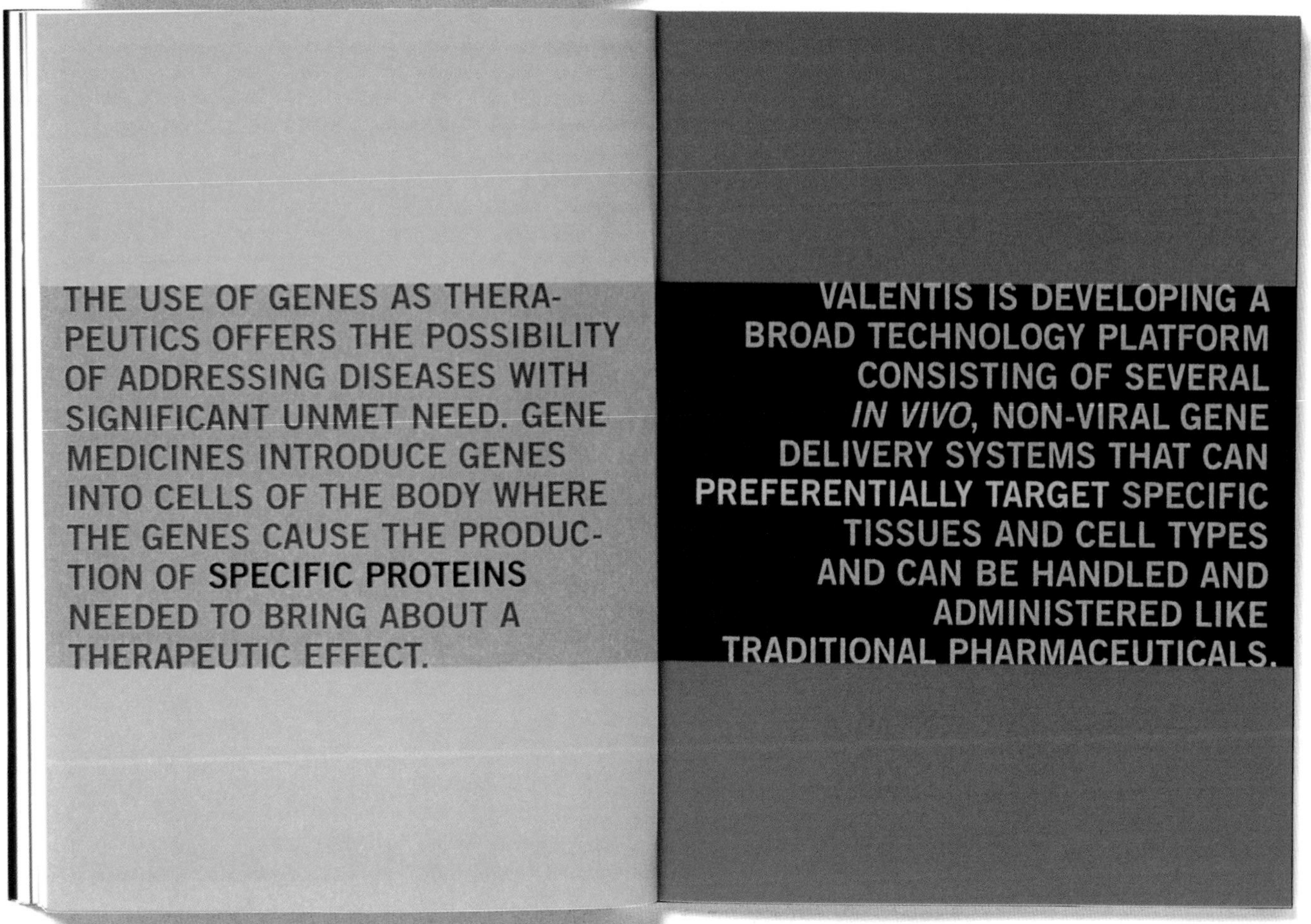
THE USE OF GENES AS THERAPEUTICS OFFERS THE POSSIBILITY OF ADDRESSING DISEASES WITH SIGNIFICANT UNMET NEED. GENE MEDICINES INTRODUCE GENES INTO CELLS OF THE BODY WHERE THE GENES CAUSE THE PRODUCTION OF SPECIFIC PROTEINS NEEDED TO BRING ABOUT A THERAPEUTIC EFFECT.
VALENTIS IS DEVELOPING A BROAD TECHNOLOGY PLATFORM CONSISTING OF SEVERAL IN VIVO, NON-VIRAL GENE DELIVERY SYSTEMS THAT CAN PREFERENTIALLY TARGET SPECIFIC TISSUES AND CELL TYPES AND CAN BE HANDLED AND ADMINISTERED LIKE TRADITIONAL PHARMACEUTICALS.

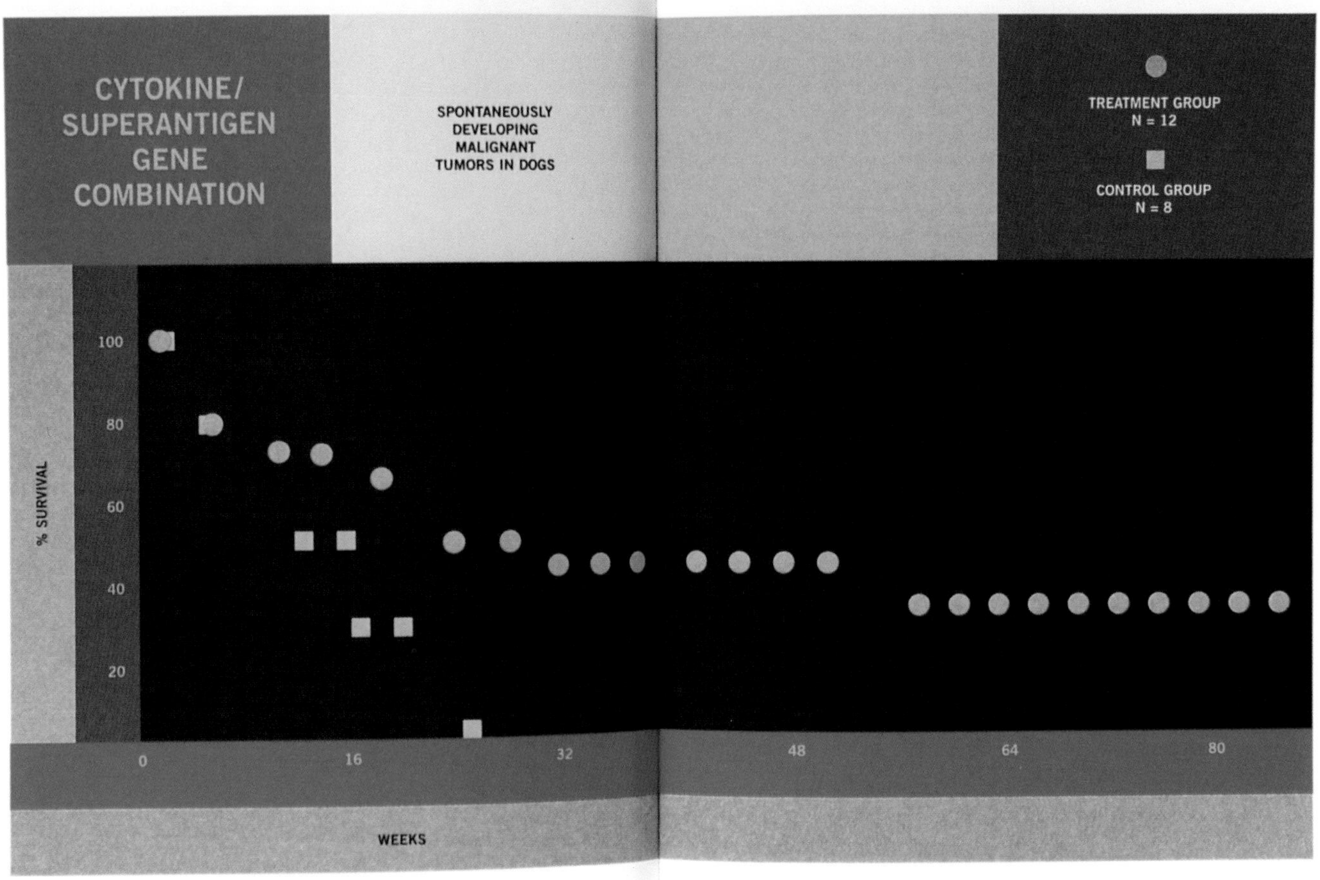
CYTOKINE/
SUPERANTIGEN
GENE
COMBINATION
SPONTANEOUSLY
DEVELOPING
MALIGNANT
TUMORS IN DOGS
TREATMENT GROUP
N = 12
CONTROL GROUP
N = 8
% SURVIVAL
100
80
60
40
20
0
16
32
48
64
80
WEEKS

Corporate Information

Officers

Benjamin F. McGraw, III, Pharm.D.
President and
Chief Executive Officer

Bennet Weintraub
Vice President Finance and
Chief Financial Officer

Rodney Pearlman, Ph.D.
Sr. Vice President
Research and Development

Kenneth Lynn
Sr. Vice President
Business Development and
Legal Affairs

Kathryn Stankis
Vice President
Human Resources

Alain Rolland, Pharm.D., Ph.D.
Vice President
Research and Development

Denny Liggitt, DVM, Ph.D.
Vice President
Pharmacology and Toxicology

Board of Directors

Benjamin F. McGraw, III, Pharm.D.
President and
Chief Executive Officer,
Valentis, Inc. and
Chairman of the Board

Patrick G. Enright
Diaz & Altschul Group, LLC

Russell M. Hirsch, M.D., Ph.D.
Mayfield Fund

Raju Kucherlapati, Ph.D.
Albert Einstein College
of Medicine

Bert O'Malley, M.D.
Baylor College of Medicine

Arthur M. Pappas
A.M. Pappas & Associates, LLC

Stanley T. Crooke, M.D.
Isis Pharmaceuticals

Gillian E. Francis, M.B., B.S.,
D.Sc., M.Sc.
PolyMASC Pharmaceuticals

Stockholder Information

Valentis

Corporate Headquarters
863A Mitten Road
Burlingame, CA 94010
Tel 650 697-1900
Fax 650 652-1990
www.valentis.com

The Woodlands Site

8301 New Trails Drive
The Woodlands, TX
77381-4248
Tel 281 364-1150
Fax 281 364-0858

PolyMASC Pharmaceuticals

Fleet Road
London NW3 2EZ
United Kingdom
Tel 44 171-284-3141
Fax 44 171-284-2212
www.polymasc.com

Corporate Counsel

Cooley Godward LLP
Palo Alto, CA

Annual Meeting

Tuesday, December 7, 1999
10:00 am
Valentis, Inc.
863A Mitten Road
Burlingame, CA 94010

SEC Form 10-K

A copy of the Form 10-K filed with the Securities and Exchange Commission can be obtained free of charge, by writing the Company at:
863A Mitten Road
Burlingame, CA 94010
Attn: Investor Relations

Transfer Agent

Boston Equiserve
Stockholder Services Division
PO Box 8040
Boston, MA 02266-8040
Tel 781 575-2000

Independent Auditors

Ernst & Young LLP

Common Stock Market Prices

Valentis, Inc. common stock is listed on the Nasdaq National Market System under the symbol VLTS. The Company's Common Stock began trading on September 15, 1997. The following table presents the quarterly high and low closing sales prices as quoted by NASDAQ.

	High	Low
1997		
Third Quarter (from 9/15)	$16.75	$12.37
Fourth Quarter	18.50	10.50
1998		
First Quarter	14.00	8.88
Second Quarter	8.88	6.38
Third Quarter	8.00	4.25
Fourth Quarter	6.94	4.00
1999		
First Quarter	6.75	4.06
Second Quarter	5.56	3.38
Third Quarter	6.50	3.75

As of September 30, 1999 there were approximately 752 stockholders of record of the Company's Common Stock.

Statements in this press release that are not strictly historical are "forward looking" statements as defined in the Private Securities Litigation Reform Act of 1995. There can be no assurance that Valentis will be able to develop a commercially viable gene-based therapeutic, that any of the programs will be partnered with a pharmaceutical partner, that necessary regulatory approvals will be obtained or that any clinical trials will be successful. The actual results may differ from those projected in the forward-looking statement due to risks and uncertainties that exist in the Company's operations and business environment. These are described more fully in the Valentis Annual Report on Form 10-K for the year ended June 30, 1999, filed with the Securities and Exchange Commission.

ANNUAL REPORT 1998 - 1999

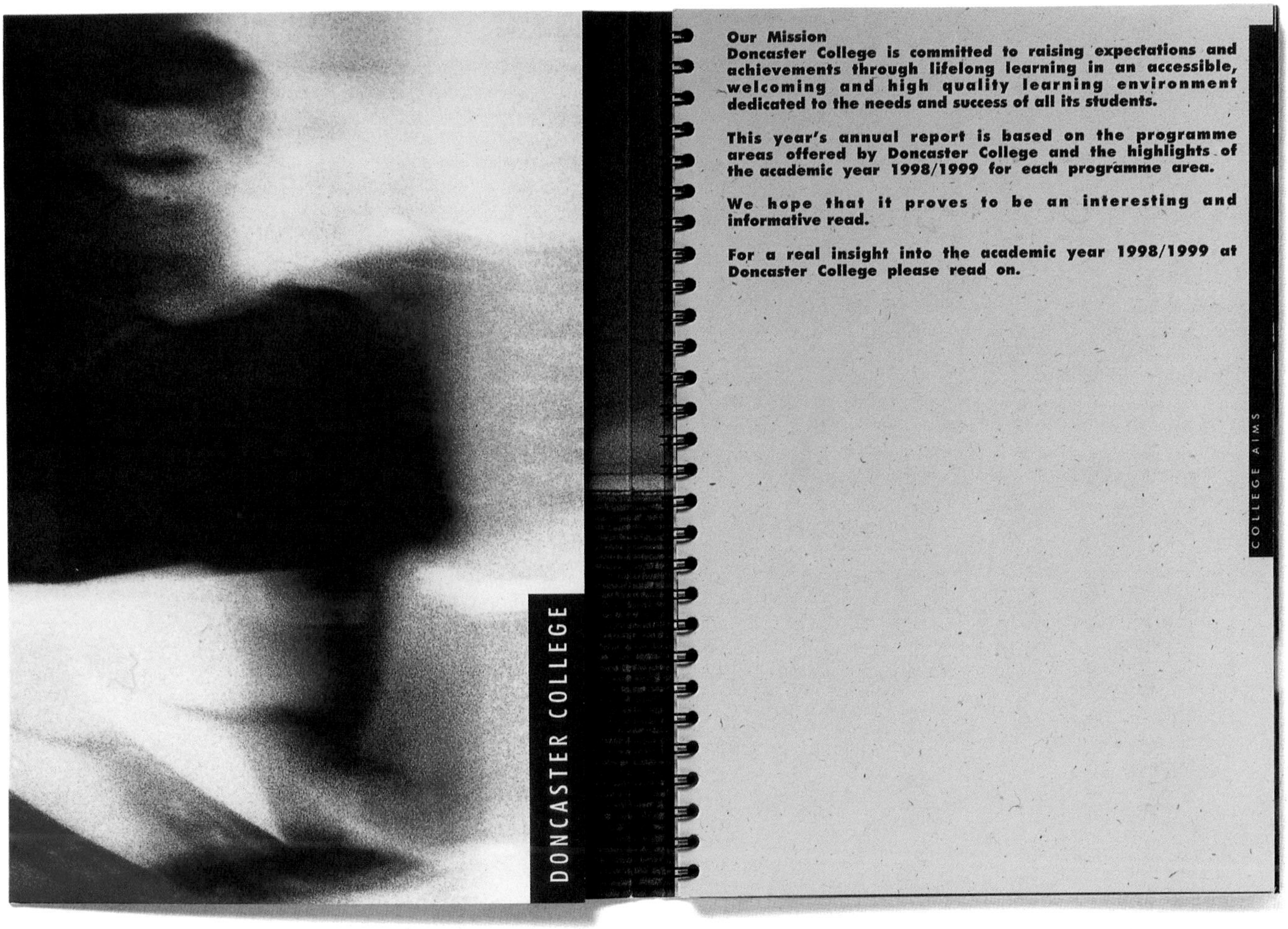

DONCASTER COLLEGE

Our Mission
Doncaster College is committed to raising expectations and achievements through lifelong learning in an accessible, welcoming and high quality learning environment dedicated to the needs and success of all its students.

This year's annual report is based on the programme areas offered by Doncaster College and the highlights of the academic year 1998/1999 for each programme area.

We hope that it proves to be an interesting and informative read.

For a real insight into the academic year 1998/1999 at Doncaster College please read on.

COLLEGE AIMS

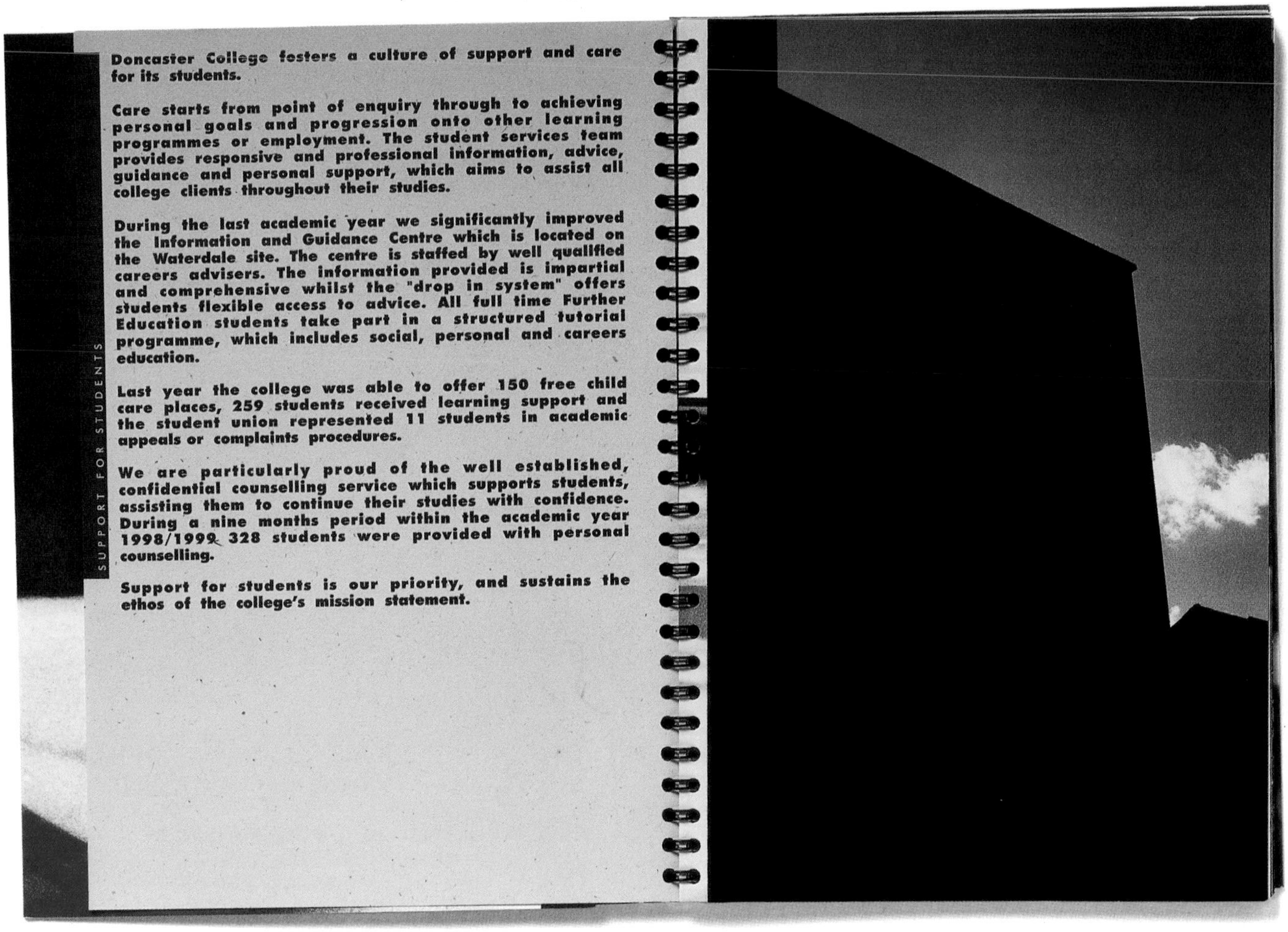

SUPPORT FOR STUDENTS

Doncaster College fosters a culture of support and care for its students.

Care starts from point of enquiry through to achieving personal goals and progression onto other learning programmes or employment. The student services team provides responsive and professional information, advice, guidance and personal support, which aims to assist all college clients throughout their studies.

During the last academic year we significantly improved the Information and Guidance Centre which is located on the Waterdale site. The centre is staffed by well qualified careers advisers. The information provided is impartial and comprehensive whilst the "drop in system" offers students flexible access to advice. All full time Further Education students take part in a structured tutorial programme, which includes social, personal and careers education.

Last year the college was able to offer 150 free child care places, 259 students received learning support and the student union represented 11 students in academic appeals or complaints procedures.

We are particularly proud of the well established, confidential counselling service which supports students, assisting them to continue their studies with confidence. During a nine months period within the academic year 1998/1999 328 students were provided with personal counselling.

Support for students is our priority, and sustains the ethos of the college's mission statement.

ART AND DESIGN

Students within the Art and Design sections consistently achieved good progression last year to both Further and Higher Education destinations.

This is borne out by the individual course records of achievement and destination, which show an 84% progression to HE. Another significant development is that courses with previously poor resources have been refurbished in line with a rolling programme of renewal. The Decorative Design section has benefited from investment during the last year and future plans include the expansion of the range of interior design courses.

To assist the teaching teams, part-time practitioners provide the necessary up-to-date commercial or professional expertise to support both the planning and delivery of the curriculum. There are many examples of joint briefs and projects across syllabus areas which enable students of various disciplines to achieve a combined and integrated experience. These projects have resulted in creative presentations to outside clients and collaborative work with schools or projects for charitable organisations.

The final show for all courses held at Church View was extremely well attended and received. Assessment and moderation reports from validating bodies confirmed the quality of both final shows and the learning experience on offer at Doncaster College.

The consolidation of the Northern Centre for Performing Arts portfolio, successes with Fashion Shows in the town centre, Hairdressing developments with the St Sepulchre Gate salon for skillshop training, and the development of hairdressing and beauty therapy at Stainforth, all contributed to widening offerings in the Arts at Doncaster College.

Success is not measured by achievement alone, but also by how the students' learning experience has been enhanced. This was recognised by the high number of nominations for the college's "Most Improved Student" award which came from the Students with Learning Difficulties and Disabilities section. SLDD students participated in the design of a memorial to mark the millennium, which is now on display in Doncaster town centre. The section is committed to providing an accessible and enriching learning environment for students of all disciplines and capabilities.

BUILT ENVIRONMENT AND MOTOR VEHICLE

The Built Environment and Motor Vehicle section is particularly proud of the excellent links that it has been developing with local schools.

Two secondary schools in the community, Balby Carr and Danum have a significant number of students studying for the GNVQ Built Environment at Foundation Level. We also have links and exchange visits with a construction college in Saint Etienne which greatly enriched the students' experience last year.

The Built Environment and Motor Vehicles section celebrated exceptional student achievements last year with formal recognition and reward ceremonies, including one sponsored by various local companies and with presentations by the Mayor. One electrical craft student received a national award and a curriculum student celebrated a "Life Time Careers" award.

In partnership with industry we hope to further develop our courses to the benefit of all of our students.

CONTACTS

GOVERNORS
Liam Hayes
David Holmes
Eric Straw
Farman Choudhry
Peter Mullinger
Peter Aldred
Peter Morley
Derek Kennedy
Jack Hobbs
Marie Hills
David Gibson
Alan Holloway
Lesley Cairns
Ted Jones
Dr Terry Ashurst

Principal and Chief Executive
Dr Terry Ashurst

Faculty Heads
Technology
Vic Briers
Client Services
Paul Barratt
Humanities
Neil Calloway
Business and Professional Studies
Chris Ball
Dearne Valley Business School
David Fell

The Principal and Governors would like to thank Viscount Catering Equipment for their financial support in the production of this report.

Doncaster College
Waterdale
Doncaster
DN1 3EX
Telephone: 01302 553553
Fax: 01302 553559
Website: www.don.ac.uk

■ DESIGN AND ART DIRECTION: ERROL MITCHELL ■ PHOTOGRAPHY: DAVE HISKEY ■ COPY: CAROL DEVINE ■ ELECTRONIC ARTWORK: ALLISON FLOWER ■ PRINT: J W NORTHEND LTD, SHEFFIELD
■ PRODUCED AND PUBLISHED BY DONCASTER COLLEGE

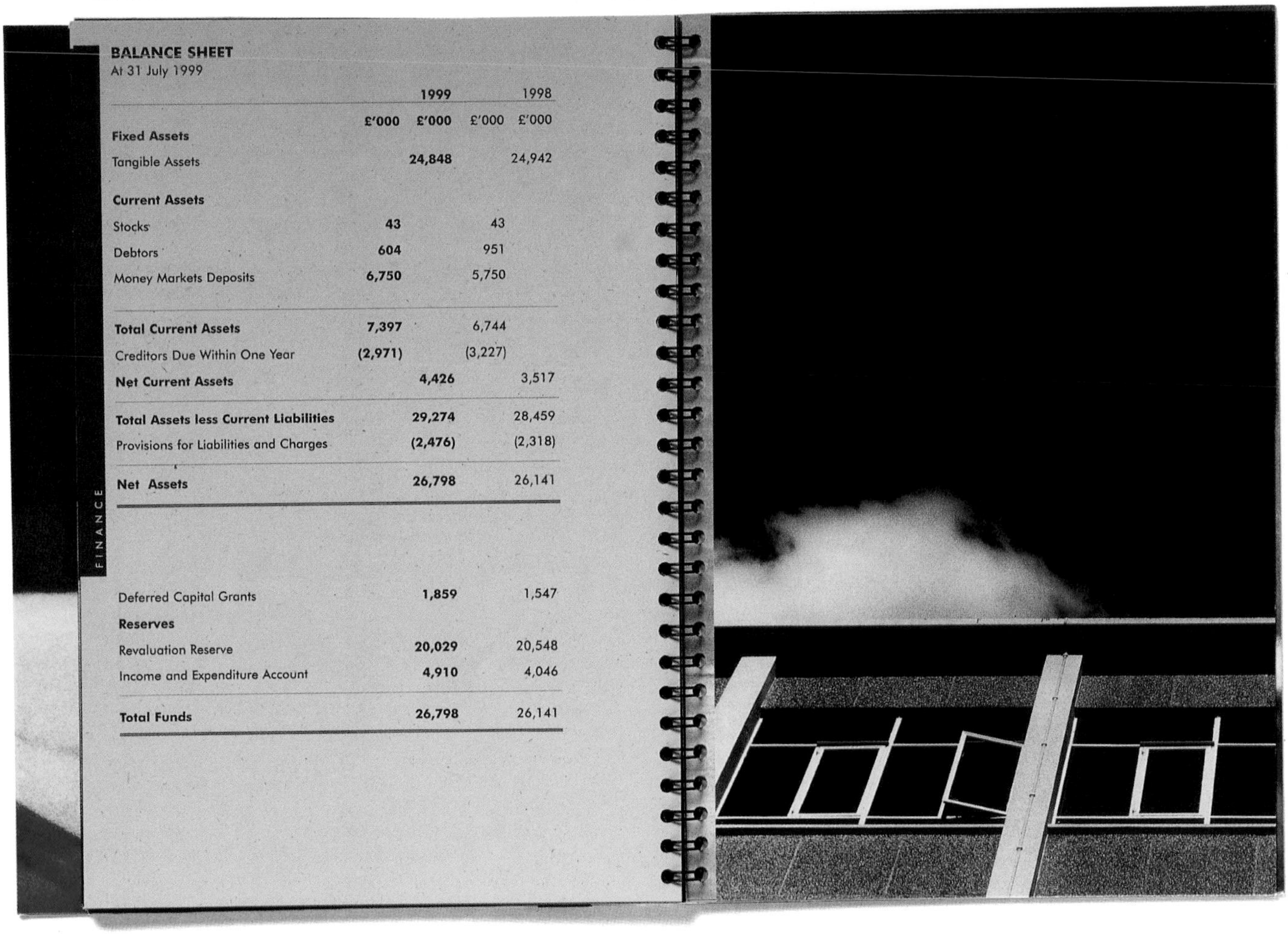

FINANCE

BALANCE SHEET
At 31 July 1999

	1999		1998	
	£'000	£'000	£'000	£'000
Fixed Assets				
Tangible Assets		24,848		24,942
Current Assets				
Stocks	43		43	
Debtors	604		951	
Money Markets Deposits	6,750		5,750	
Total Current Assets	7,397		6,744	
Creditors Due Within One Year	(2,971)		(3,227)	
Net Current Assets		4,426		3,517
Total Assets less Current Liabilities		29,274		28,459
Provisions for Liabilities and Charges		(2,476)		(2,318)
Net Assets		26,798		26,141
Deferred Capital Grants		1,859		1,547
Reserves				
Revaluation Reserve		20,029		20,548
Income and Expenditure Account		4,910		4,046
Total Funds		26,798		26,141

Big Flower Holdings

Agency: Susan Hochbaum Design
Art & Creative Director, Designer: Susan Hochbaum
Illustrator: Steven Guarnaccia
Copywriter: Rita Jacobs

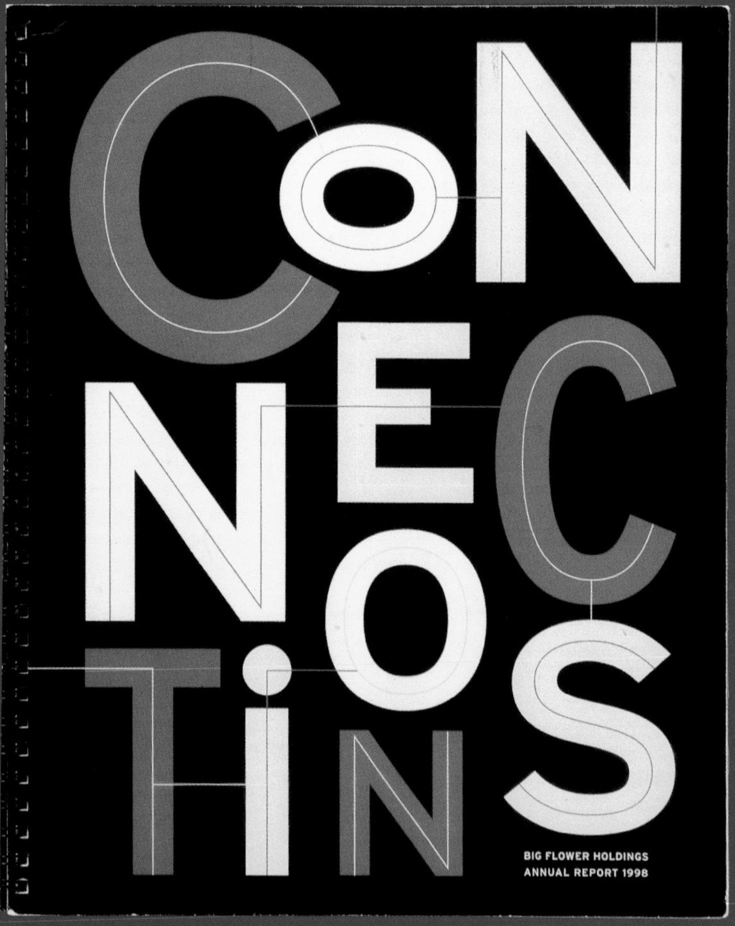
CONNECTIONS
BIG FLOWER HOLDINGS
ANNUAL REPORT 1998

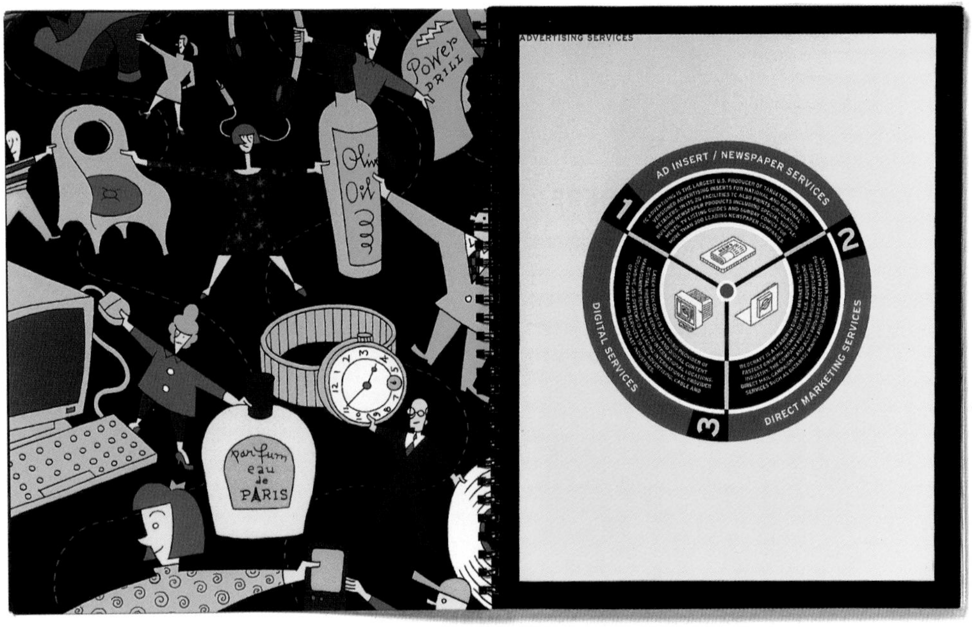
Power DRILL
parfum eau de PARIS
ADVERTISING SERVICES
AD INSERT / NEWSPAPER SERVICES
1
2
3
DIGITAL SERVICES
DIRECT MARKETING SERVICES

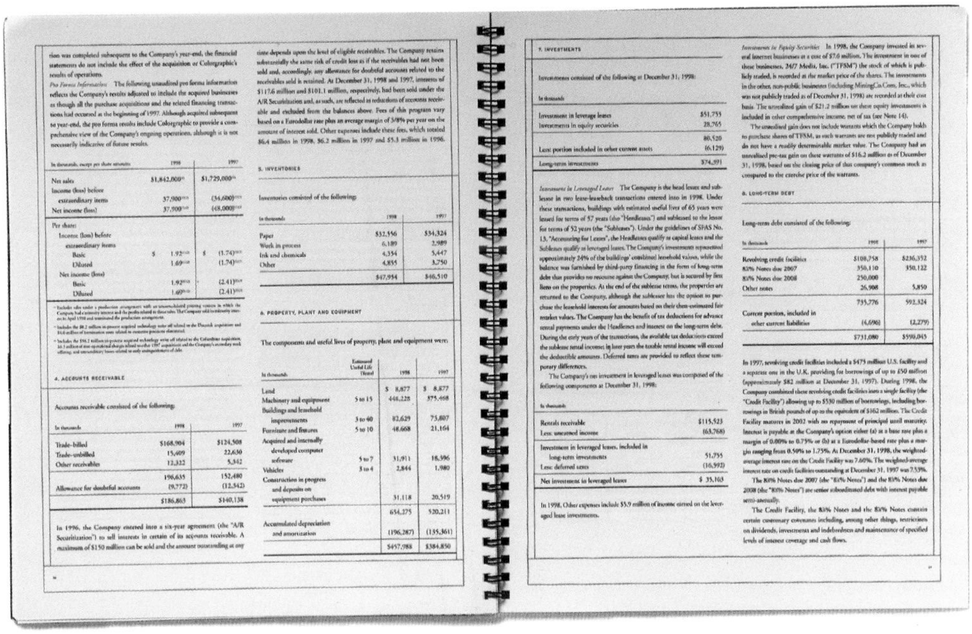
4. ACCOUNTS RECEIVABLE
5. INVENTORIES
6. PROPERTY, PLANT AND EQUIPMENT
7. INVESTMENTS
8. LONG-TERM DEBT

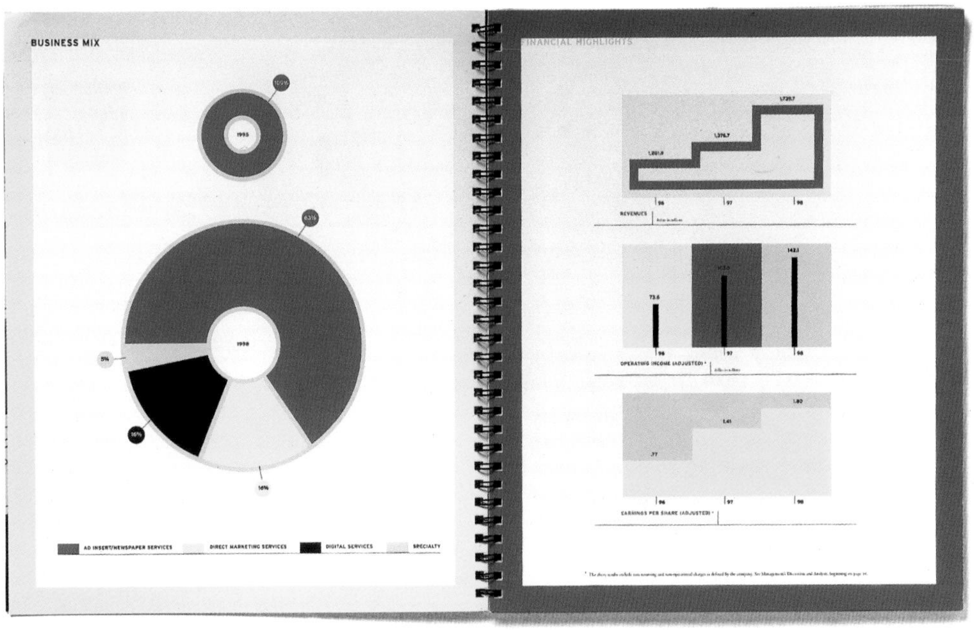
BUSINESS MIX
1998
16%
AD INSERT/NEWSPAPER SERVICES
DIRECT MARKETING SERVICES
DIGITAL SERVICES
SPECIALTY
FINANCIAL HIGHLIGHTS
REVENUES
OPERATING INCOME (ADJUSTED)
EARNINGS PER SHARE (ADJUSTED)

HONG KONG, AUGUST 27, 1998

[7:30 AM]

1998 ANNUAL REPORT, DOW JONES & COMPANY

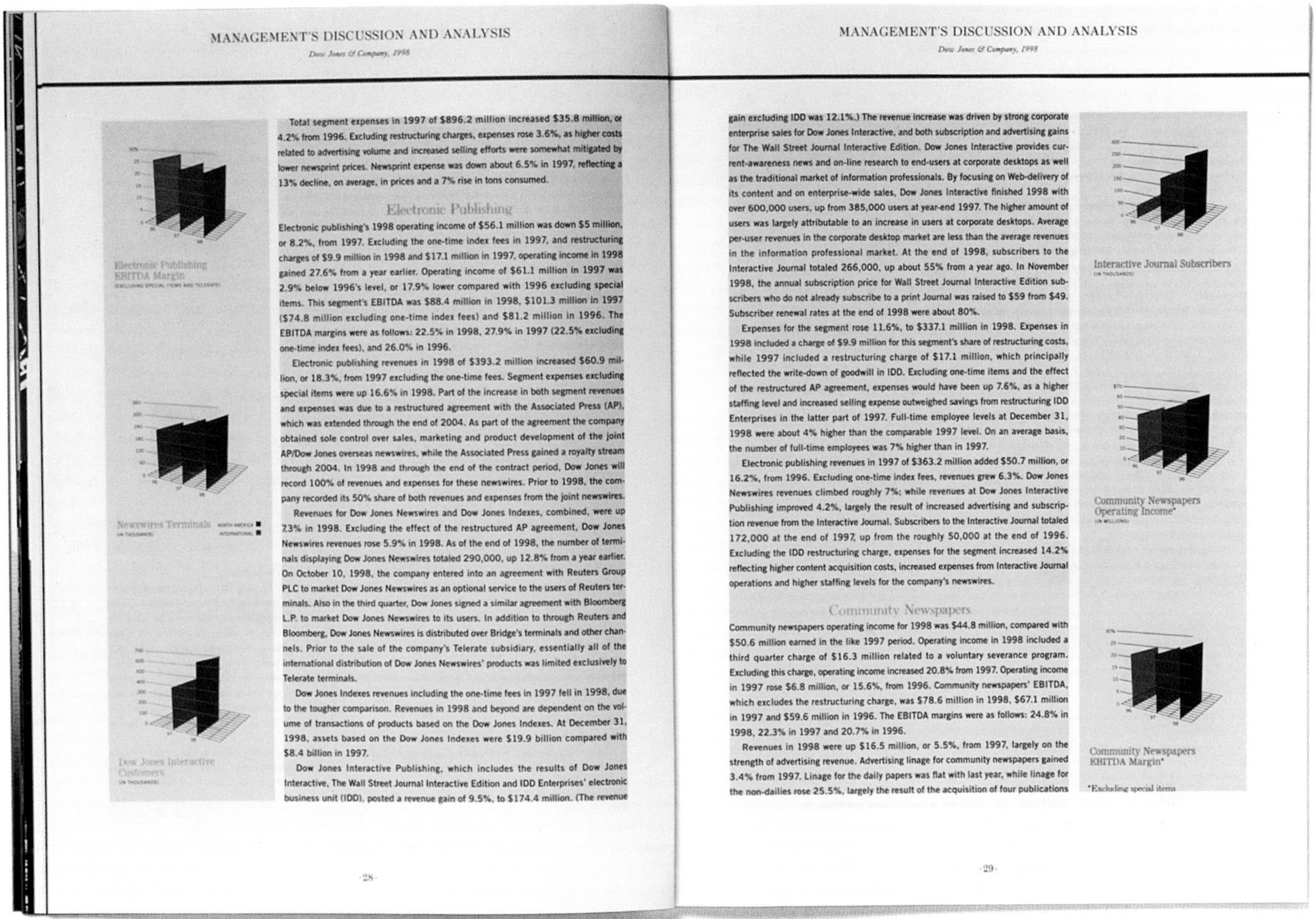

MANAGEMENT'S DISCUSSION AND ANALYSIS

Dow Jones & Company, 1998

Total segment expenses in 1997 of $896.2 million increased $35.8 million, or 4.2% from 1996. Excluding restructuring charges, expenses rose 3.6%, as higher costs related to advertising volume and increased selling efforts were somewhat mitigated by lower newsprint prices. Newsprint expense was down about 6.5% in 1997, reflecting a 13% decline, on average, in prices and a 7% rise in tons consumed.

Electronic Publishing

Electronic publishing's 1998 operating income of $56.1 million was down $5 million, or 8.2%, from 1997. Excluding the one-time index fees in 1997, and restructuring charges of $9.9 million in 1998 and $17.1 million in 1997, operating income in 1998 gained 27.6% from a year earlier. Operating income of $61.1 million in 1997 was 2.9% below 1996's level, or 17.9% lower compared with 1996 excluding special items. This segment's EBITDA was $88.4 million in 1998, $101.3 million in 1997 ($74.8 million excluding one-time index fees) and $81.2 million in 1996. The EBITDA margins were as follows: 22.5% in 1998, 27.9% in 1997 (22.5% excluding one-time index fees), and 26.0% in 1996.

Electronic publishing revenues in 1998 of $393.2 million increased $60.9 million, or 18.3%, from 1997 excluding the one-time fees. Segment expenses excluding special items were up 16.6% in 1998. Part of the increase in both segment revenues and expenses was due to a restructured agreement with the Associated Press (AP), which was extended through the end of 2004. As part of the agreement the company obtained sole control over sales, marketing and product development of the joint AP/Dow Jones overseas newswires, while the Associated Press gained a royalty stream through 2004. In 1998 and through the end of the contract period, Dow Jones will record 100% of revenues and expenses for these newswires. Prior to 1998, the company recorded its 50% share of both revenues and expenses from the joint newswires.

Revenues for Dow Jones Newswires and Dow Jones Indexes, combined, were up 7.3% in 1998. Excluding the effect of the restructured AP agreement, Dow Jones Newswires revenues rose 5.9% in 1998. As of the end of 1998, the number of terminals displaying Dow Jones Newswires totaled 290,000, up 12.8% from a year earlier. On October 10, 1998, the company entered into an agreement with Reuters Group PLC to market Dow Jones Newswires as an optional service to the users of Reuters terminals. Also in the third quarter, Dow Jones signed a similar agreement with Bloomberg L.P. to market Dow Jones Newswires to its users. In addition to through Reuters and Bloomberg, Dow Jones Newswires is distributed over Bridge's terminals and other channels. Prior to the sale of the company's Telerate subsidiary, essentially all of the international distribution of Dow Jones Newswires' products was limited exclusively to Telerate terminals.

Dow Jones Indexes revenues including the one-time fees in 1997 fell in 1998, due to the tougher comparison. Revenues in 1998 and beyond are dependent on the volume of transactions of products based on the Dow Jones Indexes. At December 31, 1998, assets based on the Dow Jones Indexes were $19.9 billion compared with $8.4 billion in 1997.

Dow Jones Interactive Publishing, which includes the results of Dow Jones Interactive, The Wall Street Journal Interactive Edition and IDD Enterprises' electronic business unit (IDD), posted a revenue gain of 9.5%, to $174.4 million. (The revenue gain excluding IDD was 12.1%.) The revenue increase was driven by strong corporate enterprise sales for Dow Jones Interactive, and both subscription and advertising gains for The Wall Street Journal Interactive Edition. Dow Jones Interactive provides current-awareness news and on-line research to end-users at corporate desktops as well as the traditional market of information professionals. By focusing on Web-delivery of its content and on enterprise-wide sales, Dow Jones Interactive finished 1998 with over 600,000 users, up from 385,000 users at year-end 1997. The higher amount of users was largely attributable to an increase in users at corporate desktops. Average per-user revenues in the corporate desktop market are less than the average revenues in the information professional market. At the end of 1998, subscribers to the Interactive Journal totaled 266,000, up about 55% from a year ago. In November 1998, the annual subscription price for Wall Street Journal Interactive Edition subscribers who do not already subscribe to a print Journal was raised to $59 from $49. Subscriber renewal rates at the end of 1998 were about 80%.

Expenses for the segment rose 11.6%, to $337.1 million in 1998. Expenses in 1998 included a charge of $9.9 million for this segment's share of restructuring costs, while 1997 included a restructuring charge of $17.1 million, which principally reflected the write-down of goodwill in IDD. Excluding one-time items and the effect of the restructured AP agreement, expenses would have been up 7.6%, as a higher staffing level and increased selling expense outweighed savings from restructuring IDD Enterprises in the latter part of 1997. Full-time employee levels at December 31, 1998 were about 4% higher than the comparable 1997 level. On an average basis, the number of full-time employees was 7% higher than in 1997.

Electronic publishing revenues in 1997 of $363.2 million added $50.7 million, or 16.2%, from 1996. Excluding one-time index fees, revenues grew 6.3%. Dow Jones Newswires revenues climbed roughly 7%; while revenues at Dow Jones Interactive Publishing improved 4.2%, largely the result of increased advertising and subscription revenue from the Interactive Journal. Subscribers to the Interactive Journal totaled 172,000 at the end of 1997, up from the roughly 50,000 at the end of 1996. Excluding the IDD restructuring charge, expenses for the segment increased 14.2% reflecting higher content acquisition costs, increased expenses from Interactive Journal operations and higher staffing levels for the company's newswires.

Community Newspapers

Community newspapers operating income for 1998 was $44.8 million, compared with $50.6 million earned in the like 1997 period. Operating income in 1998 included a third quarter charge of $16.3 million related to a voluntary severance program. Excluding this charge, operating income increased 20.8% from 1997. Operating income in 1997 rose $6.8 million, or 15.6%, from 1996. Community newspapers' EBITDA, which excludes the restructuring charge, was $78.6 million in 1998, $67.1 million in 1997 and $59.6 million in 1996. The EBITDA margins were as follows: 24.8% in 1998, 22.3% in 1997 and 20.7% in 1996.

Revenues in 1998 were up $16.5 million, or 5.5%, from 1997, largely on the strength of advertising revenue. Advertising linage for community newspapers gained 3.4% from 1997. Linage for the daily papers was flat with last year, while linage for the non-dailies rose 25.5%, largely the result of the acquisition of four publications

Electronic Publishing
EBITDA Margin
Newswires Terminals
Dow Jones Interactive Customers
Interactive Journal Subscribers
Community Newspapers
Operating Income*
Community Newspapers
EBITDA Margin*
-28-
-29-

As the sun rises in Hong Kong, the ruble falls in Russia.
"Russia Halts Ruble D
NEWSWIRE
11:26
*YELTSIN PRESS
SERVICE
CONFIRMED
GOVERNMENT
SACKED.
[1526GMT]
The immediate cause of the selloff is the firing of the Russian prime minister and his cabinet four days earlier – a story broken by Dow Jones Newswires Moscow bureau chief Alan Cullison – and the Russian government's decision today to stop supporting its currency and effectively default on its debt.

At 5:50 pm Eastern time The Wall Street Journal Report on 101 U.S. radio stations notes that:
"WALL STREET HAS OFFICIALLY ENTERED A CORRECTION AS WORRIES ABOUT THE GLOBAL FINANCIAL SITUATION PUSHED STOCK PRICES SHARPLY LOWER IN THE SECOND BUSIEST SESSION EVER."
4:00 pm
NEW YORK
USERS OF DOW JONES INTERACTIVE'S PUBLICATIONS LIBRARY WILL, BEFORE THE DAY IS OUT, CONDUCT 160,000 SEARCHES, AND RETRIEVE 225,000 DOCUMENTS.
By 8:00 pm (8:00 am August 28 in Hong Kong), the Interactive Journal contains the next day's Asian Journal.
By 10:00 pm (3:00 am in London, 4:00 am in Frankfurt), European Journal coverage is available as well.
At 11:00 pm, the content of the U.S. Journal for the next day begins to be loaded into the Interactive Journal.
As the sun sets in New York, the gale of today's news reaches its climax.

On August 27, millions of investors in the world's major stock markets saw $728 billion in market capitalization disappear, saw currencies tumble and governments tremble. Thousands of reporters, editors, broadcasters, and commentators wrote and spoke about it. Hundreds of millions of people read about it, watched it, heard about it, talked about it.

But one company made sense of it. Brought knowledge out of mere data. Provided readers, users and viewers with what they most wanted and needed to know. Published the world's most vital business and financial news and information.

Dow Jones & Company.

NEW YORK CITY, 24 HOURS LATER
[7:30 PM]
The Dow Jones Industrial Average has fallen 357 points.
The third largest point decline in history.
The globe spins on an axis of financial concern
as a chain reaction of stock market drops races the sun from Hong Kong to Europe and on to New York.
At Dow Jones, this business news is our business,
around the clock and around the world...
Witness a day in the life of business and financial news...

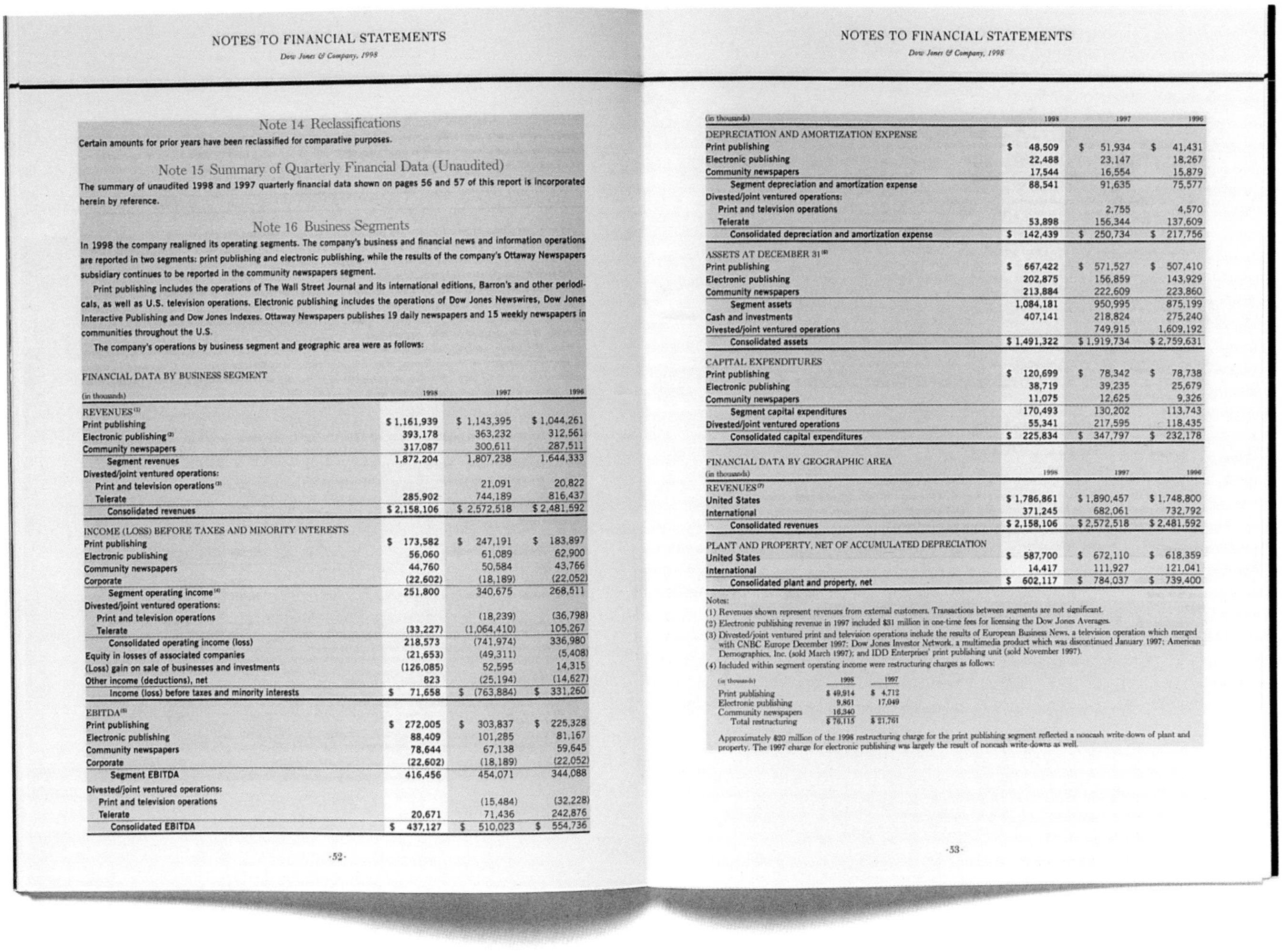

NOTES TO FINANCIAL STATEMENTS

Dow Jones & Company, 1998

Note 14 Reclassifications

Certain amounts for prior years have been reclassified for comparative purposes.

Note 15 Summary of Quarterly Financial Data (Unaudited)

The summary of unaudited 1998 and 1997 quarterly financial data shown on pages 56 and 57 of this report is incorporated herein by reference.

Note 16 Business Segments

In 1998 the company realigned its operating segments. The company's business and financial news and information operations are reported in two segments: print publishing and electronic publishing, while the results of the company's Ottaway Newspapers subsidiary continues to be reported in the community newspapers segment.

Print publishing includes the operations of The Wall Street Journal and its international editions, Barron's and other periodicals, as well as U.S. television operations. Electronic publishing includes the operations of Dow Jones Newswires, Dow Jones Interactive Publishing and Dow Jones Indexes. Ottaway Newspapers publishes 19 daily newspapers and 15 weekly newspapers in communities throughout the U.S.

The company's operations by business segment and geographic area were as follows:

FINANCIAL DATA BY BUSINESS SEGMENT

(in thousands)	1998	1997	1996
REVENUES (1)			
Print publishing	$ 1,161,939	$ 1,143,395	$ 1,044,261
Electronic publishing (2)	393,178	363,232	312,561
Community newspapers	317,087	300,611	287,511
Segment revenues	1,872,204	1,807,238	1,644,333
Divested/joint ventured operations:			
Print and television operations (3)		21,091	20,822
Telerate	285,902	744,189	816,437
Consolidated revenues	$ 2,158,106	$ 2,572,518	$ 2,481,592
INCOME (LOSS) BEFORE TAXES AND MINORITY INTERESTS			
Print publishing	$ 173,582	$ 247,191	$ 183,897
Electronic publishing	56,060	61,089	62,900
Community newspapers	44,760	50,584	43,766
Corporate	(22,602)	(18,189)	(22,052)
Segment operating income (4)	251,800	340,675	268,511
Divested/joint ventured operations:			
Print and television operations		(18,239)	(36,798)
Telerate	(33,227)	(1,064,410)	105,267
Consolidated operating income (loss)	218,573	(741,974)	336,980
Equity in losses of associated companies	(21,653)	(49,311)	(5,408)
(Loss) gain on sale of businesses and investments	(126,085)	52,595	14,315
Other income (deductions), net	823	(25,194)	(14,627)
Income (loss) before taxes and minority interests	$ 71,658	$ (763,884)	$ 331,260
EBITDA (5)			
Print publishing	$ 272,005	$ 303,837	$ 225,328
Electronic publishing	88,409	101,285	81,167
Community newspapers	78,644	67,138	59,645
Corporate	(22,602)	(18,189)	(22,052)
Segment EBITDA	416,456	454,071	344,088
Divested/joint ventured operations:			
Print and television operations		(15,484)	(32,228)
Telerate	20,671	71,436	242,876
Consolidated EBITDA	$ 437,127	$ 510,023	$ 554,736

-52-

NOTES TO FINANCIAL STATEMENTS

Dow Jones & Company, 1998

(in thousands)	1998	1997	1996
DEPRECIATION AND AMORTIZATION EXPENSE			
Print publishing	$ 48,509	$ 51,934	$ 41,431
Electronic publishing	22,488	23,147	18,267
Community newspapers	17,544	16,554	15,879
Segment depreciation and amortization expense	88,541	91,635	75,577
Divested/joint ventured operations:			
Print and television operations		2,755	4,570
Telerate	53,898	156,344	137,609
Consolidated depreciation and amortization expense	$ 142,439	$ 250,734	$ 217,756
ASSETS AT DECEMBER 31 (6)			
Print publishing	$ 667,422	$ 571,527	$ 507,410
Electronic publishing	202,875	156,859	143,929
Community newspapers	213,884	222,609	223,860
Segment assets	1,084,181	950,995	875,199
Cash and investments	407,141	218,824	275,240
Divested/joint ventured operations		749,915	1,609,192
Consolidated assets	$ 1,491,322	$ 1,919,734	$ 2,759,631
CAPITAL EXPENDITURES			
Print publishing	$ 120,699	$ 78,342	$ 78,738
Electronic publishing	38,719	39,235	25,679
Community newspapers	11,075	12,625	9,326
Segment capital expenditures	170,493	130,202	113,743
Divested/joint ventured operations	55,341	217,595	118,435
Consolidated capital expenditures	$ 225,834	$ 347,797	$ 232,178

FINANCIAL DATA BY GEOGRAPHIC AREA

(in thousands)	1998	1997	1996
REVENUES (7)			
United States	$ 1,786,861	$ 1,890,457	$ 1,748,800
International	371,245	682,061	732,792
Consolidated revenues	$ 2,158,106	$ 2,572,518	$ 2,481,592
PLANT AND PROPERTY, NET OF ACCUMULATED DEPRECIATION			
United States	$ 587,700	$ 672,110	$ 618,359
International	14,417	111,927	121,041
Consolidated plant and property, net	$ 602,117	$ 784,037	$ 739,400

Notes:

(1) Revenues shown represent revenues from external customers. Transactions between segments are not significant.

(2) Electronic publishing revenue in 1997 included $31 million in one-time fees for licensing the Dow Jones Averages.

(3) Divested/joint ventured print and television operations include the results of European Business News, a television operation which merged with CNBC Europe December 1997; Dow Jones Investor Network, a multimedia product which was discontinued January 1997; American Demographics, Inc. (sold March 1997); and IDD Enterprises' print publishing unit (sold November 1997).

(4) Included within segment operating income were restructuring charges as follows:

(in thousands)	1998	1997
Print publishing	$ 49,914	$ 4,712
Electronic publishing	9,861	17,049
Community newspapers	16,340	
Total restructuring	$ 76,115	$ 21,761

Approximately $20 million of the 1998 restructuring charge for the print publishing segment reflected a noncash write-down of plant and property. The 1997 charge for electronic publishing was largely the result of noncash write-downs as well.

-53-

Agency: Douglas Oliver Design Office
Art Director & Designer: Douglas Oliver
Photographers: Bill Livingston, Aiden Bradley

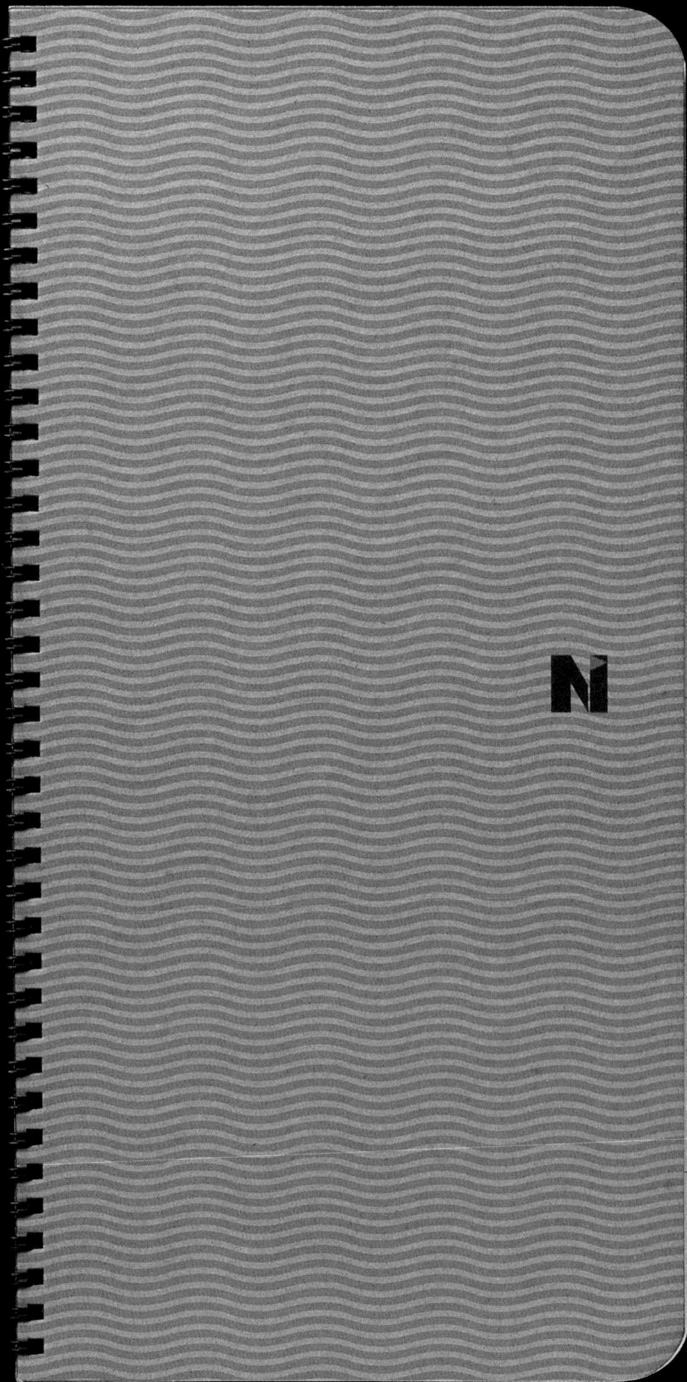

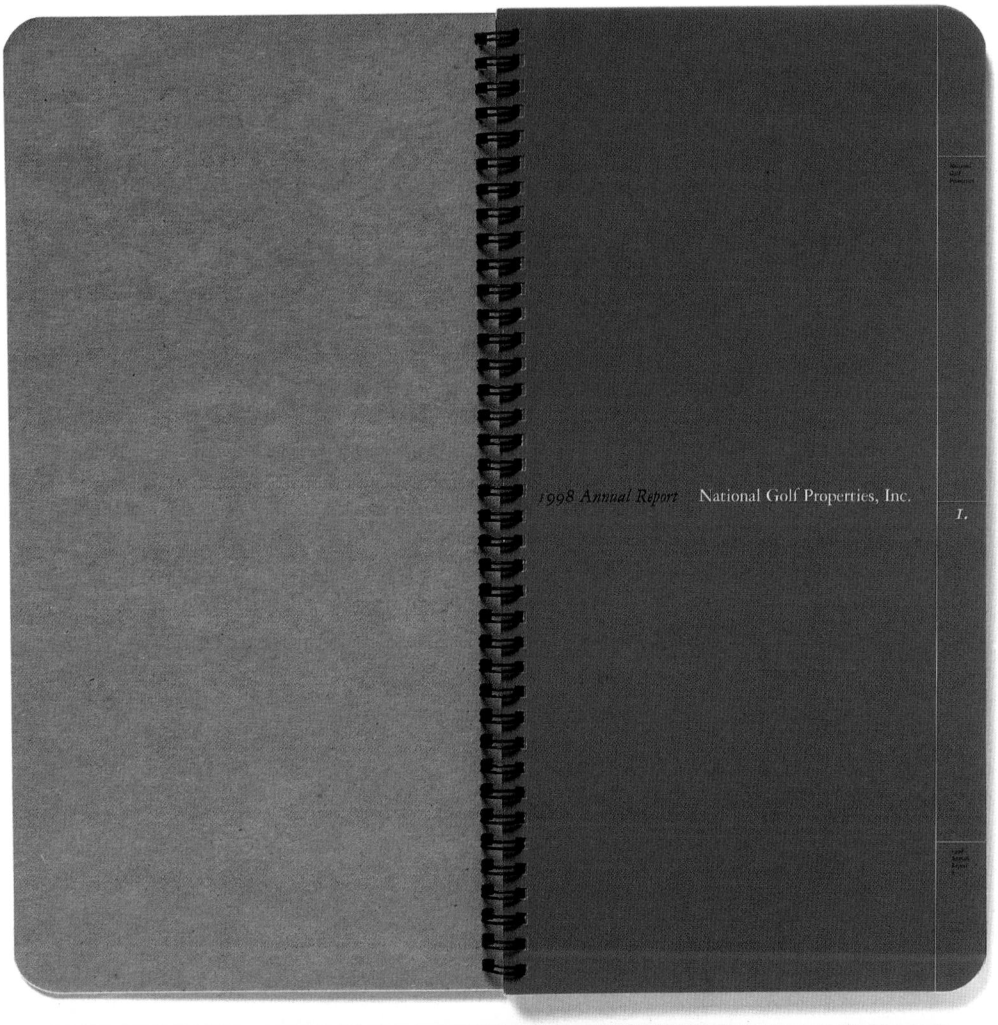
1998 Annual Report
National Golf Properties, Inc.
1.

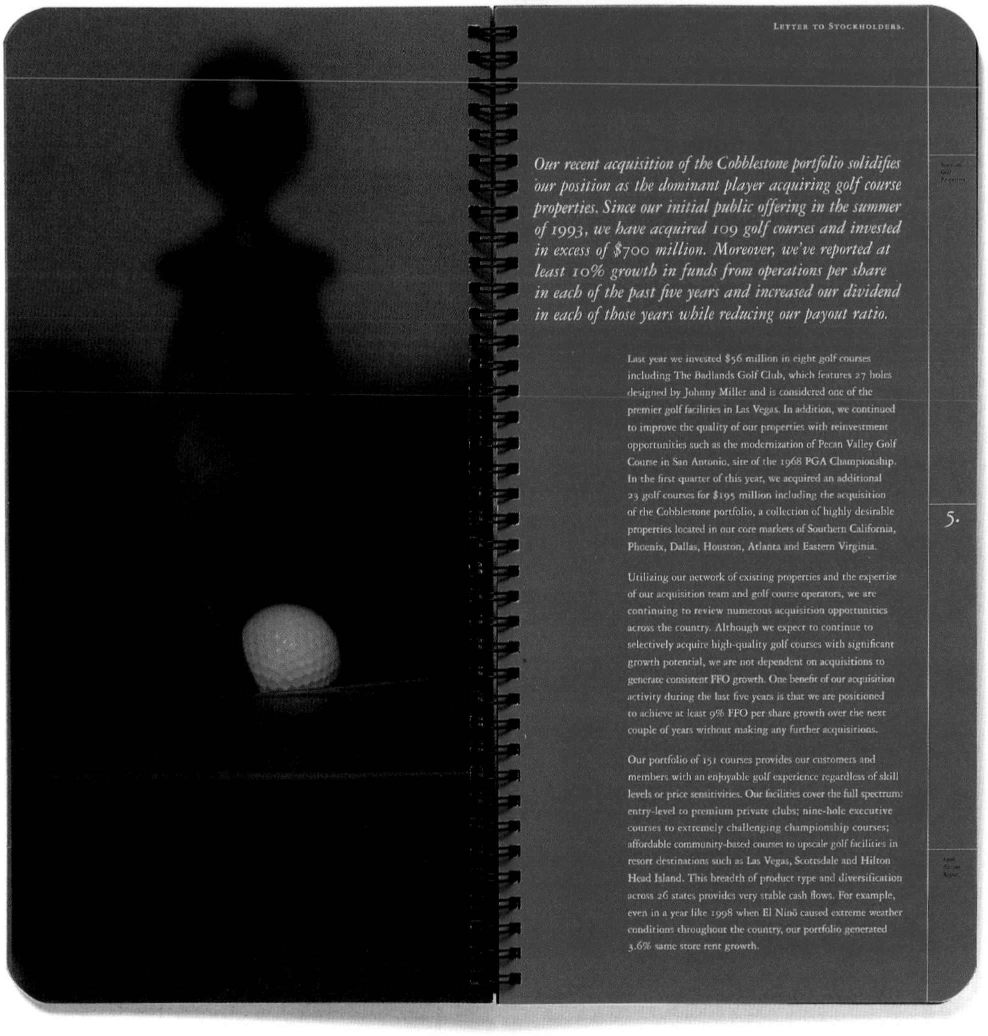
Letter to Stockholders.
Our recent acquisition of the Cobblestone portfolio solidifies our position as the dominant player acquiring golf course properties. Since our initial public offering in the summer of 1993, we have acquired 109 golf courses and invested in excess of $700 million. Moreover, we've reported at least 10% growth in funds from operations per share in each of the past five years and increased our dividend in each of those years while reducing our payout ratio.
Last year we invested $56 million in eight golf courses including The Badlands Golf Club, which features 27 holes designed by Johnny Miller and is considered one of the premier golf facilities in Las Vegas. In addition, we continued to improve the quality of our properties with reinvestment opportunities such as the modernization of Pecan Valley Golf Course in San Antonio, site of the 1968 PGA Championship. In the first quarter of this year, we acquired an additional 23 golf courses for $195 million including the acquisition of the Cobblestone portfolio, a collection of highly desirable properties located in our core markets of Southern California, Phoenix, Dallas, Houston, Atlanta and Eastern Virginia.
Utilizing our network of existing properties and the expertise of our acquisition team and golf course operators, we are continuing to review numerous acquisition opportunities across the country. Although we expect to continue to selectively acquire high-quality golf courses with significant growth potential, we are not dependent on acquisitions to generate consistent FFO growth. One benefit of our acquisition activity during the last five years is that we are positioned to achieve at least 9% FFO per share growth over the next couple of years without making any further acquisitions.
Our portfolio of 151 courses provides our customers and members with an enjoyable golf experience regardless of skill levels or price sensitivities. Our facilities cover the full spectrum: entry-level to premium private clubs; nine-hole executive courses to extremely challenging championship courses; affordable community-based courses to upscale golf facilities in resort destinations such as Las Vegas, Scottsdale and Hilton Head Island. This breadth of product type and diversification across 26 states provides very stable cash flows. For example, even in a year like 1998 when El Ninõ caused extreme weather conditions throughout the country, our portfolio generated 3.6% same store rent growth.
5.

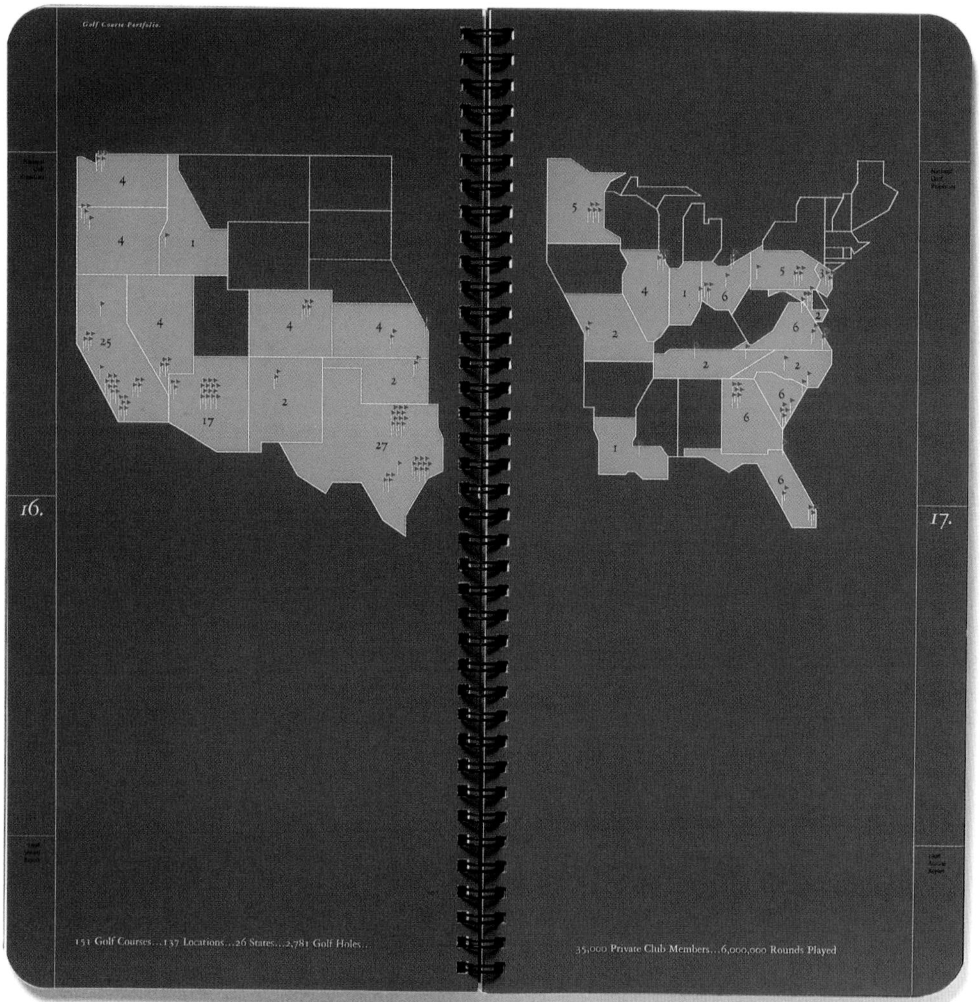
Golf Course Portfolio.
4
4
1
4
25
4
4
17
2
2
27
5
4
1
6
5
2
6
2
2
2
6
6
1
6
16.
17.
151 Golf Courses...137 Locations...26 States...2,781 Golf Holes..
35,000 Private Club Members...6,000,000 Rounds Played

The
Badlands
Golf Club
Las Vegas,
Nevada

Ruffled
Feathers
Golf Course
Chicago,
Illinois

Financial Review National Golf Properties, Inc.

Based on recent Securities and Exchange Commission pronouncements, AGC changed its accounting policy for member initiation fees to defer such revenues and recognize them on a straight-line basis over the expected average life of active membership. Accordingly, AGC's consolidated financial statements have been retroactively adjusted to reflect this change for all periods presented.

The following table sets forth certain condensed financial information concerning AGC.

	December 31,	
(In thousands)	1998	1997
Current assets	$ 82,809	$ 79,692
Non-current assets	163,629	147,423
Total assets	$ 246,438	$ 227,115
Total current liabilities	$ 84,893	$ 70,411
Total long-term liabilities	147,667	128,197
Minority interest	503	501
Total shareholders' equity	13,375	28,006
Total liabilities and shareholders' equity	$ 246,438	$ 227,115

	For the year ended December 31,		
(In thousands)	1998	1997	1996
Total revenues	$ 575,853	$ 517,131	$ 427,743
Net income	$ 4,746	$ 12,323	$ 4,343

This accounting change resulted in a decrease in AGC's retained earnings of $49,952,000, $41,172,000 and $34,315,000 as of December 31, 1998, 1997 and 1996, respectively. This impact did not have any affect on the Company's consolidated financial statements.

17. Quarterly Financial Information (Unaudited)

Summarized quarterly financial data for the years ended December 31, 1998 and 1997 is as follows:

	Quarter ended			
(In thousands, except per share amounts)	March 31	June 30	September 30	December 31
Fiscal 1998				
Revenues	$ 19,898	$ 18,797	$ 19,671	$ 25,369
Operating income	$ 11,926	$ 11,161	$ 11,658	$ 16,755
Net income	$ 3,711	$ 3,504	$ 3,094	$ 6,333
Basic earnings per share	$ 0.30	$ 0.28	$ 0.25	$ 0.51
Diluted earnings per share	$ 0.29	$ 0.28	$ 0.25	$ 0.50

	Quarter ended			
(In thousands, except per share amounts)	March 31	June 30	September 30	December 31
Fiscal 1997				
Revenues	$ 17,449	$ 18,731	$ 19,335	$ 19,078
Operating income	$ 10,317	$ 11,479	$ 11,494	$ 11,209
Net income	$ 3,278	$ 4,087	$ 3,752	$ 4,462
Basic earnings per share	$ 0.27	$ 0.33	$ 0.30	$ 0.36
Diluted earnings per share	$ 0.26	$ 0.33	$ 0.30	$ 0.36

As a result of EITF 98-9, no percentage rent and only approximately $231,000 of percentage rent was recognized in the second and third quarters of 1998, respectively. Otherwise, the Company would have recorded percentage rent in the second and third quarters of approximately $1,808,000 and $1,981,000, respectively.

18. Pro Forma Financial Information (Unaudited)

The pro forma financial information set forth below is presented as if the 1998 acquisitions (Note 2) had been consummated as of January 1, 1997.

The pro forma financial information is not necessarily indicative of what actual results of operations of the Company would have been assuming the acquisitions had been consummated as of January 1, 1997, nor does it purport to represent the results of operations for future periods.

	For the year ended December 31,	
(In thousands, except per share amounts)	1998	1997
Revenues from rental property	$ 85,897	$ 78,509
Net income	$ 16,402	$ 14,952
Basic earnings per share	$ 1.31	$ 1.21
Diluted earnings per share	$ 1.30	$ 1.20

The pro forma financial information includes the following adjustments: (i) an increase in depreciation and amortization expense; (ii) an increase in interest expense; and (iii) a decrease in income applicable to minority interest.

19. Subsequent Events (Unaudited)

On January 6, 1999, the Company purchased Beaver Brook Country Club located in Clinton, New Jersey and The Classic Golf Club located in Spanaway, Washington for a combined purchase price of approximately $10.4 million.

On January 11, 1999, the Company declared a quarterly distribution for the fourth quarter of 1998 of $0.44 per share to stockholders of record on January 29, 1999, which was paid on February 15, 1999.

On February 1, 1999, the Company extended the treasury lock until May 3, 1999.

On March 31, 1999, the Company entered into a new $300 million unsecured revolving credit facility with a group of lenders. Advances under the credit facility bear interest at the Administrative Agent's alternate base rate plus the then-applicable base rate margin or, at the option of the Company, LIBOR plus the then-applicable LIBOR rate margin. The Administrative Agent's alternate base rate for any day means the greater of (i) a rate per annum equal to the corporate base rate of interest announced by the Administrative Agent from time to time, and (ii) the federal funds rate as published by the Federal Reserve Bank plus one-half percent (0.50%) per annum. The amount of the base rate margin and LIBOR rate margin vary depending upon the amount of the Company's outstanding indebtedness compared to its capitalization. The initial rate of interest for borrowings made under the new facility as of March 31, 1999 will be equal to LIBOR plus a margin of 2.25% or the alternate base rate plus 1.00%. The credit facility replaces the Company's previous $100 million credit facility, which has been terminated.

On March 31, 1999, the Company purchased from Golf Acquisitions, L.L.C. ("Golf Acquisitions") fee interests in 15 golf course facilities and long-term leasehold interests in five golf courses and made a participating mortgage loan secured by one additional golf course for an aggregate initial investment of approximately $184.3 million, which investment was financed by approximately $178.7 million of cash and approximately $5.6 million of assumed notes. A subsidiary of AGC and a subsidiary of ClubCorp International formed Golf Acquisitions.

Microvision

Agency: The Leonhardt Group
Art Director, Designer & Illustrator: Tim Young
Creative Directors: Tim Young, Jon King
Photographer: Doug Landreth
Copywriter: Karen Wilson

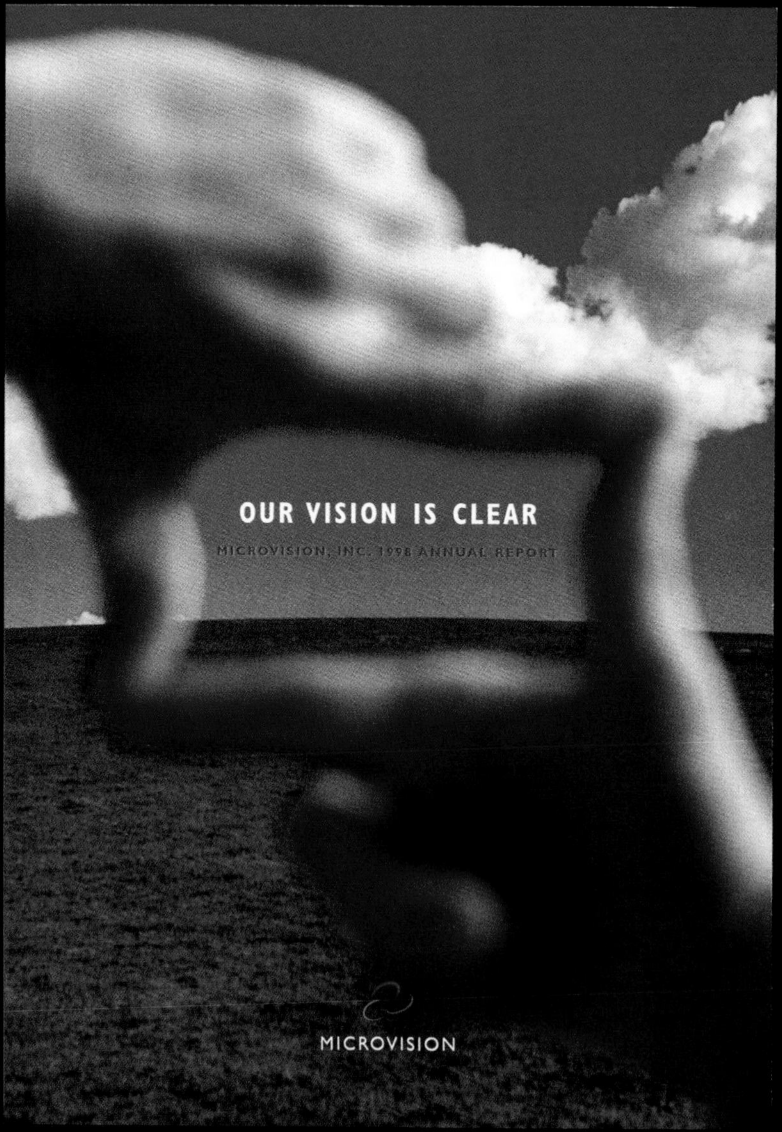
OUR VISION IS CLEAR
MICROVISION, INC. 1998 ANNUAL REPORT
MICROVISION

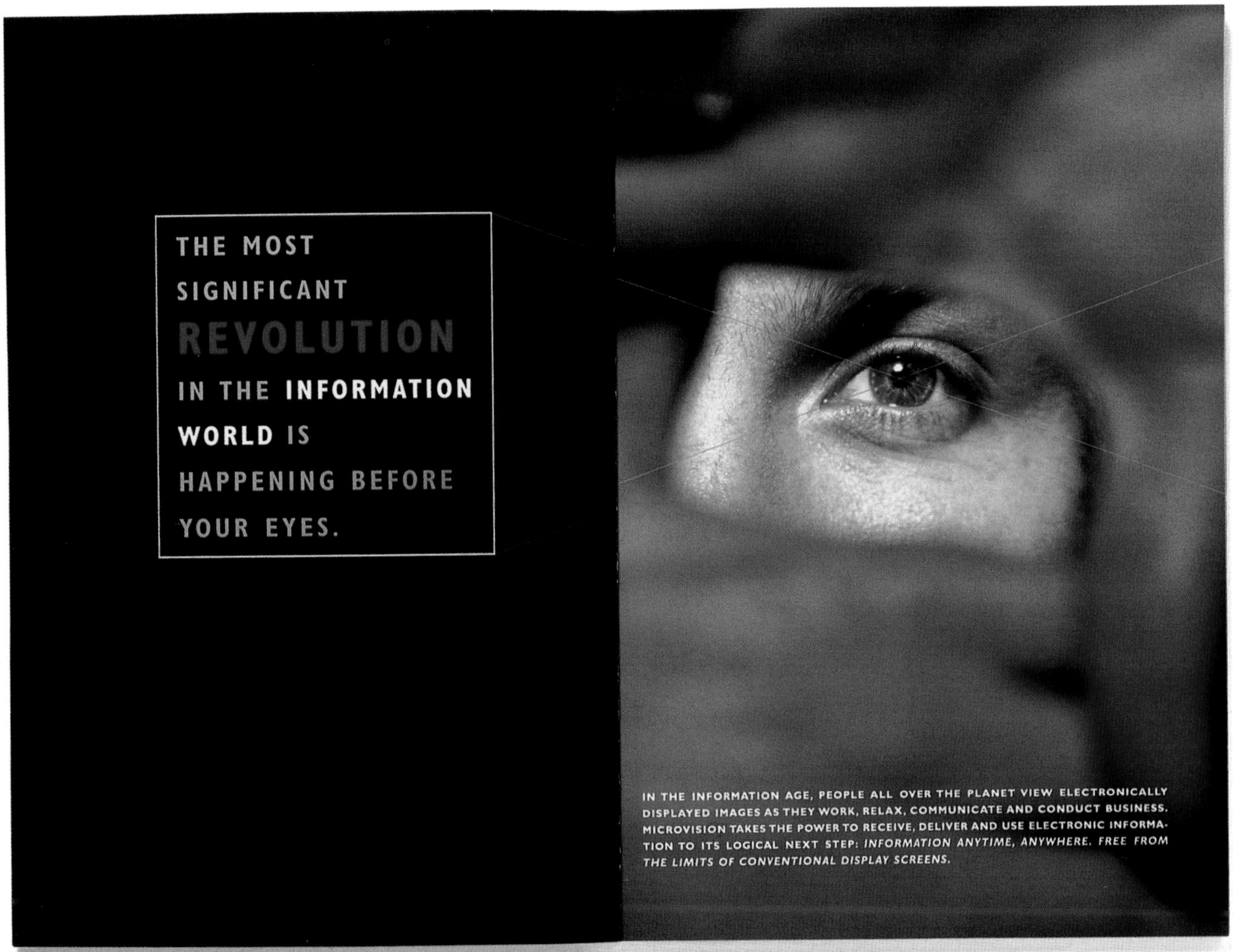
THE MOST
SIGNIFICANT
REVOLUTION
IN THE INFORMATION
WORLD IS
HAPPENING BEFORE
YOUR EYES.
IN THE INFORMATION AGE, PEOPLE ALL OVER THE PLANET VIEW ELECTRONICALLY DISPLAYED IMAGES AS THEY WORK, RELAX, COMMUNICATE AND CONDUCT BUSINESS. MICROVISION TAKES THE POWER TO RECEIVE, DELIVER AND USE ELECTRONIC INFORMATION TO ITS LOGICAL NEXT STEP: INFORMATION ANYTIME, ANYWHERE, FREE FROM THE LIMITS OF CONVENTIONAL DISPLAY SCREENS.

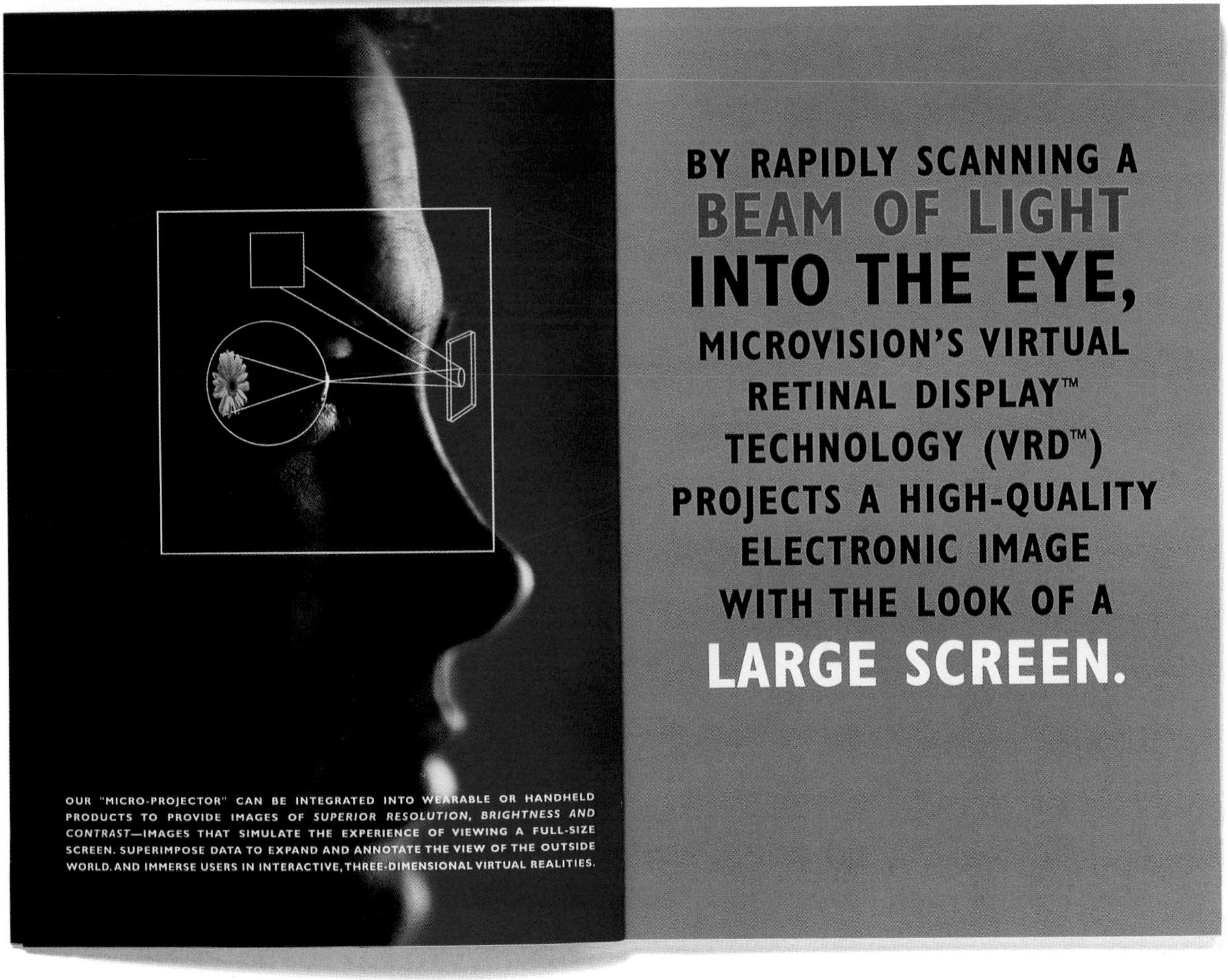
OUR "MICRO-PROJECTOR" CAN BE INTEGRATED INTO WEARABLE OR HANDHELD PRODUCTS TO PROVIDE IMAGES OF SUPERIOR RESOLUTION, BRIGHTNESS AND CONTRAST—IMAGES THAT SIMULATE THE EXPERIENCE OF VIEWING A FULL-SIZE SCREEN. SUPERIMPOSE DATA TO EXPAND AND ANNOTATE THE VIEW OF THE OUTSIDE WORLD. AND IMMERSE USERS IN INTERACTIVE, THREE-DIMENSIONAL VIRTUAL REALITIES.
BY RAPIDLY SCANNING A
BEAM OF LIGHT
INTO THE EYE,
MICROVISION'S VIRTUAL
RETINAL DISPLAY™
TECHNOLOGY (VRD™)
PROJECTS A HIGH-QUALITY
ELECTRONIC IMAGE
WITH THE LOOK OF A
LARGE SCREEN.

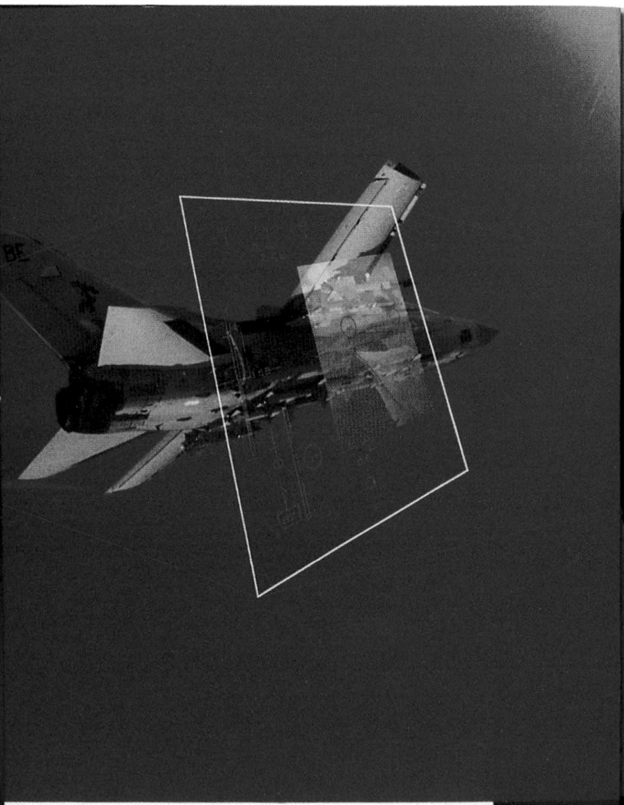

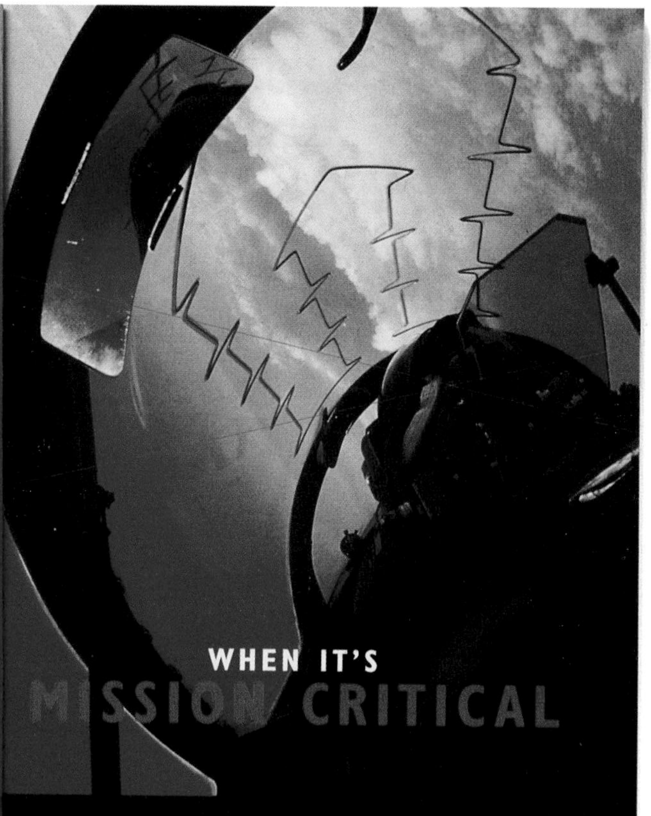

WHEN IT'S MISSION CRITICAL

DEFENSE AND AEROSPACE MARKET

1998 CONTRACTS:

Boeing Defense and Space Group
Ericsson Saab Avionics
United States Army
United States Air Force
United States Navy

Microvision meets the defense industry's pent-up demand for advanced display systems that are rugged, high-resolution and daylight-readable. In the air and on the ground, VRD technology enhances the situational awareness vital to mission success, delivering real-time data on the move. Already VRD technology is recognized as a force multiplier, extending the effectiveness of existing personnel and equipment. Our military aircraft technology is in the early stages of transfer to commercial cockpits, where improved visualization means increased safety. Together, defense and aerospace represent a total market opportunity for Microvision worth hundreds of millions of dollars annually.

At left: Helmet-mounted display demonstration system delivered to U.S. Army.

071.71
VAC
49.689
Hz
Combo
Rel
Peak
dB
Fail
AUTO

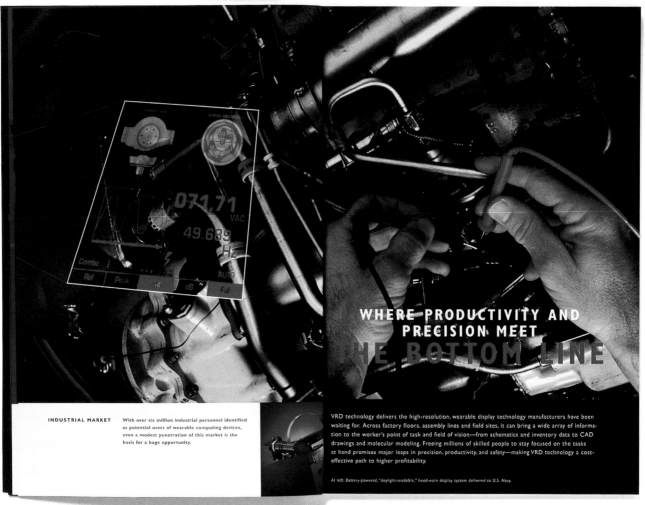

WHERE PRODUCTIVITY AND PRECISION MEET THE BOTTOM LINE

INDUSTRIAL MARKET

With over six million industrial personnel identified as potential users of wearable computing devices, even a modest penetration of this market is the basis for a huge opportunity.

VRD technology delivers the high-resolution, wearable display technology manufacturers have been waiting for. Across factory floors, assembly lines and field sites, it can bring a wide array of information to the worker's point of task and field of vision—from schematics and inventory data to CAD drawings and molecular modeling. Freeing millions of skilled people to stay focused on the tasks at hand promises major leaps in precision, productivity, and safety—making VRD technology a cost-effective path to higher profitability.

At left: Battery-powered, "daylight-readable," head-worn display system delivered to U.S. Navy.

application of our core technology to major opportunities beyond defense and aerospace—including medical, industrial and consumer segments. Microvision's strong acceptance in our entry markets and developmental momentum in a multitude of other enormous markets are the result of a strategic vision as clear as the world's need for higher-quality, more convenient and less expensive ways to access visual information anytime, anywhere. Through rigorous thinking and continual dialogue at Microvision, this vision is continuously championed, refined and deployed to leverage advances in our technology and emerging opportunities in a myriad of markets. We are happy to share some of the ongoing conversation that articulates our company-wide vision for leveraging Microvision's core technology into a wide world of personal display products—products that revolutionize the way people see in the information age.

REVOLUTIONIZING VISUAL ACCESS TO INFORMATION

RICK: In the simplest sense, Microvision provides advanced display and imaging products for customers in defense and aerospace, medical, industrial and consumer markets.

But it's also important to see the big picture. Companies gain valuable perspective when they define themselves by the value they provide. After all, people don't value technology for itself; they value what it does for them.

Microvision's big picture is about information. Our technology enables products that access information more conveniently and use it more effectively—that deliver information in a highly graphical and intuitive way. Because people see and read about information systems proliferating and advancing at an amazing pace, they quickly grasp the value of our products and why these markets have such terrific growth potential.

SIZING UP THE MARKETPLACE

STEVE: Literally anywhere people need information is a potential application for a personal display. The first markets we're targeting are categories like military and medical—each of which offers revenue potential of hundreds of millions of dollars annually. When you add the potential for industrial and consumer products, which are even larger markets, and begin to envision longer-term product potentials like laser-scanning television, you can see why Microvision offers the ability to sustain very high growth rates for a very long time.

RICHARD: Our goal is to realize those high growth rates coupled with strong gross profitability and very high productivity. This will become more apparent as our revenue stream transitions from purely contract revenue—as product revenue becomes a greater percentage of our total revenue. To really understand Microvision in 1998 and 1999, take a look at the technology and product pipelines and realize how much leverage we will get from them. The contract revenue has real immediate financial value in that it substantially offsets development and operating costs. But perhaps the greater value of these contracts is that they are feeding our product pipeline.

MARKET DEVELOPMENT

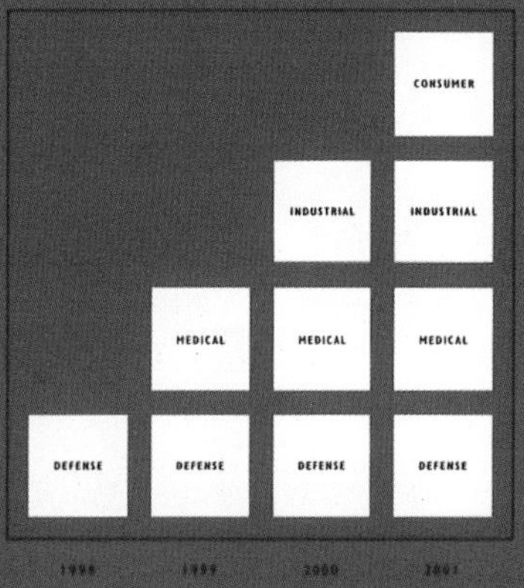
CONSUMER
INDUSTRIAL
INDUSTRIAL
MEDICAL
MEDICAL
MEDICAL
DEFENSE
DEFENSE
DEFENSE
DEFENSE

WHERE THE GROWTH IS

IN 1998, MICROVISION STRENGTHENED ITS MARKET PRESENCE AND DRAMATICALLY INCREASED REVENUES THROUGH CONTRACTS WITH THE DEFENSE AND AEROSPACE MARKETS. IN THESE ENTRY MARKETS, VRD'S BREAKTHROUGH TECHNOLOGY MEETS PENT-UP DEMAND AND DELIVERS A HIGH RETURN ON INVESTMENT. THESE SUCCESSES SUPPORT US IN LEVERAGING OUR CORE TECHNOLOGY INTO ALLIANCES AND OPPORTUNITIES IN OTHER MAJOR MARKETS—INCLUDING MEDICAL, INDUSTRIAL AND CONSUMER ELECTRONICS.

STATEMENT OF SHAREHOLDERS' EQUITY

	Preferred stock		Common stock				Unrealized holding (loss) gain on		
	Shares	Amount	Shares	Amount	Deferred compensation	Subscriptions receivable from related parties	investment securities	Accumulated deficit	Shareholders' equity
Balance at December 31, 1995	499,478	$ 2,038,900	3,098,828	$ 4,745,900	$ (42,800)	$ —	$ —	$ (7,106,900)	$ (364,900)
Issuance of stock to board members for services			22,250	110,000	(65,500)				44,500
Issuance of warrants and options for common stock				23,400					23,400
Issuance of preferred stock for cash, net of costs	360,298	1,493,900							1,493,900
Issuance of common stock and warrants for services			10,605	71,000					71,000
Exercise of warrants for common stock			50,000	40,000		(10,000)			30,000
Cashless exercise of warrants for common stock			296,875						—
Cancellation of founder's common stock			(859,375)	(66,000)					(66,000)
Amortization of deferred compensation, net					64,700				64,700
Sale of common stock and warrants in IPO			2,250,000	15,482,900					15,482,900
Conversion of convertible preferred stock	(859,776)	(3,532,800)	859,776	3,532,800					—
Collection of subscription receivable						10,000			10,000
Issuance of stock relating to retirement of 7% subordinated notes			45,000	176,200					176,200
Other			4,817						—
Net loss								(3,456,600)	(3,456,600)
Balance at December 31, 1996	—	—	5,778,776	24,116,200	(43,600)	—	—	(10,563,500)	13,509,100
Issuance of stock to board members for services			9,600	78,600	(78,600)				—
Exercise of warrants and options for common stock			56,420	348,500					348,500
Cashless exercise of warrants for common stock			75,468						
Issuance of options for services				37,200					37,200
Issuance of options for common stock				785,000	(785,000)				
Amortization of deferred compensation					206,000				206,000
Unrealized holding loss on investment securities							(1,200)		(1,200)
Other				9,800					9,800
Net loss								(4,945,000)	(4,945,000)
Balance at December 31, 1997	—	—	5,920,264	25,375,300	(701,200)	—	(1,200)	(15,508,500)	9,164,400
Issuance of stock to board members for services			24,000	120,000	(120,000)				—
Exercise of warrants and options for common stock			85,178	344,600		(78,900)			265,700
Cashless exercise of warrants for common stock			31,684						—
Issuance of stock and options for services			3,500	34,700					34,700
Issuance of options for common stock				5,300	(5,300)				—
Forfeitures of options for common stock				(137,300)	137,300				—
Amortization of deferred compensation					450,500				450,500
Unrealized holding gain on investment securities							1,200		1,200
Net loss								(7,327,500)	(7,327,500)
Balance at December 31, 1998	—	$ —	6,064,626	$ 25,742,600	$ (238,700)	$ (78,900)	$ —	$ (22,836,000)	$ 2,589,000

The accompanying notes are an integral part of these financial statements.

Platinum Technology, Inc.

Agency: Pressley Jacobs Design
Art & Creative Director, Designer: Amy W. McCarter
Photographers: Kevin Anderson, Keyvan Behpour,
Pete Eckert, Gary Faye, Karen Knover
Illustrator: Craig Ward
Copywriters: Rachel Lang, Paul McCarnas

The 1997 PLATINUM technology, inc.
ANNUAL REPORT

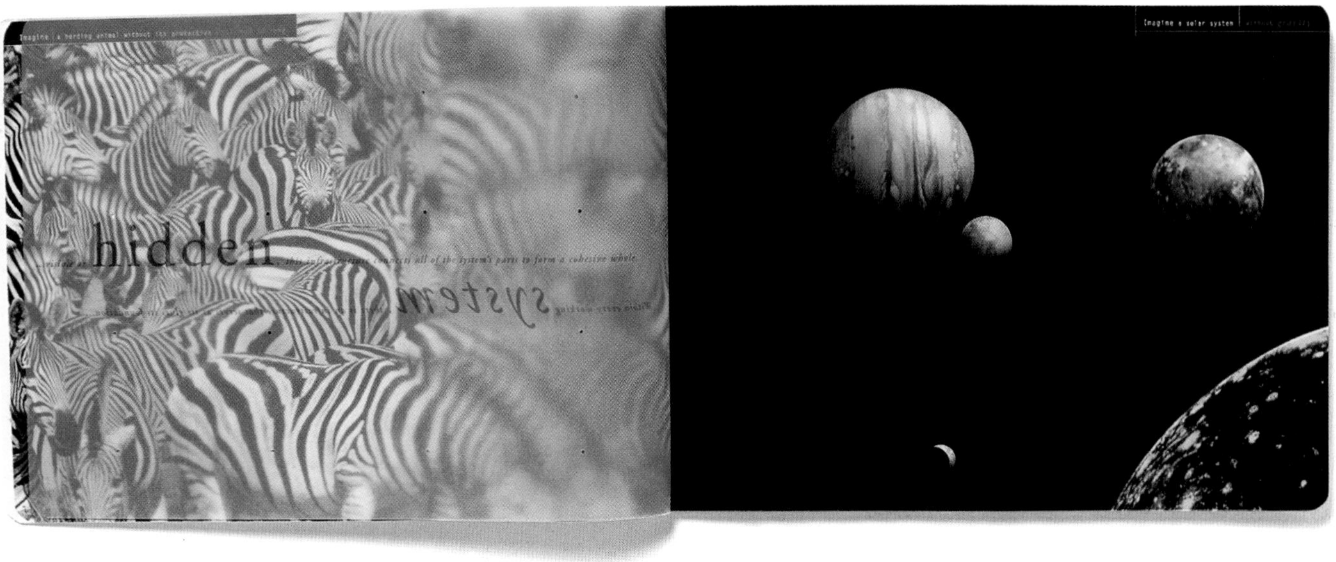
Imagine a herding animal without its protective
hidden
this infrastructure connects all of the system's parts to form a cohesive whole.
system
Imagine a solar system

How important is infrastructure?
Try to visualize the world without its oceans. A tree without roots

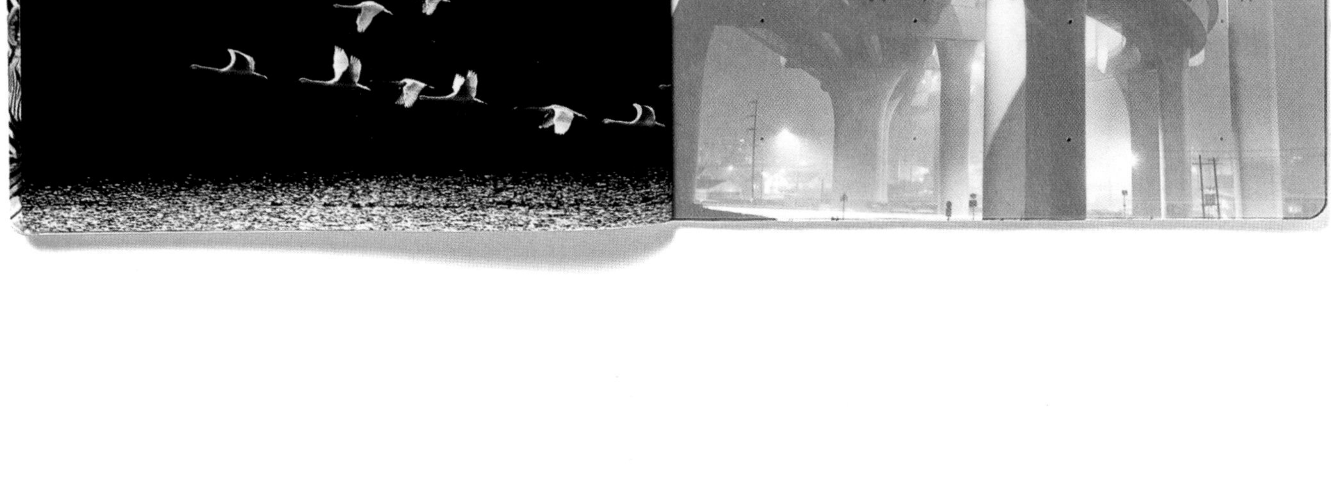
Imagine a flock
Try to visualize a building with no foundation.
success.
It isn't enough for an infrastructure,
critical
though it is, simply to exist...

...every system must be managed at an optimum level to ensure its long-term success.
Try to visualize a building with no foundation.
or with streets, but no intersections.

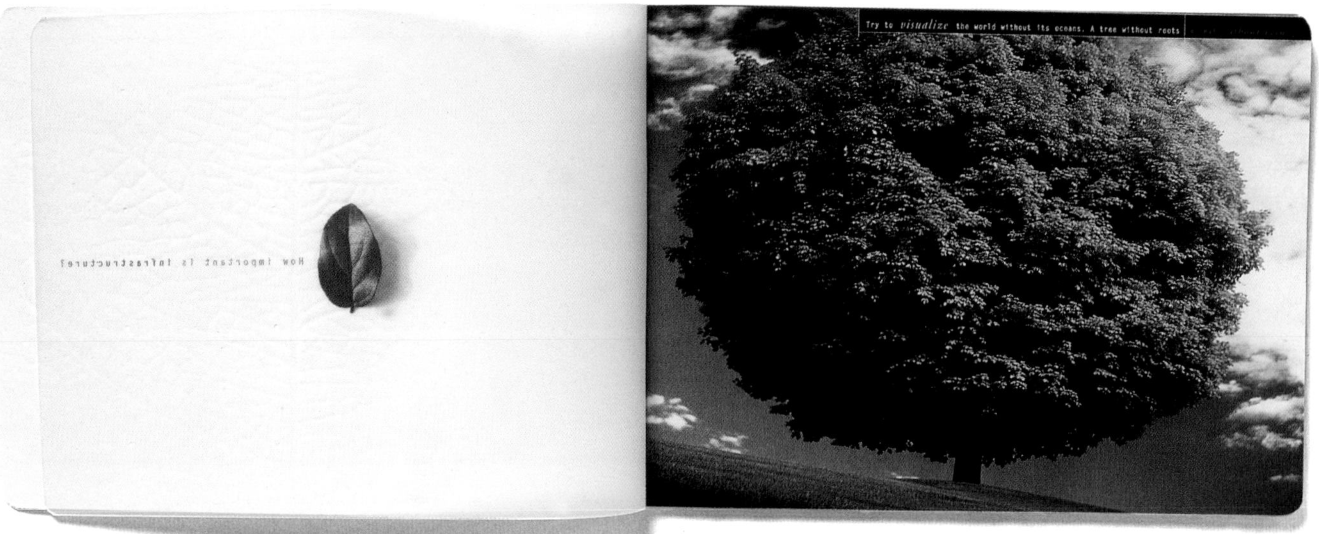
Try to visualize the world without its oceans. A tree without roots

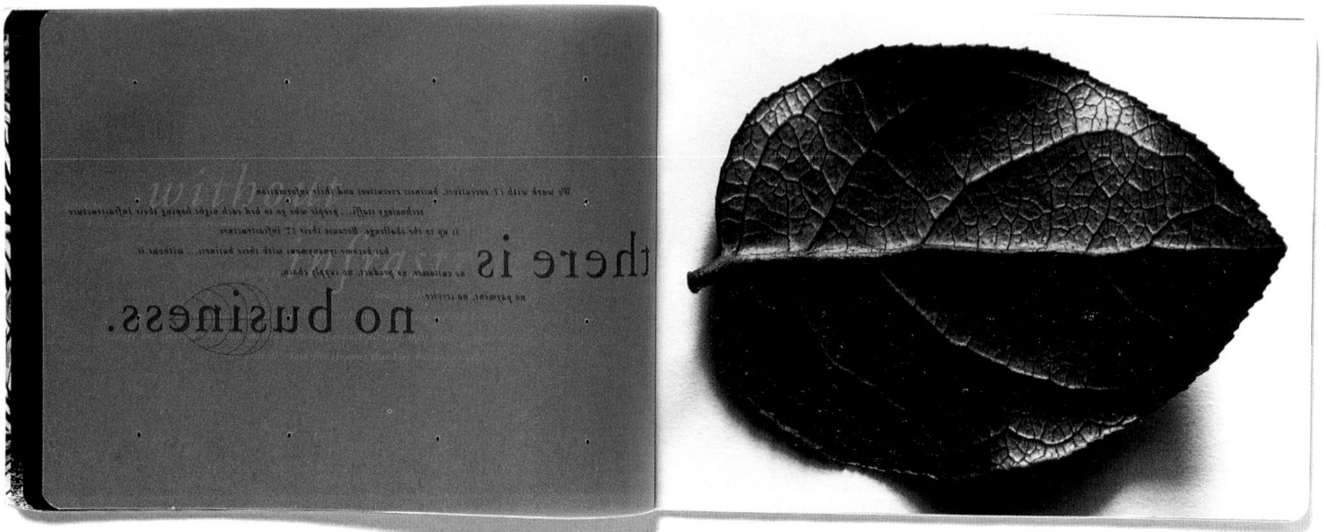

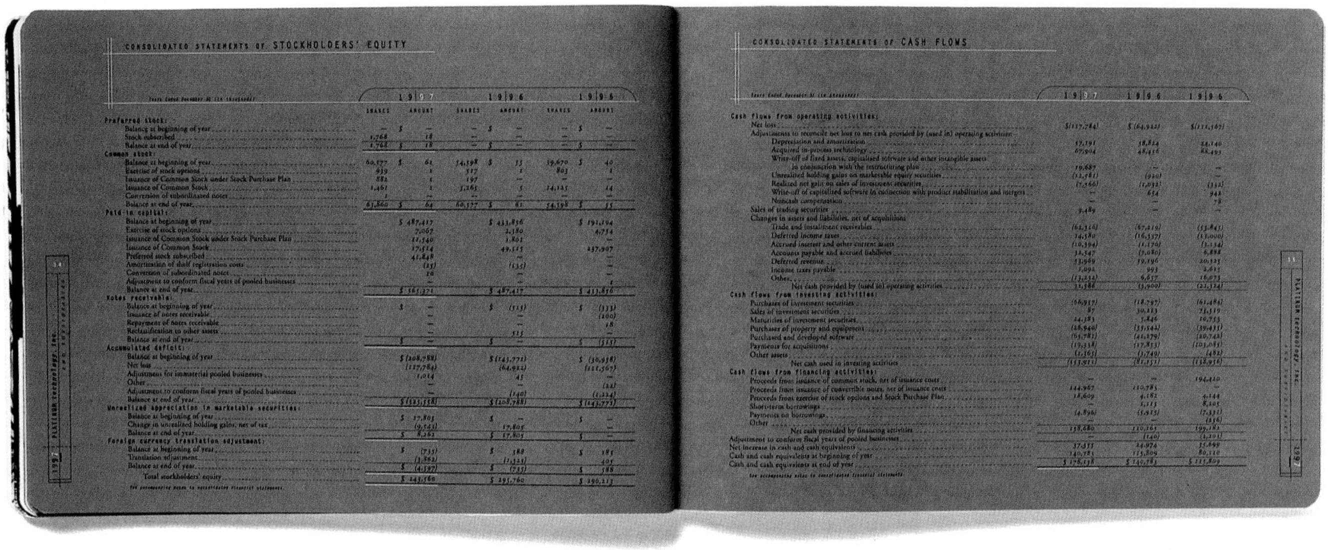
CONSOLIDATED STATEMENTS OF STOCKHOLDERS' EQUITY
CONSOLIDATED STATEMENTS OF CASH FLOWS

The financials
20 Management's Discussion and Analysis
30 Quarterly Comparisons
32 Consolidated Balance Sheets
33 Consolidated Statements of Operations
34 Consolidated Statements of Stockholders' Equity
35 Consolidated Statements of Cash Flows
36 Notes to Consolidated Financial Statements
52 Independent Auditors' Report
52 Directors and Executive Officers
53 Charitable Contributions for 1997
54 Map of Locations Around the World
56 Stockholder Information
SAFE HARBOR PROVISION

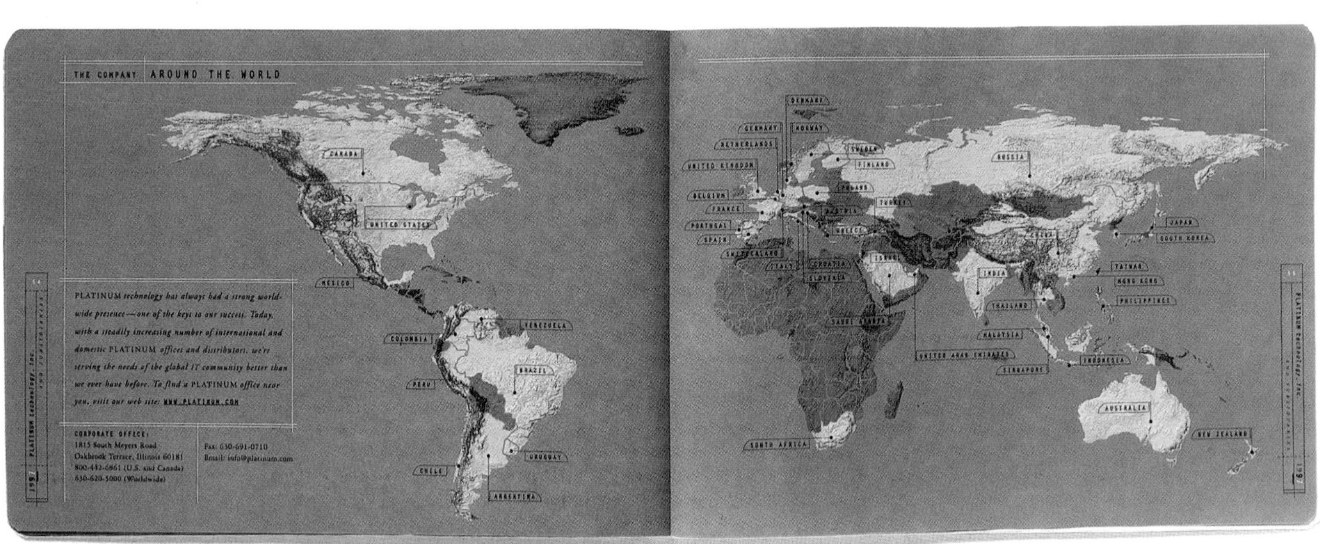
THE COMPANY AROUND THE WORLD
PLATINUM technology has always had a strong world-wide presence—one of the keys to our success. Today, with a steadily increasing number of international and domestic PLATINUM offices and distributors, we're serving the needs of the global IT community better than we ever have before. To find a PLATINUM office near you, visit our web site: WWW.PLATINUM.COM
CORPORATE OFFICE:
1815 South Meyers Road
Oakbrook Terrace, Illinois 60181
800-442-6861 (U.S. and Canada)
630-620-5000 (Worldwide)
Fax: 630-691-0710
Email: info@platinum.com
CANADA
UNITED STATES
MEXICO
VENEZUELA
COLOMBIA
PERU
BRAZIL
CHILE
URUGUAY
ARGENTINA
DENMARK
GERMANY
NORWAY
NETHERLANDS
UNITED KINGDOM
SWEDEN
FINLAND
RUSSIA
BELGIUM
FRANCE
PORTUGAL
SPAIN
SWITZERLAND
ITALY
CROATIA
SLOVENIA
POLAND
AUSTRIA
TURKEY
GREECE
JAPAN
SOUTH KOREA
INDIA
TAIWAN
HONG KONG
PHILIPPINES
THAILAND
MALAYSIA
SAUDI ARABIA
UNITED ARAB EMIRATES
SINGAPORE
INDONESIA
AUSTRALIA
SOUTH AFRICA
NEW ZEALAND

United Technologies Corp.
Agency: Ted Bertz Graphic Design, Inc.
Art Director: Richard Uccello
Creative Director: Ted Bertz
Designers: Richard Uccello, Ted Bertz
Photographers: Greg Heisler, Ted Kawalerski,
John Madera, Bill Varie, Paul Horton
Illustrators: John Harwood, Peter Krämer, Jeffrey West
Copywriter: Larry Gavrich

AIR MAIL
2000
NEXT THE
1999 Year in Review
MS. JUDITH A. BERTZ
190 WASHINGTON ST.
MIDDLETOWN, CT. 06457
United Technologies Corporation 1999 Year in Review

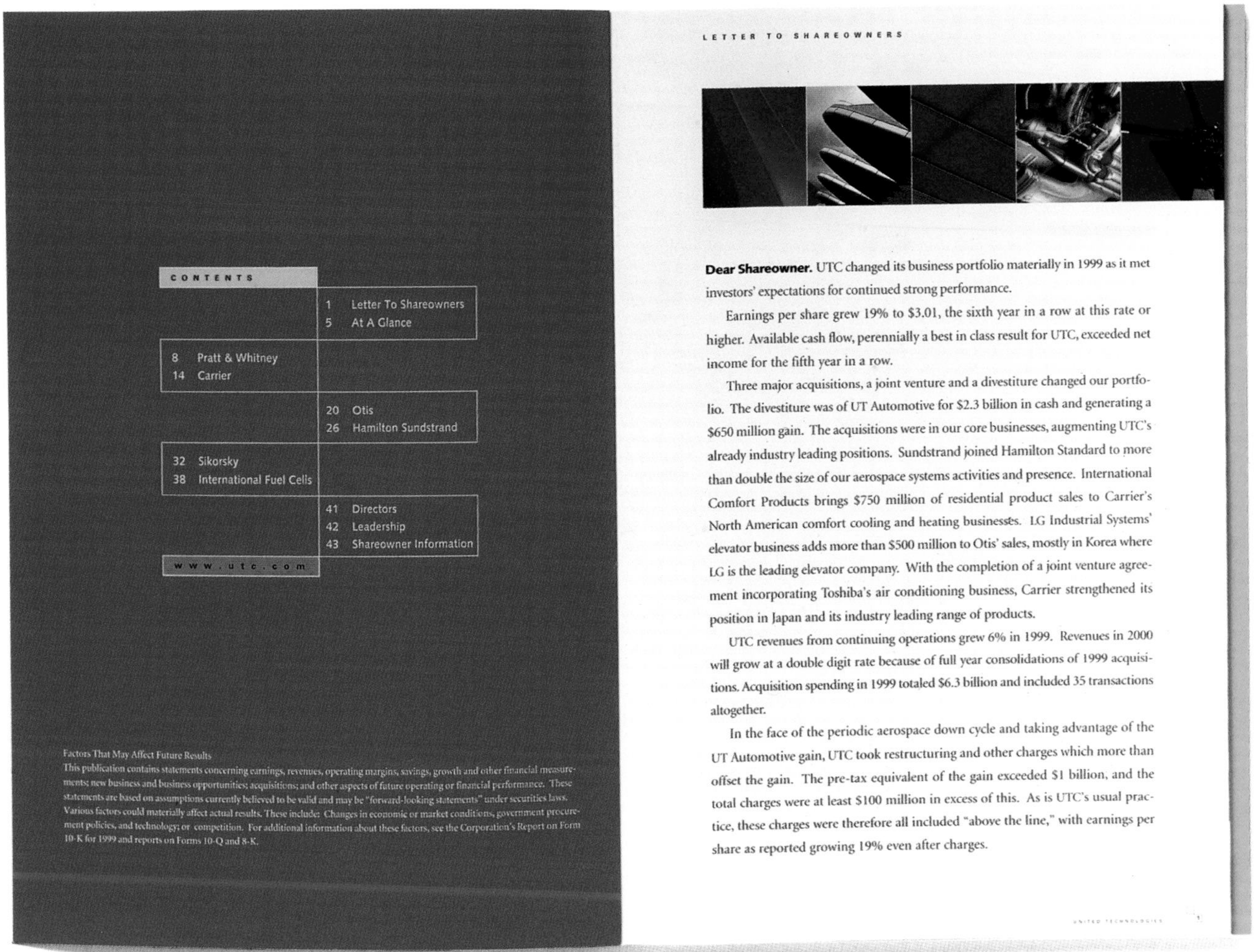

CONTENTS

www.utc.com

Factors That May Affect Future Results

This publication contains statements concerning earnings, revenues, operating margins, savings, growth and other financial measurements; new business and business opportunities; acquisitions; and other aspects of future operating or financial performance. These statements are based on assumptions currently believed to be valid and may be "forward-looking statements" under securities laws. Various factors could materially affect actual results. These include: Changes in economic or market conditions, government procurement policies, and technology; or competition. For additional information about these factors, see the Corporation's Report on Form 10-K for 1999 and reports on Forms 10-Q and 8-K.

LETTER TO SHAREOWNERS

Dear Shareowner. UTC changed its business portfolio materially in 1999 as it met investors' expectations for continued strong performance.

Earnings per share grew 19% to $3.01, the sixth year in a row at this rate or higher. Available cash flow, perennially a best in class result for UTC, exceeded net income for the fifth year in a row.

Three major acquisitions, a joint venture and a divestiture changed our portfolio. The divestiture was of UT Automotive for $2.3 billion in cash and generating a $650 million gain. The acquisitions were in our core businesses, augmenting UTC's already industry leading positions. Sundstrand joined Hamilton Standard to more than double the size of our aerospace systems activities and presence. International Comfort Products brings $750 million of residential product sales to Carrier's North American comfort cooling and heating businesses. LG Industrial Systems' elevator business adds more than $500 million to Otis' sales, mostly in Korea where LG is the leading elevator company. With the completion of a joint venture agreement incorporating Toshiba's air conditioning business, Carrier strengthened its position in Japan and its industry leading range of products.

UTC revenues from continuing operations grew 6% in 1999. Revenues in 2000 will grow at a double digit rate because of full year consolidations of 1999 acquisitions. Acquisition spending in 1999 totaled $6.3 billion and included 35 transactions altogether.

In the face of the periodic aerospace down cycle and taking advantage of the UT Automotive gain, UTC took restructuring and other charges which more than offset the gain. The pre-tax equivalent of the gain exceeded $1 billion, and the total charges were at least $100 million in excess of this. As is UTC's usual practice, these charges were therefore all included "above the line," with earnings per share as reported growing 19% even after charges.

UNITED TECHNOLOGIES 1

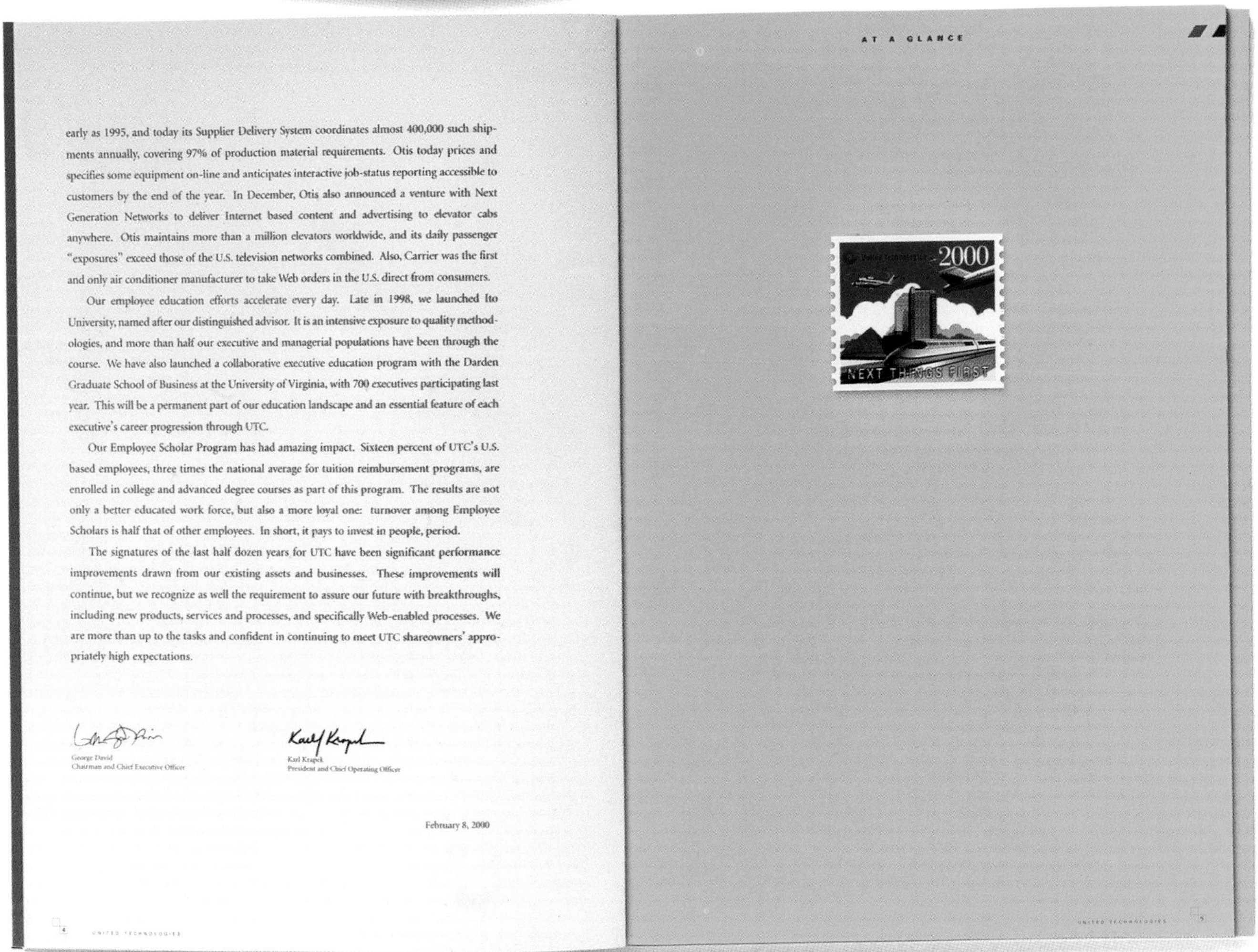

early as 1995, and today its Supplier Delivery System coordinates almost 400,000 such shipments annually, covering 97% of production material requirements. Otis today prices and specifies some equipment on-line and anticipates interactive job-status reporting accessible to customers by the end of the year. In December, Otis also announced a venture with Next Generation Networks to deliver Internet based content and advertising to elevator cabs anywhere. Otis maintains more than a million elevators worldwide, and its daily passenger "exposures" exceed those of the U.S. television networks combined. Also, Carrier was the first and only air conditioner manufacturer to take Web orders in the U.S. direct from consumers.

Our employee education efforts accelerate every day. Late in 1998, we launched Ito University, named after our distinguished advisor. It is an intensive exposure to quality methodologies, and more than half our executive and managerial populations have been through the course. We have also launched a collaborative executive education program with the Darden Graduate School of Business at the University of Virginia, with 700 executives participating last year. This will be a permanent part of our education landscape and an essential feature of each executive's career progression through UTC.

Our Employee Scholar Program has had amazing impact. Sixteen percent of UTC's U.S. based employees, three times the national average for tuition reimbursement programs, are enrolled in college and advanced degree courses as part of this program. The results are not only a better educated work force, but also a more loyal one: turnover among Employee Scholars is half that of other employees. In short, it pays to invest in people, period.

The signatures of the last half dozen years for UTC have been significant performance improvements drawn from our existing assets and businesses. These improvements will continue, but we recognize as well the requirement to assure our future with breakthroughs, including new products, services and processes, and specifically Web-enabled processes. We are more than up to the tasks and confident in continuing to meet UTC shareowners' appropriately high expectations.

George David
Chairman and Chief Executive Officer

Karl Krapek
President and Chief Operating Officer

February 8, 2000

4 UNITED TECHNOLOGIES

AT A GLANCE

2000
NEXT THINGS FIRST

UNITED TECHNOLOGIES 5

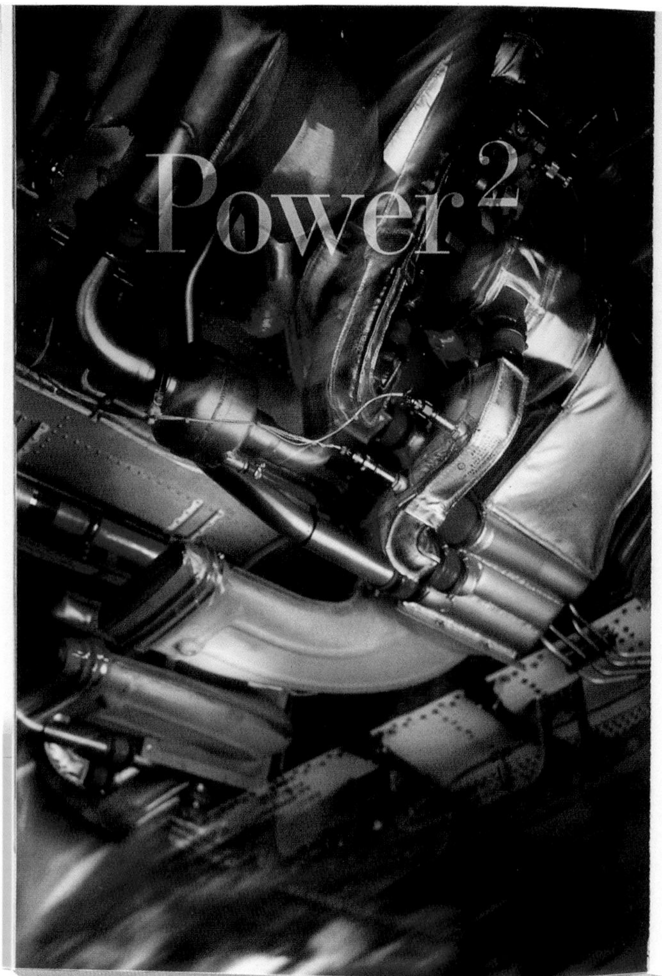
Power^2

Hamilton Sundstrand. In June, UTC made the largest acquisition in its history, purchasing Sundstrand Corporation and combining it with Hamilton Standard to form Hamilton Sundstrand. Before the acquisition, the two companies had complementary product lines; together, they form the

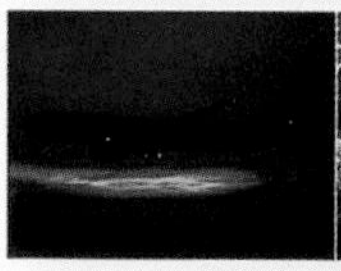

third largest supplier of aerospace products, with systems on most of the world's commercial airliners and military aircraft. Sundstrand also brought with it an annual $750 million industrial business that supports food processing, chemical, construction, mining and other industries worldwide.

Because Hamilton Sundstrand offers nose-to-tail systems and support to its aircraft maker customers, it is in an ideal position as customers reduce their supplier bases and look for lowest-cost packages. This strategy was demonstrated last year when Embraer selected Hamilton Sundstrand to supply integrated systems for several of the aircraft maker's new ERJ-170/190 family of regional aircraft, including the auxiliary power unit/tailcone, air management system, electric power generation and distribution system and actuation systems. Over the life of the program, the total contract value is expected to exceed $1 billion.

The scope of the company's aircraft business also offers insulation from aerospace cycle changes. With product on the vast majority of aircraft, declines in one segment – say large commercial jets – can be offset by growth in another, such as regional aircraft.

The new Hamilton Sundstrand provides global customer support that includes repair stations and a field service organization spreading

- **767-400, C-17, F-18**
  Hamilton Sundstrand is maintaining its leading position with numerous products on the latest aircraft.
- **Embraer**
  Hamilton Sundstrand is a long-time leader in providing the regional aircraft industry with environmental control systems, electric power systems and auxiliary power units.
- **Insert Liner Team**
  Hamilton Sundstrand's 1999 Quality Team of the Year from Grand Junction, Colo., reduced defects by 80% and cut cycle time by two-thirds for the more than 100,000 parts it makes each year.

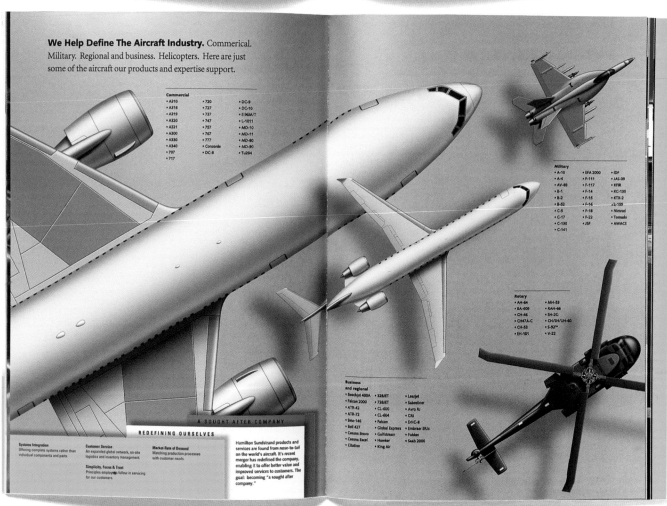

We Help Define The Aircraft Industry. Commerical. Military. Regional and business. Helicopters. Here are just some of the aircraft our products and expertise support.

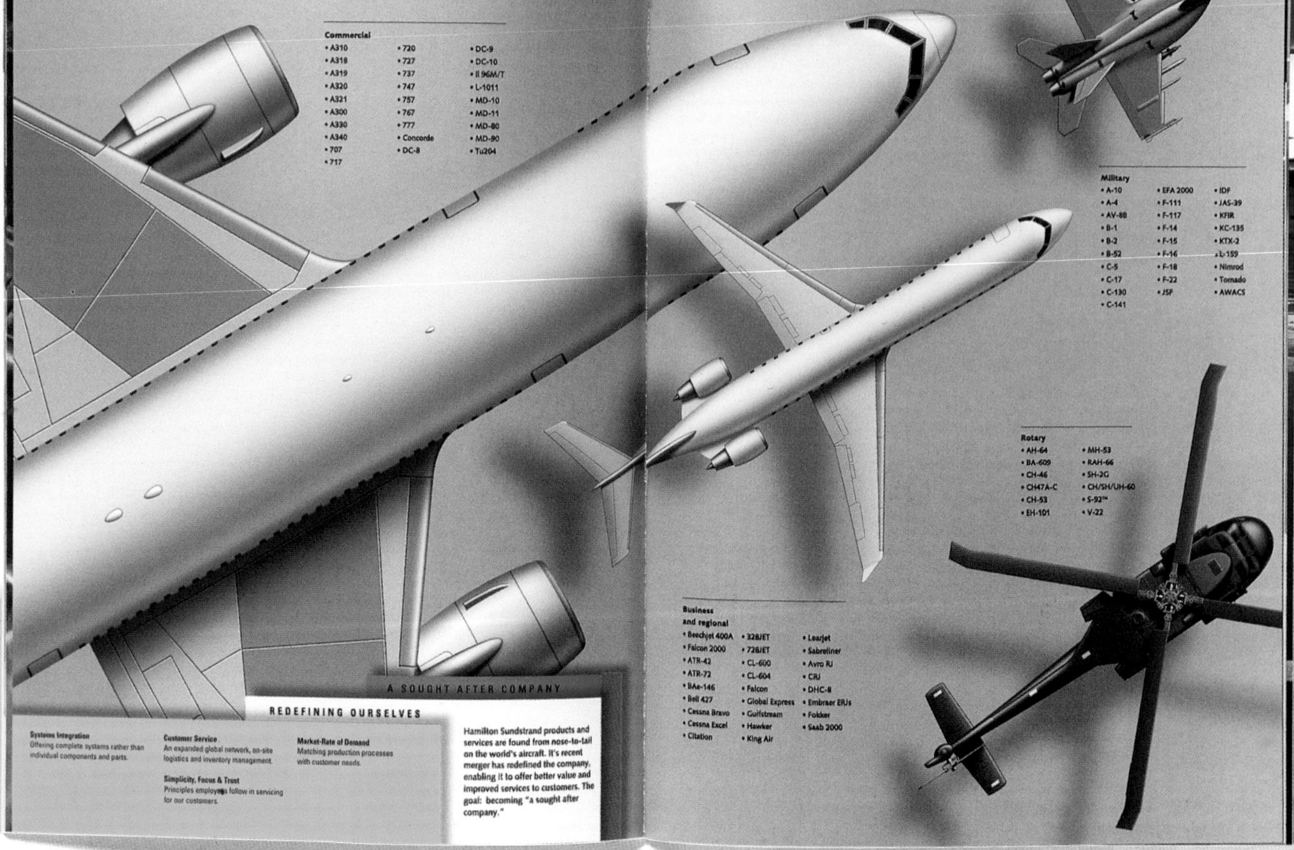

Commercial
- A310
- A318
- A319
- A320
- A321
- A300
- A330
- A340
- 707
- 717
- 720
- 727
- 737
- 747
- 757
- 767
- 777
- Concorde
- DC-8
- DC-9
- DC-10
- Il 96M/T
- L-1011
- MD-10
- MD-11
- MD-80
- MD-90
- Tu204

Military
- A-10
- A-4
- AV-8B
- B-1
- B-2
- B-52
- C-5
- C-17
- C-130
- C-141
- EFA 2000
- F-111
- F-117
- F-14
- F-15
- F-16
- F-18
- F-22
- JSF
- IDF
- JAS-39
- KFIR
- KC-135
- KTX-2
- L-159
- Nimrod
- Tornado
- AWACS

Rotary
- AH-64
- BA-609
- CH-46
- CH47A-C
- CH-53
- EH-101
- MH-53
- RAH-66
- SH-2G
- CH/SH/UH-60
- S-92™
- V-22

Business and regional
- Beechjet 400A
- Falcon 2000
- ATR-42
- ATR-72
- BAe-146
- Bell 427
- Cessna Bravo
- Cessna Excel
- Citation
- 328JET
- 728JET
- CL-600
- CL-604
- Falcon
- Global Express
- Gulfstream
- Hawker
- King Air
- Learjet
- Sabreliner
- Avro RJ
- CRJ
- DHC-8
- Embraer ERJs
- Fokker
- Saab 2000

A SOUGHT AFTER COMPANY

REDEFINING OURSELVES

Systems Integration
Offering complete systems rather than individual components and parts.

Customer Service
An expanded global network, on-site logistics and inventory management.

Simplicity, Focus & Trust
Principles employees follow in servicing for our customers.

Market-Rate of Demand
Matching production processes with customer needs.

Hamilton Sundstrand products and services are found from nose-to-tail on the world's aircraft. It's recent merger has redefined the company, enabling it to offer better value and improved services to customers. The goal: becoming "a sought after company."

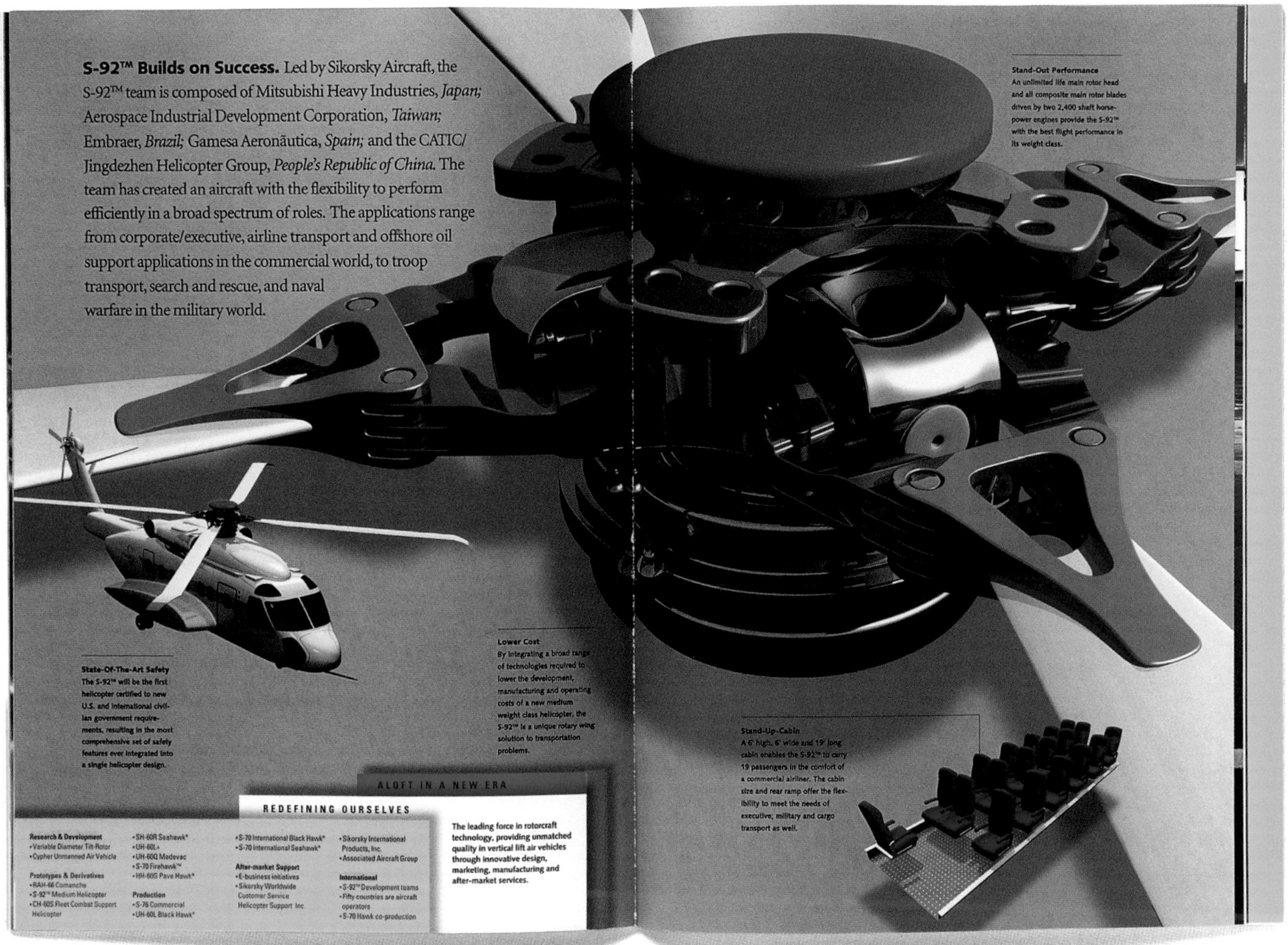
S-92™ Builds on Success. Led by Sikorsky Aircraft, the S-92™ team is composed of Mitsubishi Heavy Industries, *Japan;* Aerospace Industrial Development Corporation, *Taiwan;* Embraer, *Brazil;* Gamesa Aeronâutica, *Spain;* and the CATIC/Jingdezhen Helicopter Group, *People's Republic of China.* The team has created an aircraft with the flexibility to perform efficiently in a broad spectrum of roles. The applications range from corporate/executive, airline transport and offshore oil support applications in the commercial world, to troop transport, search and rescue, and naval warfare in the military world.
Stand-Out Performance
An unlimited life main rotor head and all composite main rotor blades driven by two 2,400 shaft horse-power engines provide the S-92™ with the best flight performance in its weight class.
State-Of-The-Art Safety
The S-92™ will be the first helicopter certified to new U.S. and International civilian government requirements, resulting in the most comprehensive set of safety features ever integrated into a single helicopter design.
Lower Cost
By integrating a broad range of technologies required to lower the development, manufacturing and operating costs of a new medium weight class helicopter, the S-92™ is a unique rotary wing solution to transportation problems.
Stand-Up-Cabin
A 6' high, 6' wide and 19' long cabin enables the S-92™ to carry 19 passengers in the comfort of a commercial airliner. The cabin size and rear ramp offer the flexibility to meet the needs of executive; military and cargo transport as well.
ALOFT IN A NEW ERA
REDEFINING OURSELVES
Research & Development
•Variable Diameter Tilt-Rotor
•Cypher Unmanned Air Vehicle
Prototypes & Derivatives
•RAH-66 Comanche
•S-92™ Medium Helicopter
•CH-60S Fleet Combat Support Helicopter
•SH-60R Seahawk*
•UH-60L+
•UH-60Q Medevac
•S-70 Firehawk™
•HH-60G Pave Hawk*
Production
•S-76 Commercial
•UH-60L Black Hawk*
•S-70 International Black Hawk*
•S-70 International Seahawk*
After-market Support
•E-business initiatives
•Sikorsky Worldwide Customer Service Helicopter Support Inc.
•Sikorsky International Products, Inc.
•Associated Aircraft Group
International
•S-92™ Development teams
•Fifty countries are aircraft operators
•S-70 Hawk co-production
The leading force in rotorcraft technology, providing unmatched quality in vertical lift air vehicles through innovative design, marketing, manufacturing and after-market services.

CONSOLIDATED

Balance Sheet

IN MILLIONS OF DOLLARS, EXCEPT PER SHARE (SHARES IN THOUSANDS)	DECEMBER 31, 1999	1998
Assets		
Cash and cash equivalents	$ 957	$ 550
Accounts receivable (net of allowance for doubtful accounts of $406 and $316)	4,337	3,417
Inventories and contracts in progress	3,504	3,191
Future income tax benefits	1,563	1,222
Other current assets	266	161
Net investment in discontinued operation	—	1,287
Total Current Assets	10,627	9,828
Customer financing assets	553	498
Future income tax benefits	873	1,093
Fixed assets	4,460	3,555
Goodwill (net of accumulated amortization of $507 and $388)	5,641	1,417
Other assets	2,212	1,377
Total Assets	$24,366	$17,768
Liabilities and Shareowners' Equity		
Short-term borrowings	$ 902	$ 504
Accounts payable	1,957	1,860
Accrued liabilities	6,023	4,719
Long-term debt currently due	333	99
Total Current Liabilities	9,215	7,182
Long-term debt	3,086	1,570
Future pension and postretirement benefit obligations	1,601	1,682
Future income taxes payable	126	143
Other long-term liabilities	2,245	1,936
Commitments and contingent liabilities (Notes 4 and 14)		
Minority interests in subsidiary companies	527	421
Series A ESOP Convertible Preferred Stock, $1 par value		
Authorized–20,000 shares		
Outstanding–12,237 and 12,629 shares	808	836
ESOP deferred compensation	(359)	(380)
	449	456
Shareowners' Equity:		
Capital Stock:		
Preferred Stock, $1 par value; Authorized–230,000 shares; None issued or outstanding	—	—
Common Stock, $1 par value; Authorized–1,000,000 shares; Issued–588,737 and 582,160 shares	4,227	2,708
Treasury Stock–114,191 and 132,056 common shares at cost	(3,182)	(3,117)
Retained earnings	6,463	5,411
Accumulated other non-shareowners' changes in equity:		
Foreign currency translation	(563)	(487)
Minimum pension liability	(41)	(137)
Unrealized holding gain on marketable equity securities	213	—
	(391)	(624)
Total Shareowners' Equity	7,117	4,378
Total Liabilities and Shareowners' Equity	$24,366	$17,768

See accompanying Notes to Consolidated Financial Statements

CONSOLIDATED STATEMENT OF

Cash Flows

IN MILLIONS OF DOLLARS	YEARS ENDED DECEMBER 31, 1999	1998	1997
Operating Activities			
Income from continuing operations	$ 841	$ 1,157	$ 962
Adjustments to reconcile income from continuing operations			
to net cash flows provided by operating activities:			
Depreciation and amortization	844	730	707
Deferred income tax provision (benefit)	4	(264)	(525)
Minority interests in subsidiaries' earnings	91	85	98
Change in:			
Accounts receivable	(256)	44	(182)
Inventories and contracts in progress	331	(113)	113
Other current assets	(66)	213	(19)
Accounts payable and accrued liabilities	595	135	331
Other, net	(74)	327	418
Net Cash Flows Provided by Operating Activities	2,310	2,314	1,903
Investing Activities			
Capital expenditures	(762)	(673)	(658)
Increase in customer financing assets	(383)	(356)	(132)
Decrease in customer financing assets	195	143	171
Acquisitions of businesses	(3,547)	(1,228)	(547)
Dispositions of businesses	43	—	36
Other, net	43	43	125
Net Cash Flows Used in Investing Activities	(4,411)	(2,071)	(1,005)
Financing Activities			
Issuance of long-term debt	1,727	402	12
Repayment of long-term debt	(557)	(146)	(129)
Increase in short-term borrowings	185	293	12
Common Stock issued under employee stock plans	354	220	143
Dividends paid on Common Stock	(353)	(316)	(291)
Repurchase of Common Stock	(822)	(650)	(849)
Dividends to minority interests and other	(159)	(138)	(95)
Net Cash Flows Provided by (Used in) Financing Activities	375	(335)	(1,197)
Net Cash Flows Provided by (Used in) Discontinued Operation	2,159	(9)	2
Effect of foreign exchange rate changes on Cash and cash equivalents	(26)	(4)	(46)
Net increase (decrease) in Cash and cash equivalents	407	(105)	(343)
Cash and cash equivalents, beginning of year	550	655	998
Cash and cash equivalents, end of year	$ 957	$ 550	$ 655
Supplemental Disclosure of Cash Flow Information:			
Interest paid, net of amounts capitalized	$ 217	$ 170	$ 162
Income taxes paid, net of refunds	368	888	859
Non-cash investing activities:			
The Corporation issued $1.9 billion of Treasury Stock in connection with the acquisition of Sundstrand Corporation			

See accompanying Notes to Consolidated Financial Statements

General Instrument
Agency: Addison
Art Director & Designer: Cindy Goldstein
Creative Director: David Kohler
Photographer: Dan Bigelow
Illustrator: James Nuel Smith
Copywriter: Colin Goedecke

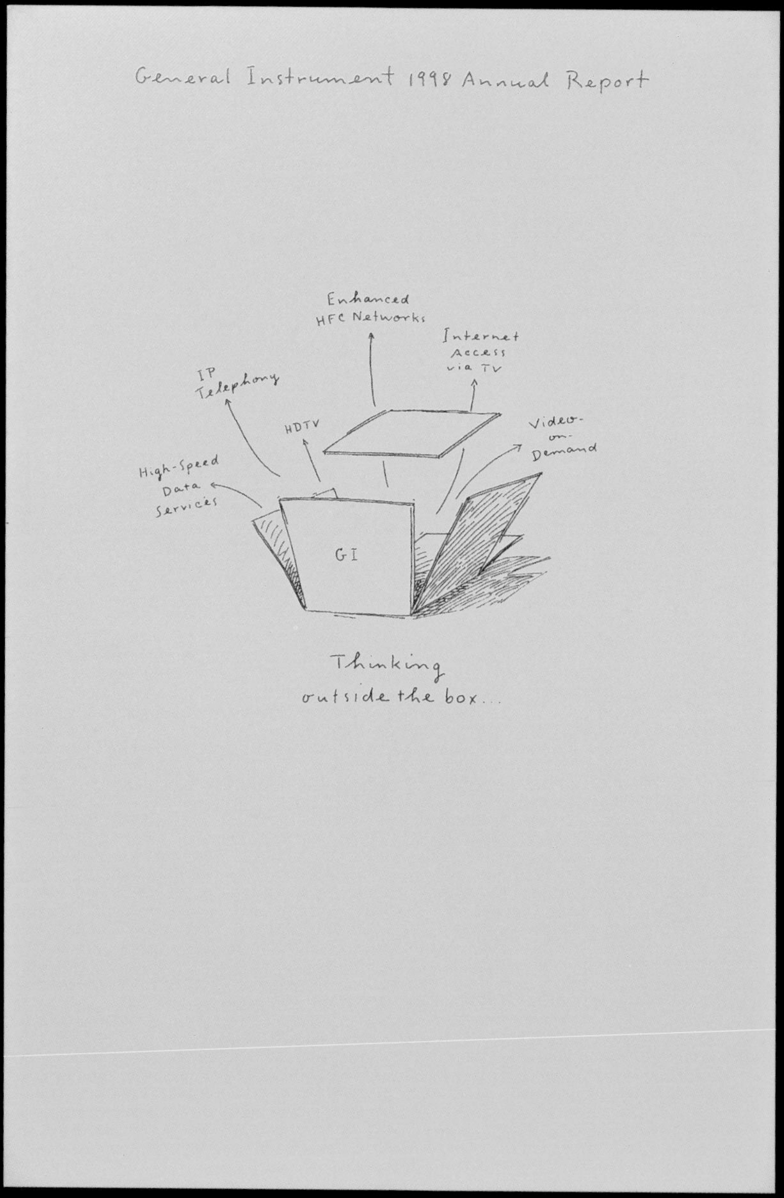
General Instrument 1998 Annual Report
Enhanced
HFC Networks
Internet
Access
via TV
IP
Telephony
HDTV
Video-
on-
Demand
High-Speed
Data
Services
GI
Thinking
outside the box...

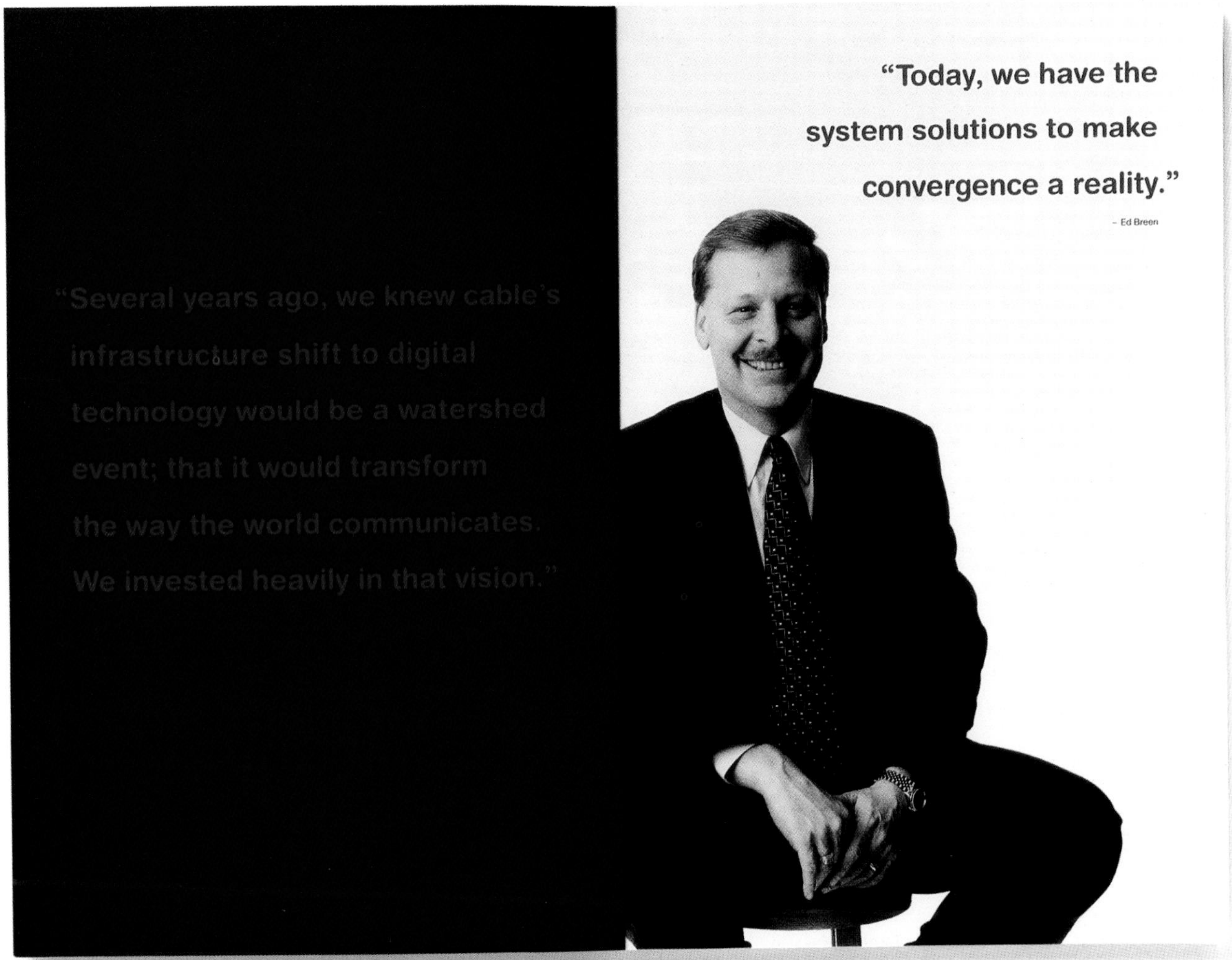
"Several years ago, we knew cable's infrastructure shift to digital technology would be a watershed event; that it would transform the way the world communicates. We invested heavily in that vision."
"Today, we have the system solutions to make convergence a reality."
– Ed Breen

Dear Stockholders,

Yesterday, cable systems delivered only analog TV, with 80 channels, simple program tiering and Pay-Per-View. Today, the digital revolution is in full swing and taking us into an exciting world of convergence: the true integration of entertainment, interactive technology and broadband telecommunications.

With convergence comes a quantum leap in communications, a new and never-before-seen level of advanced services and information, all delivered through high-capacity broadband networks: hundreds of channels, true Video-On-Demand, lightning-speed Internet access, telephony, e-mail, home networking and two-way interactivity for shopping, education, banking and games.

Broadband networks use Hybrid Fiber Coaxial (HFC) technology to create the largest capacity pipe ever available into our homes. The cable operator customers of General Instrument Corporation (GI) are upgrading and rebuilding their networks with the latest fiber optic and two-way RF technology, so they can deliver this wide range of advanced services to suscribers. They're also moving to bring these services on-stream soon, and affordably.

With digital cable and Internet protocol technologies delivered over the HFC network, the applications available to consumers become almost endless. There are over 65 million households in the U.S. currently subscribing to cable TV services, with HFC networks passing 95 percent of all American homes. The market for advanced interactive services on these networks is immense.

2

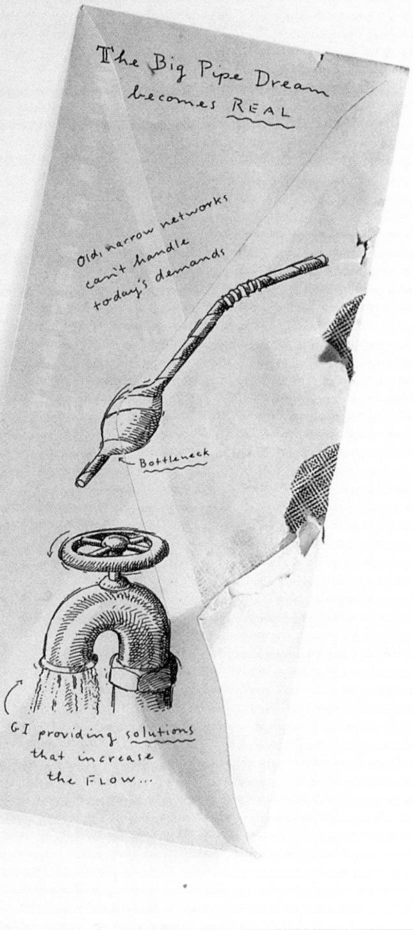
The Big Pipe Dream becomes REAL
Old, narrow networks can't handle today's demands
Bottleneck
GI providing solutions that increase the FLOW...

our customers; and Spyglass – to assist in software integration on our advanced digital platforms. In addition, through its limited partnership interest in Next Level Communications L.P., GI provides next-generation broadband access solutions for local telephone companies. The partnership's product, NLevel,[SM] permits cost-effective broadband access over twisted pair networks and can support high-speed data and video services as well as traditional telephone service over a common platform.

During 1998, our strong position was reflected in our financial performance and activities. Annual revenue grew 12.7 percent to $2 billion, and, before special charges, operating income nearly doubled, from $112 million in 1997 to $220 million in 1998. Including these charges, we generated $271 million in cash from operations. And, we repurchased 6.2 million GI shares.

Operationally, we achieved significant productivity gains through a variety of initiatives in our manufacturing facilities. We streamlined our workforce and implemented strategic procurement and product cost-reduction programs, which increased both our low-cost manufacturing advantage as well as our rates of production.

It was the hard work and expertise of our employees that led to many of the Company's most important successes and accomplishments during the year. We'll continue to make the investments necessary to hire and retain the best employees in the U.S. and around the world, building upon our strong workforce and maintaining our reputation as an "Employer of Choice."

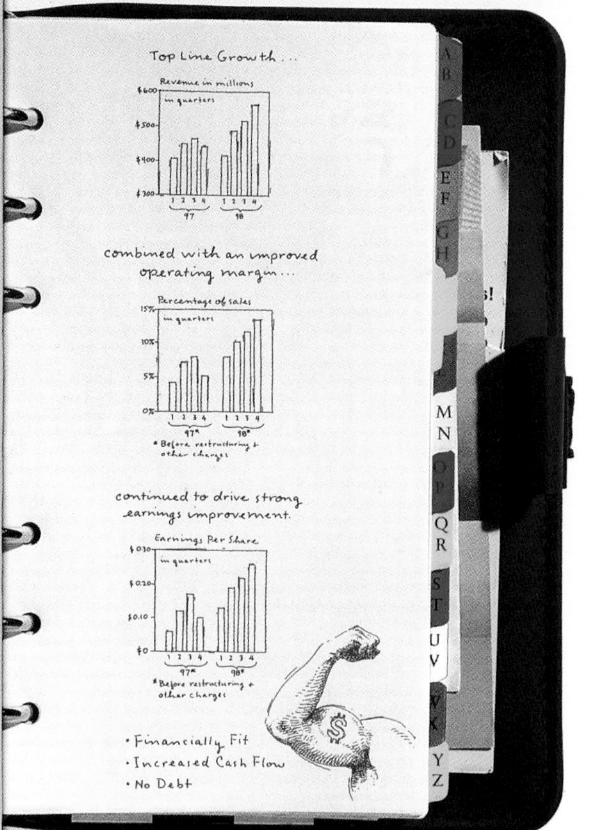
Top Line Growth...
Revenue in millions
in quarters
$600
$500
$400
$300
1 2 3 4
97
1 2 3 4
98
combined with an improved operating margin...
Percentage of sales
in quarters
15%
10%
5%
0%
97*
98*
* Before restructuring & other charges
continued to drive strong earnings improvement.
Earnings Per Share
in quarters
$0.30
$0.20
$0.10
$0
97*
98*
* Before restructuring & other charges
• Financially Fit
• Increased Cash Flow
• No Debt

General Instrument is now a comprehensive broadband systems provider, with a talented and dynamic management team seasoned in the cable business. We understand the industry and what we need to do to be successful. Drawing on this wisdom and our 50 years of cable experience, we will continue to build solutions for this ever-changing marketplace.

Now and tomorrow

Digital technology is changing the landscape and GI is using it to revolutionize communication services. As the leading innovator of cable television from its inception, and today's foremost provider of broadband cable solutions, we're enabling our customers to take full advantage of the latest developments and evolving opportunities. As we move into the future, we're extending our reach and presence. It's an exciting future that GI is entering with a powerful combination of vision, skill, alliances, research and development we need to maintain and enhance our position as the world's leading resource for integrated, interactive broadband technology.

We talk a lot about the big picture, but we never forget we're in business to create value and opportunity for you, our stockholders. I encourage your interest in GI's progress now and tomorrow, and thank you for your strong support in 1998.

Edward D. Breen

Edward D. Breen
Chairman of the Board and Chief Executive Officer

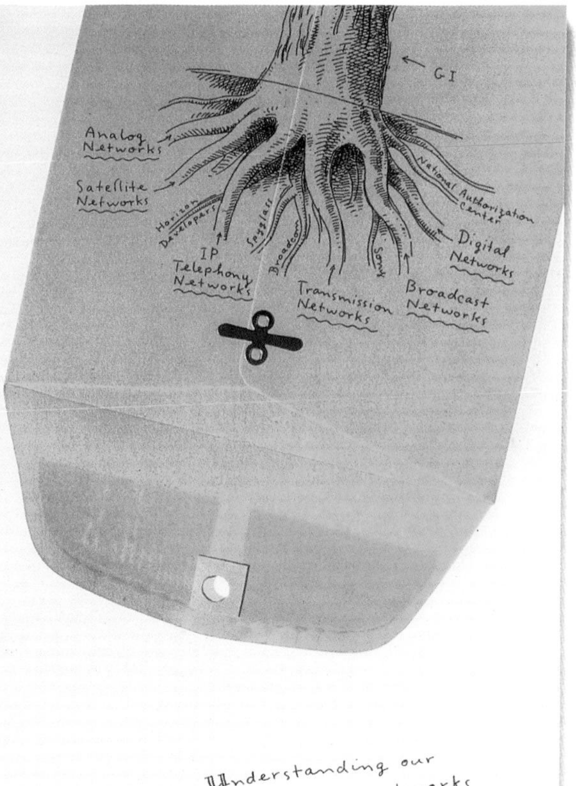
GI
Analog Networks
Satellite Networks
National Authorization Center
Digital Networks
IP Telephony Networks
Transmission Networks
Broadcast Networks

Understanding our INTEGRATED networks

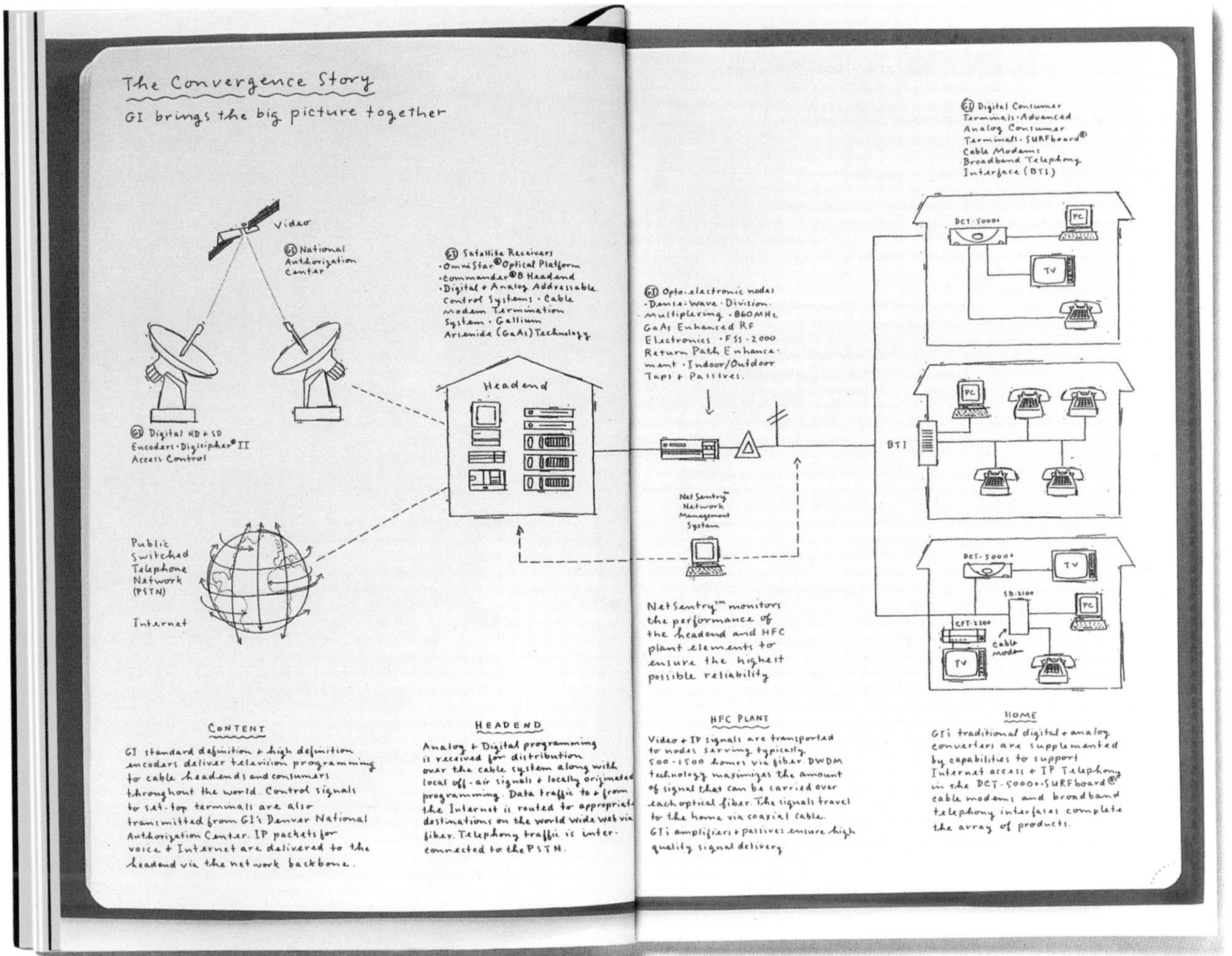
The Convergence Story
GI brings the big picture together
Video
GI National Authorization Center
GI Digital HD + SD Encoders · Digicipher® II Access Control
Public Switched Telephone Network (PSTN)
Internet
GI Satellite Receivers · OmniStar® Optical Platform · Commander® 8 Headend · Digital + Analog Addressable Control Systems · Cable Modem Termination System · Gallium Arsenide (GaAs) Technology
Headend
GI Opto-electronic nodes · Dense-Wave-Division-Multiplexing · 860MHz GaAs Enhanced RF Electronics · FSS-2000 Return Path Enhancement · Indoor/Outdoor Taps + Passives.
NetSentry™ Network Management System
NetSentry™ monitors the performance of the headend and HFC plant elements to ensure the highest possible reliability
BTI
GI Digital Consumer Terminals · Advanced Analog Consumer Terminals · SURFboard® Cable Modems · Broadband Telephony Interface (BTI)
DCT-5000+
PC
TV
SB-2100
CFT-2200
cable modem
CONTENT
GI standard definition + high definition encoders deliver television programming to cable headends and consumers throughout the world. Control signals to set-top terminals are also transmitted from GI's Denver National Authorization Center. IP packets for voice + Internet are delivered to the headend via the network backbone.
HEADEND
Analog + Digital programming is received for distribution over the cable system along with local off-air signals + locally originated programming. Data traffic to + from the Internet is routed to appropriate destinations on the world wide web via fiber. Telephony traffic is interconnected to the PSTN.
HFC PLANT
Video + IP signals are transported to nodes serving typically 500-1500 homes via fiber. DWDM technology maximizes the amount of signal that can be carried over each optical fiber. The signals travel to the home via coaxial cable. GI's amplifiers + passives ensure high quality signal delivery.
HOME
GI's traditional digital + analog converters are supplemented by capabilities to support Internet access + IP Telephony in the DCT-5000+ · SURFboard® cable modems and broadband telephony interfaces complete the array of products.

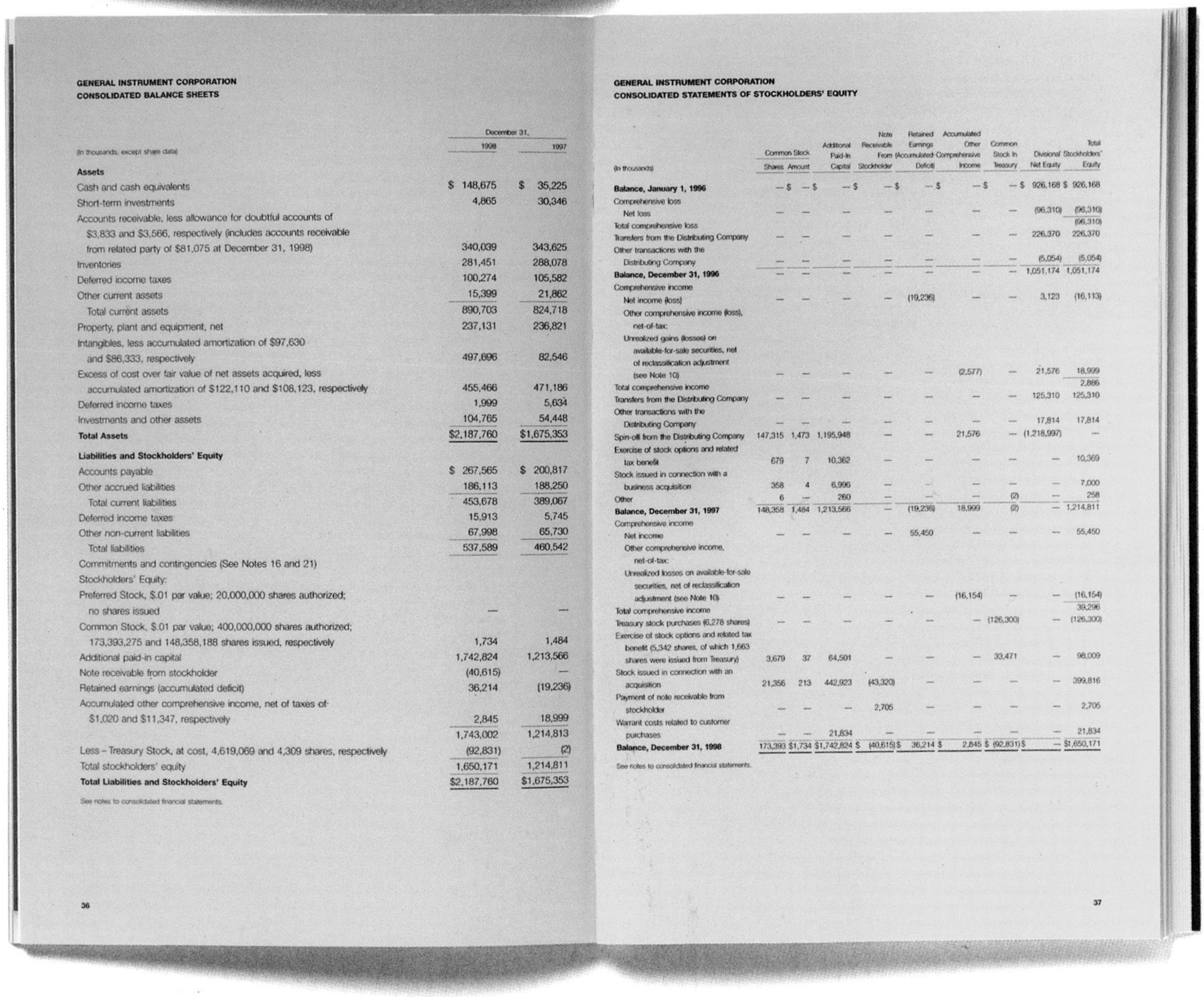

GENERAL INSTRUMENT CORPORATION
CONSOLIDATED BALANCE SHEETS

(In thousands, except share data)	December 31, 1998	1997
Assets		
Cash and cash equivalents	$ 148,675	$ 35,225
Short-term investments	4,865	30,346
Accounts receivable, less allowance for doubtful accounts of $3,833 and $3,566, respectively (includes accounts receivable from related party of $81,075 at December 31, 1998)	340,039	343,625
Inventories	281,451	288,078
Deferred income taxes	100,274	105,582
Other current assets	15,399	21,862
Total current assets	890,703	824,718
Property, plant and equipment, net	237,131	236,821
Intangibles, less accumulated amortization of $97,630 and $86,333, respectively	497,696	82,546
Excess of cost over fair value of net assets acquired, less accumulated amortization of $122,110 and $108,123, respectively	455,466	471,186
Deferred income taxes	1,999	5,634
Investments and other assets	104,765	54,448
Total Assets	$2,187,760	$1,675,353
Liabilities and Stockholders' Equity		
Accounts payable	$ 267,565	$ 200,817
Other accrued liabilities	186,113	188,250
Total current liabilities	453,678	389,067
Deferred income taxes	15,913	5,745
Other non-current liabilities	67,998	65,730
Total liabilities	537,589	460,542
Commitments and contingencies (See Notes 16 and 21)		
Stockholders' Equity:		
Preferred Stock, $.01 par value; 20,000,000 shares authorized; no shares issued	—	—
Common Stock, $.01 par value; 400,000,000 shares authorized; 173,393,275 and 148,358,188 shares issued, respectively	1,734	1,484
Additional paid-in capital	1,742,824	1,213,566
Note receivable from stockholder	(40,615)	—
Retained earnings (accumulated deficit)	36,214	(19,236)
Accumulated other comprehensive income, net of taxes of $1,020 and $11,347, respectively	2,845	18,999
	1,743,002	1,214,813
Less – Treasury Stock, at cost, 4,619,069 and 4,309 shares, respectively	(92,831)	(2)
Total stockholders' equity	1,650,171	1,214,811
Total Liabilities and Stockholders' Equity	$2,187,760	$1,675,353

See notes to consolidated financial statements.

36

GENERAL INSTRUMENT CORPORATION
CONSOLIDATED STATEMENTS OF STOCKHOLDERS' EQUITY

(In thousands)	Common Stock Shares	Common Stock Amount	Additional Paid-In Capital	Note Receivable From Stockholder	Retained Earnings (Accumulated Deficit)	Accumulated Other Comprehensive Income	Common Stock In Treasury	Divisional Net Equity	Total Stockholders' Equity
Balance, January 1, 1996	— $	— $	— $	— $	— $	— $	— $	926,168 $	926,168
Comprehensive loss									
Net loss	—	—	—	—	—	—	—	(96,310)	(96,310)
Total comprehensive loss									(96,310)
Transfers from the Distributing Company	—	—	—	—	—	—	—	226,370	226,370
Other transactions with the Distributing Company	—	—	—	—	—	—	—	(5,054)	(5,054)
Balance, December 31, 1996	—	—	—	—	—	—	—	1,051,174	1,051,174
Comprehensive income									
Net income (loss)	—	—	—	—	(19,236)	—	—	3,123	(16,113)
Other comprehensive income (loss), net-of-tax:									
Unrealized gains (losses) on available-for-sale securities, net of reclassification adjustment (see Note 10)	—	—	—	—	—	(2,577)	—	21,576	18,999
Total comprehensive income									2,886
Transfers from the Distributing Company	—	—	—	—	—	—	—	125,310	125,310
Other transactions with the Distributing Company	—	—	—	—	—	—	—	17,814	17,814
Spin-off from the Distributing Company	147,315	1,473	1,195,948	—	—	21,576	—	(1,218,997)	—
Exercise of stock options and related tax benefit	679	7	10,362	—	—	—	—	—	10,369
Stock issued in connection with a business acquisition	358	4	6,996	—	—	—	—	—	7,000
Other	6	—	260	—	—	—	(2)	—	258
Balance, December 31, 1997	148,358	1,484	1,213,566	—	(19,236)	18,999	(2)	—	1,214,811
Comprehensive income									
Net income	—	—	—	—	55,450	—	—	—	55,450
Other comprehensive income, net-of-tax:									
Unrealized losses on available-for-sale securities, net of reclassification adjustment (see Note 10)	—	—	—	—	—	(16,154)	—	—	(16,154)
Total comprehensive income									39,296
Treasury stock purchases (6,278 shares)	—	—	—	—	—	—	(126,300)	—	(126,300)
Exercise of stock options and related tax benefit (5,342 shares, of which 1,663 shares were issued from Treasury)	3,679	37	64,501	—	—	—	33,471	—	98,009
Stock issued in connection with an acquisition	21,356	213	442,923	(43,320)	—	—	—	—	399,816
Payment of note receivable from stockholder	—	—	—	2,705	—	—	—	—	2,705
Warrant costs related to customer purchases	—	—	21,834	—	—	—	—	—	21,834
Balance, December 31, 1998	173,393	$1,734	$1,742,824	$ (40,615)	$ 36,214	$ 2,845	$ (92,831)	$ —	$1,650,171

See notes to consolidated financial statements.

37

Identix

Agency: Cahan & Associates
Art & Creative Director: Bill Cahan
Designer: Michael Braley
Copywriter: JoAnna di Paolo

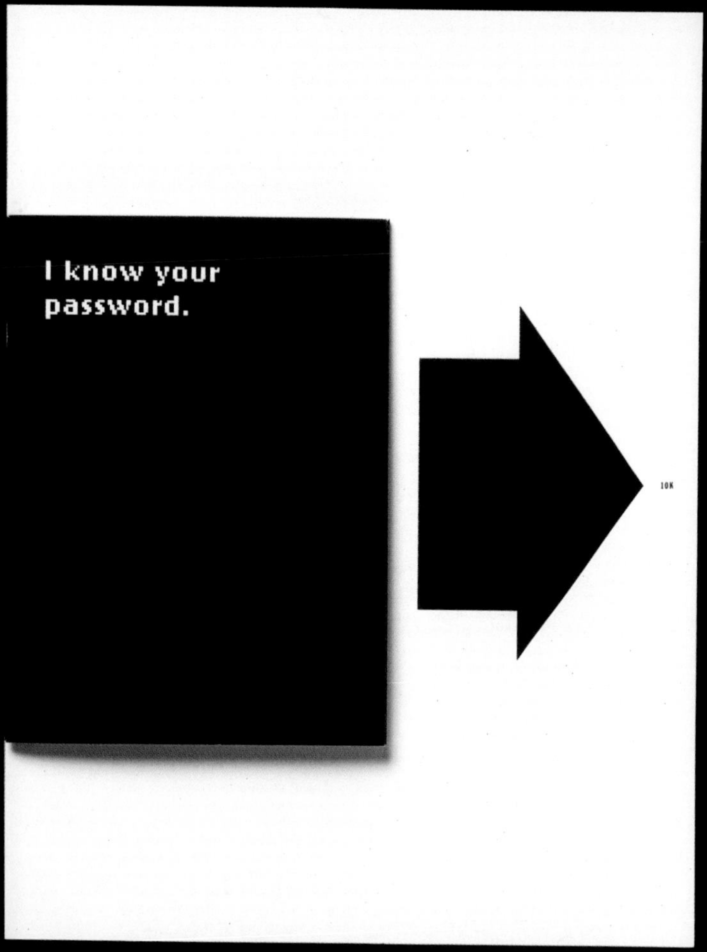
I know your password.
10K

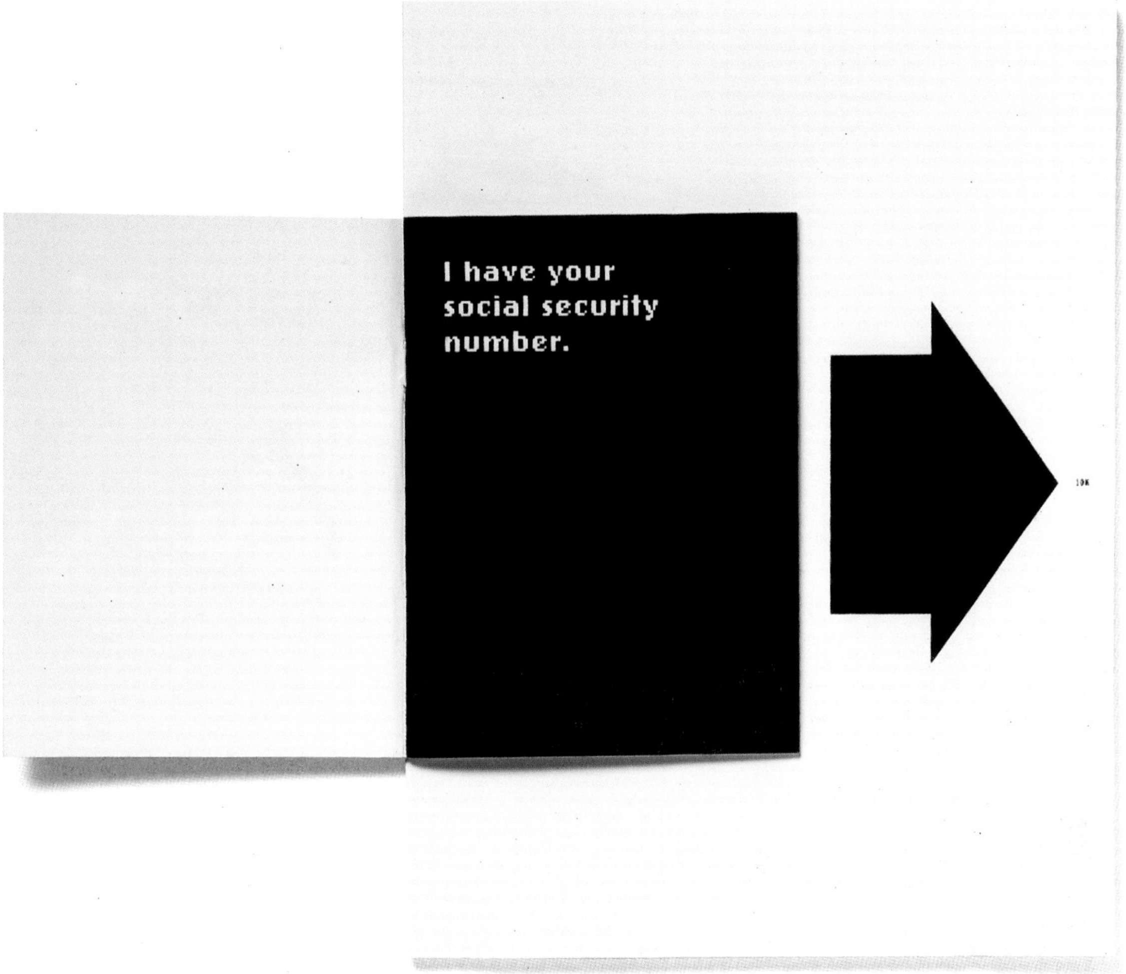
I have your
social security
number.

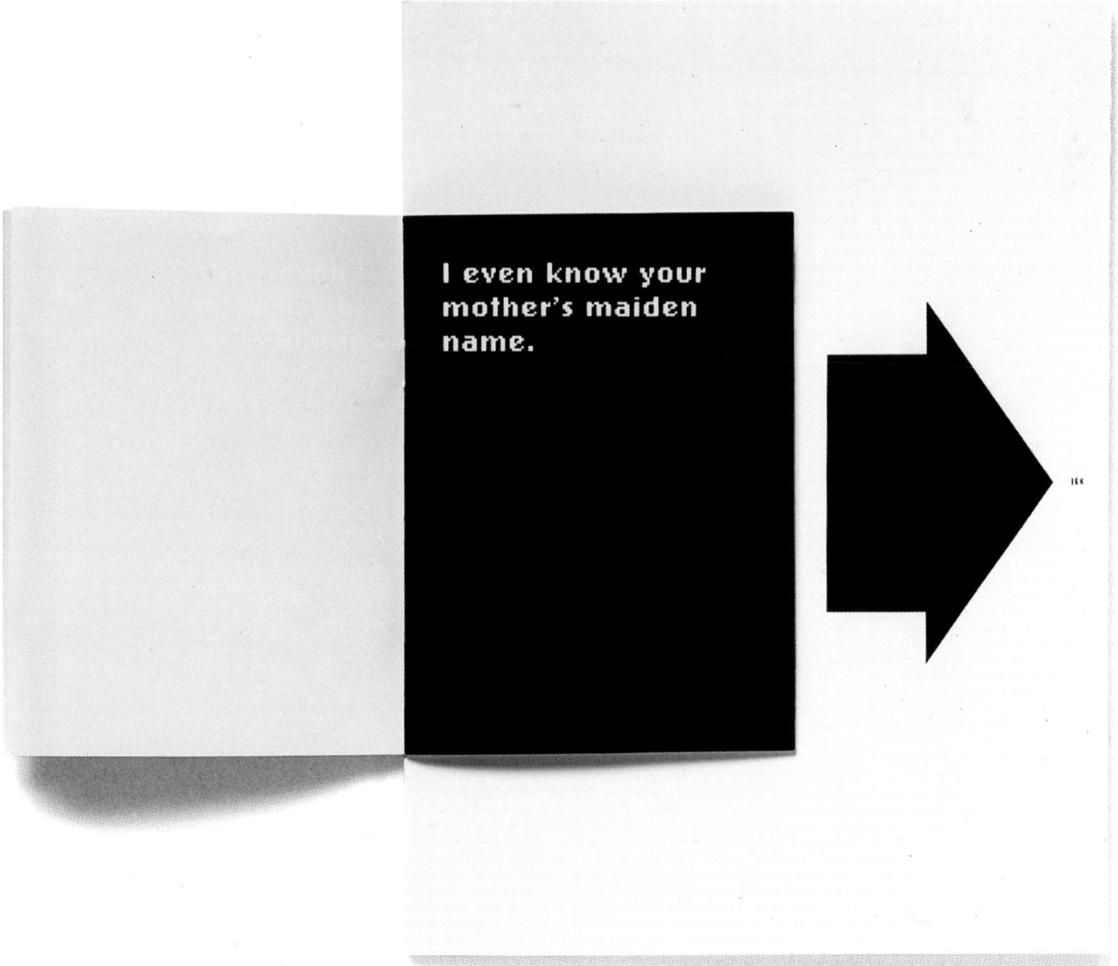
I even know your
mother's maiden
name.

IDENTIX PROVIDES
THE BIOMETRICS
TECHNOLOGY TO
PROTECT YOU IN
THE DIGITAL AGE.
10K

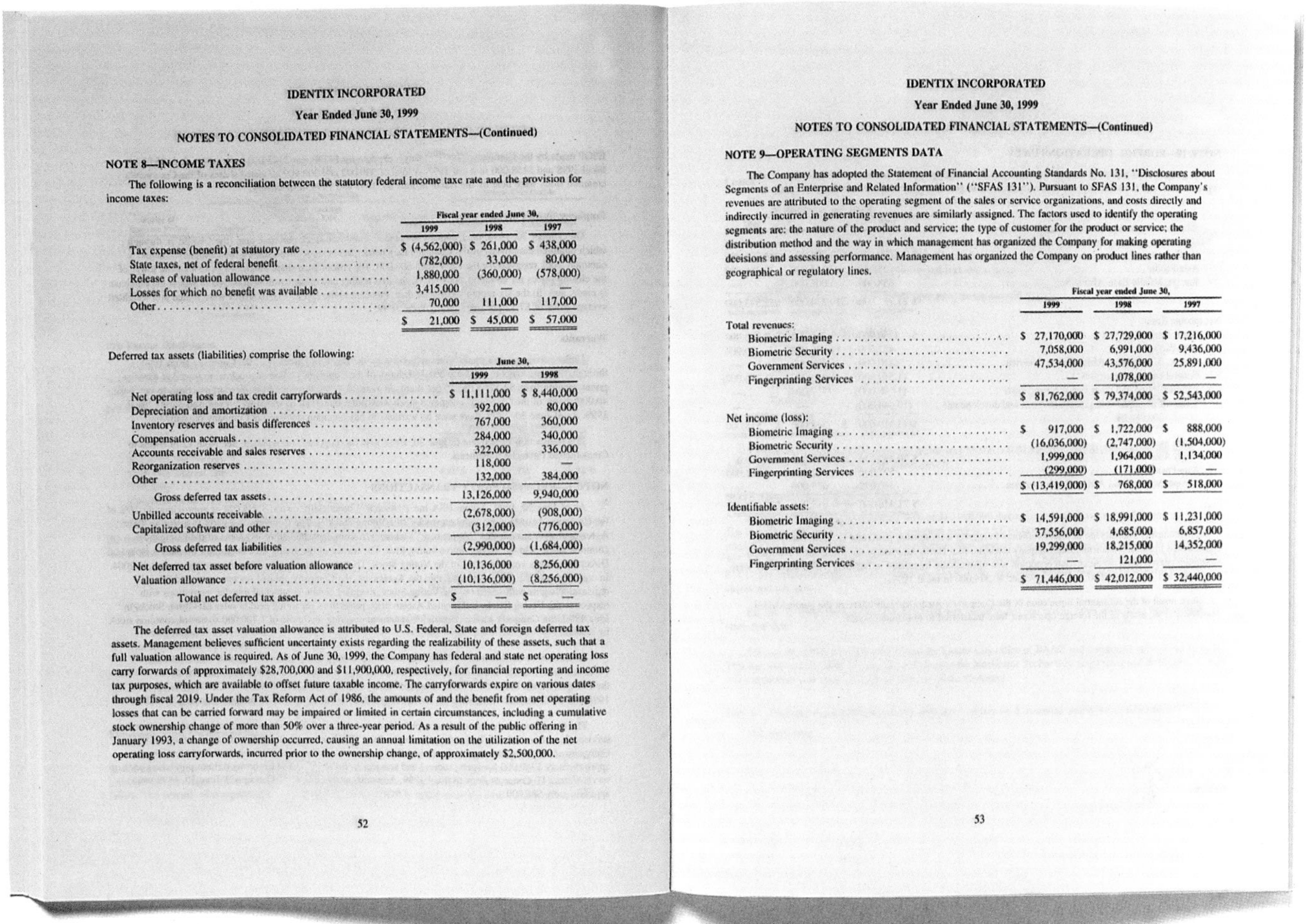

IDENTIX INCORPORATED

Year Ended June 30, 1999

NOTES TO CONSOLIDATED FINANCIAL STATEMENTS—(Continued)

NOTE 8—INCOME TAXES

The following is a reconciliation between the statutory federal income taxe rate and the provision for income taxes:

	Fiscal year ended June 30,		
	1999	1998	1997
Tax expense (benefit) at statutory rate	$ (4,562,000)	$ 261,000	$ 438,000
State taxes, net of federal benefit	(782,000)	33,000	80,000
Release of valuation allowance	1,880,000	(360,000)	(578,000)
Losses for which no benefit was available	3,415,000	—	—
Other	70,000	111,000	117,000
	$ 21,000	$ 45,000	$ 57,000

Deferred tax assets (liabilities) comprise the following:

	June 30,	
	1999	1998
Net operating loss and tax credit carryforwards	$ 11,111,000	$ 8,440,000
Depreciation and amortization	392,000	80,000
Inventory reserves and basis differences	767,000	360,000
Compensation accruals	284,000	340,000
Accounts receivable and sales reserves	322,000	336,000
Reorganization reserves	118,000	—
Other	132,000	384,000
Gross deferred tax assets	13,126,000	9,940,000
Unbilled accounts receivable	(2,678,000)	(908,000)
Capitalized software and other	(312,000)	(776,000)
Gross deferred tax liabilities	(2,990,000)	(1,684,000)
Net deferred tax asset before valuation allowance	10,136,000	8,256,000
Valuation allowance	(10,136,000)	(8,256,000)
Total net deferred tax asset	$ —	$ —

The deferred tax asset valuation allowance is attributed to U.S. Federal, State and foreign deferred tax assets. Management believes sufficient uncertainty exists regarding the realizability of these assets, such that a full valuation allowance is required. As of June 30, 1999, the Company has federal and state net operating loss carry forwards of approximately $28,700,000 and $11,900,000, respectively, for financial reporting and income tax purposes, which are available to offset future taxable income. The carryforwards expire on various dates through fiscal 2019. Under the Tax Reform Act of 1986, the amounts of and the benefit from net operating losses that can be carried forward may be impaired or limited in certain circumstances, including a cumulative stock ownership change of more than 50% over a three-year period. As a result of the public offering in January 1993, a change of ownership occurred, causing an annual limitation on the utilization of the net operating loss carryforwards, incurred prior to the ownership change, of approximately $2,500,000.

52

IDENTIX INCORPORATED

Year Ended June 30, 1999

NOTES TO CONSOLIDATED FINANCIAL STATEMENTS—(Continued)

NOTE 9—OPERATING SEGMENTS DATA

The Company has adopted the Statement of Financial Accounting Standards No. 131, "Disclosures about Segments of an Enterprise and Related Information" ("SFAS 131"). Pursuant to SFAS 131, the Company's revenues are attributed to the operating segment of the sales or service organizations, and costs directly and indirectly incurred in generating revenues are similarly assigned. The factors used to identify the operating segments are: the nature of the product and service; the type of customer for the product or service; the distribution method and the way in which management has organized the Company for making operating deeisions and assessing performance. Management has organized the Company on product lines rather than geographical or regulatory lines.

	Fiscal year ended June 30,		
	1999	1998	1997
Total revenues:			
Biometric Imaging	$ 27,170,000	$ 27,729,000	$ 17,216,000
Biometric Security	7,058,000	6,991,000	9,436,000
Government Services	47,534,000	43,576,000	25,891,000
Fingerprinting Services	—	1,078,000	—
	$ 81,762,000	$ 79,374,000	$ 52,543,000
Net income (loss):			
Biometric Imaging	$ 917,000	$ 1,722,000	$ 888,000
Biometric Security	(16,036,000)	(2,747,000)	(1,504,000)
Government Services	1,999,000	1,964,000	1,134,000
Fingerprinting Services	(299,000)	(171,000)	—
	$ (13,419,000)	$ 768,000	$ 518,000
Identifiable assets:			
Biometric Imaging	$ 14,591,000	$ 18,991,000	$ 11,231,000
Biometric Security	37,556,000	4,685,000	6,857,000
Government Services	19,299,000	18,215,000	14,352,000
Fingerprinting Services	—	121,000	—
	$ 71,446,000	$ 42,012,000	$ 32,440,000

53

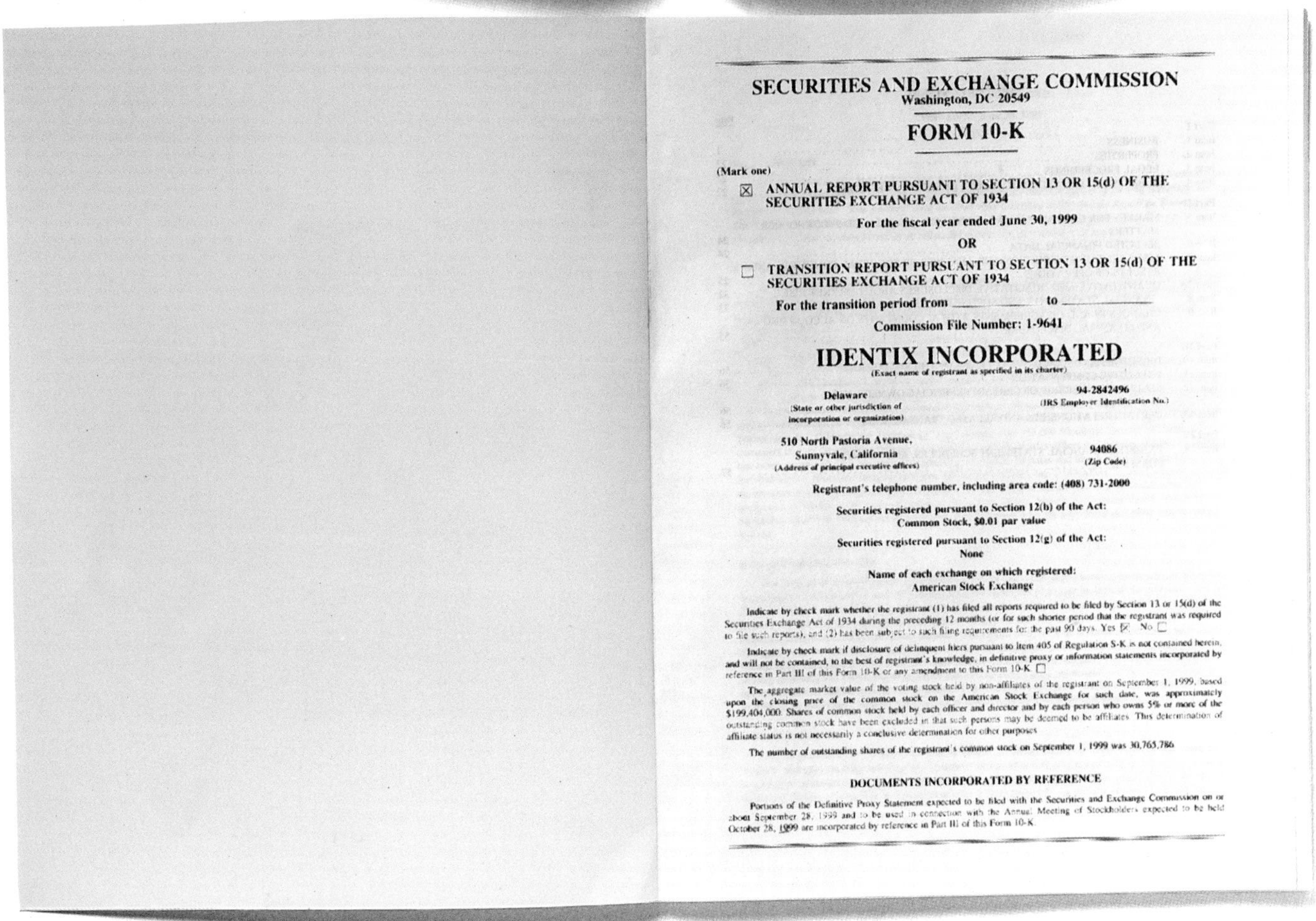

SECURITIES AND EXCHANGE COMMISSION
Washington, DC 20549

FORM 10-K

(Mark one)

☒ ANNUAL REPORT PURSUANT TO SECTION 13 OR 15(d) OF THE SECURITIES EXCHANGE ACT OF 1934

For the fiscal year ended June 30, 1999

OR

☐ TRANSITION REPORT PURSUANT TO SECTION 13 OR 15(d) OF THE SECURITIES EXCHANGE ACT OF 1934

For the transition period from ________ to ________

Commission File Number: 1-9641

IDENTIX INCORPORATED
(Exact name of registrant as specified in its charter)

Delaware (State or other jurisdiction of incorporation or organization)	94-2842496 (IRS Employer Identification No.)
510 North Pastoria Avenue, Sunnyvale, California (Address of principal executive offices)	94086 (Zip Code)

Registrant's telephone number, including area code: (408) 731-2000

Securities registered pursuant to Section 12(b) of the Act:
Common Stock, $0.01 par value

Securities registered pursuant to Section 12(g) of the Act:
None

Name of each exchange on which registered:
American Stock Exchange

Indicate by check mark whether the registrant (1) has filed all reports required to be filed by Section 13 or 15(d) of the Securities Exchange Act of 1934 during the preceding 12 months (or for such shorter period that the registrant was required to file such reports), and (2) has been subject to such filing requirements for the past 90 days. Yes ☒ No ☐

Indicate by check mark if disclosure of delinquent filers pursuant to Item 405 of Regulation S-K is not contained herein, and will not be contained, to the best of registrant's knowledge, in definitive proxy or information statements incorporated by reference in Part III of this Form 10-K or any amendment to this Form 10-K ☐

The aggregate market value of the voting stock held by non-affiliates of the registrant on September 1, 1999, based upon the closing price of the common stock on the American Stock Exchange for such date, was approximately $199,404,000. Shares of common stock held by each officer and director and by each person who owns 5% or more of the outstanding common stock have been excluded in that such persons may be deemed to be affiliates. This determination of affiliate status is not necessarily a conclusive determination for other purposes.

The number of outstanding shares of the registrant's common stock on September 1, 1999 was 30,765,786

DOCUMENTS INCORPORATED BY REFERENCE

Portions of the Definitive Proxy Statement expected to be filed with the Securities and Exchange Commission on or about September 28, 1999 and to be used in connection with the Annual Meeting of Stockholders expected to be held October 28, 1999 are incorporated by reference in Part III of this Form 10-K.

Visio Corporation
Agency: Leimer Cross Design
Art & Creative Director, Designer, Copywriter: Kerry Leimer
Photographers: Charles Blackburn, Jeff Corwin
Illustrator: Marianne Li

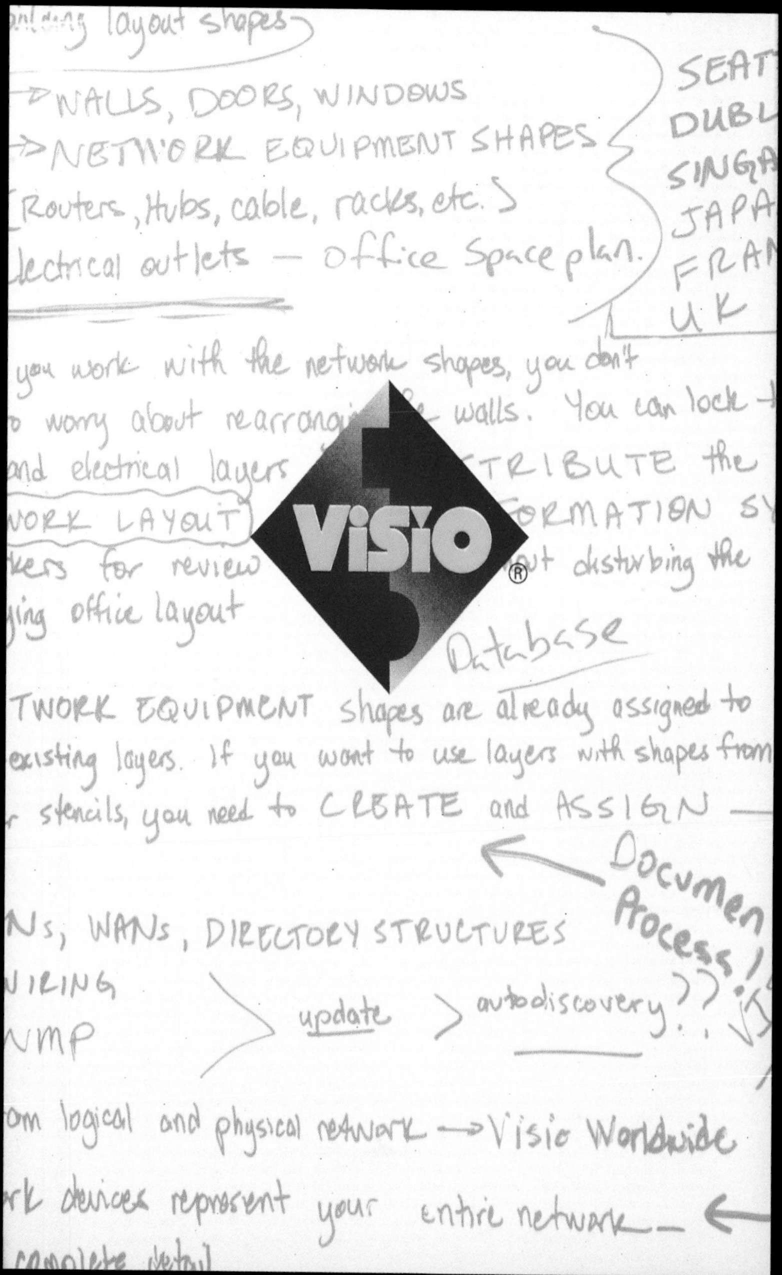
layout shapes
WALLS, DOORS, WINDOWS
NETWORK EQUIPMENT SHAPES
Routers, Hubs, cable, racks, etc.
lectrical outlets — Office Space plan.
SEAT
DUBL
SINGA
JAPA
FRAN
UK
you work with the network shapes, you don't
worry about rearranging walls. You can lock
and electrical layers
WORK LAYOUT
kers for review
ying office layout
Database
VISIO
TWORK EQUIPMENT shapes are already assigned to
existing layers. If you want to use layers with shapes from
stencils, you need to CREATE and ASSIGN
Documen
Process!
Ns, WANs, DIRECTORY STRUCTURES
WIRING
update
autodiscovery??
om logical and physical network → Visio Worldwide
rk devices represent your entire network

File Edit View Insert Format
Normal
New Media, Inc.
Product Devel

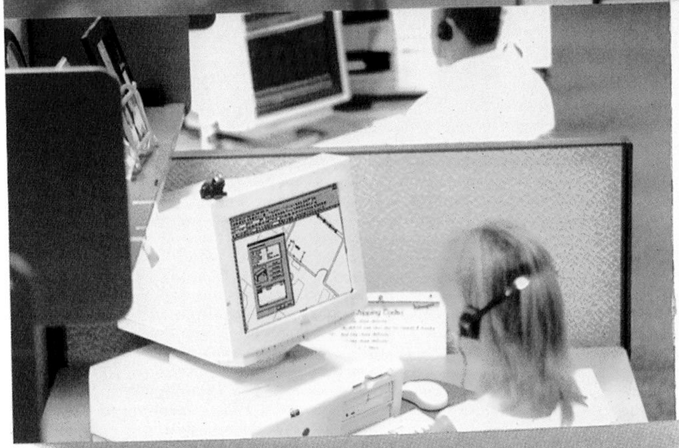

No matter what you need to visualize, our technology provides the platform. Visio Corporation succeeds because its products enable the creation of a broad range of business drawings, from simple diagrams to complex technical schematics.

11

Grow by delivering deeper drawing solutions that address the needs of engineers in strategic vertical markets: Visio Technical.

TECHNOLOGY ACQUIRED FOR VISIO TECHNICAL

1.98 MarComp, Inc.	5.98 Decision Graphics U.K. Ltd.
AutoCAD file read and write technology	computer-aided facilities management

14

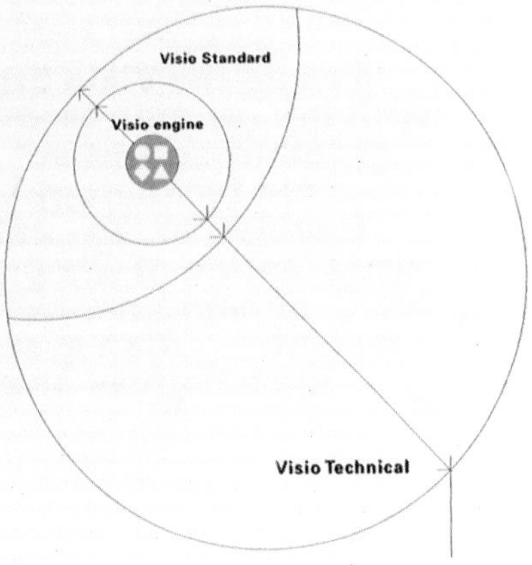
Visio Standard
Visio engine
Visio Technical

Visio Technical includes all the functionality of Visio Standard, plus specialized content for:
Mechanical engineering drawings
Space plans
Facilities management
Process plant designs
Heating, ventilation, air conditioning designs
Industrial and building automation designs
Electrical engineering schematics
Piping and instrumentation designs
Manufacturing and assembly drawings
Introduced: November 1994

VISIO

The direction for all these new products and feature sets comes from a very reliable source: our customers. We know what they want, because we listen to what they have to say.

Here's what's behind our accomplishments, and what will keep us growing in the year ahead.

Our initial vision of a huge market potential for Visio solutions is just as clear today. Each month, about 80,000 people in every kind of business all over the world adopt a new way to share ideas and distribute work—the Visio way. Business professionals are discovering a new way to draw. Products and networks are being designed. Proposals are being delivered. People and their ideas are being more clearly understood, and decisions are being made based on what Visio drawings and diagrams communicate. By the end of fiscal year 1998, our installed base had grown to 2.5 million people developing, documenting, and sharing drawings with Visio software.

Our Growth Strategy: Market Creation

While 2.5 million is an impressive number, there are 120 million Microsoft Windows business users worldwide. Our research tells us 28% of them create at least six drawings per month, or spend at least six hours per month drawing. That equates to 34 million businesspeople around the world who see drawing as a valuable part of their work. We believe that this number is a realistic marker for judging the potential size of our market. But it's important to understand that Visio Corporation is not strictly pursuing "market share." We're really in a "market creation" mode, with the express goal of owning the dominant position in the rapidly growing drawing and diagramming market. We're already No. 1 in that category, according to PC Data reports, and we are winning at "market creation." A recent survey conducted for Visio Corporation revealed that 50% of our customers had never used a PC-based drawing product before using Visio technology. The next two largest groups were Microsoft PowerPoint and Microsoft Word users, even though neither program is intended for drawing. We have created and grown a new category.

Our Growth Strategy: Evolved Products

With a new category established, we have successfully extended our core technology into new segments. We created Visio Technical, a product specifically designed for people who create technical schematics.

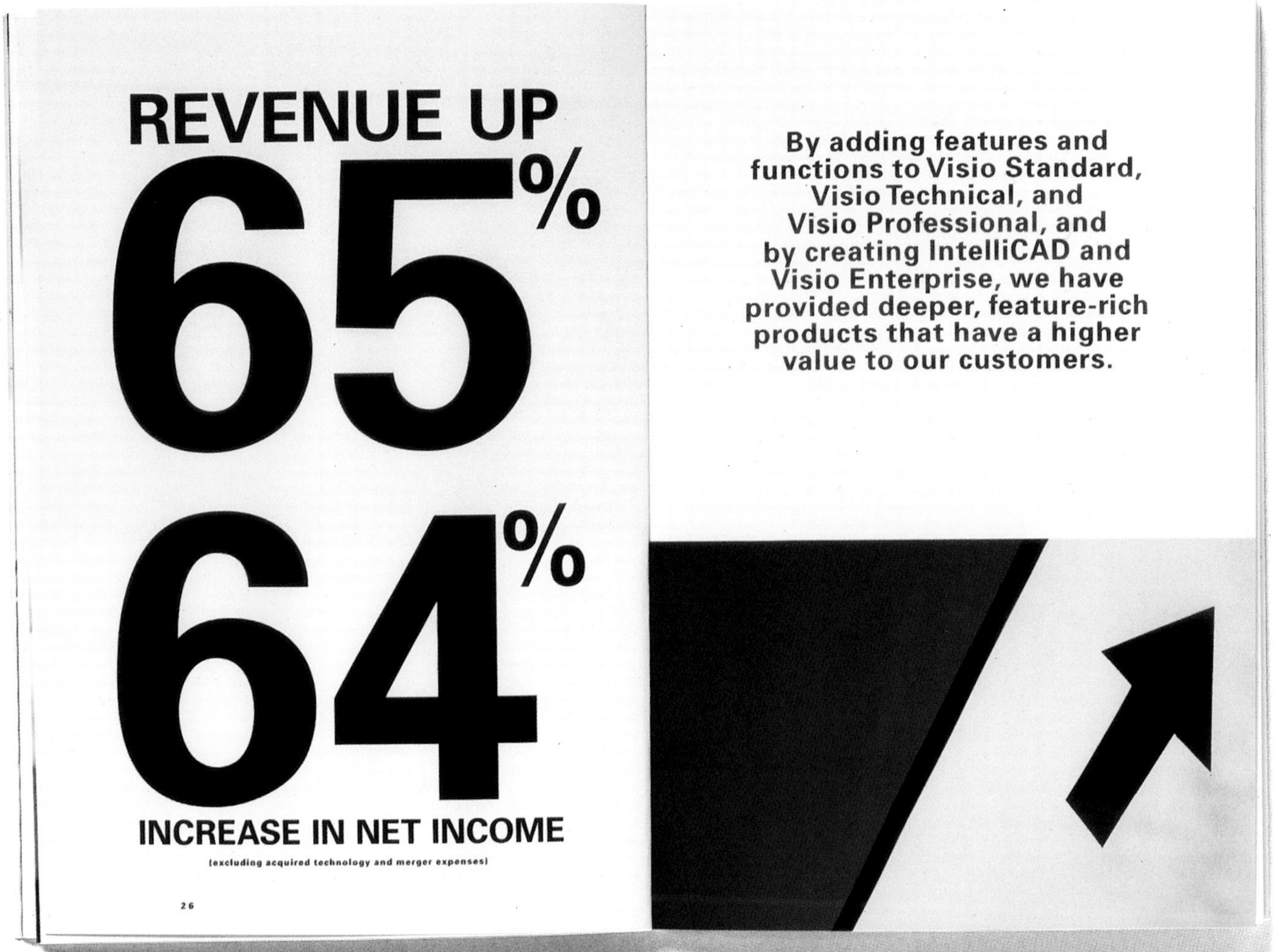

REVENUE UP 65%

64%

INCREASE IN NET INCOME

(excluding acquired technology and merger expenses)

26

By adding features and functions to Visio Standard, Visio Technical, and Visio Professional, and by creating IntelliCAD and Visio Enterprise, we have provided deeper, feature-rich products that have a higher value to our customers.

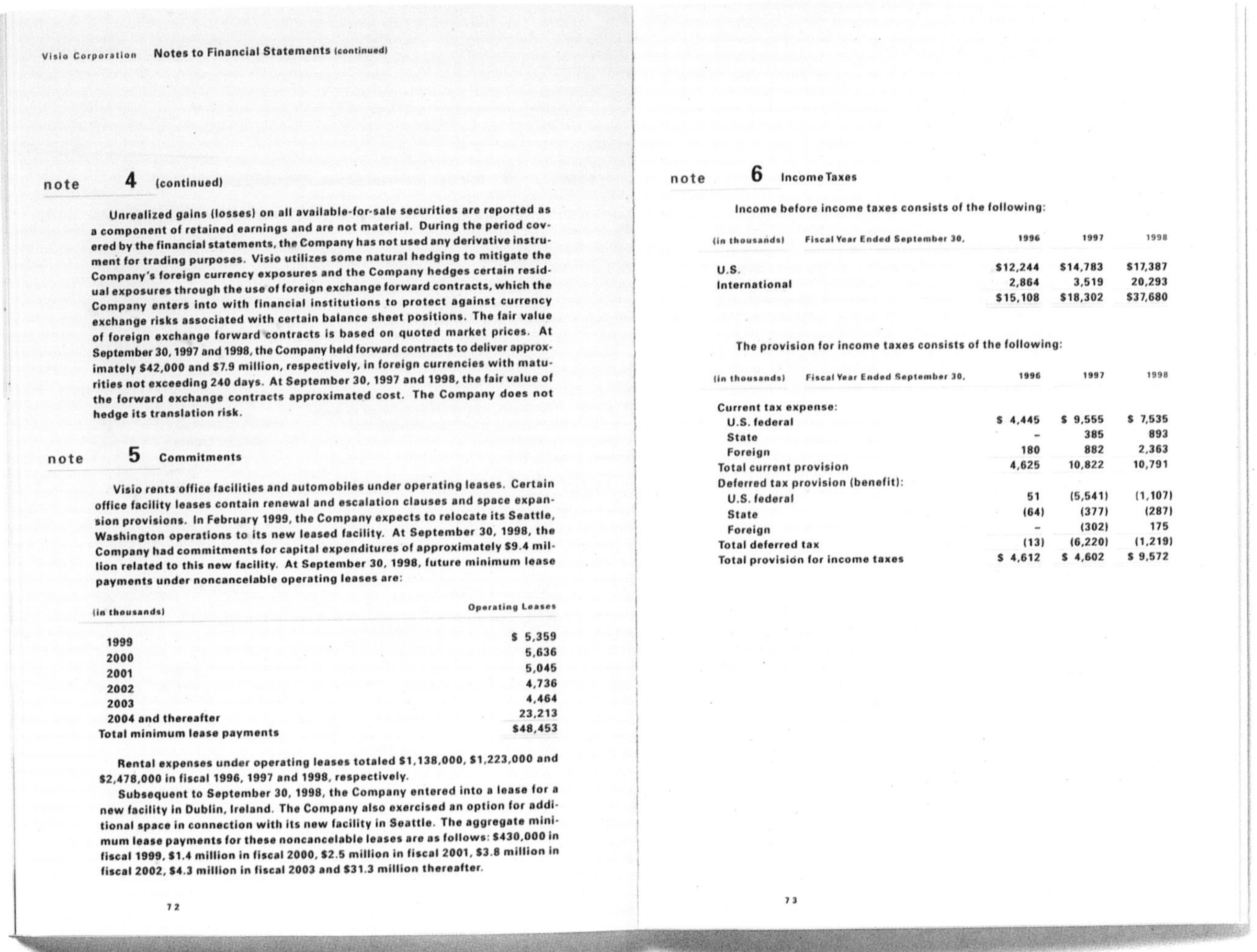

Visio Corporation **Notes to Financial Statements** (continued)

note 4 (continued)

Unrealized gains (losses) on all available-for-sale securities are reported as a component of retained earnings and are not material. During the period covered by the financial statements, the Company has not used any derivative instrument for trading purposes. Visio utilizes some natural hedging to mitigate the Company's foreign currency exposures and the Company hedges certain residual exposures through the use of foreign exchange forward contracts, which the Company enters into with financial institutions to protect against currency exchange risks associated with certain balance sheet positions. The fair value of foreign exchange forward contracts is based on quoted market prices. At September 30, 1997 and 1998, the Company held forward contracts to deliver approximately $42,000 and $7.9 million, respectively, in foreign currencies with maturities not exceeding 240 days. At September 30, 1997 and 1998, the fair value of the forward exchange contracts approximated cost. The Company does not hedge its translation risk.

note 5 Commitments

Visio rents office facilities and automobiles under operating leases. Certain office facility leases contain renewal and escalation clauses and space expansion provisions. In February 1999, the Company expects to relocate its Seattle, Washington operations to its new leased facility. At September 30, 1998, the Company had commitments for capital expenditures of approximately $9.4 million related to this new facility. At September 30, 1998, future minimum lease payments under noncancelable operating leases are:

(in thousands)	Operating Leases
1999	$ 5,359
2000	5,636
2001	5,045
2002	4,736
2003	4,464
2004 and thereafter	23,213
Total minimum lease payments	$48,453

Rental expenses under operating leases totaled $1,138,000, $1,223,000 and $2,478,000 in fiscal 1996, 1997 and 1998, respectively.

Subsequent to September 30, 1998, the Company entered into a lease for a new facility in Dublin, Ireland. The Company also exercised an option for additional space in connection with its new facility in Seattle. The aggregate minimum lease payments for these noncancelable leases are as follows: $430,000 in fiscal 1999, $1.4 million in fiscal 2000, $2.5 million in fiscal 2001, $3.8 million in fiscal 2002, $4.3 million in fiscal 2003 and $31.3 million thereafter.

72

note 6 Income Taxes

Income before income taxes consists of the following:

(in thousands) Fiscal Year Ended September 30,	1996	1997	1998
U.S.	$12,244	$14,783	$17,387
International	2,864	3,519	20,293
	$15,108	$18,302	$37,680

The provision for income taxes consists of the following:

(in thousands) Fiscal Year Ended September 30,	1996	1997	1998
Current tax expense:			
U.S. federal	$ 4,445	$ 9,555	$ 7,535
State	–	385	893
Foreign	180	882	2,363
Total current provision	4,625	10,822	10,791
Deferred tax provision (benefit):			
U.S. federal	51	(5,541)	(1,107)
State	(64)	(377)	(287)
Foreign	–	(302)	175
Total deferred tax	(13)	(6,220)	(1,219)
Total provision for income taxes	$ 4,612	$ 4,602	$ 9,572

73

Harley-Davidson Motor Company
Agency: VSA Partners, Inc.
Art Director: Jeff Walker
Creative Director: Dana Arnett
Designer: Ken Fox
Photographer: Charlie Simokaitis
Illustrator: Tom Fritz
Copywriter: Harley-Davidson

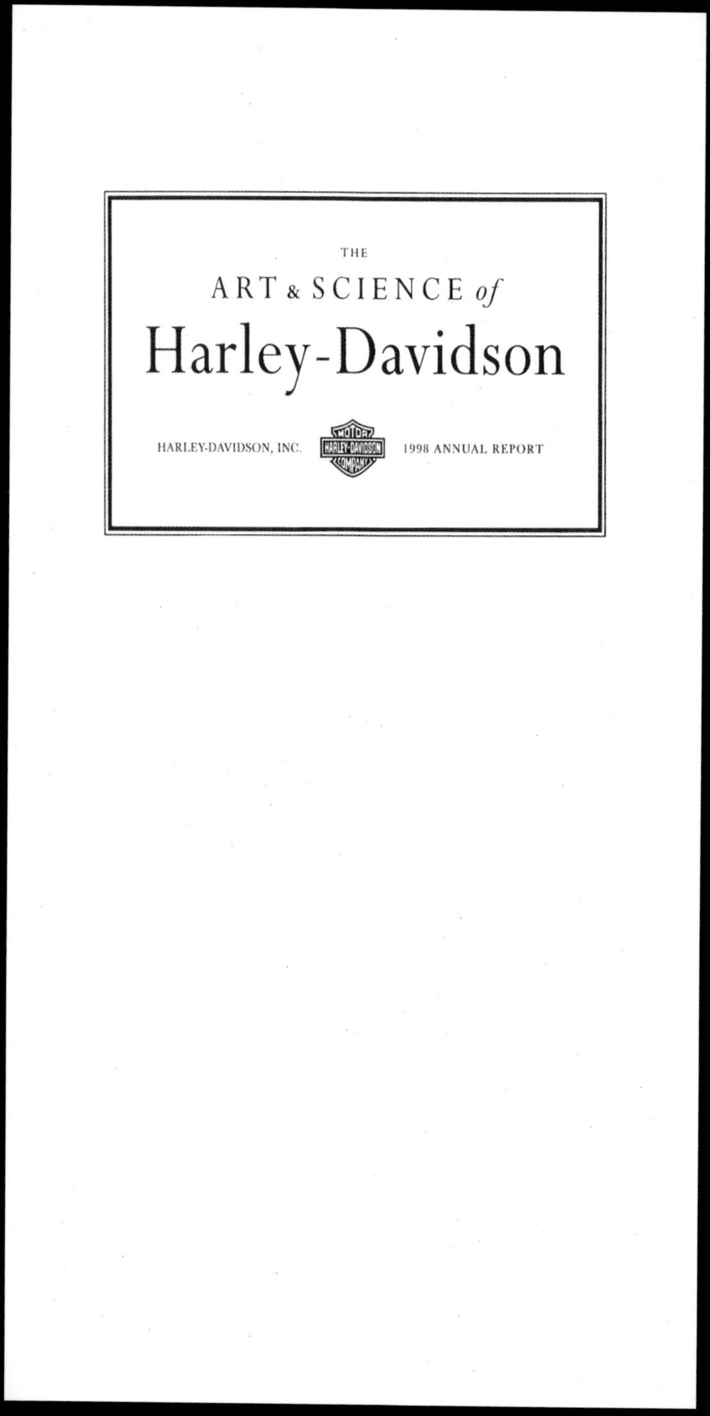
THE
ART & SCIENCE of
Harley-Davidson
HARLEY-DAVIDSON, INC.
MOTOR
HARLEY-DAVIDSON
COMPANY
1998 ANNUAL REPORT

Buell
AMERICAN MOTORCYCLES

MOTOR HARLEY-DAVIDSON COMPANY

EAGLEMARK

FINANCIAL HIGHLIGHTS

HARLEY-DAVIDSON, INCORPORATED

(In thousands except per share and shareholder data)	1998	1997	1996
Net Sales	$2,063,956	$1,762,569	$1,531,227
Income from continuing operations before provision for income taxes	336,229	276,302	227,622
Provision for Income Taxes	122,729	102,232	84,213
Income from continuing operations	213,500	174,070	143,409
Income from discontinued operations	–	–	22,619
Net Income	$ 213,500	$ 174,070	$ 166,028
Basic earnings per common share from continuing operations	$1.40	$1.15	$0.95
Diluted earnings per common share from continuing operations	$1.38	$1.13	$0.94
Weighted average common shares – basic	152,227	151,650	150,683
Weighted average common shares – diluted	154,703	153,948	152,925
Balance sheet at December 31			
Working capital	$ 376,448	$ 342,333	$ 362,031
Current Finance receivables, net	360,341	293,329	183,808
Long-term Finance receivables, net	319,427	249,346	154,264
Total assets	1,920,209	1,598,901	1,299,985
Total shareholders' equity	1,029,911	826,668	662,720
Market Price per Share	(Low-High)	(Low-High)	(Low-High)
First quarter	24 11/16 - 33 3/4	16 3/4 - 23 1/16	13 1/16 - 19 7/16
Second quarter	30 1/4 - 38	16 11/16 - 24 21/32	18 3/4 - 24 1/4
Third quarter	29 3/8 - 42	23 1/2 - 29 7/8	18 7/16 - 22 7/16
Fourth quarter	26 1/8 - 47 1/2	23 11/16 - 31 3/4	20 1/8 - 23 1/2
Dividends Paid	$0.155	$0.135	$0.110
Number of Shareholders of Record	60,503	50,374	41,483

Harley-Davidson, Inc. Year-end Stock Prices

In Dollars

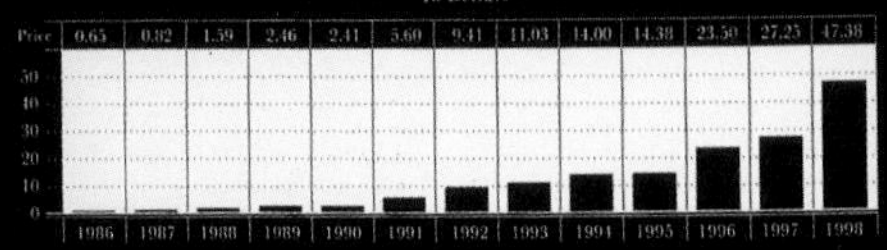
Price
0.65
0.82
1.59
2.46
2.41
5.60
9.41
11.03
14.00
14.38
23.50
27.25
47.38
50
40
30
20
10
0
1986
1987
1988
1989
1990
1991
1992
1993
1994
1995
1996
1997
1998

Throughout Harley-Davidson's 95 year history, the disciplines of art and science have harmonized to create our famous rolling sculpture and to influence every facet of our business.

DEAR FELLOW SHAREHOLDER:

As we close the books on our 13th consecutive year of record performance and a remarkable 74 percent appreciation in the market value of our company, I find myself thinking about what makes Harley-Davidson so special.

WE HAVE A POWERFUL and much admired brand centered around the experiences of motorcycling; its attributes of freedom, adventure and individuality appeal to people across a wide variety of demographic segments. We have strong relationships with all of our stakeholders– dealers, customers, employees, suppliers, governments, society and, of course, shareholders – that are grounded in trust and respect and are designed to be mutually-beneficial. We have a proven management team and empowered employees

THE

ART & SCIENCE *of*

Leadership

Harley-Davidson is one of the most admired and recognized companies in the world. We are leaders in our industry; we are leaders in relationship marketing; and we are leaders in creating consistent growth in shareholder value. That leadership position is reinforced with a unique organizational design that encourages high levels of collaboration between our inter-related businesses. By capitalizing on those synergies and effectively managing our other competitive advantages, Harley-Davidson's leadership position will be ensured for years to come.

SUSTAINED PERFORMANCE

1998 marked the 13th consecutive year of record revenue and earnings for Harley-Davidson, Inc.

GROWTH ACROSS ALL PRODUCT LINES

In 1998 all product lines significantly outpaced 1997 results. Motorcycles, Parts and Accessories, General Merchandise and Eaglemark Financial Services all grew to record levels.

INNOVATIVE ORGANIZATIONAL DESIGN

Harley-Davidson's unique circle organization at the leadership level fosters cross-functional teamwork throughout the entire organization.

THE LOOK OF A LEADER

In the early days, Harley-Davidson racers dominated the boardtracks and set the example for others to follow. The painting opposite depicts a boardtrack racer on his 1918 – J Harley-Davidson motorcycle.

A STAR IS BORN

Cycle World, the most widely read consumer magazine in the U.S. motorcycle industry, hailed the new Twin Cam 88 as "the best Big Twin ever."

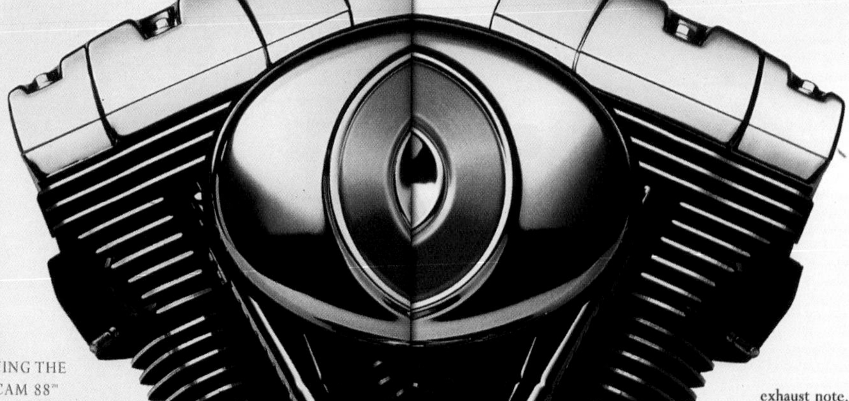

DESIGNING THE TWIN CAM 88™

The Twin Cam 88 engine signifies another milestone in the rich history of Harley-Davidson. Its immediate acceptance by enthusiasts is a tribute to the successful blending of art and science in its design.

The engineering team set out to build a new engine with even more power and durability that could be upgraded with performance packages designed, tested and perfected by Harley-Davidson. At the same time, the goal was to affirm our history of 45-degree V-Twin, air-cooled, push rod engines, and style the new heart of a Harley as an unrivaled feast for the eyes.

The 1450cc Twin Cam 88, affectionately known as the Fathead,™ continues the tradition of producing our distinct exhaust note, which is music to our customers' ears. It has more power and more torque than our 1340cc Evolution® engine. This new powerplant also underwent unprecedented testing, logging more than two-and-a-half million miles. For the 1999 model year, the Twin Cam 88 powers all of our Dyna® and touring motorcycle models.

Some call the Twin Cam 88 the evolution of the Evolution. We call it the first of many new product innovations and another great engine in the history of Harley-Davidson.

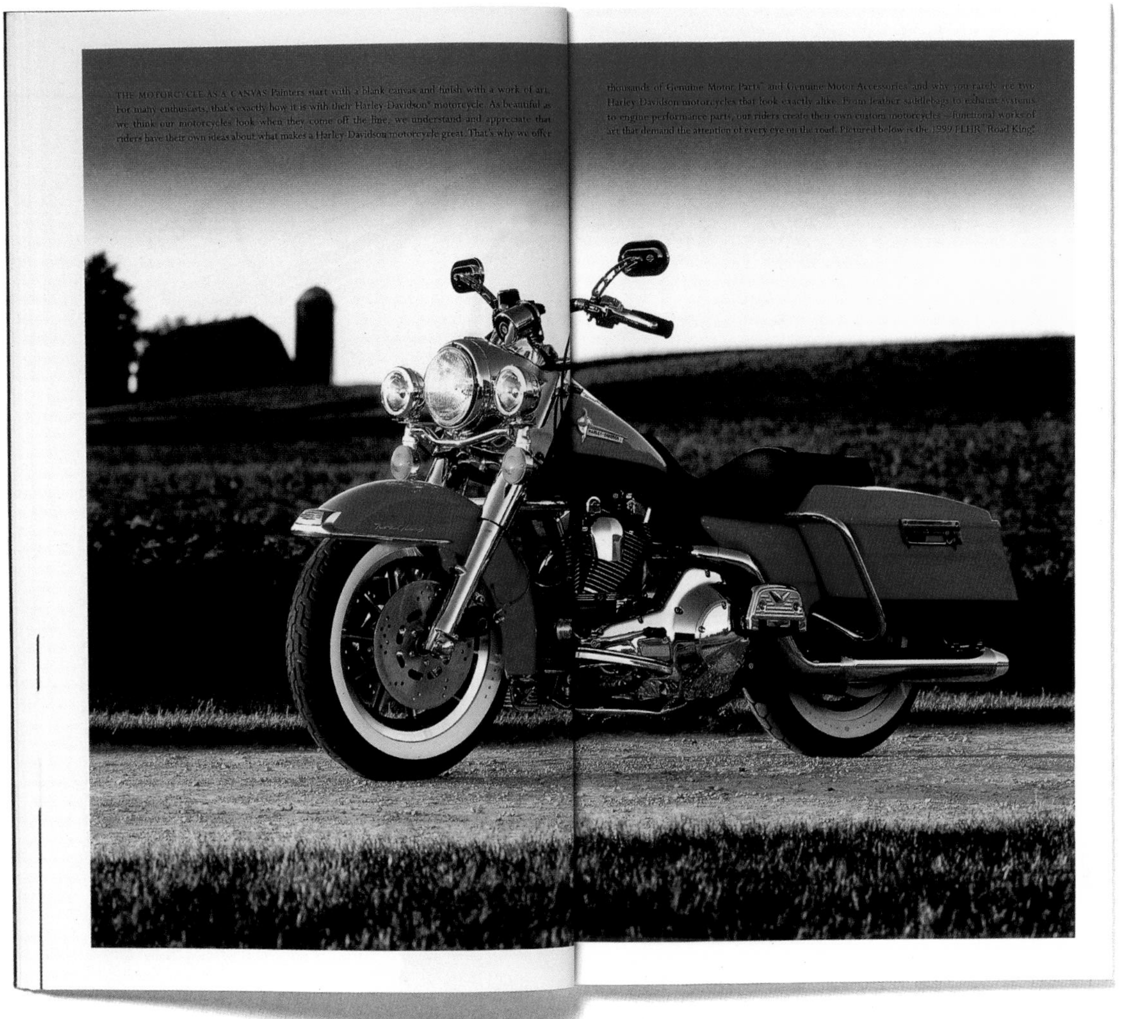

THE MOTORCYCLE AS A CANVAS Painters start with a blank canvas and finish with a work of art. For many enthusiasts, that's exactly how it is with their Harley-Davidson® motorcycle. As beautiful as we think our motorcycles look when they come off the line, we understand and appreciate that riders have their own ideas about what makes a Harley-Davidson motorcycle great. That's why we offer thousands of Genuine Motor Parts® and Genuine Motor Accessories® and why you rarely see two Harley-Davidson motorcycles that look exactly alike. From leather saddlebags to exhaust systems to engine performance parts, our riders create their own custom motorcycles – functional works of art that demand the attention of every eye on the road. Pictured below is the 1999 FLHR® Road King®.

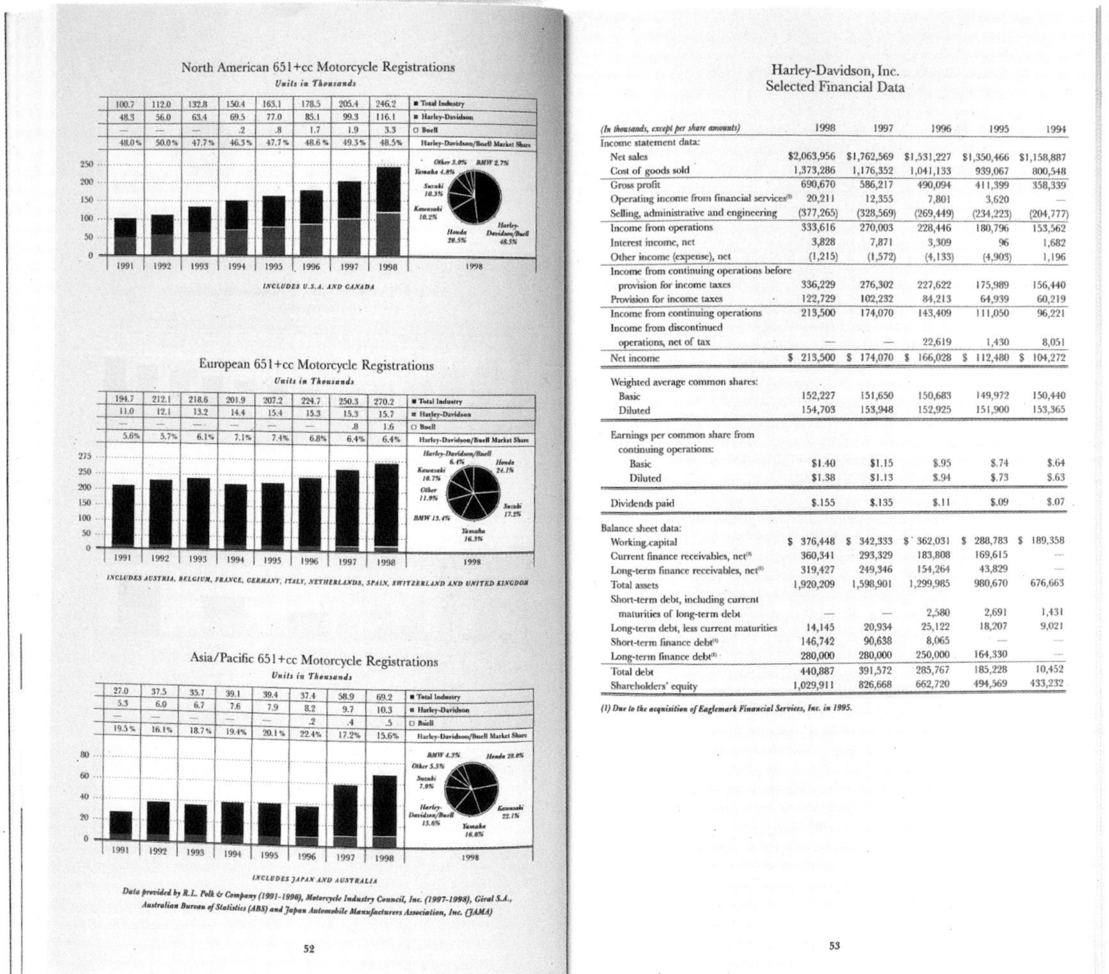

North American 651+cc Motorcycle Registrations

Units in Thousands

1991	1992	1993	1994	1995	1996	1997	1998	
100.7	112.0	132.8	150.4	163.1	178.5	205.4	246.2	■ Total Industry
48.3	56.0	63.4	69.5	77.0	85.1	99.3	116.1	■ Harley-Davidson
—	—	—	.2	.8	1.7	1.9	3.3	□ Buell
48.0%	50.0%	47.7%	46.3%	47.7%	48.6%	49.3%	48.5%	Harley-Davidson/Buell Market Share

1998
Other 3.0%
BMW 2.7%
Yamaha 4.8%
Suzuki 10.3%
Kawasaki 10.2%
Honda 20.5%
Harley-Davidson/Buell 48.5%

INCLUDES U.S.A. AND CANADA

European 651+cc Motorcycle Registrations

Units in Thousands

1991	1992	1993	1994	1995	1996	1997	1998	
194.7	212.1	218.6	201.9	207.2	224.7	250.3	270.2	■ Total Industry
11.0	12.1	13.2	14.4	15.4	15.3	15.3	15.7	■ Harley-Davidson
—	—	—	—	—	—	.8	1.6	□ Buell
5.6%	5.7%	6.1%	7.1%	7.4%	6.8%	6.4%	6.4%	Harley-Davidson/Buell Market Share

1998
Harley-Davidson/Buell 6.4%
Honda 24.1%
Kawasaki 10.7%
Other 11.9%
Suzuki 17.2%
BMW 13.4%
Yamaha 16.3%

INCLUDES AUSTRIA, BELGIUM, FRANCE, GERMANY, ITALY, NETHERLANDS, SPAIN, SWITZERLAND AND UNITED KINGDOM

Asia/Pacific 651+cc Motorcycle Registrations

Units in Thousands

1991	1992	1993	1994	1995	1996	1997	1998	
27.0	37.5	35.7	39.1	39.4	37.4	58.9	69.2	■ Total Industry
5.3	6.0	6.7	7.6	7.9	8.2	9.7	10.3	■ Harley-Davidson
—	—	—	—	—	.2	.4	.5	□ Buell
19.5%	16.1%	18.7%	19.4%	20.1%	22.4%	17.2%	15.6%	Harley-Davidson/Buell Market Share

1998
BMW 4.3%
Honda 28.0%
Other 5.5%
Suzuki 7.9%
Harley-Davidson/Buell 15.6%
Kawasaki 22.1%
Yamaha 16.6%

INCLUDES JAPAN AND AUSTRALIA

Data provided by R.L. Polk & Company (1991-1996), Motorcycle Industry Council, Inc. (1997-1998), Giral S.A., Australian Bureau of Statistics (ABS) and Japan Automobile Manufacturers Association, Inc. (JAMA)

52

Harley-Davidson, Inc.
Selected Financial Data

(In thousands, except per share amounts)	1998	1997	1996	1995	1994
Income statement data:					
Net sales	$2,063,956	$1,762,569	$1,531,227	$1,350,466	$1,158,887
Cost of goods sold	1,373,286	1,176,352	1,041,133	939,067	800,548
Gross profit	690,670	586,217	490,094	411,399	358,339
Operating income from financial services(1)	20,211	12,355	7,801	3,620	—
Selling, administrative and engineering	(377,265)	(328,569)	(269,449)	(234,223)	(204,777)
Income from operations	333,616	270,003	228,446	180,796	153,562
Interest income, net	3,828	7,871	3,309	96	1,682
Other income (expense), net	(1,215)	(1,572)	(4,133)	(4,903)	1,196
Income from continuing operations before provision for income taxes	336,229	276,302	227,622	175,989	156,440
Provision for income taxes	122,729	102,232	84,213	64,939	60,219
Income from continuing operations	213,500	174,070	143,409	111,050	96,221
Income from discontinued operations, net of tax	—	—	22,619	1,430	8,051
Net income	$ 213,500	$ 174,070	$ 166,028	$ 112,480	$ 104,272
Weighted average common shares:					
Basic	152,227	151,650	150,683	149,972	150,440
Diluted	154,703	153,948	152,925	151,900	153,365
Earnings per common share from continuing operations:					
Basic	$1.40	$1.15	$.95	$.74	$.64
Diluted	$1.38	$1.13	$.94	$.73	$.63
Dividends paid	$.155	$.135	$.11	$.09	$.07
Balance sheet data:					
Working capital	$ 376,448	$ 342,333	$ 362,031	$ 288,783	$ 189,358
Current finance receivables, net(1)	360,341	293,329	183,808	169,615	—
Long-term finance receivables, net(1)	319,427	249,346	154,264	43,829	—
Total assets	1,920,209	1,598,901	1,299,985	980,670	676,663
Short-term debt, including current maturities of long-term debt	—	—	2,580	2,691	1,431
Long-term debt, less current maturities	14,145	20,934	25,122	18,207	9,021
Short-term finance debt(1)	146,742	90,638	8,065	—	—
Long-term finance debt(1)	280,000	280,000	250,000	164,330	—
Total debt	440,887	391,572	285,767	185,228	10,452
Shareholders' equity	1,029,911	826,668	662,720	494,569	433,232

(1) Due to the acquisition of Eaglemark Financial Services, Inc. in 1995.

53

9

CORP

FreightCorp Annual Report

9

FreightCorp Profile

FreightCorp is the trading name of the Freight Rail Corporation, established on 1 July 1996 as a State Owned Corporation of the New South Wales Government. FreightCorp is an above-rail operator, providing rail and associated transport and logistics services to a range of customers including primary producers, mining companies, manufacturers, heavy industry and shipping customers. It is the largest standard gauge rail operator in Australia and approximately 90% of volumes hauled each year are for export.

FreightCorp's principal business is bulk haul of coal and grain in New South Wales. In the 3 years since corporatisation, FreightCorp has been implementing an aggressive program to establish itself as a major provider of above-rail transport and logistics services in the national market. While strengthening traditional services and customer relationships in New South Wales, FreightCorp has also extended services into Victoria, Queensland and South Australia and expanded into new business areas in intermodal freight, customised and packaged transport solutions, terminal management and container storage.

FreightCorp's goal is to succeed as the premier rail-based national freight services company in a competitive Australian transport environment.

02

03

Grain
FreightCorp delivered 4.3 million tonnes of export grain in 1998/99 and is ready to meet the transport demands of the bumper harvest forecast for 1999/00.

Initiatives such as driver only operation, through-depot crewing and the running of disciplined trains give FreightCorp a competitive edge in the delivery of cost-effective, customer responsive transport and logistics services.

8170

Customer Service
FreightCorp's customised Hunter Valley Coal Operating System (HVCOS) and Intermodal Business Information System (IBIS) are being developed jointly with clients and co-service providers. The systems offer the service supply chain immediate, common platform access to train consist and location information.

06

07

TS
CRONOS

PortLink
The PortLink disciplined train operation is the way of the future for efficient movement of export/import containers between metropolitan and regional intermodal terminals and the ports. Cooperative arrangements with the stevedores and the ports community have resulted in improved wagon turnaround and a heightened interest by customers in switching from road to rail for their container transport needs.

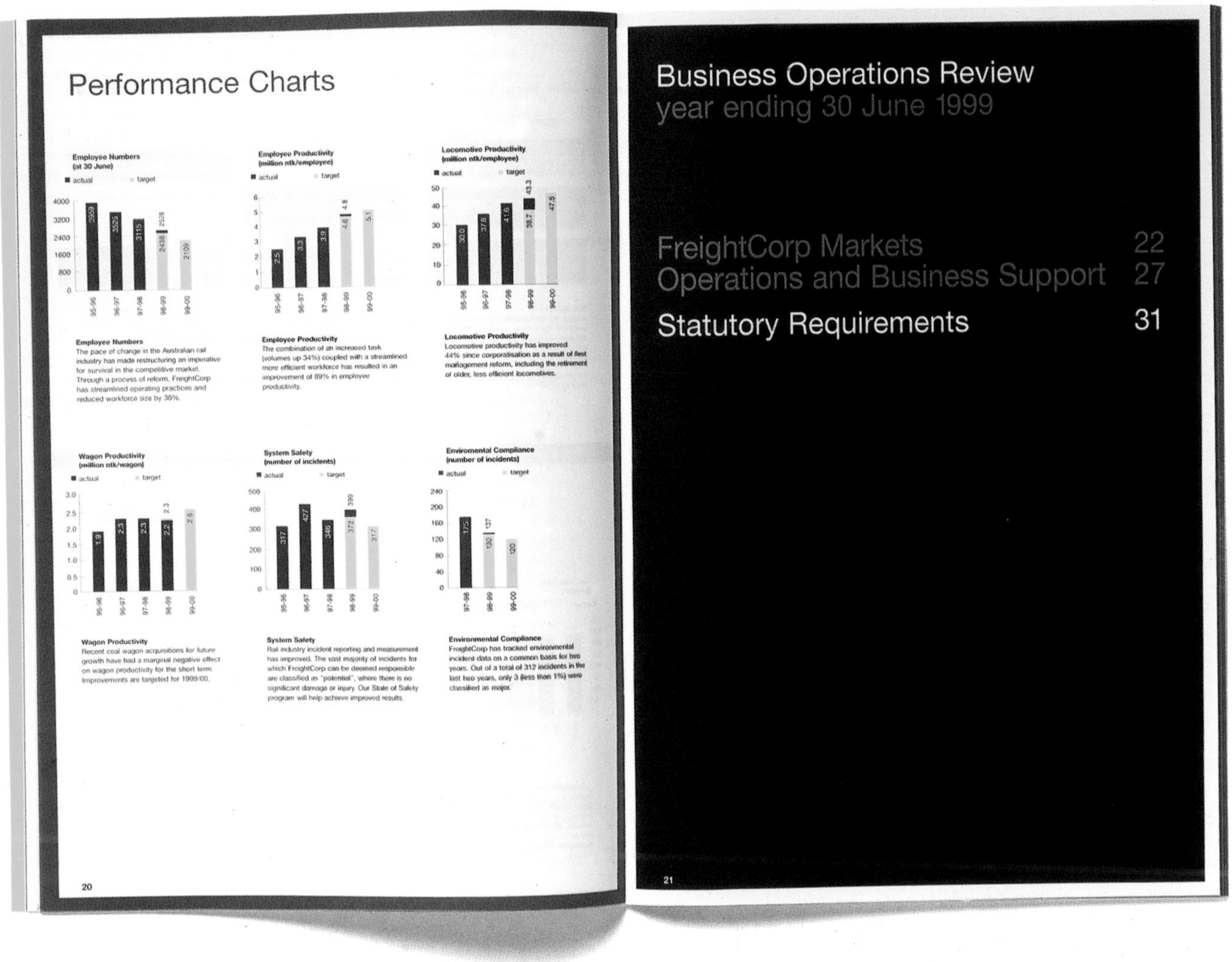

Performance Charts

Employee Numbers (at 30 June)
actual · target

Employee Productivity (million ntk/employee)
actual · target

Locomotive Productivity (million ntk/employee)
actual · target

Employee Numbers
The pace of change in the Australian rail industry has made restructuring an imperative for survival in the competitive market. Through a process of reform, FreightCorp has streamlined operating practices and reduced workforce size by 36%.

Employee Productivity
The combination of an increased task (volumes up 34%) coupled with a streamlined more efficient workforce has resulted in an improvement of 89% in employee productivity.

Locomotive Productivity
Locomotive productivity has improved 44% since corporatisation as a result of fleet management reform, including the retirement of older, less efficient locomotives.

Wagon Productivity (million ntk/wagon)
actual · target

System Safety (number of incidents)
actual · target

Enviromental Compliance (number of incidents)
actual · target

Wagon Productivity
Recent coal wagon acquisitions for future growth have had a marginal negative effect on wagon productivity for the short term. Improvements are targeted for 1999/00.

System Safety
Rail industry incident reporting and measurement has improved. The vast majority of incidents for which FreightCorp can be deemed responsible are classified as "potential", where there is no significant damage or injury. Our State of Safety program will help achieve improved results.

Environmental Compliance
FreightCorp has tracked environmental incident data on a common basis for two years. Out of a total of 312 incidents in the last two years, only 3 (less than 1%) were classified as major.

20

Business Operations Review
year ending 30 June 1999

21

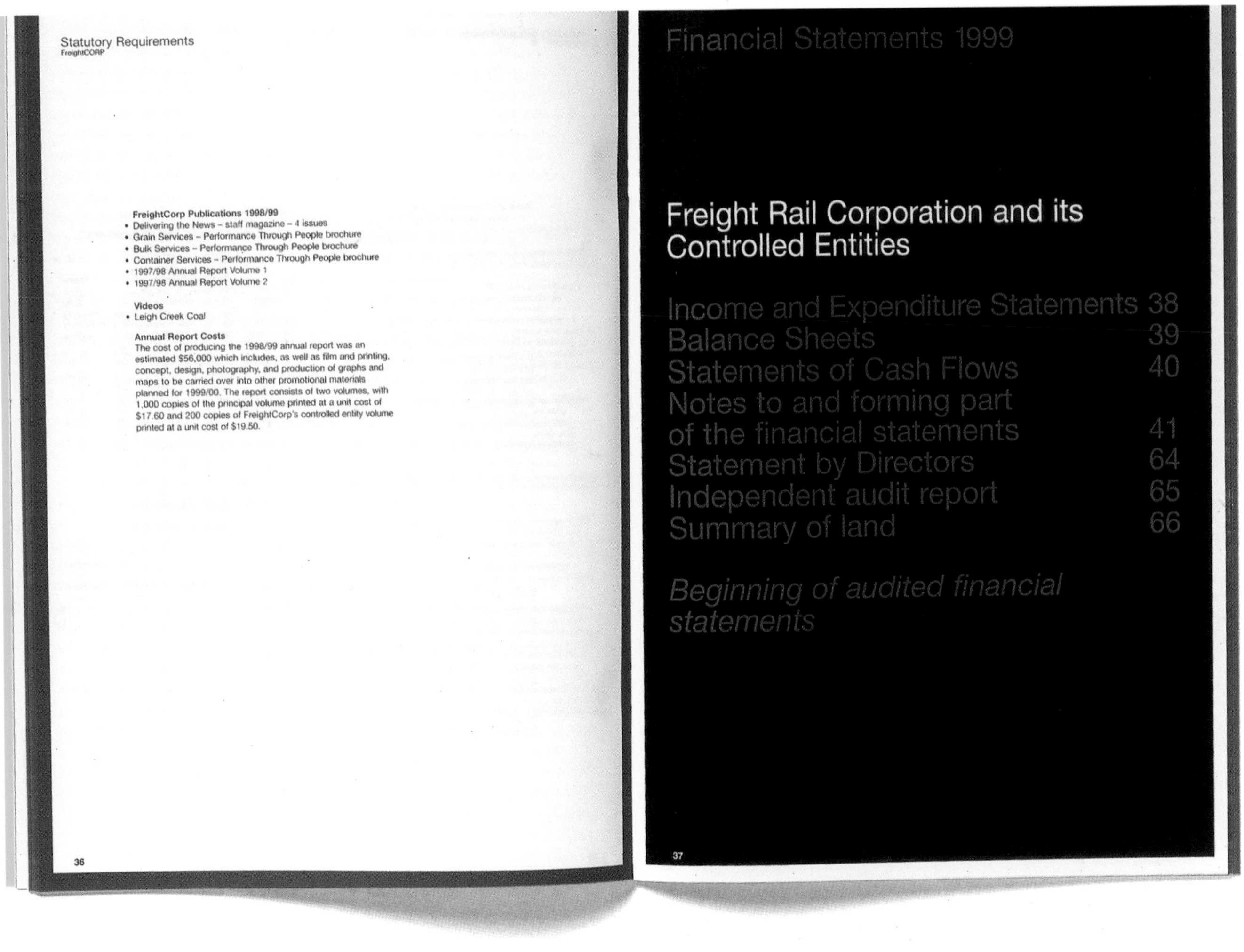

Statutory Requirements
FreightCORP

FreightCorp Publications 1998/99
- Delivering the News – staff magazine – 4 issues
- Grain Services – Performance Through People brochure
- Bulk Services – Performance Through People brochure
- Container Services – Performance Through People brochure
- 1997/98 Annual Report Volume 1
- 1997/98 Annual Report Volume 2

Videos
- Leigh Creek Coal

Annual Report Costs
The cost of producing the 1998/99 annual report was an estimated $56,000 which includes, as well as film and printing, concept, design, photography, and production of graphs and maps to be carried over into other promotional materials planned for 1999/00. The report consists of two volumes, with 1,000 copies of the principal volume printed at a unit cost of $17.60 and 200 copies of FreightCorp's controlled entity volume printed at a unit cost of $19.50.

36

Financial Statements 1999

Freight Rail Corporation and its Controlled Entities

Beginning of audited financial statements

37

BASS STRAIT OIL TRUST

1997 ANNUAL REPORT

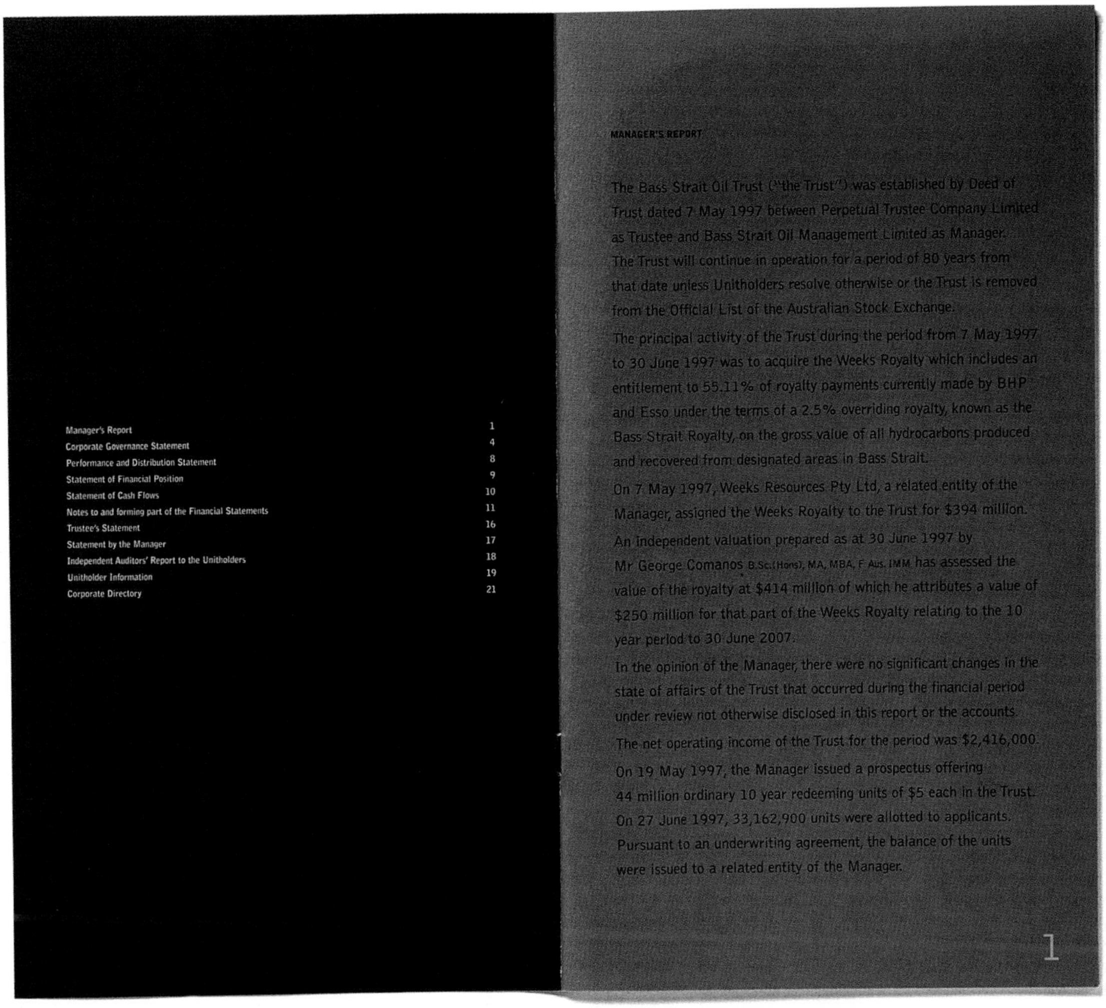

MANAGER'S REPORT

The Bass Strait Oil Trust ("the Trust") was established by Deed of Trust dated 7 May 1997 between Perpetual Trustee Company Limited as Trustee and Bass Strait Oil Management Limited as Manager. The Trust will continue in operation for a period of 80 years from that date unless Unitholders resolve otherwise or the Trust is removed from the Official List of the Australian Stock Exchange.

The principal activity of the Trust during the period from 7 May 1997 to 30 June 1997 was to acquire the Weeks Royalty which includes an entitlement to 55.11% of royalty payments currently made by BHP and Esso under the terms of a 2.5% overriding royalty, known as the Bass Strait Royalty, on the gross value of all hydrocarbons produced and recovered from designated areas in Bass Strait.

On 7 May 1997, Weeks Resources Pty Ltd, a related entity of the Manager, assigned the Weeks Royalty to the Trust for $394 million.

An independent valuation prepared as at 30 June 1997 by Mr George Comanos B.Sc.(Hons), MA, MBA, F.Aus. IMM has assessed the value of the royalty at $414 million of which he attributes a value of $250 million for that part of the Weeks Royalty relating to the 10 year period to 30 June 2007.

In the opinion of the Manager, there were no significant changes in the state of affairs of the Trust that occurred during the financial period under review not otherwise disclosed in this report or the accounts.

The net operating income of the Trust for the period was $2,416,000.

On 19 May 1997, the Manager issued a prospectus offering 44 million ordinary 10 year redeeming units of $5 each in the Trust. On 27 June 1997, 33,162,900 units were allotted to applicants. Pursuant to an underwriting agreement, the balance of the units were issued to a related entity of the Manager.

1

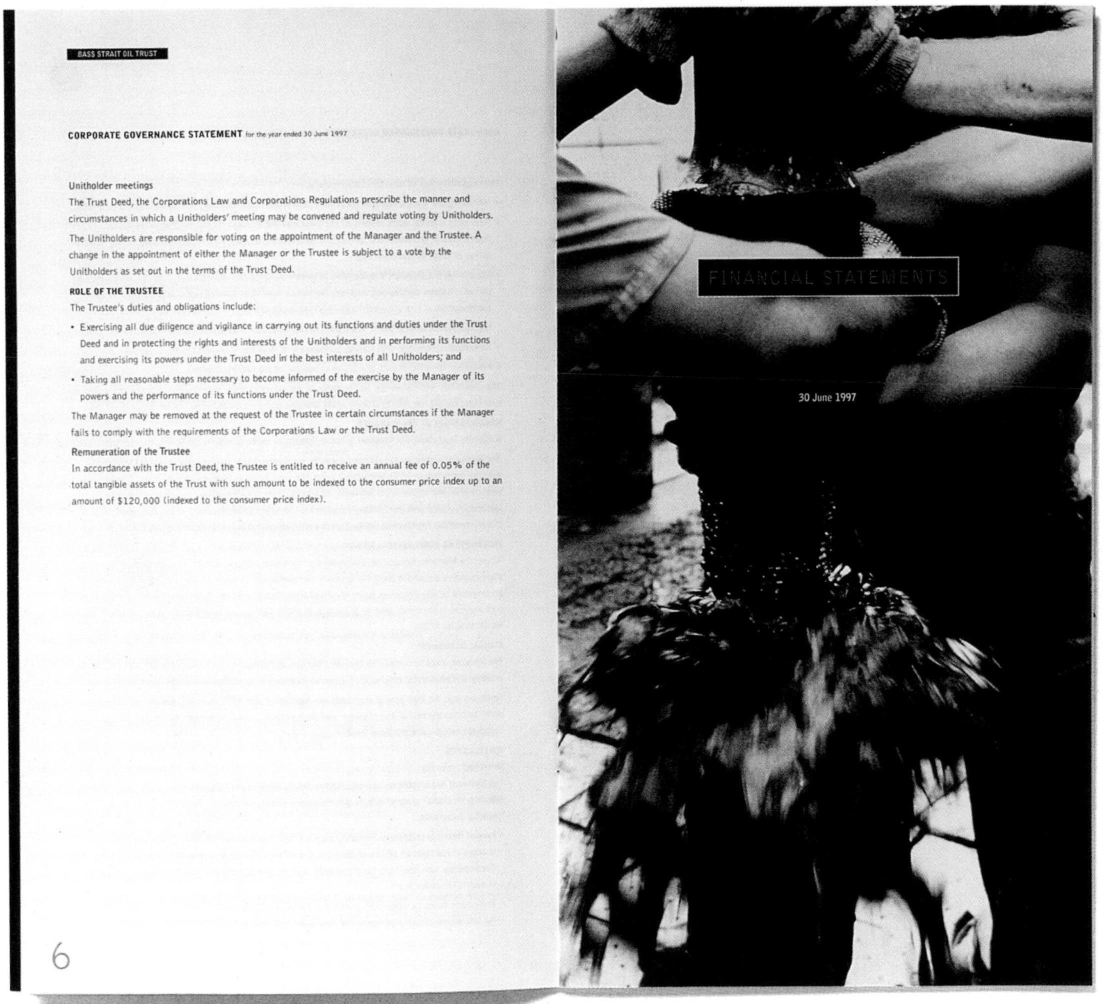

BASS STRAIT OIL TRUST

CORPORATE GOVERNANCE STATEMENT for the year ended 30 June 1997

Unitholder meetings

The Trust Deed, the Corporations Law and Corporations Regulations prescribe the manner and circumstances in which a Unitholders' meeting may be convened and regulate voting by Unitholders.

The Unitholders are responsible for voting on the appointment of the Manager and the Trustee. A change in the appointment of either the Manager or the Trustee is subject to a vote by the Unitholders as set out in the terms of the Trust Deed.

ROLE OF THE TRUSTEE

The Trustee's duties and obligations include:

- Exercising all due diligence and vigilance in carrying out its functions and duties under the Trust Deed and in protecting the rights and interests of the Unitholders and in performing its functions and exercising its powers under the Trust Deed in the best interests of all Unitholders; and
- Taking all reasonable steps necessary to become informed of the exercise by the Manager of its powers and the performance of its functions under the Trust Deed.

The Manager may be removed at the request of the Trustee in certain circumstances if the Manager fails to comply with the requirements of the Corporations Law or the Trust Deed.

Remuneration of the Trustee

In accordance with the Trust Deed, the Trustee is entitled to receive an annual fee of 0.05% of the total tangible assets of the Trust with such amount to be indexed to the consumer price index up to an amount of $120,000 (indexed to the consumer price index).

6

FINANCIAL STATEMENTS

30 June 1997

Energy Australia
Agency: Billy Blue Design and Writing
Art Director & Designer: Geordie McKenzie
Creative Director: Mick Thorp
Photographer: Graham Monro

As a result of keen pricing practices and a willingness to negotiate joint acceptable outcomes, Telstra signed an agreement for the supply of electricity for its contestable New South Wales sites.
Telstra recognises the value of dealing with Australia's largest energy supplier, while believing EnergyAustralia is a company with the capacity to meet the future challenges of the existing and emerging contestable markets.
Bruce Cornelius, National Sales Manager, responsible for leading the effort to win Telstra's business in NSW and ensuring the on-going relationship.
14
15

Directors' Report

Review of Operations

State of Affairs

In the opinion of the Directors, there were no significant changes in the state of affairs of the economic entity that occurred during the year ended 30 June 1999 not otherwise disclosed in this report or the financial statements.

Directors' interests and benefits

No Director has an interest in the share capital of the companies within the Chief Entity. Since the beginning of the year ended 30 June 1999, no Director has received, or become entitled to receive, any benefit (other than a benefit included in the total amount of remuneration) by reason of a contract made by the company, a controlled entity or a related body corporate with a Director or a firm of which the Director is a member.

Indemnities and Insurance

All Directors of the Corporation, its Secretary and executive officers are entitled to be indemnified, under Article 28 of the Corporations Constitution, to the maximum extent permitted by law unless the liability arises out of conduct involving a lack of good faith.

Since 1 July 1998, no amounts were paid under this indemnity agreement.

The Corporation has paid insurance premiums in respect of Directors' and Officers' liability insurance relating to the current and former officers of the Corporation and its controlled entities.

Since 1 July 1998, there have been no claims on Directors' and Officers' liability insurance.

Events subsequent to balance date

Since 30 June 1999, the Directors are not aware of any matter or circumstance not otherwise dealt with in the report or financial statements that has significantly or may significantly affect the operations of the economic entity, the results of those operations or the state of affairs of the economic entity in subsequent financial years.

Roundings

EnergyAustralia is exempt from clause 12 of the Public Finance and Audit (General) Regulation 1995. Accordingly, the amounts shown in the financial statements have been rounded off to the nearest tenth of a million dollars unless specifically stated to be otherwise.

Signed in accordance with a resolution of the Directors.

John C. Conde AO
Director
Sydney – 13 October 1999

Paul A. Broad
Director

46

Index to Financial Statements

47

Index

AgenciesClients

CreativeDirectorsArtDirectorsDesigners

PhotographersIllustratorsCopywriters

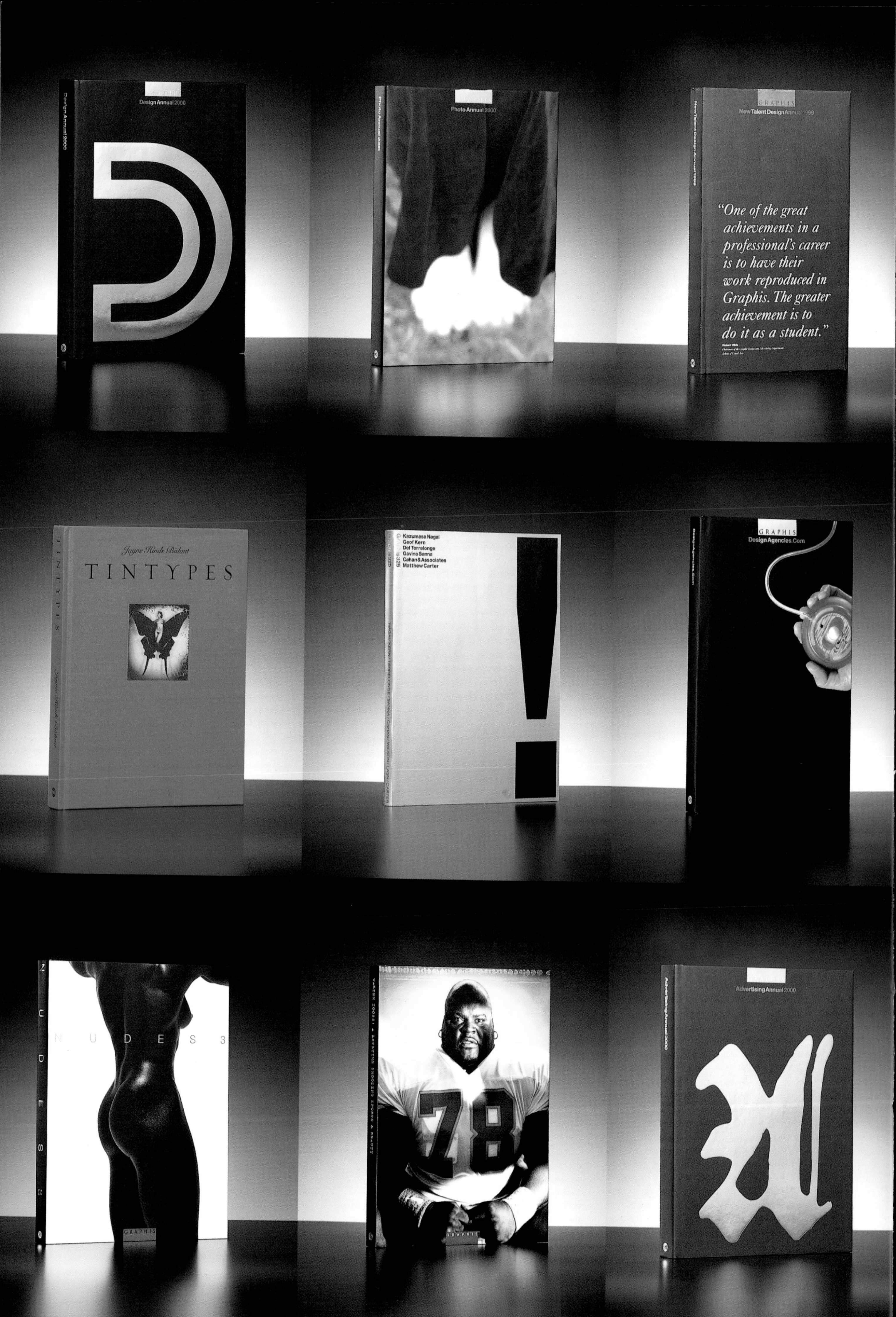
Design Annual 2000
Photo Annual 2000
GRAPHIS
New Talent Design Annual 1999
"One of the great achievements in a professional's career is to have their work reproduced in Graphis. The greater achievement is to do it as a student."
Jayne Hinds Bidaut
TINTYPES
Kazumasa Nagai
Geof Kern
Del Terrelonge
Gavino Sanna
Cahan & Associates
Matthew Carter
GRAPHIS
DesignAgencies.Com
NUDES 3
GRAPHIS
78
GRAPHIS
Advertising Annual 2000

Order Form

We're introducing a great way to reward *Graphis* magazine readers: If you subscribe to *Graphis*, you'll qualify for a 40% discount on our books. If you subscribe and place a Standing Order, you'll get a 50% discount on our books. A Standing Order means we'll reserve your selected Graphis Annual or Series title(s) at press and ship it to you at 50% discount. With a Standing Order for *Design Annual 2001*, for example, you'll receive this title at half-off, and each coming year, we'll send you the newest *Design Annual* at this low price—an ideal way for the professional to keep informed, year after year. In addition to the titles here, we carry books in all communication disciplines, so call if there's another title we can get for you. Thank you for supporting Graphis.

Book title	Order No.	Retail	40% off Discount	Standing Order 50% off	Quantity	Totals	Call for Entries
Advertising Annual 1999	1500	☐ $70.00	☐ $42.00	☐ $35.00			
Advertising Annual 2000	1550	☐ $70.00	☐ $42.00	☐ $35.00			
Advertising's Top Ten	195x	☐ $70.00	☐ $42.00	N/A			
African Journey	1992	☐ $70.00	☐ $42.00	N/A			
Annual Report 7	1895	☐ $70.00	☐ $42.00	☐ $35.00			
Apple Design	1259	☐ $45.00	☐ $27.00	N/A			
Black & White Blues	4710	☐ $40.00	☐ $24.00	N/A			
Book Design 2 (s)	1453	☐ $70.00	☐ $42.00	☐ $35.00			
Brochures 3 (s)	1496	☐ $70.00	☐ $42.00	☐ $35.00			
Corporate Identity 3 (s)	1437	☐ $70.00	☐ $42.00	☐ $35.00			
Design Annual 2001	1887	☐ $70.00	☐ $42.00	☐ $35.00			
Ferenc Berko	1445	☐ $60.00	☐ $36.00	N/A			
Graphic Art of Michael Schwab	1968	☐ $60.00	☐ $36.00	N/A			
Interactive Design 1 (s)	1631	☐ $70.00	☐ $42.00	☐ $35.00			
New Talent Design Annual 1999	1607	☐ $60.00	☐ $36.00	☐ $30.00			
New Talent Design Annual 2000	1640	☐ $60.00	☐ $36.00	☐ $30.00			
Nudes 1	212	☐ $50.00	☐ $30.00	N/A			
Photo Annual 1998	1461	☐ $70.00	☐ $42.00	☐ $35.00			
Product Design 2 (s)	1330	☐ $70.00	☐ $42.00	☐ $35.00			
Tintypes	1798	☐ $60.00	☐ $36.00	N/A			
T-Shirt Design 2 (s)	1402	☐ $60.00	☐ $36.00	☐ $30.00			
Walter Iooss	1569	☐ $60.00	☐ $36.00	N/A			
World Trademarks	1070	☐ $250.00	☐ $150.00	N/A			
Shipping & handling per book, US $7.00, Canada $15.00 USD, International $20.00 USD.							N/A
New York State shipments add 8.25% tax. All figures are in US dollars.							N/A

Standing Orders I understand I am committing to the selected annuals and/or series and will be automatically charged for each new volume in forthcoming years, at 50% off. I must call and cancel my order when I am no longer interested in purchasing the book. (To honor your Standing Order discount you must sign below.)

Signature ____________________ Date ____________________

Graphis magazine	☐ One year subscription	USA $90	Canada $125	Int'l $125
	☐ Two year subscription	USA $165	Canada $235	Int'l $235
	☐ One year student*	USA $65	Canada $90	Int'l $90
	☐ Single or Back Issues (per)	USA $24	Canada $28	Int'l $28

Calls For Entry

If you would like to receive a call for entry for any of the annuals or series please check the appropriate box, in the last column above. You can also find contest information on the Graphis website:

www.graphis.com

*All students must mail a copy of student ID along with the order form.

(s) = series (published every 2-4 years)

AR7

Name	☐ American Express ☐ Visa ☐ Mastercard ☐ Check
Company	
Address	Card #
City State Zip	Expiration
Daytime phone	Card holder's signature

Send this order form (or copy) and make check payable to Graphis Inc. For even faster turn-around service, or if you have any questions about subscribing, contact us at the following numbers: in the US (800) 209.4234; outside the US (212) 532. 9387 ext. 242 or 240; fax (212) 696.4242. Check for our mailing address or order Graphis anywhere in the world at www.graphis.com.

Poster Annual 2000
Poster Annual 2000

Graphis Books **Call For Entry**

If you would like us to put you on our mailing lists for Call for Entries for any of our books, please fill out the form and check off the specific books you would like to be a part of. We are now consolidating our mailings twice a year for our spring and fall books. If information is needed on specific deadlines for any of our books, please consult our web site: www.graphis.com.

Graphic Design Books

- ☐ Advertising Annual
- ☐ Annual Reports
- ☐ Book Design
- ☐ Brochure
- ☐ Corporate Identity
- ☐ Design Annual
- ☐ Digital Fonts
- ☐ Diagrams
- ☐ Poster Annual
- ☐ Products by Design
- ☐ Letterhead
- ☐ Logo Design
- ☐ Music CD
- ☐ New Media
- ☐ Packaging
- ☐ Paper Promotions
- ☐ Typography

Photography Books

- ☐ Digital Photo (Professional)
- ☐ Human Con. (Photojournalism)
- ☐ New Talent (Amateur)
- ☐ Nudes (Professional)
- ☐ Nudes (Fine Art)
- ☐ Photo Annual (Professional)
- ☐ Photography (Fine Art)

Student Books

- ☐ Advertising Annual
- ☐ Design Annual
- ☐ Photo Annual (Professional)
- ☐ Products by Design
- ☐ **All the Books**
- ☐ All Design Books only
- ☐ All Photo Books only
- ☐ All Students Books only

First Name: ______ Last Name: ______

Company: ______

Telephone: ______ Fax: ______

Mailing Address: ______ City: ______

State, Country: ______ Zip: ______

Mail or fax form to: Graphis, Call for Entries, 307 Fifth Ave., Tenth Floor, New York, New York 10016, USA, or fax to 212.213.3229